SLAVERY AND THE LAW

SLAVERY
& THE LAW

Edited by
PAUL FINKELMAN

MADISON HOUSE
Madison 1997

Finkelman, Paul, ed.
Slavery and the Law

Copyright © 1997 by Madison House Publishers, Inc.
All rights reserved.

LIBRARY OF CONGRESS CATALOGING-IN-PUBLICATION DATA

Slavery & the law / edited by Paul Finkelman — 1st ed.
          p.   cm.
          Includes bibliographical references and index.
          ISBN 0-945612-36-2
          1. Slavery—Law and legislation—United States —History.
     2. Slavery—Law and legislation—History. I. Finkelman, Paul, 1949–   .
KF4545.S5S577   1996
342.73'087—dc20
[347.30287]   96-8917
                                                                  CIP

Printed on acid-free recycled paper in the United States of America.

Published by Madison House Publishers, Inc.
P.O. Box 3100, Madison, Wisconsin 53704

FIRST EDITION

To David Cobin, Stephen Gottlieb, and Peter Wallenstein—
friends, collaborators, and co-conspirators in the search for
the legal history of the South and the nation

CONTENTS

ACKNOWLEDGMENTS

THIS BOOK BEGAN as a symposium at *Chicago-Kent Law Review*. The volume would not have been possible without the hard work of the many student editors on the law review. In addition, my own research assistants, John Crocitti, Lordes Sanchez, and Debra Weiss were extraordinarily helpful in finishing this book. Gregory Britton at Madison House showed great fortitude in agreeing to publish this volume. Greg embodies all that we look for in a good editor including a wonderful sense of humor. Christopher Hill was a superb copy editor. Finally, I thank my fellow scholars who cheerful complied with the competing demands of the law review editors, the press editors, and my own editing.

SLAVERY AND THE LAW

Introduction

The Centrality of Slavery in American Legal Development

Paul Finkelman

AT FIRST GLANCE SLAVERY in the United States seems anomalous, a relic of an earlier age that somehow survived the Revolution, with its emphasis on natural rights and its assertion that all people "are created equal." The title of the most influential and important history of American slavery, Kenneth Stampp's *The Peculiar Institution*, suggests the way most Americans have traditionally looked at slavery. That a neoabolitionist historian, publishing two years after *Brown* v. *Board of Education*, thought slavery was "peculiar" should not surprise us. But even antebellum Southerners often referred to slavery as their "peculiar institution." On the eve of the Civil War, white Southerners, while they extolled the value of slavery, knew their system of organizing labor and controlling race relations was unacceptable to much of the world. It was truly peculiar.[1]

In contrast to Stampp, Orlando Patterson, a sociologist, argued in 1982 that the *peculiar* institution is a misnomer for slavery. He claimed that "[t]here is nothing notably peculiar about the institution of slavery. It has existed from before the dawn of human history right down to the twentieth century, in the most primitive of human societies and in the most civilized." Patterson found slavery in every "region on earth" and concluded that "probably there is no group of people whose ancestors were not at one time slaves or slaveholders."[2]

The Peculiarity & the Centrality of American Slavery

In a number of ways Stampp and Patterson are both right. In the United States slavery was simultaneously peculiar and prosaic. Patterson has shown—and the essays by Alan Watson, Jacob Corré, and Jonathan Bush in this book reaffirm—that slavery has existed in most societies. Special-ized monographs on slavery in numerous cultures reaffirm this analy-sis.[3] Only in the last half of the twentieth century has the world been without widespread, legalized human bondage. Surely, slavery *per se* has never been a peculiar institution. However, as the great classical scholar Moses I. Finley notes, the United States South was one of only five places in the world to have developed not merely slavery but a slave society.[4] Moreover, by 1861 the racially based slavery of the American South was different—peculiar—both when compared to human bondage in other times and places and when viewed as part of the political structure of the United States.

Slavery was an oddity that ran counter to the professed ideals of the nation, and yet it was deeply embedded in the social, political, and legal structure of the nation. It undermined the "more perfect Union" cre-ated by the Constitution, but at the same time it was both protected by that Constitution and woven into the nation's political and legal fabric.[5] Slavery seemed contrary to the nation's common-law tradition, and yet it helped shape and develop much of American common law. After 1804 slavery was peculiar to the South, but much of the North shared the racial views of the South.[6] Before the Civil War the Supreme Court en-dorsed these views as the law of the land. Despite its geographical isola-tion, the influence of slavery was felt nationally and internationally. It was recognized and protected by federal laws as well as by the Constitu-tion, and it was not considered illegal under nineteenth-century notions of international law.[7]

Although apparently antithetical to American traditions of equality and democracy, antebellum Southerners, and a good many Northerners as well, had little trouble distinguishing between the rights of free white Americans and the disabilities of enslaved black Americans. Indeed, by the eve of the Civil War some Southerners claimed that democracy in America was only possible because of slavery. As William W. Fisher III demonstrates, Southerners of various social classes argued for the racial inferiority of blacks and relegated them to a permanently diminished status, thus simultaneously justifying slavery and allowing for greater de-mocracy among whites. Because they were slaves, so the argument went, blacks could never participate in politics. Instead, they provided what Senator James Henry Hammond called a "mudsill," on top of which a democracy of white men could be built.[8] Thus, the rights of life, liberty, and happiness proclaimed in the Declaration of Independence could be universally applied to white Americans precisely because they were not applied to blacks. This sort of defense was necessary because slavery was *peculiar* within the context of the natural-rights, liberal republican-ism of nineteenth-century America. Roman masters, for example, had felt no need to defend their institution. In Rome "[i]deological open-ness was facilitated by the nakedness of the oppression and exploitation:

no 'false consciousness' was necessary or possible."[9] In Rome there was nothing peculiar about slavery and therefore no need to defend it. In America slavery was very peculiar, and thus the master class felt the necessity of defending it at every turn.

Race and Slavery in the United States

The defense of slavery that allowed it to coexist with American democracy was based on race. For Americans "race has always been the central reality of slavery."[10] For most of the history of the world race was generally irrelevant to enslavement. Other New World cultures such as Brazil and Cuba had racially based slavery. But none of them maintained such rigid distinctions between the races. Even St. Domingue (present-day Haiti), arguably the most brutal slave culture in the New World, had a large class of free people of color whose part African ancestry did not prevent them from achieving some wealth and elevated status in that society. Thus, racially based slavery in the United States was both peculiar and damaging, not merely to the slaves and masters of the time but to the entire society then and now. Because slavery in the United States "was black slavery," Moses Finley has argued that "even a 'purely historical' study of an institution now dead for more than a century cannot escape being caught up in the urgency of contemporary black-white tensions."[11]

In other times and places enslavement was never confined to a single race or ethnic group. Orlando Patterson's work has shown that in most premodern societies enslavement might be the fate of anyone at any time. Historian Carl Degler has noted that "There was a time in antiquity when anyone, regardless of nation, religion, or race, might be a slave." Alan Watson's essay "Thinking Property at Rome" underscores this phenomenon, reminding us that most legal records of Roman slavery bear on the enslavement of elite slaves who were often from the same class and race as their masters. Indeed, the most striking aspect of Roman slavery for an Americanist is the extent to which enslavement had nothing to do with race. Enslavement could happen to anyone. As Finley has observed, although most classical slaves were "barbarians" from other cultures, there were also "Greek slaves in Greece [and] Italian slaves in Rome." Similarly, there were Chinese slaves in China, Africans enslaved by Africans, and Russians enslaved by other Russians.[12] Europeans enslaved each other throughout the ancient world and well into the modern period.[13]

If anyone might be a slave, freedom was a realistic possibility for slaves in many cultures. Once emancipated, a Roman slave ceased to carry the burden of his former status. "At a stroke [of the pen]," Finley writes, a slave "ceased to be a property. In juristic terms, he was 'transformed from an object to a subject of rights, the most complete meta-morphosis one can imagine.' He was now a human being unequivocally, in Rome even a citizen." Under Roman law "when a Roman citizen freed one of his slaves, barring certain circumstances the latter automatically acquired Roman citizenship himself." As Alan Watson has noted, this rule was "unique in the ancient world for its liberality."[14]

What was not unique for the ancient world, however, is the lack of racial stigma attached to enslavement. Former slaves in Rome, and in many other cultures, could rise to the highest levels of society. The biblical story of Joseph shows that in the ancient Near East it was not implausible to believe someone could rise from enslavement to the highest level of political power.[15] Unlike "Freedmen in the New World," who "carried an external sign of their slave origin in their skin colour, even after many generations," slaves in the ancient world who became free "simply melted into the total population within one or at the most two generations." In Rome "tens of thousands of freedmen's sons" rose "into a world remote from that of the masses."[16]

This was impossible—unfathomable—in the United States, where slavery was defined by race. White people[17] in the South were always free or, if held as indentured servants or apprentices, were in a position to become free in the future.[18] Only blacks could be slaves; no one else, however great their misfortune, could end up enslaved. While courts struggled at the margins to determine who might be black and therefore subject to enslavement, Southerners never doubted for a moment that, as South Carolina's highest court put it, "By law, every negro is presumed to be a slave."[19]

While some blacks in the South ceased to be slaves, freedom only relieved them of the burdens of servitude; it could never lead to full equality. Free blacks in the South were better off than enslaved blacks, but they remained second-class members of society. Even those few free blacks who owned substantial amounts of property—including slaves—faced a precarious existence that might be shattered by a change in public policy or popular sentiments.[20] The South limited the rights of free blacks much as it did slaves. Thus, as Thomas D. Morris shows in this volume, Southern states denied free blacks the right to testify against whites in court. Southern states also banned them from schools and certain professions, forbade them from owning firearms, and limited or prohibited their physical movements. On the eve of the Civil War, Arkansas moved to expel free blacks from the state.[21]

Blacks who lived in the antebellum North were far better off than their Southern counterparts, although they never had full equality. Racial prejudice growing out of slavery became rooted in the colonial period and remained strong in some parts of the North well after slavery expired in that region.[22] But after the Revolution many Northerners overcame their prejudices, at least they when faced the prospect of relegating a fellow human to slavery. As my own essay on Chief Justice Hornblower illustrates, Northern state courts and state laws often provided a shield for fugitive slaves and free blacks in the free states. Yet even where Northern states rejected much of the racism associated with slavery and offered a safe haven for blacks, that safety was limited. As James Oliver and Lois E. Horton describe, Northern blacks were never able to fully escape the danger of enslavement posed by the federal fugitive slave laws.

At the federal level neither slaves nor free blacks could hope for any protection. In *Dred Scott* Chief Justice Roger B. Taney nationalized Southern concepts of race. He found that under the Constitution blacks "had no rights which the white man was bound to respect." Applying a rigorous, although not necessarily accurate, intentionalist argument to determine the rights of blacks under the Constitution, Taney found "that neither the class of persons who had been imported as slaves, nor their descendants, whether they had become free or not, were then acknowledged as a part of the people, nor intended to be included in the general words used in that memorable instrument."[23]

Even emancipation and over a century of freedom have not removed the stigma of enslavement for African Americans. As Derrick Bell argues, to this day African Americans see their "slave heritage. . . more [as] a symbol of dishonor than a source of pride. It burdened black people with an indelible mark of difference as we struggled to be like whites."[24] In the end American slavery was peculiar because all the slaves were defined by race.[25]

American Ideology and Slavery

The nation's self-proclaimed political credo made American slavery especially peculiar. Yet Americans were able to accommodate slavery within their ideology. The ideological peculiarity of American slavery emerges out of the essential conflict between human bondage and the philosophical basis of the United States as a nation-state: "We hold these truths to be self-evident, that all men are created equal, that they are endowed by their Creator with certain unalienable Rights; that among these are Life, Liberty, and the pursuit of Happiness." On its face Jefferson's fine phrasing seems to be the essence of antislavery rhetoric. Thus, "Even the most radical abolitionists could not free themselves from the reverential awe with which their generation looked back upon the demigods of 1776." In urging slaves to throw off their chains (and urging whites to assist them), even the radical black abolitionist David Walker quoted the Declaration of Independence in his revolutionary *Appeal*.[26]

Northern Responses to the Declaration

Certainly in the northern part of the new nation, some people acted on the premises of the Declaration of Independence. During and after the Revolution various opponents of slavery relied on the language of natural rights and the experience of the war to explain or justify their views.[27] Thus, the Massachusetts Constitution of 1780 echoed Jefferson's language, declaring that "All men are born free and equal, and have certain natural and inalienable rights, among which may be reckoned the right of defending their lives and liberties; that of acquiring, possessing and protecting property, and in fine of seeking and obtaining their safety and happiness." Three years later, in *Commonwealth* v. *Jennison*, the Supreme Court of Massachusetts interpreted this clause, in light of the Revolution, to have ended slavery. Chief Justice William Cushing wrote:

> Sentiments more favorable to the natural rights of mankind, and to that innate desire for liberty which heaven, without regard to complexion or shape, has planted in the human breast—have prevailed since the glorious struggle for our rights began. And these sentiments led the framers of our constitution of government—by which the people of this commonwealth have solemnly bound themselves to each other—to declare—*that all men are born free and equal*; and that *every subject is entitled to liberty*, and to have it guarded by the laws as well as his life and property. In short. . . slavery is in my judgement as effectively abolished as it can be by the granting of rights and privileges wholly incompatible and repugnant to its existence.[28]

Pennsylvania's legislature also acknowledged the force of revolutionary ideology and rhetoric. Thus, the preamble to the Pennsylvania Gradual Abolition Act of 1780 notes:

> When we contemplate our abhorrence of that condition, to which the arms and tyranny of Great-Britain were exerted to reduce us, when we look back on the variety of dangers to which we have been exposed, and how miraculously our wants in many instances have been supplied, and our deliverance wrought, when even hope and human fortitude have become unequal to the conflict, we are unavoidably led to a serious and grateful sense of the manifold blessings, which we have undeservedly received from the hand of that Being, from whom every good and perfect gift cometh. Impressed with these ideas, we conceive that it is our duty, and we rejoice that it is in our power, to extend a portion of that freedom to others, which hath been extended to us, and release from that state of thraldom, to which we ourselves were tyrannically doomed, and from which we have now every prospect of being delivered.

The Pennsylvania legislators noted that it was their duty to end bondage because the institution deprived "Negro and Mulatto slaves . . . of the common blessings that they were by nature entitled to" and also led to the "unnatural separation and sale of husband and wife from each other and from their children, an injury, the greatness of which can only be conceived by supposing that we were in the same unhappy case."[29]

Massachusetts and Pennsylvania led the way towards abolition in the North. By 1804 Massachusetts, New Hampshire, and the new states of Vermont and Ohio had abolished slavery outright, while Pennsylvania and the rest of the North had passed gradual emancipation statutes that placed the institution on the road to extinction.[30] From the adoption of the Pennsylvania Gradual Emancipation statute until the eve of the Civil War, opponents of slavery would turn to the Declaration of Independence to support their cause. For these visionaries, at least, American slavery was peculiar because freedom and equality were the true basis of the nation.

Southern Slave Owners and the Declaration

Thus, as slavery was becoming "peculiar" in the United States during the Revolution, the contradiction between the rhetoric of freedom and the reality of bondage in the new nation was readily apparent. The author of the Declaration, after all, owned some 175 slaves and took no steps to liberate them during the contest with England or at any other time in his long life.[31] While thousands of individual Southern slaves gained their freedom during the Revolution, the states south of Pennsylvania remained committed to slavery. The best Virginia could offer was a statute allowing masters to free their slaves and an act to protect the freedom of former slaves who had served in the Revolutionary armies.[32] Moreover, with slaveholders from Virginia and South Carolina among the leaders of the struggle against Great Britain, there was little likelihood of any dramatic change in the status of human bondage in the new nation.

These ironies were not lost on British opponents of American independence. The English Tory Samuel Johnson pointedly asked, "How is it that we hear the loudest *yelps* for liberty among the drivers of negroes?" Even some of America's British friends were concerned by the hypocrisy of revolutionary slaveholders. Thomas Day, an English supporter of independence, thought it "truly ridiculous" to see "an American patriot, signing resolutions of independency with the one hand, and with the other brandishing a whip over his affrighted slaves."[33]

Southern masters fighting for their own liberty dodged such criticism. Virginia's first Constitution contained a Declaration of Rights that had a "free and equal" clause which mirrored the Declaration of Independence. However, the Virginia Declaration was carefully designed to finesse the issue of slavery. The document declared that:

> All men are by nature equally free and independent, and have certain inherent rights, of which, when they enter into a state of society, they cannot, by any compact, deprive or divest their posterity; namely, the enjoyment of life and liberty, with the means of acquiring and possessing property, and pursuing and obtaining happiness and safety.[34]

In his first draft of this clause George Mason had written that all men were "born equally free." Virginia's slaveholders were uncomfortable with this language. Robert Carter Nicholas, for example, declared this was "the forerunner or pretext of civil convulsion." Thus, the delegates replaced "born equally free" with "are by nature equally free." The legislature also added the phrase "when they enter into a state of society" to qualify when natural rights actually attached to individuals.[35] These two changes avoided declaring that slaves were free, but they implied that slaves might have some future claim to freedom that could be grounded in natural rights. Significantly, this language also implicitly acknowledged that slavery violated the natural rights doctrines at the foundation of the new nation.

Edmund Randolph noted that these changes were "not without inconsistency." However, Virginia's politicians were unconcerned about a "foolish consistency" that might imply that slavery was unconstitutional. Revolutionary-era Virginia, was, after all, a slaveholding republic.[36]

In *Hudgins v. Wrights* Virginia's highest court adopted this position, even though the author of the opinion personally would have preferred a different analysis. The case involved a family (the Wrights) of mixed racial ancestry, claimed as slaves by Hudgins.[37]

At trial Chancellor George Wythe of the Richmond District Court of Chancery declared the Wrights free on two grounds. The first was racial: they lacked any visible features of a Negro and appeared to be of white and American Indian ancestry. As such, they could not be held as slaves. In the trial Wythe also declared that slavery itself was illegal in Virginia because it violated the state's Declaration of Rights.

Virginia's highest court upheld Chancellor Wythe's decision to free the Wrights with an important analysis of the role of race in American slavery. However, Judge St. George Tucker, who was one of the few politicians in Virginia to publicly propose an end to slavery in the state, emphatically rejected Wythe's abolitionist application of the Virginia Declaration of Rights:

> I do not concur with the Chancellor in his reasoning on the operation of the first clause of the Bill of Rights, which was notoriously framed with a cautious eye to this subject, and was meant to embrace the case of free citizens, or aliens only; and not by a side wind to overturn the

rights of property, and give freedom to those very people whom we have been compelled from imperious circumstances to retain, generally, in the same state of bondage that they were in at the revolution, in which they had no *concern, agency* or *interest.*[38]

Virginia's most important modern state constitutional theorist, A. E. Dick Howard, has argued that "in Lockean terms" the changes made in the final draft of the Declaration of Rights were "hardly tenable, and the fact that revolutionary Virginians held slaves remained an anomaly." Certainly at first glance the language seems merely cumbersome rather than particularly exclusionary. But contemporary Virginians, as Judge Tucker's opinion showed, clearly understood the significance of the change. If they were out of step with Locke, they were in step with their own society. There was clearly nothing anomalous about Virginians owning slaves—they had been doing so for more than a century. However, slavery was clearly anomalous within the context of Lockean notions of natural rights, and to that extent it was "peculiar" in the new nation.[39]

Eventually Southerners went further, with some categorically rejecting the ideology of the Declaration of Independence. In 1826 John Randolph of Roanoke asserted that the Declaration was "a most pernicious falsehood." Edmund Ruffin, one of the South's earliest secessionists, thought the Declaration was a dangerous document. John C. Calhoun "labeled the idea of equality a 'false doctrine,' only 'hypothetically true,' that had been 'inserted' in the Declaration of Independence 'without any necessity.'" James Henry Hammond of South Carolina sneered at the "fine sounding and sentimental" language of the Declaration.[40]

In 1854 George Fitzhugh provided an elaborate proslavery attack on the Declaration. Fitzhugh believed that the United States was founded on "abstractions" that were "professed falsely." He candidly asserted that "men are not born physically, morally or intellectually equal," and contrary to the ideology of the Declaration, "Their natural inequalities beget inequalities of rights." Some people, including all blacks, were born "weak in mind or body." Fitzhugh believed that "Nature has made them slaves; all that law and government can do, is to regulate, modify and mitigate their slavery." He argued that on historical grounds "'Life and liberty' are not 'inalienable;' they have been sold in all countries, and in all ages, and must be sold so long as human nature lasts." Slavery, in Fitzhugh's mind, was not peculiar but fundamental to society. He believed the North, not the South, had a peculiar institution—freedom. He argued that the purpose of government was "to restrict, control and punish man 'in the pursuit of happiness.'" Thus, the preamble to the Declaration was "verbose, newborn, false, and unmeaning." The Declaration was "exuberantly false, and arborescently fallacious."[41]

As both William W. Fisher III and Ariela Gross note, Southern scientists supported Fitzhugh's racism with their own evidence. Dr. Josiah Nott, echoing the work of others, argued that blacks had smaller brains than whites. Dr. Samuel Cartwright believed "Africans are endowed with a will so weak, passions so easily subdued, and dispositions so gentle and affectionate that they have an instinctive feeling of obedience to the stronger will of the white man."[42] Fitzhugh, Cartwright, and other proslavery theorists argued that all men were not created equal, but that inequality was common, natural and universal. Rejecting the Declaration and its theories of equality, many Southerners instead developed their own proslavery arguments, ultimately asserting that slavery was a positive good for the slave and the master.

Other Southerners continued to endorse the Declaration but denied it could affect slavery. Some Southerners took the high road marked out by the Virginia Court in *Hudgins*. They argued that the Declaration, like its Virginia counterpart, only applied to citizens or members of political communities. Slaves were naturally excluded from these. One Virginia congressman argued that "no ingenuity" could "torture the Declaration of Independence into having the remotest allusion to the institution of domestic slavery." Alexander Stephens, the future vice president of the Confederacy, believed the framers had established "the first great principles of self-government by the governing race."[43]

The key for Stephens and other Southern supporters of the Declaration was of course race. Race made it possible for slaveholders to accept the credo of America because they could reject its application to their own slaves. Thus, one Louisiana slave owner affirmed that all men were created "free and equal as the Declaration of Independence holds they are." He then added, "But all men, niggers, and monkeys *aint.*"[44]

While Calhoun, Fitzhugh, and other white Southerners rejected the Declaration because it undermined slavery, other masters "frequently made the Fourth of July a holiday for their slaves."[45] It may seem ironic that masters took their slaves to barbecues and other celebrations of the signing of the Declaration of Independence, but for the master class this probably seemed appropriate. Independence, after all, allowed the American slaveholder to develop the political and legal system that perpetuated and strengthened slavery.

No one understood this better than the nation's best-known black abolitionist, Frederick Douglass. He admitted that the Declaration did not apply to him. Douglass asked, "What have I, or those I represent, to do with your national independence? Are the great principles of political freedom and of natural justice, embodied in that Declaration of Independence, extended to us?" Douglass wished "to God" that an "affirmative answer could be truthfully returned to these questions!"[46] But it could not. With a "sad sense" Douglass admitted:

> I am not included within the pale of this glorious anniversary! Your high independence only reveals the immeasurable distance between us. The blessings in which you, this day, rejoice, are not enjoyed in

common. The rich inheritance of justice, liberty, prosperity and independence, bequeathed by your fathers, is shared by you, not by me. The sunlight that brought life and healing to you, has brought stripes and death to me. This Fourth [of] July is *yours*, not *mine. You* may rejoice, *I* must mourn. To drag a man in fetters into the grand illuminated temple of liberty, and call upon him to join you in joyous anthems, were inhuman mockery and sacrilegious irony.[47]

The Isolation of American Slavery

Compounding the conflict between American ideology and slavery was the evolution of slavery as a sectional institution. Although the signers of the Declaration of Independence represented thirteen slaveholding states, by the time of the ratification of the Constitution, five states had ended slavery outright or were gradually abolishing it; by 1804 half the nation had taken steps to end slavery.[48]

This geographical isolation also led to increasing political weakness for the slave South. By 1810 the Northern population had surpassed that of the South, and thus the free states dominated the House of Representatives. In the next half century this Northern domination of the House became overwhelming. After the admission of California to the Union, in 1850, there were sixteen free states in the country and only fifteen slave states. By the time of Lincoln's election in 1860 eighteen of the states prohibited slavery, while in fifteen the institution remained legal. When the Civil War began, American slavery was geographically and culturally peculiar; more free states were on the horizon, with Kansas and Colorado joining the Union before the end of the Civil War.[49]

In addition to controlling the House, the North now controlled the Senate as well. The 1860 presidential election showed that the North could control the White House. Without getting a single electoral vote from any slave state, Abraham Lincoln won 180 electoral votes, while the combined total of his three opponents was only 123. By 1860 the South's geographical and political isolation undermined the section's political position within the country.

By this time American slavery was also peculiar because it was isolated in an international context. Orlando Patterson is clearly correct when he asserts that, with the exception of the modern era, slavery has always been widespread. Throughout most of human history there has been nothing "peculiar" about human bondage. But by 1861 the racially based slavery of the United States was "peculiar" because it could be found only in the American South, in Spain's few remaining New World colonies, and in Brazil.[50] By this time England, France, and the Netherlands had abolished slavery in their New World colonies. South of the Rio Grande Spain's once gigantic mainland empire was now independent and without slavery. In the context of the Atlantic community, slavery was increasingly considered cruel and uncivilized. Symbolic of the South's isolation was the 1856 Republican Party pledge "to prohibit in the Territories those twin relics of barbarism—Polygamy and Slavery."[51] Once the dominant form of labor in the New World, slavery was now an isolated relic of a less enlightened and more barbaric age.

The Peculiarities of American Slave Law

The political and geographic isolation of the slave South had a significant impact on the development of Southern legal culture.[52] Southern legal culture was distinctive in a variety of ways, but at the root of this distinctiveness was slavery.

As some of the essays here demonstrate, Southern courts and legislatures developed special—peculiar—legal rules to accommodate slavery to Anglo-American legal traditions.[53] Politicians also made legal and constitutional arguments peculiar to their own section to support the defining economic and social institution of the South.

Jonathan Bush, Judith Kelleher Schafer and Thomas D. Morris show how Southern jurists and legislators shaped certain aspects of the criminal and civil law not only to accommodate slavery but also to rationalize and bolster it. American slavery was sufficiently different from the common law that Southern lawmakers had to develop their own peculiar rules to accommodate the institution. Bush's article illustrates how they were able to do this in the colonial period. His analysis of English constitutional arrangements offers a startling new understanding of the ways in which law shaped and was shaped by slavery in the colonial period. Schafer reveals the willingness of Southern judges to allow treatment of slaves that violated both traditional notions of human decency and well-developed common-law rights of individuals. Morris shows how the status of slaves and the racial prejudices of whites limited the testimony of blacks and created contradictions within the common law that made it impossible to prosecute anyone for some crimes.

William W. Fisher III finds, despite internal contradictions, many "coherent" aspects of American slave law, which to a great extent defined slaves and blacks. Ariela Gross illustrates the ways in which defining slaves was tied to race but was also shaped by notions of gender. Thomas D. Russell's discussion of the role of South Carolina's courts in the sale of slaves underscores the internal rationality and coherence of American slave law by describing how the normal, everyday functioning of commercial and probate law affected slavery. Seen through Russell's lens, slavery, and especially the law of slavery, is not peculiar or strange. It is common, banal. While the whip remains the symbol of the authority of the master class for the day-to-day operations of slavery, Russell teaches us that the auctioneer's hammer is not an inappropriate symbol for the effect of law on slaves and masters alike.

Russell's article also sheds further light on the role of the slave auction in Southern society. As James Oakes has noted, slave owners "recoiled from the spectacle of the slave auction," and "masters frequently—though by no means always—faced the necessity of selling slaves with sincere if effusive hand-wringing." The courts, as Russell demonstrates, often relieved masters of the unpleasant task of selling slaves. The courts also provided an orderly mechanism to insure that slaves would be sold to satisfy debts, settle estates, and in other ways keep the system going. For the courts there was nothing peculiar about slaves: they were property to be sold like any other form of property. Oakes has argued persuasively that "Slave auctions were ceremonies of degradation, symbolic re-enactments of the violence of original enslavement, potent reminders of the slave's powerlessness and dishonor."[54]

Thus, through the mundane courthouse auction the legal system threw its weight—and its not inconsiderable symbolic representation of law, justice, and fairness—behind the buying and selling of slaves. Russell's article, combined with the analysis of Oakes and other historians of slavery, presents us with the frightening image of blind justice with the chains of a slave in one hand and an auctioneer's hammer in the other.

Despite the application of normal rules of probate, contract, and foreclosure to slavery, the use of courts to buy and sell people in United States is jarring. Still it underscores the foreignness—the peculiarity—of slavery to American legal culture. Indeed, the "coherent" American slave law that Fisher finds had one main thrust: to fit slavery into the system of Anglo-American common law, which of course had traditional restraints and rules that were absolutely antithetical to most aspects of slavery. Thus, as Fisher notes, unlike the common law rule that children follow the status of their father, the status of African American children was determined by that of their mother. Furthermore, slaves were, as Fisher asserts, "deprived of many civil rights and liberties: they could not make contracts or other legally binding choices, sue or be sued, acquire property, legally marry, or (with rare exceptions) testify against whites."[55]

Underscoring the debate about American slavery, Alan Watson's "Thinking Property at Rome" shows that in a different legal regime a slave might in fact acquire property, make a contract, and even bind his master to an agreement. Jacob I. Corré, looking at cases from Tennessee, notes in "Thinking Property at Memphis" that American judges also faced problems when slaves acted as "thinking property," but that a key difference between Rome and the United States was that Roman "slaves performed functions that slaves in the United States were likely never to have performed."[56] They could not perform these tasks because the racial basis of slavery in republican Tennessee and elsewhere in the South precluded acknowledging that slaves were capable of such tasks. If they could routinely perform "thinking" tasks, then black slaves would have been "created equal" to free whites, and thus deserving of their liberty. There were also security reasons for not allowing slaves to be involved in such professions. The master class feared that if slaves could read, write, and perform professional tasks, such as practicing medicine or pharmacy, they would be in a position to run away, poison their masters, or lead revolts. These fears, while common to all master classes, were more pronounced in the South because of the racial fears of white Southerners. Even someone as intelligent and reflective as Thomas Jefferson feared that the racial element of slavery might lead blacks to turn on whites, even if they were emancipated.[57]

Similarly, as Fisher illustrates, the peculiarity of slavery in the American South forced masters to create an ideological defense of their institution that was rooted in theories about the race of the enslaved. This defense, like the effect of slavery on Southern society, was ultimately seamless. A defense of slavery based on scientific theories of racial inequality, for example, justified the institution in the minds of those who bought the argument, but did not protect the institution from those who remained unpersuaded by the proslavery racial theory. The same was true for the elaborate biblical justification of slavery articulated by armies of Southern ministers. Southerners accepted the comforting argument that God sanctioned their behavior; Northerners generally rejected this interpretation of the Bible, and abolitionists rooted their opposition to slavery in Judeo-Christian values.[58]

Not surprisingly, Southerners developed their own peculiar notions about the meaning of the Constitution in order to defend slavery. As Michael Kent Curtis demonstrates, because they could not win the debate over slavery on the merits of the institution, Southerners sought to stop the debate altogether. Southerners would limit the First Amendment and the speech and debate clause of the Constitution to preclude any meaningful discussion of slavery. Thus, Hinton Rowan Helper, a white native son of North Carolina, could not remain in his home state after publishing his attack on slavery, *The Impending Crisis*, and Southern congressmen attempted to punish their Northern colleagues for endorsing or supporting that book.[59]

That Helper accepted prevailing Southern views of the racial inferiority of African Americans only underscored the threat his book posed to the peculiar institution. Since the creation of the American nation, thoughtful Southerners like Thomas Jefferson and less thoughtful ones like Senator James Henry Hammond had averred that race made slavery necessary, proper, and possible. Slavery, they argued, might not be peculiar, but only because the race of people who made up the slaves was peculiarly suited for enslavement. Helper threatened slavery precisely because he accepted the racism of the slave owners but turned it into an argument against the perpetuation of the institution.

Slavery and American Constitutionalism

The debate over Helper's book suggests the importance of slavery in American public law. Here we see in sharp focus the peculiarity of slavery and its simultaneous centrality to American society and American life from the Revolution to the Civil War.

Its legacy remains with us today. Judith Shklar, for example, has acknowledged the importance of sexism and the destructive results of "ungenerous and bigoted immigration and naturalization policies" in shaping American concepts of citizenship. But she has also noted that the "effects and defects" of these policies "pale before the history of slavery and its impact upon our public attitudes."[60]

Essays in this volume reach similar conclusions. Sanford Levinson powerfully argues that our constitutional structure developed around slavery and that we cannot fully understand modern constitutional law without devoting some time and effort to studying the law of slavery. Similarly, James Oliver Horton and Lois E. Horton's discussion of responses to the Fugitive Slave Law of 1850 illustrates how slavery made the Constitution come alive—in often horrible ways—for antebellum Americans who might otherwise have happily never encountered the Constitution or the legislation it spawned. Michael Kent Curtis shows how slavery collided with ideas of freedom of speech, freedom of the press, and representative government and thus helped shape the antebellum Constitution. And Derrick Bell reminds us here, and in much of his other work,[61] that the legacy of slavery and the racism it spawned continues to haunt our social and political structure as well as our legal system.

To this day historians argue about the relationship of slavery to the Constitution. The awful word does not appear in the document until the Thirteenth Amendment, which abolished the institution. Nevertheless, the main body of the document is littered with references to slaves as "other Persons," "such Persons," and "person held to Service or Labour." Through these clauses the South gained extra representation in Congress (and in the electoral college) because of its slaves; Congress was prohibited from interfering with the slave trade before 1808; and masters gained the right to recover fugitive slaves from other states.[62] Throughout the Constitutional Convention the framers talked frankly about slavery, although in the end they decided not to use the term in the final document because they feared it would undermine support for ratification in the North.

In addition to those clauses specifically relating to slavery a number of other provisions in the document protected the institution by empowering Congress to call "forth the Militia" to "suppress Insurrections," including slave rebellions; to prohibit taxes on all exports and prohibiting state taxes on imports, thus preventing an indirect tax on slavery by taxing the staple products of slave labor, such as tobacco, rice, and eventually cotton; to provide for the indirect election of the president through an electoral college based on congressional representation, thus incorporating slaves into the scheme through the three-fifths clause and thereby giving whites in slave states a disproportionate influence in the election of the president.[63]

Finally, the structure of the Constitution ensured against emancipation by the new federal government. The amendment provision of Article V requires a three-fourths majority of the states to amend the Constitution, thus ensuring that the slaveholding states would have a perpetual veto over any constitutional changes.[64] Because the Constitution created a government of limited powers, Congress lacked the power to interfere in the domestic institutions of the states.[65] Thus, during the ratification debates only the most fearful Southern antifederalists opposed the Constitution on the grounds that it threatened slavery.[66] Most Southerners, even those who opposed the Constitution for other reasons, agreed with General Charles Cotesworth Pinckney of South Carolina, who told his state's House of Representatives:

> We have a security that the general government can never emancipate them, for no such authority is granted and it is admitted, on all hands, that the general government has no powers but what are expressly granted by the Constitution, and that all rights not expressed were reserved by the several states.[67]

Conclusion

In 1863 Abraham Lincoln would reflect on the creation of the American nation. It began, according to Lincoln, in 1776 as one "dedicated to the proposition that all men are created equal."[68] Lincoln was rhetorically brilliant in reinterpreting the Declaration into a libertarian credo that supported the war effort. But as a matter of history and law, Lincoln's assertion was far from the mark.

Since the founding, slaves had constituted the second most valuable form of privately held property in the nation, after real estate. Furthermore, slaves constituted about 25 percent of the population of the South. In 1790 the census found 697,642 slaves in the United States, most living in the South. By 1860 this population had grown to 3,922,760, all of them in the South.[69]

It would have been unnatural and unreasonable for the founders, who were keenly aware of the importance of private property, not to have protected this most important kind of property in their constitutional and legal structure. The founders were not unmindful of their property interests, and they protected them at every level of their legal system.

Equally important, many of the founders, and subsequent generations of Southern judges and politicians, also understood the racial basis of slavery. Beyond the economic value of the system was its peculiar racial characteristics that prevented Southern whites from contemplating abolition. With leaders like Thomas Jefferson refusing even to consider the possibility of racial equality or emancipation within the United States, the South created a legal regime for its section—and a constitutional regime for the nation—that protected slavery at every turn. The result was a hardening of legal doctrine and constitutional interpretation that precluded any peaceful end to slavery. This made slavery peculiar in terms of American ideology and the liberalism of the mid-nineteenth-century Atlantic community; but it also made slavery a fundamental and entrenched legal and social institution that was impervious to legal or political assault.

Notes

An earlier version of this article initially appeared as "The Centrality of the Peculiar Institution in American Legal Development," *Chicago-Kent Law Review* 68 (1993) 1009–1033. I thank Peter Wallenstein, Michael Kent Curtis, and David Q. Burgess for their helpful comments on this article.

1. Kenneth Stampp, *The Peculiar Institution: Slavery in the Antebellum United States* (New York: Random House, 1956), 3; *Brown* v. *Board of Education*, 347 U.S. 483 (1954).

2. Orlando Patterson, *Slavery and Social Death: A Comparative Study* (Cambridge: Harvard University Press, 1982), vii.

3. The range of work on slavery is dramatic. For example, see M. I. Finley, *Ancient Slavery and Modern Ideology* (New York: Viking Press, 1980); M. I. Finley, ed., *Classical Slavery* (London: Cass, 1987); David Brion Davis, *The Problem of Slavery in Western Culture* (Ithaca: Cornell University Press, 1964); Ruth Mazo Karras, *Slavery and Society in Medieval Scandinavia* (New Haven: Yale University Press, 1988); Carl O. Williams, *Thraldom in Ancient Iceland* (Chicago: University of Chicago Press, 1937); William D. Phillips Jr., *Slavery from Roman Times to the Early Transatlantic Trade* (Minneapolis: University of Minnesota Press, 1985); Ehud R. Toledano, *The Ottoman Slave Trade and Its Suppression: 1840–1890* (Princeton: Princeton University Press, 1982); Léonie J. Archer, ed., *Slavery and Other Forms of Unfree Labour* (London: Routledge, 1988); Richard Hellie, *Slavery in Russia, 1450–1725* (Chicago: University of Chicago Press, 1982); Suzanne Miers and Igor Kopytoff, eds., *Slavery in Africa: Historical and Anthropological Perspectives* (Madison: University of Wisconsin Press, 1977).

4. Finley, *Ancient Slavery*, 9. The other four slave societies were classical Greece, ancient Rome, Brazil, and the Caribbean.

5. Paul Finkelman, *Slavery and the Founders: Race and Liberty in the Age of Jefferson* (Armonk, N.Y.: M.E. Sharpe, 1996), 1–33. William M. Wiecek, "Slavery

and Abolition before the United States Supreme Court, 1820–1860," Journal of American History 65 (1979): 34. See generally William M. Wiecek, *The Sources of Antislavery Constitutionalism in America, 1760–1848* (Ithaca: Cornell University Press, 1977).

6. See generally Leon F. Litwack, *North of Slavery: The Negro in the Free States, 1790–1860* (Chicago: University of Chicago Press, 1961). For a more nuanced analysis that focuses directly on the legal rights of antebellum Northern blacks and reaches a somewhat different conclusion, see Paul Finkelman, "Prelude to the Fourteenth Amendment: Black Legal Rights in the Antebellum North," 17 *Rutgers Law Journal* 415 (1986).

7. *Dred Scott* v. *Sandford*, 60 U.S. (19 How.) 393 (1857). *Prigg* v. *Pennsylvania*, 41 U.S. (16 Pet.) 539 (1842). See, for example, Chief Justice Marshall's opinion in The Antelope, 23 U.S. (10 Wheat.) 66 (1825), upholding the legality of the African slave trade under international law. For a discussion of this case, see Robert Cover, *Justice Accused: Antislavery and the Judicial Process* (New Haven: Yale University Press, 1977), 102–4. See also Wiecek, "Slavery and Abolition."

8. James Henry Hammond, Speech on Admission of Kansas, Address before the U.S. Senate (Mar. 4, 1858), in Cong. Globe, 35th Cong., No. Sess. 961–62; partially reprinted in *Slavery Defended: The Views of the Old South*, ed. Erik McKitrick (Englewood Cliffs, N.J.: Prentice Hall, 1963), 121–25.

9. Finley, *Ancient Slavery*, 117.

10. David Brion Davis, "Slavery and the American Mind," in *Perspectives and Irony in American Slavery*, ed. Harry P. Owens [hereinafter cited as *Perspectives and Irony*] (Jackson: University of Mississippi Press, 1976), 59.

11. Carl N. Degler, *Neither Black nor White: Slavery and Race Relations in Brazil and the United States* (New York: Macmillan, 1971). C. L. R. James, *The Black Jacobins: Toussaint L'Ouverture and the San Domingo Revolution* (New York: Dial Press, 1980). Finley, *Ancient Slavery*, 11.

12. Carl N. Degler, "The Irony of American Negro Slavery," in *Perspectives and Irony*, 19. M. I. Finley has argued that "racism" was a factor in ancient slavery "despite the absence of the skin-colour stigma; despite the variety of peoples who made up the ancient slave populations; despite the frequency of manumission and its peculiar consequences." See Finley, *Ancient Slavery*, 118. Thus, it was "commonplace in Roman Republican speeches that Jews, Syrians, Lydians, Medes, indeed all Asiatics are 'born to slavery.'" Ibid., 119. *Racism* in this context really refers to ethnocentrism and the attitude of masters toward the "barbarian" outsiders who made up the bulk of the slave population in the ancient world. However, despite his use of the term *racism*, Finley has noted the importance of color and "race" in the New World and how it created a slave system quite different from that of antiquity. Ibid., 118.

13. In the 1940s Germans enslaved their fellow countrymen (as well as the Russians, Poles, and other Europeans). Those sent to German industries as slaves or sent to German slave-labor camps (as opposed to death camps like Auschwitz) were often physically indistinguishable from those who commanded their labor. However, under German theories of race those enslaved were designated as members of different races or as politically corrupted.

14. Finley, *Ancient Slavery*, 97; Alan Watson, *Roman Law and Comparative Law* (Athens: University of Georgia Press, 1991), 11.

15. Gen. 39–41. Whether the story of Joseph is accurate or not (or even

happened at all) is irrelevant. My point here is that no one doubted it could have happened, despite the fact that Joseph was a "Hebrew" living in Egypt. It is of course quite impossible to imagine an African American slave gaining his freedom and becoming an advisor to a political leader at any time before the Civil War.

16. Finley, *Ancient Slavery*, 97, 98. This was also the case in Africa, where "slaves could often anticipate the gradual assimilation of their descendants into the social mainstream." See James Oakes, *Slavery and Freedom: An Interpretation of the Old South* (New York: Random House, 1990), 32.

17. It is impossible to find clear and consistent definitions of race in the colonial or antebellum South. Throughout the slaveholding South, people who had predominately European or Native American ancestors were held as slaves and considered "black," even though their outward appearance suggested otherwise. For some preliminary discussion of this, see Paul Finkelman, "The Color of Law," 87 *Northwestern University Law Review* 937, 950–57 (1993); Paul Finkelman, "The Crime of Color," 67 *Tulane Law Review* 2063 (1993).

18. North Carolina's Chief Justice Thomas Ruffin discussed at length the distinction between slaves and emancipated white children or apprentices in the famous case of *State* v. *Mann*, 13 N.C. (2 Dev.) 229 (1829). The U.S. Constitution also recognizes this distinction. In determining representation in the House of Representatives, the Constitution counts "Persons... bound to Service for a Term of Years" with other free persons, and then added to that number "three fifths of all Persons." *U.S. Const.*, art. I, § 2, par. 3.

19. *State* v. *Harden*, 29 S.C.L. (2 Speers) 151n, 155n (1832). For cases discussing race on the margins, see *Gobu* v. *Gobu*, 1 N.C. 188 (Tay.) (1802); *Hudgins* v. *Wrights*, 11 Va. (1 Hen. & M.) 134 (1806); In *Adelle* v. *Beauregard*, 1 Mart. 183 (La. 1810) the Louisiana Superior Court asserted that blacks were presumptively slaves but that free persons of color were presumptively free. No other Southern state took this position with regard to people of mixed racial heritage.

20. Ira Berlin, *Slaves Without Masters: The Free Negro in the Antebellum South* (New York: Pantheon, 1974); John Hope Franklin, *The Free Negro In North Carolina, 1790–1860* (Chapel Hill: University of North Carolina Press, 1943). Michael P. Johnson and James L. Roark, *Black Masters: A Free Family of Color in the Old South* (New York: Norton, 1984).

21. Berlin, *Slaves Without Masters*, 96–97, 304–5, Robert J. Cottrol and Raymond T. Diamond, "The Second Amendment: Toward an Afro-Americanist Reconsideration," 80 *Georgetown Law Journal* 309, 325 (1991). For example, most Southern states prohibited free blacks from entering their jurisdiction, even on a temporary basis. Most of the Southern coastal states provided for the imprisonment of free black sailors from the North or the British Empire if the sailors entered their ports. The black seamen would be released only when their ship sailed and after their captains had paid for their maintenance while in jail. The only litigation on this was *Elkison* v. *Deliesseline*, 8 F. Cas. 493, 494 (C.C.D.S.C. 1823) (No. 4,366) For discussion of this problem, see Paul Finkelman, "The Constitution and the Intentions of the Framers: The Limits of Historical Analysis," 50 *University of Pittsburgh Law Review* 349, 386–90 (1989). 1860 Ark. Acts 62, 99.

22. See Finkelman, "Prelude to the Fourteenth Amendment"; and Litwack, *North of Slavery.* Finkelman, "Color of Crime." For a discussion of the nonlegal

aspects of race and slavery in colonial America, see generally Davis, "Slavery and the American Mind"; Edmund Morgan, *American Slavery, American Freedom: The Ordeal of Colonial Virginia* (New York: Norton, 1975); and Winthrop Jordan, *White over Black: American Attitudes towards the Negro, 1550–1812* (Chapel Hill: University of North Carolina Press, 1968).

23. *Dred Scott* v. *Sandford, supra* note 7 at 407.

24. Derrick Bell, "Learning the Three *I*s of America's Slave Heritage," in this volume, 30.

25. Although most premodern societies did not define slavery by race, modern Germany's horrible use of slave labor in the 1930s and 1940s also used race (as the Germans defined it) as the criterion for enslavement and then extermination.

26. David Brion Davis, *Slavery and Human Progress* (New York: Oxford University Press, 1984), 150. David Walker, *Appeal, in Four Articles, Together with a Preamble to the Colored Citizens of the World* (Boston: David Walker, 1829).

27. See, for example, the discussion in David Brion Davis, *Slavery in the Age of Revolution, 1780–1823* (Ithaca: Cornell University Press, 1975), 332–33.

28. MASS. CONST. of 1780, art. I. *Commonwealth* v. *Jennison* [unreported] (Mass., 1783); reprinted in Paul Finkelman, ed., *The Law of Freedom and Bondage* (New York: Oceana, 1986) 35–37.

29. Act of Mar. 1, 1780, at §§ 1 and 2, ("An Act for the Gradual Abolition of Slavery"); reprinted in Finkelman, *Law of Freedom and Bondage,* 42–45.

30. Gradual emancipation laws were adopted in Pennsylvania (1780), Connecticut (1784), Rhode Island (1784), New York (1799), and New Jersey (1804). The history of this is discussed in Arthur Zilversmit, *The First Emancipation: The Abolition of Slavery in the North* (Chicago: University of Chicago Press, 1967).

31. During his life, and in his will Jefferson freed a total of eight slaves, all of them members of the Hemings family. These slaves were the children and grandchildren of Jefferson's father-in-law, John Wayles, and thus related to Jefferson through marriage. Jefferson made no effort to change the status of the three to four hundred other slaves he owned during the fifty years between the signing of Declaration and his death, on July 4, 1826. Finkelman, *Slavery and the Founders* 105, 107, 129.

32. See generally Benjamin Quarles, *The Negro in the American Revolution* (Chapel Hill: University of North Carolina Press, 1961); Berlin, *Slaves without Masters,* 16–25. "An Act to authorize the manumission of slaves," 1782 Va. Acts, ch. 61, and "An Act directing the emancipation of certain slaves who have served as soldiers in this state, and for the emancipation of the slave Aberdeen," 1783 Va. Acts, ch. 190, both reprinted in Finkelman, *Law of Freedom and Bondage,* 109–11.

33. Samuel Johnson, quoted in Donald L. Robinson, *Slavery in the Age of Revolution, 1765–1820,* (New York: Harcourt, Brace, Jovanovich, 1971), 80. Thomas Day, quoted in Davis, *Slavery in the Age of Revolution, 1780–1823,* 398–99.

34. The Declaration of Rights actually predated the Declaration of Independence. Virginia's legislators agreed to the final draft of the state bill of rights on June 12, 1776. A. E. Dick Howard, *Commentaries on the Constitution of Virginia* (Charlottesville: University Press of Virginia, 1974), 1:58 n.2. See also *The Papers of George Mason, 1725–1792,* 3 vols., ed. Robert A. Rutland (Chapel Hill: University of North Carolina Press, 1970), 1:275–77, 283–89. Va. Const. of 1776, art. I,

§ 1; reprinted in *Sources and Documents of United States Constitutions*, ed. William F. Swindler (Dobbs Ferry, N.Y.: Oceana, 1979), 10:49.

35. Mason was no abolitionist, however, and it is unlikely that he thought his expansive language would have affected slavery. See Peter Wallenstein, "Flawed Keepers of the Flame: The Interpreters of George Mason," *Virginia Magazine of History and Biography* 102 (1994): 229–60. Quoted in Howard, *Commentaries on the Constitution of Virginia*, 1:61 [footnotes omitted].

36. Ibid. "A foolish consistency is the hobgoblin of little minds, adored by little statesmen and philosophers and divines." Ralph Waldo Emerson, quoted in *John Bartlett, Familiar Quotations*, 15th ed., ed. Emily Morrison Beck (Boston: Little, Brown, 1980), 497.

37. *Hudgins* v. *Wrights, supra* note 24, at 141, 144.

38. Ibid. at 141. Wythe's opinion has not survived, but the nature of it is made clear by the majority opinion in *Hudgins*. St. George Tucker, *A Dissertation on Slavery: With a Proposal for the Gradual Abolition of It, in the State of Virginia* (Philadelphia: Mathew Carey, 1796).

39. Howard, *Commentaries on the Constitution of Virginia*, 1:62. In fact, it is not at all clear what Locke would have thought. Locke helped draft, along with his patron, Anthony Ashley Cooper, Earl of Shaftsbury, the Fundamental Constitutions of Carolina. That document provided, "Every freeman of Carolina, shall have absolute power and authority over his negro slaves, of what opinion or religion soever." The Fundamental Constitutions of Carolina, § 110 (1669); reprinted in 1 *Statutes at Large of South Carolina* 55 (Thomas Cooper and David J. McCord eds., Columbia, S.C., 1836). Tucker's opinion also hints that continued ownership of slaves was not inconsistent with regard to Lockean notions of property and the formation of political communities. *Hudgins* v. *Wrights, supra* note 24, at 141.

40. John Randolph, quoted in William S. Jenkins, *Pro-slavery Thought in the Old South* (Chapel Hill: University of North Carolina Press, 1935), 60. Ironically, Randolph freed all his slaves. See, Finkelman, *Slavery and the Founders*, 161. John C. Calhoun, quoted in Frederick Douglass, *Speeches, Debates, and Interviews, 1847–54*, ed. John W. Blassingame, 1st ser., vol. 2 of *The Frederick Douglass Papers* (New Haven: Yale University Press, 1982), 488 n.15; James Henry Hammond, quoted in Harvey Wish, *George Fitzhugh: Propagandist of the Old South* (Baton Rouge: Louisiana State University Press, 1943), 96.

41. George Fitzhugh, *Sociology for the South; or, The Failure of Free Society* (Richmond: A. Morris, 1854), 177–82. The implication of Fitzhugh's analysis is that some whites were fit for slavery as well. See generally Jenkins, *Pro-slavery Thought*; Eugene D. Genovese, *The World the Slaveholders Made* (New York: Pantheon, 1969).

42. Samuel Cartwright, "On the Caucasians and the Africans," *Debow's Review* 25 (July 1858): 45.

43. Jenkins, *Pro-slavery Thought*, 156–57. Alexander Stephens, quoted in James Oakes, *The Ruling Race: A History of Slaveholders* (New York: Vintage Books, 1982), 143.

44. Oakes, *The Ruling Race*, 143.

45. Ibid., 142.

46. Frederick Douglass, "What to the Slave is the Fourth of July? An Address Delivered in Rochester, New York, on 5 July 1852," in Douglass, *Speeches, Debates, and Interviews, 1847–54*, 359, 367.

47. Ibid., 368.

48. See generally Zilversmit, *The First Emancipation*; Paul Finkelman, *An Imperfect Union: Slavery, Federalism, and Comity* (Chapel Hill: University of North Carolina Press, 1981), chaps. 1–2. By this time Massachusetts (1780), New Hampshire (1784), and two new states, Vermont (1791) and Ohio (1803), had abolished slavery outright in their constitutions, while Pennsylvania (1784), Connecticut (1784), Rhode Island (1784), New York (1799), and New Jersey (1804) had adopted gradual emancipation statutes that would end slavery over time.

49. The whole population of the country was 9,638,453 in 1820. In that year the eleven Southern states had a population of 4,298,199. The free population in the South was 2,802,010 and the slave population was 1,496,189. The North had a free population of just under 5,340,00 people. West Virginia also joined the Union during the Civil War, but the addition of the state could not have been anticipated before the war, and indeed happened only because of the war.

50. Eugene Genovese has argued that slaveholders "stood alongside the slaveholding planters of Brazil and Cuba, alongside the Russian lords… [a]nd as late as 1861 the southern slaveholders also stood alongside such dying but still deadly landholding classes as those of Poland, Hungary, Italy, and Japan, which commanded unfree or only technically free labor in regimes even then looked upon as barbarous by both the bourgeois and laboring classes of Western Europe." Eugene D. Genovese, "Slavery—the World's Burden," in *Perspectives and Irony*, 30. He has also compared Southern slaveholders to the Junkers of Germany. But these comparisons do not work well. Certainly, most Southern masters did not see themselves in the same camp with despotic, anti-democratic landowners of Europe or Asia.

51. Republican Party Platform, 1856, quoted in James M. McPherson, *Ordeal by Fire*, 2d ed. (New York: Alfred A. Knopf, 1993), 99. The reference to polygamy was an attack on the Mormon community in Utah.

52. Paul Finkelman, "Exploring Southern Legal History," 64 *North Carolina Law Review* 77 (1985); Kermit Hall and James W. Ely Jr., eds., *An Uncertain Tradition: Constitutionalism and the History of the South* (Athens: University of Georgia Press, 1989); David J. Bodenhamer and James W. Ely Jr., eds., *Ambivalent Legacy: A Legal History of the South* (University; Miss.: University of Mississippi Press, 1984).

53. Or, in the case of Judith Kelleher Schafer's essay in this volume, to both Franco-American and Anglo-American traditions.

54. James Oakes, *Slavery and Freedom*, 22, 24.

55. William W. Fisher, III, "Ideology and Imagery in the Law of Slavery," in this volume, 43.

56. Jacob I. Corré, "Thinking Property at Memphis: An Application of Watson," in this volume, 437.

57. Jefferson wrote about the possibility of emancipation: "Deep rooted prejudices entertained by the whites; ten thousand recollections, by the blacks, of the injuries they have sustained; new provocations; the real distinctions which nature has made; and many other circumstances, will divide us into parties, and produce convulsions which will probably never end but in the extermination of the one or the other race." Thomas Jefferson, *Notes on the State of Virginia*, ed. William Peden (Chapel Hill: University of North Carolina Press, 1954), 138. See also Finkelman, *Slavery and the Founders*, Chaps 5 and 6.

58. See, for example, William R. Stanton, *The Leopard's Spots: Scientific Atti-

tudes toward Race in America, 1815–1859 (Chicago: University of Chicago Press, 1960); Josiah Nott and George Gliddon, *Types of Mankind* (Philadelphia: J. B. Lippincott, 1854); Fitzhugh, Sociology for the South; I. A. Newby, *Challenge to the Court: Social Scientists and the Defense of Segregation, 1954–1966* (Baton Rouge: Louisiana State University Press, 1967), 8–9. Thorton Stringfellow, "A Scriptural View of Slavery," in *Slavery Defended: The Views of the Old South* ed. Erik McKitrick (Englewood Cliffs, N.J.: Prentice Hall, 1963), 86. See also various articles in Paul Finkelman, ed., *Articles on American Slavery: Religion and Slavery*, vol. 11 (New York: Garland, 1989).

59. Hinton Rowan Helper, *The Impending Crisis of the South: How to Meet It* (New York: Burdick Brothers, 1857).

60. Judith Shklar, *American Citizenship: The Quest for Inclusion* (Cambridge: Harvard University Press, 1991), 13–14.

61. See for example Derrick Bell, *And We Are Not Saved: The Elusive Quest for Racial Justice* (New York: The Free Press, 1987); Derrick Bell, *Faces at the Bottom of the Well: The Permanence of Racism* (New York: Free Press, 1992).

62. U.S. CONST., art. I, § 2, cl. 3 (Three-fifths clause); art. I, § 9, cl. 1 (Migration and Importation clause). This latter clause has often been misconstrued to have required the end of the slave trade in 1808. It did not in fact require anything; it merely prohibited a ban on the trade before 1808. Article V reinforced this provision by prohibiting any amendment of the slave trade provision before 1808. Art. IV, § 2, cl. 3 (Fugitives from Labour clause).

63. U.S. CONST., art. I, § 8, cl. 15. The abolitionist Wendell Phillips considered this clause, and a similar one in art. IV, § 4, to be among the five key proslavery provisions of the Constitution. Wendell Phillips, *The Constitution, a Pro-Slavery Compact; or, Selections from the Madison Papers*, 2d ed. (New York: American Antislavery Society, 1845), vi; U.S. CONST., art. I, § 9, cl. 5; § 10, cl. 2. U.S. CONST., art. II, § 1, cl. 2.

64. Had all fifteen slave states remained in the Union, they would to this day be able to prevent an amendment on any subject. In a fifty-state union, it takes only thirteen states to block an amendment.

65. Under various clauses of the Constitution the Congress might have protected, limited, or prohibited the interstate slave trade: art. I, § 8, cl. 3; slavery in the District of Columbia or on military bases: art. I, § 8, cl. 17; or slavery in the territories: art. IV, § 3, cl. 2. None of these clauses permitted Congress to touch slavery in the states. Some radical abolitionists argued that under the Guarantee clause (art. IV, § 4) Congress had the right to end slavery in the states. See Wiecek, *Sources of Antislavery Constitutionalism*, 269–71. The delegates in Philadelphia did not debate these clauses with slavery in mind, although the Commerce clause was accepted as part of a bargain over the African slave trade. See Finkelman, *Slavery and the Founders*, 20–32.

66. One such southerner was Patrick Henry, who used any argument he could find to oppose the Constitution. Henry asserted at the Virginia ratifying convention that "among ten thousand implied powers which they may assume, they may, if we be engaged in war, liberate every one of your slaves if they please." Quoted in Jonathan Elliot, ed., *The Debates in the Several State Conventions on the Adoption of the Federal Constitution*, 2d ed. (Philadelphia: J. B. Lippincott, 1836), 3:589. Ironically, the implied war powers of the president would be used to end slavery, but only after the South had renounced the Union.

67. Elliot, ed., *Debates in the Several State Conventions*, 4:286.

68. Abraham Lincoln, "Address Delivered at the Dedication of the Cemetery at Gettysburg," in *Collected Works of Abraham Lincoln,* ed. Roy P. Basler, 9 vols., (New Brunswick: Rutgers University Press, 1953), 7:23.

69. U.S. Census Bureau, *Negro Population, 1790–1915* (Washington, D.C.: Government Printing Office, 1918), 57.

Part I

Theories of Democracy and the Law of Slavery

1

Learning the Three "I"s of America's Slave Heritage

Derrick Bell

THE YEAR IS 1993. In a first-grade classroom in rural Chester County, Pennsylvania, a six-year-old boy and girl, the only black children in the first-grade class, are summoned to the front of the room by their white teacher. To show the class how slavery worked, the teacher holds a mock slave auction.

"Teacher put us up on a table. Acted like she was selling us," the little girl later reported, adding that the teacher told her she would be sold for about ten dollars as a house cleaner.

The little boy said that the teacher used him to demonstrate how slaves, with shirts stripped off their backs, were chained to a post before a flogging. He "would have big legs and strong muscles," the teacher told the boy and his classmates.

Later, when the classroom demonstration became public, the teacher apologized. She told reporters that she was trying to teach the children about black history. "I did not view it as racial. I wanted to teach the children about prejudice. I did not do it with malice or to embarrass anyone."

The mothers of the two children rejected the apology. They and many in the black community who picketed the school wanted the teacher fired. A black high school student said she felt uncomfortable in class when teachers discussed slavery. "It's humiliating. Why do we have to be reminded of it?"[1]

The white teacher, though, had the right idea. Children do need to learn the history of slavery. It was her execution that was seriously flawed.[2] The unhappy incident illustrates that the parents, the teacher, the class, and Americans generally would benefit from a primer on the three I's of the nation's slave heritage: Information, Interpretation, and Inspiration.

Information

This collection of essays on the law of slavery serves the valuable role of presenting data about what remains an area of American history little known because the facts about—as opposed to the fact of—slavery have been systematically consigned to an era of our history that has been deemed better forgotten. As a result, slavery, though dead, has never been buried. To this day, as the misguided slave auction reveals, the nation has not come to grips with the continuing significance of its slavery origins. Blacks have continued to feel the stigma of slavery, while whites have felt neither burden nor blame.

When I was growing up in the years before the Second World War, our slave heritage was more a symbol of dishonor than a source of pride. It burdened black people with an indelible mark of difference as we struggled to be like whites. Survival and progress of the race seemed to require moving beyond, even rejecting, slavery. Childhood friends in a West Indian family who lived a few doors away often boasted—erroneously, as I later learned—that their people had never been slaves. My own more accurate, but hardly more praiseworthy, response was that my forebears included many free Negroes, some of whom had Choctaw and Blackfoot Indian blood.

In those days self-delusion was both easy and comforting. Slavery was barely mentioned in the schools and was seldom discussed by the descendants of its survivors, particularly those who had somehow moved themselves to the North. Emigration to the North; whether from the Caribbean islands or from the Deep South states—even though slavery had flourished in both the islands and in several Northern states—provided a geographical distance that encouraged and enhanced individual denial of our collective, slave past. We sang spirituals but detached the songs from their slave origins. As I look back, I see this reaction as no less sad for being so very understandable. Negroes were a subordinate and mostly shunned portion of a society that managed to lay the onus of slavery neatly on those whose forebears were slaves yet simultaneously to exonerate those whose forebears were slaveholders. All things considered, it seemed a history best left alone.

Then after the Second World War, and particularly in the 1960s, slavery became—for a few academics and some militant Negroes—a subject of fascination and a sure means of evoking racial rage as a prelude to righteously repeated demands for "Freedom *now!*" In response to a renascence of interest in our past, new books on slavery were written, and long out-of-print volumes were republished. The new awareness reached its highest point in 1977 with the television version of Alex Haley's autobiographical novel *Roots*.[3] The highly successful miniseries informed millions of Americans—black as well as white—that slavery in fact had existed and that it had been awful. Not, of course, as awful as it would have been save for the good white folks whom the television writers had created to ease the slaves' anguish, along with the evil ones on whose shoulders they placed all the guilt. Through the magic of literary license, white viewers could feel revulsion for slavery without necessarily recognizing American slavery as a burden on the nation's history, certainly not a burden requiring reparations in the present.

But the stigma associated with slavery refuses to fade, along with the deeply embedded personal attitudes and public policy assumptions that supported it for so long. Indeed, the racism that made slavery feasible is far from dead in the last decade of twentieth-century America; and the civil rights gains, so hard won, are being steadily eroded.

Because the real scope and significance of slavery in the nation's past remains repressed, most Americans cannot imagine, much less concede, that black people are now, as were our forebears when they were brought to the New World, objects of barter for those who, while profiting from our existence, deny our humanity. It is in the light of this fact that we must consider the haunting questions about slavery and exploitation contained in Professor Linda Myers's book, *Understanding an Afrocentric World View*,[4] questions that serve as their own answer.

We simply cannot prepare realistically for our future without assessing honestly our past. It seems cold, accusatory; but we must try to fathom with her "the mentality of a people that could continue for over three hundred years to kidnap an estimated fifty million youth and young adults from Africa, transport them across the Atlantic with about half dying unable to withstand the inhumanity of the passage, and enslave them as animals?"[5]

In our assessment we cannot ignore the fact that Americans did not invent slavery.[6] The practice has existed throughout recorded history, and Professor Orlando Patterson, a respected scholar, argues impressively that American slavery was no worse than that practiced in other parts of the world.[7] But it is not comparative slavery policies that concern me. Slavery as an example of what white America has done is both an explanation of the lack of concern for the dire circumstances in which so many blacks live and a constant reminder of what white America might do.

Interpretation

The second I is Interpretation, or more specifically an interpretation of slavery in American law. Most Americans likely see little present significance in the fact that the framers of this country's Constitution saw fit to recognize slavery.[8] Relatively few even know that while the Constitution is proclaimed as the model charter of individual freedom, as originally written it contained no less than ten provisions intended to recognize and protect property in slaves.[9]

How did this happen? Quite simply, the Constitution's framers felt that a government committed to the protection of property could not come into being without the race-based slavery compromises placed in the Constitution. Surely the economic benefits of slavery made a successful Revolution possible, and the political compromises of black rights that began in Philadelphia played a major role in the nation's growth and development.

But many will ask whether the history of slavery in this country has any value, beyond its guilt-evoking potential, in analyzing contemporary social policies and legal doctrine. Constitutional apologists explain away recognition and protection of slavery in the original Constitution as a historical anomaly that occurred because (1) most whites in the late eighteenth century (including many of the framers) believed that Africans were a lesser order of humans, and (2) the dire need for a strong central government committed to the protection of property pushed the framers to accept protection even of property in slaves, despite the realization by many of them that slavery was morally wrong. The rationale for many of the framers was the widespread expectation that slavery would soon die out on its own.[10]

It is clear that the fact of slavery in American law and the varying status of slaves presented dilemmas that allowed courts only the options of self-destruction or disgrace. Most chose the latter course with results that reflected the priority property held over both persons and morality.[11] Those tortured opinions of the past strike sparks of familiarity with all too many current racial decisions. Just how much reliance can we place in assurances that American slavery is an artifact of history with no contemporary relevance? Unfortunately, history contains any number of postslavery instances where black rights were sacrificed in order to protect the political or property interests of whites—or some of them.

The Constitution, with its condemnation of Africans to slavery, was written and adopted at the end of the eighteenth century. By the end of the nineteenth century, the citizenship rights won by the former slaves after the Civil War had been stripped of all but their ceremonial meaning in a series of political deals like the Hayes-Tilden Compromise of 1876. There, to settle a presidential election dispute that threatened a renewed civil war and to secure the presidency for the Republican, Hayes, the North agreed to withdraw federal troops from the South, leaving the already hard-pressed blacks to the not-too-tender mercies of former slaveowners.[12]

By 1900, when the U.S. Census reported that there were 8,833,994 Negroes, representing 11.6 percent of the population,[13] most blacks, wherever they lived in the country, had been disenfranchised either by statute or state constitutional amendment.[14] Segregation was widespread, and in 1896 its "separate but equal" status (the ultimate oxymoron) gained Supreme Court approval in *Plessy* v. *Ferguson*.[15]

Now, with the twentieth century well into its final decade, formal segregation is ended. Judicial precedent and a plethora of civil rights statutes prohibit racial discrimination. Noncompliance is more the rule than the exception, yet the Constitution's slavery provisions do seem unhappy reminders of a less enlightened era.

But are they? Racism is far from dead in modern America. Despite undeniable progress for many, no American of African descent is safe from discriminatory events, ranging from unthinking insult to career- and even life-threatening episodes. Even the most successful of us are haunted by the plight of our less-fortunate brethren, who must struggle for existence in what social scientists call the *underclass*. Burdened with lifelong poverty and soul-devastating despair, they live their lives beyond the pale of the American Dream.

Moreover, as in the eighteenth century, promising racial reforms of the 1950s and 1960s have been eroded by racial barriers more subtle but for most African Americans hardly less discriminatory than the Jim Crow laws that a century earlier mandated segregation while legitimizing deeply held beliefs in white supremacy. What no one predicted is that the semblance of equal opportunity, combined with a host of economic changes in the work force, would have a devastating effect on poor blacks, particularly those locked in the large inner cities of our major urban areas.

But black people at every economic level are caught in a double bind. We are disadvantaged unless whites perceive that nondiscriminatory treatment for us will be a benefit for them. In addition, even when non-racist practices might bring a benefit, whites may rely on discrimination against blacks as a unifying factor and a safety valve for frustrations during economic hard times.

Almost always the injustices that dramatically diminish the rights of blacks are linked to the serious economic disadvantage suffered by many whites who lack money and power. Rather than acknowledge the similarity of their disadvantage, particularly when compared with those better off, whites easily allow themselves to be persuaded that they must protect their sense of entitlement vis-à-vis blacks for all things of value. Evidently this racial-preference expectation is hypnotic. It is this compulsive fascination that seems to prevent most whites from even seeing—much less resenting—the far more sizable gap between their status and that of those who occupy the lofty levels at the top of our society.

Race consciousness of this character, as Professor Kimberlé Crenshaw suggests in her pathbreaking *Harvard Law Review* article, makes it difficult for whites "to imagine the world differently. It also creates the desire for identification with privileged elites. By focusing on a distinct, subordinate 'other,' whites include themselves in the dominant circle—an arena in which most hold no real power, but only their privileged racial identity."[16]

The critically important stabilizing role that blacks play in this society poses a major barrier in efforts to gain racial equality. Throughout history politicians have used blacks as scapegoats for failed economic or political policies. Before the Civil War rich slave owners persuaded the nonslaveholding whites to stand with them against the danger of slave revolts, even though the existence of slavery condemned whites unable to afford slaves to serious economic disadvantage.[17] After the Civil War poor whites fought social reforms and settled for segregation rather than see those formerly enslaved blacks get ahead.[18] Most labor unions preferred to allow the plant owners to break their strikes with black scab labor rather than allow blacks to join their unions.[19]

The "them against us" racial ploy—always a potent force in economic bad times—is working again in the 1990s as whites, as disadvantaged by high status entrance requirements as blacks, fight to end affirmative action policies that, by neutralizing class-based entrance requirements and requiring widespread advertising of jobs once awarded via the old-boys network, have likely helped far more whites than blacks. And today in the 1990s, as through much of the 1980s millions of Americans—white as well as black—face steadily worsening conditions: unemployment, inaccessible health care, inadequate housing, mediocre education, and pollution of the environment. The gap in national incomes approaches a chasm of crisis as those in the top fifth now earn more than their counterparts in the bottom four-fifths combined.

Shocking. And yet, conservative white politicians are able to gain and hold even the highest office despite their failure to address seriously any of these issues. They rely instead on the time-tested formula of getting working-class whites to identify on the basis of their shared skin color, and they suggest with little or no subtlety that white people must stand together against the Willie Hortons, or racial quotas, or affirmative action. The code words differ; the message is the same. Whites are rallied on the basis of racial pride and patriotism to accept their often lowly lot in life and are encouraged to vent their frustration by opposing any serious advancement by blacks. Crucial to this situation is the unstated understanding by the mass of whites that they will accept large disparities in economic opportunity in respect to other whites as long as they have a priority over blacks and other people of color for access to the few opportunities available.

This "racial bonding" by whites—as bell hooks puts it[20]—means that black rights and interests are always vulnerable to diminishment if not to outright destruction. The willingness of whites over time to respond to this racial rallying cry, far more than the failure of liberal democratic practices (re black rights) to coincide with liberal democratic theory, explains blacks' continuing subordinate status. This, of course, is contrary to the philosophy incorporated in Gunnar Myrdal's massive mid-century study, *The American Dilemma*. Myrdal and two generations of civil rights advocates accepted the idea of racism as merely an odious hold-over from slavery, "a terrible and inexplicable anomaly stuck in the middle of our liberal democratic ethos."[21] No one doubted that the standard practices of American policy making were adequate to the task of abolishing racism. White America, it was assumed, *wanted* to abolish racism. Forty years later, in *The New American Dilemma*,[22] Professor Jennifer Hochschild examined what she called Myrdal's "anomaly thesis," concluding that it simply cannot explain the persistence of racial discrimination;[23] rather, the continued viability of racism demonstrates "that racism is not simply an excrescence on a fundamentally healthy liberal democratic body, but is part of what shapes and energizes the body."[24] Under this view, "liberal democracy and racism in the United States are historically, even inherently, reinforcing; American society as we know it exists only because of its foundation in racially based slavery, and it thrives only because racial discrimination continues. The apparent anomaly is an actual symbiosis."[25]

The permanence of this "symbiosis" ensures that civil rights gains will be temporary and setbacks inevitable. Consider: In this last decade of the twentieth century, color determines the social and economic status of all African Americans, both those who have been highly successful and their poverty-bound brethren, whose lives are grounded in misery and despair. We rise and fall less as a result of our efforts than in response to the needs of a white society that condemns all blacks to quasicitizenship as surely as it segregated our parents and enslaved their forebears. The fact is that, despite what we designate as progress wrought through struggle over many generations, we remain what we were in the beginning: a dark and foreign presence, always the designated "other." Tolerated in good times, despised when things go wrong; as a people we are scapegoated and sacrificed as distraction or catalyst for compromise to facilitate resolution of political differences or relieve economic adversity.

Here, I suggest, is the place to insert the third I of slavery: inspiration.

Inspiration

Beyond the despair of the conclusion that racism is a permanent part of American society, there is the reassuring reminder that our forebears— though betrayed into bondage—survived the slavery in which they were reduced to things, property, entitled neither to rights nor to respect as human beings. Somehow, as the legacy of our spirituals makes clear, our enslaved ancestors managed to retain their humanity as well as their faith that evil and suffering were not the extent of their destiny—or of the destiny of those who would follow them. Indeed, we owe our existence to their perseverance, their faith. In these perilous times, we must do no less than they did: fashion a philosophy that both matches the unique dangers we face and enables us to recognize in those dangers opportunities for committed living and humane service.

The task is less daunting than it might appear. From the beginning we have been living and working for racial justice in the face of unacknowledged threat. Thus, we are closer than we may realize to those in slavery who struggled to begin and maintain families even though, at any moment, they might be sold and separated, never to see one another again. Those blacks living in the pre-Civil War North, though deemed "free," had to live with the ever-present knowledge that the underground railroad ran both ways.[26] While abolitionists provided an illegal network to aid blacks who escaped slavery,[27] Southern "slave catchers" likely had an equally extensive system that enabled them to kidnap free blacks from their homes or the streets and spirit them off to the South and a life in bondage.[28] In *Prigg* v. *Pennsylvania,*[29] the Supreme Court asserted that masters or their agents had a constitutional right of "self-help" to seize fugitive slaves and return them to the South, as long as they could accomplish their mission without a "breach of the peace." In reality this decision constitutionalized the kidnapping of free blacks, if it could be done quietly enough so that the surrounding white community would not be disturbed.

In those times racism presented dangers from without that were stark and terrifying, but they were hardly more insidious than those blacks face today in our inner cities—all too often from other blacks. Victimized themselves by an uncaring society, some young blacks vent their rage on victims like themselves, thereby perpetuating the terror that once whites had to invoke directly. We should not be surprised that a society that once legalized slavery and authorized pursuit of fugitive slaves with little concern about the kidnapping of free blacks now views black-on-black crime as basically a problem for its victims and their communities.

In the context of such a history, played out now as current events, is a long continuum of risks faced and survived, our oppression barring our oppressors from actually experiencing the freedom they so proudly proclaim. As the late Harvard historian Nathan Huggins points out in *Black Odyssey*, a book about slavery from the point of view of the slaves:

> Uncertainty, the act of being engaged in an unknown and evolving future, was their common fate. In the indefinite was the excitement of the possible. . . . That sense of possibility and that dream have infected all Americans, Africans no less than Europeans. . . . *Yet the dream has been elusive to us all*, white and black, from that first landfall [at Jamestown where the first twenty Africans landed].[30]

Huggins argues that Americans view history as linear and evolutionary and tend to see slavery and racism as an aberration or pathological condition: "Our national history has continued to amplify the myths of automatic progress, universal freedom, and the American dream without the ugly reality of racism seriously challenging the faith."[31] Those who accept these myths consider our view that racism is permanent to be despairing, defeatist, and wrong. In so doing they overlook the fact that the "American dogma of automatic progress fails those who have been marginalized. Blacks, the poor, and others whom the myth ignores are conspicuously in the center of the present, and they call for a national history that incorporates their experience."[32]

Such a new narrative, and the people who make it, among whom are included those who pursue equality through legal means, must find inspiration not in the sacrosanct but utterly defunct glory of ideals that for centuries have proven both unattainable and poisonous. Rather, they must find it in the lives of "an oppressed people who defied social death as slaves and freedmen, insisting on their humanity despite a social consensus that they were 'a brutish sort of people.'"[33] From that reality Huggins takes hope rather than despair. Knowing there was no escape, no way out, the slaves nonetheless continued to engage themselves. To carve out a humanity. To defy the murder of selfhood. Their lives were brutally shackled, certainly, but *not without meaning, despite being imprisoned.*[34]

We are proud of our heroes, but we must not forget those whose lives were not marked by extraordinary acts of defiance. Though they lived and died as captives within a system of slave labor, "they produced worlds of music, poetry, and art. They reshaped a Christian cosmology to fit their spirits and their needs, transforming Protestantism along the way. They produced a single people out of what had been many. . . . Their ordeal, and their dignity throughout it, speaks to the world of the indomitable human spirit."[35]

Perhaps those of us who can admit we are imprisoned by the history of racial subordination in America can accept—as slaves had no choice but to accept—our fate. Not that we legitimate the racism of the oppressor. On the contrary, we can only *de*-legitimate it if we can accurately pinpoint it. And racism lies at the center, not the periphery; in the permanent, not in the fleeting; in the real lives of black and white people, not in the sentimental caverns of the mind.

Armed with this knowledge and with the enlightened, humility-based commitment that it engenders, we can accept the dilemmas of committed confrontation with evils we cannot end. We can go forth to serve knowing that our failure to act will not change conditions and may very well worsen them. We can listen carefully to those who have been most subordinated. In listening we must not do them the injustice of failing to recognize that somehow they survived as complete, defiant, though horribly scarred beings. We must learn from their example, learn from those whom we would teach.

If we are to extract solutions from the lessons of the slaves' survival, and our own, we must first face squarely the unbearable landscape and climate of that survival. We yearn that our civil rights work will be crowned with success, but what we really want—want even more than success—is meaning. "Meaningfulness," as Stanford psychiatrist Irvin Yalom tells us, "is a by-product of engagement and commitment."[36] Engagement and commitment are what black people have had to do since slavery: making something out of nothing. Carving out a humanity for oneself with absolutely nothing to help—save imagination, will, and unbelievable strength and courage. Beating the odds while firmly believing in, *knowing* as only they could know, the fact that all those odds are stacked against them.

Both engagement and commitment connote service. And genuine service requires humility. We must first recognize and acknowledge (at least to ourselves) that our actions are not likely to lead to transcendent change and may indeed, despite our best efforts, be of more help to the system we despise than to the victims of that system whom we are trying to help. Then and only then can that realization and the dedication based on it lead to policy positions and campaigns that, instead of perhaps worsening conditions for those we would help, will alert the powers that be to the presence of persons like ourselves, who are not only *not* on their side but are determined to stand in their way.

Now, there is more here than confrontation with our oppressors. Continued struggle can bring about unexpected benefits and gains that in themselves justify continued endeavor. We can recognize miracles we did not plan and value them for what they are rather than for how they have likely contributed to our traditional goals. As a former student, Erin Edmonds, concludes, it is not a matter of choosing between the pragmatic recognition that racism is permanent no matter what we do or an idealism based on the long-held dream of attaining a society free of racism. Rather it is a question of *both, and. Both* the recognition of the futility of action—where action merely is more civil rights strategies destined to fail—*and* the unalterable conviction that something must be done, that action must be taken.[37]

This is, I believe, a more realistic perspective from which to gauge the present and future worth of our race-related activities. Freed of the stifling rigidity of relying unthinkingly on the slogan "we shall overcome," we are impelled both to live each day more fully *and* to examine critically the actual effectiveness of traditional civil rights remedies. Indeed, the humility required by genuine service will not permit us to urge remedies that we may think appropriate and that the law may even require but that the victims of discrimination have rejected.

That, I suggest, is the real Black History, all too easily lost in political debates over curricular needs. It is a story less of success than survival through an unremitting struggle that leaves no room for giving up. We are all part of that history, and it is still unfolding.

Notes

Derrick Bell is visiting Professor of Law, New York University Law School. This article is based on the text of Derrick Bell, *Faces at the Bottom of the Well: The Permanence of Racism* (New York: Basic Books, 1992).

1. Susan Weidener, "Mock Slave Auction in Class Backfires on Chesco Teacher," *Philadelphia Inquirer*, January 21, 1993, sec. A, p. 1.

2. In the antebellum period abolitionists often held a mock slave auction at meetings. The Rev. Henry Ward Beecher was particularly well-known for this theatrical tactic. For slaves and abolitionists the slave auction was perhaps the most hated symbol of the peculiar institution, not only because it embodied the dehumanization of slaves but also because it presaged the greatest personal tragedy of slavery: the destruction of families as close relatives were separated for life by the auctioneer's hammer.

3. John Hope Franklin and Alfred A. Moss, Jr., *From Slavery to Freedom*, 7th ed. (New York: McGraw-Hill, 1988), 475–76.

4. Linda J. Myers, *Understanding an Afrocentric World View: Introduction to an Optimal Psychology* (Dubuque, Iowa: Kendall Hull, 1988), 8.

5. Ibid.

6. On the origin of slavery, in what became the United States, see David Brion Davis, *The Problem of Slavery in Western Culture* (Ithaca: Cornell University Press, 1966); A. Leon Higginbotham, Jr., *In the Matter of Color: Race and The American Legal Process: The Colonial Period* (New York: Oxford University Press, 1978); Edmund S. Morgan, *American Slavery, American Freedom: The Ordeal of Colonial Virginia* (New York: W.W. Norton, 1975); Peter H. Wood, *Black Majority: Negroes in Colonial South Carolina from 1670 through the Stono Rebellion* (New York: W. W. Norton, 1974).

7. Orlando Patterson, *Slavery and Social Death: A Comparative Study* (Cambridge: Harvard University Press, 1982), 76. Professor Patterson suggests on p. 78: "The dishonor of slavery . . . came in the primal act of submission. It was the most immediate human expression of the inability to defend oneself or to secure one's livelihood. . . .The dishonor the slave was compelled to experience sprang instead from that raw, human sense of debasement inherent in having no being except as an expression of another's being."

8. But see Paul Finkelman, *Slavery and the Founders: Race and Liberty in the Age of Jefferson* (Armonk, N.Y.: M. E.Sharpe, 1996), 1–33. Donald Robinson, *Slavery in the Structure of American Politics, 1765–1820* (New York: Harcourt Brace Jovanovich, 1971); William M. Wiecek, "'The Blessings of Liberty': Slavery in the American Constitutional Order," in *Slavery and Its Consequences*, ed. Robert A. Goldwin and Art Kaufman (Washington: American Enterprise Institute, 1988), 23; Sanford Levinson, "Slavery in the Canon of Constitutional Law," in this volume.

9. William M. Wiecek, *The Sources of Antislavery Constitutionalism in America, 1760–1848* (Ithaca: Cornell University Press, 1977), 62, 63. Professor Wiecek lists ten provisions in the Constitution that provide for slavery and protect slaveowners. Paul Finkelman, *Slavery and the Founders* identifies five provisions explicitly sanctioning slavery in the Constitution and ten provisions providing indirect protection of slavery.

10. William Freehling, "The Founding Fathers and Slavery," *American Historical Review* 81 (1972): 77.

11. Robert M. Cover, *Justice Accused: Anti-Slavery and the Judicial Process* (New Haven: Yale University Press, 1975).

12. For references to writings on the Hayes-Tilden Compromise, see Derrick Bell, *Race, Racism, and American Law*, 3d ed. (Boston: Little, Brown, 1992), 32–33. See generally, Eric Anderson and Alfred A. Moss, Jr., eds., *The Facts of Reconstruction* (Baton Rouge: Louisiana State University Press, 1991); Charles A. Lofgren, *The Plessy Case: A Legal-Historical Interpretation* (New York: Oxford University Press, 1987); Rayford W. Logan, *The Betrayal of the Negro* (New York: Collier Books, 1965); Donald G. Nieman, *Promises to Keep: African-Americans and the Constitutional Order, 1776 to the Present* (New York: Oxford University Press, 1991); Paul Finkelman, ed., *The Age of Jim Crow: Segregation from the End of Reconstruction to the Great Depression*, vol. 4 of *Race, Law and American History 1700–1990* (New York: Garland, 1992).

13. Peter Bergman, *The Chronological History of the Negro in America* (New York: Harper and Row, 1969), 327.

14. J. Morgan Kousser, *The Shaping of Southern Politics: Suffrage Restriction and the Establishment of the One-Party South, 1880–1910* (NewHaven: Yale University Press, 1974); and Paul Finkelman, ed., *African-Americans and the Right to Vote*, vol. 6 of *Race, Law and American History 1700–1990* (New York: Garland, 1992).

15. *Plessy v. Ferguson*, 163 U.S. 537 (1896).

16. Kimberlé W. Crenshaw, "Race, Reform, and Retrenchment: Transformation and Legitimation in Antidiscrimination Law," *Harvard Law Review* 101 (1988): 1381.

17. Morgan, *American Slavery, American Freedom*, 295–387.

18. Derrick Bell, "The Racial Imperative in American Law," in *The Age of Segregation: Race Relations in the South, 1890–1945*, ed. Robert Haws (Jackson: University of Mississippi Press, 1978), 3.

19. Herbert Hill, *Black Labor and the American Legal System* (Washington: Bureau of National Affairs, 1977); William B. Gould, *Black Workers in White Unions: Job Discrimination in the United States* (Ithaca: Cornell University Press, 1977).

20. bell hooks, *Feminist Theory from Margin to Center* (Boston: South End Press, 1984), 54.

21. Gunnar Myrdal, *An American Dilemma* (New York: Harper and Row, 1944). "[T]he Negro problem in America represents a moral lag in the development of the nation and a study of it must record nearly everything which is bad and wrong in America. . . . [H]owever, . . . not *since Reconstruction has there been more reason to anticipate fundamental changes in American race relations, changes which will involve a development toward the American ideals.*" Ibid., xix.

22. Jennifer L. Hochschild, *The New American Dilemma: Liberal Democracy and School Desegregation* (New Haven: Yale University Press, 1984).

23. Ibid., 203.

24. Ibid., 5.

25. Ibid.

26. See Julie Winch, "Philadelphia and the Other Underground Railroad," *Pennsylvania Magazine of History and Biography* 111 (1987): 3, reprinted in Paul Finkelman, ed., *Slave Trade and Migration, Domestic and Foreign*, vol. 2 of *Articles on American Slavery* (New York: Garland, 1988).

27. Levi Coffin, *Reminiscences of Levi Coffin, the Reputed President of the Underground Railroad* (Cincinnati: Western Tract Society, 1876); Paul Finkelman, ed., *Fugitive Slaves,* vol. 6 of *Articles on American Slavery* (New York: Garland, 1989); Larry Gara, *The Liberty Line: The Legend of the Underground Railroad* (Lexington: University of Kentucky Press, 1961); William Still, *The Underground Railroad* (Philadelphia: Porter and Coates, 1872).

28. See Solomon Northrop, *Twelve Years a Slave* (Auburn: Derby and Miller, 1853); Robinson, *Slavery in the Structure of American Politics,* 286. Robinson notes that the Fugitive Slave Act of 1793, while including severe penalties for those assisting escaping slaves, "prescribed no penalties for those who sought to kidnap and re-enslave freed Negroes."

29. *Prigg v. Pennsylvania,* 41 U.S. (16 Peters) 539 (1842). For a discussion of this case see Paul Finkelman, "Sorting Out *Prigg v. Pennsylvania,*" *Rutgers Law Journal* 24 (1993): 605.

30. Nathan Huggins, *Black Odyssey* (New York: Vintage Books, 1990), 244. [Emphasis added].

31. Ibid., xvi.

32. Ibid., xiii.

33. Ibid., lvi.

34. Ibid., lxxiv.

35. Ibid.

36. Irvin Yalom, *Love's Executioner and Other Tales of Psychotherapy* (New York: Basic Books, 1989), 12.

37. Erin Edmonds, "Civil Rights according to Derrick Bell" [unpublished seminar paper].

2

Ideology and Imagery in the Law of Slavery

William W. Fisher III

In important respects, the rules used by the Southern colonies and states to administer the system of chattel slavery were consistent and coherent. For example, by the early eighteenth century, all jurisdictions had adopted the principles that a person's status as free or slave is determined by the status of his or her mother and that only persons with at least some nonwhite blood can be slaves.[1] The law governing homicide of slaves by whites was also approximately the same throughout the region: during the colonial period, killers of slaves received only modest sanctions (typically a fine or short prison term, combined with an obligation to compensate the owner of the victim); between 1790 and 1820, the penalties were increased substantially (although executions remained rare, and many substantive and procedural rules were available to killers of slaves that were not available to killers of whites or free blacks); and during the remainder of the antebellum period, the law was relatively stable in all states.[2] During the colonial period, slaves everywhere were subject to severe criminal penalties for a wide variety of offenses; by the Civil War, the relevant rules had been softened a good deal but remained harsher than those applicable to whites.[3] When dealing with sales of slaves, courts throughout the South eschewed the doctrine of caveat emptor that was coming to dominate commercial law in the North—although the rules regarding which types of defects in slaves (e.g., illness, insanity, or inclination to run away) would warrant rescission of the transaction varied significantly across the region.[4] Finally, in all jurisdictions slaves were deprived of many civil rights and liberties: they could not make contracts or other legally binding choices,[5] sue or be sued,[6] acquire property,[7] legally marry,[8] or (with rare exceptions) testify against whites.[9]

In several other respects, however, the law of slavery was inconsis-

tent or incoherent. Many issues were handled differently in the various
states. For example, in Virginia and South Carolina, slaves prosecuted
for serious crimes received few of the procedural protections available to
white defendants; in Louisiana, Georgia, Delaware, and Maryland, slave
defendants were given more protections but not as many as whites;[10] and
in Alabama, Florida, Mississippi, North Carolina, and Tennessee, the
courts could claim with some plausibility that "whenever life is involved,
the slave stands upon as safe ground as the master."[11] The rules governing manumission of slaves were equally diverse. In Georgia, for example,
the legislature severely restricted private emancipations early in the nineteenth century, and in almost all ambiguous situations, the courts ruled
against slaves whose masters had sought to free them;[12] in Tennessee, by
contrast, slaveholders until the mid 1850s continued to enjoy several
ways of freeing their slaves.[13] The legal problems associated with the increasingly important system of slave leases provoked similarly divergent
responses. In some states, if a leased slave ran away, became ill, or was
injured or killed during the lease term, the lessee (in the absence of a
relevant contractual provision) bore the resultant financial burden; in
other states, the lessor sustained the loss.[14] On the issue of a master's
financial responsibility for injuries his slaves caused to third parties, the
positions adopted by the various states ranged from absolute liability
(Louisiana) to liability only for specified sorts of misconduct by slaves
(Arkansas and Missouri) to liability only if the slaves were acting pursuant to the master's specific directions or if they had been put in positions
of public trust (South Carolina).[15] The states divided along different lines
on the question of the applicability of the fellow-servant rule to slavery:
most courts refused to exempt from liability the lessees of slaves who
were injured through the negligence of other workers, but those in North
Carolina and Alabama took the opposite stance.[16]

Doctrinal dissonance was not limited to interjurisdictional disputes;
lawmakers within a given state frequently disagreed on how major issues
involving slavery should be resolved. For example, the Tennessee courts
often upheld slave manumissions that plainly violated restrictions the
state legislature had sought to impose. In South Carolina, Mississippi,
and Virginia, the judges were divided among themselves; some upheld
highly questionable manumissions, while others denounced all efforts
to free slaves.[17] Substantive criminal law as applied to violence between
slaves and whites also provoked some degree of intrajurisdictional conflict.
In North Carolina, for example, Chief Justice Ruffin usually advocated
lenient treatment of whites who assaulted slaves and harsh treatment of
slaves who resisted such assaults; his colleagues, Justices Gaston and
Pearson, were significantly more evenhanded.[18]

Finally, the entire body of slave law was riven by three fundamental
tensions. The first concerned the legal status of slaves. In most contexts,
they were treated as things—objects or assets to be bought and sold,
mortgaged and wagered, devised and condemned;[19] sometimes, however,

they were treated as persons—volitional, feeling, and responsible for their actions.[20] In the words of the Supreme Court of Mississippi, "In some respects slaves may be considered as chattels, but in others, they are regarded as men."[21] The second tension concerned the relationship between slavery and the rule of law. In many connections, courts and legislatures took the position that the control and discipline of slaves was primarily the responsibility of their masters and that the law ought neither reinforce nor interfere with masters' exercise of their power.[22] In other settings, however, lawmakers insisted that slaves enjoyed the protection of—or were subject to punishment by—the state; private resolution of disputes with slaves was consequently discouraged.[23] The last tension pertained to interracial sexual relations. Lawmakers ostensibly sought to maintain a rigid separation of blacks and whites. Accordingly, they banned racial intermarriage, established severe penalties for interracial fornication and adultery, and frequently in related contexts expressed repugnance for "commingling" of the races. In practice, however, they typically strongly condemned and harshly punished only sexual relations between black men and white women,[24] while they commonly tolerated both consensual and forcible sex between white men and black women.[25]

This complex doctrinal pattern has elicited a variety of reactions from legal historians. Some, impressed by the variations among the rules applicable to slaves, have contended that there was no such thing as a "law of slavery"; rather, there were many incompatible laws of slavery, which can be understood only through close attention to the biographies of individual lawmakers and the socioeconomic and political forces at work in individual jurisdictions.[26] Other historians have argued that the inconsistencies and contradictions are only apparent; careful analysis will show that all aspects of slave law were shrewdly designed to serve the interests of the master class— specifically, to enable masters to extract as much labor as possible from their slaves, to enhance masters' ability to discipline their slaves, and to protect masters' property interests in their slaves.[27] Still others have acknowledged that the law of slavery was riddled with genuine inconsistencies but have contended that they were all the fruits of a single, fundamental contradiction: the incompatibility of slave socioeconomic relations (themselves the outgrowth of a mode of production centered around plantation-based cultivation of cotton and tobacco) and bourgeois socioeconomic relations (themselves the outgrowth of commercial capitalism and protoindustrialization).[28] A fourth group has proceeded on the assumption that the bulk of all legal systems are borrowed from the laws of other jurisdictions; to explain the American law of slavery, consequently, one must identify the ingredients from which it was made—a dash of villenage, a splash of Roman law (strained through the civil law tradition), a sizable dollop from the slave code of Barbados, and a large portion of the common law and equitable principles in force in England.[29]

There is much to be said for all four of these interpretations. Southern lawmakers (many of them slaveholders themselves) surely sought, among other things, to advance the material interests of the master class; local circumstances and lawmakers' idiosyncrasies were undoubtedly important in shaping the rules in force in various parts of the region; it would be surprising if the contradictory character of the Southern economy were not reflected in some way in the legal superstructure; and much of American slave law was indeed modeled on the laws of other countries. But each of the four interpretations fails plausibly to make sense of important aspects of the pattern of slave law. Rather than detail those limitations—which have been adequately discussed elsewhere[30]—this essay explores (and argues for the importance of) a set of forces all four of the prominent interpretations neglect. Specifically, it contends that we can understand better the law of slavery by examining its relationships to Southern ideology.[31]

Both the difficulty and the power of this approach arise from the fact that that ideology was neither stable nor coherent. Rather, Southerners—white Southerners in particular—struggled throughout the antebellum period to define and justify themselves and their society. Three issues provoked the most attention and debate: What are Negroes like? Why is slavery just? How should an honorable and moral person live? The following three sections describe the divergent responses Southerners developed to these questions and identify some of the ways their responses affected the rhetoric and content of the law of slavery.

Black Images in White Minds

Two radically different images of the typical male slave figured prominently in the fiction and fantasies of white Southerners. The first was the childlike and undependable but loyal and unthreatening Sambo. "Indolent, faithful, humorous,. . . dishonest, superstitious, improvident, and musical, Sambo was inevitably a clown and congenitally docile."[32] Southern social commentators repeatedly argued that the large majority of Negro men fit this image. The comments of Dr. Samuel Cartwright were typical: "Africans are endowed with a will so weak, passions so easily subdued, and dispositions so gentle and affectionate that they have an instinctive feeling of obedience to the stronger will of the white man."[33] Antebellum Southern novelists concurred. Thus, slaves are commonly depicted as lazy, immoral (e.g., mendacious, thieving, and sexually promiscuous or polygamous), highly impressionable, and easily corruptible—but also, if well treated, content, funny, musical, and fiercely devoted to their masters (willing, for example, to risk their own lives to save or protect their owners).[34] The less attractive of these various traits were generally believed to be immutable characteristics of the African race. The more appealing characteristics were described as the results of "domestication"—the displacement by the system of slavery of Africans' savage impulses with "civilized" dispositions.[35]

Unredeemed savagery was the central trait of Nat, the second, opposing image of male slaves. Less common than the Sambo image, it was equally important to the white Southern psyche. A slave in this mode was fierce, rapacious, cunning, rebellious, and vindictive. In Southern fiction "Nat was the incorrigible runaway, the poisoner of white men, the ravager of white women, who defied all the rules of plantation society. Subdued and punished only when overcome by superior numbers or firepower, Nat retaliated when attacked by whites, led guerrilla activities of maroons against isolated plantations, killed overseers and planters, or burned plantation buildings when he was abused."[36] If freed, social commentators sometimes argued, all slaves would revert to this type. William Dayton, for example, contended that emancipation would lead to servile war. "[T]he madness which a sudden freedom from restraint begets— the overpowering burst of long buried passion, the wild frenzy of revenge, and the savage lust for blood, all unite to give the warfare of liberated slaves, traits of cruelty and crime which nothing earthly can equal."[37]

The relationship between these two images was complex. Some Southerners seem to have believed that there were two types of Negro men: the majority fit the Sambo model; the minority fit the Nat model. For most white Southerners, however, the two images reflected a deep ambivalence in their attitudes toward their slaves. In their moments of confidence, they thought of them as gentle, childlike, and loyal; in their moments of doubt, they thought of them as furious, duplicitous, and homicidal.[38] Sambo, in short, was the central figure in white Southerners' fantasies of safety; Nat was the central figure in their fantasies of rebellion.[39]

Whites' images of slave women similarly revolved around two opposing stereotypes. The less threatening of the images was that of Mammy. A slave woman in this mode was loyal, trustworthy, pious, maternal, and asexual. The opposed image was Jezebel—sensual, promiscuous (willing, for example, to mate with orangutans), unrestrainable, and irreligious. Mammy lovingly cared for the master's children, honestly and efficiently managed the household, and shrewdly advised master and mistress on the management of the plantation. Jezebel lured the master into illicit sexual liaisons, corrupted the morals of the master's adolescent sons, fomented strife between master and mistress, and prevented the master from enforcing norms of chastity and monogamy within the slave quarters.[40]

White Southerners sometimes argued that Mammy and Jezebel were accurate descriptions of distinct subgroups of the female African population. The classification even had an economic function: women of the first type were said to be best used as house servants; women of the second type should be sent to the fields. As was true of their competing images of slave men, however, "many Southerners were able to embrace both images of black women simultaneously and to switch from one to the other depending on the context of their thought."[41]

As Elizabeth Fox-Genovese argues, the two stereotypes had different but equally important ideological functions:

> Mammy signaled the wish for organic harmony and projected a woman who suckled and reared white masters. The image displaced sexuality into nurture and transformed potential hostility into sustenance and love. It claimed for the white family the ultimate devotion of black women, who reared the children of others as if they were their own. . . . [Jezebel, by contrast,] legitimated the wanton behavior of white men by proclaiming black women to be lusty wenches in whom sexual impulse overwhelmed all restraint. The image eased the consciences of white men by suggesting that black women asked for the treatment they received.[42]

In view of the currency and power in antebellum Southern culture of these four images—Sambo, Nat, Mammy, and Jezebel—we should not be surprised to find that legislators and judges made frequent use of them. Sometimes when shaping legal rules, they asserted or took for granted that most male slaves conformed to the Sambo model. For example, in *State* v. *Boyce*, Chief Justice Ruffin of North Carolina relied heavily on the image in overturning a planter's conviction for keeping a disorderly house.[43] It appeared that on Christmas each year the defendant held a party for his own slaves and for a few slaves from other plantations. The revelers were permitted to drink and dance, and the defendant's daughter may have joined in the dancing. The attempt to suppress such affairs, Ruffin ruled, was entirely inappropriate. Such festivities are in no way harmful or dangerous for typical slaves. Indeed, he argued more subtly, they may help keep slaves playful and contented.

> If slaves would do nothing, tending more to the corruption of their morals or to the annoyance of the whites, than seeking the exhilaration of their simple music and romping dances, they might be set down as an innocent and happy class. We may let them make the most of their idle hours, and may well make allowances for the noisy outpourings of glad hearts, which providence bestows as a blessing on corporeal vigor united to a vacant mind.[44]

In *Roser* v. *Marlow*, Judge Charlton of the Superior Court of Georgia invoked both the image of slaves as Sambos and the conventional explanation of the social origins of their more desirable features in justifying the statutory bar against domestic manumission. Negroes, he explained, are "naturally indolent." They become and remain good workers through the efforts of their masters, who "urge them to exertion," and through the absence of bad examples. Once freed, they become "lazy, mischievous and corrupt." A sizable, visible class of free blacks in the state would thus undermine the masters' authority, "ravaging the morals, and corrupting the feelings of our slaves." Recognizing this danger, the legislature wisely "declared, that such a class should not be increased by manumission . . . or by the admission of such persons from other States to reside therein."[45]

At other times, lawmakers treated Nat as paradigmatic. Such imagery was especially common in the early, draconian slave codes. For example, a 1669 Virginia statute immunized masters from criminal liability for killing their slaves in the course of discipline partly on the ground that "the obstinacy of many [refractory servants cannot] by other than violent means [be] supprest."[46] Paranoia concerning the instincts of most slaves is even more apparent in the preamble to the 1696 Slave Code of South Carolina:

> Whereas, the plantations and estates of this Province cannot be well and sufficiently managed and brought into use, without the labor and service of negroes and other slaves; and forasmuch as the said negroes and other slaves brought into the People of this Province for that purpose, are of barbarous, wild, savage natures, and such as renders them wholly unqualified to be governed by the laws, customs, and practices of this Province; but that it is absolutely necessary, that such other constitutions, laws and orders, should in this Province be made and enacted, for the good regulating and ordering of them, as may restrain the disorders, rapines and inhumanity, to which they are naturally prone and inclined, and may also tend to the safety and security of the People of this Province and their estates; to which purpose. . . .[47]

Images of this sort by no means disappeared with the softening of slave law in the early nineteenth century; courts continued to invoke them when choosing between alternative doctrines. For example, the South Carolina Supreme Court ruled that, in view of the rebellious and vindictive impulses of blacks, masters ought not ordinarily be held liable for the torts of their slaves:

> [Negroes] were in general a headstrong, stubborn race of people, who had a volition of their own, and the physical power of doing great injuries to neighbors and others, without the possibility of their masters having any control over them; especially when they happened to be at a distance from them; and experience had taught us how little they adhered to advice and direction when left alone. It would, indeed, under these circumstances, be a most dangerous thing, to make masters liable in damages for the unauthorized acts of their slaves.[48]

In cases and contexts involving the sexuality of male slaves, the Nat image predominated. Drawing on a deeply rooted conception of Negro men as oversexed (e.g., possessing unusually large genitalia) and lustful for white women, lawmakers commonly depicted them as rapacious and predatory.[49] For example, the Supreme Court of North Carolina suggested on the following ground that the age of capacity should be lowered to permit the prosecution of Negro boys for rape:

> A large portion of our population is of races from more Southern latitudes than that from which our common law comes. We have indeed an element of great importance from the torrid zone of Africa. It is unquestionable that climate, food, clothing and the like, have a great influence in hastening physical development. Whether it may not be advisable to move down to an earlier age than 14, the period of puberty, for a portion, if not for all the elements in our population, may be a proper inquiry for the statesman.

The same anxiety concerning the sexual ambitions of black men prompted most colonial and state legislatures to mandate either death or castration for slaves convicted of raping or attempting to rape white women.[50]

In situations implicating the sexuality of female slaves, the Jezebel image predominated. For example, the supposed licentiousness and poorly developed parental instincts of Negro women were commonly invoked to justify denying them the right to marry or to retain custody of their children.[51] Similar characterizations were used to justify the failure of almost all jurisdictions to criminalize rape of a slave woman: "The regulations of law, as to the white race, on the subject of sexual intercourse, do not and cannot, for obvious reasons, apply to slaves; their intercourse is promiscuous, and the violation of a female slave by a male slave would be a mere assault and battery."[52] In a variety of other contexts, courts took for granted that Negro women had at best an "imperfect sense of the obligations of morality and common decency."[53]

The most intriguing doctrinal fields are those in which lawmakers drew simultaneously on two or more paradigms. A good example is the dissenting opinion of Chief Justice Ruffin in *State* v. *Caesar*. The holding of the case (of which more will be said below) was that a slave who, in a fit of anger, kills a white man who has just inflicted a "severe blow" on the slave's friend, is guilty of manslaughter, not murder. Ruffin argued that his colleagues were wrong to attribute to the defendant emotions and impulses a white person would have felt under similar circumstances. The large majority of slaves, he contended, are docile and obedient. Routinely humiliated by whites, they are almost impossible to provoke.

> Negroes—at least the great mass of them—born with deference to the white man, take the most contumelious language without answering again, and generally submit tamely to his buffets, though unlawful and

unmerited. Such are the habits of the country. . . . For it is an incontestable fact, that the great mass of slaves—nearly all of them—are the least turbulent of all men; that, when sober, they never attack a white man; and seldom, very seldom, exhibit any temper or sense of provocation at even gross and violent injuries from white men. . . . Crowds of negroes in public places are often dispersed with blows by white men, and no one remembers a homicide of a white man on such occasions. . . . Such being the real state of things, it is a just conclusion of reason, when a slave kills a white man for a battery not likely to kill, maim, or do permanent injury, not accompanied by unusual cruelty, that the act did not flow from generous and uncontrollable resentment, but from a bad heart—one, intent upon the assertion of equality, social and personal, with the white, and bent on mortal mischief in support of the assertion. It is but the pretense of a provocation, not usually felt.[54]

The defendant, in short, had by his violent reaction revealed himself to be a Nat, not a Sambo. He had lifted his mask, shown himself to be one of the few inherently "bad" slaves—rebellious, cunning, and homicidal. Extenuation of the crime, under such circumstances, was of course inappropriate; the sensible penalty was death.

Disputes involving alleged breaches of warranties of fitness also frequently led to deployment of two competing stereotypes. As indicated above, all Southern jurisdictions refused to apply to sales of slaves the doctrine of caveat emptor; purchasers of slaves who proved to be in some way "defective" could rescind the sales. As Ariella Gross has shown, the lawyer for the purchaser in a suit implicating this rule typically sought to portray the slave in question as rebellious, violent, vicious, dangerous, and incorrigible—in short, as a Nat. Counsel for the defendant sought instead to show that the slave was pliable, loyal, childlike, humble, and obedient—in short, a Sambo. The case then hinged on the issue of which of the two images was more accurate.[55]

Finally, the most circuitous but perhaps ubiquitous of the impacts of this imagery on the law of slavery was the use of adjectives conventionally associated with one or the other of the stereotypes to describe either a free person or an institution. For example, when a judge wished to express his contempt for a white defendant, he was likely to liken him (or compare him unfavorably) to a savage. Thus, in *State v. Hoover*, Chief Justice Ruffin denounced in the following terms a man convicted of torturing to death his female slave: "[T]he acts imputed to this unhappy man do not belong to a state of civilization. They are barbarities which could only be prompted by a heart in which every humane feeling had long been stifled; and indeed there scarcely be a savage of the wilderness so ferocious as not to shudder at the recital of them." Similarly, judges who wished to criticize a proposed legal rule or result as excessively harsh frequently would refer to it as "savage." Thus, in *State v. Jarrott*, Justice

Pearson insisted that, when assessing the guilt of a slave accused of murder, it would be wrong never to take into account the extent to which he had been provoked:

> It is [the slave's] duty to submit—or flee—or seek the protection of his master; but it is impossible, if it were desirable, to extinguish in him the instinct of self-preservation; and although his passions ought to be tamed down so as to suit his condition, the law would be *savage*, if it made no allowance for passion.

The thrust of this argument (and similar arguments by other judges in other states) is that to adopt the harsh rule would be to lower the law to the level of the people it is supposed to control—or, in other words, to deprive the law of the features that differentiated it from the slaves themselves.[56]

The Justification of Slavery

The efforts of white Southerners (and some white Northerners) to explain why it was not unjust to enslave Negroes began in the late seventeenth century. Until the early nineteenth century, they contented themselves with relatively casual and apologetic arguments. However, as abolitionist sentiment intensified in the 1820s and 30s, Southerners felt impelled to develop more formal and elaborate defenses of chattel slavery, to demonstrate that it was not merely a morally acceptable institution but a "positive good." A host of clergymen, newspaper editors, and previously alienated intellectuals took up the task—and were rewarded with popular acclaim and reasonably wide audiences.[57]

Almost all of the many theories developed by this group fell into two broad categories: paternalist arguments and racialist arguments. The key to theories of the first type was the depiction of Southern society as a whole as patriarchal and humane. Social and economic relations in the region, so the argument went, are vertical and reciprocal. Inferiors obey and respect their superiors and are rewarded with support and sustenance. Slavery is just one component (albeit an important component) of this essentially feudal system. Masters enjoy the labor and obedience of their slaves but provide them in return food, housing, moral and religious guidance, and care in their infancy and old age. The net result is a stable, familial, and mutually beneficial labor system that contrasts favorably with the brutal and tumultuous wage labor system used in the industrializing North.[58]

In its most extreme form—for example, as elaborated by George Fitzhugh—this argument was unpopular.[59] But less fiercely reactionary forms of the argument—for example, those of William Gilmore Simms,

Edmund Ruffin, Nathaniel Beverly Tucker, and George Frederick Holmes—found favor with much of the Southern intelligentsia.[60] Many planters thought of themselves as patriarchs, who controlled but were also responsible for their families and their slaves, and sought in various ways to play the role of feudal gentry in their local communities.[61]

The key to arguments of the second type was the proposition that it is morally permissible and even mandatory for Caucasians to dominate and exploit Africans. The reasons supplied by the various exponents of this approach varied considerably, but all incorporated the notion that Negroes are inherently inferior to whites and thus are properly reduced to slavery. For example, proslavery clergymen often argued that black persons had been relegated by God to the status of servants because they are descendants of either Ham (cursed for his disrespect for his father) or Cain (cursed for his fratricide). The developers of what (in retrospect) has been called the *herrenvolk* theory contended that there exists in all societies a laboring class, that it is natural that the brutish and subhuman Negroes should fill this role, and that the incidental advantages of such an arrangement for whites include democracy, solidarity, and prosperity. Josiah Nott and others supplemented both arguments with studies of the skulls and bodies of blacks, which, they contended, demonstrated blacks' inherent inferiority.[62]

As was true of the competing images of slaves discussed in the preceding section, the relationship between the two lines of proslavery argument was complex. Although not strictly speaking incompatible, they certainly pointed in different directions. The second relied heavily on the notion that blacks are inherently inferior to whites; the first did not (indeed, some of its proponents went so far as implicitly to advocate enslavement of some portion of the white population).[63] The second emphasized equality and democracy among whites; the first celebrated hierarchy and deference. Historians once thought that the two arguments appealed to reasonably distinct social groups: tidewater aristocrats found the first more persuasive, while poorer planters, particularly in the southwest, were attracted to the second. In recent years, however, most scholars in the field have concluded that "there was a good deal of interweaving of, and indiscriminate resort to, both the paternalist and the racial arguments."[64] Proslavery writers occasionally drew upon both approaches, and their readers almost certainly did.

The impact of these two lines of argument on legal doctrine was, as one might expect, equally complex. Feudal arguments and images seem to have had disproportionate sway in some contexts. For example, Chancellor Harper of South Carolina justified as follows his adoption of a rule that a contract for the sale of slaves is specifically enforceable:

> [U]nless there be something very perverse in the disposition of the master or the slave, in every instance where a slave has been reared in

a family there exists a mutual attachment between the members of it and himself. The tie of the master and slave is one of the most intimate relations of society. In every age the distinction has been recognized between the slave brought up in his master's household and one casually acquired. And it may be said that such an one is actually of more value to the master than he would be to a stranger. The owner better understands his qualities, and what he is capable of performing, and the slave will be more likely to serve with cheerfulness and fidelity. These considerations are greatly strengthened by those of humanity to the slave himself.[65]

This notion that slavery fosters (and is justified by) strong, reciprocal bonds of loyalty and affection prompted the courts in other contexts to disfavor doctrines that would facilitate the separation of slaves from their long-term masters. Thus, in *Flowers* v. *Sproule*, the Supreme Court of Kentucky justified as follows its ruling that an ambiguous loan agreement should be deemed a conditional sale rather than a mortgage:

> When a contract of this sort is construed to be a mortgage, it follows that a redemption, and that, perhaps, after a great lapse of time, must often be attended with *injurious* and *afflicting* consequences. Injurious— as it relates to the fortune and prospects of the constructive mortgagee and his family. Afflicting—as slaves, though property, are intelligent and sympathetic beings—they interchange sentiments, mingle sympathies, and reciprocate, with their possessor and the members of his family, all the social regards and kind attentions which endear the members of the human family to each other, and bind them in the social state. The agonies of feeling, as well on the part of the slaves as those of their possessors, inseparable from a sudden disruption of those social relations, ought not to be lightly regarded by the judge.[66]

In still other contexts, paternalistic conceptions of the bonds of loyalty and gratitude that characterize relations of masters and servants prompted courts to look favorably upon testators' efforts to free their slaves. In *Mayo* v. *Whitson*, for example, several slaves were ostensibly manumitted pursuant to the terms of their master's will. Fifty years later, the assignees of the master's next of kin discovered that the manumission decree had never been recorded and sought to reenslave the group. The former slaves, in response, petitioned the North Carolina courts for an order amending the record to recognize their emancipation. In upholding a grant of the former slaves' request, Chief Justice Nash of the North Carolina Supreme Court argued that the law should facilitate rather than impede the enforcement of wills of this sort.

> An aged man without children, or any descendants of such, is about to descend to the grave. Between him and his slaves exists a tie which is unknown to the master and the hireling: on the one hand, the proud

consciousness of power and protection, and on the other, the consciousness of humble submission and gratitude for kindness, which, in sickness and in health, has known no wavering. This tie is about to be
sundered; no creditor claims them; the aged man looking around him,
asks himself, "then, whose shall these be?" He does what he can to
confer upon them the boon they hold most dear![67]

Fairchild v. *Bell* provides a good example of the use of the paternalist
vision to justify imposing duties of care on abusive masters. The plaintiff,
a physician, found the defendant's slave lying in a road, badly beaten.
After nursing the slave back to health, the plaintiff sought to recover
from the defendant the value of his medical services. The defendant
acknowledged beating the slave but refused to pay. The trial judge began his charge to the jury by analogizing this situation to the refusal of a
husband to pay for his wife's "necessaries." The conduct of the defendant, he argued, was just as reprehensible.

[The master] is bound by the [most solemn] obligation to defray the
expenses, or services of another, to preserve the life of his slave, or
preserve the slave from pain and danger. The slave lives for his master's
service. His time, his labor, his comforts, are all at his master's dis-
posal. The duty of humane treatment and of medical assistance, when
clearly necessary, ought not to be withholden. That assistance was denied by the master in this case, and denied from the worst of motives.
The plaintiff rendered those services, and gave that assistance which
the master ought to have procured; and, therefore, ought to be compensated. In a case so circumstanced, the law will imply a contract,
from the reason, justice, and necessity, of the case.[68]

Analogous arguments suffuse the work of Thomas R. R. Cobb, the
foremost Southern commentator on the law of slavery. Cobb begins his
influential treatise with a forthrightly paternal defense of the institution:

That the slave is incorporated into and becomes part of the family, that
a tie is thus formed between the master and the slave, almost unknown
to the relation of master and hireling, . . . that the old and infirm are
thus cared for, and the young protected and reared, are indisputable
facts. Interest joins with affection in promoting this unity of feeling. To
the negro, [slavery] insures food, fuel, and clothing, medical atten-
dance, and in most cases religious instruction. The young child is seldom removed from the parents' protection, and beyond doubt, the
institution prevents the separation of families, to an extent unknown
among the laboring poor of the world. It provides him with a protector, whose interest and feeling combine in demanding such protection.
    To the master, it gives a servant whose interests are identical with
his own, who has indeed no other interest, except the gratification of a

few animal passions, for which purpose he considers it no robbery to purloin his master's goods.

> In short, the Southern slavery is a patriarchal, social system. The master is the head of his family. Next to his wife and children, he cares for his slaves. He avenges their injuries, protects their persons, provides for their wants, and guides their labors. In return, he is revered and held as protector and master.[69]

This conception of the nature and merits of the institution prompts Cobb, in the body of his treatise, to highlight the more humane features of slave law and to call for the amelioration of its grimmer provisions. For example, like other exponents of the neofeudal argument, he advocates tightening the restrictions on masters' power to abuse their slaves.[70] Similarly, he suggests that the state legislatures consider criminalizing rape of a slave and providing that, if a rape is committed by the slave's master, the usual penalty be supplemented with a requirement that the slave be sold to someone else. His discussion of the limitations the state legislatures had placed upon "[t]he right to manumit a slave" is uneasy; he is unqualifiedly enthusiastic only about curtailment of masters' power to free "the old and sick, who would become burdens on the community, and the young and feeble, incapable of supplying their own wants." To be sure, Cobb is no radical. For example, he tempers his proposal for the criminalization of slave rape with the assertion that "the known lasciviousness of the negro, renders the possibility of its occurrence very remote." The overall spirit of the treatise is aptly captured by the guideline he proposes for judges when interpreting statutory restrictions on manumission: "Our course shall be 'the middle way, in which is safety.'" Nevertheless, Cobb's strongly paternal outlook systematically biases—typically in the direction of a more humane regime—his treatment of almost every topic.[71]

A similar outlook helped shape the response of Chief Justice Lumpkin of Georgia to disputes arising out of leases of slaves. Lumpkin, like many of his contemporaries, believed that slaves leased to industries were often abused. For planters steeped in the paternal conception and defense of Southern culture, this belief was commonly associated with a general hostility toward industrialization and its concomitant evil—wage labor.[72] Lumpkin did not go so far. He believed that industrialization would increase employment in the South and, in general, would improve the region.[73] He was convinced, however, that hired slaves used in industry ran serious risks of injury, illness, and death. The law, consequently, must be structured so as to impel the lessees of slaves to fulfill their moral obligation to protect them. These sentiments are explicit in his famous opinion in *Gorman* v. *Campbell*, holding that, when a hirer permits a slave to engage in activities more dangerous than those contemplated by the lease and the slave is killed, the hirer is liable to the owner for the value of the slave:

> We must enforce the obligations which this contract imposes, by making it the interest of all those who employ slaves, to watch over their lives and safety. Their improvidence demands it. They are incapable of self-preservation, either in danger or in disease. —This office devolves upon those who are entrusted, for the time being, with their custody and control. And if they fail faithfully to perform it, it becomes a high and solemn duty of all courts to enforce the trust by the only means in their power—a direct appeal to the pocket of the delinquent party.[74]

The same sentiments prompted Lumpkin to refuse to abate the rent when a hired slave was disabled or killed prior to the termination of a lease and to reject application of the fellow-servant rule to slaves injured through the negligence of fellow employees.[75]

Not all courts, however, saw the problem of leased slaves through the lenses of the paternal theory. For many the notion that legal rules should be crafted to force hirers to take special care of their slave workers (better care, perhaps, than of their free workers) was altogether implausible. A lease of a slave, they contended, is no different from a lease of any other kind of property. So, for example, if the law permits abatement of the rent when "a house, leased for a year, [is] rendered untenantable by a storm," it ought to permit abatement of the rent when a slave is killed during the lease term.[76]

The racialist conception and defense of slavery that one suspects underlay the latter line of cases is more overt in many of the judicial opinions that narrowed the scope of masters' power to manumit their slaves. For example, the dramatic pair of decisions by the Mississippi Supreme Court erecting multiple barriers against all forms of emancipation were founded on blunt assertions of the profound defects of one race and the political and economic needs of the other. Negroes are "an inferior caste, incapable of the blessings of free government, and occupying, in the order of nature, an intermediate state between the irrational animal and the white man." We do and must treat them as "alien enemies." So, for instance, "[w]e enslave them for life, if they dare set their foot on our soil, and omit to leave on notice in ten days. And this not upon the principle, supposed by some, of enmity, inhumanity, or unkindness, to such inferior race, but on the great principles of self-preservation, which have induced civilized nations in every age of the world to regard them as only fit for slaves, as wholly incapable, morally and mentally, of appreciating or practicing, without enlightenment, the principles and precepts of the Divine and natural law."[77]

The Georgia Supreme Court was equally forthright:

> Neither humanity, nor religion, nor common justice, requires of us to
> sanction or favor domestic emancipation; to give our slaves their lib-
> erty at the risk of losing our own. They are incapable of taking part
> with ourselves, in the exercise of self government. To set up a model
> empire for the world, God in His wisdom planted on this virgin soil,
> the best blood of the human family. To allow it to be contaminated, is
> to be recreant to the weighty and solemn trust committed to our hands.
> Republican institutions cannot exist in Mexico, or the *commingled* races
> of South America.[78]

Vividly evident here are the central features of the second branch of the
proslavery argument: the insistence on the inherent depravity of Negroes, the celebration of democracy, and the assertion that emancipation on a substantial scale would doom it.[79] But what is most remarkable
about the passage is that it was written by Chief Justice Lumpkin, the
same judge who, in the context of leases of slaves, vigorously advanced a
paternalist conception and defense of slavery.[80] The general point suggested by this example is that the two lines of argument were not championed by discrete, rival groups of lawyers. Many (perhaps most) lawmakers invoked one of the theories at some times or in some contexts
and invoked the other at other times or in other contexts.

On occasion, a judge would even deploy both theories in the same
opinion. In *Fisher's Negroes* v. *Dabbs*, for example, the Supreme Court of
Tennessee justified on the following grounds its ruling upholding manumission of a particular group of slaves only on the condition "that they
be transported to the coast of Africa":

> The [freed slaves] residing [in Liberia] are all from the United
> States, speak our language, pursue our habits, profess the christian
> religion; are sober, industrious, moral, and contented; are enjoying a
> life of comfort and of equality which it is impossible in this country to
> enjoy, where the black man is degraded by his color and sinks into vice
> and worthlessness from want of motive to virtuous and elevated con-
> duct. The black man in these states may have the power of volition. He
> may go and come when it pleaseth him, without a domestic master to
> control the actions of his person; but to be politically free, to be the
> peer and equal of the white man, to enjoy the offices, trusts, and privi-
> leges our institutions confer on the white man, is hopeless now and
> ever. The slave who receives the protection and care of a tolerable mas-
> ter holds a condition here superior to the negro who is freed from
> domestic slavery. He is a reproach and a byword with the slave himself,
> who taunts his fellow slave by telling him "he is as worthless as a free
> negro." The consequence is inevitable. The free black man lives amongst
> us without motive and without hope. He seeks no avocation, is sur-
> rounded with necessities, is sunk in degradation; crime can sink him
> no deeper, and he commits it of course. This is not only true of the
> free negro residing in the slaveholding states of this Union. In the

non-slaveholding states the people are less accustomed to the squalid and disgusting wretchedness of the negro, have less sympathy for him, earn their means of subsistence with their own hands, and are more economical in parting with them than him for whom the slave labors; of which he is entitled to share the proceeds, and of which the free negro is generally the participant, and but too often in the character of the receiver of stolen goods. Nothing can be more untrue than that the free negro is more respectable as a member of society in the non-slaveholding than the slaveholding states. In each he is a degraded outcast, and his fancied freedom a delusion. With us the slave ranks him in character and comfort, nor is there a fair motive to absolve him from the duties incident to domestic slavery if he is to continue amongst us. Generally, and almost universally, society suffers and the negro suffers by manumission.[81]

Interwoven in this passage are important themes from both of the two lines of proslavery rhetoric. From the paternalist theory, the court has taken the contrast between the supportive, humane labor system in the South (where slaves receive guidance and support from their altruistic masters) and the hard-hearted labor system in the North (where parsimonious employers are concerned only with maximizing their own incomes). From the racialist theory, the court has taken the theme of the immutable inferiority of "the black man"—his inability ever to sustain a condition of political and social equality with whites. The arguments do not cohere well, and both are hard to reconcile with the image of prosperous, egalitarian Liberia that commences the passage. But such uneasy eclecticism was typical of the thought of many antebellum Southern judges.[82]

Codes of Conduct

The last of the three axes of ideological controversy concerned how a decent person—more specifically, a decent white man—should conduct himself. Southerners could derive answers from either of two competing worldviews: the Code of Honor and Christianity.

Until recently, the cultural power of the idea of honor in the antebellum South was not well appreciated. The work of Bertram Wyatt-Brown, Edward Ayers, and Kenneth Greenberg has largely remedied the neglect. We now know that the establishment and maintenance of personal honor was absolutely vital to the self-worth of many white men. The organizing idea of the code of conduct to which they committed themselves was that a man has only so much worth as others confer on him—or, put differently, that a man is what he appears to be. The principal guidelines for conduct that radiated from this idea were as follows: Be truthful (to call someone a liar was directly to impugn his honor); be brave (to call some-

one a coward was equally serious); defend your family and its reputation; never physically abuse the members of your household; defer to
your social superiors; and condescend to your inferiors. None of these
injunctions was observed scrupulously even by the Southerners most committed to the code, but they defined a set of expectations against which
behavior was measured and established "a framework for handling social problems."[83]

A man whose honor was impugned had to defend it in person. Not
to rise to the challenge (not to be willing, if necessary, to risk one's life to
rebut the charge) was to "lose face"—to forfeit one's claim to have honor.
The importance of this principle explains the extraordinarily high levels
of personal violence in the antebellum South—the no-holds-barred,
eye-gouging brawling among backwoodsmen; the highly ritualized dueling among gentlemen. It also helps make sense of many other distinctive aspects of Southern culture—the reluctance of white men to submit
personal disputes to the courts for resolution; the pugnacious debating
style; the vendettas; the elaborate rules of etiquette, the residues of which
we know as southern hospitality; the rapid escalation of sectional controversies such as the Nullification Crisis and the Civil War itself; and the
nearly suicidal tactics sometimes employed by Confederate soldiers.[84]

How did it come to pass that so many Southern men organized their
lives around the Code of Honor? Some historians emphasize the importance of honor (and the prevalence of violence) in the cultures of the
ethnic groups that populated the South. Others attribute the power of
the belief system to the "hothouse atmosphere" created by the system of
chattel slavery combined with the highly localized, plantation-based agricultural system. Still others contend that the Code of Honor and the
system of dueling used to maintain it were economically efficient and
survived because of their social value.[85] For our purposes, determination
of which is the best explanation is less important than recognition of the
extraordinary currency and influence of this set of interlocking ideas
and customs.

The principal ideological competitor of the Code of Honor was the
complex set of prescriptions for social and spiritual life associated with
Christianity. A broad spectrum of Christian denominations—from Catho-
lics to Quakers—had significant followings in the antebellum South, but
the largest and most culturally powerful groups were the evangelical Prot-
estant sects: Baptists, Methodists, and Presbyterians. Donald Mathews,
the leading historian of Southern religion, describes as follows the central features of the evangelical outlook:

> [T]he Christian life is essentially a personal relationship with God in
> Christ, established through the direct action of the Holy Spirit, an ac-
> tion which elicits in the believer a profoundly emotional conversion
> experience. This existential crisis, the *New Birth* as Evangelicals called
> it, ushers the convert into a life of holiness characterized by religious

devotion, moral discipline, and missionary zeal. To achieve this remarkable transformation, Evangelical preaching rejects the appeal to reason and restrained sensibilities for a direct, psychological assault upon sin and the equally direct and much more comforting offer of personal salvation. The style, suited as it is to the democracy of emotion rather than the hierarchy of intellect, destroys the psychological and social distance between preacher and people, often evoking tearful, passionate outbursts.[86]

Beginning in the mid-eighteenth century, this message found favor with growing numbers of lower-class and middle-class whites in the South. In the second quarter of the nineteenth century, the nationwide religious revival known as the Second Great Awakening accelerated the trend. By the eve of the Civil War, a substantial portion of all socioeconomic groups in the region—including slaves and planters—had committed themselves to the evangelical faith.[87]

The evangelical preachers found little of value in the Code of Honor. Many of the activities the code commended or tolerated—materialism, ostentation, drinking, gambling, and (above all) dueling—they denounced as sinful. Honor itself they characterized as a delusion and the love of it as a form of bondage. Piety, self-control, mercy, humility, and inner strength—not physical courage and self-advertisement—were the marks of a virtuous man.[88]

The impact of Evangelicalism upon Southerners' attitudes toward slavery was complex. A central tenet of the evangelical vision was the notion that God is no respecter of persons—that all men and women, slave and free, are capable of salvation. In the late eighteenth century, a substantial number of evangelical preachers took this proposition to its logical conclusion. Freeing their own slaves, they declared the institution of chattel slavery "contrary to the laws of God, man, and nature, and hurtful to society, contrary to the dictates of conscience and pure religion." After the turn of the century, however, three forces combined to blunt this abolitionist initiative. First, the reformist impulse that gave rise to the preachers' early stance was undercut by their yearning for respectability and hunger for more adherents. Second, the more members of the upper classes they recruited, the less receptive their audiences became to abolitionist arguments. Third, in ways sketched in the preceding section, Southerners as a group became more defensive of slavery as they perceived growing hostility toward it in the North. The net result was that after the 1820s, antislavery Evangelicalism was largely confined to poorer mountain regions in the South.[89]

The early emancipationist stance left two residues, however. First, evangelical Southerners were not as sanguine concerning the morality of slavery as their irreligious neighbors. In ways traced in the preceding section, "the dominant public ideology" of the region had come to be one of "arrogant assurance"; the stance of Evangelicals, by contrast, tended to be "characterized by ambivalence and guilt." Second, evangelical preachers developed and defended a "slaveholding ethic"—a set of guidelines for moral masters. Adhering to their longstanding position that slaves could and should become full members of the Christian community, they urged their parishioners to afford slaves opportunities for worship. More broadly, they insisted that respect for the humanity and dignity of slaves required that they be treated decently; that they be provided adequate food, shelter, clothing, and health care; that they not be physically or sexually abused; that they be educated; and that their family relations be protected. In the words of the Reverend Richard Fuller of South Carolina, "The right of the master places him under the deepest corresponding obligations to promote the interest, temporal and eternal, of his slaves."[90]

Both of these two competing worldviews left myriad traces on the law of slavery. Signs of the Code of Honor were everywhere. Underpinning the ban on black testimony against whites, for example, were the notions that truthfulness is a mark of honor, and that blacks—permanently, ineradicably dishonored—can be expected to lie.[91] A common justification for the rule that battery of a slave by a master (or hirer) is not a crime was that physical abuse of slaves is dishonorable behavior that will be condemned by the community, and that cruel (or potentially cruel) masters will succumb to such social pressure.[92] Similarly, the pride many Southerners took in the ability of masters and overseers to deal with most instances of slave misconduct on their plantations was based partly on their general suspicion of the legal system as a forum for the resolution of disputes—their conviction that honor entails, among other things, "policing one's own ethical sphere."[93]

The doctrinal context in which the power of the Code of Honor can be seen in most detail is the criminal law. For example, in *State* v. *Jarrott*, Justice Gaston explained as follows why the standards of provocation that would extenuate a homicide of one white man by another ought not apply when a white man kills a slave who has insulted him:

> [T]he law shews its indulgence to that frailty of human nature which urges men, before they have an opportunity for reflection, to a compliance with those common notions of honour which forbid either to give way to, or acknowledge the superior prowess of, the other. Such notions spring from a sense of equality, and the horror of personal disgrace. They do not prevail—and they ought not to exist—between those who cannot combat with each other, without degradation on one hand, and arrogance on the other.[94]

The same concepts were deployed in a different pattern in *State* v. *Caesar* to justify the requirement that slaves submit to greater insults from white persons than other whites are obliged to tolerate:

[A] blow inflicted upon a white man carries with it a feeling of degradation, as well as bodily pain, and a sense of injustice; all or either of which are calculated to excite passion; whereas a blow inflicted upon a slave is not attended with any feeling of degradation, by reason of his lowly condition, and is only calculated to excite passion from bodily pain and a sense of wrong. . . . [A]ccustomed as [the slave] is to constant humiliation, it would not be calculated to excite to such a degree as to "dethrone reason," and must be ascribed to a "wicked heart, regardless of social duty."[95]

Collating the two opinions, one gets the following rules: When one white man insults another, honor is at stake; violence is thus predictable and, to some extent, excusable.[96] When a black man insults a white man, violence is less justified because the white man under such circumstances should not feel dishonored. When a white man insults a black man, violence is also less justified because black men have no honor to be challenged.

But reasoning of this sort was by no means the only mode of analysis familiar to the Southern lawmakers; religious arguments were equally common. Statutes or judicial opinions tightening the restrictions on physical abuse of slaves, for example, frequently overtly invoked Christian principles. Thus, in *State v. Hale*, Justice Taylor, in ruling that unjustified battery on a slave is an indictable offense, sought to join "the march of benignant policy and provident humanity, which for many years has characterized every legislative act relative to the protection of slaves, and which Christianity, by the mild diffusion of its light and influence has contributed to promote; and even domestic safety and interest equally enjoin."[97]

The expansion of the defenses available to slaves accused of murdering white persons was often justified on similar grounds. So, in *State v. Will*, Justice William Gaston (a devout Catholic) insisted that a slave who kills an overseer who is attempting to kill him is guilty of no more than manslaughter. "Unless I see my way clear as a sunbeam, I cannot believe that [the contrary rule] is the law of a civilized people and of a Christian land. I will not presume an arbitrary and inflexible rule so sanguinary in its character, and so repugnant to the spirit of those holy statutes which 'rejoice the heart, enlighten the eyes, and are true and righteous altogether.'"[98]

Religious commitments were also evident in statutes and judicial opinions that sought to curb the practice of dueling. In *Commonwealth v. Hart*, for example, a Kentucky court adopted an expansive interpretation of the state statute forbidding one person to "challenge [another] to fight with deadly weapons." The court began the decisive portion of its analysis by characterizing dueling as "[a] practice originating in barbarous ages, under a superstitious notion that God would give the triumph to him who fought in a just cause; and perpetuated by chivalrous spirits, imbued with false notions of honor." Effective prevention of such behavior required, the court continued, that the statute be construed broadly: "[A]ny writing which, when connected with the circumstances of the quarrel, and conduct of the parties, shows an intention to invite or solicit a meeting or interview, in order to fight with deadly weapons, amounts to a challenge within the perview of the act."[99]

A preference for formal, legal resolution of disputes—a stance opposed to the bias in favor of plantation justice—was also commonly tied to Christian commitments. For instance, in *State* v. *Reed*, Judge Henderson responded as follows to counsel's observation that "by the laws of ancient Rome or modern Turkey, an absolute power is given to the master over the life of his slave":

> I answer, These are not the laws of our country, nor the model from which they were taken; it is abhorrent to the hearts of all those who have felt the influence of the mild precepts of Christianity; and it is said, that no law is produced to shew that such is the state for slavery in our land, I call on them to shew the law by which the life of a slave is placed at the disposal of his master.[100]

During the early nineteenth century, the distrust of slave testimony associated (in part) with the Code of Honor was offset in the minds of some judges by religious impulses. During the colonial period, Christian beliefs had tilted in the other direction. As Thomas Morris has shown, the common beliefs that witnesses must take oaths, that oath-givers must be Christian for the oaths to have any effect, that Negroes were heathens, and that their conversion would require their manumission had prompted many colonial assemblies to disable blacks from testifying—at least against whites. In the antebellum period, however, the evangelical faith in the capacity of all persons, including Negroes, to appreciate Christ's essential teachings (combined with general acceptance of the view that conversion did not necessitate emancipation) helped erode the ban on black testimony. For example, in *Lewis* v. *State*, the Mississippi Supreme Court rejected on the following grounds the prosecution's contention that the dying declaration of one slave ought not be admitted in the murder trial of another slave:

> It is true that if the declarant had no sense of future responsibility, his declarations would not be admissible. But the absence of such belief must be shown. The simple, elementary truths of christianity, the immortality of the soul, and a future accountability, are generally received and believed by this portion of our population. From the pulpit many, perhaps all who attain maturity, hear these doctrines announced and enforced, and embrace them as articles of faith.[101]

Christian arguments also helped sustain the line of judicial opinions favorable to the emancipation of slaves. For instance, in perhaps the most famous passage in this line of cases, Justice Green of Tennessee justified as follows his ruling that putatively manumitted slaves have standing to defend the will that purports to free them, despite the fact that they have not yet been declared free:

> A slave is not in the condition of a horse or an ox. His liberty is restrained, it is true, and his owner controls his actions and claims his services. But he is made after the image of the Creator. He has mental capacities, and an immortal principle in his nature, that constitute him equal to his owner but for the accidental position in which fortune has placed him. The owner has acquired conventional rights to him, but the laws under which he is held as a slave have not and cannot extinguish his high-born nature nor deprive him of many rights which are inherent in man.[102]

Last but not least, Christian commitments contributed powerfully to the mixture of anxiety, guilt, and fatalism that infused many of the harshest rulings by Southern courts. A good example is Chief Justice Lumpkin's opinion in *Moran* v. *Davis*, decided in 1855. The defendant in the case had leased a slave, Stephen, from the plaintiff's trustee. When Stephen ran away, the defendant hired another man to pursue him with dogs. Stephen was later found drowned in a creek, where he had apparently sought refuge from the dogs. In the ensuing suit by the plaintiff for the market value of Stephen, the trial judge instructed the jury that it was lawful for the owner, hirer, or overseer of a runaway slave to use dogs to pursue the slave, "provided it be done with such dogs as cannot lacerate or wound." In affirming the resultant verdict for the defendant, Lumpkin argued that the escape of slaves had become a very serious problem for the region. "The South has lost, already, upwards of 60,000 slaves, worth between 25 and 30 millions of dollars." That circumstance, he contended, justified the practice of affording considerable latitude to owners and renters in the selection of means to recover runaways. In the closing paragraph of the opinion, this relatively conventional policy argument gradually gave way to a lurid, apocalyptic vision:

> Instead . . . of relaxing the means allowed by law for the security and enjoyment of this species of property, the facilities afforded for its escape and the temptation and encouragement held out to induce it, constrain us, willingly or otherwise, to redouble our vigilance and to tighten the chords that bind the negro to his condition of servitude— a condition which is to last, if the Apocalypse be inspired, until the end of time; for the author of Revelation beheld, when the sixth seal was opened, and there was a great earthquake, and the sun became black as sackcloth of hair, and the moon became as blood, and the stars of heaven fell unto the earth, even as a fig tree casteth her untimely figs,

> when she is shaken of a mighty wind, and the heaven departed as a
> scroll; when it is rolled together and every mountain and island were
> moved out of their places; and the kings of the earth, and the great
> men, and the chief captains, and the mighty men, and every *bondman*
> (doulos, slave or servant) and every *freeman*, hid themselves in the dens
> and in the rocks of the mountains; and said to the mountains and rocks,
> fall on us and hide us from the face of him that sitteth on the throne
> and from the wrath of the lamb; for the great day of his wrath is come;
> and who shall be able to stand.[103]

The tangle of ideas and emotions in this passage—the sense that slavery
would (and was meant by God to?) last until the Day of Judgment; the
equality (in a condition of abject terror) of all men, slave and free, when
the Apocalyse arrived; and the strong suggestion that the final judgment
would include punishment for the sin of slavery—is testimony both to
the confusion and fear experienced by some of the judges who administered the system of chattel slavery and to the role of Christianity in shaping and sustaining that state of mind.

Conclusion

Two generalizations may be gleaned from the foregoing analyses. The
first and less controversial is that much of the rhetoric of the law of slavery was derived not from the English or Continental legal heritages but
from the discursive systems of other sectors of white antebellum Southern society. The vocabularies, images, and arguments developed in Southern fiction, political economy, formal defenses of slavery, and popular
political debate provided judges and legislators the materials and ana-
lytical tools from which they fashioned the rules that regulated the relations of masters and servants.

The second inference is that the content of antebellum Southern
ideology helps account for the remarkable degree of inconsistency and
instability in the law of slavery. On three questions explored in this essay—the characters and proclivities of slaves, why slavery is just, and how
a just and honorable man should behave—white Southerners were ambivalent or divided. Those divisions fostered corresponding divisions and
uncertainties in legal doctrine. Some of the views lawmakers derived from
the culture at large inclined them to be lenient or (moderately) protective on such matters as the scope of a master's power to manumit his
slaves, the protections the law of torts should (indirectly) provide leased
slaves, the exposure of slave families to breakup, and the sorts of physical or sexual abuse of slaves that would give rise to criminal liability;
other views led them to take harsher stances. Some of their commitments led them to favor private resolution of disputes and the treatment
of slaves as things; others led them to favor public, law-governed resolu-

tion of disputes and the treatment of slaves as persons. Shifts in the relative power or prominence of particular views (for example, the growing
popularity of evangelical Christianity and the efflorescence of formal
defenses of slavery) often precipitated related shifts in legal doctrine
(for example, the softening of many of the rules of criminal law).

The linkage between Southern ideology and the law of slavery should
not be exaggerated, however. Many ideas in general circulation in antebellum Southern culture did not find their way into legal discourse. For
example, the slaves themselves had strong views on many of the issues
addressed in this paper: their sense of their sexual identities and family
responsibilities differed radically from the traits ascribed to them by their
masters;[104] the Africanized versions of evangelical Christianity to which
many slaves committed themselves differed equally sharply from the versions popular among whites;[105] and slaves' beliefs concerning the morality of slavery surely were not captured by the paternalist or racialist arguments.[106] None of these attitudes found expression in statutes or judicial
opinions.[107] Nor were all aspects of white ideology equally represented.
For example, the Code of Honor was largely a construction of white
men; the doubts of many white women concerning the violence and
vanity it encouraged in men and the narrowness of the roles it assigned
women had little impact on the law.[108] Finally, lower-class whites did not
agree on all issues with their superiors; they tended to have many more
doubts concerning the merits of the institution of slavery, and although
some were ferociously racist, others found a substantial degree of social
interaction with blacks unobjectionable.[109] Again, few of these views found
favor with judges and legislators. In short, it was a highly filtered version
of Southern ideology that came to shape the law.

How did the filtration work? Some components of the process are
obvious. All of the lawyers, legislators, and judges were white men; many
were slaveowners. Inevitably, in their arguments and edicts, they gave
precedence to the beliefs of the groups from which they themselves were
drawn. Not all of those beliefs were on their face self serving; had they
been, the slaveholding class would not have been able to sustain its position as the dominant group in the society, and the lawmakers who invoked them would not have been able to sustain popular faith in the
legitimacy of the legal order.[110] Those beliefs, however, surely did not
represent a cross section of the attitudes of the community.

The foregoing account raises as many questions as it answers. How
exactly were deviant views excluded or suppressed? (For example, how
did it come to pass that lawyers and litigants—many of whom knew intimately slaves who did not conform to the Sambo or Nat stereotypes—
were induced to use those paradigms so consistently when framing their
testimony and pleas?) Did appellate opinions help to shape and sustain
the belief systems of the dominant groups, or were they merely parasitic
upon nonlegal discourse? Last but not least, if the dynamic of cultural

hegemony explains why only a subset of Southerners' views came to dominate the law, why did not the same dynamic limit the degree to which
slaveowners and lawmakers disagreed on matters of fundamental importance? Much more research must be done on the ways in which law func-
tioned in Southern culture before any of these questions can be answered.[111]

A final cautionary note: The objective of this essay is not to displace
the four interpretations that currently dominate discussions of the topics addressed herein but to supplement them. The thesis of the paper is
not that ideology alone is relevant to an understanding of the laws establishing and regulating chattel slavery in the United States. It is, rather,
that in trying to make sense of those laws, legal historians should not
limit their attention to the material interests of the dominant classes, the
idiosyncrasies of individual lawmakers, the contradictory character of
the Southern relations of production, and the laws of jurisdictions from
which Americans borrowed ideas. They should also attend to the changing ways white Southerners conceived of and sought to justify their social
world.

Notes

This essay is a revised and expanded version of an article first published in the
Chicago-Kent Law Review 68 (1993): 1051–83. The original version of this essay
was prepared while I was a Fellow at the Center for Advanced Study in the Behavioral Sciences. I am grateful for financial support provided by the Andrew W.
Mellon Foundation. Drafts of the paper were presented to the Stanford Law
School Faculty Workshop, the Stanford Legal History Group, the Harvard Summer Research Workshop, and the Yale Legal History Workshop; the reactions of
the participants in those sessions provoked significant modifications of the argument. The suggestions of Elizabeth Clark, Andrew Fede, Paul Finkelman, Robert Gordon, Joann Lisberger, Barry O'Connell, Dorothy Ross, and Richard
Yarborough also improved the paper. In revising the essay, the research assistance of Erika Frick was invaluable.

1. See Wilbert Moore, "Slave Law and the Social Structure," *Journal of Negro
History* 26 (1941): 171, 185–87. This rule represented a repudiation of the doctrine that governed the English law of villenage. For discussions of the modest
differences among the colonies and states concerning how racial status is to be
determined and how much "black blood" is essential to expose a person to enslavement (and other legal disabilities), see William W. Wiecek, "The Statutory
Law of Slavery and Race in the Thirteen Mainland Colonies of British America,"
William and Mary Quarterly 34 (1977): 238; Paul Finkelman, "The Crime of Color,"
67 *Tulane Law Review* 2063 (1993).

2. See Andrew Fede, *People without Rights: An Interpretation of the Fundamentals of the Law of Slavery in the U.S. South* (New York: Garland, 1992), 62–97; Alan
Watson, *Slave Law in the Americas* (Athens, Ga.: University of Georgia Press, 1989),
74–75.

3. See, e.g., A. Leon Higginbotham Jr., *In the Matter of Color* (New York: Oxford University Press, 1978); Philip J. Schwarz, *Twice Condemned: Slaves and the Criminal Laws of Virginia, 1705–1865* (Baton Rouge: Louisiana State University Press, 1988); Kenneth Stampp, *The Peculiar Institution* (New York: Alfred A. Knopf, 1956), 206–16.

4. For an account of the emergence of caveat emptor in the North, see Morton J. Horwitz, *The Transformation of American Law, 1760–1860* (Cambridge: Harvard University Press, 1977), 180.

For descriptions of the spectrum of positions taken by the various Southern states, see Andrew Fede, "Legal Protection for Slave Buyers in the U.S. South: A Caveat Concerning Caveat Emptor," 31 *American Journal of Legal History* 322 (1987); Judith Schafer, "'Guaranteed against the Vices and Maladies Prescribed by Law': Consumer Protection, the Law of Slave Sales, and the Supreme Court in Antebellum Louisiana," 31 *American Journal of Legal History* 306 (1987); Ariela Gross, "Pandora's Box: Slave Character on Trial in the Antebellum Deep South," in this volume. In 1899 the black writer Charles Chesnut published a book of plantation stories, the first of which revolves around a bewitched slave who during the summer was youthful and strong but during the winter was old and infirm. Each year his owner would sell the slave at the peak of his powers for a high price, then generously agree to buy him back for a low price a few months later when he seemed to be dying. That none of the purchasers of the slave sought to rescind the original sale suggests that, by the turn of the century at any rate, the warranty of fitness was not widely known. See Charles W. Chesnut, *The Conjure Woman* (Ann Arbor: University of Michigan Press, 1969), 24–28.

5. See, e.g., *Creswell's Ex'r v. Walker*, 37 Ala. 229, 234–35 (1861); A. Leon Higginbotham, Jr. and Barbara Kopytoff, "Property First, Humanity Second: The Recognition of the Slave's Human Nature in Virginia Civil Law," 50 *Ohio State Law Journal* 511, 525–28 (1989).

6. The one significant exception to this principle was that in every state slaves were permitted (usually through "next friends") to petition for freedom on the ground that they had been wrongfully enslaved. See, e.g., Act of 1740, sec. 1, S.C. Public Laws 163–64 ("An Act for the Better Ordering and Governing of Negroes and Other Slaves in this Province"); Act of June 18, 1822, sec. 76, 1882 Miss. Laws 179, 198–99 ("An Act to reduce into one the several acts, concerning Slaves, Free Negroes, and Mulattoes").

7. See, e.g., Higginbotham and Kopytoff, "Property First," 528–33; William E. Wiethoff, "The Logic and Rhetoric of Slavery in Early Louisiana Civil Law Reports," 12 *Legal Studies Forum* 441, 448 (1988); *Love v. Brindle*, 52 N.C. (7 Jones) 560 (1860). The only official exception to this rule was the willingness of some courts to defer, when administering decedents' estates, to the widespread custom of permitting slaves to keep the proceeds of crops grown on small garden plots. See *Waddill v. Martin*, 38 N.C. (3 Ired. Eq.) 562, 564–65 (1845). Slaves in ancient Rome, by contrast, had much more extensive rights. Although technically they could not own property, they frequently were permitted to earn money and thereby accumulate a fund, called *peculium*—and even to use the fund to purchase their freedom. See Alan Watson, *Roman Slave Law* (Baltimore: Johns Hopkins University Press, 1987), 90–101.

8. See Margaret A. Burnham, "An Impossible Marriage: Slave Law and Family Law," 5 *Law and Inequality Journal* 187 (1987); *Smith v. State*, 9 Ala. 990, 996

(1846): "[T]he municipal law . . . does not recognize, for any purpose whatever, the marriages of slaves, and therefore there is no prohibition against the husband and wife being witnesses for, or against each other."

9. See Eugene Genovese, *Roll, Jordan, Roll: The World the Slaves Made* (New York: Vintage, 1976), 33. The rare exceptions (seemingly inadvertent) are described in Alan Watson, *Slave Law in the Americas*, 73–74. This disability was explicitly based on race. Thus, free blacks and mulattoes typically were also forbidden to testify against whites, while slaves, free blacks, and mulattoes were able to testify against each other.

10. See Daniel J. Flanigan, "Criminal Procedure in Slave Trials in the Antebellum South," *Journal of Southern History* 40 (1974): 537, 540–46; A. Leon Higginbotham Jr. and Anne F. Jacobs, "The 'Law Only as an Enemy': The Legitimization of Racial Powerlessness through the Colonial and Antebellum Criminal Laws of Virginia," 70 *North Carolina Law Review* 969, 984–1016 (1992). In a recent article, Judith Schafer contends that in Louisiana slave defendants were treated very badly; see "The Long Arm of the Law: Slave Criminals and the Supreme Court in Antebellum Louisiana," 60 *Tulane Law Review* 1247 (1986). However, many of her examples involve aspects of the criminal justice system that Louisiana inherited from the French and that were unfavorable to all defendants (not merely slaves), and she acknowledges that convictions of slaves were overturned with approximately the same frequency as convictions of whites. See ibid., 1258–59. On balance, Flanigan's original assessment of the Louisiana system still seems accurate.

11. The quotation is from *Cato* v. *State*, 9 Fla. 163, 173–74 (1860). For documentation of the extensive protections provided slaves (especially at the appellate level) in these states, see Reuel E. Schiller, "Conflicting Obligations: Slave Law and the Late Antebellum North Carolina Supreme Court," 78 *Virginia Law Review* 1207, 1222 (1992); Flanigan, "Criminal Procedure"; A. E. Keir Nash, "The Texas Supreme Court and the Trial Rights of Blacks, 1845–1860," *Journal of American History* 58 (1971): 628–29; A. E. Keir Nash, "Negro Rights, Unionism, and Greatness on the South Carolina Court of Appeals: The Extraordinary Chief Justice John Belton O'Neall," 21 *South Carolina Law Review* 141 (1969); A. E. Keir Nash, "Fairness and Formalism in the Trials of Blacks in the State Supreme Courts of the Old South," 56 *Virginia Law Review* 64 (1970).

12. See A. E. Keir Nash, "Reason of Slavery: Understanding the Judicial Role in the Peculiar Institution," 32 *Vanderbilt Law Review* 7 (1979); Schiller, "Conflicting Obligations," 1235. But cf. David J. Grindle, "Manumission: The Weak Link in Georgia's Law of Slavery," 41 *Mercer Law Review* 701 (1990), (identifying various contexts in which the Georgia rules on manumission were not unusually harsh).

13. See Arthur F. Howington, "'Not in the Condition of a Horse or an Ox': *Ford* v. *Ford*, the Law of Testamentary Manumission, and the Tennessee Courts' Recognition of Slave Humanity," *Tennessee Historical Quarterly* 34 (1975): 249; Nash, "Reason of Slavery."

14. See David J. Langum, "The Role of Intellect and Fortuity in Legal Change: An Incident from the Law of Slavery," 28 *American Journal of Legal History* 1, 3–4, 13–14 (1984).

15. See Terrence F. Kiely, "The Hollow Words: An Experiment in Legal-Historical Method as Applied to the Law of Slavery," 25 *DePaul Law Review* 842

(1976); Thomas D. Morris, "'As If the Injury Was Effected by the Natural Elements of Air, or Fire': Slave Wrongs and the Liability of Masters," 16 *Law and Society Review* 569 (1982); Schafer, "Long Arm of the Law," 1257–61.

16. See Kiely, "Hollow Words," 871–76; Frederick Wertheim, "Slavery and the Fellow Servant Rule: An Antebellum Dilemma," 61 *N.Y.U. Law Review* 1112, 1129–36 (1986); Paul Finkelman, "Slaves as Fellow Servants: Ideology, Law, and Industrialization," 31 *American Journal of Legal History* 269 (1987).

17. See Howington, "'Not in the Condition of a Horse or an Ox'"; Schiller, "Conflicting Obligations," 1235. Until the mid 1840s, South Carolina law pertaining to manumission resembled that of Tennessee; the legislature adopted a series of statutes hostile to emancipation, which the judiciary resisted or narrowly construed. See Linda O. Smiddy, "Judicial Nullification of State Statutes Restricting the Emancipation of Slaves: A Southern Court's Call for Reform," 42 *South Carolina Law Review* 589, 598–630 (1991). After the mid 1840s, however, the consensus among the judges broke down. Compare, e.g., *McLeish* v. *Burch*, 35 S.C. Eq. (3 Strob. Eq.) 225 (1849) (upholding a bequest of a slave accompanied by instructions that he should be held in nominal service only—in defiance of an 1841 statute declaring such trusts invalid) with, e.g., *Gordon* v. *Blackman*, 18 S.C. Eq. (1 Rich. Eq.) 61, 61 (1844) (Johnston, Ch.) (bemoaning the proliferation of cases in which "the superstitious weakness of dying men, proceeding from an astonishing ignorance of the solid moral and scriptural foundations upon which the institution of slavery rests, and from a total inattention to the shock which their conduct is calculated to give to the whole frame of our social polity, induces them, in their last moments, to emancipate their slaves, in fraud of the indubitable and declared policy of the State"); see also Watson, *Slave Law in the Americas*, 75–82. For an analysis of the handling of the same problems in Mississippi, see Meredith Lang, *Defender of the Faith: The High Court of Mississippi, 1817–1875* (Jackson: University Press of Mississippi, 1977), 91–92 (concluding that "schizophrenia within the high court . . . resulted in two conflicting lines of cases on the issue of manumission: one holding the policy of the state to be merely against the increase of free Negroes in Mississippi, but not against their manumission elsewhere; and the other, opposed to emancipation in any form, anywhere)." The judges in Virginia were not so sharply divided but still differed on substantial issues. See Nash, "Reason of Slavery," 127–56.

18. See, e.g., *State* v. *Mann*, 13 N.C. (2 Dev.) 263 (1829); *State* v. *Jarrott*, 23 N.C. (1 Ired.) 76 (1840); *State* v. *Caesar*, 31 N.C. (9 Ired.) 391 (1849).

19. See, e.g., Stampp, *Peculiar Institution*, 201; Winthrop D. Jordan, *White over Black: American Attitudes toward the Negro, 1550–1812* (Chapel Hill: University of North Carolina Press, 1968), 71–82; Higginbotham, *In the Matter of Color*, 56–58. Initially slaves were classified in some colonies as real property. By the middle of the eighteenth century, however, they were treated in most jurisdictions as chattels personal. But see *Cooke* v. *Cooke*, 13 Ky. (3 Litt.) 238 (1823), treating a slave as real property for the purposes of inheritance.

20. See, e.g., *State* v. *Simmons*, 3 S.C.Law (1 Brev.) 6 (1794): "Negroes . . . have wills of their own, capacities to commit crimes; and are responsible for their offenses against society"; *United States* v. *Amy*, 24 F. Cas. 792 (C.C.D. Va. 1859) (No. 14,445); *Commonwealth* v. *Chapple*, 3 Va. (1 Va. Cas.) 184, 185, (1811), upholding the conviction of a white defendant under a statute proscribing homicide of a "person" on the ground that "a slave in this country has been fre-

quently decided to be legally and technically a person on whom a wrong can be inflicted." For secondary studies emphasizing this tension, see Moore, "Slave Law and Social Structure," 191–202; Kiely, "Hollow Words," 853–58.

21. *State* v. *Jones*, 1 Miss. (1 Walker) 83, 84 (1820). For other judicial acknowledgments of this tension, see, e.g., *State* v. *Williams*, 31 N.C. (9 Ired.) 140, 145–47 (1848); *State* v. *Jim*, 48 N.C. (3 Jones) 348, 352 (1856); *State* v. *Maner*, 20 S.C.L. (2 Hill) 453, 454–55 (1854); *Elijah* v. *State*, 20 Tenn. (1 Hum.) 102, 103–4 (1839).

22. See *Miller* v. *Porter*, 47 Ky. (8 B. Mon.) 282, 283 (1848): "The running away of a slave is not a public but a private offence, the prevention and punishment of which the law leaves to the owner, without making any provision in aid of his rights, except that when a runaway slave is taken up by a stranger, he may be placed in a county jail where he may be reclaimed by the owner; or if not reclaimed within a certain period, may be sold for his benefit. . . . The law presumes that the owner is competent to control and manage his own slave, and leaves the trouble and expense and responsibility of so doing to be borne or provided for by him."; *State* v. *Boozer*, 36 S.C.L. (5 Strob.) 21 (1850): "[A] judicious freedom of administration in our police law for the lower order, must always have respect to the confidence which the law reposes in the discretion of the master, the presence of the proprietor, his loyalty to the sympathies and the policy that involve our common interests, peace and safety"; *Ann* v. *State*, 30 Tenn. (11 Hum.) 159, 165 (1850): "[T]he charge puts the disobedience to the master's order, on the same footing with a violation of a command, or prohibition of the law. This is a great mistake. Such violation of the master's order, is not an 'unlawful act' in the sense of the rule above stated. It is no offence against the law of the land: nor is it cognizable by any tribunal created by law. It is an offence simply against the private authority of the master, and is cognizable and punishable alone in the domestic forum"; Robert Fogel and Stanley Engerman, *Time on the Cross: The Economics of American Negro Slavery* (Boston: Little, Brown, 1974), 144–47; Edward Ayers, *Vengeance and Justice: Crime and Punishment in the Nineteenth-Century American South* (New York: Oxford University Press, 1984), 133.

23. See, e.g., *Witsell* v. *Earnest*, 10 S.C.L. (1 Nott & McC.) 182, 183–84 (1818); *State* v. *Hale*, 9 N.C. (2 Hawks) 454 (1823); *State* v. *Jarrott, supra* note 18; *Doughty* v. *Owen*, 24 Miss. 404, 407–9 (1852); *Jordan* v. *State*, 32 Miss. 382, 387 (1856); *Polk, Wilson & Co.* v. *Fancher*, 38 Tenn. (1 Head) 336, 338–39 (1858). Cf. Act of 1712, sec. 19, 1712 S.C. Public Laws 18 ("An Act for the better Ordering and Governing of Negroes and Slaves in this Province"), penalizing masters for failing to impose on runaway slaves statutorily prescribed penalties.

24. See, e.g., *Armstrong* v. *Hodges*, 41 Ky. (2 B. Mon.) 69, 70 (1841); *State* v. *Fore*, 23 N.C. (1 Ired.) 378 (1841); *Midgett* v. *McBryde*, 48 N.C. (3 Jones) 21 (1855). There were, however, some exceptions to this pattern—cases in which the judges were remarkably tolerant of sexual relations between white women and black men. See, e.g., *Walters* v. *Jordan*, 34 N.C. (12 Ired.) 170 (1851); *Smith* v. *State*, 39 Ala. 554 (1865).

25. See Harvey M. Applebaum, "Miscegenation Statutes: A Constitutional and Social Problem," 53 *Georgetown Law Journal* 49 (1964); Karen Getman, "Sexual Control in the Slaveholding South: The Implementation and Maintenance of a Racial Caste System," 7 *Harvard Women's Law Journal* 115 (1984); A.

Leon Higginbotham, Jr., and Barbara K. Kopytoff, "Racial Purity and Interracial Sex in the Law of Colonial and Antebellum Virginia," 77 *Georgetown Law Journal* 1967 (1989). Cf. *Richmond* v. *Richmond*, 18 Tenn. (10 Yer.) 343 (1837), granting a divorce to a wife whose husband had committed adultery with a slave, but showing little distaste for the husband's behavior; Hubbard's Will, 29 Ky. (6 J.J. Marsh.) 58 (1831) (upholding—and commending—a bequest by a white man to his illegitimate slave daughter); *Patton* v. *Patton*, 28 Ky. (5 J.J. Marsh) 389 (1831); *Carrie* v. *Cumming*, 26 Ga. 690 (1859); *Jeter* v. *Jeter*, 36 Ala. 391 (1860), strongly condemning a husband's adultery but showing little concern for the fact that it was interracial.

The most apparent manifestation of the ubiquity of miscegenation was the growing population of mulattoes. By the Civil War, approximately 10 percent of the "black" population in the South had some white blood. See Sally G. McMillen, *Southern Women: Black and White in the Old South* (Arlington Heights, Ill.: Harlan Davidson, 1992), 22.

26. See Nash, "Reason of Slavery," esp. 141–44, 184–218; Langum, "The Role of Intellect and Fortuity," 16, contending that much of the law of slavery was determined by the personal opinions of individual lawmakers or by "fortuity".

27. See, e.g., Andrew Fede, "Legitimized Violent Slave Abuse in the American South, 1619–1865: A Case Study of Law and Social Change in Six Southern States," 29 *American Journal of Legal History* 93, 150 (1985): "[T]he changing law of white slave abusers represented the shifting accommodation of the interests of the white 'rulers' and 'despots,' and nothing more"; Schafer, "Long Arm of the Law"; Higginbotham and Kopytoff, "Property First," 525, 538. In his most recent essay on the law of slavery, Andrew Fede modifies in modest respects the stance he took in his early work—arguing that there were divisions within the master class that sometimes affected legal doctrine and that "regulations did occasionally interfere with the owner's absolute dominion over the slave, as well as the slave's economic value." Fede, *People without Rights*, 11, 52.

28. See Mark V. Tushnet, *The American Law of Slavery: 1810–1860* (Princeton: Princeton University Press, 1981); cf. Eugene Genovese and Elizabeth Fox-Genovese, "Slavery, Economic Development, and the Law: The Dilemma of the Southern Political Economists, 1800–1860," 41 *Washington and Lee Law Review* 1 (1984), commending Tushnet's analysis and arguing that the same fundamental contradiction largely paralyzed Southern political economists.

29. See, e.g., Watson, *Slave Law in the Americas*, 1–21, 63–82; Thomas D. Morris, "'Villeinage . . . as It Existed in England Reflects But Little Light on Our Subject': The Problem of the Sources of Southern Slave Law," 32 *American Journal of Legal History* 95 (1988); Arnold Sio, "Interpretations of Slavery: The Slave Status in the Americas," *Comparative Studies in Society and History* 7 (1965): 289; Bradley J. Nicholson, "Legal Borrowing and the Origins of Slave Law in the British Colonies," 38 *American Journal of Legal History* 38 (1994). Not all of the historians who adopt this approach agree, of course, on the ratios of the ingredients of American slave law; but the recipe set forth in the text would meet with at least qualified approval from most.

30. On instrumentalism, see Robert Cottrol, "Liberalism and Paternalism: Ideology, Economic Interest, and the Business Law of Slavery," 31 *American Journal of Legal History* 359 (1987). On judicial idiosyncracies, see Schiller, "Con-

flicting Obligations." On Scientific Marxism, see A. E. Keir Nash, "In re Radical Interpretations of American Law: The Relation of Law and History," 82 *Michigan Law Review* 274 (1983); Alan Watson, "Slave Law: History and Ideology," 91 *Yale Law Journal* 1034 (1982) (reviewing Tushnet, *American Law of Slavery*); Andrew Fede, "Toward a Solution of the Slave Law Dilemma: A Critique of Tushnet's 'The American Law of Slavery,'" 2 *Law and History Review* 301 (1984). On borrowing, see Richard Abel, "Law as Lag: Inertia as a Social Theory of Law," 80 *Michigan Law Review* 785 (1982).

31. The notion that ideology helped shape the institution of chattel slavery is not new, of course; it has long figured importantly in the work of nonlegal historians. See, e.g., Genovese, *Roll, Jordan, Roll*; John Blassingame, *The Slave Community: Plantation Life in the Ante-Bellum South*, rev. ed. (New York: Oxford University Press, 1979); George Fredrickson, *The Black Image in the White Mind: The Debate on Afro-American Character and Destiny, 1817–1914* (New York: Harper and Row, 1971). Only recently, however, has it begun to color the study of legal history—most notably in the work of Kenneth Greenberg and Edward Ayers. See Kenneth Greenberg, *Masters and Statesmen* (Baltimore: Johns Hopkins Press, 1985); Edward Ayers, *Vengeance and Justice*. One of the goals of this essay is to accelerate the trend.

32. Blassingame, *Slave Community*, 225.

33. Samuel Cartwright, "On the Caucasians and the Africans," *Debow's Review* 25 (July 1858), 45. Many similar comments are set forth in Blassingame, *Slave Community*, 225–28. See also Kenneth Greenberg, "The Meaning of Death in Slave Society," 8 *Research in Law, Deviance and Social Control* 113, 119 (1986). Stanley Elkins is now infamous in the historiography of slavery for assuming that this common image of slaves was accurate. See Stanley Elkins, *Slavery* (Chicago: University of Chicago Press, 1959); Ann J. Lane, ed., *The Debate over Slavery: Stanley Elkins and His Critics* (Urbana: University of Illinois Press, 1971).

34. Slave characters of this sort abound, for example, in the work of William Gilmore Simms, the most prolific and popular antebellum Southern novelist. See *The Yemassee* (New York: Harper and Brothers, 1835); *The Partisan* (New York: Harper and Brothers, 1835); *Mellichampe* (New York: Harper and Brothers, 1836); *Southward Ho!* (New York: Redfield, 1854); *The Forayers* (New York: Redfield, 1855).

35. See Julien J. Virey, *Natural History of the Negro Race* (1837), 19; Fredrickson, *Black Image in the White Mind*, 53–54.

36. Blassingame, *Slave Community*, 225. See also John Campbell, review of *Negro-Mania, Southern Quarterly Review* (1852): 163–66, depicting "the negro" as "roving, revengeful and destructive, . . . warlike, predatory, and sensual."

37. *The South Vindicated from the Treason and Fanaticism of the Northern Abolitionists* (Philadelphia, 1846), 246. This treatise, published anonymously, was apparently written by James K. Paulding, a novelist and Secretary of the Navy under Martin Van Buren. For expressions of similar sentiments, see Fredrickson, *Black Image in the White Mind*, 54–55; Schwarz, *Twice Condemned*, 194, quoting a 1785 petition submitted by the residents of Amelia County to the Virginia legislature and contending that general emancipation would unleash "the Horrors of all the Rapes, Murders, and Outrages, which a vast Multitude of unprincipled, revengeful, and remorseless Banditti are capable of perpetrating."

A powerful exploration in the fiction of the period of whites' anxieties concerning the characters of slaves may be found in Herman Melville's novella *Benito Cereno* (1855; London: Nonesuch Press, 1926). At the critical moment in the story, "scales" drop from the eyes of the credulous American, Captain Delano, and he comes to see the central figure, Babo, not as the loyal and attentive slave he had pretended to be but as a murderous rebel, whose "countenance, lividly vindictive, express[ed] the centered purpose of his soul." For a fine treatment of the story and its subtle play on Americans' perceptions of the successful slave revolt in San Domingo, see Eric J. Sundquist, *To Wake the Nations: Race in the Making of American Literature* (Cambridge: Harvard University Press, Belknap Press, 1993), chap. 2. A similar theme runs through Edgar Allan Poe's novel *The Narrative of Arthur Gordon Pym* (1838; Paris: Michael Levy Frères, 1858).

38. See Blassingame, *Slave Community*, 230–38; Genovese, *Roll, Jordan, Roll*, 361–63. For an expression of this ambivalence, see Mary Boykin Chesnut, *A Diary from Dixie* (Boston: Houghton Mifflin, 1949) 147–48:

> If they want to kill us, they can do it when they please, they are noiseless as panthers. . . .
>
> We ought to be grateful that anyone of us is alive, but nobody is afraid of their own Negroes. I find everyone, like myself, ready to trust their own yard. I would go down on the plantation tomorrow and stay there even if there were no other white person in twenty miles. My Molly and all the rest I believe would keep me as safe as I should be in the Tower of London.

Not surprisingly, the anxieties of whites concerning the character and sexuality of black men were especially strong during periods of actual or rumored slave insurrections. Whites' reports of such plots frequently accused the slaves of planning to capture and rape young white women, despite the fact that there is no evidence that slave rebels ever attempted to do so. See Jordan, *White over Black*, 398, n. 42.

39. Richard Yarborough argues convincingly that after 1850 Southerners' images of blacks became more complex and that the publication of Harriet Beecher Stowe's enormously influential novel *Uncle Tom's Cabin* helped provoke that shift in thinking. Many of the black characters in the novel—such as the bumptious Sam and Andy, the easily corrupted and easily cured Sambo and Quimbo, and the impish and heathen but redeemable Topsy—readily conform to the prevailing stereotypes. But other characters—most importantly, the dignified and Christlike Tom and the bitter, intelligent mulatto George—did not fit the extant molds. The efforts of Southern novelists and commentators (as well as Northern white and black novelists) to come to terms with these new character types set off a reconsideration of the varieties of black personality that continues today. By the Civil War, however, that process had barely begun. See Richard Yarborough, "Strategies of Black Characterization in *Uncle Tom's Cabin* and the Early Afro-American Novel," in *New Essays on Uncle Tom's Cabin*, ed. Eric Sundquist (Cambridge: Cambridge University Press, 1986), 45–84.

40. For accounts of these contrasting stereotypes and their origins, see Jordan, *White over Black*, 24–40, 154–59; Deborah Gray White, *Ar'n't I a Woman: Female Slaves in the Plantation South* (New York: Norton, 1985), 27–61; Evelyn Brooks Higginbotham, "African-American Women's History and the

Metalanguage of Race," *Signs* 17 (1992): 251, 262–66; James O. Breeden, ed., *Advice among Masters: The Ideal in Slave Management in the Old South* (Westport, Conn.: Greenwood, 1980), 242–44.

41. See White, *Ar'n't I a Woman*, 45–46.

42. Elizabeth Fox-Genovese, *Within the Plantation Household: Black and White Women of the Old South* (Chapel Hill: University of North Carolina Press, 1988), 292 (footnote omitted). See also White, *Ar'n't I a Woman*, 38–39.

43. *State* v. *Boyce*, 32 N.C. (10 Ired.) 536 (1849).

44. Ibid., 541. For other invocations of the Sambo image, see *Sarter* v. *Gordon*, 11 S.C. Eq. (2 Hill Eq.) 121, 135 (1835); *State* v. *Caesar*, *supra* note 18; Thomas R. R. Cobb, *An Inquiry into the Law of Negro Slavery in the United States of America, to Which Is Prefixed an Historical Sketch of Slavery* (Philadelphia: T. and J. W. Johnson, 1858).

45. *Roser* v. *Marlow*, 1 Ga. Ann. (R.M.C.) 542, 548 (1837). Another illustration of judicial use of Sambo imagery may be found in Chief Justice Lumpkin's opinion in *Adams* v. *Bass*, 18 Ga. 130 (1855), where he argues that interpreting a master's will in favor of sending a slave to a free state for purposes of manumission might be detrimental to the slave:

> [R]eflect upon [the] thriftlessness [of persons of color], when not controlled by superior intelligence and forethought, and what friend of the African or of humanity, would desire to see these children of the sun, who luxuriate in a tropical climate and perish with cold in higher latitudes, brought in close contact and competition with the hardy and industrious population which teem in the territory northwest of the Ohio, and who loathe negroes as they would so many lepers.

Ibid., 138–39.

46. Act of October 1669, 2 *The Statutes at Large: Being a Collection of All the Laws of Virginia* 270 (William W. Hening Comp., Richmond, 1819–23): "An act about the casual killing of slaves."

47. Quoted in John B. Boles, *Black Southerners, 1619–1869* (Lexington: University Press of Kentucky, 1983), 23.

48. *Snee* v. *Trice*, 3 S.C.L. (2 Bay) 345 (1802). For decisions in other states reaching similar results for similar reasons, see *Boulard* v. *Calhoun*, 13 La. Ann. 445, 447–48 (1858); *Parham* v. *Blackwelder*, 30 N.C. (8 Ired.) 446 (1848).

49. See Jordan, *White over Black*, 24–40, 154–59; Richard Yarborough, "The Construction of Black Sexuality in Early Afro-American Fiction" (unpublished paper presented to the European Association for American Studies Conference, Seville, Spain, April 6, 1992). For the persistence of this imagery in the postbellum period, see, e.g., Thomas Dixon Jr., *The Clansman* (1905).

50. *State* v. *Sam*, 60 N.C. (Win.) 300, 303 (1864). See Jordan, *White over Black*, 151–54; Getman, "Sexual Control," 134–42; Jennifer Wriggins, "Rape, Racism, and the Law," 6 *Harvard Women's Law Journal* 103, 105–7 (1983); cf. *State* v. *Elick*, 52 N.C. (7 Jones) 68, 70–71 (1859), depicting a slave accused of assault with intent to rape a white woman as naturally rapacious.

51. See Burnham, "Impossible Marriage," 189, 204, 208, 212; Getman, "Sexual Control," 116–17. Cf. Cobb, *Inquiry into the Law of Negro Slavery*, ccxix,

attributing "the want of chastity in female slaves" not to masters' abuse of their power, but to "the natural lewdness of the negro."

52. *State* v. *George*, 37 Miss. 316, 317 (1859) (counsel for the defendant). See also *State* v. *Sewell*, 48 N.C. (3 Jones) 245 (1855), in which a defendant accused of raping and murdering a free black woman is only charged with murder; Burnham, "Impossible Marriage," 220–21; Getman, "Sexual Control," 142–44.

The presumption that blacks are promiscuous continued to shape the content and administration of the criminal law after emancipation. Convictions of white men for raping black women remained rare, and although prosecutions of *whites* for fornication, cohabitation, and seduction were reasonably common, prosecutions of *blacks* for such offenses were unusual. See Mary Francis Berry, "Judging Morality: Sexual Behavior and Legal Consequences in the Late Nineteenth-Century South," *Journal of American History* 78 (1991): 835, 840, 849; Neil McMillen, *Dark Journey: Black Mississippians in the Age of Jim Crow* (Urbana: University of Illinois Press, 1989), 205–6.

53. *Ann* v. *State, supra* note 22, at 162. See also *Singleton* v. *Bremar*, 16 S.C.L. (Harp.) 201, 206 (1824) (argument of defense counsel): "But it may be asked, have we shown the woman to have been a prostitute in this case? Though it may sound harshly, we have shewn what is equivalent. When the intercourse commenced, she was a slave; as to whom our laws do not recognize marriage, not consequently chastity. And owing to the degraded point of view in which such persons are regarded, it was not practically an injury, as respected either her reputation or means of support."

54. *State* v. *Caesar, supra* note 18, at 421–24.

55. See Gross, "'Pandora's Box.'" For an example of a case deploying the competing images, see *Arrington* v. *Grissom*, 41 Tenn. (1 Cold.) 521, 523–25 (1860). The power of the two stereotypes was especially pronounced in appellate opinions; at trial, the lawyers would sometimes seek to demonstrate that the slaves had traits (e.g., honesty and industry) not found in either of the paradigms. See Gross, in this volume.

Kirkwood v. *Miller*, 37 Tenn. (5 Sneed) 455 (1858), exemplifies another context in which the litigants struggled over which of the two stereotypes better characterized the slave in question. The defendants sought to justify their killing of the plaintiff's slave on the ground that they reasonably believed he was engaged in an insurrection. The plaintiff and the court disagreed: at the time of the killing, the victim "had not misbehaved himself in any way, had done no wrong, threatened none, and was entirely submissive and docile." Ibid., 459. For a similar debate over a victim's character in a similar doctrinal context, see *Williams* v. *Fambro*, 30 Ga. 232 (1860).

56. *State* v. *Jarrott, supra* note 18 (emphasis in original). For similar statements, see *State* v. *Hoover*, 20 N.C. (4 Dev. & Bat.) 365, 367 (1839) (Ruffin, C.J.); *State* v. *Jones, supra* note 21, at 85–86 (Clarke, J.); *State* v. *Caesar, supra* note 18, at 406 (Pearson, J.).

57. See David Donald, "The Proslavery Argument Reconsidered," *Journal of Southern History* 37 (1971): 3; Drew Gilpin Faust, *The Ideology of Slavery: Proslavery Thought in the Antebellum South, 1830–1860* (Baton Rouge: Louisiana State University Press, 1981), 1–20; Drew Gilpin Faust, *A Sacred Circle: The Dilemma of the*

Intellectual in the Old South, 1840–1860 (Baltimore: Johns Hopkins University Press, 1977); Larry E. Tise, *Proslavery: A History of the Defense of Slavery in America, 1701–1840* (Athens: University of Georgia Press, 1987).

58. For secondary accounts of this group of theories, see Peter J. Parish, *Slavery: History and Historians* (New York: Harper and Row, 1989), 142; Faust, *Ideology of Slavery*, 12–14; Genovese and Fox-Genovese, "Slavery, Economic Development and the Law."

59. See, e.g., George Fitzhugh, *Cannibals All!; or, Slaves without Masters* ed. C. Vann Woodward (1857; Cambridge: Harvard University Press, Belknap Press, 1960). The unpopularity of this variant of the argument is documented in James Oakes, *The Ruling Race: A History of American Slaveholders* (New York: Vintage Books, 1982), chap. 2.

60. The following excerpt from William Grayson's epic poem *The Hireling and the Slave* captures the essence of the popular version of the argument:

> Taught by the master's efforts, by his care,
> Fed, clothed, protected many a patient year,
> From trivial numbers now to millions grown,
> With all the white man's useful arts their own,
> Industrious, docile, skilled in wood and field,
> To guide the plow, the sturdy axe to wield,
> The Negroes schooled by slavery embrace
> The highest portion of the Negro race.
> And none the savage will compare,
> Of Barbarous Guinea, with its offspring here.

In Eric McKitrick, ed., *Slavery Defended: The Views of the Old South* (Englewood Cliffs, N.J.: Prentice-Hall, 1963), 66–67. For documentation of the appeal of this outlook, see Genovese and Fox-Genovese, "Slavery, Economic Development, and the Law," 21; Greenberg, "Meaning of Death in Slave Society"; Parish, *Slavery: History and Historians*, 126.

61. A good early illustration of this self-image is the following excerpt from a letter written in 1726 by William Byrd (a prominent Virginia planter) to the Earl of Orrery: "I have a large Family of my own. Like one of the Patriarchs, I have my Flocks and my Herds, my Bonds-men and Bonds-women. [I must] take care to keep all my people to their Duty, to set the springs in motion, and to make everyone draw his equal share to carry the machine forward." (Byrd, quoted in Willie Lee Rose, *Slavery and Freedom* (New York: Oxford University Press, 1982), 21. For a later example, see M[oncure] D. Conway, "Testimonies Concerning Slavery" (1864), in *A Documentary History of Slavery in North America*, ed. Willie Lee Rose (New York: Oxford University Press, 1976), 406–7. Planters' efforts to live up to the patriarchal ideal prompted them frequently to make loans to their poorer neighbors to help them through difficult times, to provide assistance with the marketing and transportation of their crops, to help them with ginning and milling, to support the local schools, and to put on annual banquets for the residents of the neighborhood. See Parish, *Slavery: History and Historians*, 128–29.

62. On religious views, see, e.g., Thornton Stringfellow, *Scriptural and Statistical Views in Favor of Slavery* (1856), excerpted in McKitrick, *Slavery Defended,*

86–98; Greenberg, "Meaning of Death in Slave Society," 117–18; Thomas Virgil Peterson, *Ham and Japheth: The Mythic World of Whites in the Antebellum South* (Metuchen, N.J.: Scarecrow, 1978); Forrest G. Wood, *The Arrogance of Faith: Christianity and Race in America from the Colonial Era to the Twentieth Century* (New York: Knopf, 1990), chap. 3. On *herrenvolk* theory, see, e.g., James Henry Hammond, "Speech on the Admission of Kansas" (U.S. Senate, Mar. 4, 1858), in McKitrick, *Slavery Defended*, 122–23. Fredrickson, *Black Image in the White Mind*, chaps. 2–3; Parish, *Slavery: History and Historians*, 126. On scientific racism, see, e.g., Josiah Nott, "Two Lectures on the Natural History of the Caucasian and Negro Races" (1844), in Faust, *Ideology of Slavery*, 208–38; Josiah Nott and George Gliddon, *Types of Mankind; or, Ethnological Researches, Based upon the Ancient Monuments, Paintings, Sculptures, and Crania of Races, and upon their Natural, Geographical, Philological, and Biblical History* (1854), excerpted in McKitrick, *Slavery Defended*, 127–38; Stephen J. Gould, *The Mismeasure of Man* (New York: Norton, 1981), 69–72; William R. Stanton, *The Leopard's Spots: Scientific Attitudes toward Race in America, 1815–59* (Chicago: University of Chicago Press, 1960).

63. See Fitzhugh, *Cannibals All!*, 69, suggesting that one of every twenty people was naturally a master, the rest naturally slaves.

64. For the older view, see Oakes, *The Ruling Race*. For the newer view, see Parish, *Slavery, History, and Historians*, 143; Faust, *Ideology of Slavery*, 10; John McCardell, *The Idea of a Southern Nation: Southern Nationalists and Southern Nationalism, 1830–1860* (New York: W. W. Norton, 1979), chap. 2.

65. *Sarter v. Gordon*, *supra* note 44, at 135. For a similar argument in a similar context, see *Williams v. Howard*, 7 N.C. (3 Mur.) 74 (1819).

66. *Flowers v. Sproule*, 9 Ky. (2 A.K. Marsh.) 54, 58–59 (1819) (emphasis in original). For similar arguments in related contexts, see *Fitzhugh v. Foote*, 7 Va. (3 Call.) 13, 17 (1801); *Loftin v. Espy*, 12 Tenn. (4 Yer.) 84, 92–93 (1833); *Henderson v. Vaulx*, 18 Tenn. (10 Yer.) 30, 37–38 (1836); *Summers v. Bean*, 54 Va. (13 Gratt.) 404, 411 (1856).

67. *Mayo v. Whitson*, 47 N.C. (2 Jones) 231, 239 (1855). For a similar ruling, see *Cromartie v. Robison*, 55 N.C. (2 Jones Eq.) 218 (1855).

68. *Fairchild v. Bell*, 4 S.C.L. (2 Brev.) 129, 130 (1807). When the jury, "contrary to the judge's charge," found for the defendant, the Constitutional Court granted a new trial.

69. Cobb, *Inquiry into Law of Negro Slavery*, ccxvii–ccxviii. For a study of Cobb's life and influence, see William B. McCash, *Thomas R. R. Cobb (1823–1862): The Making of a Southern Nationalist* (Macon: Mercer University Press, 1983).

70. The helplessness of a slave "when his master is placed in opposition to him," Cobb insists, "is one of the most vulnerable points in the system of negro slavery, and should be farther guarded by legislation. Large compensation should be provided for informers, upon the conviction of the master of cruel treatment; and perhaps the best penalty that could be provided upon conviction, would be not only the sale of the particular slave cruelly treated, but of all of the slaves owned by the offender, and a disqualification forever of owning or possessing slaves." Cobb, *Inquiry into Law of Negro Slavery*, 97–98. Similar arguments by lay exponents of the paternal line of argument are discussed in Genovese and Fox-Genovese, "Slavery, Economic Development, and the Law."

71. Cobb, *Inquiry into Law of Negro Slavery*, 99–100, 279, 282, 287. A stronger bias toward a more humane regime—likewise rooted in a paternalist con-

ception of slavery—also shaped the judicial opinions and the scholarship of Chief Justice John Belton O'Neall of South Carolina. See John Belton O'Neall, *The Negro Law of South Carolina* (Columbia: John G. Bowman, 1848); *Tennent* v. *Dendy*, 23 S.C.L. (Dud.) 83, 86–87 (1837); Smiddy, "Judicial Nullification of State Statutes Restricting the Emancipation of Slaves," 635–36.

72. See Stampp, *Peculiar Institution*, 84, 318, 397–99; Robert S. Starobin, *Industrial Slavery in the Old South* (New York: Oxford University Press, 1970), 132–34.

73. See Langum, "The Role of Intellect and Fortuity," 10–11, relying on Joseph Lumpkin, "Industrial Regeneration of the South," *DeBow's Review* 12 (1852): 41. Langum goes on to argue that this attitude implies that Lumpkin's stance in cases involving slave leases cannot be explained on the basis of his affinity for the planter class and his sympathy for the ideology developed by that class (ibid., 8–11). But one need not subscribe to all portions of a belief system in order to be swayed by it. The fact that Lumpkin was not committed to "the ideology of the *agrarian* tradition" [ibid., 11 (emphasis added)] does not imply that he was unaffected by the more encompassing paternal defense of the institution of slavery.

74. *Gorman* v. *Campbell*, 14 Ga. 137, 143 (1853). For a thorough study of the case, see Tushnet, *American Law of Slavery*, 3–6, 51–54. For similar rulings in other jurisdictions, see *Lunsford* v. *Baynham*, 29 Tenn. (10 Hum.) 267, 269–70 (1849); *Bell* v. *Cummings*, 35 Tenn. (3 Sneed) 275, 282 (1855).

75. For Lumpkin's refusal to abate the rent, see *Lennard* v. *Boynton*, 11 Ga. 109, 113 (1852):

> Humanity to this dependent and subordinate class of our population requires, that we should remove from the hirer or temporary owner, all temptation to neglect them in sickness, or to expose them to situations of unusual peril or jeopardy. . . . Let us not increase their danger, by making it the interest of the hirer to get rid of his contract, when it proves to be unprofitable. Every safeguard, consistent with the stability of the institution of slavery, should be thrown around the lives of these people.

Cf. *Latimer* v. *Alexander*, 14 Ga. 259, 267 (1853), requiring a hirer to pay the medical expenses when a slave becomes ill during the lease term.

For Lumpkin's rejection of the fellow-servant rule, see *Scudder* v. *Woodbridge*, 1 Ga. 195, 199 (1846). Similar arguments underlay similar rulings in Florida, Kentucky, Louisiana, and South Carolina. See Wertheim, "Slavery and the Fellow Servant Rule," 1131–32. Cf. *James* v. *Carper*, 36 Tenn. (4 Sneed) 397, 403 (1857), insisting that the power of the hirer of a slave to discipline the slave for criminal behavior is more limited than the power enjoyed by the slave's master.

76. See *Bacot* v. *Parnell*, 18 S.C.L. (2 Bail.) 424 (1831), describing the case involving the damaged house as "a perfectly analogous decision"; *Muldrow* v. *Wilmington & Mancester R.R.*, 30 S.C. Eq. (13 Rich. Eq.) 69, 70 (1860); Wertheim, "Slavery and the Fellow Servant Rule," 1136–37. For other decisions permitting abatement of the rent in similar circumstances, see Langum, "The Role of Intellect and Fortuity," 13–14.

77. *Heirn* v. *Bridault*, 37 Miss. 209, 232 (1859); *Mitchell* v. *Wells*, 37 Miss. 235, 249, 262–63 (1859). The doctrinal history of which these cases are the terminus is described in Paul Finkelman, *An Imperfect Union: Slavery, Federalism and Comity* (Chapel Hill: University of North Carolina Press, 1981), 228–35, 285–95; and Lang, *Defender of the Faith*, 77–91.

78. *Vance* v. *Crawford*, 4 Ga. 445, 459 (1848) (emphasis in original).

79. See also *Gordon* v. *Blackman*, *supra* note 17; *Morton* v. *Thompson*, 24 S.C. (6 Rich. Eq.) 370 (1854).

80. Further evidence that Lumpkin found compelling—at least some of the time—the racialist depiction and defense of slavery may be found in his overwrought opinion in *Bryan* v. *Walton*, 14 Ga. 185 (1853). En route to his holding that a free black may not devise his own slaves, Lumpkin offers the following reflections on the institution of slavery:

> [W]e maintain that. . . the act of manumission confers no other right but that of freedom from the dominion of the master, and the limited liberty of locomotion; that it does not and cannot confer *citizenship*, nor any of the powers, civil or political, incident to *citizenship*; that the social and civil degradation, resulting from the taint of blood, adheres to the descendants of Ham in this country, like the poisoned tunic of Nessus; that nothing but an Act of the Assembly can purify, by the salt of its grace, the bitter fountain—the *"darkling sea."* . . .
>
> Our ancestors settled this State when a province, as a community of white men, professing the christian religion, and possessing an equality of rights and privileges. The blacks were introduced into it, as a race of Pagan slaves. The prejudice, if it can be called so, of caste, is unconquerable. It was so at the beginning. It has come down to our day. The suspicion of taint even, sinks the subject of it below the common level. Is it to be credited, that parity of rank would be allowed to such a race? Let the question be answered by our Naturalization Laws, which do not apply to the *African*. He is not and cannot become a *citizen* under our Constitution and Laws. He resides among us, and yet is a stranger. A *native* even, and yet not a citizen. Though not a *slave*, yet he is not free. Protected by the law, yet enjoying none of the immunities of freedom. Though not in a condition of chattelhood, yet constantly exposed to it. . . .
>
> I do not refer to these severe restrictions, for the purpose of condemning them. They have my hearty and cordial approval. The great principle of self-preservation, demands, on the part of the white population, unceasing vigilance and firmness, as well as uniform kindness, justice and humanity. Everything must be interdicted which is calculated to render the slave discontented with his condition, or which would tend to increase his capacity for mischief.

Ibid., 198, 202–3 (emphasis in original).

81. *Fisher's Negroes* v. *Dabbs*, 14 Tenn. (6 Yer.) 119, 130–31 (1834).

82. For another example of an opinion mingling the two lines of proslavery argument, see *Reeves* v. *Long*, 58 N.C. (5 Jones Eq.) 355 (1860).

83. These principles are distilled from Bertram Wyatt-Brown, *Southern Honor: Ethics and Behavior in the Old South* (New York: Oxford University Press, 1982), chaps. 2–4; John Hope Franklin, *The Militant South, 1800–1861* (Cambridge: Harvard University Press, Belknap Press, 1956); Ayers, *Vengeance and Justice*, chap. 1; Greenberg, "The Nose, the Lie and the Duel," *American Historical Review* 95 (1990): 57.

84. See Greenberg, "The Meaning of Death in Slave Society," 114–15; Wyatt-Brown, *Southern Honor*, 20–21, 40, 331–39, 350–61, 366–71, 382; Ayers, *Vengeance and Justice*, 10–12; Grady McWhiney, *Attack and Die: Civil War Military Tactics and the Southern Heritage* (University, Al.: University of Alabama Press, 1982). The reluctance of whites to use the courts to resolve personal disputes is memorialized and parodied in Mark Twain, *Pudd'nhead Wilson* (Hartford, Conn.: American Publishing, 1894). It did not deter white men from referring other sorts of disputes to the courts; antebellum Southerners were as litigious as their Northern contemporaries.

85. For the importance of ethnicity, see Wyatt-Brown, *Southern Honor*, 36–45. For the "hothouse atmosphere" hypothesis, see Ayers, *Vengeance and Justice*, 26–27; and Franklin, *Militant South*. For the efficiency hypothesis, see Warren Schwartz et al., "The Duel: Can These Gentlemen Be Acting Efficiently?," 13 *Journal of Legal Studies* 321 (1984).

86. Donald G. Mathews, *Religion in the Old South* (Chicago: University of Chicago Press, 1977), xvi.

87. See ibid., 1–80; John B. Boles, ed., *Masters and Slaves in the House of the Lord: Race and Religion in the American South, 1740–1870* (Lexington: University Press of Kentucky, 1988), 6–7; Anne C. Loveland, *Southern Evangelicals and the Social Order, 1800–1860* (Baton Rouge: Louisiana State University Press, 1980); Wyatt-Brown, *Southern Honor*, 99–105.

88. See Wyatt-Brown, *Southern Honor*, 67–68; Loveland, *Southern Evangelicals*, 180–85; Oakes, *The Ruling Race*, 105–22; Ayers, *Vengeance and Justice*, 29–30. The intensity of these sentiments is suggested by the following excerpt from an 1856 sermon by Reverend Arthur Wigfall:

> The Pagan Temple of Honour is ruled by the same spirit which teaches the Hindoo to throw himself beneath the car of the Juggernaut. . . . There exists in our country a privileged class, *soi disant* men of honor, who have established for themselves "a higher law." They put their foot upon the criminal code and trample it in the dust. They may and they do commit murder with impunity.

Quoted in Ayers, *Vengeance and Justice*, 30.

89. See Mathews, *Religion in the Old South*, 67–80; Boles, ed., *Masters and Slaves in the House of the Lord*, 8; John B. Boles, "Evangelical Protestantism in the Old South: From Religious Dissent to Cultural Dominance," in *Religion in the South*, ed. Charles R. Wilson (Jackson: University Press of Mississippi, 1985), 13–34; Loveland, *Southern Evangelicals*, 186–207.

90. See Mathews, *Religion in the Old South*, 173, 179–84; Clarence L. Mohr, "Slaves and White Churches in Confederate Georgia," in *Masters and Slaves in the House of the Lord*, ed. Boles, 153–73; Loveland, *Southern Evangelicals*, 206–11.

91. On the importance of dishonor to the status of slavery, see Orlando Patterson, *Slavery and Social Death: A Comparative Study* (Cambridge: Harvard University Press, 1982). On the supposed mendacity of slaves, see Greenberg, "The Nose, the Lie and the Duel," 65.

92. See *State* v. *Mann, supra* note 18, contending that "the frowns and deep execrations of the community upon the barbarian who is guilty of excessive and brutal cruelty to his unprotected slave" renders criminalization of such conduct unnecessary. An analogous argument was used by the South Carolina Court of Appeals to buttress its ruling that in most circumstances a master should not be liable for torts committed by his slave. The proper course for a person injured or aggrieved by a slave, the court suggested, is "to complain to the master, or other person having the charge of such offending slave, who, if he was actuated by curtesy and civility to his neighbour, would on such application, give him the necessary satisfaction for every insult or piece of improper conduct which a slave had offered." *White* v. *Chambers*, 2 S.C.L. (2 Bay) 70, 75 (1796), discussed in this connection in Morris, "Slave Wrongs," 579–80.

93. The best-known celebration of the disciplinary autonomy of the plantations is that of J. D. B. DeBow: "On our estates, we dispense with the whole machinery of public policy and public courts of justice. Thus we try, decide, and execute the sentences in thousands of cases, which in other countries would go to the courts." *The Industrial Resources etc. of the Southern and Western States* (New Orleans, 1853), 2:249; quoted in Richard C. Wade, *Slavery in the Cities: The South, 1820–1860* (New York: Oxford University Press, 1964), 249. For the underpinnings of this view in the Code of Honor, see Wyatt-Brown, *Southern Honor*, 371–77; Ayers, *Vengeance and Justice*, 135.

94. *State* v. *Jarrott, supra* note 18, at 85.

95. *State* v. *Caesar, supra* note 18, at 400, 402. Cf. *Pinkston* v. *Greene*, 9 Ala. 19, 21 (1846): "[A] provocation, which, as between free white persons, would justify or excuse a resort to force, to repel an actual or threatened injury, would afford no excuse whatever to a slave under these circumstances. . . . [H]e cannot repel force by force, but must trust to the law for his protection." (dictum)

96. The same attitude underlay the adoption by several Southern states of the rule that a person who is threatened with deadly force need not attempt to retreat but instead may defend himself—and indeed may kill his attacker—without incurring criminal liability. See Paul Finkelman, "In Search of Southern Legal History," 64 *North Carolina Law Review* 77, 104–5 (1985).

97. *State* v. *Hale, supra* note 23, at 582, 583. See also Act of 1740, 7 S.C. Public Laws 397–417 ("An Act for the Better Ordering and Governing Negroes and Other Slaves in their Province"): "And whereas, cruelty is not only highly unbecoming those who profess themselves christians, but is odious in the eyes of all men who have any sense of virtue or humanity; therefore, to restrain and prevent barbarity being exercised towards slaves, Be it enacted . . . That if any person or persons whosoever, shall willfully murder his own slave, or the slave of any other person, every such person shall . . . forfeit . . . seven hundred pounds." See also *Humphreys* v. *Utz* (La. 1854), reprinted in Judith Kelleher Schafer, "Unreported Case of *Humphreys* v. *Utz*," in this volume, wherein counsel for the plaintiff expressly invokes Christian principles to argue for harsh treatment of an overseer accused of brutal treatment of a group of slaves.

98. *State* v. *Will,* 18 N.C. (1 Dev. & Bat.) 121, 171 (1834). On Gaston's Catholicism, see J. Herman Schauinger, *William Gaston: Carolinian* (Milwaukee: Bruce Publishing, 1949), 200–209.

99. *Commonwealth* v. *Hart,* 29 Ky. (6 J.J. Marsh) 119, 121 (1831) (emphasis omitted).

100. *State* v. *Reed,* 9 N.C. (2 Hawks) 454, 456 (1823). See also *State* v. *Jarrott, supra* note 18, at 84, where Justice Gaston (whose Christian commitments were especially strong) contends:

> [I]t is not necessary . . . that a person who has received an injury, real or imaginary, from a slave, should carve out his own justice; for the law has made ample and summary provision for the punishment of all trivial offenses committed by slaves, by carrying them before a Justice, who is authorized to pass sentence for their being publicly whipped. This provision, while it excludes the necessity of private vengeance, would seem to forbid its legality, since it effectually protects all persons from the insolence of slaves, even when their masters are unwilling to correct them upon complaint being made.

See also *State* v. *Hale, supra* note 23, at 582; *Jordan* v. *State, supra* note 23, at 387.

101. See *Lewis* v. *State,* 17 Miss. (9 S. & M.) 115, 120 (1847); Thomas D. Morris, "Slaves and the Rules of Evidence in Criminal Trials," in this volume. Cf. Boles, ed., *Masters and Slaves in the House of the Lord,* 13, describing the willingness of the evangelical churches to admit the testimony of slaves in disciplinary proceedings.

102. *Ford* v. *Ford,* 26 Tenn. (7 Hum.) 91, 95–96 (1846). For another manumission case in which Christian sentiments are deployed in favor of the slave, see *Ex parte Elisha,* 57 Ky. (18 B. Mon.) 675, 676 (1857) (argument of counsel).

103. *Moran* v. *Davis,* 18 Ga. 722, 724 (1855) (emphasis in the original).

104. See Fox-Genovese, *Within the Plantation Household,* 290–333; Herbert G. Gutman, *The Black Family in Slavery and Freedom, 1750–1925* (New York: Pantheon Books, 1976), 60–75; John W. Blassingame, "Redefining *The Slave Community*: A Response to the Critics," in *Revisiting Blassingame's* The Slave Community: *The Scholars Respond,* ed. Al-Tony Gilmore (Westport, CT: Greenwood, 1978), 151–55; Jacqueline Jones, *Labor of Love, Labor of Sorrow: Black Women, Work, and the Family from Slavery to the Present* (New York: Basic Books, 1985), 29–43.

105. See Blassingame, *Slave Community,* 71–98, 130–47; Genovese, *Roll, Jordan, Roll,* 161–255; Albert J. Raboteau, *Slave Religion: The "Invisible Institution" in the Antebellum South* (New York: Oxford University Press, 1978); Lawrence W. Levine, *Black Culture and Black Consciousness: Afro-American Folk Thought from Slavery to Freedom* (New York: Oxford University Press, 1977), 3–135.

106. See Genovese, *Roll, Jordan, Roll,* 148–49; Ayers, *Vengeance and Justice,* 125–31; Levine, *Black Culture,* 54–55.

107. A much trickier question—and one beyond the scope of this essay—is whether the slaves' views on such issues forced their masters in practice to alter significantly the *administration* of the law. Cf. Genovese, *Roll, Jordan, Roll,* 30–31, suggesting that some such adjustments were made.

108. On women's roles, see Fox-Genovese, *Within the Plantation Household,* 365–71.

109. Compare Hinton Rowan Helper, *The Impending Crisis of the South: How to Meet It,* ed. George Fredrickson (1857; Cambridge: Harvard University Press, 1968), xxxi, 97, 182, with Rhys Isaac, *The Transformation of Virginia, 1740–1790* (Chapel Hill: University of North Carolina Press, 1982); Mathews, *Religion in the Old South,* 67; and Larry M. James, "Biracial Fellowship in Antebellum Baptist Churches," in Boles, ed., *Masters and Slaves in the House of the Lord,* 37–57.

110. See Antonio Gramsci, *Selections from the Prison Notebooks,* ed. and trans. Quintin Hoare and Geoffrey Nowell Smith (New York: International Publishers, 1971), 12; T. J. Jackson Lears, "The Concept of Cultural Hegemony: Problems and Possibilities," *American Historical Review* 90 (1985): 567.

111. Promising work on the second of the questions is currently being done by Ariela Gross. For a preliminary view of her findings, see her article in this volume.

Part II

Constitutional Law and Slavery

3

Slavery in the Canon of Constitutional Law

Sanford Levinson

ONE OF THE CENTRAL DEBATES in contemporary intellectual, and particularly academic, life concerns the notion of canonicity.[1] Among other things, this debate addresses the question of how disciplines, especially within the "liberal arts" and at the introductory level, become substantially defined in terms of certain subject matters that in turn are approached through the study of a limited number of what the British call *set texts*. These texts then comprise, among other things, the base of knowledge that every educated man or woman, at least within particular disciplines, is expected to know. There are many possible answers to the question of canonicity, at various levels of abstraction or reference to social theory.

In this essay I confine myself to a relatively low level of abstraction and, concomitantly, to relatively uncomplicated empirical assumptions. Whatever else might be involved in the successful construction of a canon, it is hard to imagine the process taking place without the actual presentation of the canonical issues and texts in the syllabi of relevant courses. Everyone knows the difference between *assigned* and *suggested* reading, and a necessary condition of canonicity is the appearance on the first of these two lists. What I want to do in this essay is to defend a (deceptively) simple proposition: Slavery ought to be a major topic of an introductory course in constitutional law, which is also to say that among the "set texts" assigned students, and made the subject of our class discussions, should be cases and materials involving slavery. Let me make this proposition more concrete: No fewer than six of the forty-two classes of my first-year constitutional law course are devoted to various aspects of slavery, and I shall detail below why I think they are so important and why it is worth paying undoubted costs that are involved by including them in the canon. The most obvious cost, given the inevitable limitations of time available in a course, is the necessity of omitting other valuable material in order to make way for the materials on slavery.

Before turning to the specifics of my syllabus and its rationale, it is crucial to note that teachers construct their syllabi by reference to what is easily available. It is, indeed, paradoxical to refer to an "out-of-print" canonical text, for surely one of the indicia of canonicity is that a work remains in print year after year, providing profits to its publishers by virtue of its remaining on syllabi and therefore being assigned to new generations of students. Within the legal academy, especially, the role of the *casebook* is crucial, for very few professors include in their syllabi material that is not presented in one or another of the standard casebooks.

It will surely surprise no reader that my own casebook of choice is one that Paul Brest and I coedit, *Processes of Constitutional Decisionmaking.*[2] I think it is safe to say that it is unique among currently available casebooks on general constitutional law (that is, those not devoted exclusively to the constitutional law of race relations and the like)[3] in the amount of coverage it gives slavery. The first extended section of the book is organized chronologically, and within the first three chapters can be found fairly extensive excerpts from a variety of cases involving slavery. They include *The Antelope,*[4] *Elkison* v. *Deliesseline,*[5] *Groves* v. *Slaughter,*[6] *Prigg* v. *Pennsylvania,*[7]—perhaps the farthest-reaching legitimation of implied national power in our history—and, of course, *Dred Scott* v. *Sandford.*[8] Readers will also find, just as importantly, most of the text of Frederick Douglass's speech "The Constitution of the United States: Is It Pro-Slavery or Anti-Slavery?"[9] as well as selections from exchanges between Abraham Lincoln and Stephen A. Douglas about the legitimacy of *Dred Scott.*[10] They will also read an opinion by Attorney General Caleb Cushing explaining why Southern states can legitimately prevent the delivery of abolitionist mail that calls into question the legitimacy of slavery.[11] Finally, a section on Abraham Lincoln as a war president culminates in a discussion of the Emancipation Proclamation, including a vigorous "dissent" to the Proclamation written by former Justice Benjamin R. Curtis,[12] who had, of course, just as vigorously dissented from Taney's egregious opinion in *Dred Scott.* In addition to a number of predictable Fourteenth Amendment cases that, in one way or another, make reference to the prior existence of chattel slavery,[13] we also include *Bailey* v. *Alabama,* in which the Alabama peonage laws were described by the Supreme Court (over Justice Holmes's vigorous dissent) as the kind of "involuntary servitude" outlawed by the Thirteenth Amendment.[14] Finally, students read a short discussion of an article by Akhil Reed Amar and Daniel Widawsky that argues that the issue raised in *DeShaney* v. *Winnebago County Dept. of Social Services*[15]—the liability of the state for failure to protect a child from the brutal abuse by his father—should be treated within the context of the Thirteenth Amendment and its prohibition of the complete domination of one human being by another.[16]

However, as already suggested, in the current market this emphasis on slavery is unusual. Consider, for example, five widely used casebooks in American law schools, all edited by distinguished scholars. These are the casebooks edited by Gerald Gunther;[17] by William B. Lockhart, Yale Kamisar, Jesse H. Choper, and Steven H. Shiffrin;[18] by William Cohen and Jonathan Varat;[19] by Ronald Rotunda;[20] and by Geoffrey R. Stone, Michael L. Seidman, Cass R. Sunstein, and Mark V. Tushnet.[21] I think it is only slightly hyperbolic to say that any students whose knowledge of American constitutional history will be derived from their immersion in any of the first four of these texts will have only the dimmest realization that the United States ever included a system of chattel slavery or, just as importantly, that its implications pervaded every single aspect of constitutional law (and constitutional interpretation). All of these four basically limit their recognition of slavery to very brief mention of *Dred Scott* and nothing more.

Consider, for example, the fact that, although there is an index entry for *slavery* in his book, Professor Gunther offers only three fleeting mentions, two of them in footnotes, of *Dred Scott.*[22] An attentive student will learn, for example, that the case "held unconstitutional (in part on Fifth Amendment due process grounds) the Missouri Compromise of 1820, a congressional law that excluded slavery from specified portions of American territory." True enough; but this is scarcely the most significant aspect of *Dred Scott*, especially given the repeal of the Missouri Compromise in the Kansas-Nebraska Act in 1854. Students should know that Taney in effect held unconstitutional the platform of the new Republican Party entering the American political scene insofar as it was committed to blocking the further expansion of slavery into the territories,[23] not to mention the declaration by the chief justice that, in the absence of a constitutional amendment, blacks were simply, and permanently, excluded from the American political community. Indeed, they were "so inferior" in the eyes of ruling whites "that they had no rights which the white man was bound to respect."[24] Gunther is certainly no worse than Lockhart et al., Cohen and Varat, or Rotunda, who also confine themselves to brief mention of *Dred Scott* and nothing else from or about any other materials involving slavery.[25]

Stone, et al., in comparison, offer far more, perhaps reflecting the fact that Professor Tushnet has written an important book on slavery.[26] Their text offers three pages on "Slavery and the Constitution," followed by a two-page Note on "Constitutional Attacks on Slavery."[27] This in turn is followed by two-and-a-half pages from *Dred Scott*, before the book moves on to consideration of the Fourteenth Amendment and the interpretations of racial classifications based on that Amendment. Even conceding that this constitutes a marked improvement over the other two casebooks, I would still describe it as a relatively scanty introduction to the subject of slavery and the Constitution.

I certainly realize that these distinguished editors could well do to *Processes of Constitutional Decisionmaking* what I have just done to them, for we have also omitted a number of issues that might well be thought central to a basic education in constitutional law. We do not, for example, cover many of the contemporary cases dealing with freedom of speech or press, including such fundamental modern cases as *New York Times* v. *Sullivan*[28] or *Buckley* v. *Valeo*.[29] And students looking for illumination on the issue of pornography will find nothing very helpful in our book.

As already suggested, anyone who has ever constructed a syllabus or gathered materials for a casebook is well aware that there is neither time nor paper enough to include everything that one might legitimately want to cover. Choices, almost none of them easy, must inevitably be made. What I want to do in this essay, then, is to present my reasons for allocating so much time and casebook space to slavery, even though I well know that that choice deprives my students (or the users of our casebook) of material or information in regard to other topics that would surely be desirable.

Before turning to the specifics of slavery, I should make one more obvious point: A successful defense of the inclusion of materials on slavery is not the equivalent of a justification of any given omission. One might well believe, for example, that materials on the modern interpretation of the "dormant commerce clause," somewhat copiously present in the Brest and Levinson casebook (though not, in fact, included in my course syllabus) should have been omitted instead of the materials on libel[30] or on regulation of election finance, the latter of which is, I believe, the most important contemporary First Amendment issue. That may well be true, but that is not my concern in this essay, which attempts only to make the case for including in our teaching more materials on slavery.

It may also be relevant to confront directly the possibility that many teachers might be reluctant to present materials on slavery because of the emotional valence surrounding the subject. There can be no doubt that the material is emotionally loaded, especially if one asks students, as I do, to assess the cases in terms of "thinking like a lawyer." That is, I spend relatively little time denouncing the practice of chattel slavery; much more is spent trying to determine whether one's objections to the arguments found in the legal materials themselves are "internal," based on inappropriate use of standard legal modes of analysis, or "external," based simply on the justifiability of the result in terms of morality, political theory, political desirability, or whatever.[31] I think it is important to take seriously the possibility that Taney might have been "right" in *Dred Scott*, especially if one has earlier accepted the legitimacy of *Prigg* and several other cases that will have been read earlier. Ought that to be an "unthinkable" thought for our students? And if so, by what criteria?

This cuts to the heart of the entire enterprise of legal education. Do we teach, in effect, that law is comic, that "thinking like a lawyer" is guaranteed in advance to bring one to morally admirable (or at least tolerable) results. As I have written elsewhere, too "[l]ittle recognition is given to the possibility that life under even the American Constitution may be a tragedy, presenting irresolvable conflicts between the realms of law and morality."[32] To refuse to acknowledge the possibility is irresponsible. If one wants to rebut it, what better way than an explicit confrontation with just such cases as are considered in this essay?

Whether one defines the play of law as comic or tragic, the key actors in the enactment of the play include not only judges, whose opinions are the focus of our attention, but also lawyers, who must decide whether they will indeed provide representation to all those who seek the vindication of their legal rights. What ought we be teaching our students about such such duties of representation? In two notable articles,[33] Charles Fried and Stephen Pepper both offer vigorous defenses of the lawyer's willingness to assert any and all legal rights that the system makes available to its citizenry. According to Fried, "The lawyer acts morally because he helps to preserve and express the autonomy of his client vis-a-vis the legal system."[34] Fried is fully aware that persons can be devoted to immoral ends. Still, he says,

> whatever else may stop the pornographer's enterprise, he should not be stopped because he mistakenly believes there is a legal impediment. ... [R]ights are violated if, through ignorance or misinformation about the law, an individual refrains from pursuing a wholly lawful purpose. Therefore, to assist others in understanding and realizing their legal rights is always morally worthy.[35]

Similarly, according to Pepper, "The client's autonomy should be limited by the law, not by the lawyer's morality."[36]

Fried emphasizes that he is writing only about a lawyering "within the context of just institutions."[37] An obvious question, and not only for Fried, is whether the United States prior to 1865 provided such a context so as to license an attorney in giving professional succor to slaveholders seeking the enforcement of their ostensible legal rights in regard to their property. Would Fried, for example, accept the substitution of "slaveholder" for "pornographer" in the excerpt above?[38] To be sure, such discussions present issues not only of great intellectual difficulty but also of high emotional valence. There is nothing easy about being challenged as to the way one is choosing to live one's life. But that is what serious education ultimately is about.

* * *

It is tempting to defend teaching about slavery simply by reference to certain notions of cultural (or historical) literacy or to the political importance of every American's being aware of the presence of chattel slavery in our background. I believe that both of these rationales are perfectly correct. However, one more assumption may be necessary to justify the necessity of teaching these materials in law school as part of a standard (that is, required) course on constitutional law. That assumption is that our students will not otherwise become even minimally knowledgeable about slavery if we do not take care to bring the relevant materials to their attention.

I doubt, of course, that many students are unfamiliar with the abstract fact that slavery once existed in the United States. That is not really the question. It is, rather: How many of our students have any genuine idea of how the practice of "thinking like an American constitutional lawyer" was centrally shaped by having to integrate within the fabric of our law the adoption of chattel slavery as a system of labor and social relations within much of the United States? To the degree that I think the answer is "all too few," I also think it is crucial that we, as self-conscious educators of lawyer-citizens, should try to alleviate this deficiency. I am motivated in part by a belief that this information about the American past is crucial, in a variety of ways, to understanding a number of contemporary features, including the legal dimensions, of American society.

Whatever the cogency of these rationales, they do not at all exhaust the reasons that I so emphasize slavery in my course and casebook. Indeed, I confess that I would have far more mixed feelings about my decisions were these the only reasons supporting them. The rationales sketched out may seem too overtly "political," having almost nothing to do with preparing my students for their professional roles as lawyers. Thus, I also insist that the cases and materials are excellent tools of pedagogy for raising central problems of constitutional law and theory that should be at the heart of any first-year course—though I insist as well that slavery has "surplus value," as it were, that justifies the substitution of slavery case for the contemporary cases that many students might in fact prefer.[39] What I want to do, therefore, is to discuss with some specificity the various uses I make of the slavery materials in my own course and, of course, to try to persuade my academic readers to do likewise.

* * *

Slavery overtly enters my course in its fourth week, following two classes on the place of unenumerated rights in constitutional analysis. The first class in this sequence focuses on *Fletcher* v. *Peck* and, more particularly, on the role of what Chief Justice Marshall terms "general principles which are common to our free institutions" or, even more strikingly, of what Justice Johnson describes as "the reason and nature of things: a principle which will impose laws even on the deity."[40] I use this as the occasion for mentioning an important debate in seventeenth- and eighteenth-century theology about the extent to which God is "bound" by the principles of justice, a debate that goes back at least as far as Plato's *Euthyphro*. If one meaning of popular sovereignty, a concept introduced earlier in the course via *McCulloch* v. *Maryland*,[41] is that "the voice of the people is [equivalent to] the voice of God," then it is no small matter to discuss whether either of these voices is unconstrained in the commands they might enunciate.

The second class focuses on *Griswold* v. *Connecticut*,[42] particularly Justice Harlan's invocation of American traditions to strike down Connecticut's egregious law regulating the use of contraceptives.[43] A central question is how one delineates the American political tradition. And will we necessarily be pleased by our findings? Among other things that we include in our discussion of that tradition's "fundamental values" is Garry Wills's pithy comment that "Running men out of town on a rail is at least as much an American tradition as declaring unalienable rights,"[44] as is the legally recognized freedom of some people to own others.

At this point, attention turns to John Marshall's opinion in *The Antelope*,[45] which deals, broadly speaking, with the duty of the United States to return certain slaves to their "lawful" Spanish or Portugese "owners." These slaves had been captured by pirates while in transit from Africa to some other country in which the slave trade was still legal. The pirates in turn were captured by the United States Coast Guard, which brought them and their booty, including the slaves, into the territory of the United States, which had, of course, in 1808 outlawed participation in the international slave trade. What, then, was to be done with the captured slaves?

In his opinion answering this question, Marshall draws a very sharp contrast between the *jurist* and the *moralist*. "[T]his court must not," Marshall insists, "yield to feelings which might seduce it from the path of duty, and must obey the mandate of the law."[46] Thus, at least some of the slaves were indeed returned to their owners. Yet Marshall certainly does not overtly defend slavery. On the contrary, he denounces both the international slave trade and, indeed, slavery itself as violative of natural rights, natural law, and Christian morality. Students cannot take refuge in an historicist argument that Marshall did not share, in at least some respect, our own opposition to slavery. To be sure, I scarcely believe that Marshall's world is our own, though a principal difference, ironically enough, may be that Marshall was considerably more confident about the existence of transcendental principles of justice or injustice than most of us "postmoderns." However, in this instance at least, these epistemological differences are secondary to the brute fact that Marshall had no hesitation in denouncing the morality of slavery. Far more important is that the denunciation, whatever its epistemological sources, is treated as irrelevant; contrary to what Marshall seems to have been suggesting in *Fletcher*, law and justice appear to have, in his opinion, precious little to do with one another. Indeed, much of his own argument is predicated on the international tradition of recognizing the continuing legitimacy of the slave trade (though any given nation could, of course, withdraw from the trade).

In addition to obvious questions about the relevance of morality to legal analysis, I also ask students to explain Marshall's (and Johnson's) seemingly different postures in the two cases. Is it, for example, relevant for interpretive purposes that, as a formal matter, *Fletcher* is a constitutional case, whereas *The Antelope* involves international law? This seems unlikely, unless there were some kind of particular textual provision that commanded judges to treat natural justice as part of constitutional law but not otherwise to be enforced.

More to the point, I believe, is the different thrust in the two cases of what might be termed *prudential* factors. That is, in *Fletcher* Marshall suggests that disruption of the land claims at issue in that case would have negative consequences to the pace of American economic development. Holders in due course would be ever fearful that apparent title to their property could be attacked by reference to problems much earlier in the chain of title. "General principles" of justice happily coincided with the prudential cause of economic development. In *The Antelope*, on the other hand, no such joyful congruence of deontology and consequence is present.

It takes little imagination to summon up a series of dire consequences had Marshall vindicated natural rights or natural law by freeing the hapless slaves. Portugal and Spain, however weakened as international powers, might have felt under some pressure to respond to this astounding breach in international law, whether through military response, albeit unlikely, or more plausible commercial retaliation against American interests. Far more to the point, of course, is the likely reaction of Marshall's fellow Southerners, especially South Carolinians who had already begun their baleful analyses of the necessity for secession if the Southern way of life was to be maintained.[47] Already in *McCulloch* Marshall had explicitly referred to the possibility of "hostility of a . . . serious nature" occurring within the still new nation as a result of the serious tensions present in it.[48] Again, the obvious question to ask students is whether any of these concerns is within the ambit of "thinking like a lawyer," and, if so, whether law can be so neatly separated from politics, or principles from results, as is often suggested.

This point is made with frightful clarity in *Prigg* v. *Pennsylvania*,[49] in which Justice Story, for the Court, among other things upholds the constitutionality of the Fugitive Slave Act of 1793 and strikes down Pennsylvania's Personal Liberty Law that attempted to put some constraints on the ability of slavecatchers to exercise "self-help" in the recapture of purported runaway slaves. What I find striking is the strain of instrumentalism in Story's opinion.[50] He notes, for example, that "no uniform rule of interpretation"[51] is available in regard to the construction of the Fugitive Slave Clause of Article IV,[52] though he ultimately seizes on the notion of "purpose" to give him guidance:

> How, then, are we to interpret the language of the clause? The true answer is, in such a manner, as, consistently with the words, shall fully and completely effectuate the whole objects of it. If by one mode of interpretation the right must become shadowy and unsubstantial, and without any remedial power adequate to the end; and by another mode it will attain its just end and secure its manifest purpose; it would seem, upon principles of reasoning, absolutely irresistible, that the latter ought to prevail. No Court of justice can be authorized so to construe any clause of the constitution as to defeat its obvious ends, when another construction, equally accordant with the words and sense thereof, will enforce and protect them.[53]

The great purpose of the Constitution, according to Story, was the creation of a political union, which, he says, necessitated the making of various guarantees to slaveholding interests who might otherwise have refused the invitation to union. Adherence to the purpose of maintaining the Union thus required continuing acquiesence to the interests of slaveholders lest they become antagonistic to it. As we all know, there was nothing paranoid about such concerns.

Indeed, it is worth noting that Story describes the Fugitive Slave Clause as a "fundamental article" of the Constitution, "without the adoption of which the Union could not have been formed."[54] Its status as a "fundamental" linchpin of the constitutional structure made it important that states be prevented from placing any burden on its effectuation.[55] *Prigg* may be, ironically enough, the debut in American constitutional analysis of the notion of a "fundamental interest" that would be vigilantly protected by the Court.[56]

All of this being said, I find it immensely useful, for both historiographical and pedagogical reasons, to compare the paragraph quoted above from Story's opinion to one found in Frederick Douglass's great speech, "The Constitution of the United States: Is It Pro-Slavery or Anti-Slavery?"[57] Douglass's adversary in a Glasgow, Scotland, debate had suggested that the Constitution should be interpreted by reference to the historical circumstances surrounding its adoption. Like Story, the adversary pointed to the undoubted fact that the Constitution's framers were willing to collaborate with slavery. Douglass, in contrast, emphasized the priority of what Philip Bobbitt would describe as *textualism,* a relentless focus on the words of the text quite independent of any historical referents they might be thought to have had.[58] Douglass then goes on to offer a maxim of interpretation quite different in its implications from those of Story's:

> [My opponent] laid down some rules of legal interpretation. These

rules send us to the history of the law for its meaning. I have no objection to such a course in ordinary cases of doubt. But where human liberty and justice are at stake, the case falls under an entirely different class of rules. There must be something more than history—something more than tradition. The Supreme Court of the United States lays down this rule, and it meets the case exactly—"Where rights are infringed— where the fundamental principles of the law are overthrown—where the general system of the law is departed from, the legislative intention must be expressed with irresistible clearness." The same court says that the language of the law must be construed strictly in favour of justice and liberty. Again, there is another rule of law. It is—Where a law is suceptible of two meanings, the one making it accomplish an innocent purpose, and the other making it accomplish a wicked purpose, we must in all cases adopt that which makes it accomplish an innocent purpose.[59]

To put it mildly, students (not to mention their teachers) should be encouraged to reflect on the difference it might make to adopt one or the other of these two purposive ends: maintenance of the Union, made possible according to Story only by collaboration with slavery, or respect for the principles of liberty—presumably even if risky to the maintenance of Union. Or does maintenance of the Union become a "compelling state interest" that in effect justifies chattel slavery or, more precisely, doing nothing to challenge its legal legitimacy at least in the states wherein it already existed?

The term *compelling state interest* is drawn from modern constitutional law with its emphasis on the untenability of reading any part of the Constitution as stating any absolutes. The standard example is the jurisprudence of the First Amendment, where the apparently unequivocal command that Congress and, because of the Fourteenth Amendment, state legislatures pass "no law" abridging freedom of speech has been (sensibly) interpreted to mean that speech can indeed be abridged if the state presents a "compelling interest" justifying the abridgement. The obvious issue has always been what constitutes such a compelling interest and, more particularly, if abridgement of speech as a purported defense against a perceived threat to the maintenance of basic American institutions counts as one.

I find it immensely useful to discuss such issues through presenting an 1857 opinion by Attorney General Caleb Cushing upholding the propriety of Mississippi's prohibition of the delivery of mail sent into the state by outside abolitionists.[60] One reason for assigning this opinion is simply to make the point, an important emphasis of the casebook as a whole, that many important acts of "constitutional interpretation" occur outside the courts, whether engaged in by other public officials like Cushing or by distinguished citizens like Frederick Douglass.[61] Another reason, more important in the context of this essay, is that the issues raised by Cushing's opinion continue to resonate even 135 years later, for there is a decidedly modern tone to his opinion.

Cushing emphasizes that all states must have the "power of self-preservation" and the concomitant ability to guard themselves against "insurrection." Indeed, he regards this as a basic constitutional right, "inalienable and imprescriptible." Against this background assumption he derives "the main question very much simplified. It is this: Has a citizen of one of the United States plenary indisputable right to employ the functions and the officers of the Union as the means of enabling him to produce insurrection in another of the United States?" Does a citizen of Ohio in effect have the constitutional right to conscript federal employees, such as postal officers, to aid them in their "purpose of promoting insurrection in another State?" It is this way of stating the question that, I suspect, helps to explain Cushing's utter lack of reference to the First Amendment, for even if he accepted its application to the executive branch (and not simply to congressional legislation), he almost certainly would have rejected any argument that "the freedom of speech" included the liberty (or, in the language of an earlier age, the *license*) to counsel insurrection.

As a states-rights Democrat, Cushing was intensely sensitive to local interests. Thus he goes on to assert that "the citizens of the State of Mississippi are the only competent judges of how much they may be inconvenienced by the impeded circulation among them of this or that pamphlet or newspaper." Sounding almost like Felix Frankfurter discussing the deference owed Congress upon that institution's decision to criminalize advocacy of a Communist revolution in the United States, Cushing writes that determining "inconvenience" is

> a question of self-government, which it belongs to [the citizenry of Mississippi] to answer for themselves. . . . Moreover, there is here a balance of inconveniences. Insurrections are inconvenient things. . . . If the non-circulation of this or that foreign [sic] newspaper in a particular State be an inconvenience to somebody, it is, in the aggregate of all public interests, a much less inconvenience than the occurrence, or even the danger, of insurrection in the State.

As suggested by my reference to Frankfurter and, indirectly, the Smith Act prosecutions upheld in *Dennis* v. *United States*,[62] Cushing is asking very basic questions that structure political debate even today. Most students, one suspects, will pronounce themselves horrified by the Mississippi prohibition; to the extent they are surprised by the absence of First Amendment analysis, one can note, in addition to the point made above, the Court's decision in *Barron* v. *Baltimore*[63] that the Bill of Rights applied only to the national government.

As already suggested, though, it is useful to ask precisely what difference it would have made had the First Amendment been addressed. Does the amendment truly require states to be indifferent to the possible consequences of insurrectionary propaganda? Does the Constitution, contrary to Justice Jackson's famous jibe, in fact establish a "suicide pact"[64] by which we are unable to defend our institutions against those who have announced themselves their sworn enemies and seek to enlist others in their hostility? I think it is pedagogically useful to ask students to specify exactly what does perturb—or horrify—them about Cushing's opinion. Most will surely emphasize the iniquity of slavery itself; but that is, of course, to beg the basic question fearlessly addressed by Story. Does the iniquity of slavery justify taking measures that, however favorable to liberty, threaten the maintenance of Union? If one has been able to swallow Story's invocation of "practical necessity" and "implie[d]" power in *Prigg*, then it scarcely seems very difficult to go the next step and recognize the justifications, at least from the point of view of Mississippi's ruling elites, of the policy upheld by Cushing.

One would hope that students might suggest that this perspective scarcely deserves the priority I am implicitly giving it; but that raises the whole question of the importance of perspective in the construction of our notions of rationality or "compelling" interests in regard to the regulation of speech acts. Consider also the contemporary debate about the propriety of regulating racially oriented hate speech, which Akhil Reed Amar has tried to place within the explicit context of the overcoming of the residue of slavery promised by the Thirteenth and Fourteenth Amendments.[65]

This emphasis on the role of perspective in determining constitutional norms is at the heart of much postmodernist and feminist theory,[66] and it can effectively be raised through consideration of slavery. When Marshall claims in *The Antelope* that "the world has agreed" and has given "general consent" to the practice of enslaving captives in war,[67] one might scream out the obvious questions about who constitutes the consent-giving groups.

The Antelope involved, of course, international commerce in human beings. Central to almost all first-year courses on constitutional law is the regulation of commerce, and it should occasion no surprise to discover that slavery was implicated in the controversies surrounding the limits of commercial regulation. In the nation's first century or so, states rather than Congress tended to take center stage. Marshall's invocation in *Gibbons* v. *Ogden*[68] of Congress's extraordinarily broad power over commerce was, even in the context of that case, dicta, and Congress asserted precious little of its potential reserve of power until the turn of the twentieth century. *Gibbons*, of course, only tangentially involved congressional regulation at all; the central arguments in that case concerned the exclusivity of congressional power over commerce and, therefore, whether a state retained any power to regulate commerce even in the absence of congressional regulation. Marshall, after announcing his strong inclination to adopt an exclusivity analysis, settled for emphasizing instead New York's purported conflict with a federal statute, thus transforming the case into a much tamer invocation of the Supremacy Clause.

Justice Johnson, on the other hand, articulated a strong exclusivity view in a concurring opinion in *Gibbons*, which had been presaged by his opinion a year earlier in *Elkison* v. *Deliesseline*,[69] a case involving South Carolina's Negro Seaman's Act of 1822. That Act, among other things, provided that "any free negroes [sic] or persons of color" brought by ship into a South Carolina port "be seized and confined in gaol until such vessel shall clear out and depart from this state." As suggested by its title, the law was especially concerned with the crews of ships entering Charleston harbor, and *Elkison* involved a British ship whose crew presumably included persons coming under the act's description. Johnson struck the act down as an unconstitutional regulation of commerce.

I bring up *Elkison* following my presentation of another key case on state regulation, *Mayor of New York* v. *Miln*,[70] which presents quite vividly the issue of a state's right to control what might be termed its *social character* through immigration restrictions. In this particular case, the central concern was the possible invasion (and contamination) of New York by "the moral pestilence of paupers";[71] the state, therefore, required ships' captains to prepare detailed lists of their passengers and to post security for the maintenance of anyone likely to become a ward of the city. Describing New York's law as an invocation of its "police power" in behalf of the health, safety, and welfare of the local citizenry, the majority, through Justice Barbour, upheld it. Justice Thompson characterized the law as indeed a regulation of commerce, but he deemed this irrelevant, for states had concurrent power to regulate interstate commerce in the absence of overriding congressional regulation. Justice Story agreed with Thompson's characterization but went on to argue that only Congress could regulate commerce. New York's law was, Story insisted, therefore unconstitutional.

One way of understanding both *Miln* and slavery is to ask students whether the 1822 South Carolina statute would be unconstitutional under either Barbour's or Thompson's analyses. South Carolina clearly deemed free persons of color as the equivalent of a "moral pestilence" because of the potential discontent that might be generated within the slave community simply by observing the possibility of free persons of color possessing their own dignity. South Carolinian proponents of the law in question may well have been evil, but were they irrational in deeming free blacks to be potential social dangers? If not, then why should the state be deprived of its power to protect itself, at least in the absence of explicit congressional legislation preventing this? Again, it should be obvious, students will be forced to confront the extent to which the basic decision in 1787 to enter a union with slaveholders has consequences for every aspect of American constitutional doctrine.

The racialist implications of *Miln* are further brought out by a discussion note, following that case, referring to Chief Justice Taney's opinion in *The Passenger Cases*, in which he raises the specter of the migration to the United States of "the emancipated slaves of the West Indies. . . . I cannot believe," says Taney, "that it was ever intended to vest in Congress" the power in effect to command the states to offer haven to such persons. Why not? The answer, for Taney (and for many others) was obvious: The unregulated entry of such persons into states unwilling to welcome them would "produc[e] the most serious discontent, and ultimately lead[ ] to the most painful consequences,"[72] including, presumably, secession and warfare.

Although secession may no longer threaten, debates about immigration clearly remain part of the contemporary political scene, and every one of these debates inevitably involves the basic right of a sovereign state to control its borders against those it deems threats.

Miln involves the regulation of commerce as a means to a presumed permissible purpose, the protection of the noneconomic health, safety, or welfare of the citizenry. But what if the regulation is best described as a means of protecting local economic interests? This question is directly presented by an obscure but fascinating 1841 case, *Groves* v. *Slaughter,*[73] which involves a provision of the 1832 constitution adopted by Mississippi that seemingly prohibited the importation of slaves for purposes of sale into that state. It was, however, perfectly legal to buy and sell local slaves; moreover, settlers entering Mississippi could bring with them any slaves they might possess. The prohibition was attacked as an illegitimate regulation of commerce. A majority of the Supreme Court deflected the attack by holding that the Mississippi Constitution was not self-executing and, therefore, that the failure of the state legislature to enact a law enforcing the provision deprived it of any legal force. This did not prevent three justices—Baldwin, Taney, and McLean—from conducting an important and illuminating debate.

Students should certainly realize that Justice Baldwin is stating "good" doctrine when he writes that "no state can control this [slave] traffic, so long as it may be carried on by its own citizens, within its own limits."[74] As Donald Regan has reminded us,[75] perhaps the central meaning given the Dormant Commerce Clause is the illegitimacy of a state's trying to prevent the interstate shipment of goods in order to protect a local market. As it happens, Justice Baldwin relies more on the Privileges and Immunities Clause of Article 4 than on the Commerce Clause, but the operational import is similar. Once more, students will probably want to argue that slavery is "different," as did Justice McLean, so that ordinary Commerce Clause and Privileges and Immunities analyses should not be applied to a system so monstrous. And, once more, students should be reminded of the practical impossibility of firmly differentiating legal from political analysis.

All of the questions treated above are present, of course, in what is certainly the most (in)famous of all slave cases, *Dred Scott*.[76] The crux of Chief Justice Taney's opinion is, in effect, that there can be no such category as African Americans, for membership in the American community, as recognized by the basic status of citizenship, is limited to whites. One must point out to students the extravagance of Taney's denial that blacks had been accepted as part of the political community by some states at the time of the Constitution's drafting and ratification. That being said, it should also be noted that Taney undoubtedly expressed the views of many members of America's ruling elite, and it is misleading in the extreme to assume that Taney's basic argument is foolish. *Dred Scott* obviously raises a variety of questions about what former Attorney General Meese labeled "the jurisprudence of original intent,"[77] which received its first eloquent defense in Taney's opinion. According to Taney the formally unamended Constitution "must be construed now as it was understood at the time of its adoption. It is not only the same in words, but the same in meaning." Sounding altogether like Robert Bork, who pronounced original intent the only legitimate modality of constitutional interpretation,[78] Taney goes on to insist that "Any other rule of construction would abrogate the judicial character of this court, and make it the mere reflex of the popular opinion or passion of the day."[79]

If one wishes to attack *Dred Scott*, therefore, an obvious question is whether one must go after Taney's originalist modality or, instead, after his specific historical analysis. Many students, for example, endorse Justice Curtis's dissent, which attacks Taney's history. I ask them if this means that they would in fact support Taney if further historical research called Curtis's assertions into question and supported Taney's account instead.[80] In the alternative, of course, one might decide that history should be regarded as irrelevant, though that decision itself raises all sorts of obvious questions.

As with Story's opinion in *Prigg*, Taney's opinion also raises profound questions for anyone committed to interpreting the Constitution in light of tradition-based "fundamental values." Usually, of course, the values that are mentioned are admirable ones such as liberty or equality. But Taney in substantial measure suggests that racism is a fundamental value underlying the American political tradition, as he ruthlessly dissects patterns of American law and behavior that rest on assumptions of white superiority and black inferiority.[81] How do we decide which is the authentic depiction of our tradition? Is this even a sensible question to ask?

Dred Scott, of course, was a central focus of the Lincoln-Douglas debates in 1858, not least because Lincoln strongly suggested, in effect, that he refused to treat the case as establishing what we might today refer to as the "law of the land." That is, Taney's retrospective invalidation of the Missouri Compromise would not prevent Lincoln from supporting the prohibition of further slavery in the territories. Douglas, on the other hand, proudly stood as a purported man of the law acknowledging the supremacy of the Supreme Court as a constitutional interpreter. The questions clearly resonate even today. Consider anti-abortionists who are often castigated for introducing laws that, if enacted, would almost certainly violate the Constitution as interpreted by the current Supreme Court.

A collateral issue involves the standards to be used in appointment of new members of the Court. Lincoln suggested that *Dred Scott* might well be overturned by a Court reflecting the views of new members. Douglas denounced such suggestions, accusing Lincoln of supporting the full-scale politicization of the judiciary:

> [H]e is going to appeal to the people to elect a President who will appoint judges who will reverse the Dred Scott decision. Well, let us see how that is going to be done. . . . [W]hy, the Republican President is to call up the candidates and catechize them, and ask them, "How will you decide this case if I appoint you judge." [Shouts of laughter.] . . . Suppose you get a Supreme Court composed of such judges, who have been appointed by a partisan President upon their giving pledges how they would decide a case before it arises, what confidence would you have in such a court? ["None, none."] . . . It is a proposition to make that court the corrupt, unscrupulous tool of a political party. But Mr. Lincoln cannot conscientiously submit, he thinks, to the decision of a court composed of a majority of Democrats. If he cannot, how can he expect us to have confidence in a court composed of a majority of Republicans, selected for the purpose of deciding against the Democracy, and in favor of the Republicans? [Cheers.] The very proposition carries with it the demoralization and degradation destructive of the judicial department of the federal government.[82]

Here, too, the questions resonate. How, indeed, can one have confidence in a judiciary chosen for political reasons, but how else can one imagine a judiciary being chosen? This is the perfect occasion to ask students to reflect on questions about the fealty due the Court and about the considerations that should go into appointing members of that body.

Finally, there is President Lincoln and his remarkable leadership of the nation during the events of 1861–65.[83] He used presidential power as never before (and only rarely since), and an obvious question is to ask what accounts for the veneration accorded Lincoln. Is it that he maintained the Union or, rather, that he helped to destroy slavery? In either case, what is the relationship between the end and adherence to constitutional means? The casebook includes, for example, the well-known debate between Taney and Lincoln about the latter's unilateral suspension of habeas corupus, which Taney ruled invalid in *Ex parte Merryman*.[84] Lincoln responded with the defiant, albeit plaintive question, whether "all the laws, *but one*, [are] to go unexecuted, and the government itself go to pieces, lest that one be violated?"[85]

Even more interesting in many ways, though, is the critique by former Justice Benjamin Curtis, who had written a strong dissent in *Dred Scott*, of Lincoln's assertion of presidential power in the Emancipation Proclamation.[86] Now Curtis emphasized instead the limits on executive power. "It is among the rights of all of us that the executive power should be kept within its prescribed constitutional limits, and should not legislate, by its decrees, upon objects of transcendent importance to the whole people." Curtis was fearful that the Proclamation, together with other of Lincoln's decrees, would ultimately sap the republican political order. "Among all the causes of alarm which now distress the public mind," according to Curtis, "there are few more terrible . . . than the tendency to lawlessness which is manifesting itself in so many directions."

A terrible example of this tendency was "the open declaration of a respectable and widely circulated journal, that 'nobody cares' whether a great public act of the President of the United States is in conformity with or is subversive of the supreme law of the land." Down that road, for Curtis, lay the possibility that "our great public servants may themselves break the fundamental law of the country, and become usurpers of vast powers not intrusted to them, in violation of their solemn oath of office; and 'nobody cares.'" Confirmation of sorts for Curtis's bleak view was provided by the noted diarist George Templeton Strong, who after first noting that "Respect for written law and constitutions may be excessive and no less deadly than hypertrophy of the heart," went on to write that should "learned counsel prove by word-splitting that [Lincoln] saved [the country] unconstitutionally, I shall honor his memory even more reverently than I do now."[87]

Indeed, Abraham Lincoln is in some ways the central figure of my course, in part because it is he who is honored in the most important temple of our civil religion and whose portrait is on our currency. I ask my students, "What precedent did Lincoln set?" Is it possible to cabin his assertions of a strong presidential power to the specific context of a civil war? This debate should be readily applicable to events within American life over the past decades.[88] After all, it is now standard governmental practice to proclaim "wars" on drugs, terrorists, and other social evils, not to mention more nonmetaphorical wars such as that in the Persian Gulf. It is no coincidence, then, that this chapter of the casebook concludes with the famous exchange between David Frost and Richard Nixon about presidential power:

> MR. FROST: So what in a sense you're saying is that there are certain situations . . . where the President can decide that it's in the best interests of the nation or something, and do something illegal.

> MR. NIXON: Well, when the President does it, that means that it is not illegal.[89]

Conclusion

A "purist" might well defend teaching the constitutional law of slavery for its own sake. Although I think there is much to be said for that, it should be clear that my own argument is more pragmatic inasmuch as I insist that comprehension of contemporary constitutional problems, whether of the interstate shipment of goods or of war and peace, is significantly helped by reflection on past struggles involving slavery. I strongly disagree with those who would defend their not assigning materials on slavery on the ground that, however intellectually interesting, they are simply outdated and thus disserve our students who are interested in grasping more contemporary constitutional dilemmas. This is, however, a much overdrawn contrast. Much must change in the way we teach constitutional law, beginning with the editing of our casebooks and going on to the design of our syllabi.

Notes

Sanford Levinson holds the W. St. John Garwood and W. St. John Garwood, Jr., Centennial Chair in Law, University of Texas Law School.

I am grateful to Akhil Reed Amar, Jack Balkin, Paul Finkelman, Scot Powe, Jordan Steiker, and Mark Tushnet for their comments on an earlier draft.

1. See, e.g., Henry L. Gates, Jr., *Loose Canons: Notes on the Culture Wars* (New York: Oxford University Press, 1992); Judith Resnick, "Constructing the Canon," 2 *Yale Journal of Law and Humanities* 221 (1990). Frances Lee Ansley explicitly addresses the issue of canonicity in her article, "Race and the Core Curriculum in Legal Education," 79 *California Law Review* 1511 (1991), which should certainly be read by anyone interested in the issues raised by this essay.

2. Paul Brest and Sanford Levinson, *Processes of Constitutional Decisionmaking*, 3d ed. (Boston: Little Brown, 1992) (hereinafter, "Brest and Levinson").

3. See, e.g., Derrick Bell, *Race, Racism, and American Law*, 3d ed. (Boston: Little Brown, 1992).

4. *The Antelope*, 23 U.S. (10 Wheat.) 66 (1825).

5. *Elkison v. Deliesseline*, 8 F. Cas. 493 (C.C.D. S.C. 1823) (No. 4,366).

6. *Groves v. Slaughter*, 40 U.S. (15 Pet.) 449 (1841).

7. *Prigg v. Pennsylvania*, 41 U.S. (16 Pet.) 536 (1842).

8. *Dred Scott v. Sandford*, 60 U.S. (19 How.) 393 (1857).

9. Brest and Levinson, 207–11, quoting Frederick Douglass, *Life and Writings*, ed. Philip Foner (New York: International Publishers, 1950), 2:467–80.

10. Ibid., 211–14, (quoting Paul Angle, ed., *Created Equal?: The Complete Lincoln-Douglas Debates of 1858* (Chicago: University of Chicago Press, 1958), 20–21, 36–37, 56–57, 77–78.

11. Ibid., 190–91, quoting 8 *Official Opinions of the Attorney General of the U.S.* 489 (1872).

12. Ibid., 224–26, quoting Benjamin R. Curtis, ed., *A Memoir of Benjamin Robbins Curtis* (Boston: Little Brown, 1879), 2:306–35.

13. For example, *Strauder* v. *West Virginia,* 100 U.S. 303 (1880), and the *Civil Rights Cases,* 109 U.S. 3 (1883).

14. *Bailey* v. *Alabama,* 219 U.S. 219 (1911). Given my belief that *Bailey* should become part of the standard canon of constitutional law cases, it grieves me to confess that I do not include it in my syllabus because of the pressures of time.

15. *DeShaney* v. *Winnebago Co. Dept. of Social Services,* 489 U.S. 189 (1989).

16. See Akhil Reed Amar and Daniel Widawsky, "A Thirteenth Amendment Response to DeShaney," 105 *Harvard Law Review* 1359 (1992).

17. Gerald Gunther, *Constitutional Law,* 12th ed. (Mineola, N.Y.: Foundation, 1991).

18. William B. Lockhart et al., *Constitutional Law: Cases, Comments, Questions,* 7th ed. (St. Paul: West Publishing, 1991).

19. William Cohen and Jonathan D. Varat, *Constitutional Law: Cases and Materials,* 9th ed. (Mineola, N.Y.: Foundation, 1993).

20. Ronald D. Rotunda, *Modern Constitutional Law: Cases and Notes,* 3d ed. (St. Paul: West Publishing, 1989).

21. Geoffrey R. Stone, *Constitutional Law,* 2d ed. (Boston: Little Brown, 1991).

22. Gunther, *Constitutional Law,* 12. n. 6, 23, 403 n. 2.

23. The importance of the territorial expansion of slavery is well laid out in Arthur Bestor, "The American Civil War as a Constitutional Crisis," *American Historical Review* 60 (1964): 327; portions are reprinted in Brest and Levinson, 214–16.

24. *Dred Scott* v. *Sandford, supra* note 8, at 407.

25. I should note that a good four-and-one-half page summary of *Dred Scott* leads off a chapter, "Racial Equality," in Norman Redlich et al., *Constitutional Law,* 2d ed. (New York: Matthew Bender, 1989), 566–70. See also Dan Braveman et al., *Constitutional Law: Structure and Rights in Our Federal System* (New York: Matthew Bender, 1991), 441–45 (*Dred Scott*). Finally, it is worth noting as well that the newest casebook in the field—Daniel Farber, Philip Frickey, and William Eskridge, *Constitutional Law: Themes for the Constitution's Third Century* (St. Paul: West Publishing, 1993)—which focuses strongly on contemporary cases, has as its first chapter "A Prologue on Constitutional History." Pages 11–12, part of the section "States' Rights, Slavery and Civil War," discuss *Dred Scott.*

26. See Mark Tushnet, *The American Law of Slavery* (Princeton: Princeton University Press, 1981).

27. Stone et al., *Constitutional Law,* 472–77. Included here, with great effect, is *State* v. *Post,* 20 N.J.L. 368 (1845), in which a New Jersey judge refuses to find slavery unconstitutional under the New Jersey Constitution. Discussion notes refer to *Prigg* v. *Pennsylvania.* See pp. 476–77. See also pp. 150, 268, discussing the implications of assigning Congress exclusive power over regulation of interstate commerce in the context of slavery.

28. *New York Times* v. *Sullivan,* 376 U.S. 254 (1964).

29. *Buckley* v. *Valeo,* 424 U.S. 1 (1976).

30. This might especially be the case insofar as *New York Times v. Sullivan* is best understood within the context of attempts by Southern white segregationists to defeat the "Second Reconstruction" by making it next to impossible for the national press to cover what was occurring in the Deep South. See Paul Brest and Sanford Levinson, *Processes of Constitutional Decisionmaking,* 2d ed., 1176

(1983), which notes that as of March 1964, libel suits claiming a total of $300 million in damages were pending in the South.

31. I also spend a great deal of time in effect questioning the legitimacy of the distinction between internal and external criteria.

32. See Sanford Levinson, *Constitutional Faith* (Princeton: Princeton University Press, 1988), 59.

33. Charles Fried, "The Lawyer as Friend: The Moral Foundations of the Lawyer-Client Relation," 85 *Yale Law Journal* 1060 (1976); Stephen L. Pepper, "The Lawyer's Amoral Ethical Role," *American Bar Foundation Research Journal* 613 (1986).

34. Fried, "Lawyer as Friend," 1074.

35. Ibid., 1075.

36. Pepper, "Lawyer's Amoral Ethical Role," 626.

37. Charles Fried, "Author's Reply," 86 *Yale Law Journal* 584, 585 (1977), responding to critique by Edward Dauer and Arthur Leff of "Lawyer as Friend."

38. I have no doubt, incidentally, that some opponents of pornography, especially if influenced by Professor MacKinnon—see, e.g., Catherine MacKinnon, *Only Words* (Cambridge: Harvard University Press, 1993)—might well assert that pornographers are all too similar to slaveholders.

39. I am grateful to Mark Tushnet for forcing me to address this point.

40. *Fletcher v. Peck,* 10 U.S. (6 Cranch) 87, 139, 143 (1810).

41. *McCulloch v. Maryland,* 17 U.S. (4 Wheat.) 316 (1819).

42. *Griswold v. Connecticut,* 381 U.S. 479 (1965).

43. In his concurring opinion, Justice Harlan incorporated by reference his dissenting opinion in *Poe v. Ullman,* 367 U.S. 497, 522–55 (1961), which we, like many other casebook editors, reprint as part of the *Griswold* materials.

44. Garry Wills, *Inventing America: Jefferson's Declaration of Independence* xiii (New York: Doubleday, 1978). Quoted in Brest and Levinson, 965. See also the extremely important article by Rogers Smith, "Beyond Tocqueville, Myrdal, and Hartz: The Multiple Traditions in America," *American Political Science Review* 87 (1993): 549, which argues for the co-existence in the American past of highly unattractive, illiberal traditions with more commonly recognized—because attractive—traditions of liberal tolerance and equality. For more on this point, see the discussion of *Dred Scott* below.

45. *The Antelope, supra* note 4. A rich description (and discussion) of the complicated facts and jurisprudence of this case can be found in John Noonan, Jr., *The Antelope: The Ordeal of the Recaptured Africans in the Administrations of James Monroe and John Quincey Adams* (Berkeley: University of California Press, 1977).

46. Noonan, *The Antelope,* 121.

47. See William Freehling, *The Road to Disunion: Secessionists at Bay* (New York: Harper and Row, 1990).

48. *McCulloch v. Maryland, supra* note 41, at 401.

49. *Prigg v. Pennsylvania, supra* note 4, at 539. For a superb general overview of *Prigg,* see Paul Finkelman, "Sorting Out *Prigg v. Pennsylvania,*" 24 *Rutgers Law Journal* 603 (1993) and Paul Finkelman, "Story Telling on the Supreme Court: *Prigg v. Pennsylvania* and Justice Joseph Story's Judicial Nationalism," 1994 *Supreme Court Review* 247. See also Barbara Holden-Smith, "Lords of Lash, Loom, and Law: Justice Story, Slavery, and *Prigg v. Pennsylvania,*" 78 *Cornell Law Review* 1086 (1993).

50. For a very different reading of Justice Story's opinion, see Christopher L. M. Eisgruber, "Justice Story, Slavery, and the Natural Law Foundations of American Constitutionalism," 55 *University of Chicago Law Review* 273 (1988).

51. *Prigg* v. *Pennsylvania, supra* note 7, at 610.

52. "No Person held to Service or Labour in one State, under the Laws thereof, escaping into another, shall, in Consequence of any Law or Regulation thereof, be discharged from such Service or Labour, but shall be delivered up on Claim of the Part to whom such Service or Labour may be due." U.S. Const., art. IV, sec. 2, cl. 3.

53. *Prigg* v. *Pennsylvania, supra* note 7, at 612.

54. Ibid., at 611. There is some dispute about this: "The clause was not a significant isssue in the convention. Introduced late in the proceedings by a South Carolina delegate, it aroused little debate and received unanimous approval. There is little evidence to support the assertion frequently made in later years that without the clause the constitution would have failed." Don Feherenbacher, *The Dred Scott Case* (New York: Oxford University Press, 1978), 25.

55. Although some have read Story as objecting not only to "burdens" but also to *any* participation by states in the enforcement of the clause, Paul Finkelman persuasively argues that that is a misreading of the opinion. Story does not object to state enforcement of the federal Fugitive Slave Law of 1793; in fact, he explicitly makes it clear that the states *ought* to enforce it. He just says that they cannot be *required* to do so by Congress. But Story does not indicate opposition to state legislation that authorizes state officials to act to enforce the law, so long as the legislation does not add any requirements or offer any alternative procedure to enforcement of the federal scheme. See Justice Wayne's concurrence, which stresses this point. Taney, in his own concurrence, misstates what Story said—perhaps, as Finkelman suggests, for political reasons—by describing Story's opinion as more hostile to state enforcement of the Fugitive Slave Law than is in fact the case. See Finkelman, "Sorting Out *Prigg* v. *Pennsylvania.*"

56. I owe this suggestion to my colleague Scot Powe.

57. Douglass, *Life and Writings,* 2:467–80.

58. See Philip Bobbitt, *Constitutional Fate* (New York: Oxford University Press, 1982) and *Constitutional Interpretation* (Cambridge: Basil Blackwell, 1991). Bobbitt offers six "modalities" of constitutional interpretation, of which textualism is one.

59. Quoted in Brest and Levinson, p. 210.

60. See 8 *Official Opinions of the Attorneys General of the United States* (1872), 489; reprinted in Brest and Levinson, 190–91, from which all quotations below are taken.

61. It was, of course, part of Taney's thesis in *Dred Scott* that Douglass could not be an American citizen.

62. *Dennis* v. *United States,* 341 U.S. 494 (1951).

63. *Barron* v. *Baltimore,* 32 U.S. (7 Pet.) 243 (1833).

64. *Terminiello* v. *Chicago,* 337 U.S. 1, 37 (1949) (Jackson, J., dissenting): "The choice is not between order and liberty. It is between liberty with order and anarchy without either. There is danger that, if the Court does not temper its doctrinaire logic with a little practical wisdom, it will convert the constitutional Bill of Rights into a suicide pact."

65. See Akhil Reed Amar, "Comment: The Case of the Missing Amendments: *R.A.V. v. City of St. Paul*," 106 *Harvard Law Review* 124, 151–60 (1992).

66. See, e.g., Martha Minow, "The Supreme Court 1986 Term–Foreword: Justice Engendered,"101 *Harvard Law Review* 10 (1987).

67. *The Antelope, supra* note 4, at 121.

68. *Gibbons* v. *Ogden*, 22 U.S. (9 Wheat.) 1 (1824).

69. *Elkison* v. *Deliesseline, supra* note 5.

70. *Mayor of New York* v. *Miln*, 36 U.S. (11 Pet.) 102 (1837).

71. Ibid., at 142.

72. *The Passenger Cases*, 48 U.S. (7 How.) 283, 474 (1849). Mention of The Passenger Cases for similar purposes can be found in Stone et al., *Constitutional Law*, 150 (discussing "Commerce, national power, and slavery) and 269 (discussing "'Exclusive power' and the slavery issue").

One might also note that the acknowledgement, in art. I, sec. 9, of Congress's power to bar the importation of slaves in 1808 might be taken as implied recognition of the states' retained powers to control immigration. Congress's power to prohibit the immigration of certain persons—i.e., slaves from abroad—scarcely seems to imply a power to *require* the states to accept any given category of immigrants. I owe this point to Paul Finkelman.

73. *Groves* v. *Slaughter, supra* note 6.

74. Ibid., at 525.

75. Donald Regan, "The Supreme Court and State Protectionism: Making Sense of the Dormant Commerce Clause," 84 *Michigan Law Review* 1091 (1986).

76. *Dred Scott* v. *Sandford, supra* note 8.

77. See Attorney General Edwin Meese III, Address before the D.C. Chapter of the Federalist Society Lawyer's Division (November 1, 1985), in *The Great Debate: Interpreting Our Written Constitution* (Washington, D.C.: The Federalist Society, 1986), 31–41.

78. See Robert Bork, *The Tempting of America: The Political Seduction of the Law* (New York: Free Press, 1990), 143.

79. *Dred Scott* v. *Sandford, supra* note 8, at 426.

80. For a suggestion that this might be the case, see Paul Finkelman, "The Constitution and the Intentions of the Framers: The Limits of Historical Analysis," 50 *Pittsburgh Law Review* 349, 390–95 (1989): "Those who revere the framers and the Constitution can find solace only in the fact that some of the founders in 1776 and 1787 (though probably a minority of both groups) did not intend the results that Taney reached." Ibid., 395.

81. See especially *Dred Scott* v. *Sandford, supra* note 8, at 407–17. See also Rogers Smith, "Beyond Tocqueville, Myrdal, and Hartz, *supra* note 44.

82. Angle, ed., *Created Equal?*, 57–58.

83. See Henry P. Monaghan, "The Protective Power of the Presidency," 93 *Columbia Law Review* 1, 27–28 (1993).

84. *Ex parte Merryman*, 17 F. Cas. 144 (C.C.D. Md. 1861); reprinted in Brest and Levinson, 221–22.

85. "Special Message to Congress,"July 4, 1861, in Abraham Lincoln, *Speeches and Writings, 1859–1865* (New York: Library of America, 1989), 253. Emphasis in original.

86. Curtis, *A Memoir,* 2:306.

87. Allen Nevins and Milton H. Thomas, eds., *The Diary of George Templeton*

Strong (New York: MacMillan, 1952), 4:20–21 (entry of July 15, 1865); quoted in Sanford Levinson, *Constitutional Faith*, 42.

88. See especially Monaghan's excellent article, "Protective Power of the Presidency," for a thorough discussion of the dangers of interpreting the Constitution as placing a significant degree of "inherent" untrammelled power in the hands of the president.

89. Transcript of Frost-Nixon interview, *New York Times*, May 20, 1977, sec. A, p. 16; reprinted in Brest and Levinson, 227.

4

Chief Justice Hornblower of New Jersey and the Fugitive Slave Law of 1793

Paul Finkelman

IN 1836, IN *State* v. *The Sheriff of Burlington*, Chief Justice Joseph C. Hornblower of New Jersey ordered the release of Alexander Helmsley, who was then being held as a fugitive slave in Burlington, New Jersey. In deciding this case Hornblower wrote a strongly abolitionist opinion, implying that the federal Fugitive Slave Law of 1793 was unconstitutional. However, Hornblower did not declare the federal law void, because he did not have to do so. Helmsley had been seized and incarcerated under a state law. Thus, Hornblower was able to order his release when he determined that the New Jersey law under which Helmsley was held violated the state constitution. Because neither the sheriff who held Helmsley nor the slave owner who claimed him raised the federal law of 1793, Hornblower did not have to explicitly address its constitutionality. Hornblower did not read his elaborate opinion from the bench, although he did he summarize his conclusions. Nor did Hornblower have the opinion published, either in the official reports or as a pamphlet.[1]

Some newspapers, especially the antislavery press, communicated Hornblower's decision. As far west as Ohio the antislavery attorney Salmon P. Chase, a future chief justice of the United States Supreme Court, cited it for authority in a fugitive slave case. But Chase's citation was probably an exception. Hornblower's unreported decision and unpublished opinion were initially of little use to antislavery lawyers and activists. Illustrative of the initial obscurity of Hornblower's decision is the fact that in 1838 William Jay, the abolitionist attorney and antislavery constitutional theorist, was unaware of it. Jay lived in Westchester County, New York, close to Hornblower, and Hornblower had been a personal friend of Jay's late father, Chief Justice John Jay. Yet, Jay knew nothing of the opinion.[2]

In 1851 the *New York Evening Post* resurrected the Hornblower opinion from obscurity, publishing it in pamphlet form.[3] The new Fugitive Slave Law of 1850 had revived interest in Hornblower's 1836 opinion because its principles applied to this law as well as to the 1793 act. Antislavery editors, activists, and politicians appreciated the applicability of Hornblower's conclusions to the debate over the constitutionality of the Fugitive Slave Law of 1850. In the 1850s some judges cited the previously unpublished opinion as a legal precedent;[4] but more importantly Hornblower's opinion emerged as an intellectual, moral, and political argument against the Fugitive Slave Law. The very fact that Hornblower had not published his opinion in 1836 made his arguments more valuable in the 1850s. Hornblower had not been an abolitionist when he wrote the opinion, and he had written it before fugitive slave rendition was a major political issue. Thus, his opinion was an example of a dispassionate approach to fugitive slaves by a respected state chief justice, untainted by abolitionism.

The Hornblower opinion illustrates the connection between court cases, legal theory, and antislavery politics. An understanding of this case begins with a short discussion of how New Jersey dealt with the problems posed by fugitive slaves entering that state.

Fugitive Slaves and Ending Slavery in New Jersey

The problem of fugitive slaves in New Jersey cannot be divorced from other aspects of slavery in the state. Because New Jersey was the last northern state to abolish slavery, during much of the antebellum period New Jersey was concerned about its own runaway slaves as well as those escaping from Southern bondage. This is just one of the peculiar aspects of New Jersey's relationship to the peculiar institution.[5]

In the colonial period, New Jersey was the home of one of America's most important early antislavery activists, John Woolman. In 1786 Elias Boudinot and Joseph Bloomfield organized New Jersey's first antislavery society. These men were not idealists, isolated from the mainstream. On the contrary, they were leaders in state and national politics. Boudinot was twice president of the Continental Congress, a signatory to the peace treaty with Great Britain in 1783, and a three-term congressman under the new Constitution. Bloomfield was an Admiralty judge, state attorney general, congressman, governor of New Jersey from 1801 to 1812, and a general in the War of 1812.[6]

Despite this early antislavery leadership, New Jersey was, as mentioned above, the last Northern state to take steps to abolish slavery. Not until 1804 did New Jersey enact a gradual emancipation statute. This was nearly a quarter century after Pennsylvania adopted the nation's first gradual emancipation act.[7]

There is a striking contrast on statewide abolition between New Jersey and New York. New York was also slow to join the "first emancipation," passing its Gradual Emancipation Act in 1799. But New York quickly made up for lost time. In 1817 New York adopted a law freeing all its slaves on July 4, 1827. Meanwhile, in New Jersey slavery lingered. As late as 1845, the New Jersey Supreme Court held, in *State* v. *Post*, that the "free and equal" clause of the state constitution of 1844 did not emancipate the approximately seven hundred slaves remaining in the state. Only the aged Chief Justice Hornblower supported the abolitionists who brought this case.[8]

In 1846 New Jersey took a small step toward finally ending slavery. A new law changed the status of the state's remaining slaves to "servants for life."[9] Although a "free state," New Jersey was home to some blacks still in servitude when the Civil War began. These superannuated blacks remained in a state of semibondage until the adoption of the Thirteenth Amendment ended all involuntary servitude in the nation.

Although a "free state," New Jersey was not always considered a safe haven for escaped slaves. Bondsmen from Delaware and Maryland who came into New Jersey were well advised (if they could find someone to give them such advice) to continue north. In 1846 the state's only antislavery newspaper complained that New Jersey "still continues to be the hunting ground of the kidnapper." On the other hand, in the 1830s negrophobes in southern Cumberland County complained that they were about to be overrun by fugitive slaves. One racist politician claimed these "vicious intruders" threatened the stability of the entire county, if not the state.[10] The truth no doubt lay somewhere in between these somewhat self-serving assessments.

Nathan Helmsley, whom Chief Justice Hornblower released from custody, illustrates the complexity of the treatment of fugitive slaves in New Jersey. When he resolved to leave his bondage in Maryland, Helmsley recalled, "I started for New Jersey, where, I had been told, people were free, and nobody would disturb me."[11] Once there Helmsley relocated a few times to avoid capture, and he managed to live in the state for a number of years before he was discovered and seized by a slave catcher. As the Helmsley case suggests, New Jersey was neither entirely hostile to fugitive slaves nor especially welcoming. New Jersey was no Vermont or New Hampshire; but neither was it a Maryland or a Virginia. Ironically, it was in this atmosphere that Chief Justice Hornblower would issue the most radically antislavery state supreme court opinion before the 1850s.

New Jersey, Slavery, and Early National Politics

Despite New Jersey's slow movement towards abolition, the state's representatives in the new Congress often opposed slavery and supported the
rights of free blacks. In 1793 all four of New Jersey's congressmen—Elias
Boudinot, Abraham Clark, Jonathan Dayton, and Aaron Kitchell—voted
for the Fugitive Slave Law. None of these men were supporters of slavery;
Boudinot and Dayton were known to be strong opponents of slavery. But
probably they did not see this vote as proslavery. The history of the first
fugitive slave law suggests that its supporters thought the law was a fair
compromise between the needs of slaveowners to recover their fugitives
and the needs of the Northern states to protect their free inhabitants
from kidnapping. Within a few years it became clear that the Fugitive
Slave Law of 1793 in fact offered little protection to Northern free Blacks.
In 1797 New Jersey's Isaac Smith argued in favor of federal legislation to
protect free blacks from kidnapping. Congressman Smith argued that it
"was impossible" for the states to protect against kidnapping because when
the kidnapper reached a new jurisdiction, he was safe from arrest and
prosecution. Smith was particularly worried about those free Blacks who
might be kidnapped and taken to the West Indies. He wanted a federal
inspection law to help prevent this. Smith could see no reason why such
legislation would give "offence or cause of alarm to any gentleman."[12]

Later in this session, Congressman Kitchell spoke in favor of a petition from a group of African Americans in Philadelphia who claimed to
be free but who felt threatened by the Fugitive Slave Law of 1793. During this debate Southerners argued that these blacks were in fact fugitive
slaves and that their petition was unworthy of consideration by the House.
Kitchell believed that the status of the petitioners was irrelevant. He argued that Congress should accept a petition if there was merit to the
claim. The only question for him was "whether a committee shall be appointed to inquire on the improper force of law" used against blacks
living in the North.[13]

The House of Representatives ultimately refused to modify the fugitive slave law or even to receive the petition of the Philadelphia blacks.
The votes were not entirely sectional: a number of congressmen from
New England and New York voted with Southerners on both issues. Firm
support for the rights of free blacks came from Pennsylvania, Delaware,
and New Jersey.[14] This opposition to slavery continued through the 1790s.

This relationship of slavery to national politics changed with the
Jeffersonian Revolution of 1800. Aaron Kitchell, for example, was a leader
of the Jeffersonians in New Jersey. He shared with Jefferson a negrophobia
typical of many Democrats of the era. Kitchell believed "the great evil of
slavery was the introducing a race of people of different colour from the
mass of the people. If they were the same colour, time might assimilate
them together." After 1801 he was likely to side with his proslavery South-

ern allies.[15] Thus, after 1800 New England Federalists led the opposition to slavery, while New Jersey's congressional delegation receded into the background on this issue. Opposition to fugitive slave rendition in New Jersey would not reemerge until the 1830s. The key figure at this time would be Chief Justice Hornblower, who viewed himself as a political and intellectual descendant of the Federalist Party of the previous generation.

Regulating Slaves and Freemen

The history of New Jersey's statutory and judicial regulation of slavery during and after the Revolution reveals the contradictions within the state on the issue. In 1786 New Jersey virtually abolished the further importation of slaves as merchandise from Africa or other states by establishing fines for bringing slaves into the state. However, illegally imported slaves were not freed. Furthermore, this statute prohibited free blacks from moving to New Jersey.[16] Such a provision was common in the laws of the slave states. These aspects of the law suggest a state more interested in slowing the growth of its black population than in favoring liberty. However, such an analysis may be mistaken, because the statute also encouraged private manumission and the decent treatment of slaves within New Jersey.

The 1786 statute also allowed for private manumission without requiring either that the ex-slave leave the state or that the owner give a bond to guarantee that the ex-slave would not become a public charge. This was an important inducement for those masters who wanted to free their slaves but could not afford to risk having to support them in the future or who did not want to force their slaves to choose between gaining freedom and having to abandon friends and family.

Finally, the law also subjected owners who kept their slaves to penalties if they mistreated their bondsmen.[17] This was both a step towards humanizing slavery and discouraging slaveholding.

In 1788 the legislature strengthened the prohibition on the slave trade and also attempted to prevent the kidnapping of free blacks. The statute prohibited the removal of slaves from the state without their consent. This law also removed some disabilities of free blacks while simultaneously requiring slaveowners to teach their young slaves to read and write. This statute contrasts sharply with the laws of the antebellum South, which generally made it a criminal offence to teach a slave to read. While the literacy provision was certainly "a step in preparing them for freedom," the New Jersey legislature was not ready to take the final step of adopting an emancipation scheme.[18]

These statutes made New Jersey moderately antislavery, but the legislature's actions were consistent with Madison's claim that New Jersey was not a threat to slavery in the South. This assessment of New Jersey was confirmed in 1790, when the legislature refused to adopt a gradual emancipation statute. The legislature concluded that private manumission would soon end slaveholding, and thus there was no need for a law on the subject. Indeed, the legislature perversely argued that a gradual emancipation bill would actually delay the end of slavery in the state and would "do more hurt than good, not only to the citizens of the State in general, but the slaves themselves." There was, however, little evidence to support this conclusion.[19]

In 1798 New Jersey adopted a new, comprehensive slave code as part of a general revision of the state's laws. This new law did not lead to an end to slavery, but it did contain some important modifications in how blacks and slaves would be treated in New Jersey. One significant change was to allow free Blacks from other states to enter New Jersey as long as they could produce proof of their freedom. This made New Jersey virtually unique among slave states in that it allowed the unrestricted immigration of free blacks.[20]

The 1798 law also supplemented the federal Fugitive Slave Law of 1793 by providing mandatory rewards for anyone seizing a runaway slave and by holding liable for the full value of the slave anyone harboring a fugitive slave or helping such a slave escape.[21]

In 1804 the state finally passed a gradual emancipation statute, giving freedom to the children of all slaves born in the state but requiring that they serve as apprentices, the females until age twenty-one, the males until age twenty-five. In the next seven years, the legislature fine-tuned this law, but none of these amendments and changes significantly altered the status of slaves in the state and or affected fugitives there.[22]

In 1821 New Jersey adopted a comprehensive revision of its slave laws. The provision of the 1798 law regarding fugitives remained intact. However, the 1821 law also punished severely anyone unlawfully removing a black from the state. This new provision was at least in part the result of petitions from Middlesex County calling for a law to "prevent kidnapping and carrying from the State blacks and other people of color." Slaves owned by New Jersey residents could not be sold out of the state, and only under certain circumstances could owners permanently leaving the state take their slaves with them. Persons selling a slave for illegal export were to be fined between five hundred and a thousand dollars, or sentenced to one to two years at hard labor, or both. Purchasers and exporters were to be fined one to two thousand dollars and were to spend two to four years at hard labor. Officials were empowered to search ships for blacks who were being forced out of the state, and anyone resisting faced the same penalties as exporters. This law did not apply to bona fide transients from other states nor presumably to masters recovering fugitives.[23] But the law did make fugitive slave rendition more difficult by requiring the master or his agent to make sure that the proper documentation was available before a removal took place.

The laws of 1788, 1798, 1804, and 1821 reflected the tension between the need to support the constitutional claims of Southerners and the almost universal belief in the North that slave catching was a dirty business, to be avoided by decent people. Indeed, throughout the North individual fugitive slaves often gained the sympathy of people who opposed abolitionists, believed in supporting the Union at all costs, and supported the South in politics. Thus, New Jersey's citizens were usually not inclined to support the return of fugitive slaves. Moreover, as the statute of 1798 indicates, they felt an obligation to protect both the liberty of their free black neighbors and some basic rights of the slaves living within their midst.

At the same time, however, unlike every other free state, as late as the 1830s New Jersey had a substantial slave population. New Jersey's legislators, and no doubt many of their constituents, were inclined to protect the property rights of their slaveholding neighbors. Thus, in New Jersey a tension existed between protecting local slaveowners whose human chattel might escape and protecting free blacks and fugitives from other states who lived in New Jersey. This tension is seen in the early New Jersey cases dealing with fugitive slaves.

In *The State* v. *Heddon* (1795), the New Jersey Supreme Court released Cork, a black who claimed he had gained his freedom during the Revolution. At the time, Cork was imprisoned in Essex County as a runaway slave, claimed by a man named Snowden. In a habeas corpus proceeding, the court ruled that Snowden's claim to Cork was insufficient and released the alleged slave.[24]

Heddon illustrates that before 1804 New Jersey treated blacks the way other slave states did. Officials presumed Cork was a slave, arresting him when he appeared to be wandering about without a master. The New Jersey court did not actually declare Cork to be free, but only determined that Snowden was not his owner, and since no one else claimed him, Cork had to be released from jail.

The Gradual Emancipation Act of 1804 did not end New Jersey's willingness to help in the return of fugitive slaves. In *Nixon* v. *Story's Administrators* (1813), a trial court awarded judgment against a man who had carried slaves from New Jersey to Pennsylvania. Although the Supreme Court reversed the verdict on technical grounds, the original judgment reveals the state's willingness to aid slave owners seeking their runaways.[25]

In *Gibbons* v. *Morse* (1821) and again in *Cutter* v. *Moore* (1825), the New Jersey court decided in favor of masters suing ship owners or captains who had allowed slaves to escape. New Jersey continued to enforce the provisions of the 1798 law that punished those who helped slaves escape. In both cases the plaintiffs did not allege any intent to help the slaves escape. These were not the actions of abolitionists trying to undermine slavery; rather, they were the acts of common carriers who negligently allowed slaves to escape. In these civil suits motive was not an issue. In both cases the owners recovered for the value of the lost slaves.[26]

For blacks in New Jersey—free people, local slaves, or fugitives—these two cases set ominous precedents. In *Gibbons* the chief justice of New Jersey "charged the jury, that the colour of this man was sufficient evidence that he was a slave." In upholding the jury's verdict, the New Jersey Court of Errors and Appeals also affirmed that "the law presumes every man that is black to be a slave." The headnotes to the official report of the case confirmed that "In New Jersey, all black men are presumed to be slaves until the contrary appears."

Cutter explicitly reaffirmed this analysis. Unlike all other northeastern states, New Jersey accepted the Southern view that all blacks were presumed to be slaves until they could prove otherwise.[27]

The New Jersey Personal Liberty Law of 1826

In 1826 New Jersey fundamentally altered its approach to fugitive slave rendition with the adoption of a new statute regulating fugitive slaves. This law required a claimant to apply to a judge for a warrant ordering a county sheriff to arrest the alleged fugitive slave. The judge would then hold a hearing and, if convinced that the person before him was a fugitive slave, would issue a certificate of removal. This law was designed to provide more protection for blacks living in New Jersey than was afforded by the federal Fugitive Slave Law of 1793. It was, as Chief Justice Hornblower asserted, "more humane and better calculated to prevent frauds and oppression" than the federal statute.[28] But, as Hornblower would also conclude, this law did not adequately protect against fraud and oppression.

Shortly after New Jersey adopted its 1826 act, Pennsylvania and New York passed similar laws. These laws "represent a voluntary effort to find a workable balance between a duty to protect free blacks and the obligation to uphold the legitimate claims of slave owners." While balancing interests, these laws also represented a direct challenge to federal supremacy on the subject of fugitive slave rendition. These statutes added requirements to the rendition process that had been set out in the federal law of 1793. In 1842, in *Prigg* v. *Pennsylvania*, the Supreme Court would declare such extra requirements to be unconstitutional. But before *Prigg* these laws gave some protections to free blacks and fugitive slaves in New York, Pennsylvania, and New Jersey. These laws also are early examples of state legislatures finding independent and separate state grounds for protecting the liberty of their citizens. Chief Justice

Hornblower's decision in *State* v. *The Sheriff of Burlington* similarly reflects the nineteenth-century notion that the states, and not the federal government, were the primary guarantors of individual rights.[29] The case also underscores that in antebellum America the federal government, predicated on a proslavery constitution and perpetually dominated by slaveowners, posed greater dangers to individual rights than the Northern states.

The Hornblower Decision

State v. *The Sheriff of Burlington*, an unreported case heard by the New Jersey Supreme Court in 1836, determined the meaning of the 1826 law. The case involved Alexander Helmsley, a black living near Mount Holley, New Jersey, his wife Nancy Helmsley, and their three children. Sometime around 1820 Helmsley, then a Maryland slave called Nathan Mead, escaped to New Jersey. There he married a woman who had been free in Maryland "by word of mouth" but had no free papers. In New Jersey the Helmsleys found work and raised a family of freeborn children.[30]

In 1835 John Willoughby, a Maryland attorney, purchased Helmsley "running" from the executor of Helmsley's deceased master. Another Maryland attorney, R. D. Cooper, claimed Nancy and the children as his own slaves.[31] On October 24, 1835, Willoughby and Cooper secured the arrest of the Helmsleys on a warrant issued by Burlington county judge George Haywood and had them placed in the county jail. Two days later Judge Haywood issued a writ of habeas corpus, which brought the Helmsleys into his courtroom. Following the habeas corpus hearing, Haywood recommitted Helmsley to the jail but apparently released his wife and children. At this point Helmsley's attorney applied to Chief Justice Hornblower for a writ of habeas corpus to bring the case before the New Jersey Supreme Court. While Hornblower would eventually issue this writ, he did not do so immediately. Thus, Helmsley remained in jail until November 24, when he was brought before Judge Haywood under a second writ of habeas corpus. Once again Judge Haywood returned Helmsley to the jail.

Throughout these proceedings friends of the Helmsleys provided the unfortunate family with attorneys who were abolitionists. The hearings before Judge Haywood raised numerous questions about the identity of the arrested blacks and if indeed they had been previously manumitted. A trial on the status of Helmsley finally began on December 9. After intermittent proceedings over a two week period, Haywood finally declared Helmsley to be the slave of the claimants and ordered him held in jail until he could be remanded to his owners.[32]

In early December, before Judge Haywood reached his decision on the merits of the case, Helmsley's attorneys filed for a writ of certiorari to bring the case before the New Jersey Supreme Court. This writ was in addition to the request for the writ of habeas corpus filed in November. The extant court papers do not indicate the exact procedural developments in the case. The remaining record does show that in February 1836 Chief Justice Hornblower finally issued the writ of habeas corpus that Helmsley's attorney had applied for in November.[33]

On March 3, 1836, Helmsley was brought to Trenton, where the New Jersey Supreme Court determined his status. At this point Helmsleys' abolitionist attorneys deferred to more prominent counsel, William Halsted and Theodore Frelinghuysen. Halsted had previously been the reporter for the New Jersey Supreme Court. Frelinghuysen, the mayor of Newark, was a former United States senator, a leader of the American Colonization Society, and a politician not disposed to abolition. Nevertheless, he vigorously supported the claims of this black family living in New Jersey. This suggests the potency of claims to freedom by Blacks living in the North.

Hornblower began his analysis of the case by noting that the New Jersey law of 1826 was in conflict with, although not "in direct opposition" to, the federal law of 1793. The two laws prescribed "different modes of proceedings," and so, he concluded, "both cannot be pursued at one and the same time, and one only . . . must be paramount."[34]

Hornblower concluded that the federal law provided a "summary and dangerous proceeding" that afforded "little protection of security to the free colored man, who may be falsely claimed as a fugitive from labor." The New Jersey law was "more humane." The question for the court was which law should be paramount.[35]

Hornblower acknowledged that the United States Constitution made federal laws the "supreme law of the land," but he pointed out this was only true if the law was "made in pursuance" of the Constitution. This meant that if Congress had "a right to legislate on this subject," New Jersey's law was "no better than a dead letter." Hornblower, however, was unwilling to acknowledge that Congress had this power. Instead, he offered a careful analysis of Article IV of the Constitution.[36]

Hornblower compared the Full Faith and Credit clause of section 1 with the Fugitive Slave clause of section 2. The first provision explicitly gave Congress the power to "prescribe the manner in which" acts, records, and proceedings of one state would be proved in another. Similarly, Hornblower noted that section 3 of article IV also explicitly empowered Congress to pass legislation.[37] But no such language existed in section 2 of article IV. This led Hornblower to conclude that "no such power was intended to be given" to Congress for section 2. Indeed, Hornblower argued, Congressional legislation over the Privileges and Immunities clause or over interstate rendition "would cover a broad field, and lead to the most unhappy results." Such legislation would "bring the general government in conflict with the state authorities, and the prejudices of local communities." Hornblower also noted, in a reference to the emerging proslavery argument in the South, that in "a large portion of the country, the right of Congress to legislate on the subject of slavery at all, even in the district [of Columbia] and territories over which it has exclusive jurisdiction, is denied." Thus, Hornblower found that Congress surely lacked the "right to prescribe the manner in which persons residing in the free states, shall be arrested, imprisoned, delivered up, and transferred from one state to another, simply because they are claimed as slaves." Hornblower warned that the "American people would not long submit" to such an expansive view of Congressional power.[38]

This analysis seemed to lead to only one conclusion: that the federal law of 1793 was unconstitutional. But Hornblower insisted that it was not his "intention to express any definitive opinion on the validity of the act of Congress." He thought he could avoid this grave responsibility because the case before him had been brought "in pursuance of the law of this state." However, Hornblower's position on the constitutionality of the federal law was unambiguous. His opinion explicitly argued that Congress lacked power to pass such a law.[39] The rest of his opinion dealt with the constitutionality of New Jersey's 1826 law. While not returning to the federal law, Hornblower's discussion of the state law implied that the federal law of 1793 was also unconstitutional because it did not guarantee a jury trial to putative slaves and thus violated the basic protections of due process found in the Constitution and the Bill of Rights.

Hornblower began his examination of New Jersey's 1826 law by affirming "the right of state legislation on this subject." He did not debate this question. He merely assumed the state had such a right. But the right to regulate fugitive slave rendition did not automatically make such a law constitutional. Hornblower complained that the 1826 law authorized "the seizure, and transportation out of this state, of persons residing here, under the protection of our laws." Hornblower noted that these blacks might be "free-born native inhabitants, the owners of property, and the fathers of families." Yet "upon a summary hearing before a single judge, without the intervention of a jury, and without appeal," they could be removed from the state. Rhetorically he asked, "Can this be a constitutional law?"[40]

Hornblower pointed out the possibilities for fraud and deception under the 1826 law. Under this law any free black could "be falsely accused of escaping from his master, or he may be claimed by mistake for one who has actually fled." These were issues of fact, which Hornblower believed should be decided by a jury. Indeed, he believed that the New Jersey constitution *required* that such a question come before a jury.[41]

Hornblower agreed that the Fugitive Slave clause of the Constitution had to "be executed fully, fairly, and with judicial firmness and integrity." But that did not require that "the person *claimed* shall be given up." It only required that a person who actually owed service or labor "be given up" to his or her master. But the question of whether the person before the court actually owed service or labor was a factual one that only a jury could determine.[42]

Here Hornblower made a careful distinction between the Fugitives from Justice and the Fugitive Slave clauses of article IV of the Constitution. Hornblower believed that the former required the surrender of an alleged criminal "on demand of the EXECUTIVE authority of the state" because the person delivered up was "charged with a crime." However, being charged with a crime did not guarantee a conviction. An accused person was "to be delivered up, not to be punished, not to be detained for life, but to be *tried*, and if acquitted to be set at liberty."[43]

The case of fugitive slaves was different. They would not get a trial when returned to the claimant. They would face a lifetime of bondage. With unusually passionate language, Hornblower noted that the issue was "whether he is to be separated forcibly, and for ever, from his wife and children, or be permitted to enjoy with them the liberty he inherited, and the property he has earned. Whether he is to be dragged in chains to a distant land, and doomed to perpetual slavery, or continue to breathe the air and enjoy the blessings of freedom." Hornblower had no difficulty declaring the law of his own state to be "unconstitutional on the ground that it deprives the accused of a trial by jury."[44]

Hornblower still had one more hurdle to overcome before he could free the slaves before him. By 1836 very few cases involving fugitive slaves had come before American courts. Nevertheless, one of the few precedents on this subject complicated Hornblower's decision. In 1819 the prestigious chief justice of Pennsylvania, William Tilghman, had heard a similar case, involving an alleged fugitive slave held in a Pennsylvania jail. The incarcerated black had argued that under both the Pennsylvania and the United States constitutions he was entitled to a jury trial.[45]

In rejecting this plea, Chief Justice Tilghman had asserted that "our southern brethren would not have consented to become parties to a constitution under which the *United States* have enjoyed so much prosperity, unless their property in slaves had been secured." This implication of the "original intent" of the framers of the Constitution, like so much modern intentionalist analysis, had no basis in fact. This was of little matter to Tilghman, who had concluded that "the whole scope and tenor of the constitution and act of Congress" led to the conclusion "that the fugitive was to be delivered up, on a summary proceeding, without the delay of a formal trial in a court of common law." Tilghman had naively believed, or disingenuously claimed to believe, that any slave who "had really a right to freedom" could "prosecute his right in the state to which he belonged."[46] Thus, Tilghman would not release the alleged slave before him or grant him a jury trial.

This decision was from a different state and thus was not binding on

Hornblower. Nevertheless, Tilghman was a distinguished judge from an important, neighboring state. Hornblower could not simply ignore the decision. Instead, Hornblower boldly rejected it, reiterating his demand for due process by attacking Tilghman's belief that an alleged fugitive could "be transported" to another state because "he will there have a fair trial." Hornblower declared, "So long as I sit upon this bench, I never can, no I never will, yield to such a doctrine." Indignantly the New Jersey justice asserted:

> What, first transport a man out of the state, on a charge of his being a slave, and try the truth of the allegation afterwards—separate him from the place, it may be, of his nativity—the abode of his relatives, his friends, and his witnesses—transport him in chains to Missouri or Arkansas, with the cold comfort that if a freeman he may there assert and establish his freedom! No, if a person comes into this state, and *here* claims the servitude of a human being, whether white or black, *here* he must prove his case, and here prove it according to law.[47]

With this opinion Hornblower established a right to a jury trial for any person claimed as a slave in New Jersey. He also overturned any vestiges of the notion that in New Jersey blacks were presumed to be slaves. Finally, Hornblower established himself and his court as perhaps the most antislavery justice and venue in the nation. Ironically, although New Jersey was the Northern state with the largest number of slaves, its supreme court had staked out the most progressive position on the rights of blacks claimed as fugitive slaves.

The Hornblower Opinion and Personal Liberty in the North

Hornblower's position was a remarkable response to the problem of fugitive slaves. It was the first case where a state supreme court justice demanded due process protections and jury trials for alleged fugitive slaves. Hornblower had rejected the reasoning and analysis of the Chief Justice Tilghman and the Pennsylvania Supreme Court. Similarly, he had ignored a recent New York case, even though it might have bolstered his position that New Jersey need not follow the federal law of 1793.[48] Hornblower's opinion was as radical as anything the new abolitionist movement was demanding. Equally significant, Hornblower was ahead of moderate antislavery politicians on this issue. A comparison with rulings in other states illustrates the radical position of Hornblower.

In 1826 Pennsylvania had adopted a personal liberty law that resembled the New Jersey law of the same year. Although the Pennsylvania Abolition Society thought this law was "a manifest improvement upon the previously existing laws," the law hardly offered blacks due process. A single magistrate in Pennsylvania, without the aid of a jury, would decide the status of the alleged slave. Although the law has been correctly characterized as "a compromise between what were considered the demands of the fugitive slave clause, and the responsibility to protect the personal liberty of free blacks," the 1826 act did not guarantee a jury trial, or indeed a trial of any kind, on the issue of freedom. Unlike New Jersey, Pennsylvania was unwilling to move from this position in the 1830s. In 1837, a year after the Hornblower decision, the Pennsylvania legislature overwhelmingly defeated a bill to provide jury trials in fugitive slave cases. In the Pennsylvania senate only ten of thirty-one senators present voted in favor of the bill; the Pennsylvania house defeated the proposal by a vote of seven for and ninety-three against.[49]

In 1835 Massachusetts had eliminated the common law remedy of the writ of *de homine replegiando*. This writ had allowed alleged fugitives to try their claim to freedom before a jury. With the writ gone, and no jury trial law on the books, alleged fugitives in Massachusetts were at the mercy of a single magistrate and the federal law of 1793.[50]

The situation in New York was more complicated. In 1828 New York had adopted a procedure to allow the return of fugitive slaves after a hearing before a judge. However, alleged fugitives were allowed under another statute to apply for a writ *de homine replegiando*, which would bring their status before a jury. But in *Jack* v. *Martin* the New York Supreme Court concluded that the statute allowing a writ *de homine replegiando* in fugitive slave cases was unconstitutional. On appeal to the New York Court for the Correction of Errors, Chancellor Reuben Walworth held in 1835 that the writ should apply to alleged slaves. However, Walworth, along with the rest of that court, ruled that Jack was a fugitive slave, and he was remanded to his owner. Thus, after 1835 it was impossible to know exactly what the status of a jury trial was for alleged fugitives seized in New York. In 1838, New York abolitionists questioned candidates for governor on whether they supported a jury trial in fugitive slave cases. The Democratic candidate ignored the questions, while the victorious William H. Seward was evasive. Not until 1840 did Seward sign into law a bill guaranteeing a jury trial for fugitive slaves.[51]

Within a year of Hornblower's opinion, New Jersey adopted a new law, the Personal Liberty Law of 1837, regulating the return of fugitives from the state. The law sailed through the legislature, with minimal discussion in the House and almost no debate at all in the Council. This statute allowed for a summary hearing before a state court, but instead of one judge deciding the case, a panel of three judges would be convened. The law also provided that "if either party shall demand a trial by jury, then it shall be the duty of the said judge, before whom such fugitive shall be brought," to impanel a jury to determine the black's status. This was the first statute in the North to guarantee a jury trial for fugitive slaves. It placed New Jersey in the forefront of the emerging movement to protect free blacks and alleged fugitive slaves.[52]

In 1842, in *Prigg* v. *Pennsylvania*, the United States Supreme Court ruled that state laws which interfered with the rendition of fugitive slaves were unconstitutional. Justice Joseph Story, who wrote the majority opinion, upheld the constitutionality of the 1793 law; asserted, in what may be one of the earliest uses of the "preemption doctrine" in federal constitutional law, that the law preempted the entire question; and concluded that no state could make additional regulations for the return of fugitives. Story based some of his decision on the same sort of incorrect history that Judge Tilghman had used in *Wright* v. *Deacon*. This ruling of course undermined Hornblower's opinion and the 1837 statute. Nevertheless, when New Jersey revised its statutes in 1846, the legislature included the 1837 act.[53]

The Hornblower Opinion and Antislavery Legal Theory

Although Hornblower's opinion had some impact on New Jersey law, it had little immediate effect on the rest of the nation. The opinion was never officially reported because, as Hornblower later explained, "it [was] thought best on a conference between my associates and myself not to agitate the public mind on the question of the constitutionality of the Act of Congress of 1793, then in force." As we have seen, Hornblower's opinion did not become a useful legal precedent for abolitionist attorneys. Only after it was published as a pamphlet in 1851 did the opinion become important—and then mostly as a political precedent. Moreover, Hornblower's failure to publish the opinion eventually undermined its value in New Jersey. The opinion probably set the stage for the adoption of New Jersey's Personal Liberty Law of 1837.[54] But, as knowledge of the unpublished opinion dwindled, its utility as a precedent disappeared.

The decision not to officially publish the opinion limited the public's access to newspaper accounts of the case. That had two consequences. First, it undermined the opinion as a precedent. Second, it led to conflicting understandings of exactly what was in the opinion.

The first newspaper account of the case was in *The Friend*, published by antislavery Quakers in Philadelphia. This report did not appear until June, three months after the decision. A month later the nation's leading antislavery newspaper, the *Liberator*, reprinted this article under the headline "Important Decision." *The Liberator* quoted favorably one of Helmsley's original abolitionist attorneys, who declared "this day" was "the brightest that has dawned upon this unfortunate race of beings since the year 1804," the year New Jersey had passed its Gradual Emancipation statute, "and the proudest which has occurred in our judicial history, since we became a state."[55]

At about the same time another abolitionist periodical, the *Emancipator*, reprinted of the original article in *The Friend*. The *Emancipator* added a summary of the three major points of Hornblower's decision: that the federal fugitive slave law of 1793 was unconstitutional; that all people in New Jersey had a right to a jury trial; and that "the color of a person should be no longer considered as presumptive evidence of slavery" in New Jersey. Meanwhile, the *New York Evening Star* also wrote about the decision. The *Evening Star*, basing its assessment of the case on the story in the *Emancipator*, editorialized that under this decision New Jersey had become "an asylum of fugitive slaves" where owners lacked "any hope of recovering such property."[56]

Both newspaper reports were somewhat incorrect. Hornblower had not actually declared that the federal law of 1793 was unconstitutional, although his opinion certainly implied it was. The assertions in the *Emancipator* that alleged fugitives were entitled to a jury trial and that blacks were presumptively free did accurately reflect Hornblower's opinion, but the *Evening Star* clearly exaggerated when it stated that New Jersey had become an "asylum" for fugitive slaves. However, had the principles of Hornblower's decision been vigorously adopted throughout the state, slave catching would have become quite difficult.

In August the *Newark Daily Advertiser* attacked the decision and the various newspaper accounts of it. The *Daily Advertiser* was unhappy with the decision and with public perceptions of it. The *Daily Advertiser* began its comment by quoting briefly from the stories in the *Emancipator* and the *New York Evening Star*.[57] The *Daily Advertiser* believed these newspaper reports had created an erroneous impression that needed to be countered.

But if the reports of the case in the *Emancipator* and the *Evening Star* were incorrect, so too was *Daily Advertiser*'s own account of the case. This paper asserted that the "only point *decided* by the Court was, that upon the facts of the case, . . . the prisoner was entitled to be discharged *out of jail.*" The paper conceded that all blacks in the state were presumed free, while it inaccurately denied that Hornblower had spoken to this point. The *Daily Advertiser* stressed that Hornblower's opinion had not been written and was therefore not a precedent at all. The paper complained that "an obscure partizan press" (like the *Emancipator*) was allowed to publish misleading articles about the law by "catching reports of cases . . . from the lips of lookers-on, and spreading them before the world as decisions." The *Daily Advertiser* feared that other papers would make the same mistake as the *Evening Star* and believe the report in the *Emancipator*. The Newark paper feared that this would lead to a "kindling [of] prejudice and passion" in "the Southern States, against one of the most respectable legal tribunals in the country."[58]

The *Daily Advertiser*'s fears were unnecessary. Because it was unreported, few people learned of Hornblower's decision. Moreover, shortly after the decision, abolitionists in New Jersey discovered that their victory was incomplete. In deciding the case Chief Justice Hornblower had said New Jersey's act of 1826 was unconstitutional. Other judges in the state apparently accepted this, but with ironic results.

While declaring the law violated New Jersey's constitution, Hornblower did not rule on the constitutionality of the federal law, in part because he did not have to and in part because he did not want to directly confront the national government. The result left New Jersey's free blacks and fugitives slaves in a worse position than before the Helmsley case. The 1826 New Jersey law had offered fugitive slaves more protection than the federal law, although not as much as Hornblower demanded. But with the 1826 act no longer in force, slave catchers could still use the federal law of 1793.

In August 1836 the arrest of Severn Martin, a black living in Burlington, New Jersey, revealed the irony of Hornblower's opinion. Martin had lived in the area for seventeen years, and there was little evidence that he was a slave. Only the "energy and judgment displayed by the Mayor" prevented a riot, as several hundred people "attempted to rescue" Martin. When calm was restored, a county magistrate, applying the loose evidentiary standards of the federal law of 1793, remanded Martin to the man who claimed to be his owner. The claimant quickly removed Martin. He was only freed when his New Jersey friends raised eight hundred dollars to purchase him.[59]

Because this "atrocious case occurred in New Jersey," the Philadelphia paper *Human Rights* rhetorically asked, "What has become of the decision of Chief Justice Hornblower?" The paper concluded the decision was "inoperative" because it had declared the state law, but not the federal law, unconstitutional, even though the latter also denied a right to trial by jury. The New Jersey legislature remedied this situation at its next session, when it passed the 1837 law giving alleged fugitive slaves greater legal protections than they had previously enjoyed, including the right to demand a jury trial.[60]

The Resurrection of the Hornblower Opinion

Because Hornblower's opinion was never officially reported, it was not generally cited by abolitionist lawyers in other fugitive slave cases. In Boston the nation's most prominent abolitionist, William Lloyd Garrison, urged Ellis Gray Loring, the city's most prominent abolitionist attorney, to

> assume the ground maintained by Judge Hornblower of New Jersey—
> viz.—that the law of Congress regulating the arrest of fugtive slaves, is
> unconstitutional, because no power is given by the Constitution to

> Congress to legislate on the subject—that every person in the State,
> white or black, free or slave, is entitled to a trial by jury—and that the
> color of a person should be no longer considered as presumptive evi-
> dence of slavery.

However, there is no evidence that Loring in fact ever cited the case.
The one lawyer who did use the opinion was Salmon P. Chase, the "attorney general for fugitive slaves," who cited a newspaper account of
Hornblower's opinion in attempting to free the slave Matilda, in 1837.[61]
At the time, however, Chase had not seen a complete report of the opinion. With the emergence of a new fugitive slave law in 1850, Hornblower
and his 1836 opinion gained new fame.

In April 1851 Chase, by this time a U.S. senator, sent Hornblower a
copy of his brief to the United States Supreme Court in the fugitive slave
case of *Jones* v. *Van Zandt*. Chase also sent Hornblower a copy of a speech
he had given on the new fugitive slave law. Chase did not know
Hornblower, but Chase often sent copies of his speeches and legal arguments to strangers who might agree with his position. In this letter Chase
mentioned that he had cited the 1836 Helmsley opinion in Matilda's
case, and Chase asked Hornblower for a copy of that opinion.[62]

Hornblower immediately responded with a gracious and lengthy letter thanking Chase for the material he had sent. He praised Chase for
the "noble stand" the Ohio Senator had "taken in behalf of right; in
behalf of law; of justice; humanity, of the Constitution, of patriotism, of
philanthropy, of universal emancipation of the human race in body &
mind, and of all that is calculated to elevate our fellow men, to the dignity of manhood." Hornblower complained that the "sacred . . . soil of
New Jersey, consecrated by the blood of our fathers, in their struggles
for human liberty, is now desecrated by the feet of bloodhounds pursuing their victims," and that "Jerseymen" and all "other free Americans"
faced fines or imprisonment if they refused to "join in the chase."[63]

Hornblower concluded this four-page letter by explaining to Chase
that in the Helmsley case he had prepared a long opinion but did not
actually read it from the bench. Instead, he had given an oral summa-
tion of his points. Although it now lay in his "mass of miscellaneous
unfinished" writings, Hornblower promised to find the opinion and send
it to Chase.[64]

Shortly after Chase asked for a copy of the opinion, William Dayton,
a former U.S. senator from New Jersey, also asked for a copy. Dayton had
been on the Senate Judiciary Committee during the debates over the
Fugitive Slave Law of 1850, and he regretted that he had not had access
to Hornblower's opinion then.[65]

It is unknown if Hornblower ever sent either Chase or Dayton a full
copy of the opinion. However, in 1851 the long-dormant opinion took
on a new life. That summer an antislavery convention in Ohio read

Hornblower's opinion and ordered it published.[66] This convention could have obtained the text of the opinion from Chase (who was from Ohio) or some old newspaper account.

Meanwhile, portions of Hornblower's letter to Chase appeared in newspapers and were "extensively disseminated by the press." The excerpts from the letter included references to the Helmsley case. These newspaper accounts prompted William Jay, the abolitionist attorney and son of former Chief Justice John Jay, to write Hornblower praising his antislavery position. Jay was especially pleased to find a "gentleman moving in" Hornblower's "sphere"—that is to say, a fellow bona fide upper-class American brahmin—who also opposed slavery. Hornblower then offered to send a copy of his Helmsley opinion to Jay, and by the end of July he had done so.[67]

Hornblower sent Jay the original manuscript opinion, which Jay excitedly read and then sent to New York City to have it published. On 30 July 1851 the opinion appeared on the front page of the *New York Evening Post*. In addition to publishing Hornblower's opinion in a newspaper, Jay arranged for its publication and distribution in pamphlet form. Jay told Hornblower he could have "as many copies of the pamphlet as you might desire," which made sense, since the pamphlet had been published for "gratuitous distribution."[68]

Printed with the opinion was a short unsigned commentary (actually written by Jay) quoting Massachusetts senator Daniel Webster's "Seventh of March Speech" together with a short attack on Webster for his support of the Fugitive Slave Law of 1850. Following this commentary was an extract from a letter from Hornblower to Jay, also attacking Webster and the Fugitive Slave Law of 1850.

The commentary and the quotations from Webster and Hornblower supported the notion that fugitive slave rendition should be kept in the hands of the states. The pamphlet quoted Webster's "Seventh of March" speech where he declared:

> I have always thought that the constitution addressed itself to the legislatures of the states themselves, or to the states themselves. It says that those persons escaping into other states, shall be delivered up, and I confess I have I always been of opinion that it was an injunction upon the states themselves.[69]

Jay quoted Webster on this issue to make two points. First, if the "constitution addressed . . . the states," then the federal laws of 1793 and 1850 were unconstitutional, as Hornblower had intimated in 1836, and the states should accordingly protect black rights and black freedom through appropriate legislation. Hornblower in effect held that "adequate and independent state grounds"—to use a modern concept—existed to protect free blacks from kidnapping and to insure that alleged fugitive slaves received due process.[70] Second, if this position was correct, then Webster, who had become an anathema to many Northerners—a "monster," a "fallen angel," "incredibly base and wicked"—was further exposed as a hypocrite whose only concern was his political ambition.[71]

Jay and his fellow abolitionists were willing to give away this pamphlet because they believed that Hornblower's opinion was an invaluable asset to their antislavery constitutionalism. Unlike most antislavery propaganda, this assault on the fugitive slave laws had not been written by an abolitionist. Rather, the opinion came from the respected chief justice of a very conservative northern state. This increased the credibility of the opinion and its potential impact on Northern society.

Even before the *Evening Post* printed the full text of Hornblower's manuscript, the opinion was apparently circulating within the antislavery movement. The potential of Hornblower's denunciation of the Fugitive Slave Law of 1793 and his support of due process for blacks became clear in the wake of the adoption of the Fugitive Slave Law of 1850. Finally, in early August 1851 Jay's pamphlet printing of the opinion began to circulate. Although they had asked Hornblower for a copy of the opinion before Jay did, neither Chase nor Dayton may have seen the full opinion before Jay had it published.

After reading the full opinion, Chase complimented Hornblower and expressed his regret that the opinion had not been "printed and generally circulated" when first delivered because it would "certainly have done much good." Chase thought that Hornblower's opinion might have prevented the "promulgation of the consolidation doctrines of constitutional construction" accepted by many "from whom better things might have been expected."[72]

The flurry of activity surrounding the opinion dissipated in 1851 but reemerged during the crisis over the Kansas-Nebraska Act in 1854. That year the *Trenton State Gazette* reprinted the opinion as a front-page story, noting that "Although delivered before the passage of the fugitive law of 1850, its arguments are such as will apply to that and all other laws passed by Congress for the rendition of fugitives." This paper endorsed Hornblower's argument that a jury trial was necessary for the return of a fugitive slave.[73]

A few months later Horace Greeley's *New York Tribune* cited Hornblower's opinion in arguing that judges should oppose the Fugitive Slave Law of 1850, which the paper believed violated "reason and the vital principles of the Constitution." The *Tribune* praised the the Wisconsin Supreme Court, which had declared the law unconstitutional in the case that would eventually come to the United States Supreme Court as *Ableman v. Booth.* "Chief Justice Hornblower of New-Jersey," the *Tribune* noted, "sometime ago, led the way in an elaborate opinion denying the power of Congress to legislate on the subject of fugitive slaves."[74]

In the legal conflicts caused by the Fugitive Slave Law of 1850, the

Ohio Supreme Court saw the opinion as a valid precedent, although members of that court disagreed on what it stood for. Both majority and dissenting judges cited Hornblower's opinion in *Ex parte* Bushnell, *Ex parte* Langston, a case growing out of the famous Oberlin-Wellington rescue. Simeon Bushnell and Charles Langston were in jail, under federal process, for their role in rescuing a fugitive slave. In concurring in the decision not to release the abolitionists, Justice Peck noted that in 1836

> Ch. J. Hornblower, of New Jersey . . . expressed doubts as to the validity of the act of 1793, on the ground of a want of constitutional power to pass it, and also of the validity of the act of New Jersey, but declined to declare either law invalid, and finally discharged the prisoner, because the proceedings did not conform to the requirements of the act of the State of New Jersey.[75]

In dissent, Justice Jacob Brinkerhoff, an abolitionist ally of Salmon P. Chase, found that Hornblower's opinion, along with Chancellor Walworth's of New York Court in *Jack* v. *Martin*, "shows that the question" of federal power to pass a fugitive slave law "is not settled." Justice Sutliff, also in dissent, cited both Hornblower and Walworth for the proposition that the Fugitive Slave Clause of the Constitution "vests no power in the federal government" to adopt legislation.[76]

In March 1860 Senator Benjamin F. Wade of Ohio conceded that Congressional jurisdiction over fugitive slave rendition had been accepted, "the courts having adjudicated that point against my opinions;" but he argued that "no lawyer would agree with the courts were it a case of first impression." He disputed that the courts of the nation had been unanimous on this question, as Senator Robert Toombs of Georgia had asserted. Wade pointed out that "Judge Hornblower, of New Jersey, on *habeas corpus*, held the law [of 1793] unconstitutional, and discharged the fugitive for that reason."[77] This was a slight exaggeration of what Hornblower had held. He never reached the constitutionality of the federal law because the case came before him under the state statute.

Less than a month later, New Jersey's Senator John C. Ten Eyck attempted to straighten out the facts of the case. He told the senate that Hornblower had not in fact declared the 1793 law unconstitutional but had freed the slaves before him "on the ground of defective evidence."[78] This was also an incorrect statement of what had occurred.

The speeches by Wade and Ten Eyck led to some correspondence between Hornblower and his senator. In a letter to Ten Eyck, Hornblower reaffirmed his position in the case and his opposition to remanding fugitive slaves without jury trials. Hornblower also noted that the two other judges on the court, "both of them my *political* opponents," agreed with him. One of these, Judge Ford, was himself a slaveholder, with family ties to South Carolina. Nevertheless, the New Jersey justices were unanimous in their belief that Helmsley should be discharged from custody. Hornblower believed that Senator Ten Eyck, or Hornblower's "friend," the more radical Benjamin Wade, should bring these facts before the Senate.[79]

By 1860 the Hornblower opinion had become part of the growing crisis of the Union. In 1836 Hornblower had argued that the powers of Congress in article IV were strictly limited. They did not include the right to legislate over fugitive slaves. This, he believed, was reserved for the states. That position, however, had been rejected by the Congress in 1793, by the Supreme Court in 1842, and again by the Congress in 1850.

In 1860 the eighty-three-year-old Hornblower suggested that the defeat of his position might yet help promote antislavery. Writing to Senator Ten Eyck, Hornblower suggested that someone "introduce a bill in Congress to secure to citizens of this or any other state the same 'immunities', they enjoy here, in every other state, or in other words, to carry into effect the provision of that section." Hornblower's logic was clear. *If* Congress had the power to pass legislation to enforce the fugitive slave clause of article IV of the Constitution, then Congress also had the power to enforce the Privileges and Immunities clause of article IV. Hornblower thought that a bill along these lines would "add fuel to the fire already burning in the South" and "what is now comparatively a small combustion will become a volcano."[80] The retired justice may by this time have regretted not publishing his 1836 decision, for he no longer thought that deference to the South, or federal power, was the answer to the problem of slavery in the nation.

Notes

Research for this article was funded by a grant from the New Jersey Historical Commission. The author thanks William M. Wiecek of Syracuse Law School of his helpful comments on this paper, Mary R. Murrin, of the New Jersey Historical Commission, the staffs of the New Jersey Historical Society, the New Jersey State Archives, the Library of Congress, and the Rare Book and Manuscript Library, Columbia University for their help in expediting this research. I presented earlier versions of this paper at the Seminar for New Jersey Historians at Princeton University, Seton Hall Law School, and the Organization of American Historians. An earlier version of the article, "State Constitutional Protections of Liberty and the Antebellum New Jersey Supreme Court: Chief Justice Hornblower and The Fugitive Slave Law," was published in 23 *Rutgers Law Journal* 753 (1992).

1. *State* v. *The Sheriff of Burlington*, No. 36286 (N.J. 1836) (unreported decision of New Jersey Court of Errors and Appeals, case records on file at New Jersey State Archives; hereinafter cited as Helmsley Case file.) In the Helmsley Case file this case is called *Nathan, Alias Alex. Helmsley* v. *State.*

2. Salmon P. Chase to Hornblower, April 3, 1851, Hornblower Papers, box

2, New Jersey Historical Society, Newark. Chase cited Hornblower's opinion before the Cincinnati Court of Common Pleas in the case of Matilda. Salmon P. Chase, *Speech of Salmon P. Chase in the Case of the Colored Woman, Matilda* (Cincinnati: Pugh and Dodd, 1837), 18; reprinted in *Southern Slaves in Free State Courts: The Pamphlet Literature,* ed. Paul Finkelman (New York: Garland, 1988), 2:1–40. William Jay to Hornblower, July 11, 1851, Jay Family Papers, Rare Book and Manuscript Library, Columbia University. Jay wrote: "In 1838 the question occurred to me, under what constitutional grant of power Congress has passed the fugitive slave law of 1793. I was not aware that the question had been mooted before." On the friendship between the two families, see Jay to Hornblower, August 12, 1851, Jay Family Papers, thanking Hornblower for his support "Your commendation is necessarily valuable to all who are honored by it, but to me it is peculiarly so, as coming from my Father's friend." Letters from Jay Family Papers are cited and quoted with permission of the Rare Book and Manuscript Library, Columbia University.

3. *Opinion of Chief Justice Hornblower on the Fugitive Slave Law* ([New York]: [New York Evening Post], [1851]); reprinted in *Fugitive Slaves and American Courts: The Pamphlet Literature,* ed. Paul Finkelman (New York: Garland, 1988), 1:97–104. (hereinafter cited as Hornblower Opinion). This is an incomplete report of the case but the best that exists. The text of this pamphlet is *exactly* the same as an article appearing in the *New York Evening Post* on August 1, 1851. The type and fonts for both also seem to be identical. It appears that the pamphlet was printed from the fonts of the *Post,* and logically it would have been published by the *Post.*

4. *Ex parte* Bushnell, *Ex parte* Langston, 9 Ohio St. 77, at 205, 227, 321 (1859).

5. There is no good history of slavery in New Jersey. Helpful early studies include: Henry Schofield Cooley, *A Study of Slavery in New Jersey* (Baltimore: Johns Hopkins Press, 1896); Marion Thompson Wright, "New Jersey Laws and the Negro," *Journal of Negro History* 28 (1943): 156–99; Simeon F. Moss, "The Persistence of Slavery and Involuntary Servitude in a Free State (1685–1866)," *Journal of Negro History* 35 (1950): 289–314. The most important modern contribution to this literature is Arthur Zilversmit, "Liberty and Property: New Jersey and the Abolition of Slavery," *New Jersey History* 88 (1970): 215–26; reprinted in *Slavery in the North and the West,* ed. Paul Finkelman (New York: Garland, 1989), 485, 491–96. Also useful is Francis D. Pingeon, "Dissenting Attitudes toward the Negro in New Jersey," *New Jersey History* 89 (1971): 197–220.

6. The society did not formally draft a constitution until 1793, when members of the older Pennsylvania Abolition Society came to Burlington, New Jersey, for the formal signing of the Constitution of the New Jersey Society. Arthur Zilversmit, *The First Emancipation: The Abolition of Slavery in the North* (Chicago: University of Chicago Press, 1967), 173.

7. Act of Feb. 15, 1804, 1811 N.J. Laws 103–09 ("An Act for the Gradual Abolition of Slavery"), published as *Laws of the State of New Jersey, Compiled and Published under the Authority of the Legislature* 103–09, (Joseph Bloomfield, ed., Trenton: James J. Wilson, 1811). Act of March 1, 1780, 1810 Pa. Laws 1, 492–93 (Philadelphia: Bioren, 1810).

8. Act of Mar. 29, 1799, ch. 62, 1799 N.Y. Laws 388 ("An Act for the Gradual Abolition of Slavery"). Act of Mar. 31, 1817, ch. 137, 1817 N.Y. Laws 136 ("An Act relative to slaves and servants"). See *State* v. *Post* and *State* v. *Van Beuren,* 20

N.J.L. (1 Spenc.) 368 (1845); *aff'd. o.b.*, 21 N.J.L. 699 (1848). See also Dan Ernst, "Legal Positivism, Abolitionist Litigation, and the New Jersey Slave Case of 1845," 4 *Law and History Review* 337.

9. *Statutes of the State of New Jersey. Revised and Published under the Authority of the Legislature* 567–72 (Trenton, Phillips and Boswell, 1847), later reprinted in *Digest of the Law of New Jersey* 801–10 (Lucius Q. C. Elmer ed., 3d ed., Bridgeton, Elmer and Nixon, and Trenton; C. Scott, 1861).

10. Clement A. Price, *Freedom Not Far Distant: A Documentary History of Afro-Americans in New Jersey* (Newark: New Jersey Historical Society, 1980), 92; Pingeon, "Dissenting Attitudes toward the Negro in New Jersey," 198–99.

11. Benjamin Drew, *A North-Side View of Slavery. The Refugee; or, The Narratives of Fugitive Slaves in Canada* (Boston: John P. Jewett, 1856), 33–34.

12 2 *Annals of Cong.* 861 (debate of Feb. 5, 1793). 4 *Annals of Congress*, 1767 (debate of Jan. 2, 1797); *Journal of the House*, 4th Cong., 2d Sess. 67. Paul Finkelman, *Slavery and the Founders: Race and Liberty in the Age of Jefferson* (Armonk, N.Y.: M. E. Sharpe, 1996), 80–104.

13. 4 *Annals of Cong.* 2024.

14. These states, along with Virginia, had been the only ones to consistently oppose the slave trade compromise at the Constitutional Convention. Finkelman, *Slavery and the Founders*, Chapter 1, "Making a Covenant With Death: Slavery and the Constitutional Convention," 1–33.

15 Zilversmit, "Liberty and Property," 225. On Jefferson's Negrophobia, see Winthrop Jordan, *White over Black: American Attitudes towards the Negro, 1550–1812* (Chapel Hill: University of North Carolina Press, 1968); Finkelman, *Slavery and the Founders*, 105–168. While beyond the scope of this essay, it may be noted that the change in direction for New Jersey after 1801 suggests that the slaveholding majority in Jefferson's party led to the creation of northern doughface Democrats long before the antebellum period.

16 Act of Mar. 2, 1786, 1786 N.J. Acts, published as *Acts of the Tenth General Assembly of New Jersey . . . Second Sitting* (Trenton, 1786). The fines were fifty pounds for slaves imported from Africa since 1776 and twenty pounds for other blacks. Visitors and transients were exempt from the duty as long as they removed the slave from the state. This act is discussed in Cooley, *A Study of Slavery in New Jersey*, 18–19. In *State* v. *Quick*, 2 N.J.L. (1 Pennington) 393, 413e (1807), the New Jersey court refused to free a slave who was illegally exported from New York into New Jersey.

17. Act of Mar. 2, 1786 *supra* note 17.

18. Act of Nov. 25, 1788, 1788 N.J. Acts 13, 486–88. For one example of a Southerner prosecuted for teaching free blacks to read, see *The Personal Narrative of Mrs. Margaret Douglass, A Southern Woman, Who Was Imprisoned for One Month in the Common Jail of Norfolk, under the Laws of Virginia, for the Crime of Teaching Free Colored Children to Read* (Boston: John P. Jewett, 1854); reprinted in *Slaves, Rebels, Abolitionists, and Southern Courts: The Pamphlet Literature*, ed. Paul Finkelman (New York: Garland, 1988), 2:373–439. Zilversmit, *First Emancipation*, 159, and generally, Zilversmit, "Liberty and Property."

19. An Act to Authorize the Manumission of Slaves," ch. 61, 1782 Va Laws. See Robert McColley, *Slavery in Jeffersonian Virginia* (Urbana: University of Illinois Press, 1972). Jonathan Elliot, ed., *The Debates in the Several State Conventions, on the Adoption of the Federal Constitution*, 2d ed. (Washington: Printed for the

Author, 1836), 3:422–23. The Assembly Journal is quoted in Cooley, *A Study of Slavery in New Jersey*, 25. Zilversmit, *First Emancipation*, 161–62.

    20. Act of March 14, 1798, § 27, 1798 N.J. Laws. ("An Act Respecting Slaves"). Leon F. Litwack, *North of Slavery* (Chicago: University of Chicago Press, 1961), 70, cites this law as an example of northern negrophobia. However, Litwack has failed to realize or acknowledge that at the time New Jersey adopted the law it was a *slave* state, and that for a *slave* state this was an unusually progressive law. For a discussion of the problem of understanding Northern law and race relations, see Paul Finkelman, "Prelude to the Fourteenth Amendment: Black Legal Rights in the Antebellum North," 17 *Rutgers Law Journal* 415, at 432–34 (1986).

    21. Act of Mar. 14, 1798, §27, 1798 N.J. Laws, §§4–7 ("An Act Respecting Slaves").

    22. Act of Feb. 15, 1804 ("An Act for the Gradual Abolition of Slavery"); Act of Mar. 8, 1806 ("An Act to repeal the third section of an act entitled 'An act for the gradual abolition of slavery,' passed the fifteenth day of February, eighteen hundred and four"); Act of Nov. 28, 1808 ("An additional supplement to the act entitled 'An act for the gradual abolition of slavery.'") Act of Feb. 22, 1811 ("An Act concerning the Abolition of Slavery"); Act of Dec. 3, 1804 ("An Act supplementary to the act respecting slaves") All published in 1811 N.J. Laws (*supra* note 7) 103–9, 141–43.

    23. Wright, "New Jersey Laws and the Negro," 179. Act of Feb. 24, 1820, §§ 11–21, 1820 N.J. Laws 74–80 ("An Act for the gradual abolition of slavery, and for other purposes respecting slaves"). Masters moving out of the state could take slaves with them only if they had lived in the state for the previous five years, had owned the slave during that time, and had obtained the slave's consent to the move. On slave transit in New Jersey, see Paul Finkelman, *An Imperfect Union: Slavery, Federalism, and Comity* (Chapel Hill: University of North Carolina Press, 1981), 71, 76–77, 83.

    24. *State* v. *Heddon*, 1 N.J.L. (1 Coke) 328 (1795). Heddon was the jailer who held Cork.

    25. *Nixon* v. *Story's Administrators*, 3 N.J.L. (2 Pennington) 722 (1813).

    26. *Gibbons* v. *Morse*, 7 N.J.L. (2 Halsted) 253 (1821); *Cutter* v. *Moore*, 8 N.J.L. (3 Halsted) 219 (1825).

    27. *Gibbons* v. *Morse*, *supra* note 26, at 270. *Cutter* v. *Moore*, *supra* note 26, at 225. In *Boice* v. *Gibbons*, 8 N.J.L. (3 Halsted) 324 (1826), the New Jersey court retreated slightly from this position, implying that being black might not lead to a *prima facie* assumption of slavery. See also *Fox* v. *Lambson*, 8 N.J.L. (3 Halsted) 366 (1826).

    28 Act of Dec. 26, 1826, N.J. Laws 51 ("A Supplement to an Act entitled 'An Act concerning slaves'"). *Hornblower Opinion* at 4.

    29. Thomas D. Morris, *Free Men All: The Personal Liberty Laws of the North, 1780–1861* (Baltimore: Johns Hopkins University Press, 1974), 57. Unfortunately, Morris does not discuss or analyze the New Jersey law. *Prigg* v. *Pennsylvania*, 41 U.S. (16 Peters) 536, 539 (1842). In the Constitutional Convention James Wilson of Pennsylvania asserted that one purpose of the states was "to preserve the rights of individuals." Similarly, Oliver Ellsworth of Connecticut explained that he looked to the state governments "for the preservation of his rights." Max Farrand, ed., *Records of the Federal Convention of 1787* (New Haven:

Yale University Press, 1966), 1:354, 492. Significantly, perhaps, both Wilson and Ellsworth subsequently served on the United States Supreme Court.

30. Drew, *North-Side View*, 33–34. Like many other fugitive slave cases, this one was complicated by the length of time Helmsley had lived in New Jersey, the roots he had put down, and the fact that his children had been born in a free state and thus were free persons.

31. "Upholding Slavery," 20 *The Friend* 281–82 (June 11, 1836).

32. Application for writ of habeas corpus, in Helmsley Case file. "Upholding Slavery," 281–82. Portions of this article are reprinted as "Important Decision," *The Liberator*, July 30, 1836, 124. Helmsley did not admit he was a fugitive slave until after Chief Justice Hornblower had released him and he had moved to Canada.

33. "Upholding Slavery," 281–82. Application for writ of habeas corpus in Helmsley Case file.

34. *Hornblower Opinion* at 1.

35. Ibid., at 4.

36. Ibid.

37. U.S. Const. art. IV, § 3, ¶ 2, "The Congress shall have Power to dispose of and make all needful Rules and Regulations respecting the Territory or other Property belonging to the United States. . . ."

38. *Hornblower Opinion* at 4–5.

39. Ibid., at 5.

40. Ibid.

41. Ibid., at 6.

42. Ibid.

43. Ibid.

44. Ibid., at 6, 7.

45. *Wright otherwise called Hall* v. *Deacon, Keeper of the Prison,* 5 Serg. & Rawle 62 (Pa. 1819). The United States Supreme Court would not decide a fugitive slave case until *Prigg* v. *Pennsylvania, supra* note 32.

46. *Wright* v. *Deacon* at 63–64. The fugitive slave clause was added to the Constitution late in the Convention, with little debate and with no demands made by southerners for it. Rather, it seems to have been something that a few southerners wanted and that no northerners opposed. See Finkelman, *Slavery and the Founders*, Chapter 1. For a discussion of the failure of intentionalists as historians, see Paul Finkelman, "The Constitution and the Intentions of the Framers: The Limit of Historical Analysis," 50 *University of Pittsburgh Law Review* 349–398 (1989).

47. *Hornblower Opinion* at 6.

48. In *Jack* v. *Martin,* 12 Wend. 311 (N.Y. Sup. Ct. 1834) and 14 Wend. 507 (N.Y. 1835), the New York court had denied federal power over fugitive slave rendition while acknowledging the state's obligation to return fugitives under the Constitutional clause in article IV. Despite the different outcomes of the two cases, Hornblower's position was relatively close to New York's. In finding the New Jersey law in violation of the state constitution, Hornblower implied that he might uphold a valid rendition law adopted by his state.

49. Act of Mar. 26, 1826, 1826 Pa. Laws 150–55 ("An Act to Give effect to the provisions of the Constitution of the United States Relative to Fugitives From Labor, For the protection of Free People of Color, and to Prevent Kidnapping").

Morris, *Free Men All,* 52, 53 *The Liberator,* March 24, 1837, 52, reprinting a story from the *Harrisburg Keystone.*

50. Morris, *Free Men All,* 64–65.

51. Ibid., 55–57. *Jack* v. *Martin, supra* note 48, 1834 at 327, 1835 at 512. Paul Finkelman, "The Protection of Black Rights in Seward's New York," *Civil War History* 34 (1988): 211–34.

52. Act of Feb. 15, 1837, 1837 N.J. Acts 134–36 ("A Further Supplement to an act entitled 'An Act Concerning Slaves'"). *New Jersey Assembly Minutes, 1836– 37* 331–32; *New Jersey Council Minutes, 1836–37* 192, 210–11.

53. Story wrote:

> Historically, it is well known, that the object of this clause was to secure to the citizens of the slaveholding states the complete right and title of ownership in their slaves, as property, in every state in the Union into which they might escape from the state where they were held in servi- tude. The full recognition of this right and title was indispensable to the security of this species of property in all the slaveholding states; and, indeed, so vital to the preservation of their domestic interests and institutions, that it cannot be doubted that it constituted a fundamen- tal article, without the adoption of which the Union could not have been formed.

Prigg v. *Pennsylvania, supra* note 29, at 611. *Wright* v. *Deacon, supra* note 45, at 62. For a full discussion of Story's opinion, and its implications, see Paul Finkelman, "*Prigg* v. *Pennsylvania* and Northern State Courts: Anti-Slavery Use of a Pro-Slavery Decision," *Civil War History* 25 (1979): 5–35, Paul Finkelman, "Sorting out *Prigg* v. *Pennsylvania,*" 24 *Rutgers Law Journal* 605 (1993), and Paul Finkelman, "Story Telling on the Supreme Court: Prigg v. Pennsylvania and Jus- tice Joseph Story's Judicial Nationalism," 1994 Supreme Court Review 247–94 (1995). 1847 N.J. Laws 567–72, published as *Statutes of the State of New Jersey. Revised and Published under the Authority of the Legislature* 567–72 (Trenton, Phillips and Boswell, 1847).

54. Hornblower to J. C. Ten Eyck, April 1860, Hornblower Papers, box 1, New Jersey Historical Society, Trenton. Act of Feb. 15, 1837, *supra.* note 52.

55. "Upholding Slavery," 281–82. *The Liberator,* July 20, 1836, 124.

56. "Important Decision," *Newark Daily Advertiser,* August 18, 1836, p. 2, col. 1, quoting *The Emancipator* and the *New York Evening Star.*

57. *Newark Daily Advertiser,* August 18, 1836. The *Advertiser* was apparently unaware that the story in *The Emancipator* had originally appeared in *The Friend.*

58. Ibid.

59. *New Jersey Eagle,* August 19, 1836. "The Slave Case," *Burlington Gazette,* August 20, 1836, partially reprinted as "The Slave Case," *New Jersey State Gazette,* August 26, 1836. Aristides [pseud.], "Severn Martin," *Burlington Gazette,* Sep- tember 10, 1836, p. 1, col. 2, and "Case of Severn Martin," *The Liberator,* Sep- tember 17, 1836, 151. The *New Jersey Eagle,* a Democratic paper in Newark, praised the outcome of this case and suggested that purchasing the slave, as was done by the people of Burlington, "should be imitated in all similar cases; instead of attempting to defraud the rightful owner of his property." "As It Should Be," *New Jersey Eagle,* August 26, 1836.

60. *Human Rights,* quoted in *The Liberator,* September 17, 1836, 151; Act of Feb. 15, 1837, *supra* note 52.

61. William Lloyd Garrison to Isaac Knapp, August 23, 1836, in *The Letters of William Lloyd Garrison,* ed. Louis Ruchames (Cambridge: Harvard University Press, 1971), 2:53. Chase, *Speech in the Case of Matilda,* 18. Here Chase quoted from the story about this case in *The Liberator,* July 30, 1836, 124, but did not in cite to this story. For a discussion of the Matilda case, see Finkelman, *An Imperfect Union,* 160–62.

62. *Jones* v. *Van Zandt,* 46 U.S. (5 How.) 215 (1847). Chase's brief was published in pamphlet form as Salmon P. Chase, *Reclamation of Fugitives from Service* (Cincinnati: R. P. Donough, 1847), reprinted in *Fugitive Slaves and American Courts* 1:341–448. Chase to Hornblower, April 3, 1851. Paul Finkelman, *Slavery in the Courtroom* (Washington: U.S. Government Printing Office, 1985), 74. See also, Chase Letterbook, Salmon P. Chase Papers, Manuscript Division, Library of Congress, for examples of Chase sending out his own briefs and other writings.

63 Hornblower to Salmon P. Chase, April 9, 1851, Salmon P. Chase Papers, Manuscript Division, Library of Congress.

64 Ibid.

65 William L. Dayton to Hornblower, September 9, 1851, Hornblower Papers, box 2, New Jersey State Historical Society, Trenton.

66. *New York Evening Post,* August 1, 1851.

67. William Jay to Hornblower, 17 July 185[1], typescript copy in Jay Family Papers, Rare Book and Manuscript Library, Columbia University. The letter is misdated on the typescript as 1850. See also Jay to Hornblower, 11 July 1851, 21 July 1851, and 29 July 1851, typescript copies in Jay Family Papers. In the 21 July letter Jay thanks Hornblower for a copy of the manuscript opinion, and on 29 July he indicates that the opinion has been "forwarded to. . . New York, & it will I trust be soon in print."

68. William Jay to Hornblower, September 3, 1851, typescript copy in the Jay Family Papers, Rare Book and Manuscript Library, Columbia University.

69. *Hornblower Opinion* at 7.

70. This term is used in modern constitutional doctrine to support the idea that state supreme courts may give greater protections to civil liberties and civil rights than the United States Supreme Court demands, as long as those protections are based on "adequate and independent state grounds," found within the constitution of the state. The concept first arose in *Murdock* v. *Memphis,* 87 U.S. (20 Wall.) 590 (1874). See also Martha Field, "Sources of Law: The Scope of Federal Common Law," 99 *Harvard Law Review* 881, 919–921 (1986). Under this theory the state courts can expand liberties above the minimum floor set by the United States Supreme Court's interpretation of the federal Constitution. See also the essays in Paul Finkelman and Stephen Gottlieb, eds., *In Search of a Usable Past: Liberty under State Constitutions* (Athens, Ga.: University of Georgia Press, 1991).

71. Potter, *Impending Crisis,* 132. In the poem "Ichabod" the poet John Greenleaf Whittier wrote of Webster:

> Of all we loved and honored, naught
> Save power remains;
> A fallen angel's pride of thought
> Still strong in chains.

> All else is gone; from those great eyes
>   The soul has fled;
> When faith is lost, when honor dies,
>   The man is dead!

Robert Gordon, "The Devil and Daniel Webster," 94 *Yale Law Journal* 445, at 455 (1984), has written:

> His more enduring reputation is probably the one originated by the antislavery "Conscience Whigs" of Webster's party. They pictured him as the fallen Lucifer, who, in his support of the Fugitive Slave Law in the compromise package of 1850, had sold out all his principles for the Presidency and his commercial clients.

72. Chase to Hornblower, October 21, 1851, box 2, Hornblower Papers, New Jersey Historical Society, Trenton.

73 *Trenton State Gazette,* June 15, 1854, reprinting the Hornblower Opinion from the *New York Evening Post,* August 1, 1851. As related in n. 3 above, the article in the *New York Evening Post* is identical to the seven-page pamphlet cited herein as *Hornblower Opinion.*

74. "The Fugitive Law Beginning to Tumble," *New York Tribune,* July 12, 1854. The Wisconsin case was *In re Booth and Rycraft,* 3 Wis. 157 (1854), decided in June 1854 and holding that Congress lacked the authority to pass the Fugitive Slave Law of 1850. This was appealed and reversed in *Ableman* v. *Booth,* 21 Howard (U.S.) 506 (1859)."

75. *Ex parte Bushnell, Ex parte Langston, supra* note 5, at 205 (Peck, J., concurring), at 227.

76. Ibid., (Brinkerhoff, J., dissenting), at 321 (Sutliff, J., dissenting). See generally, Jacob R. Shipherd, *History of the Oberlin-Wellington Rescue* (Boston: John F. Jewett, 1859).

77. *Cong. Globe,* 36th Cong., 1st Sess., app. 152. Debate of March 7, 1860.

78. *Cong. Globe,* 36th Cong., 1st Sess., pt. 2, 1486. Debate of April 2, 1860.

79. Hornblower to J. C. Ten Eyck, April 1860, and Hornblower to Ten Eyck, April 16, 1860, Hornblower Papers, box 1, New Jersey Historical Society, Trenton.

80. Hornblower to Ten Eyck, April 16, 1860.

5

A Federal Assault:
African Americans and the
Impact of the Fugitive Slave
Law of 1850

James Oliver Horton and Lois E. Horton

WILLIAM CRAFT WAS A SLAVE in Macon, Georgia, apprenticed to a cabinetmaker and mortgaged to a local bank to cover his master's debts. Ellen was also a slave and was the daughter of her master, a white Georgia planter. When her father's white daughter, Ellen's half sister, married, Ellen was given as a wedding present to the young couple. William and Ellen met and fell in love in the 1840s. They both longed for the far-distant freedom they knew lay a thousand or more miles to the north, but for the moment at least, they found consolation in the sort of "marriage" that slaves might enjoy with their master's consent. By 1848, their minds set on escape, they worked out a daring plan, and on the day after Christmas they set it into motion. Critical to their scheme was the fact that Ellen, with her fair skin, straight raven hair, and Roman nose, was easily mistaken for white. With her soft features, wearing men's clothing and tinted glasses, Ellen could pass for a young man. A sling around her right arm explained her inability to sign any travel documents. A face wrap feigning a swollen jaw from a toothache hid her beardlessness, and William's presence as a trusted personal servant completed the picture. Ellen appeared to be a young southern gentleman traveling to Philadelphia for medical treatment. Thus disguised, they boarded a train to Savannah and made their way by train and boat to freedom. In Philadelphia they contacted William Still and other men and women of the abolition movement, who sheltered them for a time; but all knew that to be safe they must go farther north. Boston was the location settled on for their safe haven. As a center of antislavery activity far from the border with the slave states, the city had been as safe or safer than any in the country for fugitives seeking to avoid capture. Some said that Boston was as safe as Canada, and for two years the Crafts found it so. They felt free enough, in fact, to speak out in public meetings against the slave system and even to allow their names to appear in the federal census taken for the city. But in 1850 a new federal law threatened the freedom of William and Ellen Craft and of every black American, whether fugitive slave or freeborn.[1]

This article explores the impact of the Fugitive Slave Law of 1850 on the lives of the Crafts and other African Americans living in the North before the Civil War. It also examines how black people, working as individuals and in groups, responded to the new law and the threat it posed to the freedom of all African Americans, fugitives and freepeople alike. These responses ranged from cooperation and self-help to migration and violence. In their reaction to what many viewed as an assault by the federal government, African Americans revealed much about the strength of their racial and national identity. Part 1 of this article discusses the provisions of the Fugitive Slave Law of 1850. Part 2 examines the role black youth played in antislavery resistance. Part 3 presents the case of prominent black abolitionist Henry Highland Garnet, his personal experience as a fugitive, and his opposition to the law. The militant community organization in defense of fugitives is the subject of part 4, and part 5 discusses black migration to Canada as a response to the Fugitive Slave Law. Part 6 investigates the danger of kidnapping faced by northern free blacks. The issue of violence as a form of resistance to the law is discussed in part 7, while the reemergence of emigration to Africa and the Caribbean is the subject of part 8.

The Fugitive Slave Law of 1850

In the fall of 1850 President Millard Fillmore, a native of Buffalo, New York, signed into law the strictest fugitive slave measure ever enacted. The president was not totally comfortable with the law and wondered aloud about its constitutionality. He signed it into law as part of a broad compromise that he hoped would satisfy the southern states and forestall a mounting sectional crisis.[2] The Fugitive Slave Law of 1850 expanded the power of slavery to reach into any state to retrieve those accused of fleeing from bondage. It provided that commissioners of federal circuit courts, or those acting under the authority of the federal superior court in the territories, could issue warrants under which a fugitive could be held and turned over to any claimant who could present convincing evidence that the prisoner was a runaway slave. A slaveholder might prove ownership of a fugitive by presenting an affidavit from a court in his home state that provided a physical description of the runaway. If the description fit, the federal commissioner rendered the prisoner to the custody of the claimant, who could then remove his human property from the state.[3]

The law further assisted in the capture of a fugitive by allowing federal marshals "to summon and call to their aid the bystanders . . . when necessary to ensure a faithful observance of the clause of the Constitution referred to in conformity with the provisions of this act." The law provided stiff fines and imprisonment for those who obstructed the application of the law. One portion of the law proclaimed that "all good citizens are hereby commanded to aid and assist in the prompt and efficient execution of this law, whenever their services may be required." This led blacks to argue that under its provisions any citizen could be impressed into service as a slave catcher.[4] The law also provided for federal funds covering much of the expense of recovering a fugitive. The rights and protections of those accused of being fugitives were further reduced by denying them the right to speak in their own defense, by making no provision for habeas corpus, and by not requiring that they be represented by counsel or receive a jury trial. The law also seemed to favor the interests of the slaveholders by rewarding officials with ten dollars if the accused was determined to be a fugitive and five dollars if not.[5] Although the earlier Fugitive Slave Law of 1793 had given slaveholders the right to recover their property anywhere in the country, the new law greatly enhanced their power by striking down state efforts to protect the freedom of the accused fugitive. It meant that no place, not even Boston, was beyond proslavery reach.[6]

African American Children and the Fugitive Slave Law

The tightening of federal policy regarding fugitive slaves distressed African Americans and made the work of almost every community organization more difficult. Regardless of their formal focus, virtually all free black organizations opposed slavery and supported organized resistance to laws requiring fugitives' return. Early mutual benefit societies like the African Union Society—begun in 1780 in Newport, Rhode Island—or the African Society—formed in 1796 in Boston—provided proper burials, administered the wills of their members, and cared for widows and orphans. In addition to concerning themselves with the financial needs of their free black members, they were also committed to the antislavery cause. These organizations linked the maintenance of a free society to abolition and the welfare of free blacks to the welfare of slaves, attacking the inconsistency of a "freedom-loving nation's" tolerating slavery. In an "Essay on Freedom," one member of the African Society of Boston attacked slavery and the hypocrisy of a people who "love freedom themselves . . . [but who] prevent [others] from its enjoyment."[7]

Even African American children were enlisted in the antislavery cause, and for decades the cause of the slave and the fugitive from slavery was an important part of their education. In youth associations in several northern cities, boys and girls debated the issues of racial justice and slavery and raised money for abolitionist activities. The Juvenile Garrison Independent Society, formed in Boston during the early 1830s, provided service to the local community and sponsored antislavery rallies and lectures.[8]

In New York the organizational constitution of a similar youth group included a promise to work towards "the downfall of prejudice, slavery, and oppression." At the New York African Free School, a group of grammar school boys resolved not to celebrate the Fourth of July until slavery was abolished. Years later Alexander Crummell, who had been part of the group, recalled, "For years our society met on that day [the Fourth of July], and the time was devoted to planning schemes for the freeing and upbuilding the race." The boys pledged that after their education they would "go South, start an insurrection and free our brethren in bondage."[9]

Black children in the Midwest had similar concerns. When students in Cincinnati's black schools were asked to write on the question "What do you think most about?," the impact of slavery on their young lives was clear. One seven-year-old wrote of his hope that "we get a man to get the poor slaves from bondage." A twelve-year-old claimed to speak for the children and explained that "what we are studying for is to get the yoke of slavery broke and the chains parted asunder and slaveholding cease for ever."[10]

Like their elders, many of these young people spoke from personal experience and out of concern for friends and relatives held in bondage. A ten-year-old wrote, "I have two cousins in slavery who are entitled to their freedom." He was deeply concerned because slaveholders "talk of selling them down the river," and he asked the reader, "If this is the case what would you do?" Another child wrote of his own experiences in slavery and explained that he, his mother, and his stepfather had all known bondage. Clearly, slavery was no abstract evil to these children. It was personal and was associated with the misery of loved ones. Like their parents, young blacks wondered "how the Americans can call this a land of freedom where so much slavery is?"[11]

Henry Highland Garnet: A Case Study of a Fugitive Slave

Many young people with this experience and education became the abolitionists of the 1840s and 1850s. For William Cooper Nell, Henry Highland Garnet, William H. Day, David Ruggles, and other antebellum black leaders, these groups were their first training grounds for social protest. They were generally encouraged by their parents, their teachers, and other adults active in the cause. For example, Charles C. Andrews, a teacher at the New York African Free School, was also a founder of the New York Society for the Manumission of Slaves. Along with the strong academic program at the school, he taught his students about the importance of freedom.[12]

Blacks who grew to maturity under the shadow of the eighteenth-century law, even if they themselves had not been threatened with capture, were aware that both fugitive slaves and free blacks were in danger. Many, like prominent black abolitionist Henry Highland Garnet, had personally experienced the 1793 Fugitive Slave Law's effects, and this influenced their response to the more threatening 1850 law. Garnet was born a slave in Maryland, but he escaped to freedom in New York City with his mother, father, and sister in the mid-1820s, when he was nine years old. George Garnet, Henry's father, found work as a shoemaker and enrolled Henry in New York's African Free School—at the time, one of the best educational institutions for African Americans in the country. The Garnets made friends in the community and lived in comparative comfort and freedom for five years.

In 1828 twelve-year-old Henry secured a job as cabin boy on a ship that made two voyages to Cuba, a job that kept him away from home until the next year. During his time at sea, Henry's family faced a crisis he never forgot, one that intensified his determination to work against slavery and the fugitive slave laws.

In the middle of summer 1829, George opened the door of their apartment to a white man he immediately recognized as a relative of his former master. Apparently the recognition was not mutual, for the man asked to speak to George Garnet. George promptly excused himself, pretending to go in search of the man the caller sought. After giving the alarm, George leaped through an open window to the alley twenty feet below and fled down a nearby street. Henry's mother found safety with a white neighbor, but his sister was captured and would have been sent back to slavery had it not been for friends who lied to the authorities, convincing them that she had never been a slave. The family was saved, but George was injured in his escape, almost all of their property was destroyed or taken by the slave catchers, and the Garnets were forced to leave the city. All of this young Henry learned when he returned. Thus, hunting black people and the ruin it might cause were not hypothetical issues to Henry Highland Garnet as he fought against slavery, worked in the service of the underground railroad, and opposed the even harsher 1850 law.[13]

Personal experience with slave catchers was common among northern free blacks, but from the 1830s until 1850 many states in the Northeast provided them some protection. In most of New England, and in New York, New Jersey, and Pennsylvania, officials tried to discourage the recovery of fugitives from within their boundaries by passing personal liberty laws. Generally, these laws forbade the participation of state authorities or the use of state property in the capture of a fugitive. The Pennsylvania Personal Liberty Law of 1826 went further, banning forcible seizure and removal of any fugitive from the state. In 1842, in the case of *Prigg* v. *Pennsylvania*,[14] the Supreme Court declared the Pennsylvania law unconstitutional and upheld the basic constitutionality of the Fugitive Slave Law of 1793. However, in the court's opinion, rendered by Justice Joseph Story, states were not compelled to enforce the federal law.[15] Most Northern states interpreted this ruling as allowing the continuation of a moderate version of the personal liberty laws that, while not hindering federal enforcement of the nineteenth-century Fugitive Slave Law, prohibited state facilities or officers from being used in the process. With the new Fugitive Slave Law of 1850, Congress made it considerably more difficult for states to protect fugitives through this kind of legislation.[16]

Militant Resistance to the Fugitive Slave Law

It was not long before emboldened slaveholders set out to test the effectiveness of the stronger law. Fugitives like William and Ellen Craft were vulnerable, even in abolitionist Boston. On November 1, 1850, an article in William Lloyd Garrison's *Liberator* announced "the appearance of two prowling villains . . . from Macon, Georgia, for the purpose of seizing William and Ellen Craft, under the infernal Fugitive Slave Bill, and carrying them back to the hell of Slavery."[17] The slave catchers obtained warrants for the fugitives' arrest but had trouble finding an officer who would serve it.

Meanwhile, the reaction to the presence of slave catchers in the city was intense among Boston's abolitionists, especially in the African American community. A vigilance committee with over one hundred members sprang into action. The city was plastered with signs warning of the efforts to enforce the Fugitive Slave Law. The slave catchers were arrested several times, charged with slander against and conspiracy to kidnap William Craft. In angry meetings the city's blacks made it clear that the fugitives could be taken only with considerable force. At one point, William was sheltered by black activist and former slave Lewis Hayden, who piled explosives on the front porch of his home and threatened to blow up the house and anyone who entered in pursuit of the fugitive. As it became clear that recapturing the Crafts would prove a difficult and dangerous job, the slave catchers withdrew from the city. Although they seemed safe for the moment, the Crafts, on advice from Boston abolitionists, soon booked passage for England, where they lived comfortably and securely until after the Civil War.[18]

The attempted capture of the Crafts was the first but not the last test of the new law, and not all fugitives could be saved. The first person to be returned under the 1850 law was James Hamlet, arrested in New York City, found to be a fugitive and remanded to the custody of the federal marshal, who transported him to Baltimore. Unable to prevent his return to slavery, outraged citizens contributed the eight hundred dollars demanded by his owner in order to return Hamlet to freedom in New York. In Detroit, in Boston, in New Albany, Indiana, and in other Northern communities, fugitives were arrested and returned during the first year after the law's passage. Although abolitionists raised money to purchase freedom for many returned fugitives, the federal resolve was clear. The law was applied in thirteen cases within the first three months of its passage, and all but two of those arrested were returned to slavery.[19]

Each removal of fugitives from northern communities increased the fury of the abolitionists and broadened their base of support. In many cities black and white activists cooperated in efforts to prevent the law's enforcement. In Chicago, just days after the bill was signed, blacks met to denounce the new law. The Chicago Common Council called it unconstitutional, said its supporters were traitors, and refused to require the city police to assist in the arrest of a fugitive. By 1853 in Harrisburg, Pennsylvania, enforcement of the law led to a political backlash against the Democratic officials who had supported and enforced it. By 1854 even members of the Boston police force questioned its legitimacy.[20]

Senator Stephen A. Douglas of Illinois faced constituents at home who were angry at the part he had played in crafting and shepherding through Congress the Compromise of 1850, of which the Fugitive Slave Law was a part. A Chicago Common Council resolution opposing the law had likened Douglas to Benedict Arnold and Judas Iscariot. Douglas defended the law for three and one-half hours before a crowd of four thousand. He claimed that the law would actually protect free blacks from kidnapping because, he said, it forced those claiming a fugitive to present proof of their claim. This was a curious argument, but some whites in the audience were convinced, and the city council met again to moderate their original denunciation of Douglas and the law. African Americans remained hostile, and black and white abolitionists stepped up their efforts to aid and protect fugitives, regardless of federal law.[21]

Black Migration and the Fugitive Slave Law

With the increased danger, workers on the underground railroad redoubled their efforts to move passengers to Canada. The sense of urgency was especially strong in areas within easy reach of the South. One newspaper in southern Pennsylvania reported that shortly after the passage of the Fugitive Slave Law the city was "almost deserted of black fellows, since they have heard of the new law. It is supposed that more than a hundred have left for Canada and other parts." The writer then warned black strangers of their vulnerability, saying, "They had better go—that is those who are not well known here."[22]

Even farther north, in areas less immediately vulnerable to slave catchers, many chose to migrate to Canada, and community institutions felt their loss. One African American Baptist church in Buffalo lost 130 members who crossed the Canadian border rather than risk being arrested as fugitives. Rochester's black Baptist church lost all but 2 of its 114 members.[23] Fear of kidnapping and enforcement of the Fugitive Slave Law persuaded one-third of the congregation of Boston's Twelfth Baptist Church, often referred to as the fugitive slave church, to leave for Canada. Other black churches in Boston also lost many members. One Boston abolitionist estimated that in the fifteen days between mid-February and early March of 1851, less than six months after the passage of the law, one hundred free blacks and fugitives fled the city.[24]

As an indication of these losses, historian Mechal Sobel has documented the decline in the congregational membership for some of the largest black Baptist churches in the North from the late 1840s to 1851. The declines recorded by Sobel ranged from 12 percent to 34 percent, the highest occurring at Albany, New York's Hamilton Street Church. Although the cause of this decline in black church membership can only be inferred, the testimony of the abolitionists of the period suggests that in large part their losses resulted from the Canadian migration.[25]

The upsurge in black migration was noted all over the North. Within two weeks of the signing of the law, one observer in Pittsburgh reported that "nearly all the waiters in the hotels have fled to Canada." According to his tally, "Sunday 30 fled; on Monday 40; on Tuesday 50; on Wednesday 30 and up to this time the number that has left will not fall short of 300."[26] From New Bedford came the news that "a very large number" of "fugitives" had departed for Canada and "parts unknown" with more to follow shortly.[27] The black population of Columbia, Pennsylvania, decreased by more than half as the town lost over 450 black residents in a matter of months. Detroit abolitionists guided one thousand two hundred to Canada, and Cleveland's underground railroad recorded more than one hundred emigrants per month in the year after the law's passage.[28]

On the other side of the border, estimates of black migration north were also sizable. By December one observer in St. Catharines estimated that at least three thousand blacks had taken refuge in Canada and that many more would surely follow. Within a few months of the law's passage, the Anti-Slavery Society of Canada estimated that as many as four to five thousand emigrants had come north.[29] The brisk pace of the underground to Canada continued throughout most of the 1850s and even into the 1860s. In 1859 abolitionists in Troy, New York, reported that large numbers of African Americans were moving through that station on to Canada, and in Detroit activists passed along the first contingent of northern emigration from North Carolina. Also in the late 1850s, some California blacks struck out for the freer atmosphere of Vancouver. Even as the first shots of the Civil War were being fired, the Fugitive Slave Law continued to affect African Americans. Three hundred left Chicago for the safety of Canada during the first few weeks in April 1861, it was said, because of the "vigorous enforcement" of the Fugitive Slave Law.[30]

Kidnapping: The Danger to Free Blacks in the North

Most of those who fled to Canada were fugitives and their families, but many others were free blacks afraid for their own safety. Their fear was realistic, for under the new law free people of color were more vulnerable to kidnapping by slave catchers than ever before. The danger of abduction plagued free blacks throughout the eighteenth and early nineteenth centuries, but the 1850 law increased that danger by declaring that alleged fugitives had no right to a defense or jury trial. Any black person could be judged a fugitive, taken south and sold into slavery, but the young and the naive living close to the South were especially at risk. During the winter of 1852 a young boy, John "Blackie" Johnson, disappeared from Harrisburg, Pennsylvania. Months later his distraught mother learned that Blackie had been taken to Baltimore and there bound to a master. Further, this master refused to free the boy unless he was paid the hundred dollars he claimed as transaction expenses. Blackie's mother tried to raise the money, even going door to door asking for donations. When she was only able to collect half the required sum she turned to the federal commissioner for Harrisburg, appointed by the federal court under the Fugitive Slave Law to handle fugitive cases. In part responding to the heightened tensions and increasingly militant abolitionist protest provoked by the controversial law, the commissioner interceded on the woman's behalf, and her son was returned. Yet even while Blackie's return was being negotiated, another Harrisburg black was being taken—James Phillips, a teamster in his thirties, a husband and father of two, and a twenty-year resident of the city. Despite the protests of many blacks and whites who knew him to be free, Phillips was surrendered to slave catchers, who took him to Richmond and sold him to a slave dealer. Only the payment of eight hundred dollars secured his return to Pennsylvania.[31]

Slave catching could be a lucrative undertaking, and in many northern cities bounty hunters, encouraged by the new Fugitive Slave Law, worked alone or in gangs to make easy money by kidnapping blacks and selling them south. The diary of one white Philadelphia artisan details his role in capturing blacks whenever an opportunity presented itself.

He was not troubled by the moral questions involved in slavery and had little regard for whether his victim was truly a fugitive or simply an African American who might be accepted by a slaveholder in exchange for a handsome reward.[32] Gangs like the Black Birds in New York City, the Gap Gang in Lancaster County, Pennsylvania, and many others with names like the Pug Uglies, Highbinders, and Forty Thieves terrorized black communities. The rising price of slaves in the South in the early 1850s discouraged distinctions between fugitives and free blacks.[33] Thus African American freedom was precarious even in the North, especially since most blacks captured as fugitives during the 1850s were apprehended without the aid of legal authority. Additionally, according to one historian's estimate from a survey of cases between 1850 and 1860, captured blacks were given an opportunity for a defense in fewer than three of every five cases.[34]

The vulnerability of all blacks created a widespread fear of being kidnapped. In city after city black leaders urged direct, immediate action, and some advocated carrying weapons for self-defense. Members of one group arrested for carrying guns on the Boston Common explained their actions by citing their need to protect themselves and other blacks from slave catchers. In New York black abolitionists like Henry Highland Garnet and Samuel Ringold Ward armed themselves. Even Garrisonian William Cooper Nell advised those threatened by slave catchers to act "as they would to rid themselves of a wild beast."[35] One prominent black abolitionist recalling the 1850s commented, "In [that] dark hour, when colored men's rights were so insecure, as a matter of self-defence, they felt called upon to arm themselves and resist all kidnapping intruders, although clothed with the authority of wicked law." In Pittsburgh one store reported a run on knives and handguns by the city's blacks after the passage of the Fugitive Slave Law.[36] If slave catchers could not be stopped, their work could be made more difficult and considerably more dangerous.

Violence and Self-Defense

While the new Fugitive Slave Law engendered fear, it also spawned a growing anger and an increasing militancy among African Americans. It further intensified the debate over the question of violent means for self-defense. Ultimately it spurred a shift in political strategy and rhetoric, a change perhaps most striking among those blacks who were Garrisonians. William Lloyd Garrison, who became the most influential white abolitionist of the antebellum period with the publication of his radical anti-slavery newspaper, the *Liberator*, in 1831 in Boston, was a strong advocate of nonviolence. His unswerving commitment to immediate emancipation for slaves and civil rights for free blacks made him especially popular among African Americans who had worked toward these ends for decades with only marginal assistance from white reformers. Garrison was a nonresister—a pacifist opposed to cooperation (even through voting) with any government built on slavery and compromise with slaveholders. The route to freedom, he believed, was through strength of character and moral suasion.[37]

African Americans had struggled with the ideals of nonviolence and pacifism as an antislavery strategy long before Garrison's strong commitment to these philosophies became an issue. During the eighteenth century, African Americans had been influenced by Quaker arguments for nonviolence, as of course was Garrison later. Quakers were some of the first whites to speak out as a group against slavery, and part of their antislavery fervor was based on their pacifism. Blacks who became Friends during the eighteenth and the nineteenth centuries often wrestled with the constraints of this philosophy. Although several black leaders did become Quakers, there was never a large number of black Quakers. One reason was the seeming impracticality of a nonviolent philosophy for a people violently deprived of their freedom.[38]

There was no pacifism in the analysis of slavery and the appeal issued to slaves by David Walker from Boston in 1829. "The man who would not fight, to be delivered from the most wretched, abject and servile slavery, that ever a people was afflicted with since the foundation of the world," he wrote, "ought to be kept with all his children or family, in slavery or in chains to be butchered by his cruel enemies." Walker, a free black North Carolinian who migrated to Boston, gained national attention and raised southern fears by urging slaves to take their freedom by force if necessary. "Are we Men?" he asked. "How we could be so submissive to a gang of men, whom we cannot tell whether they are as good as ourselves or not, I never could conceive." [39]

Despite the powerful influence of Walker's writing, some African Americans, especially in Garrison's Boston, remained loyal to the principles of nonviolence through the 1840s. In fact, two prominent black Garrisonians spoke eloquently against a resolution endorsing violence against slavery at an important national meeting of free blacks held in Buffalo, New York, in 1843. There Henry Highland Garnet, then a twenty-seven-year-old black abolitionist minister, echoed David Walker's exhortation, urging black males to act like men. Addressing himself to the slaves, he admonished, "It is sinful in the extreme, for you to make voluntary submission."[40]

Garnet's speech sparked a heated debate, with Frederick Douglass and Charles Lenox Remond, Garrisonians from Boston, leading the opposition to Garnet's recommendation. They spoke in favor of nonviolence as a strategy, arguing that slaves and free blacks, especially in the border states, would suffer retribution should the convention support such a radical call to violence. Nontheless, there was substantial support for Garnet's recommendations, and his call to action was only defeated by a narrow margin. For the time being, the black Garrisonians remained convinced, and they successfully blocked the open embrace of violence in the fight against slavery.[41]

The passage of the Fugitive Slave Law of 1850 changed the minds of many of those committed to nonviolence and moved most African Americans towards the position proclaimed by Garnet in the early 1840s. Even before the law had been formally adopted, many blacks reacted to it in the most militant tones. In August of 1850, reacting to congressional debate on the law more than a month before its passage, a large, boisterous group of white and black abolitionists and fugitive slaves met in Cazenovia, New York. Calling themselves the Fugitive Slave Convention, they urged slaves to rise in open rebellion. Their mood was symbolic of a growing spirit of defiance, fueled by the passage of the new law, that was spreading among antislavery supporters.[42] By 1850 Remond demanded defiance of the law, protection of all fugitives, and the withholding of federal troops should the southern slaves rise against their masters.[43]

In the late summer of 1852 Douglass spoke plainly on the question of violence before a meeting of the National Free Soil Convention in Pittsburgh, asserting that slaveholders "not only forfeit their right to liberty, but to life itself." He drew laughter and applause when he quipped that "The only way to make the Fugitive Slave Law a dead letter is to make half a dozen or more dead kidnappers." This, he argued, would do much to "cool the ardor of Southern gentlemen and keep their rapacity in check." He argued that such extreme measures were necessary so long as African Americans could not depend on the law for protection.[44] The next year Douglass advocated violence obliquely, publishing a novella in which slaves killed the captain of a slave ship and a slave owner. He continued his forthright stand on this issue when a year later he published an editorial entitled, "Is It Right and Wise to Kill a Kidnapper?" in *Frederick Douglass' Paper*. Violence, even deadly violence, Douglass reiterated, was justifiable when used to protect oneself, one's family, or one's community.[45]

Douglass's strong rhetoric reflected the anger that for some African Americans boiled over into militant action and calls for military preparedness. Ohio blacks demanded that racial restrictions be removed from the state militia so that they might take up arms in readiness for the fight that must surely come between the forces of freedom and the supporters of slavery. Boston blacks petitioned the Massachusetts legislature to charter a black military company, and they formed the Massasoit Guard without state sanction when their petition was rejected. In Cincinnati blacks formed the Attucks Guards; New York African Americans likewise invoked the name of this black Revolutionary hero, calling one of their units the Attucks Guards. In the large cities and smaller towns of the North, blacks readied themselves for self-defense, and sometimes

for much more. "Captain" J. J. Simmons of the New York unit proph-
esied that the time would soon come when northern black military units
would be called to march through the South with "a bible in one hand
and a gun in the other."[46]

Reexamining Emigration During the Dangerous Decade of the 1850s

The passage of the 1850 Fugitive Slave Law was an assault on the rights
and freedom of all black people, and it foreshadowed other attacks, which
culminated with the infamous 1857 Supreme Court decision in the case
of Dred Scott.[47] If the Fugitive Slave Law endangered the citizenship
rights of African Americans, the Dred Scott decision proclaimed that no
such rights existed. For many it was the final justification for the use of
violence for self-defense and community protection. Black anger
intensified, black rhetoric escalated, and antislavery organization increased. Many responded positively to the sentiment expressed by Charles
Lenox Remond in a crowded meeting of enraged blacks in Philadelphia: "We owe no allegiance to a country which grinds us under its iron
hoof and treats us like dogs," he said. "The time has gone by for colored
people to talk of patriotism."[48]

By the end of the 1850s there was widespread agreement that unjust
laws inflicted on the black community must be resisted. The stricter Fugitive Slave Law and Justice Taney's opinion in the Dred Scott case in
1857 lent strength to the belief that southern slaveholders could prevail
upon the federal government to ignore or abolish the rights of free blacks,
that even well-meaning state officials could not provide legal protection,
and that the "slave power" must be discouraged by violent opposition.
What free blacks had known for decades became increasingly clear. The
abolition of slavery was more than a matter of protecting family and
loved ones; it was a prerequisite to equal treatment for blacks under
American law.

Thus there was near unanimous agreement on the immorality, injustice, and intolerable nature of the Fugitive Slave Law and the racially
determined limitations imposed by the federal government that culminated in the Dred Scott decision. There was also a strong and growing
acceptance of violence as a means of defense. The stance of the federal
government in the 1850s also led some to revive plans for black emigration to places more distant than Canada. At state and regional meetings
in the early 1850s, African Americans, reacting to the Fugitive Slave Law,
also considered emigration possibilities to Mexico, Central America, Jamaica, and Haiti, all of which had by then abolished slavery. In 1851 J.
Wesley Harrison, who had recently moved to Jamaica, returned to the
United States with encouraging stories about the prospects for African

American settlement there. Although few American blacks actually migrated, there was significant interest in Jamaica as a destination. Reverend J. W. C. Pennington, who before 1850 had been a strong opponent of emigration, offered his church in New York City as a meeting place for those interested in Jamaica.

By mid-decade some blacks were also considering Haiti as an alternative to the United States. Three decades earlier several thousand African Americans had actually migrated to that nation with the encouragement of the Haitian government. Although most returned to the U.S. after a few years, interest in Haiti as an independent black nation remained. After Haitian officials assured Connecticut minister James Theodore Holly in 1855 that American blacks would be welcome, Holly conducted a series of lectures to stimulate interest in Haitian immigration. In 1858 the Haitian government sent an official commission to enlist emigrants, and by 1860 British abolitionist James Redpath was able to raise a sizable fund to support the transportation of those who might make the trip. It is a mark of the degree of blacks' disillusionment with their American prospects that Frederick Douglass, who had never supported emigration of any kind, declared at the end of 1860 that while he had never before been willing to see blacks as a "doomed race" in America, he could "raise no objection to the present movement toward Hayti."[49]

The disillusionment brought on by the Fugitive Slave Law was so powerful that it rekindled the spirit of African colonization among some free blacks. The initial efforts by the largely white American Colonization Society, established in 1816, which sponsored the emigration of hundreds of black Americans to their West African colony of Liberia, had drawn little free-black support, especially after the 1830s. Canada or even the Caribbean were close enough to allow for a continuation of the antislavery struggle. But the great distance across the Atlantic made it unlikely that blacks who emigrated to West Africa could maintain the fight. Most believed that to leave America for Africa was to abandon those left behind in bondage. Then, too, African Americans distrusted the motives of the American Colonization Society with its large slaveholding membership and its conciliatory approach to slaveholders. In 1848 Liberia became an independent nation and a source of pride for black Americans. But even its emergence from colonial status was not enough to convince most African Americans to emigrate. Despite his willingness to accept the possibility of Haitian emigration, Douglass remained dead set against African emigration. The distance, he argued, was too great for emigrants to maintain their ties with those left behind, and the reports by early migrants of disease and of warfare with native populations were discouraging. Still, there was an African emigration movement among free blacks during the mid 1850s. Blacks led by Henry Highland Garnet (who had opposed emigration during the 1840s), minister Alexander Crummell, and Pittsburgh's Martin Delany founded an emigration organization in 1858. In the late summer of that year Garnet addressed a large crowd in New York City's Spring Hall, arguing that black Americans must turn away from America's hypocrisy and toward the land of their ancestors. Citing the economic potential of African trade and the possibility for independence, he announced the formation of the African Civilization Society.[50]

Garnet's appeal to racial pride, to the prospect of expanding Christianity in West Africa, and to political and economic possibilities tempted some. But the vast majority were not willing, as they saw it, to give up their claims to American citizenship, admit that proslavery forces had won, and abandon their friends and relatives in slavery. On this last point there was the strongest feeling. As free blacks of all ages had fought against slavery throughout the antebellum period, most could not bring themselves to withdraw from the battle not yet won. They would stay and continue the fight for abolition and for their rights as free American citizens. For most these were the inseparable struggles that had defined free black life throughout the antebellum period.

Conclusion

Not all historians have appreciated this important link between free blacks and slaves, and some have depicted these two groups as more separate than they actually were. One scholar has suggested that the free blacks of the North were so immersed in the struggle to improve their own lives that they had no time and little interest in underground abolitionist activity. "Why after all, should a Northern black be an active abolitionist?" historian Frederick Cooper has asked. "Whatever feelings he had for his brethren in bonds, blacks in Northern cities still had to live their daily lives. . . . The idea of self-help was of far more relevance to their lives than the crusade against slavery."[51]

Cooper is partly correct: self-help *was* a central concern for free black people. But he draws too sharp a distinction between self-help and antislavery, assuming that commitment to one lessened involvement in the other. In doing so he fails to appreciate the bond between slaves and free blacks, a bond that manifested the African American community's propensity for collective self-help, and he fails to recognize the common danger they faced at the hands of the federal government.

Although there were frictions in black society that sometimes led to political and social fractures, slave, fugitive, and free-born blacks were bound together by blood, culture, common experience, and a recognition of the injustice of American racial inequality. At times of greatest stress the issues that bound people together became most visible. The common threat of kidnapping was an essential link in the bonds that united black people, and the passage of the Fugitive Slave Law of 1850 was the opening assault of a brutal decade. For African Americans it reinforced the reality of their shared injustice.[52]

Notes

The authors express appreciation to Michele A. Gates, Patrick Rael and Shannon Barker for editorial and research assistance.

1. William Craft, *Running a Thousand Miles for Freedom; or, The Escape of William and Ellen Craft from Slavery* (1860; reprint, New York: Arno Press, 1969); also see *U.S. Census* (Washington: U.S. Government Printing Office, 1850).

2. Robert J. Rayback, *Millard Fillmore: Biography of a President* (Buffalo: Buffalo Historical Society, 1959).

3. Jane H. Pease and William H. Pease, *The Fugitive Slave Law and Anthony Burns: A Problem in Law Enforcement* (Philadelphia: J. B. Lippincott, 1975).

4. "Document 31: An act to amend, and supplementary to, the act entitled 'An act respecting fugitives from justice, and persons escaping from the service of their masters,' approved February twelfth, one thousand seven hundred and ninety-three" reprinted in *Civil Rights and the American Negro: A Documentary History* eds. Albert P. Blaustein and Robert Zangrando (New York: Simon and Schuster, 1968), 127–33, quote 128.

5. Charles C. Andrews, ed., *Official Opinions of the Attorneys General of the United States,* vol. 6 (Washington, D.C.: Robert Farnham, 1856), 272–74.

6. Pease and Pease, *Fugitive Slave Law,* 11–12.

7. "The Sons of Africans: An Essay on Freedom," (Boston, 1808); reprinted in *Early Negro Writing, 1760-1837,* ed. Dorothy Porter (Boston: Beacon Press, 1971), 25.

8. James Oliver Horton and Lois E. Horton, *Black Bostonians: Family Life and Community Struggle in the Antebellum North* (New York: Holmes and Meier, 1979), 32.

9. *Liberator,* April 19, 1834; Alexander Crummell, *The Eulogy of Henry Highland Garnet, D.D. Presbyterian Minister* (Springfield, Mass.: John Wiley, 1891), 25–26.

10. "Report of the Condition of the People of Color in the State of Ohio," (April, 1835); reprinted in *A Documentary History of the Negro People in the United States,* ed. Herbert Aptheker (New York: Citadel Press, 1965), 157-58.

11. Ibid.

12. Charles C. Andrews, *The History of the New York African Free Schools* (New York: Negro Universities Press, 1969).

13. Joel Schor, *Henry Highland Garnet: A Voice of Black Radicalism in the Nineteenth Century* (Westport, Conn.: Greenwood Press, 1977). For a contemporary account of the attempted capture of the Garnets, see Crummell, *The Eulogy of Henry Highland Garnet.*

14. *Prigg* v. *Pennsylvania,* 41 U.S. (16 Pet.) 536, at 539, 613 (1842).

15. In 1821 New Jersey passed a law to prevent their slaves from being kidnapped and sold south before they were freed by a state law which required that slaves in the state be freed by age twenty-one for females and age twenty-five for males. For a detailed examination of the New Jersey provision and the 1793 fugitive law and a description of the case of *Prigg* v. *Pennsylvania,* see Paul Finkelman, "Chief Justice Hornblower of New Jersey and the Fugitive Slave Law of 1793" in this volume. See also Thomas D. Morris, *Free Men All: The Personal Liberty Laws of the North, 1780–1861* (Baltimore: Johns Hopkins University Press, 1974).

16. Paul Finkelman, "*Prigg* v. *Pennsylvania* and Northern State Courts: Anti-Slavery Use of a Proslavery Decision," *Civil War History* 25 (March 1979), 5–35.

17. "Slave-Hunters in Boston," *Liberator*, November 1, 1850.

18. For a more complete account of the Crafts in Boston, see Horton and Horton, *Black Bostonians.*

19. See Stanley W. Campbell, *The Slave Catchers: Enforcement of the Fugitive Slave Law, 1850–1860* (Chapel Hill, N.C.: University of North Carolina Press, 1968). Although some earlier historians have assumed that the law was not generally enforced, recent studies have made clear that the federal government was quite diligent in its enforcement. See Gerald G. Eggert, "The Impact of the Fugitive Slave Law on Harrisburg: A Case Study," *Pennsylvania Magazine of History* 109 (1985): 537–569.

20. Olivia Mahoney, "Black Abolitionist," *Chicago History* 20 (1991): 22–37; Eggert, "Impact of the Fugitive Slave Law"; Horton and Horton, *Black Bostonians.*

21. Mahoney, "Black Abolitionist"; Robert W. Johannsen, *Stephen A. Douglas* (New York: Oxford University Press, 1973).

22 *Pennsylvania Telegraph*, October 2, 1850; quoted in Eggert, "Impact of The Fugitive Slave Law on Harrisburg," 554–55.

23. A. E. Dorn, "A History of the Anti-Slavery Movement in Rochester and Vicinity" (Masters Thesis, University of Buffalo, 1932) cited in *The Life and Writings of Frederick Douglass*, ed. Philip S. Foner (New York: International Publishers, 1950), 2:545.

24. Horton and Horton, *Black Bostonians.*

25. Mechal Sobel, *Trabelin' On: The Slave Journey to an Afro-Baptist Faith* (Princeton: Princeton University Press, 1988), 216.

26. *Liberator*, October 4, 1850.

27. *Liberator*, April 25, 1851.

28. Fred Landon, "The Negro Migration to Canada after the Passing of the Fugitive Slave Act," *Journal of Negro History* 5 (1920): 22–36.

29. *Liberator*, December 13, 1850; Michael F. Hembree, "The Question of 'Begging': Fugitive Slave Relief in Canada, 1830–1865," *Civil War History* 37 (1991): 315.

30. Hembree, "Question of 'Begging,'" 327.

31. Eggert, "Impact of the Fugitive Slave Law," 537–69.

32. William Otter, *History of My Own Time*, ed. Richard B. Stott, (1835, Ithaca: Cornell University Press, 1995), 114–17.

33. See, for example, Thomas P. Slaughter, *Bloody Dawn: The Christiana Riot and Racial Violence in the Antebellum North* (New York: Oxford University Press, 1991), and Paul A. Gilje, *The Road to Mobocracy: Popular Disorder in New York City, 1763–1834* (Chapel Hill: University of North Carolina Press, 1987).

34. Allan Nevins, *The Emergence of Lincoln: Prologue to Civil War, 1850–1861* (New York: Scribner, 1950), 2:31; Campbell, *The Slave Catchers*, 137; Peter Hinks, "Frequently Plunged into Slavery: Free Blacks and Kidnapping in Antebellum Boston," paper presented at Organization of American Historians Annual Meeting, 1991; Carol Wilson, *Freedom at Risk: The Kidnapping of Free Blacks in America, 1780–1865* (Lexington: The University Press of Kentucky, 1994).

35. Horton and Horton, *Black Bostonians*, 103.

36. *Liberator*, October 25, 1850.

37. For a detailed treatment of the black response to Garrison's commitment to nonviolence, see James Oliver Horton and Lois E. Horton, "The

Affirmation of Manhood: Black Garrisonians in Antebellum Boston," in *Courage and Conscience: Black and White Abolitionists in Boston*, ed. Donald M. Jacobs (Bloomington: Indiana University Press, 1993).

38. Henry J. Cadbury, "Negro Membership in the Society of Friends," *Journal of Negro History* 21 (1936), 151–213. There was considerable controversy among the Friends over the admission of blacks to the Society. Some African Americans were rejected on account of color, even though they were considered models of Quaker virtue. It is likely that those blacks who applied for membership were likely to be at least as acceptable on grounds of principle, including that of pacifism, as whites who did so, and many blacks were accepted into the Society. See also Jean R. Soderlund, *Quakers and Slavery: A Divided Spirit* (Princeton: Princeton University Press, 1985).

39. *David Walker's Appeal*, ed. with an introd. by Charles M. Wiltse, (1830; reprint, New York: Hill and Wang, 1965), 12, 16.

40. "Speech by Henry Highland Garnet delivered before the National Convention of Colored Citizens, Buffalo, New York, 16 August, 1843" in *The Black Abolitionist Papers*, vol. 3, ed. C. Peter Ripley et. al., (Chapel Hill: University of North Carolina Press, 1991), 403–12, quotes 408–10.

41. David Blight argued that Douglass was committed to nonviolence as a tactic rather than a moral position. In this way he was never a nonresistant in the Garrisonian sense of that term. See David Blight, *Frederick Douglass' Civil War: Keeping Faith in Jubilee* (Baton Rouge: Louisiana State University Press, 1989).

42. Paula J. Priebe, "Central and Western New York and the Fugitive Slave Law of 1850," in *Afro-Americans in New York Life and History* 16, 1 (1992): 19–29.

43. Horton and Horton, *Black Bostonians*.

44. *Frederick Douglass' Paper*, August 1852.

45. William S. McFeely, *Frederick Douglass* (New York: W.W. Norton, 1991); *Frederick Douglass' Paper*, June 2, 1854.

46. Ripley, *The Black Abolitionist Papers*, 4:319.

47. *Dred Scott v. Sandford*, 60 U.S. (19 How.) 393 (1857).

48. *The Liberator*, April 10, 1857. For a analysis and interpretation of the Dred Scott decision and general information on the proslavery stands taken by the court during the antebellum period, see Paul Finkelman, *An Imperfect Union: Slavery, Federalism, and Comity* (Chapel Hill: University of North Carolina Press, 1981).

49. Quoted in Philip Foner, *History of Black America* (Westport, Conn.: Greenwood Press, 1983), 3:163. See also *Frederick Douglass' Monthly*, January 1861.

50. Wilson Jeremiah Moses, *The Golden Age of Black Nationalism, 1850–1925* (New York: Oxford University Press, 1978); Schor, *Henry Highland Garnet*.

51. Frederick Cooper, "Elevating the Race: The Social Thought of Black Leaders, 1827–50," *American Quarterly* 24 (1972): 604–25. For an insightful critique of Cooper's thesis, see Peter P. Hinks "'We Must and Shall Be Free': David Walker, Evangelicalism, and Antebellum Black Resistance" (Ph.D. diss., Yale University, forthcoming).

52. For a more detailed treatment of the link between northern free blacks and slaves, see James Oliver Horton, *Free People of Color: Inside the African American Community* (Washington, D.C.: Smithsonian Institution Press, 1993).

6

The Crisis Over *The Impending Crisis:* Free Speech, Slavery, and the Fourteenth Amendment

Michael Kent Curtis

IN 1859 THE UNITED STATES OF AMERICA stood on the verge of civil war. One Southerner after another rose in Congress to announce that the election of a "Black Republican" president would justify secession. Republican congressmen answered that secession would be met with coercion. The divisive issue was slavery. Congress convened in December 1859, shortly after John Brown's unsuccessful October raid on Harper's Ferry, a raid designed to free slaves by force of arms. Democrats announced that Brown's raid was the natural consequence of Republican and antislavery agitation.[1]

Exhibit 1 in the case against the Republicans was an antislavery book written by Hinton Rowan Helper, *The Impending Crisis of the South: How to Meet It.*[2] In this book Helper, a North Carolinian, appealed for political action by nonslaveholders of the South to eliminate slavery. Although isolated passages from the book were ambiguous and could be read in a more sinister way, at the least the book suggested that if the channels of peaceful political change were closed to opponents of slavery by violence and repressive laws, then resort to counterviolence was justified. Here, supporters of slavery suggested, was the blueprint for the infamous John Brown raid. Republicans were implicated in the raid, they insisted, because more than sixty Republican congressmen had endorsed Helper's book.[3] Later in the session, faced with an explicit choice of protecting slavery or endorsing the principle of freedom of speech on all political matters including slavery, Democrats in the Senate chose slavery.

By 1859 the controversy over slavery had become the consuming issue of American politics. A focus of dispute was slavery in the territories.[4] Would slavery be planted in the soil of new territories or would it be excluded?

The contest over slavery during 1859 and 1860 included another battle: a battle over the meaning of political liberty, focused on freedom of speech and of the press. The institution of slavery had a pervasive impact on law and ideology, and in the years before the Civil War, it undermined support for basic liberties of speech, press, and political action. Reaction to the "slave power's" suppression of political liberty in the years before the Civil War shaped the guarantees of liberty added by the Fourteenth Amendment after the Civil War.

In 1859 and 1860 the conflict between slavery and antislavery forces produced debates on free speech in Congress and repression of antislavery speech and press in much of the South, including a prosecution of an antislavery minister in North Carolina for circulating Helper's book. Together these events cast light on how slavery shaped Republican ideas of free speech, press, and religion and on the duty of states to respect these liberties.

The events of 1859 are a crucial part of the background that shaped the worldview of the people who wrote, proposed, and adopted the Fourteenth Amendment, and particularly its clause prohibiting states from denying the privileges or immunities of citizens of the United States. Because the Fourteenth Amendment today forbids states from abridging freedom of speech, press, and religion, and because this development has had its share of critics, the uproar of 1859 is pertinent to understanding the purposes of those who framed its first section. Today we continue to struggle to assure equal protection for African Americans. The role of free speech on questions related to race and other group characteristics remains very much with us. The events of 1859 are an important part of that story.

The conflict between free speech and slavery revived the issue of the relation of free speech to republican government previously raised by the 1798 Sedition Act, but with a significant difference. In this second crisis of free speech, suppression came from the states, not from the national government. The crisis over slavery and free speech also highlights the crucial importance of the "incorporated" Bill of Rights as a whole to republican government. For example, Republicans invoked rights referred to in the First Amendment (here involving antislavery speech, press, and religion), the Fourth Amendment (involving unreasonable searches and seizures aimed at antislavery activists and publications), and the Eighth Amendment (involving cruel and unusual punishments for opponents of slavery) in the years 1859 to 1866 to criticize state political repression that the "slave power" aimed at opponents of slavery. In this respect the battle between antislavery and slavery replicated historical battles for political liberty in which dissenters invoked basic liberties, including criminal procedure guarantees, later set out in the American Bill of Rights.[5] In 1859 criminal procedure guarantees were especially pertinent because some Democrats implied that the Republican party was not a normal political party but instead was a criminal conspiracy.

The 1859 controversy over *The Impending Crisis* provides a case study of conflicting ideas of freedom of expression and of the liberties of American citizens. The debate that swirled around slavery and free speech and press casts some light on early Republican understanding of the concept of freedom of expression. Was freedom of the press limited to protection against restraint before publication, or did it also protect some expression from subsequent punishment? Should political speech believed to have bad tendencies be banned, or does the very notion of free speech have a hard, central meaning that protects political speech from suppression?

The Southern rejection of free speech about slavery was not as unique as it first appears. In World War I the Court upheld criminal convictions for criticism of the war thought to have a tendency to interfere with the draft.[6] In the 1950s the Court allowed punishment for Communist advocacy of revolution, although the revolution was not to be effectuated immediately but as soon as circumstances would permit. The main opinion in that case, *Dennis* v. *United States*, balanced the gravity of the evil against its improbability.[7] To Southerners a slave revolt was a grave evil indeed and, as the Nat Turner Rebellion showed, not all that improbable. Still the demand to suppress antislavery speech was remarkable and the most profound threat to civil liberty since the Sedition Act: it was aimed at peacetime advocacy of political change by peaceful means.

The controversy over free speech and slavery is also an important part of the history of the Fourteenth Amendment, an amendment shaped by the conflict between slavery and civil liberty. Events of 1859 help us to understand what Republicans meant when they provided in section 1 of the Fourteenth Amendment that "No state . . . shall abridge the privileges or immunities of citizens of the United States." Did they intend that state observance of the commands of the Bill of Rights would remain[8] a matter of state option? Was there anything like a consensus on the issue? Since the meaning of words depends on their context, the historical context in which section 1 was adopted sheds further light on the original meaning of the words used. The 1859 crisis over *The Impending Crisis* is a crucial part of that context. It provides some additional evidence from which to evaluate two contending theories about section 1 of the Fourteenth Amendment.

One theory insists that section 1 was originally designed only to guarantee limited equality of treatment under state law; the other insists that it was also designed to prevent states from denying some additional national personal liberties, including those in the Bill of Rights. Two themes run through this story about free speech and slavery—the need to require states to respect the commands of the Bill of Rights, and the need to protect speech and press even when political speech seems to threaten grave public danger.

The uproar over the *Impending Crisis* is a significant moment in the history of free speech in the United States and of the application of free speech guarantees to the states through the Fourteenth Amendment, a history too often forgotten by lawyers.[9]

Historical Overview

THE FIRST BILL OF RIGHTS

By the time of the American Revolution, American revolutionaries appealed to the basic rights of Englishmen, including habeas corpus, jury trials, protection against ex post facto laws and unreasonable searches, and other procedural rights. They also appealed to freedom of speech, press, and religion, and the right to counsel. These appeared in bills of rights in many state constitutions. The omission of many of these basic rights from the American Constitution was one of the major arguments against its adoption.

When James Madison proposed the Bill of Rights in 1789, he cautiously expressed his expectation for the role to be played by guarantees of liberty. Madison hoped the Bill of Rights would limit abuses of power by the legislature, the executive, and most of all by the majority against the minority. By declaring guarantees of liberty, a bill of rights would have "a tendency to impress some degree of respect for them, to establish the public opinion in their favor." The judiciary would "consider themselves in a peculiar manner the guardians of those rights; they will be an impenetrable bulwark against every assumption of power." Madison noted that in the British system declarations of rights "have gone no farther than to raise a barrier against the Crown; the power of the legislature is left altogether indefinite. . . . The freedom of the press and rights of conscience, those choicest *privileges* of the people, are unguarded in the British constitution."[10]

In addition to the rights that did make it into the Bill of Rights, Madison had also proposed "that no State shall violate the equal right of conscience, freedom of the press, or trial by jury in criminal cases." "[E]very Government should be disarmed," he insisted, "of powers which trench on those particular rights." Though some state constitutions secured the rights, there was no reason not to have "a double security on those points. . . . State Governments," Madison said, "are as liable to attack the invaluable *privileges* as the General Government is." When a critic suggested that the matter should be left to the states, Madison responded that the limitation on the states was "the most valuable amendment in the whole list." While Congress accepted most of Madison's proposals, the Senate rejected his proposal for explicit limitation on the states. The Bill of Rights, the Supreme Court ruled in 1833, did not limit state or local governments.[11]

THE SEDITION ACT

The Sedition Act of 1798 put the Bill of Rights to its first major test.[12] The act made false and malicious criticism of the president a crime. Political motives for the act were clear. It protected the president, John Adams, from criticism, but not the vice president, Thomas Jefferson, his likely opponent in the election of 1800. The act was set to expire by the time the new president was in office. Federalists used the act to prosecute supporters of Thomas Jefferson for political criticisms of President Adams.[13]

Much of the Jeffersonian attack on the Sedition Act was based on federalism: the Constitution gave Congress no power over speech and press, and the First Amendment explicitly denied such power. The Virginia Resolutions, penned by Madison, made a more fundamental criticism: the Sedition Act should "produce universal alarm, because it is levelled against that right of freely examining public characters and measures, and of free communication among the people thereon, which has ever been justly deemed the only effectual guardian of every other right." Charles Black calls such arguments structural: a conclusion drawn from how republican governments have to function to fulfill their design.[14] The argument suggested an area of political speech that should be beyond the power of government to suppress.

This response to the Sedition Act built on and elaborated the Leveller and Radical Whig tradition. By that tradition the people were the master, government officials were the agent, and free speech was an essential mechanism by which the master could control the agent. While Blackstone's *Commentaries*, the leading English text, defended parliamentary sovereignty and the idea that freedom of the press was limited to a protection against prior restraint, the attack on the Sedition Act emphasized popular sovereignty and a broad concomitant right to criticize government measures and officials. Although the federal courts sustained the Act, Jefferson was elected president, the Sedition Act expired, and Jefferson pardoned those convicted under it.[15]

A SOUTHERN QUARANTINE ON ANTISLAVERY SPEECH

Although the nation repudiated the Sedition Act, the controversy over antislavery publications in the 1830s raised the issue of "dangerous" political speech again, this time on both the state and national levels. In the 1830s a slave revolt in Virginia produced a state legislative debate on slave emancipation and deportation. Opponents of emancipation insisted that antislavery expression was a threat to safety. North Carolina, Virginia, and other Southern states passed laws aimed at antislavery expression. The North Carolina and Virginia laws led to prosecutions for antislavery speech and press, including 1859 prosecutions aimed at distributors of *The Impending Crisis*. In the 1830s Southerners demanded similar laws in the North, and the governor of New York proposed a limited version of one. In 1859 some Democrats in Congress advocated reviving his plan for Northern state laws aimed at antislavery speech.

By the mid 1830s much of the South was quarantining antislavery expression.[16] This left abolitionists in a curious position. The slaves and slaveholders were in the South. Abolitionists had hoped to persuade slaveholders to abandon slavery, but increasingly they found themselves unable directly to address them. That left them to persuade the often hostile masses of the North, who, however, had no slaves. According to Charles Sydnor, in the mid 1830s Whig Congressmen began pressing the slavery issue by presenting antislavery petitions in an effort to split the Northern and Southern wings of the Democratic party. Congress, over Whig protests, passed the "gag rule," laying all abolitionist petitions on the table without discussion or printing. Because political leaders used congressional publication and dissemination of events in Congress as a major source of public information, the gag rule closed one important channel of communication. As slavery became increasingly politicized, antislavery congressmen emerged in Congress.[17]

The intellectual quarantine in North Carolina became ever more strict. One case shows how times were changing. In 1856 Benjamin Hedrick, a talented professor of chemistry at the University of North Carolina, was driven first from his job and then from the state for supporting John C. Frémont, the Republican presidential candidate. Laws against antislavery expression were merely the tip of an iceberg, and conformity was, in Hedrick's case, enforced by public opinion expressed through mob action. Hedrick was "exposed" in the *Raleigh Weekly Standard*. At the end of the affair, the *Standard* exalted:

> We may have aided to *magnify* him somewhat in the public eye, but that was one of the unavoidable incidents, and not the object. Our object was to rid the University and the State of an avowed Frémont man; and we succeeded. And we now say, after due consideration . . . that no man who is avowedly for John C. Frémont for President ought to be allowed to breathe the air or to tread the soil of North Carolina.[18]

Hedrick became a close friend of another exile from North Carolina, Hinton Rowan Helper, the author of *The Impending Crisis*.

ABOLITIONIST CONSTITUTIONAL DOCTRINE

The congressional gag rule; the 1837 murder of Elijah Lovejoy, an Alton, Illinois, abolitionist editor, by a mob seeking to destroy his press; the suppression of free speech in the South; and the congressional battle over antislavery and the mails all enhanced the prestige of abolitionists, who began to appear as champions of civil liberty. Starting in 1837 an increasing faction of abolitionists favored political action, and by 1840 they even created an antislavery political party.[19]

As abolitionism developed and as states like North Carolina and Virginia quarantined themselves to protect against the contagion of abolition, abolitionist legal theory also began to change. The changes are significant for our story because parts of radical abolitionist legal theory were embraced by mainstream Republicans.

In spite of a lack of enthusiasm by some Southern courts for enforcing laws against antislavery expression,[20] the prospect of broad protection of free speech for abolitionists under Southern laws and court decisions looked bleak. One group of radical political abolitionists began to appeal to the federal Constitution for protection of civil liberties against state action.[21] For radical political abolitionists the Constitution protected civil liberties against both state and federal action.

Joel Tiffany, author of an 1849 *Treatise on the Unconstitutionality of American Slavery*, was a lawyer and reporter for the New York Supreme Court who grew up in a hotbed of antislavery sentiment in Ohio. Tiffany believed that the guarantees of liberty in the original Constitution and in the Bill of Rights limited the states and protected all citizens of the United States from state action infringing their rights. In this, his views, though unorthodox, were not unique. Citizens were entitled to "all the privileges and immunities . . . guaranteed in the Federal Constitution," which included all its "guarantys . . . for personal security [and] . . . liberty." These were protected from hostile state legislation. Some of the privileges guaranteed were listed by Tiffany: for example, the right to petition, to habeas corpus, to keep and bear arms, and to not be subject to unwarrantable searches and seizures. As between citizen and citizen, Tiffany thought protection of rights was left largely to the states. Although the Bill of Rights limited the states, where states fulfilled their duty of protection of citizens' rights, the Bill of Rights typically did not provide a remedy for one citizen wronged by another private citizen. As a result, Tiffany insisted that his theory charted a middle course between states' rights and consolidation.[22]

Then, in a dramatic leap of faith, Tiffany concluded that slaves, like all persons born or naturalized in the United States, were citizens. Although few antislavery politicians agreed that slaves were citizens, Tiffany's other constitutional doctrines became increasingly influential. Congressman John Bingham of Ohio was one person influenced by a view of civil liberty like that espoused by Tiffany. Bingham, unlike Tiffany, did not assert that slaves were citizens. Bingham was to become the main author of section 1 of the Fourteenth Amendment.

Even before the Civil War, Bingham read Article IV, section 2, as directing states to respect all constitutional guarantees of liberty. One orthodox reading of Article IV limited it to protecting temporary out-of-state visitors from discrimination in certain basic rights. Article IV provides: "The citizens of each State shall be entitled to all Privileges and Immunities of Citizens in the several states." Bingham read it as containing an ellipsis, as implicitly containing the material added here in brackets: "The Citizens of each State shall be entitled to all Privileges and Immunities of Citizens [of the United States] in the several States." He read "Privileges" as dictionaries of that time and today do: as meaning rights.[23] Included were those rights in the Bill of Rights.

In using the word *privileges* in this way, Bingham was using it as members of the revolutionary generation often had used it and as James Madison used the word in the debate on the Bill of Rights.[24] Bingham believed that states were morally obligated to obey the guarantees of the Bill of Rights by the oath state officers took to support the Constitution. Still, he believed the Article IV, section 2, obligation was not legally enforceable. Although this reading seems strange to us today, it was a federalism-based reading of Article IV that fit well with interpretations the Court had put on other provisions of the Article.[25] This interpretation preserved an appeal to the moral authority of the Bill of Rights, and that moral authority was one way Madison hoped the Bill would function to protect liberty.[26] But if moral suasion failed, judicial protection was not available.

The range of constitutional thinking before the Civil War was quite broad. Some followed the orthodoxy of *Barron* v. *Baltimore*, which held that the Bill of Rights did not limit the states. Some, like Bingham, believed that in some sense states were obligated to obey the guarantees of the Bill of Rights. Some, including many Southern and Northern Democrats, believed that slaves were property and that the Due Process Clause guaranteed the right to take them into federal territories. So antislavery territorial legislation was unconstitutional. In 1856 and 1860 the Republican platform said that slaves were persons and the Due Process Clause banned slavery in federal territories, though not in the states.[27]

A similarly broad range of ideas existed on the subject of slavery and free speech. For some the issue was simply up to the states; for others state statutes banning free speech and press on the subject of slavery violated constitutional obligations. Although much attention was devoted to the subject in Congress in 1859 and 1860, there was little discussion of the speaker's underlying legal theory. Still, the debate that swirled around the topic on the eve of the Civil War gives us some guidance as to different theories people held at that time about the First Amendment, free speech, and free press. It also sheds light on whether the speaker thought local option on the issue of free speech was acceptable.

The centerpiece of the debate on free speech in Congress in 1859-60 was Hinton Rowan Helper's *Impending Crisis of the South*. The debate on Helper's book took place in the context of growing sectional antagonism over slavery.

SECTIONALISM AND SLAVERY, 1830–60

In the 1830s slavery became an increasingly divisive political issue. In the Northwest Ordinance of 1787 Congress prohibited slavery in every part of the west then under congressional jurisdiction.[28] After that, Congress, faced with increasing Southern demands, compromised the policy of exclusion of slavery from the territories. The Louisiana Territory was acquired without an antislavery restriction. In 1820 Missouri was admitted as a slave state, but slavery was prohibited in the remainder of the Louisiana Purchase lying north of latitude 36 degrees, 30 minutes. Although the Kansas and Nebraska territories were included in the Missouri compromise as areas where slavery was forbidden, in 1854 Congress abrogated the compromise, bowing to further Southern demands. The Kansas-Nebraska Act provided for the admission of Kansas and Nebraska with or without slavery, as their constitutions might provide.

The Kansas-Nebraska Act struck the political world like a giant asteroid and so changed the environment that some older forms of political life gradually became extinct. The Whig party disintegrated. Thirty-seven of the forty-four Northern Democratic House members who voted for the Kansas-Nebraska Act were defeated in the next election. The Republican party, founded in 1854 largely on hostility to the Kansas-Nebraska Act, made a strong run for the presidency in 1856. In 1857, in *Dred Scott* v. *Sandford*, the Court ruled that Americans had a federal constitutional right to hold slaves in all territories, a right whose exercise Congress lacked the power to prevent.[29] Since the keystone of the Republican platform was exclusion of slavery from the territories, *Dred Scott* implied that the Republican party platform was itself an unconstitutional proposal.

After *Dred Scott,* Republicans feared a slave-power conspiracy to nationalize slavery, planting it not only in all the territories but in the free states as well.[30] And slavery, as many Republicans saw it, inevitably required the suppression of liberty. As Senator Charles Sumner put it in 1860, denial of rights to the slave "can be sustained only by disregard of other rights, common to the whole community, whether of person, of the press, or of speech. . . . [S]ince slavery is endangered by liberty in any form, therefore all liberty must be restrained." Tobias Plants, a conservative Republican congressman, would make essentially the same point in 1866.[31] It was part of the common faith of the Republican party. The progression seemed clear and grim. From enslaving blacks to limiting the free-speech rights of Southerners and Northerners in the South; from censorship in the South to censorship in slave territories and demands for censorship in the North; from demands for Northern censorship to the clubbing of Senator Sumner in the Senate; from slavery in the Southern states with a ban on slavery in national territory to a constitutional requirement that slavery be tolerated in all national territory and next, Republicans feared, in Northern states also.[32]

The Kansas territory showed just what the rules against antislavery expression meant in practice. Slaveholders and opponents of slavery poured into Kansas, and the territory literally became a battleground in the sectional conflict. The proslavery government of the territory enacted a slave code. It made expressing antislavery opinions a crime, provided the death penalty for helping slaves escape, and required voters to take an oath to support these laws.[33]

One critic of the Kansas laws was John A. Bingham, the antislavery congressman from Ohio who, as was mentioned above, would author most of the first section of the Fourteenth Amendment, proposed in 1866.[34] Bingham's 1856 speech in the House of Representatives bristles with antipathy to the Kansas statute:

> Congress is to abide by this statute, which makes it a felony for a citizen to utter or publish in that Territory "any sentiment calculated to induce slaves to escape from the service of their masters." Hence it would be a felony there to utter the strong words of Algernon Sidney, "resistance to tyrants is obedience to God"; . . . a felony to read in the hearing of one of those fettered bondsmen the words of the Declaration, "All men are born free and equal, and endowed by their Creator with the inalienable rights of life and liberty"; . . . Before you hold this enactment to be law, burn our immortal Declaration and our free-written Constitution, fetter our free press, and finally penetrate the human soul and put out the light of understanding which the breath of the Almighty hath kindled.[35]

As in earlier and later cases of suppression of political speech, laws against antislavery speech and press were often explicitly framed or justified in terms of the bad tendencies the speech was thought to have.[36] Bingham's invocation of the Declaration showed the havoc that a theory justifying suppression of political speech because of "bad tendencies" could play with the protection of political speech. But Bingham underestimated the potential reach of laws suppressing antislavery expression because of its perceived bad tendencies. By 1860 the North Carolina Supreme Court would hold that the incendiary statements need not initially be heard by or directed to slaves or blacks to justify conviction of those circulating them. Suppression of distribution to whites was required because of the danger the statements would eventually reach blacks.[37]

The Kansas statute was much like those enacted in Southern states. Since Kansas was a federal territory, Bingham insisted, the limitations of the First Amendment clearly applied to it. Under the decision in *Barron* v. *City of Baltimore*, the guarantees of the Bill of Rights did not prevent the states from enacting such statutes. There was significant dissent from *Barron*, however. Indeed a significant minority of state supreme courts held that the rights in the Bill of Rights limited state legislation, *Barron* to the contrary notwithstanding.[38]

The Impending Crisis *and the Free Speech Issue in Congress*

HELPER AND HIS BOOK

Hinton Rowan Helper was born to a farm-owning family in Davie County, North Carolina, in 1829. Except for a foray into California and South America in an unsuccessful attempt to make his fortune, Helper lived in North Carolina until publication of *The Impending Crisis* in 1857.[39]

The book was an appeal for antislavery political action by non-slaveholders of the South. Helper supported forming an antislavery party, refusing to vote for slaveholders, socially ostracizing slaveholders, boycotting proslavery newspapers, and boycotting slave labor.[40] Helper's plan involved no compensation for slave owners; instead, they would be taxed to pay the costs of colonizing or resettling their former slaves. Helper sought to prove, with assistance from census data, that the South had become an economic disaster area because of slavery. He saw slavery as especially inimical to the interests of nonslaveholding whites. Much of the book consisted of charts, tables, and statistics from the census to demonstrate Southern backwardness, statements from men of the revolutionary generation to show the evils of slavery, and excerpts from the Virginia abolition debates of 1832.[41]

Helper was a self-described abolitionist (free soilers, he said, were just abolitionists in the tadpole stage),[42] and he faced the same dilemma other abolitionists faced. He sought to speak emancipation to the South and the South refused to listen. Abolition expression was silenced by laws and mobs.

The most sympathetic interpretation of the violence suggested by some of Helper's rhetoric is that it was contingent and designed to demonstrate Helper's willingness to meet violence with violence to protect access to the channels of political expression for supporters of emancipation. He repeatedly noted that free speech was denied to opponents of slavery in the South, and he protested mobbings and tar-and-featherings. "Free speech," Helper wrote, "is considered as treason against slavery: and when people dare neither speak nor print their thoughts, free thought itself is well nigh extinguished. . . . Give us fair-play," he demanded, "secure to us the right of discussion, the freedom of speech, and we will settle the difficulty at the ballot box, not on the battleground— by force of reason, not force of arms."[43] Critics of the book did not usually cite such statements. Instead, like the *Richmond Whig*, they quoted other parts of the book, including the following passage:

> So it seems that the total number of actual slave owners, including their entire crew of cringing lickspittles, against whom we have to contend,

is but three hundred and forty-seven thousand five hundred and twenty-five. Against this army for the defense and propagation of slavery, we think it will be an easy matter—independent of the negroes, who, in nine cases out of ten, would be delighted with an opportunity to cut their masters' throats . . . —to muster one at least three times as large, and far more respectable for its utter extinction. . . . We are determined to abolish slavery at all hazards—in defiance of all opposition, of whatever nature, which it is possible for the slavocrats to bring against us.[44]

These sentiments were followed by a plea for a peaceful and political resolution of differences,[45] but the *Whig* did not reprint those statements.

The sentiments quoted in the *Whig* would have enraged Southern supporters of slavery in the calmest of times. In fact, however, most of the controversy about *The Impending Crisis* occurred during a period of great alarm and excitement in the South—after John Brown's raid at Harper's Ferry, a raid that was designed to free slaves by force of arms.

Helper's book was first published in 1857, on the heels of Frémont's defeat. Many Northern opponents of slavery praised the book, which enjoyed significant but limited success. Opponents of slavery and Republican politicians hit upon the idea of publishing an abridgment, a "compendium" of the work and circulating it as a campaign document. This project was advertised and well underway before Brown's October 1859 raid. Over sixty Republican members of Congress had endorsed the project.[46]

Context for Congressional Discussion, 1859–60

On October 18, 1859, the *New York Herald* reported, "Negro Insurrection at Harper's Ferry. Strange and Exciting Intelligence. . . . [R]egular negro conspiracy." The *Herald*'s editor saw the event as a potent means of discrediting the Republican party. This, the Democratic spin doctors of the day announced, was the natural consequence of Republican doctrine. On the next day, together with more news of Harper's Ferry, the *Herald* reprinted a speech by Senator Seward of New York, a leading contender for the Republican nomination.[47] Seward had suggested an "irrepressible conflict" between slavery and freedom. "No reasoning mind," the *Herald* announced, "can fail to trace cause and effect between the bloody and brutal manifesto of William H. Seward . . . and the terrible scenes of violence" at Harper's Ferry. Later the *Herald* printed a list of Republican endorsers of Helper's book together with what it claimed were inflammatory passages from the book. "Text Book Revolution," screamed the headline; "Republican Congressmen Franking Revolutionary Appeals." Here was another "Black Republican" blueprint for Harper's Ferry. In December 1859 a grand jury in Wilson County, North Carolina, added a literal indictment to the political ones: it branded *The Impending Crisis* treasonous to North Carolina and called on New

York Republican Governor Edwin Morgan to deliver "to indictment and punishment" Republican endorsers of the book, including himself.[48] Of course, no trial followed the indictment because the defendants were beyond the power of the court.

THE DEMOCRATIC ATTACK

When Congress convened in December 1859, the Democrats attempted again and again to nail John Brown's raid to the Republican party. Democrats, particularly Southern congressmen, cast themselves in the role of prosecutor and judge. They cast Republicans as criminal defendants— accessories before the fact to the Harper's Ferry raid. Helper's book tended to cause violence; the violence of John Brown's raid followed publication of the Helper book; Republicans had endorsed the book; therefore the Republicans had endorsed violence. At a minimum, violence was the natural consequence of their doctrines. To support this charge Democrats offered the expert opinion of a veteran abolitionist agitator. John Brown's raid, they quoted Wendell Phillips as saying, was "the natural result of anti-slavery teaching. For one, I accept it; I expected it."[49] Although the debate on *The Impending Crisis* began in the House, it soon spilled over into the Senate.

John Sherman, Republican candidate for Speaker of the House of Representatives, like nearly half the Republican congressional delegation, had endorsed publication of an abridged version of Helper's book. A resolution proposed by Democratic representative John Clark of Missouri announced that no endorser of Helper's book was fit to be speaker.[50] After forty-four ballots Republicans fell just short of electing John Sherman as Speaker. Finally Sherman withdrew in favor of a compromise candidate.

Between ballots Democrats in the House (and also in the Senate) discussed slavery, Senator William Seward, and most of all *The Impending Crisis*. Democrats, by placing the worst possible construction on Helper's (or Seward's) words, sought to reap the benefits of linking that construction with the actions of their political opponents. Fire was the dominant metaphor. Senator Alfred Iverson of Georgia announced that Helper's book "inculcates incendiary sentiments." Republicans, said Representative Roger Pryor of Virginia, had applied "the spark, and then affect astonishment at the explosion." Congressman Clark of Missouri emphasized Helper's announcement that nonslaveholders should act peaceably if they could, forcibly if they must, to strike against slavery. "Do these [Republican] gentlemen expect that they can distribute incendiary books, give incendiary advice, advise rebellion . . . ?" "Such advice," he thundered later, "is treason . . . rebellion." Those knowingly giving it deserved a fate it would not be respectful to announce.[51]

Concern for such civilities did not last long. Helper's book, said Senator Iverson, returning to the attack, advised "our slaves to fire our dwellings and put their knives to our throats." We "ought to hang every man who has approved or indorsed it." Senator Seward shared the billing with Helper as an incendiary. Senator Jefferson Davis of Mississippi, after noting the law of accessories before the fact, cited Seward's irrepressible conflict speech: "That Senator made his speech before the event; he may not have contemplated the fruit it bore—if, indeed, it bore this." But, Davis said, when Senator Lyman Trumbull of Illinois defended the speech after the Harper's Ferry raid (arguing that it was being misconstrued), he was "far more guilty" than Seward. Representative Reuben Davis, also from Mississippi, later suggested that Seward "deserves, I think the gallows." John Brown, announced representative Thomas Hindman of Arkansas, "was the tool of Republicanism, doing its work; and now, that the work is done, Republican politicians cannot skulk the responsibility." The country would "gibbet them for it," and the hemp that strangled Brown would strangle the instigators.[52]

So it went, week after week, as Republicans repeatedly fell a few votes short of the majority required to make Sherman the Speaker. Congressmen came to the floor armed, and some Southerners contemplated coups and blood baths and wondered about the best way to launch secession. Slave-state Democrats announced that the election of a "Black Republican President" would be good cause for secession. One suggested that the Union could be preserved only if the essentially criminal Republican party disbanded.[53]

THE REPUBLICAN RESPONSE

Most Republicans in the House concluded that discussion of substantive issues was improper before the election of a Speaker. So they sat in silence. Sherman announced that he had no recollection of endorsing Helper's book and in any case had not read it. He had relied on the suggestion of a friend. He disavowed any action by the North to interfere with the domestic institutions of the South. A letter from one of the sponsors of the compendium project indicated that the compendium was supposed to delete offensive passages.[54] Republicans worried that the Democratic effort to link them to Harper's Ferry might work, and a few rushed to dissociate themselves from Helper's book.

A few conservative Republicans were the first to respond to the Democratic indictment. Several recanted their endorsements, pleading ignorance, and repudiated the book. Representative Lucius Q. C. Lamar of Mississippi suggested that the effort at repair came "too late for the victims of the Harper's Ferry tragedy." Republicans were guilty of the blood spilled on that occasion. Several House Republicans said that the Democrats had grossly misrepresented Helper's book and, after the eight-week speakership deadlock was broken, more did so.[55]

The early Republican reticence is curious. They were a few votes short of what they needed, and perhaps conciliation by conservative members and silence by the rest was intended to be reassuring. At any rate, the lack of a vigorous defense disgusted the *New York Tribune* and some party activists. William Herndon, Abraham Lincoln's law partner, suggested Republicans in Congress were "grinding off the flesh from their knee caps."[56] Eventually, after a speaker was finally selected, Republicans spoke powerfully and explicitly to the issues of the day. Then Republican after Republican roundly condemned the South for its repression of free speech. All in all, the session was remarkable for its lengthy discussions of slavery, the territories, natural rights, the views of the founding generation, the Declaration of Independence, secession, and free speech. The debate on free speech was a centerpiece of the session.

THE DEBATE ON FREE SPEECH: POLITICS AND THEORY

The 1859 congressional debate was conducted by politicians, not by jurists, legal theorists, or political philosophers. As a result, theories, to the extent they were present, were often implicit rather than explicit. Some Democrats suggested that Helper's book and Seward's "irrepressible conflict" speech had incited the Harper's Ferry raid and that the inciters were as guilty as the perpetrators. Still, they did not frame their analysis in terms of the limits on free speech. Nonetheless, they necessarily, though implicitly, embraced the theory that political speech with "bad tendencies" could be suppressed.[57] When they supported silencing abolitionists in Southern states, they were, at least, making implicit statements about the reach of guarantees for free expression under both state and federal constitutions.

The Democrats focused the debate on Helper and Seward, as examples of the evil tendency of Republican doctrine, a doctrine said to be capable of producing horrible acts of violence. There were curious aspects to the attack. The official justification for suppression of antislavery speech in the South was that it had the tendency to cause violence and insurrections by the slaves. The slaveholder was particularly vulnerable, Jefferson Davis noted, because "The negroes, as domestics, have access at all hours through the unlocked doors of their master's houses." Still, for important and "proper" political purposes, Southerners and Democrats were republishing the very statements thought to be too dangerous to tolerate. Democratic and Southern newspapers were spreading excerpts from Helper's "incendiary" book throughout the North and South, as they had done with Seward's speech.[58] Indeed, when Republicans complained that their doctrines were not permitted to circulate in the South, Southern members of Congress pointed to Southern papers that had reprinted Seward's "irrepressible conflict" speech.

Senator Benjamin F. Wade of Ohio, a strong foe of slavery, thought he saw a curious paradox. If incendiary matter was dangerous, asked Wade, was not the "most dangerous" of all that "which went to teach the people [of the South] that a great party, controlling all the free States, were sympathizing with raids upon the South; were ready to lend themselves to any uprising that might be got up there." Still, this "most dangerous of all" incendiary speech was carried into Southern states by the Democratic version of Republican ideas, without Republican antidote or explanation. This was so because Republican papers were not permitted to circulate there.[59]

A final irony was that the attack on Helper's book transformed it from a moderate success to a raging best-seller. One hundred and forty-two thousand copies of the book had been distributed by the fall of 1860. In December 1860 the *New York Tribune*, which was promoting the book, cheerfully reported that Southern "Fire-eaters" and Northern "Doughfaces" had by their persistent discussion of *The Impending Crisis* generated a circulation rapidly approaching that of *Uncle Tom's Cabin.*[60]

The opponents of slavery were quick to see a political agenda in the paradoxical Democratic approach to the problem. Early in the session Senator John P. Hale of New Hampshire suggested that Northern Democrats, decimated by their support of the Kansas-Nebraska Act, were weeping crocodile tears for the victims of the Harper's Ferry raid. Some Northern Democrats, he said, "whom the tender solicitude of their constituents had left in the retirement of private life, free from the corroding cares of public station . . . received the news of this outbreak in Virginia with a perfect yell of delight." They hoped to use it as "something they could catch hold of to ride into power." Abraham Lincoln, in his Cooper Institute speech, suggested Democrats were trying to use "John Brown, [the] Helper book, and the like [to] break up the Republican organization."[61] Political implications were never far from the center of the controversy. Southern nationalists used Helper, Seward, and Harper's Ferry to show why secession was imperative if a "Black Republican" were elected President; Northern Democrats used the same events as a stick with which to beat the "sectional" Republican party; and Republicans used the secessionist speeches to discredit Northern Democrats.

In the controversy over antislavery expression, Republicans thought they heard the jingle of gold coins. John Bingham suggested that a powerful slave-owning plutocracy sought to protect slavery in order to protect its economic interests. "These gentlemen apprehend," said Bingham, "that if free speech is tolerated and free labor protected by law, free labor might attain . . . such dignity . . . as would bring into disrepute the system of slave labor, and bring about if you please, gradual emancipation, thereby interfering with the profits of these gentlemen."[62] Abraham Lincoln warned of the "proneness of prosperity to breed tyrants."[63]

Although one complaint about Helper's book was that it would lead the slaves to violence, another concern was clearly present. Some Democrats warned of means "other than those which John Brown resorted to." Helper and Republicans, Democrats insisted, were trying to develop a local opposition among the nonslaveholding white majority of the South. Ultimately, Democratic Senator George Pugh of Ohio charged, they hoped "to strike down slavery [in the South] by changing state constitutions."[64] Indeed, Republicans did hope to use nonslaveholders as a great lever to achieve emancipation in the South. In particular, Republicans planned to use patronage, free speech, and free access to the mails to develop this local opposition after a Republican was elected President. John Sherman wrote Lydia Child suggesting that within two years of the election of a Republican president, there would be a Republican party in every Southern state. A Republican victory, Sherman insisted, would encourage emancipation by the Southern states themselves. In this sense the Southern fear of an attack on slavery in the South was well-founded. Republican postmasters would not be likely to censor Republican or antislavery literature. Democratic Senator William Gwin of California suggested that Southern states would not tolerate Republican postmasters.[65] (In those days, of course, postmasters were key political operatives and organizers, not just deliverers of mail.)

Some Republican complaints about suppression of speech in the South could be handled by constitutional doctrine that was consistent with *Barron*. Some Southern laws and actions explicitly discriminated against out-of-state "agitators" or publications. Those might be answered by a conventional reading of Article IV, section 2 that prohibited discrimination against out-of-staters. Democrats had long pointed out, however, that laws in the South typically did not discriminate against those from other states. Antislavery expression was equally forbidden for Southern opponents of slavery.[66] Sometimes Southerners suppressed supporters of the national Republican party or its candidates. Such actions might be dealt with not by invoking a broad view of free speech but by insisting that the republican nature of the national government meant that such behavior was unconstitutional.[67] Such limited responses might have been the main ones made, but they were not.

Because Republicans thought free speech on the subject of slavery in the South was essential to the development of a Republican party there, Republicans did not embrace a view of free speech that limited it to "legitimate" subjects of national legislation. Slavery in the states, most Republicans conceded, was not such a subject.[68] Because they insisted on the right of people in the South to discuss slavery, they did not embrace the view that the privileges of American citizens were limited to protection of national political speech or to protection of out-of-staters against discrimination. So the Republican demand for free speech on slavery was a seamless fabric, moving without any marked transition from complaints about suppression of free speech on national topics and complaints about suppression of speech of Northerners to complaints about the suppression of antislavery expression by Southerners on both state and national topics. Nor was freedom of expression aimed at slavery limited to political speech, narrowly defined; it included antislavery religious expression by ministers who discussed the theological aspects of slavery and antislavery artistic expression, like the best seller *Uncle Tom's Cabin.* Similarly, appeals to the privileges and immunities of citizens of the United States, which Republicans thought were protected by Article IV, often moved seamlessly from complaints about discrimination against citizens from other states to complaints about violation of the "absolute" rights of American citizens to free speech.[69]

THE REPUBLICAN DEMANDS FOR FREE SPEECH

From the beginning, Republicans had made demands for free speech a centerpiece of their political program. Their campaign slogan in 1856 had been "Free Speech, Free Press, Free Men, Free Labor, Free Territory, and Frémont."[70] When Republicans embraced "free speech" in the context of the struggle over slavery, that decision also implied ideas about the role and limits of free speech. Implicitly, and sometimes explicitly, most who spoke to the issue repudiated the bad-tendency test by appealing instead to a core area of speech beyond government's power to suppress.[71]

Early in the 1859 congressional session, Democratic Senator Albert Brown of Mississippi pointed out that Republican Senator Henry Wilson of Massachusetts had attended an antislavery meeting. The sponsors of the meeting passed a resolution declaring the right and duty of slaves to resist their masters and of Northerners to incite them to resistance. Brown asked if Wilson had spoken against the resolution. Wilson explained that he had spoken a few days before to a large meeting where he had condemned John Brown's raid. He had been invited to the second meeting to hear from the other side, and he had attended.[72]

Senator Brown's question to Senator Wilson opened a running discussion of free speech, North and South. The debate took place in the context of a resolution passed by a meeting in Massachusetts that was a clear call to resistance by slaves. It was the very sort of incitement the Democrats were trying, with the use of less promising material, to pin on the Republicans. "Senators should remember," Wilson said, "that the right to hold meetings and to utter opinions upon all matters of public concern is an acknowledged right in my section. . . . I wish the people of other sections of the country would thus cherish the sacred right of free discussion." Senator Fessenden, later chairman of the Joint Committee on Reconstruction in the 39th Congress (the committee that proposed the Fourteenth Amendment), made much the same point. He refuted the claim that the resolution urging resistance by slaves was proof that public opinion in the North approved the Brown raid. "[W]e allow everybody to hold a public meeting that wants one, and he may say what he pleases. . . . We are not in the habit of interfering with the expression of opinion by anybody; persons may say what they like."

That freedom of speech was denied to opponents of slavery in the South struck Republicans as an outrage against the principles of liberty. Senator Trumbull discussed Republican support for a ban on slavery in the territories and compared it to the chameleonlike Democratic approach to the issue. "We do not preach popular sovereignty in the North, and scout it as a humbug in the South," Trumbull announced. "You do not preach it in the South at all," interjected Senator Pugh, Democrat of Ohio. Trumbull retorted that "the men who do not allow our principles to be proclaimed in the South talk about sectionalism. A sectionalism, so pure . . . that it will not tolerate the exposition of the principles of its opponents at all where it is in power, talks to the other party about sectionalism!"

In the Lincoln-Douglas debates, Lincoln made a similar point. Douglas argued that the Republicans were a sectional party because they could not proclaim their doctrines in the South. Lincoln responded that the exclusion of Republicans from the South was the result of despotism; Douglas also could not go to czarist Russia to proclaim democracy and denounce monarchy.[73] Senator Wilson protested that there was not a Republican Senator who could send his frank into Southern states without subjecting "his letter to be opened, examined, and destroyed." Southern papers and some Southern legislatures had offered rewards, he noted, for the heads of opponents of slavery, including some Republican members of Congress.[74]

Senator Wilson engaged in a lengthy dialogue with Southern senators on free speech in the slave states. He was not discussing, Wilson insisted, the merits of inciting slaves to rebellion. Southerners held such men "amenable to their laws." But, said Wilson, "throughout a large portion of the South," men who entertain opinions on slavery like those of Washington, Jefferson, and Patrick Henry, "cannot reside, . . . cannot exist, in safety." Senator Brown of Georgia said that Wilson could go into his state and avow "any sentiments which he has a right to entertain." He would not, however, be permitted to urge Brown's slaves to cut Brown's throat. Wilson insisted that was not the issue. He noted that Professor Hedrick had been driven from North Carolina because he supported Frémont and that John Underwood was compelled to leave Virginia because he attended the Republican national convention of 1856. Senator Brown replied that support for Frémont was, indeed, a far different matter:

[T]here was a great deal more involved in the . . . election of Mr. Frémont . . . beyond the mere avowal of that sentiment [that Kansas should be a free state]. . . . I would not myself tolerate any man who would go to my State and avow his preference for the election of Mr. Seward upon the program he laid down in his Rochester speech.

Seward would not be permitted to teach his irrepressible conflict doctrine "because our safety, . . . our peace, the peace of our hearths, depends upon the repression of such doctrines with us."[75]

Wilson said that Brown had conceded his point. "Mr. Stanard was driven from Norfolk for simply attempting to vote for Frémont. . . . In the [South], where we have an inbred constitutional right to advocate these doctrines, it is confessed that we will not be permitted to do it." "Every American citizen," Wilson later insisted, had a right "to advocate exclusion of slavery from the Territories. . . . Slavery will not tolerate free speech and a free press." Wilson also defended Helper's book. It contained "the most valuable information" together with a few phrases those who had recommended it would disavow.

Earlier in his remarks Wilson had made a ringing defense of free speech: "[I]n Massachusetts we have absolute freedom of speech and of the press. We deal with all public questions, all social questions, all questions that concern the human race. We have nothing there that prevents the fullest and boldest discussion." The Senator from Georgia could go there and advocate slavery, the dissolution of the Union, or re-opening the slave trade, and he would be "listened to in peace" and "received kindly." Wilson knew that this was hard for senators to understand who came from a section where "freedom of speech on some political, moral, and social subjects is not tolerated."

Most Republicans denied that Helper's book was incendiary. After the controversy erupted over Helper's book, Senator Wade said he had studied it in detail. By rhetorical questions he suggested that nothing in the book was "dangerous to the people of any section." It contained nothing that "could not safely be entrusted to the hands of any freeman." It was simply composed of arguments addressed by a nonslaveholder to his fellow non-slaveholders. "Unless such arguments are unlawful there, I see nothing in the book but what is just, right, and proper for the consideration of all men who take an interest in these matters." Wade clearly thought the book *should* be protected expression:

> [H]as it come to this, in free America, that there must be a censorship of the press instituted; that a man cannot give currency to a book containing arguments that he thinks essentially affect the rights of whole classes of the free population of this nation? I hope not, and I believe not.[76]

Senator Seward also made a defense of the principle of free speech, and he mixed references to why national action to suppress speech was inappropriate with a more general statement of principle. Southerners had complained, he said, that Republicans

> sanction too unreservedly books designed to advocate emancipation. But surely you can hardly expect the Federal Government or the political parties of the nation to maintain a censorship of the press or of debate. The theory of our system is, that error of opinion may in all cases safely be tolerated where reason is left free to combat it.[77]

According to Congressman Sidney Edgerton of Ohio, Republicans were being denounced as traitors for adopting the antislavery opinions of Jefferson, Washington, Madison, and Henry. There had been a complete suppression of free speech in the South. "For years," he said,

> in most of the slaveholding states, the most sacred provisions of the Constitution have been wantonly and persistently violated. Where is the liberty of speech and of the press in the slaveholding states? Can a northern man . . . print and speak his opinions? Not if he believes in the Declaration of Independence.

Nor could preachers "discuss the moral bearings of slavery."[78]

Threats against opponents of slavery and arrests for selling Helper's book illustrated the denial of free speech and press. Southerners had said Reverend Beecher would be hung if he came South. "And the gentleman from South Carolina informed the House that . . . they had arrested a man for selling Helper's book" and had said they would hang him. Edgerton said he had studied Helper's book. It did not, as charged, advise "insurrection, treason, servile war, arson, and murder." Those who made such charges had "never read the book. And yet to sell this harmless book in a slave State is considered a crime. Where is your constitutional liberty?" The "liberty of South Carolina" was equivalent to the "despotism of Austria." "Gentlemen of the South," Edgerton exclaimed, "the North demands of you the observance of constitutional obligations. She demands that her citizens be protected by your laws in the enjoyment of their constitutional rights. She demands the freedom of speech and of the press; and if your peculiar institution cannot stand before them, let it go down."

Representative Henry Waldron of Michigan reached similar conclusions:

> This slave Democracy tramples [the Constitution] under foot. We have sacred guarantees in that instrument in behalf of free speech, free thought, and a free press, and yet today Democratic postmasters rifle mails and violate the sanctity of private correspondence. Today a system of espionage prevails which would disgrace the despotism and darkness of the middle ages. The newspaper which refuses to recount the

blessings and sing the praises of slavery is committed to the flames. The press that refuses to vilify the memory of the fathers is taken by a ruthless mob and engulfed beneath the waters. The personal safety of the traveler depends not on his deeds, but upon his opinions. And these outrages are daily committed under the rule of the Democracy, because that party has taken under its guardian care an institution which can only exist and prosper at the sacrifice and expense of the constitutional rights of the citizen. Where slavery is there can be no free speech, no free thought, no free press, no regard for constitutions, no deference to courts.[79]

Other Republican members of Congress also complained that slavery caused suppression of free speech and press—by actions of state, federal, or territorial governments, and by mob action. They expressed concern for free speech directed to state as well as national issues. John Bingham said, "[T]oday, it would cost a man his life to rise deliberately in the Legislature of Virginia and announce a sentiment in favor of emancipation, such as [were] announced by some of her most distinguished sons in the memorable debate of 1832."[80]

One Republican objection to permitting slavery in the territories was that slavery inevitably would bring its despotic practices with it. Slaveholders would pass territorial laws that denied freedom of speech and press. "They claim the right to seal every man's lips, and stop every man's mouth, on questions of great national interest," complained Congressman Cydnor Tompkins of Ohio. They would "condemn as a felon the man who dares proclaim the precepts of our holy religion." They would "strip naked and cut into gashes the back of the man who utters opinions" that did not square with those of the slaveholders.[81]

While Republicans protested the slave states' system of censorship in the interests of slavery and warned that it would inevitably spread to all slave territories, some Democrats advocated extending the suppression of antislavery sentiments to the free states. Representatives Daniel Sickles of New York and Muscoe Garnett of Virginia suggested that Governor Marcy of New York had been correct in 1836 when he advocated legislation to limit abolitionist expression designed to reach the South. Sickles implied that such expression should have been "put down" by law because it "lead[s] to bad consequences." Now that the North was learning that men in their states planned to carry "discord, invasion, and danger" to the South, Sickles said, the North was going to recur to the "wise and patriotic recommendation of Governor Marcy."[82] In February and March of 1860 Abraham Lincoln warned that the "slave power," along with other demands, insisted that "Senator Douglas's new sedition law must be enacted and enforced, suppressing all declarations that slavery is wrong, whether made in politics, in presses, in pulpits, or in private."[83]

In June 1860, after Lincoln's nomination, the Senate considered a series of resolutions on slavery offered by Jefferson Davis of Mississippi, the future president of the Confederate States of America. One resolution said that slavery, "as it exists in fifteen states of this Union, composes an important portion of their domestic institutions." Slavery, the resolution continued, was recognized by the Constitution as "constituting an important element in apportionment of powers among the states." Nothing could justify "open or covert attacks [on slavery] with a view to its overthrow." Such attacks, the resolution declared, were a "breach of faith" and a violation of the national "compact."[84] Senator James Harlan of Iowa proposed a free-speech amendment to the resolution:

> But free discussion of the morality and expediency of slavery should never be interfered with by the laws of any State, or of the United States; and the freedom of speech and of the press, on this and every other subject of domestic and national policy, should be maintained inviolate in all the States.

The Senate defeated the amendment on a straight party vote, with every Republican on the floor voting for it. The resolution is strong evidence that Republicans were calling for free speech on all issues of policy—local as well as national.

The word *domestic* in the resolution meant "local to the states." Slavery, according to Jefferson Davis's resolution, was an important part of the "domestic" institutions of fifteen states. Republicans sought to amend the resolution by calling for free speech on all issues of policy, "domestic" as well as national. The word *domestic* here takes its meaning from the use of the same word earlier in the resolution to refer to the "domestic" institutions of fifteen states. The meaning of the word *domestic* in the free speech resolution is also illuminated by the larger context in which it was used, the context of uproar over a book advocating political action in the Southern states themselves to end slavery.

Democrats in the Senate rejected the free-speech amendment. The party of James Madison rejected a demand for free speech on all political issues, including slavery. The institution of slavery reshaped ideas of liberty to suit its needs.

On April 5, 1860, Owen Lovejoy bitterly condemned slavery. Lovejoy was a congressman from Illinois, a supporter of Lincoln, an intense critic of slavery, an outspoken proponent of assisting fugitive slaves escaping from bondage, and the brother of Elijah Lovejoy, the antislavery newspaper editor who had been killed defending his press from a proslavery mob. Denouncing slaveholding as "the sum of all villainy," he came close to causing a riot on the floor of the House. On the issue of free speech, however, Lovejoy's position was close to that of most Republicans who spoke on the issue. He supported, he said, Helper's object: organizing a party in the slave states against slavery. Those objecting to the book were insisting that "an American citizen, address[ing] himself to his fellow-citizens, in a peaceful way, through the press . . . must be hanged."

Like John Bingham, Lovejoy invoked the privileges and immunities of citizens of the United States as protecting basic rights, including free speech and press: "I do claim the right of discussing this question of slavery anywhere, on any square foot of American soil over which the stars and stripes float, to which the privileges and immunities of the Constitution extend." "[T]hat Constitution, which guaranties to me free speech" protected his right to criticize slavery. Just as the invocation of Roman citizenship protected ancient Romans, so American citizenship should protect Americans in their rights. "That is my response to the question of why I recommended circulation of the Helper book." Lovejoy claimed "the privilege of going anywhere . . . as a free citizen, unmolested, and of uttering, in an orderly and legal way, any sentiment that I choose to utter." Among his other complaints Lovejoy protested that Southern states "imprison or exile preachers of the Gospel."[85]

Lovejoy's speech ended on a somber note. Representative Elbert Martin of Virginia announced, "And if you come among us we will do with you as we did with John Brown—hang you up as high as Haman." "I have no doubt of it," replied Lovejoy.[86]

The Impending Crisis in North Carolina: The Trial of Reverend Daniel Worth

WORTH'S ARREST AND NORTH CAROLINA'S REACTION

On the day that Congressman Lovejoy spoke and complained about Southern states that "imprison or exile preachers of the Gospel,"[87] the *New York Times* reported that Reverend Daniel Worth, Wesleyan Minister, was convicted in North Carolina of circulating Helper's book. He was sentenced to a year in prison.[88] Worth's arrests in two counties for circulating the Helper book had been reported earlier in the antislavery press. The *National Era* had reported it wearily on January 12, 1860: "We should literally have no room for anything else," the paper reported, "if we were to publish all the details of whippings, tar-and-featherings, and hangings, for the utterance of Anti-Slavery opinions in the South." It expected that Worth would be convicted and suffer "fine, imprisonment, and whipping."[89]

Worth had been born in 1795 in Guilford County, North Carolina, to a devout Quaker family. He and his family migrated to Indiana in 1822, as many southern Quakers had done. Worth was active in the Indiana anti-slavery society in the 1840s and later supported the Republican party.

In 1857 Worth, by this time a Wesleyan minister, returned to Guilford County, North Carolina, where he began to preach his antislavery ver-

sion of the gospel. The American Missionary Association, a strongly antislavery organization, supplied him with financial support and fifty copies of Helper's book. Worth sold all fifty copies of Helper's book and
ordered more, and he secured subscriptions for the *New York Tribune*,
the same antislavery newspaper that was seized from the mail and burned
in Virginia in 1859.[90]

Worth was aware that his work was dangerous. "I can preach," he
reported to his nephew with satisfaction, "and have done it, as strong
and direct against slavery as ever you heard me in the north, and I believe that there is not another man that could." He attributed his success
to his age, Southern birth, and his influential family connections.[91]

After the Harper's Ferry raid, pressure to suppress Worth increased.
On November 26, 1859, the *North Carolina Presbyterian* warned that "so-
ciety must be protected against cut-throats and assassins" and demanded
that an unnamed fanatic abolitionist preacher be removed from the state.
The North Carolina *Raleigh Weekly Standard* asked for the name: was he
the fanatic Daniel Worth, the minister who had even been referred to in
Helper's book as a Southern minister preaching against slavery? On
December 17, 1859, the *North Carolina Presbyterian* obligingly supplied
Worth's name. "[I]t is notorious," the paper wrote, "that [Daniel Worth]
has been inculcating, publicly and privately, his incendiary doctrines in
Randolph and Guilford counties, and the time has come when he should
be compelled to abandon this work." On December 10, 1859, the Council of State passed a resolution saying postmasters who delivered incendiary books or newspapers to the addressee should be prosecuted as
circulators of the item. Another resolution enjoined all public officers
to subject out-of-state merchants, book dealers, tract distributors, and
lecturers to "the strictest scrutiny."[92]

On December 21, 1859, Worth wrote to the American Missionary
Association forecasting "times of trial." "Since the unfortunate affair at
Harper's Ferry, the county is in a tremendous ferment. Threatenings
reach me from various quarters."[93] The North Carolina papers were filled
with denunciations of Helper's book and of the sixty-eight Republican
congressmen who endorsed it. The *Raleigh Register* reprinted excerpts
from *The Impending Crisis* to show the enormity of the offense. It quoted
a passage in which Helper demanded

> as the only true means of attaining to a position worthy of sovereign
> States . . . an energetic, intelligent, enterprising, virtuous, and unshack-
> led population, an untrammelled press, and the freedom of speech.
> For ourselves, as white people, and for the negroes and other persons
> of whatever color or condition, we demand all the rights, interests and
> prerogatives that are guaranteed to corresponding classes of mankind
> in the North.[94]

By Christmas Daniel Worth was under arrest.

The North Carolina press reported Worth's arrest and preliminary hearing. Raleigh and Greensboro papers of all political persuasions were unanimous in their condemnation of Worth.[95] In the *Greensboro Patriot's* account of the preliminary hearing, the editor said he had not read Helper's book, "but from extracts which were read on the trial" it was "infamous" and should "consign to infamy" all who circulated it. "[T]hey will most assuredly receive condign punishment."[96] To the extent that Helper's book was a political issue, each party used it in an attempt to tar the other. Democrats charged that Whig Congressman John Gilmer had been mailed a copy by Helper. Gilmer denied knowing possession. Gilmer's supporters then claimed that Governor Ellis had received a copy of the book. Ellis responded that he had thrown the first copy he received out the window, and when a second copy of the book was sent to him, he used its incendiary pages to light his pipe.[97]

The *Raleigh Standard* noted efforts to circulate Helper's book and called for increased vigilance. "We would," it sternly lectured, "again remind Postmasters of their duties in this respect. Let every copy of Helper's book, and every copy of the New York Tribune, and every document franked by Seward, Wilson, Burlingame, John Sherman, and other abolitionists which may come to their offices, *be committed to the flames.*"[98]

Politicians, judges, and ordinary citizens united in their effort to suppress Worth and his associates. John T. Harriss, a farm laborer in Randolph county, wrote Governor Ellis "a fiew lines concerning Daniel Worth he has bin circulating a seditious Book . . . by the title of Helpers impending Crisis one Jacob Briles, senr has one [as did Jacob, junior] . . . and it can bea proven that they got them of this same Daniel Worth." The governor promptly wrote an irate letter to Judge Dick, a superior court judge. "The local magistrates," the governor protested, "have been, up to this time wholly remiss in suppressing the most flagrant violations of Law—the circulation of incendiary books & papers, and the use of language calculated to incite slaves to insurrection." Upon receiving Harriss's letter from the governor, Judge Dick wrote the governor to say that he "forthwith issued a warrant for Jacob Bryles [Briles] senr," instructing the sheriff "to search for books." The judge assured the governor that all that properly could be done was being done, "and I fear that more will be done than ought to be done." Had Worth been released on bail, the judge said, he would have been hung. No one, the judge promised, would escape against whom evidence could be obtained.[99] Following this promise, the press reported the arrest of a number of others suspected of involvement with the Helper book.[100]

At least one North Carolinian did criticize the prosecutions, but he wrote from the safety of his exile in New York City. Benjamin Hedrick, the deposed and exiled chemistry professor, wrote to his old friend Thomas Ruffin, formerly chief justice of North Carolina. He asked Ruffin to use his influence to "arrest the terrorism and fanaticism which now so much disturbs the South. . . . Some of the men recently arrested are among the best men in the state." Their persecution could only be stopped by intervention of upright citizens. Hedrick continued:

> In order that you may have an opportunity to know also what offense is laid to some of these men I send you a copy of Helper's book. You will find not a word in it is addressed to either free or slave negroes, That [sic] most of the sentiments that are current in the state and attributed to this book, are the fabrications of the New York Herald. Please examine the book and see if there is any thing in it that one free-man may not properly address to any other. For myself I am free to admit that I do not approve of every proposition advocated in the book, nor with the manner in which some good propositions are maintained. But unless we tolerate difference of opinion we must have despotism at once.

Hedrick also sent Ruffin a copy of a searing indictment of slavery published in Greensboro in 1830. It argued that slaves were entitled to state constitutional protections of liberty and that they were the victims of kidnapping. Hedrick also alluded to an 1832 speech by Judge William Gaston of the North Carolina Supreme Court to show "It was not then treason to discuss slavery, and to print opinions adverse to the system." Hedrick later engaged counsel for Worth and raised money for his defense.[101]

Meanwhile, Judge Ruffin received correspondence about Worth from Reverend George McNeil, the editor who had "exposed" Worth. McNeil passed on a letter from Jonathan Worth, Daniel's influential cousin. "In addition to the horror of having a minister of the Gospel, aged 68 years [sic] whipped," Jonathan Worth warned, "[t]he abolitionists at home and abroad will turn it to account." Jonathan Worth also complained about the statute under which Worth had been convicted:

> Judge Shepherd held at Montgomery last week, that an article in the religious creed of a Society declaring that Slavery is inconsistent with Christian religion, if printed and circulated among its members, would make the person circulating it indictable under this Statute, because all religious societies admit slaves as members and such an article would have an "evident tendency to make them dissatisfied with their social condition." This reasoning seems to be clear. It follows that all Quakers are indictable under this Statute and liable to ignominious punishment. . . . Its execution, according to this interpretation would produce general horror.

Jonathan Worth would have limited the statute to those intending to "produce dissatisfaction among slaves" and said his cousin, except for his age and otherwise "exemplary character," was a fit case for the execution of the statute. All things considered, he hoped the whipping would be omitted and Daniel Worth would be permitted to leave the state.[102]

The Trials of Daniel Worth

Daniel Worth was charged with violating section 16 of chapter 34 of the North Carolina statutes, passed originally in the 1830s and revised in 1854. Section 16 made it a crime to circulate "any written or printed pamphlet or paper . . . the evident tendency whereof is to cause slaves to become discontented with the bondage in which they are held . . . and free negroes to be dissatisfied with their social condition." For the first offense persons violating the statute were to be whipped, put in the pillory, and imprisoned for not less than a year. For the second offense the punishment was death.[103]

At his preliminary hearing Worth admitted selling Helper's book but denied that his object was to stir up insurrection. His was a mission of peace. Worth was bound over for trial in Superior Court. He remained incarcerated pending trial. Meanwhile, an additional shipment of Helper's book was seized and publicly burned.[104]

At Worth's first trial, in Randolph County, the prosecutor read the jury the indictment, containing lengthy extracts from *The Impending Crisis*. The Guilford indictment (which is probably similar) quoted Helper's argument that slavery was a nuisance and nonslaveholders were concerned with it just as they would be in the case of mad dogs; that slavery was worse than stealing; and that slave and free-negro victims of crimes were not permitted to testify against white oppressors. The indictment also quoted the passage in which Helper compared, in the event of violent confrontation, the number of slaveholders who would be arrayed against nonslaveholders—those totals being independent of the slaves who would often be "delighted with an opportunity to cut their masters throats." Unlike the *New York Herald*, the indictment quoted the rest of the passage: a hope and belief that the matter would be adjusted without violence; a desire for peace, not war; and finally Helper's plea to give us "freedom of speech, and we will settle this difficulty at the [ballot] box, not on the battleground by force." Though the indictment went on for some eighteen pages, the passages referred to are representative. Jury selection was difficult because so many potential jurors were already convinced of Worth's guilt.[105]

At trial the state proved that Worth sold the book. Jacob Briles, uncovered as a result of the letter from the farm laborer to Governor Ellis, became a witness for the state and testified against Worth. Counsel stipulated that the book need not be read. Worth offered no evidence. Unfortunately, the local newspaper did not report the "able and sometimes truly eloquent" arguments on both sides. The court charged the jury that a book was within the reach of the statute even though the statute specifically listed only papers and pamphlets. Whether the book was incendiary was left to the jury to determine. The jury retired at 11 P.M. and returned a guilty verdict at 4 A.M. the next morning. Judge Bailey sentenced Worth to a year in prison and excused the whipping.[106]

The Guilford trial was a repeat performance with the same lawyers and judge, but this time the jury convicted in fifteen minutes.[107] Worth appealed, his bond was reduced, and he quietly slipped out of North Carolina. The authorities apparently wanted to avoid not only the provocative spectacle of an elderly minister of the gospel placed in the pillory and whipped—an outcome the judge had apparently foreclosed— but also wanted to avoid the spectacle of Worth's imprisonment. Worth went on a speaking tour of the North to raise the funds necessary to reimburse his bondsmen. If he could not raise the funds and if he lost his appeal, he said he would return to be imprisoned.

In a speech in New York, Worth insisted that Helper's book was not "addressed to the colored people" and that he had never given the book to them. Worth said he had defended himself at the preliminary hearing, making what "they said was a regular abolitionist harangue." "I quoted from Mr. Helper's book the language of Thomas Jefferson" to the effect that in a contest between slave and master, God would be on the side of the slave. Worth reported that his friend Hinton Helper had contributed fifty dollars to his bail fund.[108]

The North Carolina Supreme Court affirmed Worth's conviction. It was not necessary to prove, the supreme court held, that the book was delivered to slaves or free Negroes or was read in their presence. "The circulation, within the State, is alike prohibited, whether it be amongst whites or blacks," Justice Charles Manly wrote. "The Legislature seems to have assumed, that if a circulation, within the State, was once established, that its corrupting influence would inevitably reach the black." Guilt turned on intent. A copy could be delivered by one person to another without incurring guilt, when it was delivered to gratify curiosity, "both parties to the act being equally opposed to the design." With this observation, perhaps, Manly had solved the paradox of why it was lawful for North Carolina papers to publish extracts from Helper's book but criminal for the book's proponents to circulate it. Finally, Manly had no problem finding the work inflammatory. Every passage of it, "in the most inflamatory [sic] words," declared that "the slave ought to be discontented with his condition, and the master deposed from his, and that the change should be effected, even at the cost of blood." Worth's counsel seems not explicitly to have raised, nor did the court explicitly consider, claims that the statute violated free press or free speech. The North Carolina Constitution had no explicit protection for free speech, but it did provide that "the freedom of the Press is one of the great bulwarks of liberty, and therefore ought never to be restrained."[109]

In 1860 the North Carolina legislature amended the incendiary document statute. Worth's crime, circulating an "incendiary" book on the subject of slavery, was henceforth punishable by death for the first offense.[110]

A New Birth Of Freedom

THE IMPENDING CRISIS AND THE BILL OF RIGHTS

James McPherson has suggested that the Civil War was a second American Revolution.[111] Democrats repeatedly insisted that the Republicans were a revolutionary party. Indeed one of the characteristics of the Helper book that critics found outrageous was his suggestion that slavery was the unfinished business of the first American Revolution. In 1860 Senator James Chestnut, Jr., of South Carolina said the Republican party was governed by the Red Republican principles of France, though it had "changed its complexion" and "blacked its face." The fundamental fallacy of the Republican party was that it held "that the Declaration of Independence is the basis of the Constitution." When they considered the power and duties of the Government with reference to the domestic affairs of the states, Republicans, Chestnut said, "string their sophistical arguments" on the "abstract opinions" of the Declaration. "This fatal error arises . . . out of the untenable postulate that all men, under all governments, are naturally and equally entitled to liberty, without reference to the well-being of society or to their own fitness to enjoy and preserve it."[112]

In response to charges like those of Chestnut, Republicans insisted they were the true conservatives, conserving the heritage of liberty espoused by the Declaration of Independence and the leaders of the American Revolution. In 1860 Republicans repeatedly invoked the anti-slavery expressions of the Revolutionary fathers. They cited antislavery statements of Thomas Jefferson, James Madison, and George Washington and early antislavery resolutions from Georgia and other colonies. And they cited Luther Martin, delegate from Maryland to the Constitutional Convention, again and again: slavery was incompatible with republicanism and had the tendency to destroy those principles on which it was supported.[113]

Southern secession was a preemptive counterrevolution. As Southerners saw it, Republicans would not be content with banning slavery from the territories. Republicans were insisting generally, with Lincoln, that Americans should never forget that slavery was wrong everywhere. They hoped that the election of a Republican president and the use of patronage would establish an antislavery party in the Southern states. That party would then abolish slavery on a state-by-state basis. Senator Seward suggested that if free speech were restored in the South, the Republicans promptly would have as many supporters there as the Democrats did in the North. Democrats insisted that election of a Republican president could never be accepted by all the states. Southern states would never tolerate Republican officeholders and postmasters who could not be expected to eliminate antislavery publications from the mails.[114]

Secession did inaugurate the second American Revolution. Within five short years slavery had been abolished and Republicans had proposed an amendment to make blacks citizens and to secure civil liberty for all American citizens. The basis of their philosophy was, as Senator Chestnut suggested, the idea of the Declaration of Independence that government was established to secure individual rights. Republicans were no longer willing to allow local denials of basic rights. The need to protect citizens against state denials of their rights was reiterated time and again by the Republicans in the congresses that proposed the Thirteenth and Fourteenth Amendments. They insisted on giving all citizens the "shield" of "all the guarantees of the Constitution."[115] In the same debates Republicans recurred again and again to denials of civil liberty that had characterized the pre-Civil War years. The main exhibits in their litany of horrors were state denials of freedom of speech, press, and religion. The controversy surrounding the Helper book and the trial of Daniel Worth help us understand, from a distance of many years, what Republicans were talking about.

During debates on abolition, James Wilson, chairman of the Judiciary Committee in the 38th and 39th Congresses, cited the privileges and immunities clause of Article IV, section 2 to illustrate slavery's denial of constitutional rights. "Freedom of religious opinion, freedom of speech and press, and the right of assemblage for the purpose of petition belong to every American citizen, high or low, rich or poor, wherever he may be within the jurisdiction of the United States. With these rights no State may interfere." Still, slavery had suppressed free exercise of religion for those who took the golden rule as a rule for conduct. It had destroyed free speech and press. "The press has been padlocked, and men's lips have been sealed." Many other Republicans also recalled slavery's denials of free speech.[116]

In 1866, as Republicans saw it, a new spirit of recalcitrance was evident in the South. Andrew Johnson wanted immediate readmission of the Southern states to Congress, but Congress balked. Southern states passed Black Codes that discriminated against blacks' right to own property, to testify, and to contract; the states also denied blacks fundamental rights referred to in the Bill of Rights. Congressmen complained that constitutional rights of Unionists and blacks were once again being violated. Southerners were once again suppressing free speech and other constitutional rights.[117]

In this situation Congressman John Bingham insisted that a constitutional amendment was needed to give Congress the power to enforce all the "guaranties of the Constitution." In 1859 some Republican members of Congress insisted that the protection of the citizen's liberty depended on the action of his state and was beyond the power of the federal government. By 1866, before ratification of the Fourteenth Amendment, some leading Republicans were insisting that Congress could correct state legislation violating citizens' rights through its power to enforce the Bill of Rights. Bingham, to the contrary, insisted a constitutional amendment was necessary for that purpose. In 1866 no Republican in Congress said it was desirable to allow a state the "right" to deny individual rights. In 1866 Republicans explicitly provided that no state shall "abridge the privileges or immunities of citizens of the United States."[118]

As we have seen, Madison himself had described the freedom of the press and the rights of conscience as the "choicest *privileges* of the people" and again as "invaluable *privileges*,"[119] and to secure them he advocated federal as well as state constitutional guarantees. John Bingham repeatedly indicated that his purpose was to draft a constitutional amendment to enforce all the "guarantees of the Constitution" and to require the states to obey them. The Fourteenth Amendment did not purport to create new rights but, in the fashion of state and federal bills of rights, to secure those rights assumed to belong to the citizen from invasion by the states. The 1789 Congressional Resolution submitting to the states the *original* proposal for a Bill of Rights similarly described the Bill not as creating rights but as "further declaratory and restrictive clauses."[120]

Justice Black championed John Bingham as the father of incorporation and described Bingham as the James Madison of the Fourteenth Amendment.[121] Some scholars have answered Black's comparison of Bingham with Madison with ad hominem attacks on Bingham, with suggestions that a plan to require states to obey the Bill of Rights heralded the destruction of federalism, and with incredulity.[122] Still, Bingham did follow Madison's plan of a double security for basic constitutional rights, including those in the Bill of Rights. He used the word *privileges* to describe constitutional rights, including those in the Bill of Rights. That was one of the two words Madison used to describe such rights in Congress in 1789.

Like Madison, Bingham was concerned with protecting minorities against the tyranny of the majority. Yet he went further than Madison and included other constitutional privileges as well, like the protection against cruel and unusual punishment and against unreasonable searches and seizures. Perhaps experience with statutes that allowed whipping ministers who advocated an antislavery gospel and experience with searches of the mail and of travelers for incendiary documents led him to conclude that double security for these privileges was also required. Perhaps in 1866, when Bingham said that section 1 of the Fourteenth Amendment was needed to prevent states from inflicting cruel or unusual punishments,[123] he thought of the whip and the pillory, the punishments provided for outspoken opponents of slavery. There is much to be said for Justice Black's comparison of John Bingham to James Madison.

If the Civil War was the second American Revolution, the Thirteenth and Fourteenth Amendments gave birth to a transformed Constitution and Bill of Rights. The most revolutionary aspect of the change was the attempted transformation of the African American population from slavery (with badges of slavery for free blacks) to citizenship and equal civil rights. In another sense the change was less than revolutionary. It simply amended the Constitution to reflect the principles of the Declaration.

Compared to changes in the legal status of the race, proposed changes in the means of protecting basic liberties were far less revolutionary. The basic rights of the English people and the rights of freedom of speech, press, and religion had been assumed to be the possession of all American citizens. These rights had been "protected" by the Bill of Rights against the federal government and, to some extent at least, by state guarantees against the states. The Declaration of Independence indicated that government was organized to protect basic rights. So the idea that states should be permitted to violate such fundamental rights struck Republicans as absurd. The Fourteenth Amendment merely added a new enforcement mechanism—a "double security," to use Madison's phrase. The ship of liberty would henceforth have lifeboats as well as a double hull.[124] Perhaps that is why the change was so noncontroversial and was assumed to have been effectuated by so many leading Republicans at the time.[125] It is much like the system the Supreme Court, following a curious path, has finally arrived at today. There were four constitutional law treatises written shortly after the Fourteenth Amendment was proposed. Three of these, as Richard Aynes has noted, said that the amendment was designed to require states to obey Bill of Rights guarantees.[126]

Shortly after Congress proposed the Fourteenth Amendment to the states, it amended the federal Habeas Corpus Act to allow federal judges, acting "within their respective jurisdictions . . . to grant writs of habeas corpus in all cases where any person may be restrained of his or her liberty in violation of the constitution . . . or law of the United States."[127] The object of the statute, according to Senator Trumbull, chairman of the Senate Judiciary Committee, was to protect a person held under *state* law in violation of the Constitution or laws of the United States.[128] Of course, the act says nothing about which constitutional rights would be protected against state action. Still, it further protected federal constitutional rights from state denial. The Habeas Corpus Act provided a mechanism by which a plan to require states to obey the Bill of Rights could be enforced and realized. As John Bingham said in 1871:

> Sir, before the ratification of the fourteenth amendment, the State could deny to any citizen the right of trial by jury, and it was done. Before that the State could abridge the freedom of the press, and it was done in half the States of the Union. . . . Under the Constitution as it is . . . no State hereafter can imitate the bad example . . . of Georgia and

send men to the penitentiary, as did that State, for teaching the Indian
to read the lessons of the New Testament.[129]

In 1866 many in Congress seemed poised to readmit the Southern
states upon their ratification of the Fourteenth Amendment.[130] The Republican party was not yet ready to insist on black suffrage. Republicans
knew that without the black vote, their chances of controlling governments in the Southern states were slim. That meant, in effect, that the
only security for the rights of Republicans and their allies in the South
might be the guarantees of the Thirteenth and Fourteenth Amendments.
Nothing heightens respect for the guarantees in the Bill of Rights so
much as the recognition that one may be the subject of prosecution. In
1859–1860 Republican signers of the endorsement for a compendium
of Helper's book were being treated as criminals in the South. In February 1860 Abraham Lincoln exhorted Republicans not to be "frightened
[from our duty] by menaces of destruction to the Government nor of
dungeons to ourselves."[131] Indeed, a major factor protecting Republicans from prosecution was the fact that they were beyond the physical
power of the Southern states. By 1866 an endorser of the Helper book
had become the Speaker of the House of Representatives. Three of the
seven Republican House members of the Joint Committee that reported
the Fourteenth Amendment had endorsed the book.[132] One of these
three was John Bingham. John Bingham and the other endorsers of the
book had personal and concrete experience with the importance of guarantees of free speech and the other guarantees of the Bill of Rights.
When Bingham said that states would henceforth be required to respect
these guarantees, it is likely that he meant what he said. To most Republicans at least, such a "completion" of the constitutional plan was unlikely to be controversial.[133]

The Impending Crisis and Free Speech

The controversy over Helper's book also gives some insight into early
Republican understanding of the guarantees of freedom of speech, press,
and religion. By the 1860s there was scholarly support for the idea that
the freedom of the press meant a guarantee against prior restraint.[134]
Under that theory government could not censor books in advance of
publication but could punish the author after circulation. In the cases of
denial of free press complained of by Republicans, and certainly in the
case of Helper's book, the problem that confronted Republicans was
subsequent punishment not prior restraint. Yet they repeatedly insisted
that such subsequent punishment also violated the rights to freedom of
speech and of the press.

After the Civil War and the ratification of the Fourteenth Amendment, the Supreme Court suggested that the Constitution protected the right to assemble and to petition the Congress from interference from any quarter but did not protect free speech, assembly, or petition with reference to state concerns. The Court made a structural argument, indicating that republican government by its very nature implied a right to petition.[135] Some have suggested that Republican arguments for free speech similarly might be limited to matters within the sphere of the national government.[136] It is hard to see how free speech could be isolated into state and national boxes so as to eliminate free speech on matters of state concern. No state, after all, is an island isolated from national issues, nor is the nation isolated from state issues, as the battle over slavery shows. The power to amend the Constitution means that all local issues are potentially national ones. With the passage of the Fourteenth Amendment, Republicans in the Senate explicitly indicated that states should not be permitted to deny free speech on domestic (local) as well as national issues.

On balance, the debates from the 36th, 38th, and 39th Congresses do not support the idea that most Republicans thought a bifurcated reading of freedom of expression was accurate or desirable. Republican complaints about denial of free speech and press rights included matters both directly related to the national government and those not directly related. Helper's book basically addressed how to eliminate slavery in the South. Most congressmen agreed that slavery as a domestic issue in the Southern states was peculiarly a matter of state concern, a matter over which Congress had no power. But the suppression of Helper's book in the South, a book addressed to a matter of uniquely state concern, was seen by Republicans as a flagrant denial of free speech and free press.

Finally, in 1859 and 1860 many Republicans championed a robust view of free speech in the controversy over Helper's book. Like James Madison at the time of the Sedition Act, they suggested a hard central core to the First Amendment that included the right to discuss public measures and public questions. And they supported this right even for those who advocated conduct they considered barbarous and horrible— human slavery and reopening the African slave trade. Implicitly at least they rejected the idea that speech on such matters should be suppressed because of its bad tendency. Indeed, one Republican showed Democrats how easily the bad-tendency test could be manipulated to make Southerners guilty of the kidnapping of free blacks in the North. He did so, however, not to embrace the bad-tendency argument but to support his rejection of it.[137] Of course, history is rarely uniform. During the Civil War Abraham Lincoln justified the arrest, military trial, and exile of a Democratic politician who had made an antiwar speech. Lincoln suggested that war-time emergency justified suppression of political expression with a tendency to cause desertion. Some post-Civil War judicial decisions invoked the bad-tendency test to punish political expression that did not advocate violence. Suppressions of free speech by the Lincoln administration produced some protests within the Republican party.[138]

Conclusion

The laws protecting slavery from criticism were really sedition acts broadly defined. That, indeed, was how supporters and opponents saw them. They made it a crime to criticize one legal and social institution and to advocate its abolition. Harry Kalven has suggested that freedom cannot survive sedition acts—acts that make some political speech criminal.[139] The controversy over *The Impending Crisis* suggests that his view is correct. This second controversy over seditious speech, however, was far different from the first. This time the threat came from the states, not from the national government, and for that reason arguments about the lack of federal power to suppress speech were irrelevant. What was needed to help prevent other episodes like the suppression of Helper's book and other core political speech, was a set of national privileges which no state could abridge.[140] Section 1 of the Fourteenth Amendment was designed to meet that need.

Notes

I wish to thank Professors Akhil Amar, Paul Escott, Paul Finkelman, David Logan, Alan Palimiter, Wilson Parker, Jefferson Powell, David Shores, Harry Watson, Ronald Wright, and Michael Zuckert for comments on an earlier draft of the article. The mistakes are, of course, my own. I also wish to thank Jeffrey Scott Tracy, Edwin G. Wilson, Jr., Owen Lewis, Paul M. Goodson, and R. Bruce Thompson and Wake Forest Law librarians John Perkins and Martha Thomas for assistance with research.

1. See, e.g., *Cong. Globe*, 36th Cong. lst Sess. 124 (1859–60) [hereinafter *Globe* 36(1)] (Sen. Gwin), at 272 (Rep. Rust), at 455 (Sen. Clingman), at 881–82 (a collection of these statements by Republican Rep. McPherson), at 932 (Rep. Edgerton); at 94 (Rep. Curry); at 27–28 (Rep. Mallory); at 49 (Rep. Pryor).

2. Hinton Rowan Helper, *The Impending Crisis of the South: How to Meet It*, ed. George Fredrickson (1857; reprint, Cambridge: Harvard University Press, 1968).

3. In addition to the speeches listed in note 1, see, e.g., *Globe* 36(1) at 43 (Rep. Garnett). For examinations of other responses to John Brown, see Paul Finkelman, ed., *His Soul Goes Marching On: Responses to John Brown and the Harpers Ferry Raid* (Charlottesville: University Press of Virginia, 1995).

4. See, e.g., *Globe* 36(1) at 58 (Sen. Trumbull), at 1836–37 (Rep. Bingham); *Cong. Globe*, 36th Cong., 1st Sess. appendix, at 136–40 (1860) [hereinafter *Globe* 36(1) app.] (Rep. Corwin).

5. Zechariah Chafee, Jr., *Free Speech in the United States* (1964; reprint, New York: Atheneum, 1969), 21, 499, 501, 522; Michael Kent Curtis, "In Pursuit of

Liberty: The Levellers and the American Bill of Rights," 8 *Constitutional Commentary* 359 (1991).

6. See, e.g., *Debs* v. *United States*, 249 U.S. 211, 216–17 (1919).

7. *Dennis* v. *United States*, 341 U.S. 494 (1951).

8. See *Barron* v. *City of Baltimore*, 32 U.S. (7 Pet.) 243 (1833).

9. Some historians have focused on free speech about slavery. Deeply researched studies to which I am indebted include Clement Eaton, *The Freedom-of-Thought Struggle in the Old South* (1940; reprint, New York: Harper and Row, 1964), focusing on events in the Southern states; Russell B. Nye, *Fettered Freedom: Civil Liberties and the Slavery Controversy, 1830–1860* (East Lansing: Michigan State College Press, 1972); W. Sherman Savage, *The Controversy over the Distribution of Abolition Literature, 1830–1860* (1938; reprint, Washington, D.C.: The Association for the Study of Negro Life and History, 1968). For two fine studies that bear directly on the Worth case, see Clifton H. Johnson, "Abolitionist Missionary Activities in North Carolina," *North Carolina Historical Review* 40 (1963): 295–301, and Noble J. Tolbert, "Daniel Worth: Tar Heel Abolitionist," *North Carolina Historical Review* 39 (1962): 284–90.

A number of legal studies have focused on the historical background of the Fourteenth Amendment with regard to guarantees of civil liberty. Typically these have built on prior work and offered new evidence and interpretation as well. Richard H. Sewell, *Ballots for Freedom: Antislavery Politics in the United States, 1837–1860* (New York: Oxford University Press, 1976) provides an excellent survey of the rise of the political antislavery movement. For a very important study of early antislavery legal thought, see William M. Wiecek, *The Sources of Antislavery Constitutionalism in America, 1760–1848* (Ithaca: Cornell University Press, 1977). Pioneering works on incorporation of the Bill of Rights in the Fourteenth Amendment are Charles Fairman, "Does the Fourteenth Amendment Incorporate the Bill of Rights?: The Original Understanding," 2 *Stanford Law Review* 5 (1949), and William Winslow Crosskey, "Charles Fairman, 'Legislative History' and Constitutional Limitations on State Authority," 22 *University of Chicago Law Review* 1 (1954).

My own work was heavily influenced by Crosskey, and my understanding of the subject evolved over time. See Michael Kent Curtis, "The Bill of Rights as a Limitation on State Authority: A Reply to Professor Berger", 16 *Wake Forest Law Review* 45 (1980); Michael Kent Curtis, "The Fourteenth Amendment and the Bill of Rights", 14 *Connecticut Law Review* 237 (1982); Michael Kent Curtis, "Further Adventures of the Nine Lived Cat: A Response to Mr. Berger on Incorporation of the Bill of Rights", 43 *Ohio State Law Journal* 89 (1982). For a critique of Mr. Berger's work, see Aviam Soifer, "Protecting Civil Rights: A Critique of Raoul Berger's History", 54 *New York University Law Review* 651 (1979). For two important recent articles on incorporation, see Akhil Reed Amar, "The Bill of Rights and the Fourteenth Amendment," 101 *Yale Law Journal* 1193 (1992), and Richard Aynes, "On Misreading John Bingham and the Fourteenth Amendment," 103 *Yale Law Journal* 57 (1993).

For important scholarship denying application of the Bill of Rights to the states under the Fourteenth Amendment, see Raoul Berger, *The Fourteenth Amendment and the Bill of Rights* (Norman: University of Oklahoma Press, 1989), William E. Nelson, *The Fourteenth Amendment: From Political Principle to Judicial Doctrine* (Cambridge: Harvard University Press, 1988), and Jonathan Lurie, "The

Fourteenth Amendment: Use and Application in Selected State Court Civil Liberties Cases, 1870–1890", 28 *The American Journal of Legal History* 295 (1984).

10. Bernard Schwartz, ed., *The Bill of Rights: A Documentary History* (New York: Chelsea House Publishers, 1971), 1028, 1030–31 (Madison in the first Congress), [hereinafter Schwartz, ed., *The Bill of Rights*]. For recent commentary, see Akhil Reed Amar, "The Bill of Rights as a Constitution," 100 *Yale Law Journal* 1131 (1991); Paul Finkelman, "The First Ten Amendments as a Declaration of Rights", 16 *Southern Illinois University Law Journal* 351 (1992); Paul Finkelman, "James Madison and the Bill of Rights: A Reluctant Paternity," 1990 *Supreme Court Review* 301 (1990).

11. *Documentary History*, 1033, 1113 (emphasis added); *Barron v. City of Baltimore, supra* note 8.

12. Act for Punishment of Certain Crimes (Sedition Act), 1 Stat. 596–97 (1798).

13. James Morton Smith, *Freedom's Fetters: The Alien and Sedition Laws and American Civil Liberties* (Ithaca: Cornell University Press, 1966).

14. James Madison, "Virginia Resolutions," Dec. 21, 1798; reprinted in Melvin I. Urofsky, ed., *Documents of American Constitutional and Legal History* (Philadelphia: Temple University Press, 1989) 1:159, 160; Charles L. Black Jr., *Structure and Relationship in Constitutional Law* (Baton Rouge: Louisiana State University, 1969), 9–15, 40–42.

15. See John Trenchard and Thomas Gordon, *Cato's Letters: Essays on Liberty, Civil and Religious, and Other Important Subjects* (1755; reprint, New York: Da Capo Press, 1971), 96–103, 249–50, 253; Curtis, "In Pursuit of Liberty," 367–68; David M. Rabban, "The Ahistorical Historian: Leonard Levy on Freedom of Expression in Early American History," 37 *Stanford Law Review* 795, 823 (1985). For early understandings of free speech, see also Donna L. Dickerson, *The Course of Tolerance* (New York: Greenwood Press, 1990); Leonard W. Levy, *The Emergence of a Free Press* (New York: Oxford University Press, 1985); David A. Anderson, "The Origins of the Press Clause," 30 *University of California in Los Angeles Law Review* 455 (1983). Sir William Blackstone, *Commentaries on the Laws of England* (Philadelphia: R. H. Small, 1825), 4:151–52. On enforcement of the act, see *United States v. Cooper*, 25 F. Cas. 631 (C.C.D. Pa. 1800) (No. 14,865).

16. Eaton, *Freedom of Thought*, 88, 335–52.

17. Charles S. Sydnor, *The Development of Southern Sectionalism, 1819–1848* (Baton Rouge: Louisiana State University Press, 1962) 232–42.

18. "Mr. Hedrick, Once More," *Raleigh Weekly Standard*, Nov. 5, 1856, 1. For other articles in the same paper, see "Professor Hedrick, of the University," *Raleigh Weekly Standard*, Oct. 8, 1856, 1; "Professor Hedrick's Defence," ibid., 4. See also John Spencer Bassett, *Anti-Slavery Leaders of North Carolina* (1898; reprint, Baltimore: Johns Hopkins University Press, 1973), 29–47.

19. See Sydnor, *Development*, 233–45; Sewell, *Ballots for Freedom*, 43–72.

20. See, e.g., *Bacon v. Commonwealth*, 48 Va. (7 Gratt.) 602 (1850). For other prosecutions, see *State v. Read*, 6 La. Ann. 227 (1851); *State v. McDonald*, 4 Port. 449 (Ala. 1837).

21. Curtis, *No State Shall Abridge*, 42–44.

22. Curtis, *No State Shall Abridge*, 24–25, 46–56; Amar, "The Bill of Rights and the Fourteenth Amendment," 1205–14. Joel Tiffany, *A Treatise on the Unconstitutionality of American Slavery* (1849: facsimile, Miami: Mnemosyne, 1969), 56–57, 57–58, 84–89, 93–94, 97, 99.

23. *Cong. Globe,* 35th Cong., 2d Sess. 983–4 (1859). Curtis, *No State Shall Abridge,* 60–63. "Privilege . . . 1. a right, immunity or benefit enjoyed by a particular person or a restricted group of persons. . . . 5. any of the rights common to all citizens under a modern constitutional government." *Random House Webster's College Dictionary* (New York, 1991), 1074. An 1851 law dictionary included among other definitions "a right peculiar to some individual or body." *A New Law Dictionary and Glossary* (New York: J. S. Voorhies, 1851), 2:828.

24. Curtis, *No State Shall Abridge,* 64–65, 67, 75–76 (Blackstone describing English liberties as "privileges" and "immunities"). For the mixed heritage of the words, see ibid., 67–68. For Madison's use of the word *privilege* to describe Bill of Rights liberties, see text accompanying notes 11 and 12.

25. See *Kentucky v. Dennison,* 65 U.S. (24 How.) 66 (1861); *Prigg v. Pennsylvania,* 41 U.S. (16 Pet.) 536, 539 (1842). Curtis, *No State Shall Abridge,* 63–64, and Paul Finkelman, "Sorting Out *Prigg v. Pennsylvania,*" 24 *Rutgers Law Journal* 605–65 (1993).

26. *Documentary History,* 1030.

27. Curtis, *No State Shall Abridge,* 27–28, 46–47.

28. Kentucky, Tennessee, Mississippi, and Alabama were not yet under federal control. A proposal to apply the ban on slavery to all new American territory, north as well as south, had been defeated in 1784. See William W. Freehling, *The Road to Disunion: Secessionists at Bay,* (New York: Oxford University Press, 1990), 138.

29. *Dred Scott v. Sandford, supra* note 23, at 425–26. Don E. Fehrenbacher, *The Dred Scott Case* (New York: Oxford University Press, 1978), 188, 192.

30. Paul Finkelman, *An Imperfect Union: Slavery, Federalism and Comity* (Chapel Hill: University of North Carolina Press, 1981), 313–24.

31. *Globe* 36(1) at 2595–97; *Cong. Globe,* 39th Cong., 1st Sess. 1013 (1866) [hereinafter *Globe* 39(1)].

32. Abraham Lincoln, *Speeches and Writings, 1859–1865* (New York: Library of America, 1984), 53, 57–58; James M. McPherson, *Battle Cry of Freedom: The Civil War Era* (New York: Oxford University Press, 1988), 178–88.

33. McPherson, *Battle Cry,* 147.

34. The citizenship clause was added in the Senate and was not written by Bingham.

35. *Cong. Globe,* 34th Cong., 1st Sess. app. 124 (1856).

36. See, e.g., ch. 34, sec. 16, 1855 N.C. Rev. Code (referring to circulation of matter "the evident tendency whereof is to cause slaves to become discontented.").

37. *State v. Worth,* 52 N.C. (7 Jones) 488, 492 (1860).

38. *Barron v. Baltimore, supra* note 8, at 250–51. Curtis, *No State Shall Abridge,* 22–56; Amar, "The Bill of Rights and the Fourteenth Amendment," 1205–16, 1223–38. *Nunn v. Georgia,* 1 Ga. 243 (1846); *Cockrum v. State,* 24 Tex. 394, 401–2 (1859); *Rinehart v. Schuyler,* 7 Ill. (2 Gilm.) 473, 522 (1846). Most state courts followed *Barron.*

39. Bassett, *Anti-Slavery Leaders,* 11–12.

40. Helper, *The Impending Crisis,* 155–56; Bassett, *Anti-Slavery Leaders,* 23–24.

41. See, e.g., Helper, *The Impending Crisis,* 35–39, 62–66, 175–79.

42. Ibid., 116.

43. Ibid., 149, 409; Bassett, *Anti-Slavery Leaders,* 23.

44. Helper, *The Impending Crisis*, 149; quoted in "A False and Genuine Helper," *Richmond Whig*, Jan. 8, 1860, 4.

45. Helper, *The Impending Crisis*, 151.

46. David M. Potter, *The Impending Crisis, 1848–1861* (New York: Harper and Row, 1976), 387. "Revolutionary Designs of the Abolitionists—New York Names Endorsing Treason," *New York Herald*, Nov. 26, 1859, 4.

47. *New York Herald*, Oct. 18, 1859, 1. "The 'Irrepressible Conflict,'" Wm. Seward's Brutal and Bloody Manifesto," *New York Herald*, Oct. 19, 1859, 2 [hereinafter "Irrepressible Conflict"].

48. William H. Seward, "Speech by Governor Seward," (delivered Oct. 25, 1858), in *Collection of Anti-Slavery Propaganda in the Oberlin College Library* (Louisville: Lost Cause Press, 1964), microfiche reprint, SLB 1255. "Irrepressible Conflict," 2. "Text Book of Revolution," *New York Herald*, Nov. 28, 1859, 1. North Carolina grand jury action reported in *New York Weekly Tribune*, Dec. 24 and 31, 1859, cited in Earl Schenck Miers, Introduction to Helper, *The Impending Crisis* (New York: Collier Books, 1963), 13.

49. See, e.g., *Globe* 36(1), at 17 (Rep. Clark), at 21 (Rep. Millison), at 24 (Rep. Keitt), at 28 (Senator Mallory), at 29–30 (Senator Iverson), at 45 (Rep. Lamar), at 49 (Rep. Pryor), at 61–62 (Rep. Davis), at 94–96 (Rep. Curry), at 110–11 (Rep. Stewart), at 121 (Senator Clay), at 281–82 (Rep. Pryor).

50. Ibid., 3; Ollinger Crenshaw, "The Speakership Contest of 1859–60," *Mississippi Valley Historical Review* 29 (1942): 323, 323–24.

51. *Globe* 36(1), at 14, 17, 281.

52. Ibid., at 30, 43, 62–63, 69, 524. See also ibid. at 71, 94, 104–5.

53. Crenshaw, "The Speakership Contest," 332–37. *Globe* 36(1), at 819 (Rep. Anderson); see also ibid., at 841 (collection by Rep. Clark).

54. Ibid. at 346 (Rep. Wells), at 21 (Rep. Sherman), at 74 (Rep. Stanton). Crenshaw, "The Speakership Contest," 325.

55. *Globe* 36(1), at 4 (Rep. Kilgore), at 40 (Rep. Kellogg), at 394 (Rep. Morris), at 45 (Rep. Lamar), at 826 (Rep. Fenton), at 930–31 (Rep. Edgerton), at 1887–88 (Rep. Alley).

56. Ibid. at 40 (Rep. Kellogg, quoting from *New York Weekly Tribune*, Dec. 6, 1859). Sewell, *Ballots for Freedom*, 357.

57. The Southern "bad tendency" approach was later followed in Massachusetts and in the United States Supreme Court. See, e.g., *Commonwealth* v. *Karvonen*, 106 N.E. 556, 557 (Mass. 1914); *Debs* v. *United States*, *supra* note 6.

58. *Globe* 36(1), at 63. See, e.g., "Revolutionary Designs of the Abolitionists," *New York Herald*, Nov. 26, 1859, 4, and Nov. 28, 1859, 1; "Incitement to Treason and Civil War," *Raleigh Weekly Standard*, Dec. 7, 1859, 1.

59. *Globe* 36(1), at 141; see also ibid. at 58 (Sen. Trumbull).

60. Joaquin J. Cardoso, "Lincoln, Abolitionism, and Patronage: The Case of Hinton Rowan Helper," *Journal of Negro History* 53 (1968): 144, 147. "Helper's Crisis," *New York Tribune*, Dec. 27, 1859, 4.

61. *Globe* 36(1), at 7. Abraham Lincoln, *The Collected Works* ed. Roy Basler (New Brunswick: Rutgers University Press, 1953), 3:541.

62. *Globe* 36(1), at 1861.

63. Lincoln, *Collected Works* 2:406.

64. *Globe* 36(1), at 240–41 (Rep. Smith), at 407 (Sen. Pugh).

65. Eric Foner, *Free Soil, Free Labor, Free Men: The Ideology of the Republican Party before the Civil War* (Oxford: Oxford University Press, 1970), 122, 207; *Globe*

36(1), at 240 (Rep. Smith), at 282 (Rep. Pryor), at 462 (Rep. Underwood), at 95 (Rep. Curry), at 912 (Sen. Seward, asserting that freedom of speech and ballot would produce a large Republican party in the South), at 125 (Sen. Gwin), at 407 (Sen. Pugh).

66. *Cong. Globe*, 24th Cong., 1st Sess. app. at 9 (1835) (report of Postmaster General Kendall).

67. See, e.g., *United States* v. *Cruikshank*, 92 U.S. 542, 552 (1875); Black, *Structure and Relationship*, 33–50.

68. *Globe* 36(1), at 54 (Sen. Trumbull), at 66 (Rep. Leach); Lincoln, *Speeches and Writings, 1859–65*, 61.

69. See, e. g., infra nn. 75–81, 84, 85, 113, 115–19, 129.

70. Sewell, *Ballots for Freedom*, 284.

71. For a discussion of two approaches to the free-speech issue, see Hugo L. Black, "The Bill of Rights," 35 *New York University Law Review* 865, 867 (1960); Laurent B. Frantz, "The First Amendment in the Balance," 71 *Yale Law Journal* 1424, 1430–32 (1962).

72. *Globe* 36(1), at 12. Quotations from this congressional discussion of free speech, given in the next two paragraphs, are found in ibid., at 12, 31, 57.

73. Paul Angle, ed., *Created Equal?: The Complete Lincoln-Douglas Debates of 1858* (Chicago: University of Chicago Press, 1958), 290–91, 300.

74. *Globe* 36(1), at 128.

75. Ibid. at 64. The remarks of Senators Brown and Wilson in this and the subsequent two paragraphs are found in ibid., at 63–65.

76. Ibid. at 144.

77. Ibid. at 913.

78. Edgerton's remarks in this and the next paragraph are found in ibid., at 930–31.

79. Ibid. at 1872.

80. Ibid. at 1031–32 (Rep. Van Wyck), at 1039–40 (Rep. Perry, appealing also to a somewhat more conventional reading of the interstate privileges or immunities clause to bolster his complaint of lack of protection for visitors from the North), at 1585 (Rep. Wells), at 1861–62 (Rep. Bingham), at 1861 (Rep. Bingham).

81. Ibid. at 1857.

82. Ibid. at 133 (Rep. Sickles), at 44 (Rep. Garnett).

83. Lincoln, *Speeches and Writings, 1859–65*, 128 (Address at Cooper Institute), 149 (Address at New Haven).

84. Statements by Senators Davis and Harlan in this paragraph are found in *Globe* 36(1), at 2321. On the usage of *domestic*, see below.

85. *Globe* 36(1) app., at 202, 205.

86. Ibid. at 207.

87. Ibid. at 205.

88. "Case of Reverend Daniel Worth," *New York Times*, Apr. 5, 1860, 5; see also ibid., Apr. 6, 1860, 6.

89. "Freedom of Speech in the South," *National Era*, Jan. 12, 1860, 6.

90. Tolbert, "Daniel Worth," 284–90. For a second powerfully researched article dealing with Worth, see Johnson, "Abolitionist Missionary." (Note 9)

91. Daniel Worth to Aaron Worth, Apr. 30, 1858, in Tolbert, "Daniel Worth," 290.

92. Ibid., 291. "An Abolition Emissary," *Raleigh Weekly Standard*, Dec. 14,

1959, 1, quoted in Tolbert, "Daniel Worth," 291. "The Abolition Emissary," *North Carolina Presbyterian*, Dec. 17, 1859, 1. "The Council of State," *Raleigh Weekly Standard*, Dec. 14, 1859, 1.

93. Daniel Worth to American Missionary Association, Dec. 21, 1859, in Johnson, "Abolitionist Missionary," 312.

94. "Hinton R. Helper's Infamous Book—What the Sixty-Eight Demand," *Weekly Raleigh Register*, Dec. 14, 1859, 1.

95. "Arrest of Reverend Daniel Worth," *Raleigh Weekly Standard*, Dec. 28, 1859, 3; "Arrest of Reverend Daniel Worth," *Weekly Raleigh Register*, Jan. 4, 1860, 1; "Arrest and Trial of Reverend Daniel Worth," *Greensboro Patriot*, Jan. 6, 1860, 3.

96. "Arrest and Trial of Reverend Daniel Worth," 3.

97. See, e.g., *Globe* 36(1), at 188 (Rep. Gilmer); "Helper's Book," *Greensboro Patriot*, Aug. 12, 1859, 2.

98. "Incendiary Documents," *Raleigh Weekly Standard*, Jan. 4, 1860, 1.

99. John T. Harriss to John W. Ellis, Dec. 30, 1859, *Papers of John W. Ellis* (Raleigh: State Department of Archives and History, 1964), 1:340; Judge Dick to John W. Ellis, ibid., 342–45.

100. "The Abolitionist George W. Vestal," *Daily Progress*, Jan. 3, 1860, 2; "The Abolitionists Worth and Turner," *Daily Progress*, Jan. 3, 1860, 2; "Abolitionists Worth and Turner," *Raleigh Weekly Standard*, Jan. 4, 1860, 1; "Arrest of A Suspicious Character," *Weekly Raleigh Register*, Jan. 4, 1860, 1.

101. Benjamin S. Hedrick to Thomas Ruffin, Jan. 16, 1860, *Papers of Thomas Ruffin*, ed. J. G. de Roulhac Hamilton (Raleigh: Edwards and Broughton, 1920), 3:64, 65. For the antislavery pamphlet, see *Address to the People of North Carolina on the Evils of Slavery* (1830; reprint, Greensboro: Manumission Society of North Carolina, 1860), 5, 9, 13, 15. Tolbert, "Daniel Worth," 298.

102. George McNeill, Jr., to Thomas Ruffin, Mar. 12, 1860, *Papers of Thomas Ruffin* 1:73. Jonathan Worth to George McNeill, Jr., Mar. 10, 1860, ibid., 1:74.

103. "Act to Prevent Circulation of Seditious Publications," ch. 34, § 16, 1854 N.C. Rev. Code (revising 1830 N.C. Sess. Laws ch. 5, at 10–11).

104. "Arrest and Trial of Rev. Daniel Worth," *Greensboro Patriot*, Jan. 6, 1860, 3. The following account of Worth's trial comes from fragmentary press accounts and from the few surviving appellate papers. These do not include the defendant's brief. Johnson, "Abolitionist Missionary," 315.

105. Indictment, *State v. Worth*, Guilford County, North Carolina, Department of Archives and History, 1–8 (1860). See Johnson, "Abolitionist Missionary," 317; "Randolph Superior Court," *Greensboro Patriot*, April 6, 1860, 2.

106. "Randolph Superior Court," *Greensboro Times*, April 7, 1860, 6. "Randolph Superior Court," *Greensboro Patriot*, April 6, 1860, 2.

107. "Trial of Reverend Daniel Worth," *Greensboro Times*, May 5, 1860, 6.

108. "Daniel Worth in New York," *Greensboro Times*, May 19, 1860, 2–3; "A Christian Minister in the South: The Story of Reverend Daniel Worth," *New York Tribune*, May 8, 1860, 5. See also "Church Anti-Slavery Society," *New York Times*, May 7, 1860, 8.

109. *State v. Worth*, *supra* note 37, at 490–93. N.C. Const. Declaration of Rights, § 15, quoted in 1836 *Proceedings and Debates of the Convention of North-Carolina Called to Amend the Constitution of the State* 410.

110. 1860 N.C. Sess. Laws ch. 23, at 39.

111. James M. McPherson, *Abraham Lincoln and the Second American Revolution* (New York: Oxford University Press, 1991), 23–42, 131–52. The extent to

which the second American Revolution envisioned consolidation of power in the federal government is subject to dispute, and any theory of full consolidation is hard to square with the evidence.

112. E.g., *Globe* 36(1), at 1617 (Sen. Chestnut), 1618–19.

113. E.g., ibid. at 822–26 (Rep. Fenton).

114. Lincoln, *Speeches and Writings*, 129–30; *Globe* 36(1), at 912–13 (Sen. Seward). Ibid. at 125 (Sen. Gwin), at 455 (Sen. Clingman).

115. *Globe* 39(1), at 728 (Rep. Welker), at 586 (Rep. Donnelly), at 632 (Rep. Kelley), at 1088 (Rep. Woodbridge on the need to keep states within their orbits), at 1088 (Rep. Bingham), at 1183 (Rep. Pomeroy), at 1152 (Rep. Thayer), at 1263 (Rep. Broomall), at 1629 (Rep. Hart), at 1832–33 (Rep. Lawrence), at 2542 (Rep. Bingham), at 1072 (Senator Nye); *Cong. Globe*, 39th Cong., 1st Sess. app. 67 (1866) (Garfield); at 256 (Rep. Baker); Curtis, *No State Shall Abridge*, 49–56, 59, 63–91.

116. *Congr. Globe*, 38th Cong., 1st Sess. 1202 (1864) (Rep. Wilson) [hereinafter *Globe* 38(1)]. For example, see ibid. at 1313 (Sen. Trumbull), at 1439 (Sen. Harlan), at 2615 (Rep. Morris). *Globe* 39(1), at 1013 (Rep. Clarke), at 1263 (Rep. Bromall), at 1072 (Sen. Nye). Cf. *Globe* 38(1), at 114 (Rep. Arnold), at 1971–72 (Rep. Scofield); *Congr. Globe*, 38th Congr., 2nd Sess. 138 (Rep. Ashley), at 193 (Rep. Kasson); *Globe* 39(1), at 157–58 (Rep. Bingham), at 1617 (Rep. Moulton), at 1627 (Rep. Buckland), at 1627–29 (Rep. Hart); *Congr. Globe*, 39th Congr., 1st Sess. app. 255–56 (Rep. Baker). See also Curtis, *No State Shall Abridge*, 27–59, 131–53.

117. Petitions presented by lawmakers from citizens demanded protection for rights of speech, press, assembly, and the right to bear arms. *Globe* 39(1), at 337 (Sen. Sumner), at 494 (Sen. Howard). See also ibid. at 462 (Rep. Baker: "[T]he American citizen shall no more be degraded . . . by being required to surrender his conscience as a peace-offering to . . . an . . . aristocracy of class"), at 1617 (Rep. Moulton, complaining of outrages against Union men and freedmen: "There is neither freedom of speech, of the press, or protection to life, liberty, or property."), at 1629 (Rep. Hart, insisting on the need to ensure that rebel states have a government that respects guarantees in the Bill of Rights), at 1837 (Rep. Clarke on need for "irreversible guarantees" of civil liberty including for rights recognized and secured by the Constitution). For a fuller review, see Curtis, *No State Shall Abridge*, 34–91.

118. *Globe* 39(1), at 432. Curtis, *No State Shall Abridge*, 34–130.

119. Schwartz, ed., *The Bill of Rights*, 1028, 1033 (Madison in the first Congress); Curtis, *No State Shall Abridge*, 64–65, 74–77; Curtis, "A Reply to Professor Berger," 48.

120. See, for example, *Globe* 39(1), at 432. Resolution of Congress March 4, 1789, transmitting proposed amendments to the states describing them as "declaratory and restrictive clauses." *The Constitution of the United States and The Declaration of Independence*, vol. 20 (Washington, D.C.: Commission on the Bicentennial of the United States Constitution, 1991). Cf. Howard Jay Graham, "Our 'Declaratory' Fourteenth Amendment," 7 *Stanford Law Review* 3, 37 (1954–55); Amar, "The Bill of Rights and the Fourteenth Amendment," 1205–12.

121. *Adamson* v. *California*, 332 U.S. 46, 74 (1947) (Black, J., dissenting).

122. Raoul Berger, *Government by Judiciary: The Transformation of the Fourteenth Amendment* (Cambridge: Harvard University Press, 1977), 145–46; Charles Fairman, *Reconstruction and Reunion*, vol. 6 of *History of the Supreme Court of the*

United States (New York: Macmillan, 1971), 462, 1289. For an important and thoughtful defense of Bingham from the ad hominem attacks of his critics, see Aynes, "On Misreading John Bingham," n. 16. For a careful analysis of the post-Civil War constitutional amendments in light of the original Constitution and federalism, see Michael P. Zuckert, "Completing the Constitution: The Fourteenth Amendment and Constitutional Rights," 22 *Publius* 69 (Spring, 1992); Michael P. Zuckert, "Completing the Constitution, The Thirteenth Amendment," 4 *Constitutional Commentary* 259 (1987); see also Michael P. Zuckert, "Congressional Power Under the Fourteenth Amendment—The Original Understanding of Section Five," 3 *Constitutional Commentary* 123 (1986).

123. *Globe* 39(1), at 2542.

124. The metaphor comes from Randy E. Barnett, "Reconceiving the Ninth Amendment," 74 *Cornell Law Review* 1, 23–34 (1988).

125. Curtis, *No State Shall Abridge*, 131–70; Michael P. Zuckert, review of *The Politics of Judicial Interpretation,* by Robert Kaczorowski; *No State Shall Abridge,* by Michael Kent Curtis; and *The Fourteenth Amendment and the Bill of Rights,* by Raoul Berger, 8 *Constitutional Commentary* 149–63 (1991).

126. See Aynes, "On Misreading John Bingham." Judge Timothy Farrar, an abolitionist legal theorist, published *Manual of the Constitution of the United States of America* (Boston: Little, Brown, 1867). George W. Paschal, a respected and conservative lawyer and law teacher, published *The Constitution of the United States Defined and Carefully Annotated* (Washington, D.C.: W. H. and O. H. Morrison, 1868), 290. John N. Pomeroy, the respected New York University professor of law, said that the Fourteenth Amendment would correct both *Dred Scott,* by securing constitutional protection to blacks, and *Barron,* by requiring the states to obey the guarantees of the Bill of Rights. John Norton Pomeroy, *An Introduction to the Constitutional Law of the United States* (New York: Hurd and Houghton, 1868), 147–53. See also Curtis, *No State Shall Abridge*, 173. Thomas Cooley, the most important and respected constitutional commentator of his day, seems not to have addressed the meaning of section 1 in his *Constitutional Limitations* (1868; reprint, Birmingham: Legal Classics Library, 1987).

127. Act of February 1, 1867, 14 Stat. 385 (1867).

128. *Globe* 39(1), at 4229.

129. *Globe,* 42(1) app., at 84.

130. Joseph B. James, *The Ratification of the Fourteenth Amendment* (Macon: Mercer University Press, 1984), 2–9; Eric L. McKitrick, *Andrew Johnson and Reconstruction* (Chicago: University of Chicago Press, 1960), 359–61, 448–85.

131. Lincoln, *Speeches and Writings, 1859–65,* 130, 150.

132. Schuyler Colfax was Speaker of the House. Ellihu B. Washburne, Justin S. Morrill, and John A. Bingham were members of the joint committee who had endorsed the compendium. *Report of the Joint Committee on Reconstruction at the First Session, Thirty-ninth Congress,* vol. 3 (1866; reprint, Washington, D.C.: Government Printing Office, 1969). For a list of congressional endorsers, see, e.g., "Hinton Helper's Infamous Book—What the Sixty-Eight Demand," *Raleigh Register,* Dec. 14, 1859, 1.

133. Curtis, *No State Shall Abridge*, 48–49, 53, 90; Fehrenbacher, *Dred Scott,* 27.

134. See Paschal, *The Constitution,* 256. Joseph Story seems both to embrace Blackstone's analysis of prior restraint and to justify suppression of items adjudged at trial to have a "pernicious tendency." Joseph Story, *Commentaries on*

the Constitution of the United States (1833; reprint, Durham: Carolina Academic Press, 1987) 703–7. For a more libertarian approach to the subject and a rejection of the idea of freedom of expression limited to protection against prior restraint, see Cooley, *Constitutional Limitations* (Cambridge: Little, Brown, 1868), 414–30.

135. *United States* v. *Cruikshank, supra* note 67, at 552 (1949).

136. Fairman, "Fourteenth Amendment," 2 *Stanford Law Review* 96–97 (1949). The first purely textual problem with this argument is that the Constitution provides in Article IV, section 4 that the United States shall guarantee to each state a "Republican Form of Government." Leading Republicans in 1866 insisted that free speech and other Bill of Rights guarantees were essential to a truly republican government. *Globe* 39(1), at 1072 (Sen. Nye). See also ibid. at 1629 (Rep. Hart).

137. *Globe* 36(1), at 763 (Sen. Hale).

138. McPherson, *Abraham Lincoln*, 58–60. For some postwar "bad tendency" cases, see, e.g., *Commonwealth* v. *Karvonen*, 106 N.E. 556, 557 (Mass. 1914); *Fox* v. *Washington*, 236 U.S. 273, 276–77 (1915); *Patterson* v. *Colorado*, 205 U.S. 454 (1907). Mark M. Krug, *Lyman Trumbull: Conservative Radical* (New York: A. S. Barnes, 1965), 207–8; Paludan, *Covenant with Death*, 149.

139. Harry Kalven, *The Negro and the First Amendment* (Columbus: Ohio State University Press, 1965), 15–16, 63–64.

140. Curtis, *No State Shall Abridge.* Akhil Reed Amar, "The Case of the Missing Amendments: *R.A.V.* v. *City of St. Paul*," 106 *Harvard Law Review* 124, 140–42 (1992). For the retrospective views of Republicans who mentioned Worth's case, see George W. Julian, *Political Recollections (1840 to 1872)* (1883; reprint, Miami: Mnemosyne, 1969), 171–73; Henry Wilson, *History of the Rise and Fall of the Slave Power in America* (1872; reprint, New York: Greenwood Publishing, 1969), 2:668.

Part III

Criminal and Civil Law of Slavery

7

Slaves and the Rules of Evidence in Criminal Trials

Thomas D. Morris

*The negro, as a general rule, is mendacious**

IN 1853 WILLIAM GOODELL searingly observed that the slave "becomes '*a person*' whenever he is to be *punished!* . . . He is under the control of law, though unprotected by law, and can know law only as an enemy, and not as a friend." Goodell's argument that slaves were outside the protection of the law rested upon two legal rules, one evidentiary and one substantive. The substantive rule was the simple assertion, as articulated by South Carolina's Judge John Belton O'Neall in *State* v. *Maner,* that the slave was outside the protection of the common law. The evidentiary rule was another matter. Slaves could not testify against whites. As Chief Justice Drewry Ottley of St. Vincent noted, the result of exclusion was that "the difficulty of legally establishing facts is so great, that White men are in a manner put beyond the reach of the law." This was changed in the West Indies during the 1820s, as the British colonies inched toward abolition. Whites would receive the testimony of slaves who could show they were Christians and understood the significance of an oath. Even then, there remained a vital exclusion: the testimony would be excluded if the white were on trial for his life.[1] No comparable shift in policy occurred in the American South. The wholesale exclusion remained in force to the end of slavery.

A major change, however, did occur in the rules when slaves had evidence to offer in cases involving free blacks and Indians. From the Revolution to the 1820s, the evidence of slaves began to be admitted against such people of color in capital as well as noncapital cases. Prior to that, slaves could not testify in capital trials, although there is evidence

* Thomas R. R. Cobb, 1858. See *infra,* n. 14, for full citation.

their testimony was received, even though reluctantly, in noncapital cases. For instance, in Maryland as of 1717 the evidence of slaves was received in cases against any black or Indian as long as it was a case that did not involve depriving them "of Life or Member." At the same time their testimony against "any *Christian,* White Person" was excluded.[2]

In 1777 North Carolina became one of the first states to expand the rule on the admissibility of slave evidence to include capital cases. A typical statute was that of Mississippi (1822): "[A]ny negro or mulatto, bond or free, shall be a good witness in pleas of the state, for or against negroes or mulattoes, bond or free, or in civil pleas where free negroes or mulattoes shall alone be parties, and in no other cases whatever."[3] The deterioration in the legal position of free blacks was a product of the revolutionary generation. But in practice there were not all that many cases in which the testimony of slaves figured prominently in indictments against free blacks.

Race, as well as status, had become the basis for exclusion, and the exclusion of the testimony of slaves against any white understandably was scored by critics of the laws of slavery such as George M. Stroud and William Goodell.[4] On the other hand, what was the case when the slave was not the victim of violence but rather was the person charged with the criminal offense? In many cases that person never reached the courts at all. Occasionally slaves were victims of mob violence. An example occurred in 1843 near Copiah, Mississippi. A group of whites took off the plantation and summarily hanged two slaves who had allegedly raped a white woman. According to the newspaper account, they were "hung according to a statute of Judge Lynch, 'in such cases made and provided.'" When slaves were indicted in the public courts, they normally were charged with capital offenses, not with such petty crimes as thefts of chickens and fights among themselves. These lesser offenses were handled on the plantations.[5]

Once slaves got to court, what rules of evidence applied? There is a fine debate about the history of evidentiary rules for the exclusion of certain kinds of testimony such as hearsay testimony or the evidence of prior convictions. James Bradley Thayer contended that the rules emerged during the eighteenth century in order to control the discretion of juries. Recently, John Langbein has suggested that they arose to control lawyers.[6] But neither jury discretion nor unethical lawyers mattered that much to slaves during the eighteenth century. Of much more moment were the rules that concerned the competency of someone to testify at all and the credibility to be given to their testimony if they were ruled competent.

Two rules used in seventeenth-century English criminal trials were of significance in the trials of slaves. Both derived from Christian doctrine. The first was the two-witness rule found in Deuteronomy. The second was the rule that a person had to take an oath before he would be admitted to testify. In the seventeenth century, the theory behind the oath was that it was a way to bring forth immediate divine vengeance upon false swearing. This was a time when the belief in divine, as well as devilish, intervention in the affairs of men was very deep. By the nineteenth century, when such beliefs were less secure, the oath had become a way to remind the oath-taker of a future punishment for false swearing. As Simon Greenleaf, a master of the law of evidence, put it in 1842: "[O]ne of the main provisions of the law, for the purity and truth of oral evidence, is, that it be delivered under the *sanction of an oath.* Men in general are sensible of the motives and restraints of religion, and acknowledge their accountability to that Being, from whom no secrets are hid." The oath then was used to lay "hold on the conscience of the witness."[7]

Not everyone, however, was allowed to take an oath. The opinion of Sir Edward Coke was that only a person who believed in a Christian God could take a valid oath, and therefore the only competent witness was a Christian. Sir William Holdsworth believed this view was breaking down because of "commercial considerations." The work of Sir Matthew Hale at the end of the seventeenth century reflected transformation. He believed that an oath other than that required of Christians was acceptable "in cases of necessity, as in forein [sic] contracts between merchant and merchant." Hale also was disturbed by the notion that a murder might not be punishable if it were committed "in presence only of a Turk or a Jew, that owns not the Christian religion." Hale would allow non-Christians to testify under an oath that derived from their own religion. He did this grudgingly, however, and ended with the observation "that the credit of such a testimony must be left to the jury."[8] Still, there had to be an oath of some sort.

While the demands of market capitalism opened the courts to some, social status closed them to others. Holdsworth, for instance, noted that the person who had been reduced to villenage had "lost his law." Thomas R. R. Cobb made much of this. Only free men, he wrote, were "*othesworth,*" and wherever villenage or slavery existed in the past, the testimony of those in the "menial" or degraded social position was excluded altogether. Cobb, in fact, came very close to saying that *law* was a system only for the free. One theory behind the exclusion, according to him, was reflected in the assertion of the early Jewish historian, Josephus, that the testimony of servants was not admitted "on account of the ignobility of their soul."[9] Masters, moreover, were ever reluctant to give up their property interests lightly, and especially to have them subject to the testimony of the ignominious. This presented a serious problem for the legal order. As the Maryland lawmakers observed in 1717: "[I]t too often happens that Negro Slaves, *&c.* commit many Heinous and Capital Crimes, which are endeavoured to be smothered, and concealed, or else such Negroes, *&c.* are conveyed to some other Province, and Sold by their Owners, who for the sake of the Interest they have in their Lives and Services, suffer them to escape Justice." The answer was not to admit the testimony of slaves but instead to provide compensation to the owners of slaves who were executed.[10] If the social position of slaves, as well as the property interests of their masters, generally barred slaves from the public courts as witnesses *altogether,* we have missed something.

The first Virginia statute that dealt with evidence in slave trials is conclusive of the fact that we have. It was a law of 1692 "for the more speedy prosecution of slaves committing Capitall Crimes."[11] The rules of evidence concerned testimony in capital cases. There is no indication of what rules applied in noncapital trials before the county Gentlemen Justices. In capital cases the only testimony of a slave ever mentioned is the confession of the accused. The other evidence is the "oaths of two witnesses or of one with pregnant circumstances." According to Hale's 1678 treatise, the evidence for the prisoner in English courts was often not under oath, and the examination of the prisoner prior to trial also was "not upon Oath." The 1692 Virginia law went further. It excluded all testimony not under oath except for the confession of the defendant. By the time the English colonies established slavery in the seventeenth century, the exclusion was not expressly social as it had been in the case of villenage. The exclusion now was religious. As Sir William Hawkins observed in the 1720s in his *Treatise of the Pleas of the Crown,* it was a good reason to exclude a witness because he was "an Infidel; That is, as I take it, that he believes neither the Old nor New Testament to be the Word of God; on one of which our Laws require the Oath should be administered." The evidentiary rule in the 1692 law referred first to the "oaths of two witnesses," and second it mentioned "or of one with pregnant circumstances." In either case a person had to take an oath, and the overwhelming majority of slaves at that time were non-Christians. They could take no oath in an English court. And seventeenth-century slaveholders notoriously obstructed efforts to proselytize amongst them for fear that conversion would lead to emancipation.[12]

As early as 1680 the Reverend Morgan Godwyn complained about this. Savage black slaves could not testify in Christian white English courts in cases where slaves were on trial for their lives, except to confess. Wholly consistent with this conclusion was an evidentiary rule buried deep within an elaborate 1705 statute establishing and regulating the proceedings in the General Court. It read "that popish recusants convict, negroes, mulattoes and Indian servants, and others, not being christians, shall be deemed and taken to be persons incapable in law, to be witnesses in any cases whatsoever."[13]

Whites, of course, never viewed slaves as paragons of truthfulness. Landon Carter, for example, wrote in 1777: "Do not bring your negroe to contradict me! A negroe and a passionate woman are equal as to truth or falsehood; for neither thinks of what they say." And Cobb, in the next century, argued "[that] the negro, as a general rule, is mendacious, is a fact too well established to require the production of proof, either from history, travels or craniology."[14]

The result of such beliefs, and of the corresponding legal rules, was that until 1723 slaves could not testify (except to confess) in any capital case in a Virginia court. They were largely outside the legal order except as objects of the rules of property. But in that year the rule was changed, and the reason shows that evidentiary rules could arise directly from a concern to maintain domination as much as to assure justice. The preamble to the statute made clear the reason for changing the evidentiary rule: it was to remove the difficulties of punishing secret plots and conspiracies "known only to such, as by the laws now established, are not accounted legal evidence." Governor Sir William Gooch some years later, explained that one of the problems facing white Virginians in many slave cases before 1723 was that "there could be no legal proof, so as to convict them." The change in the evidentiary rule was occasioned by white fears over slave insurrections, but it was not limited to rebels. It applied to all capital cases. In any event the burgesses dropped the two-witness requirement but added that the trial court could accept "such testimony of Negroes, Mulattos, or Indians, bond or free, with pregnant circumstances, as to them shall seem convincing."[15] Even in England the two-witness rule was transformed during the eighteenth century. By the century's end it was retained only in cases of perjury and treason.[16] The requirement that the evidence of blacks be supported by pregnant circumstances, however, was the functional equivalent of the two-witness rule.

Once the testimony of slaves was admitted, the problem of perjury arose. Coke defined the crime of perjury at common law in such a way that it could not apply to the testimony of the overwhelming majority of slaves in colonial Virginia. It was bound with the oath. "Perjury," he wrote, "is a crime committed, when a lawfull oath is ministered by any that hath authority, to any person, in any judiciall proceedings, who sweareth absolutely, and falsly in a matter materiall to the issue."[17] This definition would not do: nor would the normal punishment for perjury, which was a fine and/or imprisonment. The law of 1723 therefore provided a charge from the court that included the penalty which was designed to assure that slaves as non-Christians would be under "the greater obligation to declare the truth." The charge was this:

> You are brought hither as a witness; and, by the direction of the law, I am to tell you, before you give your evidence, that you must tell the truth, the whole truth, and nothing but the truth; and that if it be found hereafter, that you tell a lie, and give false testimony in this matter, you must, for so doing, have both your ears nailed to the pillory, and cut off, and receive thirty-nine lashes on your bare back, well laid on, at the common whipping-post.[18]

Six years after the adoption of this law, Toney and Jone, slaves in Richmond County, learned its bloody seriousness as they lost their ears. So did the slave Mary in Lancaster County in 1752. However, by that time there is evidence that this law was not always strictly followed. In Lancaster County in 1754, Alec, who was found guilty of having given false evidence against two fellow slaves, received only six lashes. And in that same county in 1756, Will received thirty-nine lashes for "letting a Lye in his Evidence Relating to Sambo," on trial for hog stealing.[19] The 1723 law remained the basis for the admission of evidence in capital trials of slaves in Virginia to the end of slavery in 1865, despite the vagaries of enforcement.

Before the rules in other colonies and states are taken up, a word about the phrase *pregnant circumstances.* The legal treatises Virginians used, such as Michael Dalton's, or Hales's, or Hawkins's, did not use the phrase.[20] J. H. Baker, in his study of the criminal courts and procedure from 1550 to 1800, has noted that "strong and pregnant presumption" was all that was necessary, according to some, to show that Crown evidence was sufficiently "meet" or "fit" to proceed to trial. He did not say it was sufficient or necessary to convict. Hale referred to strong presumptive evidence, but he warned against it. He gave as an example a case in which a man was found riding a horse that had been stolen. This created a strong presumption that he stole the horse, and in the case Hale related the man was executed. Later the real thief confessed.[21]

Sir William Blackstone discussed what he called "*circumstantial* evidence or the doctrine of *presumptions.*" His categorization includes violent, probable, and light, or rash presumptions. The first is "many times equal to full proof; for there those circumstances appear, which *necessarily* attend the fact." It is unlikely that the Virginians had this in mind. A violent presumption can be full proof, and then it would not be necessary to admit the testimony of a savage black slave at all. The next category comes closer. Probable presumptions arise from a set of circumstances that "*usually*" attend a fact and should be given "due weight." This kind of circumstantial evidence could be used to lend credibility to the testimony of a slave precisely because the last category, light, or rash, was not entitled to any consideration whatsoever.[22]

Now to return to the rules in the colonies. The rules in Delaware are not clear. The law simply authorized the court to "acquit or condemn according to their Evidence" and to condemn "upon due Proof to them made." In Maryland a similar evidentiary history to that in Virginia developed. The first mention of the testimony of slaves has been noted. Inferentially, at least, the testimony of slaves was inadmissible in capital slave trials. The first mention of separate capital trials was a law of 1729, nearly contemporary to the critical Virginia law. It refers only to a slave "convict, by confession, or verdict of a jury." There is no reason to believe that slaves testified in such trials in Maryland any more than in

Virginia. Aside from the evidence from the 1717 law, and from the fact that the basic common-law system prevailed, there is additional evidence in the colonial perjury law of 1699. The Maryland law punished perjury by fines, a year in jail, and exclusion in perpetuity from being sworn as a witness; if a person could not pay his fine, he was to have his ears nailed, but not cut off. There was no other perjury statute, and this one did not embrace non-Christian slaves, who could not swear an oath. The Delaware law provided that those guilty of perjury would be punished according to the law of Great Britain. The language in the first direct law in Maryland on slave testimony in capital cases lends more support insofar as Maryland is concerned. A law of 1751 referred to a conviction of a slave "upon his, her or their voluntary confession, or the verdict of a jury, upon the testimony of one or more legal or credible witness or witnesses, or even the testimony or the evidence of other slaves, corroborated with such pregnant circumstances as shall convince and satisfy" those hearing the case. The punishment for perjury by a slave followed Virginia. To the south the colony of North Carolina adopted the Virginia law in 1741.[23]

The evidentiary history in South Carolina differed. Its law of 1690 mentioned only that a magistrate was to conduct a *preliminary examination* where he was to have "all persons to come before him that can give evidence." It is not certain that this meant only those persons who could give evidence in an English court. The trial that followed was to be based upon the testimony of the "evidences." In English West Indian colonies, according to Elsa Goveia, "at the discretion of the courts, the evidence of slaves was admitted for or against other slaves" during the eighteenth century. But, according to Cobb, this was similar to the rule in the French colonies where judges could use such testimony only to "illustrate other testimony." The evidence for South Carolina is inconclusive. The next law was one of 1712 that charged the court trying a slave with "diligently weighing and examining all evidences, proofs and testimonies." "Violent presumption and circumstances" could be considered in cases of murder. In petty larceny cases slaves could be found guilty by "confession, proof, or probable circumstances." Finally, in a separate part of the statute, this appeared:

> That the confession of any slave accused, or the testimony of any other slave, that the justices and freeholders shall have reason to believe to speak truth, shall be held for good and convincing evidence in all petty larcenies or trespasses, not exceeding forty shillings; but no negro or other slave shall suffer loss of life or limb, but such as shall be convicted, either by their own free and voluntary confession, or by the oath of christian evidence, or, at least, by the plain and positive evidence of two negroes or slaves, so circumstantiated as that there shall not be sufficient reason to doubt the truth thereof, and examination being always made, if the negroes or slaves that give evidence, do not

bear any malice to the other slave accused; excepting in the case of murder, in which case, the evidence of one slave, attended with such circumstances as that the justices and freeholders shall have no just reason to suspect the truth thereof, of which they are hereby made judges, or upon violent presumption of the accused person's guilt.[24]

This was a complex effort to construct different layers of evidentiary rules depending upon the seriousness of the offense. In minor crimes, the rule resembles the Virginia law of 1723 on major slave crimes. The two-witness rule, possibly reenforced by something like a "pregnant circumstances" rule, applies to slave testimony in major crimes, except for murder, where once again the rule resembles the Virginia law of 1723. South Carolina abandoned this confusing effort in 1735. By then the evidentiary rule was basically the same as elsewhere: "[T]he confession of any slave accused, or the testimony of any other slave or slaves, attended with circumstances of truth and credit, shall be deemed good and convincing evidence on the trial of any slave or slaves for any of the crimes aforesaid, or any other crimes, capital or criminal; of the strength of which evidence, the said justices and freeholders who try the same, are hereby made sufficient and competent judges."[25]

By 1740 the rule took its final form in South Carolina. Now the evidence "of any slave, without oath, shall be allowed and admitted in all causes whatsoever, for or against another slave accused of any crime or offence whatsoever; the weight of which evidence being seriously considered, and compared with all other circumstances, attending the case, shall be left to the conscience of the justices and freeholders."[26] There was no oath, no two-witness rule, and no requirement that the testimony of slaves be corroborated by "pregnant circumstances."

The only voice raised in protest against this 1740 law was that of John Belton O'Neall, and that was not until 1848, by which time many slaves were Christians. O'Neall argued for the propriety of taking slave testimony under oath: "Negroes (slaves or free) will feel the sanctions of an oath, with as much force as any of the ignorant classes of white people, in a Christian country."[27] The legislature did not agree.

Virginia and South Carolina displayed a legal atavism found nowhere else in the antebellum South. Both retained evidentiary rules framed between 1720 and 1740. In 1808 Maryland provided that the testimony of slaves was admissible either for or against a slave defendant in all criminal prosecutions. There was no reference to "pregnant circumstances." Georgia modified its rule slightly in 1816: "[O]n the trial of a slave or free person of colour, any witness shall be sworn who believes in God and a future state of rewards and punishments."[28]

Without a doubt, however, the most interesting transformation occurred in 1821 in *State* v. *Ben*, where the issue of slave testimony, and especially the pregnant-circumstances standard, came before the North

Carolina Supreme Court. Here different views, missing from the black letter of a statute, were articulated by the judges. Daniel Flanigan, one of the few to analyze this decision, has condemned the reasoning of the majority opinion of Chief Justice John Louis Taylor, which overthrew the pregnant-circumstances rule, and led to the execution of Ben for burglary. It was based upon a "superficial equalitarian rhetoric" blind to the realities of slavery and to the fact that the pregnant-circumstances rule was actually both a "relic" and an "important statutory protection" for slaves. There are some important assumptions in Flanigan's analysis. One of those was that the rule should have been retained. But why? The assumption that this was an important protection for slaves may rest upon the notion that Southern whites were correct, after all: slaves could not be trusted to tell the truth because they were not free agents, and therefore no slave should ever be condemned on the testimony of slaves alone, without some corroboration. This was the view of the abolitionist critics Stroud and Goodell. They had argued that the testimony of slaves against slaves was especially suspect because Southern law allowed the emancipation of slaves for "meritorious services," one of which was *"giving information of crimes committed by a slave."*[29] This is fanciful except in the case of insurrections, where it does hold true.[30] But it also rests upon a pejorative view of slaves themselves, of their sense of community and solidarity. Susan Rhodes, a former slave, recalled, for example, that "People in my day didn't know book learning but dey studied how to protect each other, and save 'em from such misery as they could."[31] I do not mean to suggest that Flanigan had in mind a negative view of the sense of community among the slaves, only that it lay beneath the surface of the abolitionist argument. Another possible unwritten assumption, which I do not share, could be that because of the cruelty of human bondage, almost all slave offenses should be viewed as "political." From this standpoint, they were protests against degradation, and therefore rather ordinary rules of law used to convict rather ordinary felons should not apply.

Whether one assumes that slaves could not be trusted to tell the truth or takes all slave offenses to be "political," the result seems to be the same: Slave testimony should not be tested by the ordinary rules. In any event, Taylor's 1821 opinion did not proceed upon such assumptions. He argued that from 1793 forward basic, common-law rules of evidence applied in the trials of slaves. The law of that year granted trial by jury to slaves, and Taylor argued that it drew "after it, as an incident, the common-law principles of evidence and all the consequences of common-law proceedings."[32]

Taylor admitted one exception, and it is ironic. A law of 1802 retained the evidentiary rule from 1741 in cases of trials of slaves for insurrection, or conspiracy to rebel. This was a narrow exception in his view and was "passed soon after some disturbances had arisen among the slaves in the lower part of the State, and the clause was probably re-enacted for the purpose of tempering that excess which public excitement had produced in the trials for these offenses."[33] The irony, of course, is that the rule originally had been tied to a law designed to uncover slave insurrections, but was retained in order to protect slaves against white hysteria about such insurrections.

Judge John Hall vigorously dissented. "That the policy of the law of 1741," he wrote, "was founded on a sense of the degraded state in which those unhappy beings existed, no doubt, will be ceded. Being slaves, they had no will of their own, and a humane policy forbade that the life of a human being [one of themselves] should be taken away upon testimony coming from them, unless some circumstance appeared in aid of that testimony."[34] The testimony of social subordinates simply was not to be believed. They lacked free will. The majority of the court, however, disagreed with Hall's analysis based upon social status.

Outside of the older colonial slave societies, the pregnant-circumstances requirement appeared for a time in Kentucky, Tennessee, Mississippi, and Alabama. It did not appear in other states, and these four dropped the rule between the 1830s and the 1850s. Elsewhere the evidence of slaves was sufficient to convict or acquit, and in Georgia and Louisiana it could be testimony taken under oath.[35]

Whether sworn or not, and it usually was not, by the nineteenth century the evidence of slaves could be sufficient to convict or acquit slaves. The problem of perjury was universally dealt with by corporal punishment. Most states had substituted whipping for the mutilation adopted in Virginia, but it could be severe. In some states the number of lashes was thirty-nine, and in Alabama the number could reach 100, and the perjurer would then be branded with a P.[36]

* * *

While the rules of evidence regarding the admissibility of the testimony of slaves in the trials of slaves had changed considerably by the nineteenth century the question remains, how did it work in practice? Was it common for slaves to be convicted, or acquitted solely on the basis of the testimony of other slaves? Betty Wood, in her study of a handful of slave trials in Georgia, for example, has suggested that it was not. She found only one in which the verdict was "[at least in theory] entirely dependent upon evidence supplied by other slaves." The accused was convicted, hanged, and his head was put up on a pole.[37] This case does not show that a slave had been convicted solely on the testimony of other slaves: they had attempted to establish his innocence.

While slaves often tried to help one another with their testimony, it was not always so. In 1746 in Lancaster County, Virginia, the slave Guy was convicted—on the testimony of three slaves, two of whom were slaves of Guy's owner, Landon Carter—of stealing breeches valued at one shilling. He was given thirty-five lashes. In 1750 in the same county, Sarah at first pleaded not guilty when placed on trial, but later she pleaded guilty to having "rec'd Sundry" goods. She then implicated seven slaves in all, and only one of them was discharged. Sarah apparently testified in order to minimize her own punishment.[38]

Some slaves turned state's evidence in capital burglary trials in order to save their lives. In 1741 Ben and Dedan were indicted for breaking and entering the public warehouse and stealing a hogshead of tobacco. The evidence against Ben was given by Jacob, George, and Dedan, all slaves. Dedan was "released from his tryal" because he had become "a material evidence for our Sovereign lord the King." Ben was found guilty, but he was not executed because he was granted his clergy.[39] Slaves were no more heroic or ignominious than anyone else, and to overlook this obvious fact is to slip into romanticism.

Similar impressions emerge from the nineteenth-century records. In Fairfield County, South Carolina, for example, four slaves and a free black were tried for "violating the peace" in 1849. The testimony came from two slaves, Tom and William. Tom testified that George and Levy "were Quarreling at the time he Saw George have a knife in his hand and open and heard him say to Levy that if he did not Stand away from him he would Cut or Stick him he saw Levy go to the fence and Get a piece of a Fence Rail he was persuaded to and did lay the Rail down." William testified that Elijah Bond, the free black, "commenced the Quarrel with George."[40] It was when conflicts erupted within the slave or black community that one could expect cases to rest solely upon the testimony of slaves.

One special category of crime was the conspiracy to commit an insurrection. This was precisely the crime that had led Southern whites to admit slave testimony in the first place. Clearly, such testimony was critical in convicting the slave defendants. It was critical, for instance, in the insurrection panic that hit the iron fields in Tennessee in 1856. But in insurrection conspiracy cases, slave testimony was often obtained in clear violation of normal common-law rules. It came as the result of confessions or accusations that followed torture. Torture was commonplace in civil law systems such as in Spanish Louisiana. In 1771, for instance, a Louisiana slave was ordered to "be tortured to make him confess who were his accomplices."[41] The use of torture was not a feature of the common law, however. Southern whites nonetheless were not squeamish about the use of the whip despite the common-law tradition, and this was especially true in cases involving charges of insurrection.

The major insurrection cases are well known.[42] But the use of force to obtain evidence or confessions was also used on lesser occasions. In Spartanburg County, South Carolina, for example, a number of slaves were "tried" at Otts Bridge on September 24, 1860. A number of whites conducted this ad hoc trial. They even kept written testimony, which was turned over to the lawful authorities. After slaves such as John and Glenn testified about some mysterious white man, seven slaves were ordered blindfolded and whipped between thirty and eighty-five lashes apiece. On September 28 there was a formal indictment against Jerry, Anderson, Ellis, Andy, and Steve for a conspiracy to raise an insurrection in the neighborhood. The trial before the magistrate-freeholders began on October 2, 1860. The primary testimony came from the same John who had been tried and found guilty at Otts Bridge. He testified that he had not told the whole truth there because he was afraid. His current evidence came after he was "whipped in jail and made to tell it." What he testified to was that he was at a cave where there were some runaways. According to John, "Anderson was talking about being set free—people wer [sic] coming from the North to set them free said he expected the black people would have to fight and he would fight if he was obliged to. Ellis said about the same." There was virtually nothing said about the other slaves, and on the testimony of John the magistrate-freeholders reached this verdict: "[T]he boys Anderson and Ellis they think are guilty to some extent." The members of the court added that "they think that they may have had some thought and made some preparation of an insurrectionary tendency." The magistrate-freeholders ordered them to receive fifty lashes each.[43]

Despite such occasional reliance on the "evidence" of slaves, the overwhelming majority of criminal trials of slaves in the South did not turn on the testimony of slaves alone.[44] The testimony of whites was necessarily involved for some crimes, such as rapes, assaults on whites, or attempts to kill whites. The few crimes that did involve only the testimony of slaves were slave-insurrection conspiracies, crimes that arose out of some disruption within the slave community itself, or, finally, the handful of criminal cases when slaves turned state's evidence in order to minimize or escape punishment.

*   *   *

The major exception was the "confession," which had always been admitted into evidence. Greenleaf has noted that confessions of guilt were to be received with considerable caution. Among the reasons were the fact that a prisoner might be "oppressed by the calamity of his situation" and influenced by motives of "hope or fear." Nevertheless, if the threshold problem of admissibility were crossed, "deliberate confessions of guilt" were to be viewed as "the most effectual proofs in the law." This rested upon the view that "they are deliberate and voluntary, and on the presumption, that a rational being will not make admissions prejudicial to his interest and safety, unless when urged by the promptings of truth and conscience."[45]

A suggestive view of lower-class defendants is that they often behaved with submissiveness and deference when brought into court before their social "betters."[46] One test of this view when applied to slaves would be the commonness of confessions. By this test slaves must have been a dis-

appointment. They rarely confessed. In eleven Virginia counties examined for eighteenth-century cases, for instance, I found only fifteen confessions.[47] The relative numbers of confessions did not rise in the next
century, either.[48] One of the early Virginia cases, moreover, is not truly a
confession at all. In 1730 Harry lost his ears in Richmond County for
stabbing another slave. The only evidentiary entry was that he was adjudged guilty "not Denying What is laid to his charge."[49] This is a case of
a slave whose refusal to plead was taken as a confession of guilt.

One of the more interesting cases involved a murder. It is interesting both because it is so rare and because it was one of the only cases that
arose before the admission of slave testimony in 1723. It was in the trial
of Wapping in 1722 in Lancaster County for the murder of Guy, another
slave. He had assaulted him with "Axes Clubs &c." If slaves could not
testify against each other before the 1720s, and if almost none "confessed" like Wapping, how much criminal conduct by slaves was not punished in public courts as a practical matter before that time? Scholars
have often claimed that slave crime increased by the middle of the eighteenth century,[50] but they have failed to see that one reason for the statistical increase is the earlier exclusion of slave testimony. This skews the
picture and may well present a false impression of the magnitude of the
increase.

* * *

We know, of course, that owners often punished offenses on the plantation; but what happened if the offender or the offense never came to
the attention of the whites? Was there some mode of social control among
the slaves in their conduct toward one another? Were they in the process
of creating a body of norms for conduct within the quarters in terms of
respect for possessions, or norms that regulated sexual relationships
which, if broken, brought out some sanction by the slaves themselves?
Scholars have recognized the degree to which slaves created first a pid-
gin and then a creolized language within the quarters, and the fact that
they firmly grasped, even when they modified, the various elements of
African culture. This included such things as rhythmic patterns, religious
practices, and folk tales.[51] But if they retained all of this in syncretic forms,
why should we assume that they failed to retain any of the various African notions of legal right and wrong and legal ways of social control?
Unfortunately, the degree to which slaves might have held on to ways to
define acceptable behavior within the quarters, and to sanction devia-
tions, is beyond recall. Nonetheless, there is one very suggestive piece of
evidence recounted by Thomas Webber in his work on the significance
of the "spirit world" among the slaves. It concerns the manner of uncov-
ering thieves within the quarters:

> The third way of detecting thieves was taught by the fathers and moth-
> ers of the slaves. They said no matter how untrue a man might have

been during his life, when he came to die he had to tell the truth and had to own everything he had ever done, and whatever dealing those alive had with anything pertaining to the dead, must be true, or they would immediately die and go to hell to burn in fire and brimstone. So in consequence of this, the graveyard dust was the truest of the three ways in detecting thieves. The dust would be taken from the grave of a person who had died last and put into a bottle with water. Then two of the men of the examining committee would use the same words as in the case of the Bible and the sieve, "John stole that chicken," "John did not steal that chicken," and after this had gone on for about five minutes, then one of the other two who attended to the Bible and the sieve would say, "John, you are accused of stealing that chicken that was taken from Sam's chicken coop at such a time." "In the name of the Father and the Son and the Holy Ghost, if you have taken Sam's chicken don't drink this water, for if you do you will die and go to hell and be burned in fire and brimstone but if you have not you may take it and it will not hurt you." So if John had taken the chicken he would own it rather than take the water.[52]

Such a "trial," with its rules of evidence, shows it is a reasonable speculation that the slaves maintained a quasi-legal order among themselves despite their exclusion for most purposes from the courts of the whites. Surely the legal notions of Africans did not suddenly disappear any more than their view of appropriate family relationships or the significance of magic.

*   *   *

There was, then, enormous complexity and ambivalence in the ways slave conduct was controlled and sanctioned if it fell outside accepted norms, and public law was only one level of control. Offenses might be dealt with outside the public courts by the whites on the plantations or by the blacks themselves outside the observation of the whites; there was also the discipline that existed within the Southern churches.[53] But the immediate question is that of slave evidence in the courts of the whites. With the evidence in the public courts, there were serious problems presented—above all by the confession. They focus around the question of "voluntariness."[54] In some cases there is no doubt whatever that the confession was not the result of a voluntary act by the accused. For instance, in 1818 in Richmond, Virginia, the Common Council verified a charge that an "engine of torture," which turned out to be a finger screw, had been used by public authorities to extort confessions from black defendants, regardless of the crime. Or consider the matter-of-fact entry in the case of the trial of Ben for burglary in Southampton County, Virginia, in 1821. After his arrest he "was . . . taken out and with small cords Suspended by the thumbs for about one minute, but the prisoner made no confession he was then tied by the toes and drawn up but not entirely off the ground," but he still did not confess. After he spent the night in the custody of a young man, he did confess, although the record does not show why. He was sentenced to hang with a recommendation that he be transported. His counsel made no complaint.[55]

But there is an even deeper question about "voluntariness" that arose because of the use of violence. If slaves were without wills of their own, how could their confessions ever be voluntary, and therefore admissible? This question surfaced within the context of both judicial and extrajudicial confessions. Cobb, for one, argued that extrajudicial confessions, when made to masters, should not be admissible as evidence. According to him, the slave "is bound, and habituated to obey every command and wish" of the master. The slave

> has no will to refuse obedience, even when it involves his life. The master is his protector, his counsel, his confidant. . . . Every consideration which induces the law to protect from disclosures confidential communications made to legal advisers, applies with increased force to communications made by a slave to his master. Moreover, experience shows, that the slave is always ready to mould his answers so as to please the master, and that no confidence can be placed in the truth of his statements.[56]

Southern jurists usually did not go that far. Nearly all the appellate cases came during the 1850s, but the first notable one was decided in 1830 in North Carolina in *State* v. *Charity*. This case turned on the admissibility of evidence of a master. Judge Thomas Ruffin focused upon the question of whether a master could testify for or against his slave, but in the course of his analysis he mentioned that confessions "being to the master, may or may not be of that voluntary character which the law, not less in wisdom than humanity, requires"; but this case did not require an examination of that problem, which presented "not a little difficulty." Judge Hall remarked that the slave might object to her master giving as evidence her confession to him because "he is authorized to defend her; and because she is his slave, and by various means, against which slavery could make but little resistance, he might exact from her any confessions he pleased." He added, however, that "upon this part of the case I give no opinion." Chief Justice Leonard Henderson believed that the confessions of slaves to masters ought always to be excluded from evidence. "The master," he noted, "has an almost absolute control over both the body and mind of his slave. The master's will is the slave's will. All his acts, all his sayings are made with a view to propitiate his master. His confessions are made, not from a love of truth, not from a sense of duty, not to speak a falsehood, but to please his master."[57]

Courts that faced the issue later did not go as far as Henderson urged in 1830, or as Cobb suggested in his late-1850s treatise. Still, judges often were suspicious of confessions made by slaves to those with direct authority over them. Edwin and Nelson, for instance, were tried for murder in Louisiana in 1848. The court overturned the guilty verdict against Nelson and affirmed that against Edwin. Judge George Rogers King held that Edwin had made his confessions repeatedly, and voluntarily, and that the only constraint upon him was that necessary "for his safe custody." Nelson's case was different. He confessed to the overseer, who was the owner's son, while he "was in the stocks" and after the son declared that "it would be better for him to tell what he had done." The court was not disturbed by the fact that Nelson was in stocks. This did not "authorize the conclusion that, threats or violence were used to extort confessions." He was in stocks "only for safekeeping." The problem concerned the remark made by the overseer. The confession to him came "strictly within the rules which should have excluded it from evidence. It was made to his young master . . . to whose authority he habitually submitted, to whom he would naturally look for protection. . . . [T]he admonition coming from such a source was well calculated to inspire the slave with the hope of protection from the consequences of his act if fully confessed," and it should have been excluded.[58]

An Alabama court reached a similar conclusion in an arson case against the slave Wyatt. Chief Justice William P. Chilton did not contend that all confessions made to masters by slaves should be excluded, but he did argue that the court should examine "with caution, whether the confessions of guilt made by a slave in interviews had with his master, or one having dominion over him, were not elicited or controlled by the relation, and predicated upon the fear of punishment or injury, or upon the hope of some benefit to be gained by making them." The Alabama court ruled the confession to the master in this case was not voluntary, and should have been thrown out.[59]

A final example should do. It concerns an arson case, *Simon [a slave] v. State*. In this case Simon was examined by the mayor of Pensacola, who told him that if he had burned the house "he would be put upon his trial and would be certainly hung; that if he had any accomplices he would, by testifying against them, become State's evidence, and they would be put upon their trial and not him." The mayor noted that there was a loud crowd outside and that they said the prisoner should be hung. Simon asked for his master, to whom he would tell the whole truth. He confessed. According to his master he "was under a great state of excitement . . . was laboring under great terror, and . . . he never saw any one more terrified." Judge Albert Semmes, for the majority of the Florida court, ruled this and subsequent confessions inadmissible. "Independent of these confessions," Semmes wrote, the fact that the accused was a slave who had confessed to his master was "entitled to the most grave consideration; the ease with which this class of our population can be intimidated, and the almost absolute control which the owner . . . [has] over the will of the slave, should induce the courts at all times to receive their confessions with the utmost caution and distrust."[60]

A major exception to this line of cases came in Mississippi in 1857 in *Sam [a slave]* v. *State.* Sam's owner had captured his slave, "chained his legs together, and brought him home in the stage-coach." He asked him why he burned the gin house, and Sam allegedly replied, because he "wished to be hung." Judge Alexander Handy, for the court, upheld the conviction based in part on the confession. His reasoning was that "The relation which the slave bears to the master, is certainly one of dependence and obedience, but it is not necessarily one of constraint and duress." Patriarchalism had a severe price, not the least of which was this characterization of the master-slave relationship. "It is not to be presumed," Handy continued, "that the master exercises an undue influence over his slave to induce him to make confessions tending to convict him of a capital offence, because besides the feelings of justice and humanity, which would forbid such efforts, it would be against the interest of the master that the slave should make confessions which would forfeit his life; for he would thereby sustain a loss to the amount of one-half of the value of the slave." It would be extremely dangerous to exclude the confessions of slaves to masters:

> Such confessions are not incompetent upon any sound legal principle; and to establish the rule that they are incompetent, would be highly impolitic and dangerous; because, from the nature of the connection between master and slave, if confessions fully made to him should not be admissible, they would not be likely to be made to any others; and thus, however true the confessions, and however strongly corroborated by circumstances, all violations of law committed by slaves, the proof of which depended on that sort of evidence, would go unpunished in the courts of justice. And the consequence of this would be, that a disposition would be created to punish slaves, otherwise than according to the rules and restraints of the law, which should operate, both in its protection and in its punishments, upon them, as well as upon white men.[61]

Obviously, a different legal problem was presented when slaves "confessed" to the murder of those with direct authority over them. Now the significance of subordination or deference to those to whom confessions were given became murky. All of the appellate cases in which the problem was considered arose after 1850. That the issue arose at all and when it did reflected a heightened concern on the part of Southern jurists with fairness in slave trials.

One of the first cases in which the problem was considered was *Alfred* v. *State,* a Tennessee case decided in 1853. The court upheld the convictions of the slaves for the murder of their master despite objections to the admissibility of certain evidence. Under the law of Tennessee a magistrate before whom defendants were brought was to "record the examination of the party" and transmit the written record to the trial court. It appears that there was a confession made by each slave to someone other than the committing magistrate. These confessions, the court noted, "were attended by such circumstances as to render them incompetent." The lower court had held them to be so but permitted them to go to the jury. But the real question for the appellate court concerned the confessions taken by the magistrate. These were "competent." The court argued that if a defendant "be cautioned by the magistrate that whatever he may say may be used against him, and that he is not bound to criminate himself, but that it is his privilege to submit to an examination or not, at his option, there certainly can be no good reason why any statements or confessions he may make under such circumstances should not be good evidence against him." Slaves possessed a right against self-incrimination and were to be warned by a committing magistrate of this right.[62] At least they possessed the right in the abstract.

Three years later the Georgia court confronted this problem in *Rafe [a slave]* v. *State*. The slave Rafe confessed to the sheriff of Liberty County, who was bringing Rafe back from Savannah. On the way back the sheriff met others, and an interrogation followed. During the course of it the sheriff told Rafe that the people of the county believed he had killed his master. The sheriff then said that "if he did do it he had better acknowledge it, but if he did not do it not to acknowledge it; that if he lied, it would be adding sin to sin; that the people of Liberty were so satisfied he did it they would hang him any how." After that Rafe confessed, but as the sheriff put it, "Prisoner has confessed and denied several times since to me and others." The court ruled the confessions admissible since they were "not elicited by promises or threats; and although they may have been induced by the remarks and interrogation of the Sheriff, the record shows that they were voluntarily made." The court, through Judge Charles J. McDonald, hastened to add that it disapproved "of the manner in which they were obtained—spiritual exhortations had better be left to the clergy."[63]

That same year the Mississippi high court also ruled on an important confessions case, *Dick [a slave]* v. *State*. This case involved the confessions made to white persons who did not have authority over the slaves as either magistrate or master. The slaves were found guilty of the murder of their master, whom they allegedly had choked to death. Counsel for the slaves made a bold effort to invalidate their confessions. They had come late in the evening after some whites had been with the slaves all day, and it was not until there were about eighteen to twenty whites surrounding them, and after they were arrested, chained, and told to confess, that they did so. "The man who is born a slave, raised a slave, and knows, and feels his destiny and lot is to die a slave," counsel argued, "always under a superior, controlling his actions and his will, cannot be supposed to act or speak voluntarily and of his free will, while surrounded by fifteen or twenty of those to whom he knows he is subservient, and by the law bound to obey." He continued by asserting that,

> Such a being, in his physical, moral, and intellectual faculties, is, and must ever be, more or less subservient to the will and wishes of the freeman having the control over him; and when in chains, and informed that it would be better for him to confess, is under duress. Place man physically and morally, in perpetual slavery, and how can the intellectual man be free? Perpetual slavery and free will are incompatible with each other.

Cobb agreed—but then, so did Rousseau.[64] Precisely because of their speaker's social status, the confessions of slaves should always be suspect—and to the point of total exclusion.

The Mississippi court, however, did not rise to this challenge in 1856, any more than it would a year later in Sam's case. It focused on the fact that the confessions were not made before an officer during a judicial examination. It admitted that "No warning of any kind whatever, was given to the prisoners of their rights—and that they were not bound to make any confession, by which they would criminate themselves." But this was a right that existed only in the context of an official examination. As long as no effort was made by private parties to induce the slaves to confess by "threats or promises," the confessions would be held to be "perfectly voluntary." Subordination, even to all whites, did not preclude "voluntariness" in Southern courts. The court, of course, did not discuss the notion that from the point of view of slaves, all whites were persons in "authority." This is a question of considerable significance. Goodell, for instance, has cited a number of Southern statutes to show that slaves were held to be in subjection to all white persons. And the South Carolina Supreme Court held in *Ex parte Boylston* that it was a criminal offense, triable in a magistrate-freeholders court, for a slave to be insolent to a white.[65] Would not such a view of the relationship between slaves and all whites necessarily raise a serious question about the "voluntariness" of any confession given by a slave to any white? And would that not in turn bring us back to the notion that because of the "ignominy of the soul" that flowed out of social degradation, the testimony of slaves, including their confessions, should be excluded?

Mark Tushnet has suggested that courts began to recognize that coerciveness was essential in the master-slave relationship and that this was "ultimately subversive of the general rule of voluntariness." The rule could be preserved only if it were preserved for third parties, "particularly representatives of the state," who were independent of the master class. This proved impossible, in Tushnet's view, because "of the threat to public order and self-conception" that a special slave law created. I agree up to a point. But this view overlooks the significance of race. It was impossible to completely preserve "voluntariness," not solely because of the threat to public order—and that was genuine—but also because whites in general were not always conceptually separated from the "master class." Slaves were considered to be subordinate to all whites, and therefore voluntariness could not have been preserved even for third parties. But this would not necessarily mean that all confessions had to be excluded from evidence, even though that was one strong answer. Another might have been to admit all confessions and leave it to the court or jury to give them what weight they deserved in the circumstances. This was the approach of Scottish law, as Tushnet noted, and was applauded by Chief Justice Joseph Henry Lumpkin, an opponent of legal technicality, in *Stephen* v. *State*.[66] This would have amounted to treating slave confessions in a fashion similar to slave testimony generally in the West Indies during the eighteenth century. It was ultimately a matter of policy, and Southern whites had always shown themselves to be quite supple about such matters. Nonetheless, in this case it seems likely that the weight of legal traditions and learned practice blunted any widespread move toward the Scottish solution.

Conclusion

Legal traditions, religious values, the imperatives of social subordination, racism, and even property interests, then, could determine whether a person would be admitted as a witness in a criminal case, and they could determine the way evidence was weighed if it were received. But this was contingent. Down to the 1720s slaves generally were excluded from Southern courts except in noncapital cases, with the possible exception of South Carolina. Fear of the violent resistance of the slaves compelled the admission of their testimony, even though with conditions and restraints. As in the West Indies, the testimony would be accepted, but the weight of it was for the triers of fact to determine, and it had to be corroborated, at least in capital cases. For slaves, law was more often the rules of the plantation, or even their own norms and sanctions. As Judge David Wardlaw of South Carolina observed in a leading slave insolence case, the law as to slaves was but "a compact between his rulers" with which the slaves had nothing to do.[67] On occasion this meant, especially before the 1720s, that some slave "crime" was not punishable in the public courts of the South. It was a price Southern whites paid for refusing to allow the testimony of pagan blacks. Slaves then existed in a sort of limbo, the abode of souls barred from heaven because of not having received Christian baptism. They were also barred from Southern courts at times and existed only in the shadows of the legal order. It was fear of violent resistance coming from those shadows that finally overcame legal traditions derived from England.

As the Civil War approached there was evidence that the testimony of slaves would be taken more seriously, either by being taken under oath or by being allowed without the requirement that it be corroborated by pregnant circumstances. This was another dimension of the fact that slaves were increasingly drawn into the normal criminal justice system. The end result of this line of legal development could have cut very deeply into the claims and prerogatives of masters—with very serious consequences. In the face of such developments and threats, Southern whites erected ideological defenses of their social order,[68] which brought to the fore the problem of social subordination. This, in turn, raised serious questions about slave confessions, questions that had never been openly asked or considered before.

Forced to confront a relationship that ultimately rested upon the whip, some argued in the nineteenth century that confessions of slaves to masters were suspect and ought to be wholly excluded. The logic of this position could not have been kept within bounds since Southern whites argued that black slaves were to show deference to all whites. There was no principled way to limit the analysis as long as the slave system was inextricably tied in Southern white discourse with the problem of race. The result could have been a swing back to the medieval view that had excluded the evidence of villeins. This, however, was in tension with the modern legal developments whereby slaves were granted more and more procedural rights in Southern courts, including such legal securities as the right to a jury trial, the right to counsel, and the right to an appeal.[69]

There clearly were contradictory tendencies at work in Southern criminal law as it applied to slaves, and there was no inevitable resolution of the tensions. The resolution came as a result of the bloodbath that began in 1861, but it was far from certain before that. One thing, however, was certain. Rules of evidence—rules fashioned to control juries and lawyers—were also constructed to assure the property interests of slaveholders, and the domination of blacks by whites. Some of the rules of evidence might have been evenhanded for those who possessed property—or at least who were entitled to acquire it—but generally those examined here would never be fair for persons of color, and especially for those who were held as property. There had even been times when slaves were unprotected at law—they were not even admitted to the mysteries of the criminal side of the legal order, unless the case were minor or unless they confessed. As Cobb had observed, law was for the "*othesworth,*"[70] and that meant it was for the free.

Notes

1. William Goodell, *The American Slave Code in Theory and Practice: Its Distinctive Features Shown by Its Statutes, Judicial Decisions, and Illustrative Facts* (1853; reprint, New York: Negro Universities Press, 1969), 309. *State v. Maner,* 20 S.C.L.

(2 Hill) 453 (1834). Drewry Ottley, quoted in Elsa V. Goveia, *The West Indian Slave Laws of the Eighteenth Century* (Lodge Hill, Barbados: Caribbean Universities Press, 1970), 31, 33. See, for example, the law of Jamaica of 1826 "An Act to regulate the admission of the Evidence of Slaves," in *British Parliamentary Papers: Slave Trade* (Shannon: Irish University Press, 1969), 73:39–40.

2. Act of 1717, *The Laws of the Province of Maryland* 199–200 (John D. Cushing, ed., 1978) This law was not repealed until "An Act relating to the law of Evidence," ch. 27, 1847 Md. Laws.

3. 1 *Revised Statutes of the State of North Carolina*, 583 (Raleigh, Turner and Hughes, 1837); *The Revised Code of the Laws of Mississippi* 373 § 21 (Natchez, 1824).

4. George M. Stroud, *Sketch of the Laws Relating to Slavery in the Several States of the United States of America* (Philadelphia: Kimber and Sharpless, 1827); 1856 edition reprinted in Paul Finkelman, ed., *Statutes on American Slavery*, 2 vols. (New York: Garland, 1988). Stroud notes (reprint, X:44) that it was "the cause of the greatest evils of slavery." Goodell, *American Slave Code*, 303, observes, "A community or a Government that could tolerate such rejection of testimony– the testimony of the defenseless against those holding and daily exercising despotic power over them–must be resolutely bent on oppressing instead of protecting them."

5. *Mississippi Free Trader* (Natchez), February 24, 1843. James H. Hammond, "Letter to an English Abolitionist," in Dred Gilpin Faust, ed., *The Ideology of Slavery: Proslavery Thought in the Antebellum South, 1830–1860* (Baton Rouge: Louisiana State University Press, 1981), 190. On the capital trials of slaves, see, for example, Michael S. Hindus, *Prison and Plantation: Crime, Justice and Authority in Massachusetts and South Carolina, 1767–1878* (Chapel Hill: University of North Carolina Press, 1980); Philip J. Schwarz, *Twice Condemned: Slaves and the Criminal Laws of Virginia, 1705–1865* (Baton Rouge: Louisiana State University Press, 1988).

6. James Bradley Thayer, *A Preliminary Treatise on Evidence at the Common Law* (1898; reprint, Little, Brown, 1969), 180. John H. Langbein, "The Criminal Trial before the Lawyers," 45 *University of Chicago Law Review* 263, 306 (1978).

7. *Deut.* 17:6. *The Book of the General Lawes and Libertyes Concerning the Inhabitants of the Massachusetts* 54 (Thomas G. barnes ed., San Marino, Cal., Huntington Library, 1975, originally published 1648). Sir William Holdsworth, *A History of English Law*, 16 vols. (London: Methuen, 1903–66), 9:189. Even though the depth of religious belief might have been somewhat shallower in the colonial South before the Great Awakening than it was in New England, it certainly was pervasive. One illustration might be the daily diary entries of William Byrd. Maude H. Woodfin and Marion Tinling, eds., *Another Secret Diary of William Byrd of Westover for the Years 1739–1741* (Richmond: Dietz Press, 1942). Consider the charge to the county officers in Prince Georges County, Maryland, in March 1735. They were enjoined to uncover "all manner of felonies Witchcrafts Enchantments Sorceries Arts Magick Trespassess." Entry for March 1735, in Prince Georges County Court Record, March 1735–March 1738, Maryland Hall of Records, [hereinafter MHR]. Holdsworth, *History of English Law*, 9:189–90. Simon Greenleaf, *A Treatise on the Law of Evidence*, 4 vols. (Boston: Little, Brown, 1842), 1:473.

8. Sir Edward Coke and Sir Matthew Hale, cited in Holdsworth, *History of English Law*, 9:190–92.

9. Ibid., 191–92; Cobb, *Law of Negro Slavery,* 227-29. Cobb observes at p. 227 that "the term 'law,' according to the common law, is defined to be 'a freeman's privilege of being sworn in Court as a juror or witness.'"

10. "A Supplementary Act to the Act relating to Servants and Slaves" on May 1717 *The Laws of the Province of Maryland* 200 (John D. Cushing ed., 1978) (repealed 1847). All jurisdictions at one time or another provided some compensation, usually partial compensation, to the owners of slaves executed by law. See the pathbreaking article, Marvin L. M. Kay and Lorin L. Cary, "'The Planters Suffer Little or Nothing': North Carolina Compensation for Executed Slaves, 1748-1772," *Science and Society* 40 (1976): 288–306.

11. "An act for the more speedy prosecution of slaves committing Capital Crimes" on April 1692 *The Statutes at Large: Being a Collection of all the Laws of Virginia, from the First Session of the Legislatures in the Year 1619* 103 (William H. Hening comp., Richmond, 1819–23) (hereinafter cited as Va. Stat. (1619–1820)).

12. Sir Matthew Hale, *Pleas of the Crown* (London: Richard Tonson, 1678), 262, 264. This was virtually an outline of the Hale's larger study published posthumously in 1736. See Sir Matthew Hale, *The History of the Pleas of the Crown,* W. A. Stokes and E. Ingersol, eds., 2 vols. (Philadelphia: R H. Small, 1847). This is the first American edition of this work. 3 Va. Stat. (1619–1820) 103. William Hawkins, *A Treatise of the Pleas of the Crown,* 2 vols. (London, 1724–26; reprint, New York: Arno Press, 1972), 2:434. Winthrop D. Jordan, *White over Black: American Attitudes toward the Negro, 1550-1812* (Chapel Hill: University of North Carolina Press, 1968); Michael Anesko, "So Discreet a Zeal: Slavery and the Anglican Church in Virginia, 1680-1730," *Virginia Magazine of History and Biography* 93 (1985): 247–78.

13. Morgan Godwyn, *The Negro's & Indians Advocate* (London: Printed for the Author by J. D., 1680), 36. "An act for establishing the General Court, and for regulating and settling the proceedings therein," 3 Va. Stat. (1619–1820) 298.

14. Jack P. Greene, ed., *The Diary of Landon Carter of Sabine Hall, 1752-1778,* 2 vols. (Charlottesville: University Press of Virginia, 1965) 2:1107. In 1766 Carter had made the point more succinctly: "A negroe can't be honest." Ibid, I:310. For Cobb's nineteenth-century example, see Thomas R. R. Cobb, *An Inquiry into the Law of Negro Slavery in the United States of America. To Which Is Prefixed, an Historical Sketch of Slavery* (1858; reprint, New York: Negro Universities Press, 1968), 233. There is, of course, an extensive scholarly literature. One might begin with Eugene D. Genovese, *Roll, Jordan, Roll: The World the Slaves Made* (New York: Random House, 1974), and George M. Fredrickson, *The Black Image in the White Mind: The Debate on Afro-American Character and Destiny, 1817-1914* (New York: Harper and Row, 1971).

15. "An Act directing the trial of Slaves, committing Capital Crimes, and for the more effectual punishing Conspiracies and insurrections of them; and for the better government of Negros, Mulattos, and Indians, bond or free" May, 1723, 4 Va. Stat. (1619–1820) 126-7. Sir William Gooch, quoted in Herbert Aptheker, *American Negro Slave Revolts* (New York: Columbia University Press, 1943), 177–178.

16. William Blackstone, *Commentaries on the Laws of England,* 4 vols. (Oxford: Clarendon Press, 1765–69), 3:370.

17. Sir Edward Coke, *The Third Part of the Institutes of the Laws of England: Concerning High Treason, and Other Pleas of the Crown, and Criminall Causes* (London: M. Flesher, 1644), 164.

18. Act of May, 1723, *supra* note 15, at 128.

19. Peter C. Hoffer and William B. Scott, eds., *Criminal Proceedings in Colonial Virginia: Records of Fines, Examinations of Criminals, Trials of Slaves, etc., from March 1710/1711 to 1754* (Richmond County, Virginia), Vol. 10 of American Legal Records, (Athens, Ga.: University of Georgia Press, 1984), 120. "Trial of Davie, Robin, Daniel, and Moll," May 25, 1752; "Trial of Dick and Tom," January 17, 1754; and "Trial of Sambo," March 19, 1756/7, Lancaster County Order Book No. 10 (1752-1756), Virginia State Library, Richmond [hereinafter VSL].

20. Michael Dalton, *The Countrey Justice, Containing the Practice of the Justices of the Peace out of Their Sessions* (1622; reprint, New York: Arno Press, 1972); Hale, Pleas of the Crown; Hawkins, *Treatise on the Pleas of the Crown*.

21. J. H. Baker, "Criminal Courts and Procedure at Common Law, 1550–1800," in *Crime in England, 1550–1800,* ed. J. S. Cockburn (Princeton: Princeton University Press, 1977), 19; Barbara J. Shapiro, *"Beyond Reasonable Doubt" and "Probable Cause": Historical Perspectives on the Anglo-American Law of Evidence* (Berkeley:University of California Press, 1991) is a superb study of the epistemological problem of the probabilities associated with human knowledge, and of how philosophical notions in England were intertwined with and supported legal solutions to the problem of knowing something at the various stages of the criminal trial process. Hale, *History of the Pleas of the Crown,* 2:288–89.

22. Blackstone, *Commentaries,* 3:371, 4:350.

23. "Laws of the Government of New-Castle, Kent and Sussex upon Delaware," in *The Earliest Printed Laws of Delaware, 1704–1741,* ed. John D. Cushing (Wilmington: Michael Glazier, 1978), 74. "An Act for the more effectual punishing of negroes and other slaves, and for taking away the benefits of clergy from certain offenders," *The Laws of Maryland* 191 (Virgil Maxcy, ed., Baltimore, Philip H. Nickin, 1811) (hereinafter cited as 1811 Md. Laws). "An Act for Punishment of Persons suborning Witnesses or committing Willful and Corrupt Perjury," *The Laws of the Province of Maryland* 2. This penalty followed the common law; see Blackstone, *Commentaries,* 4:137. Nailing the ears of free persons was only an alternative if the person were unable to pay his fine. In this sense, the perjury punishment for slaves in Virginia was similar to that of the common law, except that the ears were cut off, and there was a whipping instead of a fine—which, of course, slaves could not pay in any event. *First Laws of the State of Delaware,* 4 vols., ed. John D. Cushing (Wilmington: Michael Glazier, 1981), 1:65–66. Act of May, 1751, 1811 Md. Laws 1, 237. "A Collection of all the Public Acts of Assembly of the Province of North-Carolina," *The Earliest Printed Laws of North Carolina, 1669-1751* 171–72 (John D. Cushing, ed., 1977). The exact language was that the court was "to take for Evidence, the Confession of the Offender, the Oath of one or more credible Witnesses, or such Testimony of Negroes, Mulattoes, or Indians, bond or free, with pregnant Circumstances, as to them shall seem convincing, without the Solemnity of a Jury." The penalty for perjury was the same as in Virginia, but this 1741 law did not require the justice to charge the slave the same way as in Virginia. In North Carolina the "first Person in Commission" who sat on the trial of the slave was to charge any black or Indian, "not being a Christian . . . to declare the truth."

24. Act of February, 1690, 7 "An Act for the Better Ordering of Slaves," *Statutes at Large of South Carolina* 345 (Thomas Cooper and David J. McCord eds., Columbia, S.C., 1836–41) (hereinafter cited as 1836–41 S.C. Stat.) For a general discussion of the early development of South Carolina slave law, see M. Eugene Sirmans, "The Legal Status of the Slave in South Carolina, 1670–1740," *Journal of Southern History* 28 (1962): 462–73. Goveia, *West Indian Slave Laws*, 34. Cobb, *Law of Negro Slavery*, 229: "By the Code Noir, the evidence of slaves was excluded in all cases in the French Colonies, whether for or against freemen or slaves. The Judges were allowed to hear their evidence, as suggestions to illustrate other testimony, but they were prohibited from drawing thence, '*aucune presomption, ni conjecture, ni adminicule de preuve.*' The same rule obtained in the British West Indies, and it is a little remarkable that the commissioners appointed to inquire into their condition, with a view to meliorating the status of the slave, hesitated to recommend a different rule, except in criminal cases." 1836–41 S.C. Stat. 7, 355, 356–57.

25. Act of March, 1735, 1836–41 S.C. Stat. 7, 389.

26. Act of May, 1740, 1836–41 S.C. Stat. 7, 401. Georgia followed in 1770 with a slave code patterned on South Carolina's 1740 statute. An excellent study of the adoption of slavery and of the code in Georgia is Betty Wood, *Slavery in Colonial Georgia, 1730-1775* (Athens, Ga.: University of Georgia Press, 1984). In particular, see chapter 7, "'The Better Ordering and Governing of Negroes.'"

27. John B. O'Neall, *The Negro Law of South Carolina* (Columbia, S.C.: John G. Bowman, 1848) 14. His general attitude toward the mode in which slaves were tried is summed up in his remark that it was the "worst system which could be devised." Ibid., 35. See also A. E. Keir Nash, "Negro Rights, Unionism, and Greatness on the South Carolina Court of Appeals: The Extraordinary Chief Justice John Belton O'Neall," 21 *South Carolina Law Review* 141–90 (1969).

28. See, for example, the Virginia law of 1819 that codified the slave law of the state: Act of March, 1819, 1 *The Revised Code of the Laws of Virginia* 422, 431 (Richmond, Thomas Ritchie, 1819). Virginia's law could be a bit misleading to the unwary. Two sections in the 1819 code are relevant, sections 5 and 44. Section 5, based upon a law adopted in 1785, provides that "Any negro or mulatto, bond or free, shall be a good witness in pleas of the Commonwealth for or against negroes or mulattoes, bond or free, or in civil pleas where free negroes or mulattoes shall alone be parties, and in no other cases whatever." Section 44 concerns "legal evidence" and provides that "the court may take for evidence the confession of the offender, the oath of one or more credible witnesses, or such testimony of negroes or mullatoes, bond or free, with pregnant circumstances, as to them shall seem convincing." Ibid., 431. The South Carolina rule is discussed in O'Neall, *Negro Law,* 14. "A Further supplement to the act, entitled An act relating to servants and slaves," 3 Maxcy 389. "An Act for the Trial and punishment of Slaves and Free People of Colour," *A Compilation of the Laws of the State of Georgia* 805 Lucius Q. C. Lamar, comp.,(Augusta, T. S. Hannon, 1821).

29. *State v. Ben*, 8 N.C. (1 Hawks) 434 (1821). Daniel J. Flanigan, "The Criminal Law of Slavery and Freedom," (Ph.D. diss., Rice University, 1973), 124–25. Flanigan considered this case "a classic of the law of slavery" because it "illustrated the Orwellian world the slave endured even when he approached equality with whites." Goodell, *American Slave Codes*, 315, merely following Stroud's earlier statement in *Sketch of the Laws Relating to Slavery*, 93. (This pagination is from the 1856 edition of Stroud's book).

30. A very early example of this practice was the grant of freedom to Will in 1710. The burgesses granted him his freedom because he was "signally service-able in discovering a conspiracy of diverse negroes" in Surry County who intended upon "levying war in this colony." 3 Va. Stat. (1619–1820) 537. Will got his freedom for his "fidelity and for encouragement of such services." One frustrating aspect of this case is that, according to the lieutenant governor, the "chief conspirators" were "tryed this General Court, found guilty, and will be executed." The records of the General Court have not survived, so it is not possible to know what evidence was used to convict the two "chief conspirators." Given the existing rules of evidence, it is not likely that Will's testimony would do. It is more likely that confessions were extorted from the slaves. Aptheker, *American Negro Slave Revolts*, 170–71.

31. Quoted in Thomas L. Webber, *Deep Like the Rivers: Education in the Slave Quarter Community, 1831–1865* (New York: W.W. Norton, 1978), 63–64.

32. One scholar who tends to view slave crime in a political sense is Philip J. Schwarz. In a very useful article, for example, he refers to a hog-stealing case as one in which slaves "consciously challenged the system of slave control." "Gabriel's Challenge: Slaves and Crime in Late Eighteenth-Century Virginia," *The Virginia Magazine of History and Biography* 90 (1982): 284. See also Philip J. Schwarz, "Forging the Shackles: The Development of Virginia's Criminal Code for Slaves," in *Ambivalent Legacy: A Legal History of the South*, ed. David J. Bodenhamer and James W. Ely, Jr. (Jackson: University Press of Mississippi, 1984); and Schwarz, *Twice Condemned*. For a critical review of this position, see Paul Finkelman, "Prosecutions in Defense of the Cornerstone," *Reviews in American History* 17 (1989): 403. *State* v. *Ben*, *supra* note 56, at 436.

33. Ibid., at 437–38. This provision on pregnant circumstances remained part of the law of North Carolina. See *Revised Code of North Carolina* 572 Bartholomew F. Moore and Asa Biggs eds., (Boston: Little, Brown, 1855).

34. *State* v. *Ben*, *supra* note 56, at 437.

35. The rule in Tennessee was set by the law of 1815 on the trial of slaves, "An act to repeal so much of the forty-eighth section of an act now in force in this state, as provides for the trial of slaves, for capital offenses, and directing the mode of trial in future," *Tenn. Sess. Laws* 175, but by 1857 the state's code read simply that "the trial of a slave for a capital offence shall be conducted in the same manner as that of a free person." *The Code of Tennessee* 510 (J. Meigs and William F. Cooper eds., Nashville, 1858). Mississippi, in its massive 1822 code, followed the Virginia pattern of 1819. Section 21 provides that blacks can testify, and section 58 considers "legal evidence" in terms of the testimony of blacks, slave or free, along with a pregnant-circumstances requirement. Act of June, 1822 §§ 21, 58, *The Revised Code of Mississippi* 373, 382 (Natchez, 1824). By 1857, however, the pregnant-circumstances requirement had disappeared. *The Revised Code of the Statute Laws of State of Mississippi* (Jackson, 1857) (hereinafter 1857 Miss. Rev. Code), art. 62, p. 249. The 1798 law of Kentucky that required the corroboration was patterned after the Virginia law. 2 *A Digest of the Statute Laws of Kentucky* 1475 (C. S. Moorhead and Mason Brown eds., Frankfort, Ky.: Albert G. Hodges, 1834). By the 1850s slaves were to be tried for offenses punished with death "in the same mode and manner as free persons are tried." 2 *The Revised Statutes of Kentucky*, 377 (Richard H. Stanton ed., Cincinnati, Robert Clarke, 1860) (hereinafter cited as 1860 Ky. Rev. Stat. [Stanton]).

Alabama followed the pregnant-circumstances rule as late as 1836. *A Digest of the Laws of the State of Alabama* 123 (2d ed., John D. Aiken ed., Tuscaloosa, 1836). By 1852 the state provided that, in general, the trials of slaves was to be "in the mode provided by law for the trial of white persons." *The Code of Alabama* 595 (John J. Ormond et al. eds., Montgomery, 1852). *The Revised Statutes of Louisiana* 58 (U. B. Phillips, comp., New Orleans, 1856).

36. An example of the thirty-nine-lashes approach is 1860 Ky. Rev. Stat. (Stanton) 377. 1852 Ala. Code 595. Mississippi continued to provide for the mutilation of slaves by cutting off ears. 1857 Miss. Rev. Code 249.

37. Betty Wood, "'Until He Shall Be Dead, Dead, Dead:' The Judicial Treatment of Slaves in Eighteenth-Century Georgia," *Georgia Historical Quarterly* 71 (1987): 391. See also John C. Edwards, "Slave Justice in Four Middle Georgia Counties," *Georgia Historical Quarterly* 57 (1973): 265. Royce Gordon Shingleton, "The Trial and Punishment of Slaves in Baldwin County, Georgia, 1812-1826," *Southern Humanities Review* 8 (1974): 67. *Lord Proprietary* v. *Kate*, June Court, 1755, Talbot County Court Criminal Judgments, 1751-1755, MHR.

38. "Trial of Guy," March 25, 1746, Lancaster County Order Book No. 9 (1743-1752), VSL. Greene, ed., *Diary of Landon Carter,* 1:370–71, 415; Trial of Sarah, September 6, 1750, Lancaster County Order Book No. 9 1743-1752, VSL.

39. "Trial of Ben and Dedan," September 11, 1741, Charles City County Order Book, 1737–1751, VSL. See also "Trial of Ned and Bob," January 26, 1762, Charles City County Orders, 1758–1762, and "Trial of David, Robin, Daniel, and Moll," May 25, 1752, Lancaster County Order Book No. 10 (1752–1756), VSL.

40. "Trial of George et al.," Jan. 27, 1849, Fairfield District: Records of Magistrates and Freeholders Courts, 1846-1851, Trial Papers, South Carolina Department of Archives and History [hereinafter cited as SCDAH]. See also "Trial of Martin and Dave," February 26, 1857, Spartanburg District, Records of Magistrates and Freeholders Courts, Trial Papers, SCDAH (involving the accidental killing of a slave in a fight that erupted over a card game). In another case, Balaam was prosecuted for breaking into the dwelling of Wade Dennis, a free black. The slave Brad testified that Balaam had claimed that he had had "Dennis's papers," but that he later burned them. The slave Dover testified that Dennis had offered him ten dollars to find out who burned his fodder stack and robbed him. He said that Balaam "told him that he burn'd Wade Dennis' fodder." Balaam was acquitted when a number of whites provided him with an alibi. "Trial of Balaam," May 7, 1856, Anderson District, Records of Magistrates and Freeholders Courts, Trial Papers, SCDAH. Slaves, of course, did not usually turn to the public courts. An example of a different approach occurred on the Dabney plantation in Mississippi where a number of slaves succeeded in having their owner sell a slave woman who had been a frequent thief in the quarters. Susan Dabney Smedes, *Memorials of a Southern Planter,* ed. Fletcher M. Green (Jackson: University Press of Mississippi, 1965), 90. Genovese, *Roll, Jordan, Roll,* 606-7, notes that while we can never really know how often slaves stole from one another, it was a problem on some plantations.

41. See Charles B. Dew, "Black Ironworkers and the Slave Insurrection Panic of 1856," *Journal of Southern History* 41 (1975): 321–38. Laura L. Porteous, "Torture in Spanish Criminal Procedure," *Louisiana Historical Quarterly* 8 (1925): 16.

This case involved slaves who murdered their master, Juan Baptiste Cezaire Lebreton.

42. Records of the trials in New York and Charleston are published. Daniel Horsmanden, *The New-York Conspiracy,* ed. with an introd. by Thomas J. Davis (1810; reprint, Boston: Beacon Press, 1971); Lionel H. Kennedy & Thomas Parker, *An Official Report of the Trials of Sundry Negroes, Charged with an Attempt to Raise an Insurrection in the State of South Carolina* (Charleston: James R. Schenck, 1822). On the Vesey conspiracy in Charleston, see also John Lofton, *Insurrection in South Carolina: The Turbulent World of Denmark Vesey* (Yellow Springs, Ohio: Antioch Press, 1964). On the Gabriel conspiracy, see Gerald W. Mullin, *Flight and Rebellion: Slave Resistance in Eighteenth-Century Virginia* (London: Oxford University Press, 1972); Schwarz, "Gabriel's Challenge," at 283–309; and Douglas R. Egerton, *Gabriel's Rebellion: The Virginia Slave Conspiracies of 1800 and 1802* (Chapel Hill: University of North Carolina Press, 1993).

43. In addition to the works cited in note 42, see Peter H. Wood, *Black Majority: Negroes in Colonial South Carolina from 1670 through the Stono Rebellion* (New York: W. W. Norton, 1974); Henry I. Tragle ed., *The Southampton Slave Revolt of 1831: A Compilation of Source Material* (New York: Random House, 1973); Stephen B. Oates, *The Fires of Jubilee: Nat Turner's Fierce Rebellion* (New York: Harper and Row, 1975). Trial of Jerry et al., October 2-11, 1860, Spartanburg District, Records of Magistrates-Freeholders Courts, Trial Papers, SCDAH.

44. This is a firm impression based upon reading the lower court records, as lean as they often are, for over fifty counties in all of the slave states.

45. Greenleaf, 1 *Treatise on Evidence* 250, at §§ 214–15.

46. Hoffer and Scott, *Criminal Proceedings in Colonial Virginia,* xxxi, for instance, notes that defendants in Richmond County were often quite submissive. They even declined to demand a jury trial when entitled to one. A similar observation in New York led Julius Goebel, Jr., and T. Raymond Naughton, *Law Enforcement in Colonial New York* (1944; reprint, Montclair, N.J.: Patterson Smith, 1970) 78, to suggest that in misdemeanor cases upper-class judges rarely confronted lower-class suspects who demanded trials.

47. The eleven counties are Caroline, Charles City, Essex, Fauquier, King George, Lancaster, Orange, Princess Anne, Richmond, Southampton, and Sussex. The periods covered ranged from ten to fifty years. Of the fifteen confession cases only five involved capital sentences: four were burglaries, and one was a murder. One of the slaves convicted of burglary received benefit of clergy. A murder case, discussed below, is recorded in "Trial of Wapping," May 30, 1722, Lancaster County Order Book No. 7 (1721-1729), VSL. A number of burglary cases were all in Richmond County. "Trial of Harry," July 1738 (he received clergy); "Trial of Dick," September 1749; "Trial of Newman and Sam," September 1749; "Trial of Daniel," November 1753, all in Hoffer and Scott *Criminal Proceedings in Colonial Virginia,* xlix–l, 187, 240–42, 244–46. Newman and Sam pled as follows: they "Confessed that they were in some part guilty of the said felony and burglary but not of the Whole." They put themselves on the court for trial, were found guilty, and sentenced to death. Ibid., 242. Aside from the murder case there was only one other case of violence. Harry stabbed another slave in 1730. Ibid., 123. This case is discussed below in the text. All the remaining cases were property crimes. One involved receiving stolen goods. "Trial of Sarah," September 6, 1750, Lancaster County Order Book No. 9, (1743-1752),

VSL. This case was discussed above in the text. The remaining eight cases all were charges of hog stealing. They were as follows: "Trial of Will," August 12, 1748, Caroline County Order Book, 1746–1754; "Trial of Jones," March 19, 1748/9, Caroline County Order Book, 1746-1754; "Trial of Citto," June 4, 1752, King George County Order Book, 1751-1765; "Trial of Aaron," September 24, 1767, Orange County Order Book 7, 1763-1769; "Trial of Ned," November 7, 1771, Princess Anne County Minute Book 9, 1770-1773; "Trial of Rippon," January Court, 1742, Charles City County Order Book, 1737–1751; "Trial of Harry and Jack," December Court, 1746, Charles City County Order Book, 1737-1751; and, finally, "Trial of Dick," October 4, 1758, Charles City County Court Orders, 1758-1762, VSL.

48. A couple of illustrations should suffice. I found no confessions in Elbert County, Georgia, between 1837 and 1849 (the years for which full records are extant), and but one in Chatham County, Georgia, which included Savannah, between 1813 and 1827 and between 1850 and 1859. On February 11, 1857, William pled guilty to voluntary manslaughter. Chatham County, Georgia, Superior Court Minutes, 1855-1859, Georgia Department of Archives and History. A final example might be the confession of Ned in Jessamine County, Kentucky, in 1842. He was the only slave I found in the county's records for the years 1800-1849 who confessed. He admitted to his master that he had sold some goods taken in a burglary, and had left some at his wife's home. Papers in Ned's case filed in box no. 8, 1840-42, Circuit Court Clerk, Circuit Court Indictments, Jessamine County, Kentucky, 9 boxes, Kentucky State Archives, Frankfort.

49. "Trial of Harry," February 1729/30, in Hoffer and Scott, *Criminal Proceedings in Colonial Virginia,* 123.

50. "Trial of Wapping," *supra* note 80. See, for example, Hoffer and Scott, *Criminal Proceedings in Colonial Virginia,* l–li.

51. Among the fine studies that might be consulted are Genovese, *Roll, Jordan, Roll;* Lawrence W. Levine, *Black Culture and Black Consciousness: Afro-American Folk Thought from Slavery to Freedom* (New York: Oxford University Press, 1977); Herbert G. Gutman, *The Black Family in Slavery and Freedom, 1750-1925* (New York: Pantheon Books, 1976); John Blassingame, *The Slave Community: Plantation Life in the Antebellum South* (New York: Oxford University Press, 1972); Charles Joyner, *Down by the Riverside: A South Carolina Slave Community* (Urbana: University of Illinois Press, 1984); Margaret Washington Creel, *"A Peculiar People": Slave Religion and Community-Culture Among the Gullahs* (New York: New York University Press, 1988); Sterling Stuckey, *Slave Culture: Nationalist Theory and the Foundations of Black America* (New York: Oxford University Press, 1987).

52. Webber, *Deep Like the Rivers,* 120–21 quoting Jacob Stroyer, *Sketches of My Life in the South.* This might be compared to some of the samples discussed in E. Adamson Hoebel, *The Law of Primitive Man: A Study in Comparative Legal Dynamics* (1954; reprint, New York: Athenaeum, 1972).

53. On church discipline, see Donald G. Mathews, *Religion in the Old South* (Chicago: University of Chicago Press, 1977), 146–48. One interesting case arose in the Salem Baptist Church in Marlborough County, South Carolina, in the 1850s. A master charged his slaves with theft of hams from the smokehouse. The charge was before the church, not the local magistrate. The slaves unsuccessfully tried to defend themselves with the argument that since they had con-

tributed to the preparation of the hams by their labor, they had merely taken what was theirs.

54. One of the fullest accounts of the voluntariness problem in confessions is Mark Tushnet, *The American Law of Slavery, 1810–1860: Considerations of Humanity and Interest* (Princeton: Princeton University Press, 1981), 127–37.

55. See Marianne Burloff Sheldon, "Black-White Relations in Richmond, Virginia, 1782–1820," *Journal of Southern History* 45 (1979): 32. "Trial of Ben," 1821, Southampton County Court Order Book, 1819-1822, at 341, VSL.

56. Cobb, *Law of Negro Slavery*, 272.

57. *State* v. *Charity*, 13 N.C. (2 Dev.) 543, 545, 547, 548 (1830).

58. *State* v. *Nelson*, 3 La. Ann. 497, 499, 500 (1848).

59. *Wyatt [a slave]* v. *State*, 25 Ala. 9, 14–15 (1854).

60. *Simon [a slave]* v. *State*, 5 Fla. 285, 286–87, 296 (1853).

61. *Sam [a slave]* v. *State*, 33 Miss. 347, 351, 351–52 (Ct. Err. & App. 1857).

62. *Alfred and Anthony* v. *State*, 32 Tenn. (2 Swan) 581, 589–90 (1853). One case that emptied this right of any significance was *Seaborn and Jim* v. *State*, 20 Ala. 15, 18 (1852). Justice Chilton remarked about the confessions that they "were made to the examining magistrate, who did not previously caution them, as he undoubtedly ought to have done, as to the effect of such admissions, would not justify the court in excluding them. We find no case excluding confessions for want of such caution."

63. *Rafe (a slave)* v. *State*, 20 Ga. 62, 63, 68 (1856). See also *Mose [a slave]* v. *State*, 36 Ala. 211 (1860). Mose had confessed to the murder of a white man to two separate men, and one condition that preceded the confessions had been that he had been handed over to a "vigilance committee," some of whom suggested that they collect a fund to pay for him and execute him themselves. On this aspect of the case Chief Justice A. J. Walker commented as follows: "His confessions seem to have been prompted by a sense of religious duty, awakened by the apprehension of a speedy execution at the hands of lawless violence, and were not the result of the slightest hope of temporal benefit on account of the confession." Ibid., at 228. They were held admissible.

64. *Dick, Aleck, and Henry [slaves]* v. *State*, 30 Miss. 593, 595 (1856). Jean Jacques Rousseau, *The Social Contract and Discourses,* trans. G. D. H. Cole (London: Dent, 1968), 5: Rousseau argued that "Aristotle was right: but he took the effect for the cause. Nothing can be more certain than that every man born in slavery is born for slavery. Slaves lose everything in their chains, even the desire of escaping from them: they love their servitude, as the comrades of Ulysses loved their brutish condition. If then there are slaves by nature, it is because there have been slaves against nature. Force made the first slaves, and their cowardice perpetuated the condition."

65. *Dick, Aleck, and Henry [slaves]* v. *State, supra* note 64, at 598. Two cases in which confessions were thrown out because they were obtained by violence inflicted by third parties who were not magistrates were *Jordan [a slave]* v. *State*, 32 Miss. 382, 386–88 (Ct. Err. & App. 1856), and *Simon [a slave]* v. *State*, 37 Miss. 288 (Ct. Err. & App. 1859). Both cases involved the killing of slaves rather than whites. Goodell, *American Slave Code*, 305–8; *Ex parte Boylston*, 33 S.C.L. (2 Strob.) 41 (1847).

66. Tushnet, *American Law of Slavery*, 127; *Stephen* v. *State*, 11 Ga. 225, 235 (1852).

67. *Ex parte Boylston, supra* note 103.

68. Flanigan, "Criminal Law of Slavery and Freedom," *passim.* There has been superb work on the proslavery argument and some excellent collections. One of the more controversial among the former is Larry E. Tise, *Proslavery: A History of the Defense of Slavery in America, 1701–1840* (Athens: University of Georgia Press, 1987), 232–37. Tise grounds many of the significant proslavery arguments in the conservative political philosophy of New England Federalism and the conservative theology of New England congregationalism. An excellent collection of primary materials is Faust, *The Ideology of Slavery.*

69. The relevant statutory extensions can be followed conveniently in John C. Hurd, *The Law of Freedom and Bondage in the United States,* 2 vols. (Boston: Little, Brown, 1858) 2:2–200.

70. Cobb, *Inquiry into Law of Negro Slavery,* 227–29.

8

"Details Are of a Most Revolting Character": Cruelty to Slaves as Seen in Appeals to the Supreme Court of Louisiana

Judith Kelleher Schafer

WHEN LOUISIANA BECAME an American possession in 1803, the territory's approximately 38,000 slaves had rights unknown in any state of the American South. Most important of these were the right of self-purchase and the right to petition to be sold away from a cruel master. American rule instituted an era of diminished protections for slaves as Louisiana planters found themselves for the first time in a position to make their own laws. In 1806 the territorial legislature passed a new *Black Code (Code Noir)* that greatly reduced the rights of slaves in American Louisiana.[1] They lost the right of self-purchase, unless their owner voluntarily permitted it. Furthermore, the new code mandated that juries had to criminally convict slaveholders of cruelty before they could be forced to sell an allegedly abused slave. Slaves had not only lost the rights to petition the courts for sale away from an abusive master, but the right to initiate any legal action, except for suing for their freedom.[2]

One of the primary purposes of the *Black Code* was to create a legal apparatus for the control and discipline of slaves. Slavery, by its very nature, required such regulation. Discipline was an essential element of the slave system if slaves were to earn a profit for their owners. Control of slave behavior also maintained the image of white superiority and the prescribed and delicate etiquette of relations between the races. In addition, whites believed that making slaves "stand in fear"[3] was a necessary precaution to prevent slave insurrections.

Breaches of discipline necessitated punishment, which was most often physical in nature. All such punishments were inherently cruel; if the chastiser were a martinet, extreme—even barbarous—cruelty was always possible. The *Black Code* prohibited treatment harsher than what was acceptable in American Louisiana, but recalcitrant slaves and hot-tempered masters were a combination that could convert control into brutality. According to the *Black Code*, slaves were "passive" creatures, whose subordination to their master and "to all who represent him" was "not susceptible of any modification." Hence, even minor insubordination might occasion excessive punishment. The *Digest of 1808*, a compilation of the civil law in territorial Louisiana, reinforced the *Black Code*: "The slave is entirely subject to the will of his master who may correct him and chastise him, though not with unusual rigor, nor so as to maim or mutilate him, or expose him to the danger of loss of life, or to cause his death." The *Digest of 1808* also provided, if the presiding judge so ordered, for the court-ordered sale of slaves whose owners had been convicted of cruel treatment. No other American state had such a provision.[4]

The *Black Code* also prohibited the maiming or killing of slaves by their owners or others. Persons who treated slaves with cruelty risked a fine of between two hundred and five hundred dollars. The code excepted certain types of physical chastisement from its definition of cruel punishment: "flogging, or striking with a whip, leather thong, switch or small stick." Other exceptions included placing a slave in fetters or in confinement. It is indicative of legislative sentiment concerning cruelty to slaves that Louisiana lawmakers passed an act in 1821 mandating a fine of two hundred dollars or imprisonment for six months for a person convicted of "wantonly or maliciously kill[ing] any horse, mare, gelding, mule, or jack-ass." Those convicted of this crime were also liable to the owner of the animal for its value. To "cruelly beat, maim, or disable" an animal subjected the offender to a hundred dollar fine and liability for damages to the animal.[5]

Evidence that excessive violence and cruel treatment of slaves was not uncommon in Louisiana abounds in plantation diaries and other manuscript sources. The most famous case involved the notorious Madame Lalaurie. A New Orleans court found this sadistic woman guilty of abusing her slaves and ordered the sale of the slaves away from her. Lalaurie's relatives purchased the slaves and returned them to her. She chained them to the walls of her Royal Street home, where she reportedly alternated between striking them and harsher forms of torture. On April 10, 1834, an elderly slave, fettered in a garret, somehow managed to set fire to Lalaurie's house. The New Orleans *Bee* described the events that followed:

> The conflagration at the house occupied by the woman Lalaurie . . . has been the means of discovering one of those atrocities, the details of which seem to be too incredible for human belief. We would shrink from the task of detailing the painful circumstances connected therewith, were it not that a sense of duty . . . renders it indispensable to do so.

The flames having spread with alarming rapidity, and the horrible suspicion being entertained among the spectators, that some of the inmates of the premises . . . were incarcerated therein. Upon entering one of the apartments, the most appalling spectacle met their eyes. Seven slaves more or less horribly mutilated, were seen suspended by the neck, with their limbs apparently stretched and torn from one extremity to the other. The slaves were the property of the demon, in the shape of a woman. They had been confined by her for several months . . . and had been merely kept in existence to prolong their sufferings and make them taste all that the most refined cruelty could inflict.

Those who came to fight the fire turned into an angry mob when they observed the pitiful condition of the slaves. Madame Lalaurie barely escaped the city just ahead of a furious band of pursuers who had seen the horror. The angry crowd destroyed her furniture by dropping it from the balcony to the courtyard below, and then proceeded to demolish most of the house.[6]

Section 16 of the *Black Code* authorized criminal prosecution for mutilation, severe ill-treatment, or killing of a slave. Section 17 held that if a slave were "mutilated, beaten or ill-treated" when no witnesses were present, the owner or person responsible for managing the slave would be prosecuted for cruelty unless he or she could produce evidence to the contrary. Since slaves could not testify in court against whites, this provision was intended to protect slaves in situations in which they were the only witnesses to the cruel treatment. However, the creators of the *Black Code* left a loophole: an owner prosecuted under such circumstances could also clear himself "by his own oath." Although this provision drastically weakened the law, and although few slave owners were ever prosecuted for cruelty, neither Louisiana law nor the state's courts ever ruled out this possibility—as did North Carolina Judge Thomas Ruffin, writing for the court, in *State* v. *Mann*. In this often quoted decision, Ruffin held that slaveholders could not be held criminally responsible for an assault and battery on one of their own slaves because such a ruling contradicted the absolute power of the slaveholder, which was necessary "to render the submission of the slave perfect."[7]

Plenty of evidence of ill-treatment exists in the records of appeals of civil cases to the Louisiana court. At times the cases reveal unprovoked or senseless violence on the part of owners, overseers, or strangers. In many instances, cruelty to a slave resulted from a white's overreaction to a slave's minor infraction.

Three factors prevented the Supreme Court of Louisiana from hearing many appeals from criminal trials for cruelty to a slave during the antebellum period. The most obvious is that there were few prosecutions of this nature at the lower level. Since slaves were often the only witnesses to such incidents, and since Louisiana law prohibited them from testifying against whites, finding legally competent witnesses was difficult. Often, white witnesses, many of whom felt that slave discipline was a private matter between slaveholders and their property, were reluctant to testify. A second factor is that such prosecutions as occurred in the lower court probably often ended in acquittals. As we will see, white juries simply refused to convict despite overwhelming evidence of brutality. Of course, prosecutions that ended in acquittal were not appealed and therefore do not appear in the records of the Supreme Court of Louisiana. The third reason for the scarcity of criminal appeals is technical. The first constitution of the State of Louisiana (1812) limited the jurisdiction of the state supreme court to civil appeals. Until the Constitution of 1845 gave the high court criminal jurisdiction, the court heard no criminal appeals. Appeals of criminal prosecutions for cruelty to slaves were therefore limited to the sixteen-year period 1846–62, although the court heard appeals of civil suits that involved death or injury to slaves throughout the antebellum period.[8] The court was quite willing to sustain the property rights of slaveholders in civil suits when their slaves were injured or killed by others, but the justices had little opportunity to affirm convictions of whites in criminal prosecutions. There were only six criminal appeals of cruelty convictions to the court between 1846 and 1862. Each involved a slave who died from the abuse he received.

Criminal Convictions for Cruelty

The first appeal of a criminal conviction for cruelty to a slave occurred in *State* v. *Morris* (1849). The defendant allegedly beat his slave to death "in a cruel and barbarous manner . . . causing sundry dangerous and severe bruises and wounds upon the thigh, loins, and other parts of the body." A hole in the abdomen, the size of a dollar and appearing to have been "gouged out," was the immediate cause of death. No one witnessed this treatment of the slave, and Morris presented his oath in an affidavit denying his responsibility for the alleged cruelty. The district judge instructed the jury that the oath was not conclusive evidence of the defendant's innocence. The jury found Morris guilty. He appealed, claiming that section 17 of the *Black Code* held that the owner's oath could not only repeal the presumption of guilt created by the same section, but was intended to be conclusive proof of innocence. Justice George King, writing for the court, denied this interpretation of section 17:

> Such does not appear to us to be a just interpretation of the act. The law creates a presumption of the master's guilt, which, in the absence of this express legislation, would not arise. It is founded upon the relation of master and slave, and the power of the former to maltreat the latter secretly and without the possibility, in many instances, of otherwise establishing his guilt.

He is consequently held answerable for the cruel treatment received by his slave while under his charge, and when no person is present, and is presumed to be guilty of the offence [sic], "unless," in the words of the act, "he can prove the contrary."

It has been correctly urged by the Attorney General, that the interpretation contended for by the defendant would enable the master to escape punishment by interposing his oath, when his guilt could be satisfactorily established by other testimony which could not have been contemplated by the legislature. . . . [I]n such cases the legislature could not have intended that the owner should escape punishment by interposing his own oath; or that the jury should acquit, notwithstanding their convictions, from the testimony, of the guilt of the accused.[9]

State v. *Morris* is one of only a handful of cases in the appellate court records of the American South in which a state supreme court upheld the conviction of a slaveholder for cruelty to his slave. Overseers, poor whites, and free persons of color were more likely to be successfully prosecuted for abuse of slaves than slave owners.[10]

Seven years elapsed before the court heard the next appeal of a conviction for cruelty, *State* v. *Bass and McNabb* (1856). William Bass and his stepfather, Harry McNabb, both described as yeomen, were convicted of killing a slave named Joe, allegedly a runaway. Bass shot Joe out of a tree with a shotgun loaded with "divers leaden bullets." The slave had climbed the tree in order to escape pursuing hounds. Bass's primary defense was that "he was but a boy" and also an orphan. The prosecutor charged McNabb with aiding and abetting Bass in the shooting. The jury acquitted McNabb but found Bass guilty with a recommendation of clemency, as Bass was an "orphan boy of tender age." The Morehouse District Court judge sentenced Bass to only thirty days in jail and a fine of three hundred dollars. The State appealed to the supreme court on the basis that the district court judge had erred in giving Bass such a light sentence because the judge had allowed Bass's counsel inappropriately to introduce damaging testimony about the character of the victim in an attempt to justify the shooting. However, Justice Henry Spofford, writing for the court, upheld the decision of the trial court.[11]

Two of the other four criminal prosecutions for killing a slave involved free blacks. In *State* v. *Taylor, f.m.c.* (1856), the first District Court of New Orleans found the free man of color (f.m.c.), Joseph Jerry Taylor, guilty of manslaughter in the death of Henry Cruize, a slave. Taylor had killed Cruize by throwing a brick at his head. The judge sentenced him to the penitentiary for seven years at hard labor, and his attorneys appealed. The primary witness at the trial had been a mulatto named Charles Robinson, who said that he had been a slave but that his mistress had freed him upon her death. Attorneys for Taylor objected to his testimony, saying that Robinson had offered no proof that he was free, and if he were a slave, he could not testify. Justice Spofford rejected this argument, stating that the objection to Robinson's testimony came only after the testimony, too late to sustain such an objection. The court affirmed the judgment of the lower court.[12]

The other criminal appeal involving a free man of color, *State* v. *Populus, f.m.c.* (1857), occurred the following year. The Rapides Parish District Court convicted Joseph Populus of killing the slave David by stabbing him with a "dirk knife." The convicting jury recommended him to the mercy of the court, and the judge sentenced him to twelve months at hard labor. His attorneys appealed on the grounds that the judge had not sequestered the jury after he had charged it. The jurors had gone home for the night and had returned the next morning to render their verdict. The supreme court found this irregularity sufficient grounds to grant the petition for a new trial.[13] No record of the subsequent proceeding exists.

During the next term, in *State* v. *Ward and White* (1858), the court heard an appeal from two defendants in the second criminal conviction for cruelty to a slave by those who owned him. The St. Martin Parish jury found George White and Clarence Ward guilty of "inflicting inhuman and cruel treatment" on a slave under sections 16 and 17 of the *Black Code*, and the judge fined each four hundred dollars. The slave had died from his wounds. White appealed the conviction on a legal technicality, asserting that an 1855 legislative act relative to crimes had repealed sections 16 and 17 of the *Black Code*. White also asserted that if not repealed, sections 16 and 17 did not require a criminal prosecution for cruelty. He claimed that he was entitled to a civil trial for damages rather than a criminal prosecution. Chief Justice Edwin Merrick rejected these arguments. He found that the act of 1855 did not repeal sections 16 and 17, and he wrote a strong opinion in favor of criminal prosecution:

> We know no law which requires the prosecution under these sections of the Act of 1806 to be conducted as a civil suit. On the contrary, we think that the terms, conviction and offence, used in them, imply a prosecution by information or indictment. Moreover, the first offence [sic] specified in section 16, viz, the offence [sic] of killing the slave of another, could be prosecuted in no other manner.[14]

The last criminal prosecution for killing a slave, *State* v. *Davis*, occurred in 1859. The record of the lower court no longer exists. The opinion of the Louisiana Supreme Court indicates that a grand jury indicted W. H. Davis for felonious assault on a slave "by willfully shooting at him with a shotgun loaded with gunpowder and divers leaden shot." Davis's attorneys filed a motion to quash the indictment, asserting that no law existed that forbade a free person from purposefully shooting at a slave with intent to kill. The Morehouse Parish District Court ordered Davis's indictment quashed, but the supreme court reversed this order, reinstated the indictment, and remanded the case to the lower court for prosecution. Associate Justice James Cole wrote for the court: "Slaves are treated in our law as property, and, also as persons; this section [of the Act of 1855 pertaining to crimes] then applies to an assault upon a slave or upon a free person."[15]

Civil Suits Involving Cruelty

Owners of slaves abused by others often chose to bring a civil action for the value of the slave in question if he were dead, or for the amount the injury had diminished his value. It is in these cases that evidence of cruel treatment most often appears, and it is clear that the property value of the slave took precedence to obtaining a just punishment for the perpetrator of the barbarous treatment. Even a purely civil matter would have brought the incident to the attention of the public prosecutor, who could have chosen to begin a criminal prosecution. The scarcity of criminal prosecutions was the result of solidarity among whites and especially among slave owners, which often prevented whites who witnessed the atrocities or who had seen the physical evidence of them, from pressing charges or even reporting the abuse to the authorities.[16]

Appeals to the Supreme Court of Louisiana in civil cases involving cruel treatment or senseless, unprovoked violence against slaves can be divided into three categories: abuse by strangers, by overseers, and by owners. The last classification was the least frequent, no doubt because slaves, who could not testify in court, were often the only witnesses to such incidents, and owners would be unlikely to report the abuse themselves. On the other hand, owners were much more likely to report acts of violence by others that injured or killed their valuable slave property.

Slaves who stole animals and produce risked gunshot wounds and even death, though their infractions might have been minor. In *Allain, f.m.c.* v. *Young* (1821), the Louisiana Supreme Court heard an appeal from a free black slave owner named François Allain, whose slave Régese had such a bad character, so witnesses testified, that no one would accept him as a gift. Régese regularly stole cattle and hogs from neighboring farms, slaughtered them, and sold the meat. From the record it is not clear whether Régese acted without his master's knowledge, or whether Allain, too, profited from the sale of the stolen meat. When a man named Young caught Régese with some stolen animals, Régese attempted to seize Young's gun, and Young shot and killed him. Allain sued Young for Régese's value, which he estimated at two thousand dollars. The judge of the lower court held for the defendant, reasoning that Régese died while committing a felony. Allain appealed, but Chief Judge George Mathews affirmed the decision: "If a slave of a bad character is pursued on suspicion of felony, attempts to seize a gun, flies, and is killed in the pursuit, the supreme court will not disturb a verdict for the defendant, who killed him."[17]

Régese had been involved in an extensive scheme to steal from others. In most other cases involving animal stealing, thieves were committing petty larceny, usually pilfering chickens for their own use. The court did not condone excessive violence in these instances. *Déslonde, f.m.c.* v. *LeBréret* (1833) involved a free man of color who sued Pierre LeBréret for shooting and killing his slave Isaac for attempting to steal one of LeBréret's chickens. LeBréret caught the slave in the act, bound him with a rope, and shot him, execution-style. LeBréret claimed the act was justified, saying that Isaac was "in the habit of stealing and carrying away the defendant's property in the night." The supreme court remanded the case to the lower court to ascertain the value of Isaac, presumably to award damages to Déslonde.[18] There is no record of subsequent action by the lower court.

In the 1850s the Supreme Court of Louisiana heard several appeals in which owners sued others for shooting their slaves for stealing animals or produce. Stealing sugarcane resulted in the death of a slave, which instigated the lawsuit *Carmouche* v. *Bouis* (1851). Narcisse Carmouche brought a civil action against his neighbors, Francis P. Bouis and his son Louis, for the value of a slave named John. Testimony indicates that a gang of slaves had been making nightly raids on Bouis's sugar plantation to steal cane. Determined to put an end to the depredations, Bouis ordered his son and his overseer to arm themselves and keep watch over his fields. Both were instructed not to shoot at trespassing slaves but merely to fire warning shots to frighten them. When Bouis's son saw John climbing the sugarcane field's fence, he fired without taking aim and by chance mortally wounded the slave. The Pointe Coupée Parish Court awarded Carmouche eight hundred dollars, and Bouis appealed. Bouis contended that he had the right to defend his property. However, the justices of the supreme court ruled that he was liable for the death and resulting property loss to Carmouche. The difference between this case and the decision in *Allain, f.m.c.* v. *Young* lies in the nature of the slaves' acts: Régese's attempt to seize a firearm was a felony; John's offense was petty theft. Justice Isaac Preston, writing for the court, held that homicide was not necessary to prevent a misdemeanor and that the killing of John was unnecessary for the defense of Bouis's person, family, or property.[19]

Eight years later the court heard an appeal from the District Court of Plaquemines Parish, *McCutcheon* v. *Angelo* (1859), which involved the shooting and blinding of a slave named John Hall, the property of S. D. McCutcheon. The plaintiff brought a civil action for three thousand dollars, two thousand of which was the alleged value of the slave, the remaining thousand being for his future maintenance, as McCutcheon claimed that John was worthless as a result of his injuries. Angelo claimed that he shot the slave because he had observed him lurking about his chicken house. When the slave realized that Angelo had seen him, he fled, ignoring Angelo's order to stop, whereupon Angelo shot him. The attending physician testified that Hall had been wounded eight times, including one shot in one eye and two in the other. The lower court judge awarded McCutcheon fifteen hundred dollars, stating that Angelo had used "excessive force for petty larceny." In his appeal Angelo asserted that his actions were justified since the slave was in the act of committing a felony and had refused to obey Angelo's order to halt. The supreme court ordered Angelo to pay the damages assessed by the lower court. Chief Justice Edwin Merrick wrote the opinion dismissing the defendant's assertion that chicken-stealing was a felony and rejecting Angelo's contention that the shooting was justified by the slave's refusal to stop when commanded:

> It is true that it is provided by law that "if any slave shall be found absent from his usual place of working or residence, without some white person accompanying him, and shall refuse to submit himself to examination, any freeholder shall be permitted to seize and correct him; and if he should resist or attempt to escape, the freeholder is authorized to make use of arms, but to avoid killing the slave; but should the slave assault and strike him, he is authorized to kill him."[20]

Justice Merrick's opinion made no mention of an 1818 case, *Jourdan* v. *Patton* (1818), in which the court ordered an owner who was fully compensated for the blinding of her slave to transfer title to the owner of the slave who caused the injury. That the supreme court considered the well-being of the slave, who had been owned by the same mistress for many years, but denied that the slave's future situation had relevance under the law. The difference was that in *Jourdan* the slave was injured by another slave, while in *McCutcheon* the slave was gravely wounded by the very person to whom title would have transferred. Although in *Jourdan* the court stated that "Cruelty and inhumanity ought not to be presumed against any person," Angelo's excessive punishment for chicken stealing went far beyond the mere presumption that further abuse of the slave might occur.[21]

During the same term that the court decided *McCutcheon*, it also heard the appeal of *Gardiner* v. *Thibodeau* (1859), a civil suit in which Edward C. Gardiner sought to recover the value of his slave Charles. The slave had been in the act of stealing chickens when Jean Thibodeau shot and killed him. A witness stated that after the shooting "There were chicken feathers from the [chicken] yard to the place where the negro was lying." Thibodeau admitted that he had shot Charles because he ordered the slave to halt, but the man continued to flee. The District Court of St. Landry Parish found for the defendant, and Gardiner appealed. Citing an 1857 act, which provided that "It shall be lawful to fire upon runaway negroes, who may be armed, when pursued, if they refused to surrender," Thibodeau contended that he was justified in shooting Charles because he was running away and was armed. Chief Justice Merrick, writing for the court, rejected this argument:

> It is proved that a knife was found in the pocket of his coat after the body of the negro was removed to the residence of the plaintiff. The coat was lying at the feet of the boy, and the knife was a butcher knife, six or seven inches long. This does not bring the case within the statute. The defendant did not pretend (as we have seen), that he killed the slave because he was a runaway and armed, but because he was stealing his chickens, and run [sic], and did not stop when commanded.
>
> If it be assumed, that the negro had his coat on when he was stealing the chickens, and the knife was in the pocket, the defence [sic] still fails, because it is now shown that the slave was a runaway. So far from being a runaway, the proof makes it sufficiently certain that he was out for no other purpose than that of stealing chickens; two of which were found by his house. The proof shows, that he was addicted to theft; but there is none tending to show that he was a runaway. Our law does not justify the killing of any one for a theft, and the defendant is left without sufficient justification.

The supreme court reversed the decision and awarded Gardiner $1,150. Citing *McCutcheon* v. *Angelo* in his ruling, Merrick ordered Thibodeau to reimburse Gardiner for Charles's value.[22]

In *Dupérrier* v. *Dautrive* (1857) the owner of another slave who disobeyed an order to halt was unable to recover from those who shot the luckless man. Dupérrier claimed that the defendants had "wantonly shot and mortally wounded" his slave while they were riding patrol for the city of New Iberia. When the patrol spotted the slave, they ordered him to halt, but he galloped away on a horse, whereupon members of the patrol fired upon him. Testimony established that his master had sent him into town on horseback to run an errand. When the patrol ordered him to stop, his horse, which was newly broken, bolted; members of the patrol fired at him three times with shotguns. The slave returned home and died of his wounds the next day. The District Court of St. Martin Parish held for the defendants, who, the court reasoned, believed the slave was a fugitive and were only doing their duty. Unrest among the slaves in and around New Iberia and rumors of slave insurrection had caused the patrols to take their responsibilities more seriously than usual. The supreme court affirmed the judgment, stating that recent disorders among the slaves in New Iberia called for the strict enforcement of laws for policing of slaves. The justices cited Section 65 of the act of 1855, "An Act Relative to Slaves and Colored Persons," which provided that any white who found a slave away from his usual residence who resisted arrest might "make use of arms" to seize and subdue him. The use of weapons, the justices reasoned, implied the risk of killing, and therefore applied to this case.[23]

Civil Suits against Overseers for Cruelty

The Louisiana Supreme Court heard several appeals involving slaveholders who sued their overseers for brutality and injury to their slaves. Slaves' hatred toward overseers in the American South is legendary. Historians have charged that overseers had a marked preference for using physical force in managing their charges. Since slaves did not accord overseers the same respect they gave owners, physical coercion was often necessary to induce obedience. Details from the lower-court cases reveal that many overseers deserved their reputation for harsh and often excessive measures to maintain discipline and maximize productivity. The *Black Code* provided for criminal prosecution of persons who beat slaves belonging to others without sufficient provocation: section 33 provided not only for financial compensation if a slave were injured or killed but also criminal prosecution of the offender. Yet not one case of abuse by an overseer that was appealed to the supreme court involved criminal prosecution; all were civil suits to regain the value of the lost labor of slaves temporarily incapacitated by mistreatment, or the full value of slaves permanently disabled or killed. Often the slaveholder asked merely that the court reduce the overseer's salary as compensation for the loss. The lack of criminal prosecutions despite overwhelming evidence of barbarous treatment demonstrates both the failure of slave law to provide protection for the basic right to be treated humanely and the resultant inadequacy of the courts in dealing with cruelty to slaves.[24]

It is also worth noting that in these cases the supreme court ruled overwhelmingly in favor of the slaveowners, regardless of the decision of the lower court. There is no evidence of a shift in jurisprudence during the antebellum period: despite changing times and personnel, the court almost always supported the property interest of the masters against their overseers. Only unusual circumstances produced any other result.

The earliest case involving an overseer killing a slave is an exception to the court's more ordinary practice of maintaining an owner's financial interest in his slaves. In *Martineau* v. *Hooper* (1818, 1820), the plaintiff sued his overseer for killing one of his slaves. Initially the jury found the overseer blameless and ruled against Martineau. On appeal the supreme court refused to rule because the clerk of the district court had failed to provide a transcript of one witness's testimony. The district court retried the case in 1820, the jury again found for the defendant, and Martineau appealed. Witnesses testified that Harry, the slave at issue, was so insubordinate that his master was afraid to return to his plantation, and he ordered the overseer to subdue him. Evidence indicated that the slave was so out-of-control that he had laid hands on his master. Believing that the slave would resist him, the overseer took the precaution of loading his gun, although he left it in the house before going outside to whip the recalcitrant slave. Harry resisted, as predicted, and a scuffle ensued, during which the overseer threatened to kill the slave. Harry took flight, and Hooper ran to the house, got his gun, and fatally wounded the slave. The Louisiana Supreme Court, in an opinion written by Chief Justice Mathews, held Hooper blameless, as the slave was "in an actual state of rebellion." It was imperative, the court ruled, that a slave who set such an example not go unpunished. The court reasoned that Hooper had acted as though the slave were his own and that two juries had excused him for refusing to allow "this rebel slave" to escape with impunity.[25]

Martineau v. *Hooper* was an exceptional decision based on the interest of the slaveholding community in maintaining slave discipline by not allowing an ungovernable slave to go unpunished. The court was willing to allow a slaveholder to suffer a loss of his property for the general safety of the community. Otherwise, however, the justices ordinarily ruled in favor of slave owners. In 1827 the court heard an appeal involving an overseer, *Perrie* v. *Williams and Adams*. Lucy Perrie, an absentee owner, sued her overseer, James Williams, and her neighbor Arthur Adams, both of whom had allegedly shot her slave Milo, killing him. In her petition Perrie claimed that Williams was an incompetent overseer who "cruelly treated and unnecessarily abused her slaves, . . . drove them off the plantation, and made a poor crop." She alleged that Williams and Adams had severely whipped and shot at two other slaves on her plantation. Adams, for his part, admitted the shooting, but said it was justified because Perrie's slaves often stole his cattle for food; their rations, he added, were so meager. The trial-court jury found Williams and Adams liable, and the judge awarded Perrie $900, $450 each from Williams and Adams. Only Williams appealed. Chief Judge Mathews affirmed the judgment of the lower trial court on the grounds that Perrie had a reasonable claim for damages because of the "unjustifiable violence and injury done directly to the property of the plaintiff."[26]

Womack v. *Nicholson* (1842) was a civil action brought by Abraham Womack, the owner of a slave named Nancy, against Peter Nicholson for the value of Nancy and other damages. Womack had hired Nancy to Nicholson, whose overseer had beaten the pregnant slave woman so severely that she delivered her baby prematurely, and she and the infant subsequently died. Nicholson denied the allegations stating that Womack had represented Nancy as being "humble, tractable, and healthy," when in fact she was not only sickly, but "insolent, disobedient, and in the habit of running away." The defendant claimed that Womack owed him five hundred dollars for days of lost labor as well as maintenance and medical care for the slave. The Caddo Parish jury found in favor of the plaintiff for the sum of $558, and the defendant appealed. The testimony of witnesses established that Nancy was an intractable slave and that she had run away several times from the defendant. One of the witnesses stated that Nancy "required more whipping than ordinary negroes," and that another planter who had hired her returned her to

Womack because of "her vicious and unmanageable character." When Nicholson found Nancy so insubordinate that she was useless, he ordered Mr. Churchman, his overseer, to return Nancy to her owner. A neighbor subsequently found her lying by the side of the road, her head gashed, bruised and swollen, with both old and fresh marks of the lash on her body. The neighbor who discovered her summoned a physician, who found symptoms of dropsy (congestive heart failure), as well as evidence of a severe beating. Womack brought Nancy to his plantation, where she continued to exhibit symptoms of dropsy. He never summoned a physician, and Nancy died two months later. The Caddo Parish jury believed that the beating Nicholson's overseer administered to Nancy had caused her death, but the supreme court reversed the decision, stating that although the beating most likely caused the death of Nancy's baby, Nancy herself had died of a preexisting disease, dropsy. The court held that Womack's neglect in failing to call a physician cost him full recovery of Nancy's value. The court lowered the award to $158.50, the cost of medical care for Nancy at the neighbor's house as a result of the overseer's beating. In modifying the trial court's judgment, Associate Judge Alonzo Morphy, writing for the court, held that the decision of the jury was a "manifest error," contrary to the evidence as to the cause of Nancy's death. Although the Supreme Court of Louisiana could review both law and fact, it could not overturn or modify the verdict of a lower court on the basis of fact unless, as in this case, the decision was judged clearly wrong, i.e. a "manifest error."[27]

Occasionally, a master who believed that his overseer had abused a slave retaliated by withholding the overseer's salary. In *Hendricks* v. *Phillips* (1848) the overseer Hendricks sued Phillips, his employer, for back wages. Phillips admitted that Hendricks had been his overseer but stated that Hendricks had treated his slaves with such cruelty that he made a reconventional demand (a civil-law term for countersuit) for the amount of the overseer's wages. Witnesses testified that Hendricks was a capable overseer who made a good crop, but they admitted that he had treated one slave woman with great brutality. Condemning the conduct of the overseer, Justice Thomas Slidell observed "the details are of a most revolting character, and exhibit conduct on the part of the overseer utterly undefensible." Since the lower court record no longer exists, we do not know what the "revolting" details were, except that witnesses' testimony was "extremely unfavorable to him [the overseer] with regard to the cruel treatment of the negro." Citing article 173 of the *Civil Code*, which prohibits masters, and by implication, those to whom masters delegate power, from inflicting excessively rigorous punishment, as well as the *Black Code*, section 33, which made anyone cruelly chastising the slave of another liable for the value of the slave, Justice Slidell's opinion modified the decision of the Catahoula Parish District Court, which had lowered the overseer's salary by the amount of the value of labor lost during the slave woman's convalescence. The supreme court ruled that testimony in the case established that the overseer had permanently disabled the slave, and that Phillips was entitled to her value as well as medical expenses. The court awarded Phillips the entire amount of the overseer's wages plus one hundred dollars.[28]

The following year the court heard another appeal involving an overseer, *Blanchard* v. *Dixon* (1849). In this civil suit Blanchard alleged that Dixon, who was the overseer of the plaintiff's neighbor, had shot one of Blanchard's slaves without provocation. The overseer had seen the slave on the road in front of Blanchard's residence. He demanded a pass from the slave, who answered in French, which the overseer did not understand. However, Dixon believed from the tone of the reply that the slave was insolent, whereupon, he demanded that the slave halt. In response to this order the slave took flight, and the overseer ran to his house for his gun, mounted a horse, and pursued the slave until he was sufficiently close to shoot him, fracturing his knee. Witnesses testified that the slave had been well-behaved and submissive before the incident. The overseer cited the *Black Code*, sections 30 and 32, to justify the use of force in arresting a slave absent from his master's premises without a pass. The district court found for the overseer, but the supreme court reversed the judgment. Associate Justice George Rogers King compared the case with *Allain, f.m.c.* v. *Young*, in which a white man had shot a slave who was out without a pass. The difference between the two cases, he reasoned, was that in *Allain* the slave had attempted to seize a firearm and was in the act of committing a felony whereas in *Blanchard* the slave was guilty of no crime but failing to halt and be examined. As a physician had declared the injury to be permanent, the court awarded Blanchard seven hundred dollars in damages, two-thirds of his slave's value, plus fifty dollars in medical expenses.[29]

The supreme court cited both *Allain* and *Blanchard* in the next appeal it considered of a case in which an overseer had shot a slave without provocation. *Arnandez* v. *Lawes* (1850) involved two slaves belonging to Jean Baptiste Arnandez. They were catching driftwood at their master's order when the overseer of a plantation across the river called them ashore and demanded their passes. Although both slaves produced written permits from Arnandez to be on the river, the overseer, Thomas B. Lawes, ordered two armed men standing nearby to restrain both slaves. One of the slaves, William, became frightened and fled. He had gone only a few feet when he apparently realized that running might make the situation worse; he turned to submit to Lawes, just as the overseer fired several times, mortally wounding William. The lower court ruled in favor of the owner and awarded him a thousand dollars in damages; Lawes appealed on grounds that under section 32 of the *Black Code* it was not a crime to shoot a slave who refused to halt. Associate Justice Pierre Adolphe Rost rejected this argument, calling Lawes's actions "useless, barbarous, unjustified violence." In a rare action, Rost amended the judgment and raised the award to Arnandez to twelve hundred dollars.[30]

The following year the court heard another appeal from an overseer who shot a slave for a minor offense. In *Benjamin* v. *Davis* (1851) Herman P. Benjamin sued his overseer for the value of his slave Ned. The slave had misbehaved and had subsequently fled because Davis planned to whip him. The following day the overseer armed himself and a companion; the two mounted horses and tracked Ned down with "negro dogs." After bragging to witnesses that they were off to hunt runaways, they returned with a mortally wounded Ned across Davis's saddle. Davis claimed the slave was a fugitive and, as such, could be shot with impunity according to the *Black Code*. The West Feliciana District Court jury found for the defendant, and Benjamin appealed. Justice Rost, writing for the court, reversed the decision of the lower court, calling the shooting "totally unjustified." Citing *Carmouche* v. *Bouis*, he questioned what excuse two able-bodied, armed, and mounted men with dogs might have had in firing upon an old, unarmed slave. Calling the verdict of the lower court "clearly erroneous," the court awarded Benjamin $350.[31]

Six months later, Justice Rost wrote another decision involving an overseer's cruel treatment of the slaves in his charge, *Dwyer* v. *Cane* (1851). The overseer, Samuel E. Dwyer, sued his former employer, who had fired him and refused to pay his back wages. Despite the fact that Dwyer had made a good crop, "he inflicted cruel and unusual punishments upon the male slaves, and . . . his conduct with the women of the plantation was grossly and openly immoral." Dwyer lost in the district court and appealed to the supreme court. Justice Rost, writing for the court, acknowledged that Dwyer was not guilty of such mismanagement and that he should not have been dismissed because he "made a good crop of cotton." However, Rost rejected the overseer's demand for reinstatement and back wages: "Cruelty to slaves is a sufficient cause of dismissal, and *honeste vivere* [a Roman law term meaning "to live virtuously"] forms part of the duties of an overseer."[32]

In 1855 the supreme court heard two appeals from judgments in which owners claimed that overseers caused the loss of one of their slaves through excessive punishment. In *Kennedy* v. *Mason* the plaintiff claimed six hundred dollars from the estate of the owner of the plantation as the final amount due for his wages. The agent of the owner filed a reconventional demand for one thousand dollars, the value of a slave named Jim Crack, who allegedly died at the hands of the overseer as a punishment for having run away. Witnesses stated that despite extremely cold weather, Kennedy stripped the slave, tied him "with his belly down to the cold ground," and beat him steadily for an hour and a half with a handsaw and a whip. Following the beating, Kennedy rubbed the slave with a mixture called "No. 6" and administered a dose of castor oil. Fellow slaves put Jim Crack in his bed, where he died within a few hours. The lower court found in favor of the unpaid overseer, but the supreme court reversed the decision. The physician who conducted the post mortem exam had concluded that the whipping alone did not cause Crack's death but that the combination of the whipping and exposure to the frigid weather was fatal:

> [The physician testified,] "I saw that he had been whipped and considerably bruised on his buttock, and each side of his shoulders. The buttock and sides of the shoulders did not appear much cut, but considerably bruised, from which the blood oozed and stuck to the shirt in a few places. That amount of whipping under ordinary circumstances, would not produce death. I thought it imprudent to whip the boy at that time and under the circumstances. From internal and external indications, I think it more likely that death was caused by a congestive chill, than by the whipping; but more likely death in this case was caused by a combination of all the circumstances." Under this state of facts we do not think it is unreasonable to infer that the slave's death was caused by the severity of the punishment inflicted upon him, combined with his exposure to the weather. Had the plaintiff taken proper care of him after he retired to his cabin, he might have averted the unfortunate consequence: but he did not. This was gross negligence on his part.

The high court allowed the reconventional demand of the owner's agent for the full value of Jim Crack. The overseer requested a rehearing on the grounds that Jim Crack had been a frequent runaway and was therefore virtually of no value. A witness testified that she had known the slave since he was a child, and "with his character and habits he was entirely worthless." Notwithstanding the testimony, the court refused to grant him a rehearing.[33]

During the same month, the supreme court heard a similar case, *Kemp* v. *Hutchinson*. The overseer had whipped a slave named "Big Nancy" twice in one day for stealing, and was threatening a third flogging if she did not produce the allegedly stolen articles. She denied the theft but said she would try to find the articles. Instead, she threw herself into a river and was drowned. The difference between *Kemp* and *Kennedy* v. *Mason*, Associate Justice Alexander Buchanan reasoned in the court's opinion, was that there was no proof that the overseer caused Big Nancy's death, which was what Justice Buchanan termed a "voluntary act." The court ruled that the overseer was not responsible for the slave woman's death:

> The power of correction of a slave, vested in his master by our law, was held, in the case of *Kennedy* v. *Mason*, to be delegated to an overseer, from the nature of his employment. In the exercise of that power, the

owner of the slave or his delegate, is only to be held responsible for the immediate and necessary consequences of his acts.

Buchanan ordered Hutchinson to pay the overseer the wages he had withheld.[34]

The following year the court heard the appeal that most clearly demonstrates the inability of the legal system to deal with excessive cruelty to slaves. The unreported case of *Humphreys* v. *Utz* (1856)[35] is remarkable for several reasons, among them for providing compelling evidence that the Supreme Court of Louisiana had an unspoken policy of underreporting or omitting entirely from its official reports certain kinds of cases involving cruelty to slaves. Cases of flagrant sexual abuse were one category that made the justices reticent. For example, in *Hendricks* v. *Phillips* (1848), the court stated that the overseer's behavior with a slave woman was "of a most revolting character, and exhibited conduct on the part of the overseer utterly indefensible," but we are not given the "revolting" details, and the record of the trial court has vanished. In *Dwyer* v. *Cane*, the court again relied on generalizations—"He inflicted cruel and unusual punishment upon the male slaves . . . and his conduct with the women of the plantation was grossly and openly immoral"—and again the trial-court record, where we might learn specifics, has disappeared. In citing "cruel and unusual punishment," though, the justices touched on a second phenomenon they disliked to report: extreme (and almost certainly sadistic) physical brutality. Several appeals involving beatings of slaves, even to death, were dutifully reported, but when the issue was torture, not merely harsh discipline, things were different. *Humphreys* v. *Utz* was a torture case that speaks volumes about the court's tacit policy on reporting. For here, at last, the grisly details have somehow survived: we have the complete trial-court record, the briefs to the supreme court, the court's handwritten decision, even a sheet of scratch paper on which the trial jury figured the amount of damages—and the case went unreported. *Humphreys* was a suit for civil damages of five thousand dollars brought by J. C. and G. W. Humphreys, absentee owners of the Burkland plantation in Madison Parish, against Henry Utz, their overseer, for damages he allegedly caused "by inflicting unusual unnecessary and cruel punishment." In the petition the Humphreys brothers allege that Utz inflicted "cruel treatment of an unusual inhuman and outrageous nature . . . upon two of the negroes placed under his care." The Humphreys brothers charged that one of the slaves, named "Ginger Pop," died from Utz's cruelty. Specifically, the Humphreys charged that Utz had killed Ginger Pop by "nailing the privates of said negro to the bedstead and then inflicting blows upon him until said negro [sic] pulled loose from the post to which he had been pinned by driving an iron tack or nail through his penis." The Humphreys further alleged that Utz had "inflicted a similar outrage upon a certain negro boy named Dave," who also belonged to them.

Utz denied the allegations of cruelty. He claimed that the brothers had hired him to manage the plantation for the year 1853 for a salary of eight hundred dollars. He said he had served as overseer until he was "wrongfully discharged" on August 19, 1853, and he made a reconventional demand for his salary. He stated that he "was at all times attentive to his business, kind to the sick and humain [sic] to all" and that the plaintiffs were bent on ruining his reputation as "a careful manager of negroes, and a good cultivator of the soil." He alleged that the slaves of Burkland plantation "had the reputation of being difficult to manage, and several of them were habitual runaways." Utz asked for $6,000 in damages from the Humphreys for the damage done to his reputation.

A witness to the incident testified that Ginger Pop was a habitual runaway, and apparently Utz had tried to discipline him in other ways, once attempting to nail his ear to the gallery of the plantation house and once "took the butt end of his cow hide and whipped—on the head as long as he could stand over him." Gabriel Utz, brother to the defendant and himself an overseer on a neighboring plantation, testified that Ginger Pop was always running away: besides, Gabriel added, Henry Utz had told him that he only tacked Ginger Pop's penis to the bedpost to scare him, "that it had done more good than all the whipping[,] that it had calmed him."[36] Gabriel Utz also testified that Ginger Pop would have been worth from eight hundred to one thousand dollars if he were not a habitual runaway; but with his character, he was "worth little or nothing."

On the night Ginger Pop died, Utz told a witness "that he was *damd* [sic] glad of it and he wished he could get clear of Shed and Maria, [other slaves on the plantation], deft [sic] told witness next morning that he had Slept the happiest night [sic] Sleep he had Slept Since he had been on the place."[37] Ginger Pop died on 10 June; the Humphreys called a physician to conduct a post mortem examination on 20 August, but the decomposition of the body prevented him from coming to any conclusion regarding the cause of death. Utz claimed Ginger Pop had died of a "congestive chill," although he admitted that "he had worn him out." The Humphreys brothers fired Utz the same day.

The trial-court jury found for Utz in the amount of $388.86. They arrived at this amount by calculating Utz's wages from 1 January to 20 August—$508.83—and then deducted damages to Ginger Pop of $120. Why did the Madison Parish jury find for Utz despite overwhelming evidence to the contrary? Why was Utz never convicted of cruelty in a criminal trial? The answer to both questions lies in the brief to the supreme court by the Humphreys' attorney, Andrew R. Hynes:

> It will be remembered that the Mssrs. Humphreys reside in the State of Mississippi and seldom visit the Burkland plantation, and were not present at the trial of this suit in the District Court. The Grand Jury

acting in and for the Parish of Madison, indicted the defendant for cruel treatment of the slaves of the plaintiff, and the Jury empanelled to try the case brought in a verdict of "Not Guilty," although the proof was direct and overwhelming. It will be remembered that in a sparsely peopled country, where the owners of property are non-residents, the Jurors of the country are almost entirely made up of Overseers, and that perhaps no class is so clannish or so disposed to protect each other in their difficulties. Whenever a planter shall in a contest with an overseer resort to a jury, there can be no doubt as to what the verdict will be, and the only hope left to the country is that the purity of the Bench will correct the evil.[38]

Justice Alexander Buchanan wrote the decision of the court. He acknowledged that Ginger Pop was "an incorrigible runaway . . . a very vicious & worthless subject,"[39] and he further acknowledged that there was no proof that the actual death of the slave had been caused by Utz's cruel treatment. However, Buchanan did not allow Utz to avoid the consequences of his actions:

[Y]et acts of revolting brutality have been proved, which entirely exceed the limits of that repressive and correctional discipline which is necessary to the management of the agricultural laborers of the South . . . [which] should be strict . . . but . . . tempered with mercy. The evil passions of men become infuriated to reckless ferocity by unbridled indulgence: and the very helplessness of the slave . . . is sometimes found to encourage . . . cold blooded refinements of torture. He who cannot protect himself has a double claim to protection.

Buchanan reversed the decision of the trial court, and ruled that the Humphreys' discharge of Utz was justified. Ordering Utz to pay his wages to the date of his discharge to the plaintiffs—$508.83—the supreme court also ruled that Utz pay costs in both courts.[40]

Humphreys v. *Utz* provides rare documentary evidence, originally considered too horrible to be published, of the barbarous treatment that some slaves endured. It also reveals a jury unwilling to award to the owner of such a slave more than token damages for such abuse. From the appellate brief we learn that Utz was the defendant in a criminal trial as well as in the civil suit for damages. The result of this trial is a clear illustration of a criminal justice system that utterly failed to protect slaves from even the most savage treatment: Utz was acquitted; despite overwhelming evidence against him, the jury simply refused to convict.

The following year, in *Miller* v. *Stewart* (1857) another overseer sued his employer for his wages of eight hundred dollars for two years' service, and the owner filed a reconventional demand for $1,250, claiming the overseer was liable for the death of one of his slaves. In the appeal the overseer claimed that the slave, Tom, had attacked him, was incorrigible, and had resisted when he had attempted to whip him. During the scuffle Tom bit off the tip of Miller's finger and scratched his face. Finally Miller subdued the slave, loaded him with chains, staked him to the ground, and gave him a severe lashing. An eyewitness claimed that Miller had whipped Tom from his neck to his heels, and that the stripes were so close together that a person could not put a finger between them. This witness testified that he had never seen a slave whipped with such brutality. The two physicians who conducted the post mortem exam agreed that either the flogging itself or exhaustion and overexertion from the scourging caused Tom's death. The Carroll Parish jury awarded Miller $344.15, the wages he had earned from the time of his employment to the time of his discharge, and Stewart appealed. Citing *Kennedy v. Mason*, and describing the overseer's actions as "gross negligence," the supreme court awarded Stewart twelve hundred dollars—the assessed value of the slave—deducting $344, wages Stewart owed the overseer. In his decision Voorhies quoted section 16 of the "Crimes and Offences" section of the *Black Code* and questioned the overseer's allegations that Tom was a troublemaker:

> The overseer may correct and chastise the slaves of the planter who employs him, but he cannot do so "with unusual rigor, nor so to maim or mutilate them, or to expose them to the danger of loss of life, or to cause their death." . . . [T]here is not a scintilla of evidence showing that the slave *Tom* was vicious or that his character was bad; nor was there any attempt to show the nature of the offence [sic] which brought upon him such severe punishment.[41]

The supreme court heard the last case involving improper conduct by an overseer to a slave in *Kessee v. Mayfield & Cage* (1859). Kessee sued the defendants for his wages of eight hundred dollars for one year as overseer of their plantation. The owners had employed him on April 10, 1856, and discharged him, Kessee alleged, for no reason on June 22, 1856. Kessee's attorneys cited *Civil Code* article 2720, which requires an employer who fires an employee without cause to honor the terms of the contract of hiring, paying wages for the entire time provided for in the agreement. The defendants asserted that they fired Kessee for good cause: incompetence, disregarding defendant's instructions, and cruelty to the slaves. Mayfield and Cage were willing to pay Kessee for the two months he had worked for them, but Kessee claimed wages for the whole year. Although the owners introduced no evidence to prove their allegations that the overseer was cruel or incompetent, evidence supported their claim that he disregarded their instructions. The defendants had strictly ordered Kessee not to discipline the slaves with his own hand. Drivers were to flog the slaves if they should need chastisement. Witnesses stated that Kessee ignored these instructions and lashed the slaves himself. The District Court of Terrebonne Parish found that the owners had discharged

Kessee for good cause and denied him any wages whatever. As the defendants had been willing, despite Kessee's actions, to pay the overseer wages for the actual time worked, this award was more favorable than the defendants had demanded. The supreme court reversed this ruling and granted Kessee wages for the period he had actually worked. In its ruling the court stated that although article 2720 applied only to persons fired with no cause, it seemed unfair not to grant Kessee wages to the time of his discharge.[42]

Civil Suits against Owners for Cruelty

Cases in which masters were accused of abusing their own slaves reached litigation infrequently during the antebellum period. The supreme court heard only three appeals of such civil suits during the whole time. In the first, *Markham* v. *Close* (1831), the plaintiff presented a petition to the District Court of Opelousas in which he alleged that his neighbor, Close, had cruelly beaten his own slave, Augustin. Markham requested that the court take the slave away from Close and sell him. Close did not deny the beating but claimed that the slave had been a fugitive for some time and deserved the punishment. Witnesses testified that the flogging was so severe that Augustin was incapable of sitting or lying on his back, and that Close had lashed him on three separate occasions. His back was "very much cut and skinned . . . the weather being warm, the wounds smelled badly." The district court judge placed the case on its docket as a civil action, and although Close protested that the proceedings were unknown to the law and that Markham had no right to institute such a suit, the lower court ordered Close to sell the slave. He appealed to the Louisiana Supreme Court.

The supreme court, in a decision written by Associate Judge Alexander Porter, found that Markham's petition was "an anomalous action, instituted in *civil* form to punish a *criminal* offense." Porter stated that Markham had no interest in the slave but had presented himself to the court as a public prosecutor. Porter acknowledged that evidence supported Markham's claim that Close had been excessively cruel to the slave, and he added: "It is greatly to be deplored, that owners of slaves should abuse their authority," However, Porter denied that Markham had any right to institute such a suit. Excessive cruelty, the court reasoned, was a public offense that had to be prosecuted criminally, according to section 16 of the *Black Code.* The court also cited article 192 of the *Civil Code,* which states that a master can not be compelled to sell his slave unless he is actually convicted of cruel treatment. In such cases the judge can order the sale of a slave at public auction "in order to place him out of the reach of the power which his master has abused." Without a criminal conviction, no court could order the sale of the slave.

Markham could not take the law into his own hands in this manner, Porter ruled. Reversing the lower court's decision, Porter found that while Markham's motives might have been admirable, in another instance, a person bringing a similar suit might be motivated by "envy, malice, and all uncharitableness."[43] There is no record of any subsequent criminal prosecution against Close.

In 1857, the court heard *Barrow* v. *McDonald*, a lawsuit for damages for the "malicious killing" of a slave by one of his owners. The plaintiff, Robert Ruffin Barrow, owned a three-fourths interest in the slave; the defendant, who managed one of Barrow's four sugar plantations, owned one-fourth. Barrow estimated his losses at fifteen hundred dollars. Barrow and McDonald were business partners and owned the sugar plantation where the killing occurred in the same proportions in which they owned the slave. The judge in the Terrebonne District Court ruled that the damages should properly be a part of the action (which was in progress) to dissolve the partnership between the two men and not a separate action. The supreme court agreed with this assessment and affirmed the judgment.[44]

The high court heard the last appeal involving cruelty to a slave by a master in *Ney* v. *Richard*. This case was a civil action that arose because of the improper handling of a criminal case. The sheriff of St. Landry Parish arrested Adele Roy Ney for cruel treatment of her slave Frozine. The parish court judge released Ney after she posted bail. At the same time, he ordered Frozine to be incarcerated in parish prison pending the outcome of the trial. His purpose was to furnish the slave protection from Ney. Ney's husband filed an action against the parish judge and the sheriff. The district-court judge ruled that sequestering the slave to remove her from Ney's power was the proper action under the circumstances. The supreme court ruled that the district court had erred in its ruling because no law existed to remove a slave from the power of his or her master without a criminal conviction for cruelty. The court ordered the release of the slave to the Neys.[45] No record exists of an appeal of the criminal prosecution.

Conclusion

Louisiana law provided slaves few protections against cruel treatment, although the legal machinery was in place had witnesses, prosecutors, judges, and juries chosen to use it. Evidence in appeals to the Supreme Court of Louisiana shows that strangers, neighbors, overseers, and owners abused slaves at times, ignoring such protective laws as existed. Most of these cases involved irate owners bringing civil actions to recover damages for slaves injured or killed by others. The court heard no criminal appeals until after 1846 because it lacked jurisdiction, and even after

1846 the court heard few criminal appeals of this nature. Masters were apparently more interested in financial compensation than justice. Since most lower-court records of criminal prosecutions are not accessible or have not survived, these appeals are the only solid evidence of prosecutions for cruelty to slaves in Louisiana. Of course, we have no way of knowing how many persons accused of brutal cruelty and incontrovertibly guilty of it were acquitted because, as with Henry Utz, a jury simply refused to convict. Certainly though, *Humphreys* v. *Utz* demonstrates the failure of the law to provide even the most basic protection for slaves.

Slave owners created the legal system that prohibited cruel treatment, and the judiciary as a whole seems to have been very reluctant to interfere with what many judges perceived as a matter between owners and their property. The courts were quite willing to support the slave owners' financial interest in injured or dead slaves, which was a simple issue of awarding property damages, but only the most atrocious crimes occasionally resulted in criminal prosecutions; in all criminal prosecutions of a slave owner, the cruel treatment had caused the death of the slave. Ironically, even though the legal status of slaves in Louisiana was insignificant compared to that of their powerful owners, the law abundantly protected the slaveholders *from* their slaves. The paradox of the slave's being at once person and property often disappeared when he or she committed a crime. In that instance the slave was almost invariably a person in the eyes of the law. By contrast, when a slave was victimized by an owner's cruelty, Louisiana was far more cognizant of the slave as property. Thus, again, the legal system was rendered inadequate to protect slaves' most basic rights; for when the limited right of slaves to life conflicted with the property interests of slaveholders, the outcome was seldom in doubt.

Notes

This article is drawn from the author's book, *Slavery, the Civil Law, and the Supreme Court of Louisiana* (Baton Rouge, La., 1994). The author is grateful to the Louisiana State University Press for permission to publish this portion of her book. Both this piece and the book-length study are based on the manuscript records of the Supreme Court of Louisiana, which are housed in Account No. 106 in the Earl K. Long Library of the University of New Orleans. Although scholars have had access to the printed reports of the decisions of the court, the original handwritten decisions have only recently become available. This is the first book-length study of these incredibly rich and valuable records. The printed reports usually contain a brief and often sparse recitation of the facts of the case, the decision of the court, and the legal reasoning on which the court based the decision. The case files ordinarily include a handwritten copy of the lower court case, including attorneys' arguments, depositions, written interrogatories, and the clerk's summary of the testimony. Thus the handwritten case record ordinarily contained fifty to one hundred pages, and included a wealth of detail only suggested by the brief printed report of the case. Before these records became available, students of slave law had only legal indexes, such as the *Louisiana Digest: 1809 to Date* (St. Paul, Minn., 1959) and Helen T. Catterall, *Judicial Cases Concerning American Slavery and the Negro* (New York, 1926), to guide them to judicial decisions involving slavery. The index in the *Louisiana Digest* is based on the reports of cases and is far from complete, and Catterall was forced to base her work on the reported cases, as she did not have access to the original manuscripts of the court. Furthermore, there are a number of appeals involving slavery that were never reported and are therefore only available in manuscript form. These unreported cases are invisible in Catterall's work and in all legal indexes. For the convenience of those readers who may wish to access the manuscript records previously mentioned, we have included the docket number where applicable in the case citations.

In this chapter I use "Black Code" to refer to the codes written after statehood by the Louisiana legislature; "Code Noir" refers to the code written while Louisiana was a French Colony; "Codigo Negro" refers to the code written when Louisiana was a Spanish colony.

The author wishes to thank the Dean of the Tulane Law School, John R. Kramer, for his support and encouragement.

1. Act of June 7, 1806, § 16 *Orleans Territory Acts, 1806*, 150, 206–7, ("An Act Prescribing the Rules and Conduct to Be Observed with Respect to Negroes and Other Slaves of This Territory": hereinafter referred to and cited as *Black Code* to distinguish it from the 1724 French *Code Noir*). The Supreme Court of Louisiana refused to allow a free black woman to sue for cruelty on behalf of her slave daughter. *Dorothée* v. *Coquillon*, no. 1649, 7 Mart. (n.s.) 350 (La. 1829).

2. Hans Baade, "The Law of Slavery in Spanish Luisiana, 1769–1803," in *Louisiana's Legal Heritage*, ed. Edward F. Haas, Jr. (Pensacola, Fla., 1983), 74–75.

3. Kenneth Stampp, *The Peculiar Institution: Slavery in the Antebellum South* (New York, 1956), 141.

4. *Black Code*, "Crimes and Offences," § 16, pp. 206–7. Moreau Lislet, *A Digest of the Civil Laws Now in Force in the Territory of Orleans* (New Orleans, 1808), tit. VI, art. 16, p. 40, and tit. IV, art. 27, p. 42. Hereinafter cited as *Digest of 1808*. Along with acts of the Louisiana legislature, the *Digest of 1808* served as law in Louisiana until replaced by the *Civil Code of 1825* (New Orleans, 1825). Hereinafter cited as 1825 La. Civ. Code. William Goddell, *The American Slave Code* (London, 1853), 149. Goddell points out that masters had only to repeat excessive punishments until they became "usual."

5. *Black Code*, "Crimes and Offenses," § 16, 208. Act of January 31, 1821, §§ 1–2, 1821 La. Acts, 24 ("An Act Concerning Crimes and Misdemeanors").

6. New Orleans *Bee*, April 11–12, 1834. See also Stampp, *Peculiar Institution*, 182, 188; Joe Gray Taylor, *Negro Slavery in Louisiana* (Baton Rouge, La., 1963), 225–27. Fred Darkis contends that Mme. Lalaurie was the victim of a "bad press." Fred R. Darkis, "Madame Lalaurie of New Orleans," *Louisiana History* 23 (fall 1982): 383.

7. *Black Code*, "Crimes and Offenses," §§ 16–17, pp. 206–8. *State* v. *Mann*, 13 N.C. (2 Dev.) 263 (1829). South Carolina was the only other state with the provision that slaveholders could clear themselves from a charge of cruelty to their slaves by a personal oath. Goddell, *American Slave Code*, 280; *State* v. *Raines*,

14 S.C.L. (3 McCord) 533 (1826). For an overview of prosecutions for cruelty to slaves in common law states, see Andrew Fede, "Legitimized Violent Slave Abuse in the American South, 1619–1865: A Case Study of Law and Social Change in Six Southern States," 29 *American Journal of Legal History*, 93 (1985).

8. 1812 La. Const. art. IV, § 2; tit. IV, art. 63, in *Constitutions of the State of Louisiana* 503, 514 (Benjamin Wall Dart ed., Indianapolis, 1932).

9. *State* v. *Morris*, no. 1293, 4 La. Ann. 177 (1849).

10. Fede, "Legitimized Violent Slave Abuse," 96, 133. For cases in other states involving convictions of masters see *State* v. *Hoover*, 21 N.C. (4 Dev. & Bat.) 365 (1839); *Souther* v. *Commonwealth*, 48 Va. (7 Gratt.) 672 (1851).

11. *State* v. *Bass and McNabb*, no. 4603, 11 La. Ann. 478 (1856).

12. *State* v. *Taylor, f.m.c.*, no. 4132, 11 La. Ann. 430 (1856).

13. *State* v. *Populus, f.m.c.*, no. 250, 12 La. Ann. 710 (1857).

14. *State* v. *Ward and White*, 13 La. Ann. 573 (1858). *Black Code*, "Crimes and Offenses," §§ 16–17, pp. 206–8.

15. *State* v. *Davis*, 14 La. Ann. 678 (1859). Act of March 14, 1855, § 9 1855 La. Acts, 131 ("An Act Relative to Crimes and Offenses"). The judge in *State* v. *Hale*, a North Carolina case, ruled that assault on a slave by persons other than the slave owner was an indictable offense. *State* v. *Hale*, 9 N.C. (2 Hawks) 582 (1823).

16. *Black Code*, "Crimes and Offenses," § 16, pp. 206–8. Fede suggests that slaveholders chose civil remedies if the offender had the financial means to compensate for the damages to or loss of the slave but chose criminal prosecution to serve as a deterrent to poor whites, who would have been unable to come up with a sufficient amount to justify a civil suit for the value of the slave. Fede, "Legitimized Violent Slave Abuse," 113.

17. *Allain, f.m.c.* v. *Young*, no. 537, 9 Mart. (o.s.) 221 (La. 1821). For a similar case, see *Hébert* v. *Esnard*, no. 1818, 8 Mart. (n.s.) 498 (La. 1830). It was against the law for slaves to sell or barter produce without permission from their masters. *Black Code*, § 14, pp. 156–58.

18. *Déslonde, f.m.c.* v. *LeBréret*, no. 2300, 5 La. 96 (1833). For a similar case, see *Richardson* v. *Dukes*, 15 S.C.L. (4 McCord) 156 (1827).

19. *Carmouche* v. *Bouis*, no. 2032, 6 La. Ann. 95 (1851). For a similar case involving a slave shot in the act of stealing a hog, see *Bibb* v. *Hébert*, no. 753, 3 La. Ann. 132 (1848). See also *Jennings* v. *Fundeburg*, 15 S.C.L. (4 McCord) 161 (1827).

20. *McCutcheon* v. *Angelo*, no. 5425, 14 La. Ann. 34 (1859).

21. *Jourdan* v. *Patton*, no. 304, 5 Mart. (o.s.) 615 (La. 1818). Mark Tushnet discusses *Jourdan* v. *Patton* in his book *The American Law of Slavery: Considerations of Humanity and Interest* (Princeton: Princeton University Press, 1981). Tushnet states (66–71) that in *Jourdan* the supreme court recognized the "sentiment that slavery could generate between master and slave" but denied that those ties were relevant because there was no reason to presume that the owner of the slave who blinded the plaintiff's slave would be cruel. But this analysis does not take into account the possibility that if the "sentiment" between the mistress and her slave were so strong, she could have accepted less than the full value of her slave, and title would not have transferred.

22. *Gardiner* v. *Thibodeau*, 14 La. Ann. 732 (1859). Act of March 19, 1857, § 41, 1857 La. Acts, 233 ("An Act Relative to Slaves").

23. *Dupérrier* v. *Dautrive,* 12 La. Ann. 664 (1856). St. Martin Parish and neighboring parishes were shaken by rumors of slave revolts in the fall of 1856. In *Dupérrier* the patrol shot the slave in August 1855. See Harvey Wish, "The Slave Insurrection Panic of 1856," *Journal of Southern History* 5 (May 1939): 217–18. Act of March 15, 1855, § 65, 1855 La. Acts, 386 ("An Act Relative to Slaves and Free Colored People"). See also *Witsell* v. *Earnest,* 10 S.C.L. (1 Nott & McC) 182 (1818).

24. Stampp, *Peculiar Institution,* 183; Alton V. Moody, "Slavery on Louisiana Sugar Plantations," *Louisiana Historical Quarterly* 7 (April 1924): 210; William Kaufman Scarborough, *The Overseer: Plantation Management in the Old South* (Athens, Ga., 1984), 78–79; *Black Code,* "Crimes and Offenses," § 33, pp. 176–78.

25. *Martineau* v. *Hooper,* no. 49, 5 Mart. (o.s.) 661 (La. 1818).

26. *Perrie* v. *Williams and Adams,* no. 1444, 5 Mart. (n.s.) 694 (La. 1827).

27. *Womack* v. *Nicholson,* no. 949, 3 Rob. 248 (La. 1842). 1812 La. Const. tit. IV, art. 63; art. LXII, in Dart, ed., *Constitutions of the State of Louisiana,* at 514, 528.

28. *Hendricks* v. *Phillips,* no. 98, 3 La. Ann. 618 (1848). A *reconventional demand* is the civil-law equivalent of a counterclaim in common law. The court heard an appeal in an almost identical case in which an overseer shot the slave Alfred: *Taylor* v. *Patterson,* no. 3473, 9 La. Ann. 251 (1854). 1825 La. Civ. Code, art. 173, p. 27. *Black Code,* § 33, pp. 176–78.

29. *Blanchard* v. *Dixon,* no. 1135, 4 La. Ann. 57 (1849). *Black Code,* "Crimes and Offenses," §§ 30, 32, pp. 172–76.

30. *Arnandez* v. *Lawes,* no. 1572, 5 La. Ann. 127 (1850). *Black Code,* "Crimes and Offenses," § 30, p. 176.

31. *Benjamin* v. *Davis,* no. 2141, 6 La. Ann. 472 (1851). *Black Code,* "Crimes and Offenses," § 35, p. 180.

32. *Dwyer* v. *Cane,* no. 222, 6 La. Ann. 707 (1851). Cruelty to slaves was not an uncommon cause of dismissal. Scarborough, *Overseer,* 96.

33. *Kennedy* v. *Mason,* no. 362, 10 La. Ann. 519 (1855). "No. 6" may refer to one of the six basic medicines of the "system," which was brandy or wine fortified with herbs, roots, bark, and other natural ingredients, thought to strengthen "the internal system and the weakened patient." Todd L. Savitt, *Medicine and Slavery: The Diseases and Health Care of Blacks in Antebellum Virginia* (Urbana, Ill., 1978), 170 n.37. Another court record states that a sick slave was rubbed down with brandy and cayenne pepper. Cayenne pepper was No. 2 of the system. *Buddy* v. *Vanleer,* no. 1901, 6 La. Ann. 34 (1851).

34. *Kemp* v. *Hutchinson,* no. 452, 10 La. Ann. 494 (1855).

35. *Humphreys* v. *Utz,* no. 3910 (La. 1856) (unreported decision of Louisiana Supreme Court, case records on file at Earl K. Long Library, University of New Orleans). The full case record is published herein as a supplement to this essay.

35. Ibid., at MS 448.

36. Ibid., at MS 442.

37. Ibid., at MS 460–61.

38. Ibid., at MS 466–67.

39. Ibid., at MS 467.

40. Page numbers refer to the present volume. It is unclear whether Utz actually nailed the slave's penis to the bedpost or whether he nailed only the

foreskin. One witness said that Utz "had drove a tack through the skin of his penis to the Bed Rail and hit him two or three licks until he pulled loose." Either way, Utz's actions were barbarous. Hynes's assessment of the cause of Utz's acquittal from criminal charges may well be accurate. The census of 1850 for Madison Parish lists only 404 persons qualified to vote, meaning white males of twenty-one years or more. The census also indicates that there were sixty-six overseers. Although we cannot know how many overseers were in the jury pool at any given time, the census would indicate that the possibility of getting several overseers on any given jury was high. The total population of Madison Parish in 1850 was 8,773, of whom 1,416 were white and 7,353 were slaves. Only four free persons of color resided in Madison Parish in 1850. Superintendent of the United States Census, *The Seventh Census of the United States, 1850* (Washington, D.C., 1850).

41. *Miller* v. *Stewart,* no. 4946, 12 La. Ann. 170 (1857). *Black Code,* "Crimes and Offenses," § 16, pp. 206–7.

42. *Kessee* v. *Mayfield,* no. 6022, 14 La. Ann. 90 (1859). 1825 La. Civ. Code, Art. 2720, p. 418. Disobeying orders not to whip slaves was another common cause of dismissal for overseers. Scarborough, *Overseer,* 93–94.

43. *Markham* v. *Close,* 2 La. 581 (1831); *Black Code,* "Crimes and Offenses," § 16, pp. 206–8; Civil Code, Art. 192, pp. 29–30.

44. *Barrow* v. *McDonald,* no. 4854, 12 La. Ann. 110 (1857). Barrow was a wealthy Terrebonne Parish slaveholder who owned four sugar plantations: "Residence," Myrtle Grove," Caillou Grove," and "Point Farm." Scarborough, *Overseer,* 187.

45. *Ney* v. *Richard,* 15 La. Ann. 603 (1860).

The Unreported Case of *Humphreys* v. *Utz* (1856)

[The following materials were transcribed from the original handwritten records. Original spelling and word usage were retained. Original page numbers are indicated. Editor's comments are contained in footnotes.]

The Trial Court Record: Humphreys v. Utz

STATE OF LOUISIANA }
PARISH OF MADISON }

TENTH JUDICIAL
DISTRICT COURT

Pleaz before the Honorable the Tenth Judicial District Court of the State of Louisiana in and for the Parish of Madison,

Be it known and remembered that, on the 17th day of September A D 1853, J C & G W Humphreys by this attorney filed this petition in this Court, and it is in the words and figures following to wit.

PETITION

To the Honorable the Judge of the Tenth Judicial District Court holding session in and for the Parish of Madison.

The Petition of John C Humphreys and George W Humphreys who reside in the State of Mississippi

———————————— Respectfully Represent ————————————

That Henry Utz a resident of Madison Parish was employed by your petitioners as an Overseer or manager upon the Burkland Plantation owned by them, and Situated in said Parish, during the year 1853.

Shows—that during the year 1853 the Said Utz whilst acting as overseer on Said Plantation cruelly abused the negroes attached to said plantation, and owned by your petitioners by inflicting unusual unnecessary and cruel punishment to them.

They charge the Said Utz with having whipped the negroes belonging to [page 2] and attached to Said Plantation, to such an unnecessary and cruel degree as to materially injure their worth and to occasion loss to your petitioners.

They particularly charge cruel treatment of an unusual inhuman and outrageous nature perpetrated by the Said Utz upon two of the negroes placed under his care, protection and management.

They alleged that one of said negroes whose name was *"Ginger Pop"* died from the effect of cruelties inflicted upon him by the Said Utz in nailing the privates of Said negro to the bedstead and then inflicting blows upon him until Said negro pulled loose from the post to which he had been pinned by driving an iron tack or nail thorough his peniss or privates.

Petitioners further charge that Said Utz inflicted a similar outrage upon a certain negro boy named Dave or David also the property of your petitioners and under the control or management of Said Utz as Overseer on the Burkland Plantation.

Petitioners aver that they have sustained damage from the wrongful acts of the Said Utz to the full amount of Five Thousand dollars.

Wherefore the premises considered petitioners pray that Henry Utz be cited to answer this petition and served with a copy of the Same, and upon final hearing thereof, that they have judgment against him for Five Thousand Dollars damages, for [page 3] costs and for trial by jury and for relief generally.

A R Hynes, Atty.

Endorsed:
2327. J C & G W Humphreys vs. Henry Utz.
Petition Filed Sept. 17 1853 M Wallace Clerk.

Citation

J C & G W Humphreys ⎫
vs. No. 2327   ⎬
Henry Utz. ⎭

STATE OF LOUISIANA
TENTH DISTRICT
COURT
PARISH OF MADISON

To Henry Utz residing in the Said Parish of Madison.

You are hereby cited either to comply with the demand contained in the petition of the Said J C & G W Humphreys, of which a copy accompanies this citation, or to deliver your answer to the Said petition, at the office of the clerk of Said Court, held in the Town of Richmond, in Said Parish, within ten days after Service hereof.

Witness the Honorable A Snyder Judge of Said Court and the Seal thereof this 17 day of September AD 1853.

Seal   M Wallace Clerk of Said Court.

Sheriffs Return

Recd Sept 17th 1853 and served a certified copy of the Original petition, and a certified copy of this Citation, by handing the Same [page 4] to Henry Utz, in Person, in the Town of Richmond La, on the 22d day of Same Month & year.

Sheriffs Office

Jas L Crandell Sheriff
By J.A. Fleetwood Dept Sheriff

Sept 23d 1853

Endorsed: 2327. J C & G W Humphreys vs Henry Utz,
Citation. Filed September 24th 1853 M Wallace Clk by F M Cinch Dyck [Deputy Clerk]

Answer
J C & G W Humphreys ⎫
vs 2327   ⎬
Henry Utz ⎭

10TH DISTRICT COURT
PARISH OF MADISON
LA

The Said defendant for answer to the demand of the plaintiffs 1st Denies the allegations of the plaintiffs petition, except that he was employed by them to Oversee on the Said Burkland Planation for the Year 1853 for which he was to receive the Sum of Eight Hundred dollars. 2nd. This Respondent alleges that at the earnest Solicitations of the Said plaintiffs he engaged to Manage for them the Said plantation for the sum of eight hundred dollars for the year 1853. That in compliance with his part of the agreement, he went upon the Said plantation on the 1st day of January 1853 and continued to discharge his duty as overseer up to the 19 day of August 1853 and was still ready and willing to go on and discharge his duty of Overseer for and during the time agreed on, but he was [page 5] not permitted so to do by the wrongful acts of the plaintiffs, who without any just Cause dismissed this respondent and would not permit him to perform his part of the Said Contract, Whereby the Said Plaintiffs became liable to pay to this Respondent, at the time he was thus wrongfully discharged, the Sum of Eight Hundred dollars, which Sum he demands and prays judgment for in reconvention against the Said Plaintiffs with five per cent interest from the rendition of Such Judgment until paid.

Third. This Respondent further alleges that for the last five years he has been engaged in Overseeing and had established a reputation for being a careful manager of negroes, and a good Cultivator of the Soil, all of which was well known to the plaintiffs, and it was only at their urgent Solicitations that he agreed to take charge of the Said Burkland Plantation in the capacity of Overseer.

Respondent had been employed by one of the plaintiffs, towit George W Humphreys, to oversee for him during the year 1848. From experience he knew it was difficult to Manage negroes to Suit him—that he required of them more than ordinary labor, and often inflicted on them ordinary punishment.

For this reason this respondent did not like to undertake the management of Said Burkland Plantation. [page 6]

Respondent further alleges that—Slaves on Said Plantation had the reputation of being difficult to Manage, and Several of them were habitual runaways. But notwithstanding the Said negroes had such reputation and had for years previous been used with great Severity, yet respondent did agree to Oversee for them for the year 1853. The Said Plaintiffs agreeing & promising to appoint Gabriel Utz,—who lived nearby— their agent to advise with and watch the Management of Respondent.

Respondent alleges that he never heard of any complaint of his management as an Overseer until about the 19 of August 1853 when he was discharged by them, although they and their agent were often times upon the plantation.

Your Respondent will show that up to they [sic] verry day that he was discharged that Said Plaintiffs approved of his entire management as Overseer for them—that up the 19 August the Crop on Burkland was better than any previously raised on Said place—that he was at all times attentive to his business, kind to the Sick and humain to all.

Respondent alleges that about the time he was discharged by the plffs, the plffs with the malicious intent and purpose of injuring him and destroying his reputation as an Overseer, did falsely assert and Cause to be circulated throughout this Parish and [page 7] elsewhere, divers false and slanderous reports to wit: That Respondent had treated their negroes with cruelty and inhumanity—that he had cut and mutilated them and had caused the death of one of them, by which false and slanderous reports, so uttered and circulated by the plaintiffs, this Respondent has suffered damages to the amount of Six Thousand dollars which amount he demands in reconvention & prays Judgment in Solido[1] against them for the Said Sum with five per cent interest from the rendition thereof until paid. Respondent prays that the demand of the plffs be rejected at their costs & for general relief.

Short & Parham,

Endorsed 2327. J C & G W Humphreys vs Henry Utz.
Answer Filed 15 Nov 1853 John T Mason Clk

Evidence

J C & G W Humphreys ⎫
vs 2327   ⎬
Henry Utz.   ⎭

   Joseph Reimer Sworn for plff—Says—he knows the plaintiffs and he also knows the deft Henry Utz. Witness has been living about 2 years on the Burkland Plantation with the exception of about five months, Says he knew the Boy Ginger Pop before his death, that Ginger Pop runaway [sic], and when witness came in from his work, that deft told [page 8] him that he had caught Ginger Pop, and had drove a tack through the skin of his penis to the Bed Rail and hit him two or three licks and he pulled loose, this took place in February, about eight weeks before the death of Ginger Pop, he had runaway again and was caught and Mr Utz had him brought up on the Gallery, He took a ten penny nail and made Several licks at it to drive it through, his ear but did not get it through he then got a hand vice and screwed it on his ear several times and made the Boys Ear bleed, Utz then Said to the Boy; I mean to knock a tooth out of your head every time you runaway or else I will burry you, he then got a nail and made several attempts to put it through his ear, but did not do it. Witness held the Boy, deft then took the but end of his cow hide and whipped—on the head as long as he could stand over him. Deft then sent one of the Boys for a wash pan and assisted him with something witness does not know what it was. On the night that Ginger Pop died deft told witness that he was dead and that he was *damd* glad of it and he wished he could get clear of Shed and Maria, deft told witness next morning that he had Slept the happiest night Sleep he had Slept Since he had been on the place. On the Morning of the day that Bob died Witness Seen deft going down to the quarters when he returned he Said to witness I have been wearing Bob out I think there is nothing [page 9] the matter with Bob but what is usual. Witness has often Seen deft whip the Boy Bob or Ginger Pop, he died about three o'clock in the evening and he was buried at Seven next Morning, there were no other white persons on the place except deft & witness.

CROSS EXAMINED

Witness has been living on that place—last October, except five months, that Edward Rundell was the Overseer previous to Mr Utz. that boy runaway about every month, and he had great difficulty in managing him. Says when the Boy Runaway that Rundell would give him a light Brushing, Sometimes with a Cowhide and Sometimes with Switches, when the Boy was caught at the upper place and taken home the nigroes would ask Rundell for five dollars for taking him and Rundell replied; he would not give five dollars for him, Witness Says he never heard of Ginger Pop being Sick one hour from the effect of driving the tack through the Skin of his peniss, Witness, Says that John Humphreys came to the place in February or March, that William Humphreys came to the place early in the Spring, Witness seen William Humphreys and deft riding over the plantation, he never heard a word between them, witness Says he was present when deft took a ten penny nail, and he Seen the boy against the post, did not See the nail on the Ear of the boy, and did not See the Ear against the post but he heard the boy hollow [sic], deft then requested witness to hold the boy which witness did, Witness held the head of the Boy against the post of the chair that deft had a nail and made Several [page 10] licks at it, does not know that the nail was on the Ear, cant tell whether the nail damaged the Ear or not as there was blood on it produced from the hand Vice, never hear of the Boy being Sick a moment or confined afterwards, Witness Says deft was as far as he knows, always Kind and attentive to the Sick on the place and humain to the other negroes, and he was attentive to his business as an Overseer, he heard no complaints, witness did not know that Bob was Sick, Witness says when he came home at night deft told him Bob was dead and he was glad of it, and deft told him he had died of *"Infective"* chills, witness did not think about the Boy being killed, the boy died about the first of June, Witness Says that John Humphreys came up about one month after the death of the boy, witness did not go to see the boy before he was buried, Witness did not tell Humphreys any thing about the affair, Witness Says that before this affair took place John Humphreys told him—witness—had a home and a home with him as long as he wanted, but on the day of the trial Humphreys did not Say any thing to him about a home for life. that he did not on that day [sic] any thing to him about living on the place, Witness is living on the Place at this Time.

:IN CHIEF:

Witness is watching on the place and has two of the hands on the place assisting him, that on the day of the death of Ginger Pop there was no physician called on the place.

John Bartlett Sworn for plff—Says he heard Henry Utz Say that he Stretched the Skin of the peniss of Ginger Pop and took [page 1 1] a nail and drove through it on to the Bed Rail and hit him two or three licks & he tore loose, and before he finished the Conversation he remarked that it was a shoe makers tack.

CROSS EXAMINED:

Witness had known Ginger Pop a long time and he was a great run-away.

J S Alexander Sworn for Plff makes the Same Statement made by John Bartlett in chief.

CROSS EXAMINED:

Witness lives on the plantation adjoining the one deft lived on and he never has known any cruelty on his part towards the Slaves on the place.

R W Burney Swown for plff Says he took up three negroes this year about Scraping Cotton time and put them in Jail at Vicksburg he afterwards Saw one of the Mr Humphreys with the same three negroes tied, Witness says one of them was verry badly whipped when he took him up. Says Mr Humphreys was on the Ferry Boat coming on this Side of the River.

CROSS EXAMINED:

Witness did not know the name of the negroe that was badly whipped, Some of the marks were fresh and Some of them were cured up, Witness distinctly recollects that in a Verry few days after he put them in Jail that he saw Mr Humphreys taking them to the plantation, in this Parish.

:IN CHIEF:

Witness says he thinks the name of the Boy was Ginger Pop but is not certain and will not Swear to it positively.

John H Calloway Sworn for deft. [page 1 2] Says that they were working on the Road and the Conversation in relation to the negroe was introduced by Mr Gabriel Utz in Joking his Brother, Witness Gabriel Utz Said what an idea it was to tack a negroes peniss to the bed post for running away, at that moment Witness was called away and heard nothing more of it that day, Witness is Overseeing about half a mile from the place where Utz the deft lived, Witness rode over the crop once during the Summer and thought the place was well managed, that he never saw any cruelty on the place, witness was present at the trial before the magistrate, witness Says he heard John Humphreys Say to Mr Puller the Magistrate that he wanted Mr Reimer to give in his testimony without any fear and that he wanted him protected in it and he also Stated to Puller that Reimer could have a home with him as long as he wanted it, That the Plantation belonged to him (Humphreys) Witness Says on the Monday after the inquest John Humphreys proposed to Henry Utz to compromise "the Matter and we will leave it to two men and I will assist you in getting a Situation next year," Witness has known deft since 1850 that he was absent in the year 1852, became acquainted with him when he was Overseeing for Mr Mims in 1850 about three or four miles a cross the Swamp from the residence of witness.

Witness says when John Humphreys made use of the observation to Mr Puller in relation to the testimony of Reimer and also in relation to giving him a home that Reimer was about four or five feet from Humphreys and witness was about twelve feet from Humphreys and distinctly heard him. [page 13] Witness Says about two or three weeks before the inquest he Saw one of the Mr Humphreys going towards the 'Bend' in company with Gabriel Utz.

:Cross Examined:

Witness knew the Boy Ginger Pop, that he was small and about thirty years old, and Such a boy now under a good character would be worth from $800. to $1000 if he was a healthy boy as far as he knew.

:In Chief:

Witness Says the boy under the character he had was worth little or nothing.

Dr Charles J Mitchell Sworn for deft says on the 20 August he was sent for by Mr Humphreys and a Boy was taken up that had been buried as they Said about Six weeks. John Humphreys was present at the examination and John Humphreys directed the attention of witness to the head to ascertain if there was a fracture and witness discovered none afterwards to the ribs and the examination of the ribs was not complete, the Stench of the Body was Such that it was unpleasant to make a further examination, and the floating ribs were all Sound. Witness's attention was called to the peniss, that it maintained it natural size and rounded form that he observed no obraisures and cannot Say there were none:

Witness Says from the examination he was not led to the conclusion that the Boy came to his death by cruelty, Witness is the attending physician on Humphreys place, witness never knew of any cruelty on the part of Mr Utz towards the negroes, the Crop had the appearance of being a good one, about as good as witness had seen on the place, thinks Utz was sufficiently attentive [page 14] to the Sick on the Place, Witness has met with Mr Humphreys from time to time on the place.

CROSS EXAMINED:

Witness resides about four miles from the place where Utz was Overseeing, don't remember ever Seeing the Boy Ginger Pop, thinks he was not sent for at the time of his death, Witness says from the decayed Situation of the Body it was impossible to tell whether he came to his death by Violence or not, he might have been beat with a Stick or Stabed to the heart, the examination of the ear not minute but it presented its natural form.

Gabriel Utz Sworn for deft Says; that both the plaintiffs had been after him to act as agent for the place to advise his brother in the management of the place, Witness always refused to do it as the negroes were hard to manage, always running away. That last fall William Humphreys Spoke to Witness to act as agent and he consented to do So, that Humphreys told him he had already hired Henry Utz, he Said he was going to give him Twelve Hundred dollars, and that he wanted the negroes managed on the Burkland place as they were on the Dalkeath, Witness Told Humphreys that when ever they were made work as they did on Dalkeath they would always be running away and he preferred that Henry Utz Should not take the place, he Said if they did runaway he would bring them back and *stick up* to Henry and try and break them, that they had never been managed, Witness was there verry [sic] week and at one time remained a week and Saw no cruelty nor heard of none; the Boy Ginger Pop was always running away, that Henry was [page 15] laughing and Swearing and Said he believed he had broke Ginger Pop, Witness heard Henry Utz tell Wilson Humphreys that he believed that he had broke Ginger Pop, that he took a tack and with his thumb and finger he had pressed it through the skin of his peniss to the Bed Post and Told Mr Humphreys why he done it, that he merely done it to Scare the Boy and to Keep from whipping him, that it had done more good than all the whipping that it had calmed him, Humphreys replied; any way So he did not abuse the property, deft told him he would not abuse the property and if Humphreys though So he would call Bob up and let him examine him, Humphreys replied No and Smiled and that was all that was Said about it. Witness says Willson Humphreys brought the three negroes that Bunny took up to wit Emanuel, Pass and Jo Bass to the Burkland Plantation and Stripped and examined them, he had the three laid out and he whipped them, he made one hold the other, he had them put in the Stocks and told deft to whip them again and deft replied he did not think they needed any more, he then told deft to iron them and deft and Witness beged Jo Bass off, his order was to keep irons on them until he returned and deft in a week or two took them off from Emanuel, Humphreys then came up Some time in July and insisted upon witness to go to Burkland with him as he understood that deft had cut the backs of Pass and Ginger Pop badly and he did not wish it done, [page 16] Witness told him that he could See Pass but that Ginger Pop had been dead three or four days,

Humphreys rode up to Pass and asked him how much deft had whipped him and he replied only three or four licks over his clothes, he then told Pass he heard he was badly whipped and examined him and there was no fresh marks upon him, deft then asked Humphreys his brother, and he replied he was pledged and could not tell him, deft then told Humphreys to have Ginger Pop taken up and Send for Doctor Mitchell and if he could find any fresh marks upon him he would abide the Consequences, deft insisted upon Mr Humphreys having the Boy taken up and examined and he offered to pay the expenses and told him now is the time to have this matter Settled, this was about three or four days after the Boy died, the Boy died about the 10 or 15 of July, two weeks afterwards John Humphreys came up and insisted on witness going with him to Burkland and Witness Went it was about 12 Oclock and as the negroes were passing deft told John Humphreys of the reports in circulation and requested him to examine all the negroes and he examined two or three, and Said there is nothing to make a fuss about, deft then asked him to Send for Doct Mitchell and Some of the neighbors and have the Boy taken up & his reply was that he would not as it was all a pack of lies, deft then asked Humphreys to get another place—to live as he did not wish to remain on the place, and Humphreys replied that he might Consider himself engaged for the next year, and deft [page 17] replied he would not stay on these Terms, John Humphreys then remarked; I will raise your wages make yourself Satisfied, deft replied that Willson Humphreys was always complaining about the expenses of the place, but they made no bargain for the next year, Witness Says the Conversation between Willson Humphreys and deft was Some Time in February, Witness Says that Ginger Pop, Pass and many others on the place were badly scared before deft went on the place, Witness says a good many bad negroes were sent up from the other plantations to Manage, Witness has been Overseeing 17 or 18 years, that the Crop on the place this year is as good as he has ever Seen on it.

CROSS EXAMINED:

Witness is the brother of the defendant.

Admitted that Henry Utz was discharged by John Humphreys on the 19 of August 1853 and that the disinternment of the negroe was at the instance of the deft.

The evidence is here closed on both sides.

I certify the foregoing is all the evidence received on the trial of this Cause.

Witness my Signature this 18 Nov 1853.

John T Mason Clerk

Endorsed: 2327. Humphreys vs Henry Utz.
Evidence Filed 18 Nov 1853 John T Mason Clk.

EVIDENCE OF J REIMER

J C & G W Humphreys vs Henry Utz. [page 18]

Joseph Reimer witness Says. when he returned from his work deft told him that he had caught Ginger Pop, he then called another Boy, and he took Ginger Pop on the Gallery and got a hand vice and screwed it on his ear, he then took a nail and put his head against a chair "and Took a nail and place it against his head, did not see him strike the nail, the Boy hollered, Says the Boy died about Six or eight weeks afterwards, Says the treatment of deft to the negroes was as kind as any other Overseer he was with, that the plffs were over on the places every two or three weeks and never heard any complaint made by them and never heard any thing of the Killing of Ginger Pop until the day of the inquest, did not See the Boy after his death, had no idea at the time that the Boy was whipped to death Says the Boy died about 10th of June and the inquest was about 20 August. Says John Humphreys came up before the inquest or just after witness does not know which, Witness Says he was before the examining Magistrate does not recollect Mr John Humphreys on the day of the Magistrates trial Saying "Reimer go on and Swear what you please, you can have a home as long as you want it" Witness Says between the death of the Boy and the inquest Willson Humphreys did not come up. Witness Says deft left a better Crop on the place than was ever made on it before, Says when deft told him that the Boy was dead he Said he had died with a congestive chill, Never heard or knew of Mr Utz to be cruel to any other of the Negroes on the place, and that if there had been any [page 19] unkind treatment on the place he would have known it.
State of Louisiana
Parish of Madison

I certify the foregoing evidence was this day Taken down in Open Court on the Trial of this case,
April 27 1854.   John T Mason Clk.

Endorsed. 2327 J C & G W Humphreys vs Henry Utz
Evidence of Joseph Reimer. Filed 27 April 1854 John T Mason Clk.

MINUTES

On the 26 day of April 1854 the following entry was made upon the minutes of the Court Book C page 608.

J C & G W HUMPHREYS
2327 vs　　　　　　　　 } 　　　This case came regu-
HENRY UTZ　　　　　　　　　　　larly up for trial.

Whereupon came the following jurors To Wit A Peel. W A Evans. Durden Davis. F Heilderband. Thos Jewell, Thos R Davis. S. B. Cameron. P. E. White. J W Couch Jr. W, E Phillips. W A Jackson. B B Franklin.[2] The case not being finished the Court adjourned till tomorrow morning 8 Oclock.

Minutes:

On the 27th day of April 1854 the following entry was made upon the Minutes of the Court Book C page 609

J C & G W HUMPHREYS
2327 vs　　　　　　　　 } 　　　This case was again
HENRY UTZ　　　　　　　　　　　taken up for trial,
　　　　　　　　　　　　　　　　　[page 20]

The jury were called and it appeared that Frederick Heilderbrand failed to appear and the counsel for the Plaintiffs and defendants consented to go into the trial with Eleven jurors. By consent the parties agreed to use the evidence taken down at the last term of the Court with the priviledge to call any of the witnesses of they think Proper.

The evidence was closed and after the argument of counsel the Court appointed P E White Foreman. The Jury having received the charge of the Court retired to their room to deliberate upon their Virdict. The Jury returned into Court and delivered the following Virdict which is ordered to be Recorded and is in the words and figures following to wit: "We the Jury find a virdict in favor of the defendant for the sum of $388.86 P E White Foreman."

Whereupon the Court received the following

Judgment:

By reason of the law and the Evidence in this case being in favor of the defendant and by the further reason of the Verdict of the Jury it is ordered that the defendant have Judgment against the plaintiffs in Solido in the sum Three Hundred and Eighty Eight dollars and Eighty Six cents, and that the Said Plaintiffs pay the costs of this Suit.

Thus done and Signed in Open Court this 29 day of April 1854.

　　　　　　　　　　　　　　　　　Alonzo Snyder Judge
　　　　　　　　　　　　　　　　　Tenth District.

MINUTES

On the 28th day of April 1854 [page 21] the following entry was made upon the minutes of the Court Book C page 609 To Wit:

J C & G W HUMPHREYS ⎫
2327 VS ⎬   Motion for new trial
HENRY UTZ ⎭   filed by plaintiffs, and

Motion for new trial
filed by plaintiffs, and
Motion Overruled.

On motion of plaintiffs Counsel made in Open Court and in presence of defendants Counsel It is ordered that a devolutive[3] appeal be granted in this case. Returnable into the Supreme Court at New Orleans on the Second Monday in February 1855. And the bond be posted at One hundred dollars Continued according to law.

MOTION FOR NEW TRIAL

HUMPHREYS ⎫
VS ⎬
UTZ ⎭

The plaintiffs moves the Court for a new trial upon the ground that the Virdict of the Jury is contrary to the law and the Evidence. Wherefore they pray for a new trial.

And R Hynes attny for plffs.

Endorsed: 2327. Humphreys vs Henry Utz
Motion for new trial Filed 28 April 1854
John F Mason Clerk.

APPEAL BOND

J C & G W HUMPHREYS ⎫
VS 2327 ⎬   State of Louisiana
HENRY UTZ ⎭   Parish of Madison

State of Louisiana
Parish of Madison
Tenth District Court

Know all men by These presents [page 22] that John Humphreys as principal and Andrew R Hynes as Security are held and firmly bound unto Henry Utz in the sum of One hundred dollars good and lawful money of the United States, for the payment of which will and truly to be made we hearby bind ourselves our heirs Executors and administrators firmly by these presents. Witness our hands this 8 day of May AD 1854.

The condition of the above obligation is such that whereas a final Judgment was rendered in the above entitled Suit in favor of the deft

Henry Utz and against the plffs J C and G W Humphreys from which Judgment So rendered the Said Humphreys have taken a devolutive appeal to the Supreme Court of Louisiana, Returnable on the Second Monday of February AD 1855 into Said Court Sitting in the City of New Orleans.

Now if the Said J C & G W Humphreys Shall prosecute their Said appeal with effect, and Shall pay and Satisfy such Judgment as may be rendered against them if they be cast in Said appeal, or if the Same Shall be Satisfied by the proceeds of the sale of their estate real or personal, then this Obligation to be Void, otherwise to remain in full force and Virtue.

John Humphreys
by And R Hynes atty
And R Hynes Security.

Endorsed: 2327. Appeal Bond Filed May 8, 1854 Jno T. Mason Clerk
By F M Couch
Dy [Deputy] Clerk.

CLERKS CERTIFICATE. [PAGE 23]

STATE OF LOUISIANA ⎱   Tenth District Court
PARISH OF MADISON ⎰   Clerks Office

I hereby certify the foregoing Twenty two Pages from one to twenty two inclusive to contain a true and correct copy of all the pleadings and documents filed in the case, and all the evidence adduced and documents offered and received upon the trial of the Suit J C & G W Humphreys vs Henry Utz No 2327. And further certify the foregoing Twenty two pages to contain copies of all the entries upon the minutes of the Court and all the proceedings had upon the final Trial of Said Cause in testimony of all which I hereunto sign my name and affix the seal of said court at Richmond La for this the Twenty fifth day of May AD 1854.

John T Mason
Clerk [page 24]

INDEX[4]

J C & G W Humphreys
  vs
Henry Utz.
No 2327.

HUMPHREYS V. UTZ[5]

1 January 10 19 Aug (incl.) 7 mon. & 19 days
12/$800.00—per annum
   66.66—per month
    x 7
   466.62
    33.33
     6.66
     2.22
 $508.83—wages to 19th Aug inclusive
 $388.86—verdict of the jury [in] favor [of] deft
 $120.— amt. deducted from wages by the jury

APPELLANT'S BRIEF.

J. C. & G. W. HUMPHREYS, VS. HENRY UTZ. *No. 2327.*

The defendant was employed by the plaintiffs as an overseer for the year 1853, on the Burkland plantation. During his management the slaves of the plaintiffs received *unusual, unnecessary* and *cruel* treatment, and for which they instituted this suit for damages. The petition charges generally cruel treatment to all the slaves under his management, but particularly cruel treatment of an *unusual, inhuman,* and *outrageous* nature, perpetrated by the defendant upon two of the negroes placed under his care, protection and management. That one of said slaves, whose name was "Ginger Pop," died from the effect of cruelties inflicted upon him by the defendant, in nailing the privates of said negro to the bed-stead, and then inflicting blows upon him until said negro pulled loose from the post to which he had been pinned, by driving an iron tack or nail through his penis or privates. That the defendant perpetrated a similar outrage upon a certain other slave named David, placed under his management by the plaintiff.

The petition claimed $5,000 damages for the wrong and injury sustained, and prayed for trial by jury. The answer denies generally the allegations of the petition, and avers that he was discharged on the 19th day of August, 1853, without *any just cause,* and claims the sum of $800 00-100 wages for the entire year of 1853, for which he was employed. The answer further charges "that the plaintiffs discharged him with the malicious intent and purpose of injuring him and destroying his reputation as an overseer, and falsely asserted and caused to be circulated throughout the Parish and elsewhere divers false and slanderous reports, to wit: "That the defendant had-treated their negroes with cruelty and inhumanity—that he had cut and mutilated them and had caused the death of one of them, by which false and slanderous reports defendant has suffered damages to the amount of $6,000, for which he prays judgment." The case was submitted to a jury whose verdict reads as follows "We the Jury, find a verdict in favor of the defendant for the sum of $388 86-100."

The testimony of Joseph Rimmer, proves "that the defendant acknowledged to him that he drove a nail or tack through the privates of the negro "Bob or Ginger Pop," and whipped him until he broke loose. This was in February—(see Record, page 8.) That the defendant, on another occasion, took a ten-penny nail and attempted to drive it through the ear, and then got a hand-vice and screwed it upon the ear several times, until it was covered with blood—then told the boy that he would nock a tooth out every time he ran away, or he would *bury* him—then took the but-end of his cow-hide and whipped the boy over the head as long as he could stand over him, and then anointed the boy's back with something in a wash-pan."

"On the night that Ginger Pop died defendant told witness that he was *damned* glad of it, and he wished he could get clear of *Shed* and Maria in the same way. The defendant told witness the next morning that he had *slept* the happiest nights' *sleep* since he came on the place. On the morning of the day, that Bob, or Ginger Pop died, witness saw defendant going down to the quarters; when he returned, he said to witness that he had been *wearing Bob out:* the boy died about 6 o'clock of that evening—(see testimony of Reimer, Record pages 8 and 9.)

John Bartlett, a witness, proves that he heard the defendant say that he stretched the skin of the penis of the negro, and took a nail and drove through it to the bed-rail, and hit him two or three licks, and he broke loose—(see testimony in Record pages 10,11.)

The testimony of J. H. Calloway and J. S. Alexander, proves the same acknowledgment.

The testimony of Dr. C. J. Mitchell, who made the post mortem examination, states that the body was so far decomposed and so offensive having been buried six weeks, that it was impossible to tell whether he came to his death by violence or not, as he might have been beat with a stick or stabbed to the heart; that he was not sent for to see the negro before his death, and that he was the attending physician on the place."

The only testimony of the defence relied upon, is the witness Gabriel Utz, a brother of the defendant Henry Utz. The attempt to, show that Wilson Humphreys, one of the plaintiffs, sanctioned all that the defendant did, is unworthy of credence, when it is remembered that he is one of the best and purest of men in the State of Mississippi. It is not to be believed that an owner of slaves would, if informed of the cruelties practiced upon them, such as this record exhibits, sanction either by words or acts, such outrages upon decency and humanity; much less that after having sanctioned it, he would bring this suit for damages. It will be remembered that the Messrs. Humphreys reside in the State of Mississippi and seldom visit the Burkland plantation, and were not present at the trial of this suit in the District Court. The Grand Jury acting in and for the Parish of Madison, indicted the defendant for cruel treatment of the slaves of the plaintiff, and the Jury empanelled to try the case brought in a verdict of "Not Guilty," although the proof was direct and overwhelming. It will be remembered that in a sparsely peopled country, where the owners of property are non-residents, the Jurors of the country are almost entirely made up of Overseers, and that perhaps no class is so clannish or so disposed to protect each other in their difficulties. Whenever a planter shall in a contest with an overseer resort to a jury, there can be no doubt as to what the verdict will be, and the only hope left to the country is that the purity of the Bench will correct the evil. Such is the hope of all good citizens in reference to this case. The judicial records of our country presents no parallel in turpitude, baseness and lowness, to the case which is presented to the consideration of this Court, and which it will be your duty to decide. The instincts of all good men, of all right thinking persons, revolt at the perpetration of such an outrage upon decency and humanity as the defendant in this case confesses to have been guilty of. Slavery in our country is not the irresponsible right of the master or overseer over the slave, but our laws have clearly laid down and our courts will rigidly enforce certain duties due slaves from their masters and managers. The Civil Code, article 173 says, "the slave is subject to the will of the master, who may correct and chastise him, though not with unusual rigor, nor so as to maim or mutilate him, or expose him to the danger of loss of life." Our laws have wisely and humanely thrown a shield of its protection around not only its citizens but its slaves. The acts of 1806, 1816, in addition to the security given by the Code to our slaves against unusual rigors that owners and managers might inflict upon them, has provided severe penalties for those who inflict cruel and unusual punishments upon them. Thus we see that our express legislation upon the subject of slaves, is dictated by considerations of humanity, and restricts the authority of the master; and although juries may fail through prejudice to enforce its plain provisions, we have an abiding faith that their errors will meet with the proper correction at the hands of the Judiciary. We are unwilling to believe that southern people are more willing to tolerate wrong and injuries to negroes than our northern brethren—but if the Courts of the country shall finally decide that the defendant has done nothing to be condemned in the cruelties perpetrated upon the plaintiffs negroes, then indeed has slavery wrongs deep—deeper wrongs than we have heretofore believed. But it is impossible that christian Judges can acquit one who has proved himself a monster in cruelty! To dwell upon the testimony is sickening indeed, but duty impels me, however unpleasant the task. The witness Rimmer, informs us that on the morning of the death of the negro Utz came in and said in his brutal language "I have been wearing Ginger Pop out; I fastened him to the bed-rail, by driving a nail through his penis, and then whipped him until he broke loose!" Yes, *he had worn him out."* This was said with all the self-complacency with which a good man would have boasted of some noble charity by which he had relieved suffering humanity from further woe. Yes, he had literally *worn out* a poor, helpless negro; he had robbed of life, by his merciless cruelties, a human being with all the power of sense and suffering that you or I possess. He had sent into the presence of God, who will be the Judge of the victim and the victor, a poor helpless and unoffending negro. If slavery can sanction such acts, it is the most monstrous curse that ever stained our earth, the greatest blur and blot of sin that man ever perpetrated or Heaven permitted. But thanks to the civilization and christianity of the age, our laws sanction no such wrongs, and our peculiar institution is provided with protection against such monsters. What did the defendant do when he found life was extinct in the poor victim of his cruelties? Did he express any anxiety and uneasiness in thus having hurried into eternity this poor creature? Did his hard heart relent? and as he looked upon death, a picture that mollifies and softens the most addurate, did he feel remorse for his deep and damning wrongs? No, the witness informs you that he boasted "that he would sleep well to-night, and he wished he could only get rid of Shed and Maria in the same way." Is there any horror beyond this? and can such a monster ever sleep well? It may be that the defendant will escape justice in this world, but surely He who will maketh inquisition for blood and forgeteth not the cry of the humble, will remember and rebuke the wrongs of the defenseless.

It remains for this unprejudiced tribunal to do duty that a prejudiced Jury failed to do. To say whether in this land of law such cruelties shall go unpunished, unrebuked—whether the property of individuals entrusted to agents shall be abused, wasted and destroyed, without hold-ing them to a strict accountability. Our law holds in such abhorrence cruelties of any and all kinds, that severe penalties are enacted against all persons who inflict unusual punishments upon animals of any kind. The act of 1821 provides that any one guilty of any cruel treatment to a horse, mare, gilding, jack, milch cow, or even dog, shall be fined and imprisoned. Shall it be said that our law, which protects even a dog from the brutal violence of his master, shall not throw the aegis of its protec-tion around a human being, —one who although a slave, is made after the image of God and stamped with the dignity of soul and intellect which exalts human nature above the level of other created beings. For the sake of humanity, for the sake of religion, for the sake of God, place the seal of your condemnation upon such conduct and let your judg-ment be one that when it is recorded upon the imperishable records of our country, that your children and your children's children, may not blush at the recollection of what their forefathers may have done.

The tone of this Court, as shown in 3 An. 618 and 132, 4 An. 177, we feel will not be departed from in a case meriting your severest condem-nation. Respectfully submitted.

And. R. Hynes,
Attorney for Appellant.

[Judgement of The Appelate Court]

J.C. & G.W. Humphreys[6]
v.
Henry Utz }

Plaintiffs, the owners of a cotton plantation in the parish of Madi-son, hired defendant to oversee said plantation for the year 1853, com-mencing the 1st January. The salary agreed on was eight hundred dol-lars for the year. On the 19th August they discharged him, and have brought this suit against him for damages, which they allege they have suffered by abuse of the slaves attached to their plantation, while under the charge of the defendant. Plaintiffs charge that defendant inflicted unusual, unnecessary and cruel punishments on said slaves; that he whipped them to such an unnecessary & cruel degree as to materially impair their value; that one of their slaves named "Ginger Pop" died from the effect of cruelties inflicted upon him by defendant; that he inflicted similar cruelties upon another slave of plaintiffs, named Dave or David.

Defendant pleads the general issue; that the plaintiffs had violated their contract with him by discharging him without cause, and were, in consequence, liable to him for the full amount of his years' salary, eight hundred dollars, which he claims. Defendant further charges that plaintiffs have circulated false and slanderous reports that he had treated their slaves with inhumanity and cruelty, in order to injure his reputation, and for which he claims damages.

Upon this issue, the parties went to trial before a jury of the vicinage, who found a verdict for defendant in the sum of three hundred and eighty-eight dollars and eighty-six cents. A new trial was asked by plaintiffs and refused; and plaintiffs appealed.

As a calculation shows, the defendants salary, at the rate of eight hundred dollars a year, would have amounted to five hundred & eight dollars & eighty-three cents, for the portion of the year which has elapsed at the time of his discharge and as nothing is proved to have been paid him by pl'ffs we may interpret the verdict as having awarded to defendant his wages to that time, with a deduction of one hundred and twenty dollars, in the nature of damages allowed to plaintiffs. Juries are not required, like judges, to give reasons for their judgments; and in investigating the motives of a verdict, we are compelled to narrow a posteriori— to arrive as we best may, through the conclusion, at the premises.

Of this verdict the defendant does not complain; and it becomes our duty to determine whether it has done full justice to the plaintiffs, under the evidence.

The legislation of Louisiana has always been characterized by humanity to slaves. The statute of 1806 [the Black Code], in force when this suit was instituted (Bullard & Curry's Digest, page 61, sec. 55 and 56,) provided as follows "___ If any person shall wilfully kill his slave, or the slave of another person, the said person being convicted thereof, shall be tried and condemned agreeably to the law of the territory; and in case any person or persons should inflict any cruel punishment, except flogging or striking with a whip, leather thong, switch or small stick, or putting in irons or confining such slave, the said person shall forfeit and pay for every offence, a fine not exceeding five hundred and not less than two hundred dollars." "If any slave be mutilated, beaten or ill treated, contrary to the true intent and meaning of this act, when no one shall be present, in such case the owner or person having the charge or management of the slave thus mutilated, shall be deemed responsible and guilty of the said offence, and shall be prosecuted without further evidence, unless the said owner or other person, so as aforesaid, can prove the contrary by means of good and sufficient evidence, or can clear himself by his own oath, which said oath every Court under the Cognizance of which such offence shall have been examined and tried, is by this act authorized to administer."

Again, by the act of 1855, page 379, section 18, "whoever shall inflict, or cause to be inflicted, any cruel treatment upon any slave, whether by mutilating, flogging, failing to clothe and feed in a proper manner, by imprisoning, by putting in irons, or by ill treating in any other manner, to be judged of by the court and jury, shall be fined not less than fifty nor more than two hundred dollars. The court and jury shall have power in all cases, whether they convict or not, to decree the sale of the slave at public auction. The owner shall not be allowed to purchase either directly or indirectly, or to have under his control the said slave, under the penalty of one thousand dollars. The price of the slave thus sold shall be paid over to the owner, after deducting all costs. It shall be the duty of the committing magistrate, to whom complaint shall be made, to notify the district attorney of the district, whose duty it shall be forthwith to prosecute the owner of the slave."

A proof that the humane spirit of the legislation is in consonance with the sentiments of the slave owners of Louisiana, is found in the fact, that the present is the third prosecution of an overseer by a planter, for ill treatment of slaves under the care of the former, which has come under our cognizance within the past year; the two others being at the last term in the Western circuit.

It is due to the defendant to say, that the charge of causing Ginger Pop's death, is not made out by the evidence. It is proved, that Ginger Pop was an incorrigible runaway; and that on one occasion of his being caught & brought home, in the month of February 1853, he was very severely beaten and otherwise ill treated, by the defendant. But the death of Ginger Pop did not take place until four months afterwards; to wit, on the 10th June 1853. And it is disproved, that his death was occasioned by the ill treatment received from defendant or that he was even confined to his bed in consequence of it. The defendant represented him as having died of congestive chills; and the physician who made a post mortem examination of Ginger Pop, at the insistence of the defendant, discovered no marks of laceration or ill usage upon any part of his body or members. It is true, that this post mortem examination was only made some six or eight weeks after the death of Ginger Pop, to wit, on the 20th August, the next day after defendant was discharged by plaintiffs. But it is in evidence, that defendant had several times previously urged plaintiffs to have the slave disinterred, for the purpose of refuting the sinister rumors as to the cause of his death; and the first of those occurring was written three days after the death of the slave.

Upon a review of the whole evidence, although the charges of the petition are exaggerated, and we must acquit the defendant of homicide; although the negro Ginger Pop is proved to have been a very vicious & worthless subject; yet acts of revolting brutality have been proved, which entirely exceed the limits of that repressive and correctional discipline which is necessary to the management of the agricultural laborers of the South—a discipline which all, who are qualified by experience to speak upon this very important subject will acknowledge should be strict, in the interest of the bondsman himself; but which the law of Louisiana, and the precepts of religion and morality no less imperiously demand, should be tempered with mercy. The evil passions of men become infuriated to reckless ferocity by unbridled indulgence: and the very helplessness of the slave, which inspires generous natures with compassion and sympathy, is sometimes found to encourage those of an opposite organization, to cold blooded refinements of torture. He who cannot protect himself, has a double claim to protection from the ministers of the law.

We think such an abuse of the plaintiffs property entrusted to defendants care has been proved, as justified plaintiffs in discharging defendant before the expiration of the term for which they had hired him. The verdict of the jury, as we understand it, has allowed plaintiffs a deduction of about one fourth of defendants wages to the time of discharge, by reason of such abuse. This allowance appears to us too small. An entire forfeiture of the wages due does not exceed the limits of a legal distinction, and while it does no more than justice between the parties, may serve as a salutary example.

It is therefore adjudged and decreed that the verdict and judgment appealed from be reversed; that plaintiffs recover of defendant five hundred and eight dollars, eighty three cents damages in full satisfaction of wages earned by defendant in the plaintiffs employ as owners of the Burkland plantation; and that defendant pay costs in both courts.

Notes

1. *In Solido* is a Louisiana law term which means that each party is liable for the whole amount of the judgment.

2. W. A. Evans, Durden Davis, Thomas R. Davis, P. E. White, William Phillips and B. B. Franklin were listed as overseers in the 1850 and 1860 census, proving Andrew Hynes's assertion in the appellant's brief that juries were often composed of a large proportion of overseers.

3. A devolutive appeal is a civil-law term which means an appeal that does not suspend the execution of a judgment.

4. This is a transcription of the original index. It retains references to the page numbers of the handwritten record.

5. This is a transcription of a piece of scratch paper used by the jurors to determine the amount of the award to Henry Utz. They calculated the amount of wages owed for the seven months and nineteen days Utz worked on Burkland, and then subtracted $120.00, the amount of damages they decided to award to the plaintiffs, to arrive at the amount of judgment.

6. This is a transcription of Justice Buchanan's handwritten decision for the Louisiana Supreme Court.

9

Pandora's Box:
Slave Character on Trial in
the Antebellum Deep South

Ariela Gross

THOMAS READE COBB expressed an ancient theme of slave law when he
wrote that slaves in the American South had the "double character of
person and property" under the law, which generally meant that slaves
were persons when accused of a crime and property the rest of the time.
Indeed, when slave buyers felt their newly acquired human property to
be "defective" physically or morally, they sued the seller for breach of
warranty—just as they would over a horse or a piece of machinery. Similarly, slave owners sued hirers, overseers, and others for damaging their
property when they beat or neglected slaves.[1] Yet in these mundane civil
disputes, the parties in the courtroom brought into question, and gave
legal meaning to, the "character" as well as the resistant behavior of enslaved people who persisted in acting as people.[2]

Of course, horses could run away or be recalcitrant without being
human, leading legal historian Andrew Fede to suggest that slaves
influenced the law merely the way horses influenced the law. However,
in these cases slaves influenced the law far more than things or horses
ever could, because these disputes, by forcing "the law" to consider slaves'
character, also challenged slaveholders' self-conception as masters and
statesmen. In 1821 South Carolina Judge Abraham Nott warned that
extending an implied warranty of soundness to a slave's moral qualities
would be "worse than opening Pandora's box upon the community."[3] By
this he acknowledged the dangers of litigating slave character to a system based on denying the personhood of human property.[4]

The issue of slave character arose most directly in suits for breach of
warranty. While sellers rarely warranted a slave's good character in writing, these cases reached the courts frequently in actions for fraud or
deceit, when buyers charged that sellers had orally vouched for the slave.

Moral qualities included not only the general character of the slave but also his or her "habits" of drinking, stealing, and running away.[5] Slave character also went on trial whenever a slave's runaway habit or other "vice" became an excuse for a white person to take some action such as shooting the slave; owners or hirers might also give a slave's character as an excuse for why a slave died or got sick.

These disputes over the nature of an individual slave's character brought forth many of the racial theories at large in Southern culture, but they also helped to define which images of the black man and woman would prevail in the legal arena, which in turn influenced the culture as a whole. The law created the meaning of race most obviously in statutes and cases that drew the color line, defining blackness in terms of fractions or drops of "black blood." But the law also established racial meanings through the ideology and imagery of race, not only by promulgating specific stereotypes of black people but also by painting a picture of black character development that differed from Southern white accounts of white moral character development. Thus, even the "private law" of slaves as property contributed to the construction of "race" in Southern culture.

What is a Good Slave?

As William W. Fisher III shows, self-conscious legal writers of treatises as well as appellate judges drew heavily on the images of the black slave as a happy, docile Sambo, a rebellious Nat, or a sensuous Jezebel. Other images emerged at the trial level. As George Fredrickson has pointed out, Southerners needed a spectrum of images to deal with individual slaves in their daily lives.[6] Witnesses in trial testimony talked about slaves in ways that did not fit into the simple stereotypes ideologues propagated, particularly in recognizing the personalities, human motivations, and skills of individual slaves. For example, the good slave, at the trial level, often had qualities Sambo did not have, such as honesty and industry, and attributes beyond those of which Sambo was capable. Other narratives also governed the way Southern whites talked about slave character. Probably the most important were stories about the slave as valuable capital and as skilled or unskilled worker. Ultimately, whites understood an enslaved person's character in terms of his or her value—whether in dollars or in labor.

Slave sellers generally advertised their slaves with highly favorable language: "a No. 1 boy," "honest, industrious and free from vice," or "honest, sober, humble and not given to be a runaway." In one Louisiana case, the seller's witnesses proved William's honesty by testifying that he was "a boy of good character perfectly honest and sober" who "used to be sent to the house of the most respectable men in [town] to shave them when they did not like to come to the shop." Not only that, William "was well informed and well acquainted with amounts and generally managed [his owner's] affairs." Likewise, an overseer testified that Aglae was "very industrious very clean," and Lucinda's owner advertised her as "an honest trusty servant" who "always brought her wages in." Honesty and industry were qualities both male and female slaves might exhibit.[7]

Very occasionally, witnesses referred to slaves' intelligence or morality, implicitly or explicitly raising them to a level with whites. Not infrequently, parties spoke of slaves as "men" and "women" or "persons" rather than "boy," "girl," or "wench." For example, in one slave inventory all adult slaves (over the age of eighteen) were designated "man" or "woman," while all children were designated "boy" or "girl." In *Pilie* v. *Lalande*, one witness reported that a female slave was "quick and intelligent," another that she was "of good disposition intelligent and a good servant." In tort cases in which the court had to decide whether to hold a white person responsible for injury to a black slave, judicial comments about the volition of the slave were sometimes accompanied by the recognition that a slave is "a moral agent." On the other hand, black intelligence could be a negative attribute from a white point of view, particularly in a woman. In one case, Farmer tried to return Kitty because "she knew too much . . . the essence of Farmer's objection was that the slave was too smart."[8]

A bad slave had the opposite characteristics: faithlessness, dishonesty, indolence, and insubordination. The same slaves whom sellers portrayed as honest and trustworthy were accused by slave buyers suing for character defects of being "vicious and worthless, habitual and dangerous runaway[s]," "ill disposed, faithless, inconstant, unsteady, disobedient, and bad in all respects," or "dishonest, lazy and vicious." A particularly bad slave, Lawson, "was violent and headstrong and abused the smaller negroes." Another witness in Adams County (Mississippi) Court described his former slave Jesse as one he "bought . . . in chains . . . and sold . . . in the stock, as a notorious scoundrel." Such vehement denunciations of the slave's whole character as degraded and vicious almost always attached to male slaves. Witnesses might characterize enslaved women as lazy, but the same stereotype of savagery did not form on their lips to describe rebellious women. For example, in one case over a runaway woman slave, the buyer's most detailed complaint about her character was that she was "as smart a negro as any, if she would stay." In other cases the buyer merely argued that the female runaway was crazy or idiotic.[9]

It is striking how frequently vice in enslaved men was connected with dishonesty and faithlessness—suggesting that masters could normally expect honesty and loyalty from slaves. If all slaves were mendacious Sambos, this expectation would make no sense. Sometimes one party, usually the seller, would invoke the Sambo stereotype, arguing that one cannot expect too much even from good slaves; "it [is] very common amongst Negroes to steal a little and run away." This bore out the stereotype of slaves as mendacious and mischievous, though generally harmless. Yet there was a strong counterstory which insisted that, in fact, well-treated, good slaves were both honest and trustworthy. Indeed, in the same case the witness being deposed made plain that he "Don't believed most negroes would [steal and run away.]" Thus, while Southerners in court spoke of bad slaves as dishonest and vicious, they usually meant to distinguish these individuals from the general character of all black slaves.[10]

The emphasis on honesty and industry also suggests that these were characteristics whites highly prized in slaves. As we saw in the earlier example of William, an honest, industrious slave was one who could be trusted to go out and do a job and come home again. In a market economy, these were particularly important attributes. Legal disputes over slave character took place in a market context, in which the slave's value as a worker was foremost in the parties' minds.

Because slaves were, next to land, the most important form of capital in the antebellum South, positive descriptions of a slave's character were often accompanied by an estimate of value, such as "being a fine fellow honest industrious free from vice and such an one as would command a good price" or "a Negro woman slave whose character was exceptionable and was considered not so valuable on account of her bad qualities but was worth as he considered $400."[11] Constantly putting a numerical value on a slave's character meant that whenever slaves were viewed as people, their property aspect also intruded. Commodification meant always thinking about slave character in dollar terms.

Witnesses and sellers also described good or bad slaves in terms of their work skills or the jobs they performed. Women were disproportionately represented in both warranty and hire disputes over skilled slaves. Indeed, if a buyer sued a seller for a breach of warranty in the sale of a woman slave, and if the case did not involve physical illness or death, the complaint was most likely that she did not perform sufficiently well as a house servant. Thus, it appears that behavior on the part of a woman that might have been interpreted as deficiency in character in a man was more often portrayed as deficiency in skill.

In valuing slaves, skills could weigh in the balance against qualities considered to be defects, such as old age or high temper. Philander, for example, "was an old man about 50 years old; he was represented as a very good carpenter; though he was old, yet he might be more valuable on account of being a mechanic." In another warranty case, Sally "was a pretty good looking old woman—was a House servant, and capable, but very high tempered—she was an *excellent* Cook—she was put into the work house for her impudence." The defendant told one witness that he could not manage her, and a former owner testified "that Sally was a very capable servant and objectionable only as respected her temper—which was intolerable."[12]

In order to recover the price of a slave, it was rarely legally sufficient to prove that a slave did not have the skills she was represented to have. However, a skills claim could supplement another claim of unsoundness to the benefit of the buyer. Evidence that a seller had lied about a slave's skills, for instance, tended to prove to the trier of fact that the seller had also lied about other things. At times the skills claim itself may have carried some weight as a redressable injury, but not enough to stand alone. For example, in *Brocklebank* v. *Johnson* the buyer's chief claim was that Romeo was a drunkard and suffered illness from his drinking, but, secondarily, he wanted to prove that Johnson had misrepresented Romeo as a good bricklayer. The trial judge instructed the jury to consider both claims but said that for the skills claim "the Plaintiff could only recover the difference in value between a Bricklayer and a common negro." Brocklebank won both a jury verdict and an appellate judgment that he could recover for deceit even if Johnson had given no written warranty of Romeo's character or his skills as a bricklayer.[13]

The Louisiana Supreme Court heard several of these mixed-claim cases involving women sold to do housework. The facts of the cases, as set out in the trial testimony, highlight the different ways parties characterized women and men who refused to work. For example, Grenier Petit sued Jean Laville because Aglae "was neither a washer nor a good subject." The plaintiff brought forth witnesses who testified that they had tried the slave Aglae as a washer and "she did not appear to understand any thing about washing." One, Mme. Felix, "gave her two shirts to wash and after keeping them during four hours she returned them without having finished them." She testified on cross-examination that "she can say in an hour if a person is a washer or not." A woman who worked for Mme. Felix testified that she had been obliged to rewash the two shirts Aglae washed and that, although she "is not a washer by trade," she "is a good judge of washing." It is impossible for us to determine whether Aglae did not know how to wash shirts or simply decided not to wash them as a form of resistance; but it is significant that all the witnesses agreed that Aglae's defect was her lack of washing skills rather than her rebelliousness or even laziness. This is in stark contrast to cases in which male slaves failed to complete work and were branded rebels of bad character and habits.[14]

The debates over a slave's skills often revealed low judicial standards for what level of skill or what amount of work might reasonably be expected of a slave. In *Chretien* v. *Theard*, William Rogers, a carpenter, testified that the slave Lafortune was "expert in neither trade of Carpenter or Joiner, that he said Lafortune is not more expert in them than an intelligent man who has never learnt said trade." Despite the fact that several other witnesses corroborated this testimony, the judge gave great weight to the testimony of two witnesses who had known Lafortune many years earlier and who said "that he was capable of executing work when market [sic] out to him." The judge wrote, "[T]his I think is as much as could be expected of an unlettered slave. It could not be supposed that he could calculate the dimensions and proportions of a building. It was not to be expected that a slave should be a master workman."[15]

It is clear that William Rogers believed that Lafortune, sold as a "carpenter and joiner," should have had the skills of a carpenter and been able to perform his work better than even an "intelligent man" without training. By contrast, the judge implied that a slave carpenter could meet a lower standard than a "carpenter"; the judge did not consider an "intelligent man" to be the appropriate reference point for "an unlettered slave." While ordinary Southern whites expected slaves to meet a level of skill as well as industry, judges justified their decisions in these cases in a way that avoided inscribing in the law too high a standard for slaves, one that might too greatly contradict the Sambo stereotype.

Finally, the slave's identity as capital and as labor intersected. Litigants argued vehemently over a slave's skills in determining the slave's dollar value. For example, in *Stone & Best* v. *Watson*, the buyer succeeded in proving a slave unsound because of illness, but he also wanted to show that her "value if sound" should take into account that she was reputed to be "a No. 1 seamstress" and in fact was not. In *Campbell* ads. *Atchison*, one witness testified that "he would not have given a Dollar for" Salley, for whom the buyer had paid $350, "but that she ought to have brought $250." His reason for considering her worthless was her temper, but he recognized that her skills would bring money on the market. Another witness testified that Salley "would *at the present time be worth $350*, but for her temper. . . ." In *Porcher* ads. *Caldwell* a witness testified "that a first rate cook would be worth $500" but that because of the slave's poor cooking skills, he "dont [sic] think the negro worth $350 if she had been sound."[16]

The cases involving slaves' skills show several, sometimes contradictory, impulses: witnesses' attribution of intelligence, ability, and efficiency to enslaved people; judges' unwillingness to set high standards for slaves' labor; the constant juxtaposition of paternalist rhetoric with discussions of slaves in terms of dollar value; a focus on women's inability as opposed to men's insubordination. Yet for the most part, disputes over skilled slaves avoided the starkest contrasts between the good slave and the bad slave for the very reason that they presupposed a stereotype-breaking competency on the slave's part.

Origin and Development of Slave Character

Disputes involving runaway slaves, on the other hand, highlight the schizophrenic racial ideology of white Southerners: the hope that slaves were happy Sambos and Mammys always balanced by the fear that if the bonds of slavery were loosened, the childlike slave would revert to a savage beast. The trials help to illuminate this child-savage duality by demonstrating a multiplicity of stories about what made a slave into a child or a savage and about which slaves were one and which the other. Slave buyers and sellers, hirers and owners told different stories about the dependence of slave character on masters' influence and about the immutability of slave "vice."

George Fredrickson has shown that Sambo and Nat were two sides of the same coin: according to Southern white racial theory, "the Negro was by nature a savage brute. Under slavery, however, he was 'domesticated' or, to a limited degree, 'civilized.' Hence docility was not so much his natural character as an artificial creation of slavery." As Dr. Samuel Cartwright put it, "the negro must, from necessity, be the slave of man or the slave of Satan." White Southerners believed that black character was plastic; one Virginia planter wrote, "[T]he character of the negro . . . is like the plastic clay, which may be moulded into agreeable or disagreeable figures according to the skill of the moulder." But they did not think it was "infinitely plastic": "innate racial traits limited his potential development to a more or less tenuous state of 'semi-civilization.'"[17]

This picture of black character as malleable up to a certain point should be contrasted with Southern ideas of white character development. To some extent Southern ideals of white character depended on slavery and, implicitly, on a contrast between black and white. As James Oakes and other historians of Southern culture have explained, the South was a society based on both honor and slavery; slaves were those who could have no honor, whereas all white men could potentially take part in the code of honor. White Southerners accepted the idea that the "moral sense" was an innate faculty of all white men. This moral sense could be developed through education, or it could be left in the rough; but all white men had it.[18]

By the nineteenth century, most white Southerners believed that blacks were bereft of the moral sense to be educated. While proslavery writers did not put their conviction of black moral inferiority in terms of "the moral sense," they so frequently asserted that blacks could not benefit from moral education because they lacked the necessary prerequisites, that this equation can be inferred.[19] Therefore, the plasticity of slave "character" did not necessarily equate with moral development as understood by educated whites. Rather, Southern ideologues emphasized the *imitative* abilities of the black slave. As Dr. Cartwright wrote, "When made contented and happy, as [slaves] always should be, they reflect their master in their thoughts, morals, and religion, or at least they are desirous of being like him. They imitate him in everything, as far as their imitative faculties, which are very strong, will carry them."[20] Thus, a slave well governed might *mimic* moral development without actually having the moral faculty to develop himself.

"Like Master, Like Man"

In warranty cases the malleability of slave character was essentially a seller's story. Only a seller would suggest that the slave's character depended on good government by a master. The buyer unhappy with a runaway or "vicious" slave preferred to portray the slave's character as immutable. This particular slave, according to the typical buyer, was an incorrigible savage under any circumstances. Buyers painted a world in which slaves were born with particular characteristics, just as whites were. On the other hand, while malleable character made slaves seem childlike but human, immutable viciousness could render an enslaved person subhuman.

The seller's story of malleability also played into the paternalist defense of slavery by shifting the focus from the slave's character to the master's treatment of the slave. One South Carolina case, decided on appeal by Chief Justice John Belton O'Neall, illustrates this transference. In *Johnson* v. *Wideman* the buyer (Wideman) portrayed Charles as an insubordinate and vicious drunkard and runaway, while the seller (Johnson) claimed that he behaved badly only under bad government.[21] The South Carolina Supreme Court, in an unusual opinion, reprinted the report of the trial judge, including the testimony and briefs.

Wideman's witnesses testified that Johnson had represented Charles to be sober, honest, and humble; that Johnson had said "he would trust him with money"; and that "a boy of ten years old could control him." Instead, according to Alexander Cummins, "Charles would get drunk; he would not work; he let his coal kiln burn up; was insolent; he was very often drunk; he saw him once lying behind the shop, and at another time in the woods. He (Charles) stayed with the defendant about two months and then ran away."[22]

According to the buyer-defendant, not only was Charles lazy and insolent, he cursed his overseer and attacked or threatened other white men. "He was saucy: [one witness] saw him shove a white man, named Cramer, down. He did not bring much custom to the shop: he threatened to beat another white man named Wells," testified one. Another witness reported that "Charles and Norris (a white man) were gambling— he struck Norris. At a race, Berry [Charles's former owner, before Johnson] and another white man were quarrelling. Charles came up behind his master, shut up his fist and swore that he wished he was a white man." Several witnesses testified to Charles's drinking, swearing, laziness, and general insolence. One witness even recounted a story of Charles pulling a knife to prevent the witness from pulling Charles's two big dogs off his own little dog.[23]

The defense maintained that Charles had been a runaway and a drunk when Johnson, the seller, had owned him. John Wideman (relation to defendant unclear) testified that

His brother (who as well as he, was a boy) was once about whipping Charles' wife: she broke and run, crying and calling for her husband. Charles came to her and asked what was the matter: she said William, the witness' brother, was whipping her: he swore he would mash him to the earth. At another time, he and his brother chased Charles from the kitchen; he turned and offered to fight them.[24]

Other witnesses who lived near Johnson told stories of Charles swearing that he would not live with Johnson, hiding in a willow thicket when there was work to be done, and asking a storekeeper for a ticket (a pass). Major William Eddings estimated Charles's value at one thousand dollars when Johnson bought him from Berry, "taking him *as he was*" because of his skill as a blacksmith. On the day of the sale, according to James Spikes, "Charles quarrelled with Berry: charged him with keeping his wife, shut up his fist and was walking towards Berry, when Johnson prevented him." When the plaintiff-seller tried to argue that a firmer master could have reined in Charles's misbehavior, defense witness Sherwood Corley testified that "he had often helped to tie and whip [Charles]" when Berry owned him; "it had no effect on him; he would curse his master as soon as taken down."[25]

In short, according to the buyer-defendant in this case, Charles was everything that struck terror into slaveholders' hearts about slaves: he owned a dog (against the law); he was married (unrecognized by law); worse, he tried to defend his wife's honor against white men; he not only acted as though he was equal to a white man, he *said he wished he were a white man*; he threatened white men with violence; he refused to work unless he wished to; he did not respond to whipping; and he ran away at will. In all of these offenses, according to the buyer-defendant, Charles was impervious to good or bad treatment; he was immutably vicious.

The plaintiff-seller's witnesses, however, told a different story. According to them Charles was a drunkard and an insolent negro only when he lived with Wiley Berry, a "drinking, horse-racing" man himself (from whom Johnson bought Charles). As Lewis Busby explained, "He had heard of [Charles's] drinking. He had borne the character of an insolent negro: but not in the time he belonged to the Johnsons." Others testified that Charles was humble and worked well; that when Johnson owned him, "he was not so indolent as when he belonged to Berry." Berry had exposed him frequently to spirits and had whipped him frequently. Alexander Presley testified that Wideman knew Charles's reputation and told Presley that Charles "was under a bad character . . . as he could out-general old Wiley Berry, he must be bad." Thus, Johnson's case rested on the contention that Charles was a good slave when managed well, and that the only evidence of his insolence came from his behavior under Berry and under Wideman himself. In the alternative Johnson argued that Wideman knew Charles's bad character before he bought him.[26]

The circuit judge, instructing the jury, asked, "[W]hat moral qualities would be so material, as that a misrepresentation of them would
have the effect to rescind the contract?" And he answered "that any quality represented to exist, which, if it did not, would have the effect of
diminishing in a considerable degree, the usefulness and value of the
slave, would have that effect."[27] He went on to enumerate those of
Charles's vices that might qualify:

> Habitual drunkenness was I told them, such a vicious habit as would
> justify them in rescinding the contract, if they should believe that it
> existed, that the plaintiff knew it, and so knowing, deceived the defen-
> dant by informing him that the negro was sober. I told them that occa-
> sional intoxication, not amounting to a habit, would not justify them
> in rescinding a contract.
>
> An habitual runaway was, I thought, a material defect, which might
> justify them in finding, for the defendant, if there was on the part of
> the plaintiff a wilful misrepresentation. *Occasional flights of a slave from
> his master's service for special causes would not constitute any material moral
> defect.*
>
> Honesty, I said to them, was a material moral quality in a slave: but
> nothing short of general dishonesty would show a defect in this behalf.
> For occasional thefts among the tolerably good slaves may be expected.[28]

But the judge added a strong caveat. While all of these qualities in a slave
might justify not paying a note, "generally, I said, the policy of allowing
such a defence might be very well questioned. For, most commonly such
habits were easy of correction by prudent masters, and it was only with
the imprudent that they were allowed to injure the slave. *Like master, like
man* was, I told them, too often the case, in drunkenness, impudence,
and idleness."[29]

The bad slave, as Wideman portrayed Charles, had two particularly
dangerous traits: first, insolence, which meant that he threatened white
men; second, the runaway habit, which meant that he threatened the
institution of slavery. Charles, in the courtroom, was indeed both child
and savage; but Wideman claimed that he was a savage *no matter what,*
whereas Johnson made the claim Fredrickson documents: that Charles
was "a child *in his place,* and a savage *out of it.*"[30] Johnson's argument,
largely accepted by the trial judge and Chief Justice O'Neall, was that
Charles's misbehavior could be attributed to the freedom Berry gave
him and the bad example Berry set. This theory of slave "vice"—*like master, like man*—removed agency from the slave and portrayed the slave as
the extension of his master's character.

The judge's instructions contain, in microcosm, several of the stories about slave character development. He draws several dichotomies:
"occasional intoxication" vs. "habitual drunkenness"; "occasional
flights . . . for special causes" vs. "habitual runaway"; "occasional thefts"

vs. "general dishonesty." Like Sambo, the typical slave could be expected to drink, run away, and steal a little; only when these acts came to define his character could he be considered defective. On the other hand, black character, like white character, was formed through habit, and masters were responsible for slaves' habits.[31]

By contrast, slave buyers, hirers from whom slaves ran away, or persons accused of shooting runaway slaves emphasized slaves' immutable viciousness and their own proper exercise of control over the slaves. In *Moran* v. *Davis,* the slave Stephen ran away from Davis, who had hired him from Moran for the Montpelier Institute. Moran then sued Davis for the price of Stephen; in answer, Davis replied that Stephen "was of bad and insubordinate character and difficult to manage and keep in proper subjection. . . . [D]efendant says he used only so much and such means as were necessary to keep said negro under control . . . was unruly and insubordinate and would not submit to the control of the defendant." The jury agreed that Davis should not have to reimburse Stephen's mistress for her loss.[32]

Buyers rejected any evidence of mutable character. Because a slave could have no reason to want her freedom, she must simply have a runaway vice or habit. As John Staples, a witness for the buyer in *Hagan* v. *Rist,* explained, "I do not know why he runaway [sic] he certainly had no reason I think it is a natural vice with him." John Staples believed John to be immutably vicious. William J. Ethridge, the overseer, corroborated this testimony by saying that John "ranaway [sic] without any cause whatever," in contrast to a slave who was cruelly whipped or had other reasons. Therefore John must *be* a runaway. Likewise, Abram Taylor complained, Pompey was "ill disposed, faithless, inconstant, unsteady, disobedient, and bad on all respects," and "John Cochran and Peter Watts well knew him to embrace the earliest opportunity to return to his old masters. . . . Pompey never would remain or live with any other person or master than [Cochran and Watts.]"[33]

Run Away or Runaway?

"Some months after the said Negroe man had run away he learned . . . that the same Negro was a runaway," explained one witness in a Louisiana case.[34] The distinction between the act and the character, drawn at length by the trial judge in *Johnson* v. *Wideman,* had several impulses. On the one hand, it was a simple recognition of masters' lack of absolute control over their slaves; to define runaway character or dishonesty by a single act would open the floodgates, because resistant acts simply happened *too* often. But it was more than that: the exercise of proving a runaway character or habit defined the slave by his vice, and made the vice into an immutable essence. An Alabama case may illustrate the point.

In 1849 Walker Reynolds sued William Ward for payment of an eight hundred dollar note, given for the purchase of a slave named Bill.[35] In defense Ward claimed that Bill was a runaway and that Reynolds had deceitfully represented Bill as "a negro of excellent character and recommended him in every particular extolling him both as to character and value." Indeed, according to Ward, Reynolds had explained that the only reason he was selling Bill was "that there had been a disturbance between the negro and another about a negro woman the wife of the other."

Reynolds, the seller, called witnesses to show that Bill was a good slave when he owned him. William Wilson testified that "I never knew or heard of said negro Bill to resist or rebel against his owner or any other person who had authority to control him." On cross-examination Wilson made a good start, reiterating that Bill was "active, able, and willing," but then added that "with this exception that he would occasionally run away." Wilson probably lost his value as a plaintiff's witness when asked "Had the said Bill the reputation of the Red fox and was not that reputation acquired by his running away and the difficulty in his being caught?" Wilson answered, "He had the name of the Red fox and was hard to catch when out." On reexamination, the plaintiff-seller's attorney asked Wilson, "Do you not believe the habit of running away by which Bill acquired the reputation of Red fox arose from imprudence of the plaintiff by his making unnecessary threats?" Wilson explained that "if Bill had belonged to some persons he would not have run away, and it was well understood that if he expected to get a whipping beforehand he would leave." In this case, the plaintiff's counsel was in the odd position of arguing that his own client's slave management had been so deficient—in "making unnecessary threats"—that the slave had run away from his seller, but that that did not prove he would run away from his buyer.

Several witnesses testified both that they knew Bill as "Red fox" because of his skill at evading the slave patrol *and* that he was an excellent worker. William Mecham, who described Bill as a "stout, active and good-looking negro," claimed that he only knew Bill to have run away once, "one time he came to me one morning and said his master had got mad with him, he wished me to go home with him which I did." Micajah Lisle, who thought Bill a "*pert* active negro," also knew of only one runaway episode, when "I came across the boy Bill once in the woods." Cunningham Wilson stated that Bill was "in mind and body as far as I know as sound as any man—black or white." On cross-examination, Wilson admitted that "I did know him to run away, I cannot state how often, several times, one time he went out a horse hunting and staid some time, how long am unable to say." He also said that the name Red Fox "was acquired from a race one night with dogs having run well but was caught."

However, Wilson concluded that Bill's value was "set with full knowledge of his character he having worked for me at harvest . . . and a better hand I would never desire." The plaintiff-seller sought to prove that Bill's selling price had already been discounted for his runaway habit. Each witness was asked to estimate Bill's value, and explain whether their estimate included a discount for the Red Fox reputation.

In this case, the seller argued that Bill only ran away when he was afraid of being whipped or when his master acted unreasonably, but that Bill had a good character. The buyer argued that being a runaway *was* Bill's character; Bill was a red fox. Many warranty-and-hire disputes over runaway slaves hinged on just this distinction between the act of running away and the *character* or *habit* of a runaway. To some extent this distinction, particularly as it was codified in Louisiana law, amounted to tacit recognition of the area of rights slaves had carved out for themselves, and of masters' lack of absolute control over slaves. Despite increasingly strict statutory restrictions on slaves' movements, many slaves continued throughout the antebellum period to "go abroad" at night, to visit wives on other plantations, to hire themselves out, and even to live in town apart from their masters.

Yet the *run away/runaway* distinction was more than just accommodation on the part of whites; it was an effort to define slave character in terms of habits. If a slave ran away once, it was acceptable to attribute that action to a rational motive; but if this dangerous habit became routine, then slaveholders treated that habit as a vicious character trait or a disease. Without such a distinction a line like "some months after the said Negroe man had run away he learned . . . that the same Negro was a runaway" would make no sense.

Again, issues of dollar value always arose at moments of character determination. In one Natchez case Jonathan Guice sued John Holmes for possession of a slave he claimed Holmes had illegally detained. Guice's lawyer questioned several witnesses about the slave John: "[W]hat is his character, was he in the habit of running away?" Holmes's lawyer then cross-interrogated: "What was the value of such boy when addicted to running away? What is the difference between the value of slaves who are confirmed runaways and those not having this vice, all other things being Equal?" The witnesses all agreed that John had a good character and was not a runaway but that a runaway was worth less than half "as he otherwise would be if not a runaway."[36]

Witnesses frequently mentioned a slave having run away once, and called her a good slave at the same time. Henry Doyle testified that Captain Samuel Cotton had told him that Mary "was dissatisfied at living in the county and that she had run away from Mr. Rogillio. . . . He also stated that she was among the best servants he had ever owned." James Wallace, a witness for John Morton in a suit to retrieve damages for a runaway slave shot in flight, testified that Spencer was "a likely boy worth twelve or fourteen hundred—never heard anything against his character except that he had run away."[37]

The Medicalization of Vice: "Habit" and "Disease"

Buyers realized that if a slave's vice was a "habit" akin to a disease, she was reduced to a status closer to animal than if her vice were a purposeful one; sellers knew, similarly, that if she was merely the product of her owner's management, that brought her closer to a child. Both of these "insights" implicitly contrast with some conception of immanent human "character." Complete malleability and immutable "addiction" to vice both negate the idea that a slave behaved a certain way out of the conscious choice of a rational mind or the yearnings of a human soul.[38]

The legal tendency to medicalize slave vice by portraying character defects as "habits" or "addictions" drew its inspiration from mid nineteenth-century versions of biological racism. Perhaps the most active expositor of these pseudoscientific theories was Dr. Samuel Cartwright, who acted as a physician-witness in slave cases in Natchez, Mississippi, before moving to New Orleans to begin his better-known career as a medical propagandist for slavery. Cartwright promulgated the notion that Negroes were not only inferior but in fact constituted a different, subhuman species, and he propounded what historians have called *states'-rights medicine*, giving "medical" justification for the Southern way of life.[39] In a series of articles in *DeBow's Review*, Cartwright propounded theories that intertwined polygenesis, the physiological bases of black inferiority, and "negro diseases" of which the causes were physiological, the symptoms behavioral, and the cures a combination of behavioral and physical measures.

Cartwright located the central distinction between blacks and whites in a complicated feedback between the nervous system, blood, and lungs. "The great development of the nervous system . . . would make the Ethiopian race entirely unmanageable. . . . [D]efective hematosis . . . is the true cause of that debasement of mind which has rendered the people of Africa unable to take care of themselves." Black people, Cartwright contended, rebreathed their own air, unlike whites: "In bed, when disposing themselves for sleep, the young and old, male and female, instinctively cover their heads and faces, as if to insure the inhalation of warm, impure air. . . . The natural effect of the practice is imperfect atmospherization of the blood—one of the heaviest chains that binds the negro to slavery." Blacks needed slavery, Cartwright explained, because they needed white men's authority to "vitalize and decarbonize their blood by the process of full and free respiration, that active exercise of some kind alone can effect."[40]

Cartwright argued that medically slaves were like children: in their susceptibility to scrofulous diseases, their anatomy (livers, veins, sensitive skin), their fear of the rod, and in the fact, according to him, that they were "easily governed by love combined with fear" and "required government in every thing." Cartwright also enumerated the Negro diseases, including "negro consumption" (what is now known as *miliary tuberculosis*, a deadly form of the disease). Cartwright wrote that, contrary to popular opinion, dirt-eating was a symptom, not the cause, of "negro consumption." Further, he drew the connection between the physician's diagnostic role with respect to "negro diseases" and their role in litigation:

> It is of importance to know the pathognomonic signs in its early stages, not only in regard to its treatment, but to detect impositions, as negroes afflicted with the complaint are often for sale; the acceleration of the pulse on exercise incapacitates them for labor, as they quickly give out and have to leave their work. . . . [T]he seat of negro consumption is . . . in the mind, and its cause is generally mismanagement or bad government.[41]

Two other diseases were of paramount importance to this medical handbook for slave owners: "drapetomania" (the disease of running away) and "Dysthesia Ethiopica, or Hebetude of Mind" ("what overseers call Rascality"). Cartwright explained that drapetomania was caused by masters who did not recognize that Negroes are by nature "knee-benders," from whom "awe and reverence must be exacted . . . or they will despise their masters, become rude and ungovernable, and run away." To cure drapetomania required keeping slaves in "that submissive state which it was intended for them to occupy . . . and treat[ing them] like children, with care, kindness, attention, and humanity."

Rascality could also be attributed to lax management or excess freedom: "Dysthesia Ethiopica . . . attacks only such slaves as live like free negroes in regard to diet, drinks, exercise, etc." The proper treatment, in order to stimulate the liver, skin and kidneys, was to wash and oil the slave, then to slap his skin with a broad leather strap and put him to hard work, which would increase his circulation. There was no danger in keeping the slave hard at work, because, conveniently, according to nature's laws, it was impossible to overwork a Negro. Cartwright wrote, "A white man, like a blooded horse, can be worked to death. Not so the negro. . . . The white men of America have performed many prodigies, but they have never yet been able to make a negro overwork himself."[42]

Samuel Cartwright has been dismissed by some historians as a marginal thinker in the American South, whose ideas were accepted only on the fringe. William Stanton portrays Cartwright as "that brutal Louisiana physician and publicist . . . with his banana-skin humor, who appeared only on the periphery of the controversy to comment, cheer, or make impolite noises of disapproval." There is validity to this viewpoint only with respect to Cartwright's theories on polygenesis. Few Southerners accepted Cartwright's attempt to reconcile the separate origins of blacks with the Bible by showing that Eve was tempted in the Garden of Eden not by a serpent but by a "negro gardener," and few believed that blacks outside slavery were slaves to a serpent/Satan. However, the idea that there were "distinctive peculiarities and diseases of the negro race" was far more widespread. Articles by other authors, whose titles allude to such diseases, appeared not only in *DeBow's* but in a number of other Southern periodicals.[43] And the links between body and behavior were widely accepted by antebellum Southerners. While few Southerners may have used the technical terminology of *drapetomania*, they did refer to *dysthesia ethiopica* and *cachexia africana* (dirt-eating) in court and were accustomed to talking about running away and other slave behaviors in terms of "addiction" and "habit."

In the Louisiana Civil Code, theft was an "addiction" and running away a "habit." To prove a slave a runaway or a thief, thus, it was necessary to prove that this "condition" was of long standing and had manifested itself a certain number of times and for a given duration. Because Louisiana was the only state that codified slave vices of character, perhaps it is understandable that it was the only state in which there was such an impulse to reduce moral qualities to medical bases. Certainly, it had the effect of reducing the slave to something more animal than human. Yet the description of running away or other vice (such as theft or disobedience) as a "character," a "habit," or an "addiction" was widespread in other states. It was also common to characterize slaves with the phrase "his habits were very bad."[44]

The Medicalization of Vice: Madwomen and Idiots

The tendency to treat moral questions as medical ones seems to have been even stronger when the slave at issue was a woman. There was no female Nat in the Southern lexicon. When a woman resisted or refused to work, it did not conjure the same fears in the white mind as did a rebellious black man. In court, buyers or hirers of runaway women were more likely to question their sanity or mental capacity than their character.

On January 3, 1834, Rose Icar, a New Orleans free woman of color, bought from Anthony Abraham Suares a twenty-year-old slave, Kate. Icar paid five hundred dollars cash for her slave and, by all accounts, bought Kate for her labor, not to gain her freedom. Not one month later, Icar was in district court, suing Suares for selling her a runaway. Rose Icar's petition to the court complained that "three or four days after the said slave had been taken possession of . . . it was discovered that said Slave was crazy, and she also ran away from her new mistress."[45]

The witnesses for the plaintiff all described Kate's "craziness" in terms that raise the possibility that she was as sane as a slave could be, rationally resisting her position. Jean Dinot testified that said Slave is not worth much. When she is asked to fetch one thing she fetches another. . . . She is capable of setting fire to [a house], as she does not know what she is about. . . . Witness has seen said Slave when sent by her mistress go away in quite a different direction talking to herself and gesticulating.

Witness on one occcasion met her going toward the Lake and asked her where she was going when she answered she did not know.

On cross-examination Dinot admitted that he had seen Kate only three times before seeing her in court, and he revealed one other important fact: Kate spoke only English. Dinot did not know whether Rose Icar understood or spoke English.

Kate ran away, but she did not get far. She was caught and brought to the police jail of Jefferson, a neighboring county. She managed to frustrate her jailor as well; she told him that she belonged to a Doctor Sealden. He asked where this doctor lived, and she told him, "Down there, down that Street." He was unable to extract any other information from her and came to the conclusion that "said slave is not of sound mind." The sheriff testified that he had seen Kate "act as a crazy person—she holloed danced all night and could hardly answer when spoken to"; although he threatened her often to be quiet, "the threats availed nothing," which led him to "the opinion that said Kate was crazy."

Two other witnesses reached the same conclusion. One based his diagnosis on the fact that "She is of no use in a house—when her mistress told her to do one thing she did another," although he too noted that Rose Icar spoke only a few words of English. On cross-examination the witness explained that "when the Plaintiff told the slave Kate to do any work she spoke to her in English in the best manner she could." He never saw Kate do any work; in fact, "Witness was present when Plaintiff told said slave to go and wash her clothes. She took her clothes and went out of the House and ran away."

By contrast, the only defense witness told the court that when Rose Icar had "informed [him] that Kate had absconded . . . [he] observed to her that inasmuch as the Slave was a stranger and unacquainted with the city, it was probable that she had lost her way, and that no doubt she had been taken up and put in jail." When he suggested that Kate might be found at the Jefferson parish jail, Icar told him that it was up to Mr. Suares to hunt for her, but "in none of the conversations which Witness had with the Plaintiff in relation to this Slave, did she allege the slave to be crazy; that during the whole time the Slave was under the superintendence of the Witness, he observed nothing in her behaviour to induce him to believe that she laboured under any . . . derangement."

The trial-court judge granted Icar a rescission of the sale on the ground that Kate was a habitual runaway. The judge applied the January 20, 1834 act of the legislature, which created the presumption that a newly imported slave who ran away within two months after sale had had the redhibitory vice of running away at the time of the sale. (Redhibitory vices were those which justified rescission of the sale.) Furthermore, the judge ruled that "the evidence of a personal inspection of the Slave satisfy the Court that the Slave is . . . destitute of mental capacity." Suares appealed on the ground that neither Kate's running away nor her craziness were sufficiently established; "the utmost that can be inferred from the testimony is that she was rather stupid: this is an apparent defect, if a redhibitory defect at all." Suares also complained that the judge erred in basing his judgment on his own impression of the slave. However, the supreme court was "satisfied from the evidence in the record, independently of the impression made on the mind of the judge, by personal inspection, that the slave in question was wholly, and perhaps worse than useless."[46]

Kate acted as though she did not understand her French, colored mistress speaking English, disobeyed orders, avoided work, tried to escape, and lied to her jailers. This behavior convinced her mistress and the witnesses for the plaintiff, as well as the judge, that Kate was crazy. If we compare her behavior to that of the runaway male slaves who came before trial courts in these cases, it is hard to distinguish what made her crazy and them vicious. Had Kate been a man, her refusal to take orders and her efforts to escape might have been seen as rebelliousness or viciousness; her owners would have feared violence or insurrection. Her drinking might have been emphasized more as evidence of intractable vice. But being a woman, "moral qualities" vices were not seen as applicable to her; her actions did not instill a fear of violent rebellion. Insubordination must be lunacy.

Other cases involving "craziness" or "idiocy" of female slaves bear many similarities to cases in which male slaves were accused of vice. For example, witnesses for the buyer of the slave Melly testified that she whistled after answering any question put to her by a white person, that she was "much whipmarked and . . . did not seem to enjoy senses enough for common purposes;" and that she seemed to be an "imbecile." However, defense witnesses found Melly to have "common sense enough for a field hand"; "she did like any other person she did her work well and obeyed well orders." These witnesses commented that, although Melly talked to herself, "white persons are more apt to speak to themselves than negroes," so that could hardly be a sign of idiocy![47] The Louisiana court, in ruling that idiocy was an apparent vice, vented their frustration with deciding questions of slaves' minds and morals: "It is very difficult, if not nearly impossible, to fix a standard of intellect by which slaves are to be judged."[48]

In another Louisiana case, *Buhler* v. *McHatton*, the buyer, Buhler, tried to have the sale set aside on two counts: first, "because said Jane has proved entirely useless as a cook"; and second, "because she is *addicted to madness*" (emphasis added). Buhler tried to show Jane's insanity with evidence of her burning up her clothes, an act "utterly irreconcilable with the idea of deception"; refusing to eat meat on Friday or Saturday; and "frequent paroxysms of weeping, superstition, and violence." Witnesses ascribed Jane's odd behavior to "religious enthusiasm and grief at being separated from her children." Buhler characterized her "weeping and lamenting a separation of children" as "superstitious monomania." The jury, unimpressed, found for the seller, McHatton. Justice Campbell, in affirming the lower-court judgment, noted that Jane's behavior "did not attract particular attention, and was not noticed for a month or more," and attributed it to her "religious scruples."[49]

One attorney's brief gave a particularly revealing soliloquy on the impossibility of imagining an enslaved woman taking moral action or having moral dilemmas. In *Walker* v. *Hayes*, the woman sued upon had drowned herself and her child soon after being sold. The seller's witness, J. D. Hair, called Agnes "a girl of unusual good sense," and the jury gave a judgment for the seller. On appeal the buyer's attorney argued that, by itself, the fact that Agnes committed suicide proved that she was "addicted to madness." He went on to consider all the rational reasons a person might commit suicide and concluded that none of them could apply to an enslaved woman:

> When it is done to avoid disgrace by the man sensitive about his honor, or in accordance with the prevailing custom of a people, whose minds are darkened by superstition or when it is done from motives of patriotism to retrieve a nation's honor, or rescue it from ruin, or in despair of the liberties of one's country, or to avoid a more cruel fate, in a death of torture, as illustrated by the heroes of antiquity, rendered immortal by their wisdom and their valor; it is not for a moment contended that it proceeds from insanity.
>
> But how different all these classes of suicide from the one for our consideration: here is a poor slave with no patriotic designs or interests to subserve, no national custom to conform to, no disgrace to avoid, no terrible punishment to escape, who buries herself and helpless child in a common grave.[50]

In other words, an enslaved woman could have no *honor*: no nation, no tradition, no courage. The only possible reason she could take her life was insanity.

Opening Pandora's Box

SLAVE AGENCY

In contrast to the explanations of slave character and behavior as functions of slave management or as habit or disease, some witnesses told stories that attributed more agency to enslaved people themselves, suggesting, for example, that slaves ran away for their own, rational rea-

sons—because they disliked an owner, were amusing themselves, or
wished to return to a family member. While occasionally the courts explicitly recognized the human motivations or intentions of the slave as
the cause of a slave's "vices," more often these stories, appearing in the
trial transcripts, were weeded out of the appellate opinion. Just as judges
were reluctant to recognize slaves' skills and abilities, so did they fear
giving legal recognition to slaves as moral agents with volition, except
when it suited very specific arguments or liability rules.

For example, in one Louisiana case a witness for the plaintiff-seller,
while testifying that the slave Caleb was "punctiliously honest and trustworthy," explained that he had never heard of "Caleb absenting himself
from the plantation but once, there being no white persons on the plantation he and his wife had a quarrel and he (Caleb) was out, I believe all
night." Another witness testified to a conversation in which the slave seller
explained that although the slave had run away four or five times, "it was
generally for the fear of being whipped."[51] The appellate court referred
to the latter comment, but not to the former. If a slave ran away for fear
of being whipped, it suggested a mechanical reaction to stimuli within a
master's control; fear of whipping could be easily integrated into a theory
of vice as the function of slave management. However, running away
because of a quarrel with one's wife connoted a slave's control over his
own family life and his own decision making, an implication that fit poorly
into accepted theories of slave behavior.

In *Reynolds* v. *White*, the buyer-plaintiff complained that Sam was a
runaway and a thief; his witness, George Malcolm, testified that Sam
"stay[ed] away sometimes one day, sometimes more" and that the "plaintiff was obliged to tie up said boy and nail up his gates to keep him at
home." On the other hand, White's witness, C. J. Cook, knew Sam to be
"absent" when White owned him only once:

> to wit; the boy's mother was sick and the physician left a prescription
> for her; the boy was sent out with other prescription to the Druggists
> after candlelight that boy did not return for 24 or 48 hours . . . and Mr.
> White and family thought the boy was lost and witness was of the same
> opinion. The boy was in the constant habit of getting out to play when-
> ever he could and would return.

This "play" Cook did not consider to be running away.[52]

Similarly, in *Anderson* v. *Dacosta*, a witness for Mathilda's seller described her as one who "liked to play and amuse herself" but nevertheless "bore a good name and character and was of a mild disposition."
Another witness who spoke well of Mathilda denied that she was a runaway, explaining that she was only "in the habit of going back to the
places where she was hired before," and that "all she wanted was a master to look to her and not to allow her privileges to run about." Another

slave seller described the slave Charlotte as "a good girl, only quarrel-some at times. . . . [S]he did not believe the girl had run away," although the buyer claimed Charlotte was "addicted to running away."[53]

At the level of witness testimony, hire cases often brought forth evidence of enslaved people's acting of their own volition. For example, one owner sued a railroad for taking his hired slave to Brunswick, when he had been hired to work on the South Western Road or the Muscogee Road. The railroad's lawyer cross-examined one witness to suggest that the change in work assignment came of the slave's own volition not the needs of the railroads: "Do you know defendant carried said negro to Brunswick? Did not the negro run away and go towards Brunswick? Did defendant ask leave to carry said negro to Brunswick, or did he not say to you that the negro wanted to go there. And did he not tell you that he ran away?" The witness replied that "I do not recollect that he said the negro wanted to go. After the negroes death Deft said something in regard to the negroes having become attached to some of the negro women that went to Brunswick and this being a reason why the negro went off with them. I do not think Deft said he ran away, but that he went along with the other hands and overseer."[54]

Witnesses often presented evidence of slaves trying to go back to former masters or, when hired out, to their present owners. Judge Hackleman sold a slave "because he said he wanted another master—said he thought he ought to be allowed to go to preaching when he wanted to. He ran away from witness once. Got dogs and caught him. Told him I would whip him if he did not finish his task the day before—He did quite finish it and went off." Another slave ran away because, one witness reported, "he did not wish to go to Texas." Mary, a Natchez slave, ran away because she "was dissatisfied at living in the country," although she had been purchased "to satisfy a negro boy . . . named Henry who wanted her for a wife. Mary reported to a witness that she had "taken *some medicine to clear herself*," which he took to mean "thereby to produce abortion."[55]

Abram Martin sued Charles Bosley when they could not agree on how to divide a lot of slaves they had bought together. According to a witness present at the "division," two slaves asserted their own, contradictory preferences for the transaction: "the fellow said if he was parted from [a certain woman slave] he would destroy himself he further observed that if he did not get her for a wife he would destroy the girl or himself and the girl would not live with him or have him for a husband and they were then parted and had been parted for the voige [sic]."[56]

The Louisiana Court was the only Deep South court that seemed to occasionally accept evidence of the slave's own motivations to explain her running away. This was probably because Louisiana had such strict codified parameters for the "habit of running away"—up to a certain point, a slave's behavior might be only "petit marronage"; after that point, the slave was a runaway. Because the definition of the runaway habit was strictly set out in the Civil Code, it may have been easier for judges to recognize a slave's personhood when his or her behavior fell outside the strict definition.[57]

For example, the New Orleans parish court did not consider the slave a runaway if the slave ran away to visit a spouse after a sale. Ludger Fortier sued for the rescission of a slave sale because the slave left for several hours three days after the sale. According to defense witnesses, the slave had a good character, had never been whipped by his former owner, and had run away only to visit a slave woman on a neighboring plantation. The court denied Fortier's claim, finding that "Negroes sometimes absent themselves from their masters in the night without being runaway."[58]

Similarly, in *Bocod* v. *Jacobs* the supreme court noted that a slave's running away "may be the consequence of the displeasure of being sold— of his dislike of the new owner"; in *Nott* v. *Botts* the trial judge found "nothing extraordinary in the fact of a negro coming from Kentucky, where they are treated almost on an equality with their master, running away in Louisiana," implying a slave's desire for greater autonomy.[59] All of these characterizations of slave motivation aver reasons that are rational, not products of "disease" or even immutable viciousness.

The fact that Louisiana's definition of a runaway led to greater recognition of slaves' human agency did not escape the notice of litigants in nearby states. One Natchez, Mississippi, case became a referendum on the applicability of Louisiana law to local conditions. John D. James, a local slave trader, sold nine slaves to Joseph J. B. Kirk in 1848 at a slave market that had apparently been part of Pointe Coupee Parish, Louisiana at one time. In 1849 Kirk filed suit against James for $750 on the basis of James's warranty, executed under Louisiana law, that "said Slaves were free from the redhibitory vices and diseases." Kirk complained that one of the slaves, Simon, had run away repeatedly and had finally drowned in an escape.[60]

Both James and Kirk asked for jury instructions based on Louisiana law. Judge Posey refused to give several of James's instructions, but he did explain the Louisiana code on redhibition to the jury. James appealed the lower-court decision on the ground that the jury had applied an "arbitrary rule of evidence of another state." James argued that Louisiana was travelling down a slippery slope towards recognition of slaves' personhood and protection of slave buyers. Mississippi should not follow. "For illustration, suppose that by the laws of Louisiana negro slaves are competent witnesses to prove the vice in a companion. . . . Again, let us suppose that one of the redhibitory vices warranted against was a habit of drinking." Equally outrageous as admitting slave testimony, argued James, was warranting that a slave would not run away.[61]

John D. James's argument about the dangers of accepting Louisiana's protections for slave buyers in Mississippi reveals general fears about the slippery slope of implied warranty. While a buyer's rule that strictly codified vices as "habits" made it possible to treat slaves as subhuman, buyer-claimants also introduced arguments about slaves' human agency, which threatened a law of sales in which slaves were property only.

Judges resisted extending protections to buyers because they did not want to open the Pandora's box of putting slave character on trial. Going to trial risked long, involved proceedings (and possible hung juries) on the question of masters' treatment of slaves. In *James* v. *Kirk*, the testimony dwelt on whether a master was "as good a disciplinarian . . . as any of his neighbours." Other cases put masters' character on trial in other ways—for example, judging the savviness of the slaveholder in the marketplace. Because these market transactions were risky and slaveholders became personally invested in the outcome, slaves had the most chance to influence them by their behavior.

Judges recognized slave agency most directly in tort cases, in which one slaveholder sued another for damage to a slave when under the other's control. Most commonly, the defendant in such a case was an industrial hirer, or a common carrier, usually a ferryboat. Common carriers were generally held responsible for damages to property on board, which they insured. In *Trapier* v. *Avant*, the trial judge tackled the question of "whether negroes, being the property damaged, they should form an exception to the general rule of liability in the carrier." He determined that slaves should not be an exception. "Negroes have volition, and may do wrong; they also have reason and instinct to take care of themselves. As a general rule, human beings are the safest cargo, because they do take care of themselves." According to the judge, the humanity of the slaves did not present enough of a problem to alter the general property rule. "Did this quality, humanity, cause their death? certainly not—what was the cause? The upsetting of the boat. who is liable fore the upsetting of the boat? The ferriman; there is an end of the question."[62]

The dissenting judge, however, pointed out the problem created by slaves' human agency: if the slaves had run away or thrown themselves overboard before the ferryman had a chance to reach them, then holding Avant responsible would amount to converting his contract into a guarantee of the slaves' "good morals and good sense." To the dissenting judge, the slaves' humanity—their desire to escape and even to commit suicide—prevented the application of the usual liability rule. He explained:

> These people like ourselves possess volition and physical powers which nothing short of the [illegible] can contain. Fetters may restrain their physical powers and the [illegible] may suppress the visible emotions of the will. But these restraints once removed, nothing short of omnipotence can infallibly circumscribe or put bounds to their powers.[63]

Thus, some judges were most receptive to claims about slaves' human agency at the moment when a white person's dollars were at stake. Yet it is important to recognize that *some* white person's money was at stake in all these cases. Torts pushed the logic of the black slave's dependent character to its outer limit; the position that won out in this case accepted that logic—but the dissent suggests the strains it caused.[64]

Another boat case illustrates the *Avant* dissenter's position that whites could not be held responsible for actions taken by enslaved blacks of their own "free will." In a Georgia case of a slave drowned as a hired boathand, the ferry owner claimed it was Landon's own fault that he died; Landon's owner claimed that the boat owner must be held liable because he was responsible for the slave and improperly employed him in clearing the river of logs.[65] Richard Bishop testified for the Thomas Gorman, the slave owner, that

> it is not the custom of the . . . rivers to employ negroes hired for Boat Hands in clearing obstructions from the river or opening new passages for the Boats [added later] unless it is unavoidable at the time or necessary. . . . The boy Sam [Landon] of his own accord, in presence of the captain went into the river and commenced cutting a log. That he was about half an hour cutting the log in two—and the captain present during the time —that the water was very swift at the place he was cutting, and when he had cut the log—to save himself from being carried down stream he jumped upon another log which projected into the water, but which gave way and was carried down stream by the current with the boy on it—that in floating down his hat fell off, and in endeavoring to recover it, he sank suddenly, and was soon found, a short distance below.[66]

The captain and engineer of the boat testified that "the boy Landon was not drowned from the improper management of the owners of the Boat—Express orders being given by the witnesses for the negroes to engage in the work of choosing[?] the river." The court charged the jury that if they believed the negro was engaged in the work of his own free will, the boat owner was not liable. The jury found for the boat owner. The plaintiff appealed, on the ground that the court's instructions amounted to a statement "[T]hat it was not necessary to use coercion with this kind of property." The plaintiff clearly understood that recognizing a slave's agency threatened the bonds of slavery.[67]

On the other hand, judges in hire disputes frequently used legal analogies to horses or real estate, which had the effect of minimizing the person/thing distinction and deemphasizing slaves as moral agents.[68] This may be because suits over hire fell under the law of bailment, or rental property, which meant that they were classified more closely with real property, especially real estate. Courts compared a slave falling ill or running away during the hire term to "the loss of the house by fire"; they compared the injunction not to treat a hired slave cruelly to the requirement that "after [a hired horse] is exhausted, and has refused its feed, the hirer is bound not to use it."[69] Through the abstraction of claims about slaves into general property claims, judges made it possible to think of slaves less as human agents and more as things.

TRICKERY

To whites, the worst part about slaves' acting for themselves was the possibility that they might deceive their masters. Slaveholders were constantly on the lookout for trickery by slaves, and their fear lent greater urgency to the project of proper slave "management." A master who could not read slaves well ran the risk of being duped by them, and nothing was less honorable than being fooled by a slave.

The most common mention of a slave's deceit was to characterize a slave as feigning illness—"lazy . . . and affected to be sick"—when in fact "little was there and then the matter with him, the said slave, and only needed whipping to make him work well." Hardy Stevenson complained that he had only bought the slave Esther because "the defendant represented said slave to be sound and to be deceitful in pretending to be sick frequently and . . . said all that she needed was a master who would drive her."[70] Slaveholders constantly feared that slaves were feigning illness or otherwise trying to manipulate their masters; a good master was one who could see through this deceit and make a slave work.

Doctors sometimes told a slave's master that a slave was "practicing a deception on the family . . . and [I] treated her accordingly." One doctor, who sold an old woman slave as sound, told the buyer that "she complained of being sick but that she was able to do the house work." Her former owner also testified at the trial that although Fanny complained of rheumatism, "it was more from an unwillingness to work than from want of ability."[71]

Slaves could also feign insanity by putting on fake fits or acting as though they could not understand what was said to them. These stories about deceitful pretense of insanity mirror the same fears as those of feigning physical illness. Even when the parties generally agreed that a slave was insane, they felt it necessary to point out that her symptoms were "utterly irreconcilable with the idea of deception."[72] In a breach of warranty case for an allegedly insane slave, the seller often suggested that the insanity was feigned, as did this seller's lawyer on cross-examination of the buyer's overseer:

> 3. What were the symptoms of insanity, if any, which you discovered about the negro Lawson? Were they constantly on him, or did they return only occasionally? Was not the said Lawson an artful designing fellow and do you not believe he *affected* to be deranged? Do you not remember that he pretended to be in love, and did he not state *that* as the cause of his derangement, and did not the plff order him to be

whipped saying he pretended only to be deranged, and that he would
whip him out of his love fit, or words to that effect?[73]

But the most terrifying deceit by a slave was not to pretend illness or
even insanity but to pretend to be a white man. This issue arose in lawsuits by owners against railroads or ferryboats for transporting a runaway slave. The common carrier's defense was often that a reasonable
person would have taken the slave for a white man. In one Georgia case
the owner introduced a witness who had seen Sam in Chicago, "passing
as a white-man. . . . Saw him take drinks at the bar with white men." Although "to a casual observer," this witness said, Sam "did not show any
negro blood, he shewed the negro from the nose down." The railroad
put on witnesses who "swore that they had *seen* Sam about plffs store for
a year or more and considered him a *white man*—that they had dealt
with him in the store as a clerk of the plffs bought goods of him and paid
him money—that his complexion was light his hair straight and his general appearance to ordinary observation that of a white man one offered had been in the habit of calling him Mr Wallace and regarded him
as a member of the firm."[74]

SLAVE TESTIMONY

The one area in which judges did travel down the slippery slope of recognizing slaves' personhood was in the acceptance of slaves' own statements as evidence in the courtroom. It was a cardinal rule of slave law in
every state that slaves could under no circumstances testify against a white
man; this rule applied to out-of-court nonhearsay as well as live testimony. The rationale for the rule was simple: slaves were mendacious
and unworthy of taking the oath to testify; their words could not be the
basis of liability or culpability of a white person. Yet time and again in
warranty cases, slave statements regarding his or her own condition were
allowed, almost always against a white man, the slave seller. Thomas R. R.
Cobb notes in his treatise that this was the main exception to the rule,
due to "the necessity of the case."[75] Here, again, this mostly happened at
the witness level, and passed without judicial comment.

It was common for witnesses to refer to slaves' statements in their
testimony without either party objecting. If no party objected, evidence
of the use of slave testimony did not appear in the appellate opinion.
For example, in *George v. Bean*, several witnesses testified that "the girl
complained of a pain in her head and side" and "complained . . . of de-
bility . . . of being overcome by hurt." The Mississippi High Court granted
the plaintiff-seller a new trial on other grounds, never mentioning the
admission of slave statements in its opinion.[76]

In one South Carolina case, one witness testified that "the Negro
said he had eaten dirt," another that Romeo "after a drunking frolic

would complain of a stoppage in his water," to which no one objected. In a case that involved competing medical testimony, one doctor testified that a slave "said she was unable to attend to her duties about the house" because of an "enlargement of the tendons of her ankle." The other doctor, who argued that the swelling was only mild rheumatism, testified that "she said she had runaway, and took a cold, and that the swelling arose from that."[77]

The reported statements sometimes went beyond mere medical symptoms. One Natchez witness reported that an enslaved woman "had a short time before [she was sold] taken *some medicine to clear herself* (meaning thereby to produce abortion as this affiant understood)." Another testified to a slave's statements about his ownership: "the overseer went with him to the negroe's cabbin [sic], where he was sick, saw and spoke to [the slave], asked him who he belonged to, and answered, to Mr Sauve and that said Barnaby sold him to him."[78]

Often the opposing party objected to the admission of slaves' words at trial, but the judge overruled the objection. In the Pickens County, Alabama, Circuit Court, William Murrah's attorney asked Dr. Jesse Peebles about Phoebe's illness, including the following interrogatories:

> 11. State what account the negro woman Phoebe gave to you of the causes and length of her diseased state? How long she had been laboring under a cough and difficulty of respiration? Whether she had been cupped blistered or scarified and what for? Who had been the physician . . . Whether she had ever afterwards felt well? State what she described her feelings to be and to have been since said former sickness? 13. State how the symptoms [she] described accorded with your own opinion.

Despite the fact that the defendant excepted to the eleventh and twelfth interrogatories "because predicated on the sayings of a slave," Dr. Peebles answered the questions.[79] In one Adams County, Mississippi, case the defendant based his motion for a new trial on the judge's ruling allowing "so much of the deposition of said Collins as relates to and is founded upon hearsay and the statements of the negro Caroline." The judge allowed the jury to hear the deposition that "the girl Caroline stated that she was sickly and had been in bad health for several years, and had been sold several times and taken back," and the jury found for Caroline's buyer. The defendant lost his case and his motion for a new trial.[80]

When these cases reached a higher court, judges invented creative excuses for what seemed like a long step out-of-bounds: first, they took care of any hearsay objections on the grounds that the statements were verbal acts, or *res gestae*; second, they ruled that since doctors routinely used a slave's statements about her own condition as one criterion on which to base their medical opinions, such statements could be admitted in the context of the doctor's opinion. Yet, eventually, even sick slaves' declarations to laymen were allowed. It was impossible to hear suits about the condition of human beings without hearing from the human beings themselves.[81]

The Mississippi case *Fondren v. Durfee* decreed that a sick slave's declarations to his master about his present illness were admissible as "verbal acts, indicating the nature and character of the disease under which the slave is laboring," and then arrived at the dubious conclusion that "being made to the master, who is interested in the welfare of the slave, [the slave's declarations] are presumed to be honest." This was a far cry from the expectation that a slave will dissemble illness to get out of work. The court also rationalized the presumption of slave honesty by the fact that slaves' declarations were "constantly acted upon by medical men as true statements."[82]

In one Alabama case Dr. Peterson testified, "In conversation with the negro, I learned from him, although he made the statement with extreme reluctance, that he had been subject to similar attacks before." In another case Mary Treadwell explained that Toney "made frequent suggestions as to the treatment to be used, which led to inquiries on my part, as to whether he had been before afflicted in the same way. He replied that he had been subject to similar attacks and had generally been relieved by drinking soap suds . . . [and] by being put in a barrel of warm water." Sarah Stephens added that she heard Toney "suggest the use of red pepper, which he generally carried in his pocket. . . . [H]e often asked for syrup and said meat would hurt him."[83]

Despite the defendant-seller's objections to this testimony, the Alabama court ruled that slaves' declarations "are admissible evidence upon the principle of *res gestae* as well as from the necessity of the case." However, slave statements regarding previous illness would only be admissible if made to a physician. The court cautioned that if it went too far in allowing statements as reported to other witnesses, such as "the female witnesses who disposed in this case, . . . it would be an easy matter to prove slaves unsound by their declarations of their unsoundness, oftentimes feigned as an excuse to avoid labor, or to procure a change of masters." Thus, the Alabama Supreme Court ruled in *Blackman v. Johnson* that a witness could not testify that a slave prayed or called on others to pray for him as evidence of sickness.[84]

Conclusion

The introduction of slave testimony threatened slavery because it introduced right into the courtroom the specter of the deceitful slave manipulating whites. The possibility that a slave might deceive one into believing in his illness, idiocy, or whiteness, impugned a white man's honor in the deepest way. More than any other kind of dispute, those invoking whites' fear of being tricked by blacks demonstrate why it cannot be true that "the slaves' influence on sales law . . . was akin to that of horses, rather than to that of persons."[85] Slaves *were* people, whether or not "the law," as constituted by legislatures and appellate judges, recognized them as such. As people, they behaved in ways, consciously and unconsciously, that wreaked havoc with judges' efforts to treat them as things or horses. If a horse turned out to be lame or vicious, it did not create a trial scene in which a man's neighbors came out to accuse him of being unable to control his plantation.[86] A horse could not provide a challenge to a white man's honor.

Furthermore, a horse could not provide a challenge to the system of slavery the way a resistant slave could. As James Oakes has shown, "liberalism . . . provided the slaves with the crack into which their acts of resistance drove the decisive wedge."[87] Runaway slaves forced conflict to the surface in cases of comity—but they did so in more mundane disputes as well. Slave resistance assumed political significance in Southern courts because the courts were an arena in which Southerners faced the most difficulty in reconciling slavery to their liberal institutions. The "tone of desperation" Oakes found "hover[ing] over the case law of slavery in the Old South" is apparent in the appellate decisions of "moral qualities" warranty cases, as judges tried to shut Pandora's box.[88] Lawyers and judges confronted slave resistance by promoting stories about the origins and development of slave character and behavior that removed rational agency from slaves. In this way the law created an image of blackness as an absence of will, what Patricia Williams has called "antiwill."[89]

Yet reading trial records shows how incomplete a picture of "the law" appellate opinions provide. If what happened in courtrooms, in the common experience and consciousness of ordinary people, was "law"— if "law" is one of the "great cultural formations of human life"—then it is impossible to pin down one integrated version of "the good slave" under "the law."[90] Buyers, sellers, hirers, owners, and overseers all told different stories about why slaves behaved as they did and had the "character" they had. The portrayal of slave character as malleable, dependent on a master's management, benefited slave sellers and owners; "medicalizing" slave vices as "habits" or "addictions" benefited buyers and nonowners who damaged slaves. Because the conflict devolved so often into a debate over mutability or immutability of character, the focus inevitably shifted from slaves to masters. These cases mattered in Southern culture precisely because putting black character on trial put white character on trial.

Notes

I want to thank Robert Gordon, Janet Halley, George Fredrickson, Paul Finkelman, Winthrop Jordan, Samuel Gross, Thomas Grey, Patricia Williams, Terry Fisher, Armstead Robinson, Gwendolyn Hall, Jon Goldman, Wendy Lynch,

Leslie Harris, Alice Yang Murray, Karen Dunn-Haley, and the members of the U.S. History Workshop at Stanford for invaluable comments on drafts of this article. This article was prepared while I was a fellow at the Stanford Humanities Center and is a selection from a dissertation-in-progress by the same title. I am grateful for research funds provided by the American Historical Association, the Stanford Humanities Center, and the Center for Research on Legal Institutions. An earlier version of this chapter appeared in *Yale Journal of Law & Humanities* 267–316 (1995).

1. Thomas R. R. Cobb, *An Inquiry into the Law of Negro Slavery in the United States of America* (1858; reprint, New York: Negro Universities Press, 1968), p. 83. As Alan Watson notes in his article in this volume, the "thinking property" in Rome could act as a person in a variety of contexts that were not open to American slaves. Most sales contracts for slaves included a declaration that a slave was "sound in body and mind and a slave for life," so these suits were for breach of an express contract. If there was no express contract, the states varied in their approach. South Carolina followed the old rule, "a sound price implies a sound article," while most other states were moving to a rule of "caveat emptor" ("buyer beware"). *Timrod v. Shoolbred*, 1 S.C.L. (1 Bay 324) (1793). Louisiana's Civil Code included strict consumer protections providing for rescission (or "redhibition") of slave sales in the event of "redhibitory" defects such as illness, madness, addiction to theft, or the habit of running away. 1824 La. Civ. Code, chap. 6, § 3, "Of the Vices of Things Sold," art. 2496–2505. See also Andrew Fede, "Legal Protection for Slave Buyers in the U.S. South: A Caveat Concerning Caveat Emptor," 31 *American Journal of Legal History* 322 (1987); Judith K. Schafer, "'Guaranteed against the Vices and Maladies Prescribed by Law': Consumer Protection, the Law of Slave Sales, and the Supreme Court in Antebellum Louisiana," 31 *American Journal of Legal History* 306 (1987); Judith K. Schafer, "'Details Are of a Most Revolting Character': Cruelty to Slaves as Seen in Appeals to the Supreme Court of Louisiana," in this volume.

2. This article is based on a review of published state supreme court reports of civil disputes involving slaves in South Carolina, Georgia, Alabama, Mississippi, and Louisiana, 1800-1870 (about six hundred cases); all of the available trial records of those cases in South Carolina, Georgia, Alabama, and Mississippi (about two hundred) and all those directly involving slave character in Louisiana (about seventy); as well as a survey of the unappealed cases in Adams County, Mississippi, 1798–1861 (ten thousand out of a total of thirty thousand causes of action; one hundred seventy-seven were full-blown trials involving slaves).

3. *Smith v. McCall*, 12 S.C.L. (1 McCord) 220, 224 (1821).

4. Andrew Fede, "Legal Protection for Slave Buyers," 323. Indeed, some legal historians have denied the existence of a "person/property" tension in the law of slavery at all, arguing that slaves were simply property that had human qualities. See, e.g., Andrew Fede, *People without Rights* (New York: Garland, 1992); Leon Higginbotham and Barbara Kopytoff, "Property First, Humanity Second: The Recognition of the Slave's Human Nature in Virginia Civil Law," 50 *Ohio State Law Journal* 511 (1989). Kenneth Greenberg has shown the symbiosis of ideals of mastery and statesmanship in antebellum Southern culture. Kenneth Greenberg, *Masters and Statesmen* (Baltimore: Johns Hopkins University Press, 1985). *Smith v. McCall, supra* note 3, at 224. See Mark Tushnet, *The American Law*

of Slavery, 1810–1860 (Princeton: Princeton University Press, 1981) for a discussion of this attempted separation, which he calls the division of "law" and "sentiment."

5. The term *character*, in the antebellum period, was sometimes used to mean "reputation," as in, "he gave his good character," or "he had the character in the neighborhood as a ———." This usage does not necessarily mean, however, that *character* referred to something less important because exterior. While New Englanders recognized a strong division between external appearances and one's inner, "true" self, so that reputation could serve only as *evidence* of character, Kenneth Greenberg has recently shown the extent to which, for nineteenth-century Southerners, appearances *were* what mattered. Kenneth S. Greenberg, "The Nose, the Lie, and the Duel in the Antebellum South," *American Historical Review* 57, 63 (1992).

6. William W. Fisher III, "Ideology and Imagery in the Law of Slavery," in this volume. George Fredrickson, *The Arrogance of Race* (Middletown, Conn.: Wesleyan University Press, 1988), 211.

7. *White v. Cumming*, docket #357, Alexandria series, 1826, La. Supreme Court Archives, Earl K. Long Library, University of New Orleans (hereinafter cited as SCA-UNO), appeal reported in 5 Mart. (n.s.) 199 (La. 1826); testimony of William Rudder, *Castillanos v. Peillon*, docket #944, New Orleans, May 1824, SCA-UNO, appeal reported in 2 Mart. (n.s. 466) (La. 1824); testimony of Etienne Girard, *Petit v. Laville*, docket #4660, New Orleans, June 1843, SCA-UNO, appeal reported in 5 Rob. 117 (La. 1843); *Pahnvitz v. Fassman*, docket #512, New Orleans, June 1847, SCA-UNO, appeal reported in 2 La. Ann. 625 (1847).

8. See, e.g., *Chretien v. Theard*, docket #612, New Orleans, Feb. 1822, SCA-UNO, appeal reported in 11 Mart. 11 (La. 1822); *Lewis v. Casenave*, docket #2559, New Orleans, Dec. 1833, SCA-UNO, appeal reported in 6 La. 437 (1833); *Pilie v. Lalande*, docket #1724, New Orleans, Mar. 1829, SCA-UNO, appeal reported in 7 Mart. (n.s.) 558 (La. 1829). See also *Walker v. Hays*, docket #6606, New Orleans, Feb. 1860, SCA-UNO, appeal reported in 15 La. Ann. 640 (1860) ("The plaintiff . . . established by Mr. Hair that [Agnes] was a very intelligent servant" [plaintiff's brief]); see, e.g., *Horlbeck v. Erickson*, 39 S.C.L. (6 Rich.) 154, 158 (1852); *Farmer v. Fiske*, docket #5248, New Orleans, Dec. 1844, SCA-UNO, appeal reported in 9 Rob. 351 (La. 1844).

9. Complaint, *Taylor v. Cochran*, drawer 7 #1441, June 1802, Adams County Court, Mississippi Territory, Historic Natchez Foundation (hereinafter cited as *HNF*); memo (by judge?), *Perkins v. Hundley*, drawer 91 #25, May 1819, Adams County Cir. Ct., Miss., HNF; deposition of William Shaffer, *Tull v. Walker*, drawer 70, May 1830, Adams County, Miss. Cir. Ct., HNF; see, e.g., *Laurence v. McFarlane*, docket #1722, New Orleans, *SCA-UNO*, Mar. 1829, appeal reported in 7 Mart. (n.s.) 558 (La. 1829) ("sold [Fanny] because she was lazy"); *Romer v. Woods, f.w.c.*, (free woman of color), docket #1911, New Orleans, Jan. 1851, SCA-UNO, appeal reported in 6 La. Ann. 29 (1851); see, e.g., *Icar v. Suares*, docket #2649, New Orleans, Jan. 1835, SCA-UNO, appeal reported in 7 La. 517 (1835); *Briant v. Marsh*, 19 La. 391 (Sept. 1841).

10. *Cozzins v. Whitacker*, docket #1261, book 34, Jan. 1833, Ala. Supreme Court Records, Alabama Department of Archives and History (hereinafter cited as ADAH).

11. Ibid.

12. Testimony of Thomas N. Gadsden, *Gantt* v. *Venning*, City Court of Charleston, box 34, Jan. 1840, S.C. Supreme Court Records, South Carolina Department of Archives and History (hereinafter cited as SCDAH), appeal reported in 25 S.C.L. (Chev.) 87 (1840); *Campbell* ads. *Atchison*, box 21, Mar. 1827, S.C. Supreme Court Records, *SCDAH*. The word *old* in the first quotation from *Campbell* was added to the transcript in a different ink.

13. *Brocklebank* v. *Johnson*, box 28, Apr. 1834, S.C. Supreme Court Records, *SCDAH*, appeal reported in *Johnson* v. *Brockelbank*, 20 S.C.L. (2 Hill) 353 (1834); see also *Nowell* v. *Gadsden*, City Court of Charleston, box 42, May 1848, S.C. Supreme Court Records, *SCDAH*, appeal unreported (breach of warranty for Lander because of illness and lack of skill as blacksmith); *Chretien* v. *Theard*, *supra* note 8 (buyer "instantly discovered that [Lafortune] was neither a carpenter nor joiner . . . a drunkard and a thief and also an insubordinate slave"); *Athey* v. *Olive*, 34 Ala. 711, 712–13 (1859) (defendant refused to pay note because Matilda was crazy and because "Matilda . . . was represented by the plaintiff to be a good cook, washer and ironer, and seamstress, that she came up to neither of these representations").

14. *Petit* v. *Laville*, *supra* note 7. See also *Buhler* v. *McHatton*, docket #3448, New Orleans, Mar. 1854, *SCA-UNO*, appeal reported in 9 La. Ann. 192 (1854) ("Jane has proved entirely useless as a cook, and 2d, because she is addicted to madness, insanity, or habitual craziness.").

15. *Cretien* v. *Theard*, *supra* note 8.

16. *Stone & Best* v. *Watson*, 37 Ala. 279 (1861); *Campbell* ads. *Atchison*, *supra* note 12; *Porcher* v. *Caldwell*, box 37, Mar. 1842, S.C. Supreme Court Records, *SCDAH*, appeal reported in 27 S.C.L. (2 McMul.) 329 (1842).

17. George M. Fredrickson, *The Black Image in the White Mind: The Debate on Afro-American Character and Destiny, 1817–1914* (New York: Harper and Row, 1971), 53–54, 52. Dr. Samuel Cartwright, "Negro Freedom an Impossibility under Nature's Laws," *DeBow's Review*, 30 (1860): 651; H., "Remarks on Overseers, and the Proper Treatment of Slaves," *Farmers' Register* 5 (1837): 302.

18. James Oakes, *Slavery and Freedom: An Interpretation of the Old South* (New York: Knopf, 1990), chap. 1; Orlando Patterson, *Slavery and Social Death* (Cambridge, Mass.: Harvard University Press, 1982); see also Fredrickson, *Arrogance of Race*, 159; Kenneth Greenberg, *Masters and Statesmen*, 65. The dishonor of slaves played out in the law, as, for example, when slave testimony was barred because slaves could not be trusted to tell the truth, unlike honorable men. Fisher, "Ideology and Imagery." On the history of the idea of moral sense in the South, see E. Brooks Holifield, *The Gentleman Theologians: American Theology in Southern Culture, 1795–1860* (Durham, N.C.: Duke University Press, 1978), chap. 5.

19. See, e.g., the articles collected in J. D. B. DeBow, ed., *The Industrial Resources, Statistics, etc., of the United States, and More Particularly of the Southern and Western States*, [3d ed.] (1854; reprints, New York: A. M. Kelley), vol. 2, including John Campbell, "Negro-Mania: Being an Examination of the Falsely-Assumed Equality of the Various Races of Men" ("Lawrence remarks, that the difference of color 'between the white and the black races is not more striking than the preeminence of the former in moral feelings and in mental endowments'"); "Negro Slavery—Memoir on, by Chancellor Harper; Prepared for, and Read before, the Society for the Advancement of Learning, of South Carolina" ("Objection answered—'The slave is cut off from the means of intellectual, moral,

and religious improvement, and in consequence his moral character becomes depraved, and he addicted to degrading vices'"—arguing that the slave cannot improve himself because he has not the capacity for moral character development). See also Cobb, *Law of Negro Slavery*, 37–38 (considering "[T]he development of his moral character, when in contact with civilization," and finding that blacks "exhibit the same characteristics" of moral degradation, whatever the circumstances).

20. "Dr. Cartwright on the Caucasians and the Africans," *DeBow's Review* 32 (1861): 53–54. See also Cobb, *Law of Negro Slavery*, 35 ("[T]he negro . . . is imitative, sometimes eminently so, but his mind is never inventive or suggestive. Improvement never enters into his imagination").

21. *Johnson* v. *Wideman*, 24 S.C.L. (Rice) 325 (1839). In this case the seller sued the buyer because he did not pay his note.

22. Ibid. at 326–28.

23. Ibid. at 330–35.

24. Ibid. at 332–33.

25. Ibid. at 334–40.

26. Ibid. at 337–39.

27. He began by instructing the jury that the defendant could not recover tort damages for the plaintiff's deceit; the only question would be whether the defendant was obligated to pay the hundred-dollar note. Ibid. at 342. This is a legal issue that cropped up frequently: the distinction between *breach of warranty*, a contract action, which could only result in a return of the slave and/or refund of the price, and *deceit*, a tort action, for which the injured party could recover damages. However, the judge, having settled the legal issue, made it clear that the moral issues would decide the case. He also instructed the jury that they must find evidence of fraud in order for the buyer-defendant to win.

28. Ibid. at 342. Emphasis added.

29. Ibid. at 342–43. The jury found for the seller-plaintiff, Johnson; Wideman appealed on the grounds that the judge's instructions had biased the jury for the plaintiff by ruling out damages for the defendant. In a per curiam opinion, Chief Justice O'Neall affirmed the lower-court judgment. Ibid. at 344–45.

30. Fredrickson, *Arrogance of Race*, 215.

31. See also *Cozzins* v. *Whitacker, supra* note 10 ("[plaintiff's w]itness Mr. Henry Fort proved . . . that he Anthony would steal chickens &c and run away and that, that was his character"; but defendant's witness, Mr. Madden, testified "that it was very common amongst Negroes to steal a little and run away, it was greatly owing to the kind of master or owner they had"); *Perkins* v. *Hundley*, drawer 91 #25, May Term 1819, Adams County, Miss. Cir. Ct., *HNF* (Lawton was a good slave under his master, but "after his master died [Lawton] became a little unruly which was the reason of his being sold").

32. *Moran* v. *Davis*, docket #1561, Apr. 1855, Ga. Supreme Court Records, *GDAH*. Appeal reported in 18 Ga. 722 (1855). In *Thornton* v. *Towns* Jesse Thornton charged that Andrew Towns had violated a hire contract by his cruel treatment of several slaves. Towns argued that "Golding is bad and idle and troublesome and complainant confessed to Respondent that he was an idle and careless negro and would stay out from his work." Golding's bad character, according to Towns, fully justified his harsh treatment. Docket #3869, Jan. 1865, Ga. Supreme Court Records, *GDAH*. Appeal reported in 34 Ga. 1225 (1865).

33. *Hagan* v. *Rist,* docket #4503, eastern district, June 1844, 8 Rob. 106 (La. 1844); *Taylor* v. *Cochran,* drawer 7 #1441, June 1802, Adams Cty. Ct., Miss., *HNF.*

34. *Castillanos* v. *Peillon, supra* note 7.

35. *Ward* v. *Reynolds,* docket #4181, book 221, Perry Cty. Cir. Ct., Jan. 1858, *ADAH,* appeal reported in 32 Ala. 384 (1858).

36. *Guice* v. *Holmes,* drawer 347, 1854, Adams County, Miss., *HNF.*

37. *Cotton* v. *Rogolio,* drawer 202 #143, Apr. 1837, Adams Cty. Cir. Ct., Miss., HNF; *Morton* v. *Bradley,* docket #4175, book 215, June 1857 4–5, no. 2, Ala. Sup. Ct. Records, ADAH, appeal reported in 30 Ala. 683 (1857).

38. White supremacists often gave immutable viciousness, or at least underlying savagery, as proof of the subhumanity of the entire Negro race. See Fredrickson, *Black Image.*

39. James O. Breeden, ed., *Advice among Masters: The Ideal in Slave Management in the Old South* (Westport, Conn.: Greenwood Press, 1980), 139.

40. *DeBow's Review* 11 (1842): 65, 209, 331, 504; reprinted in *Industrial Resources,* vol. 2, 318–19, 325.

41. This extract and the following paragraph drawn from ibid., 320–23.

42. Ibid., 323; Cartwright, "On the Caucasians and the Africans," 51.

43. William Stanton, *The Leopard's Spots: Scientific Attitudes toward Race in America, 1815–1859* (Chicago: University of Chicago Press, 1960), vii. See Cartwright, "Negro Freedom an Impossibility, 648 (on identity of Negroes and serpents); Samuel Cartwright, "Unity of Human Race Disproved," *DeBow's Review* 29 (1860): 129; and the responses to it: "Dr. Cartwright on the Serpent, the Ape and the Negro," *DeBow's Review* 32 (1861): 507; "Dr. Cartwright Reviewed—The Negro, Ape and Serpent," *DeBow's Review* 32 (1861): 238; "Dr. Cartwright on the Negro, Reviewed," *DeBow's Review* 32 (1861): 54; "Dr. Cartwright on the Negro—Reviewed," *DeBow's Review* 33 (1861): 62. See, e.g., A. P. Merrill, M.D., "Plantation Hygeine," *Southern Agriculturist* 267 1 (Sept. 1851): 267; Dr. J. S. Wilson, "Peculiarities and Diseases of Negroes," *DeBow's Review* 28 (1860), 29 (1860): 112; see generally Todd L. Savitt, *Medicine and Slavery: The Diseases and Health Care of Blacks in Antebellum Virginia* (Urbana: University of Illinois Press, 1978), 1–184, and numerous articles by Southerners on black medical distinctiveness cited therein.

44. 1824 La. Civ. Code, Bk. III, Tit. 7 chap. 6, § 3, art. 2505. "The slave shall be considered as being in the habit of running away, when he shall have absented himself from his master's house twice for several days, or once for more than a month." The statutory rule was varied by case law when a slave was new to the state. See Judith Schafer, "'Guaranteed against the Vices and Maladies Prescribed by Law.'" See, e.g., *Ward* v. *Reynolds, supra* note 35 ("addictedness to running away"); *Mizell* v. *Sims,* 39 Miss. 331, 333 (1860) ("not a runaway nor in the habit of running away" vs. "a habitual runaway"); *James* v. *Kirk,* drawer 348 #55, May 1853, Adams Cty. Miss., *HNF,* appeal reported in 29 Miss. 206 (1855) ("the character of a runaway" and "the habit of running away"); *Tull* v. *Walker,* drawer 70 #2744, 1830, Adams Cty., Miss., *HNF; Campbell* v. *Kinloch,* Charleston, Fall 1857, S.C. Supreme Court Records, *SCDAH,* appeal unreported.

45. *Icar* v. *Suares, supra* note 9.

46. *Suares* v. *Icar,* 7 La. at 518.

47. *Chapuis* v. *Schmelger,* docket #2328, New Orleans, Dec. 1851, SCA-UNO. Dismissed, unreported.

48. *Briant* v. *Marsh*, 19 La. 391, 392 (1841). See also *Nelson* v. *Biggers*, docket #428, Ga. Sup. Ct. Records, *GDAH* (breach of warranty for "Betty, from imbecility of mind . . . a slave incapable of performing ordinary work and labor"). Witnesses for the buyer testified that the seller had said that Betty "had not sense to raise her child and they took it from her and raised it in the house for she had overlaid her first one"; Osborn Unchurch, the buyer's overseer, "put her Betty to dropping corn and she could not do it for she had to be shown the place to drop and I put her to cover corn with manure and she did not have sense to do that"; however, the seller's witness, James Heagans, testified that while Betty was not "as bright as some negroes," she was capable of the ordinary work of field hands. The lower court judge excluded this testimony; the buyer won. On appeal, the Georgia Supreme Court found error in the interpretation of the word *healthy* in the warranty as applying to mind as well as body, and reversed.

49. *Buhler* v. *McHatton*, *supra* note 14.

50. *Walker* v. *Hays*, *supra* note 8.

51. *Thomas* v. *Selser*, docket #4774, New Orleans, Mar. 1842, SCA-UNO, appeal reported in 1 Rob. 425 (La. 1842).

52. *Reynolds* v. *White*, docket #3982, New Orleans, Jan. 1849, SCA-UNO, unreported.

53. *Anderson* v. *Dacosta*, docket #996, New Orleans, Feb. 1849, SCA-UNO, appeal reported in 4 La. Ann. 136 (1849); *Romer* v. *Woods, f.w.c., supra* note 9.

54. *Collins* v. *Lester*, docket #1349, May 1854, Ga. Sup. Ct. Records, *GDAH*, appeal reported in 16 Ga. 410 (1854).

55. *Maury* v. *Coleman*, docket #3063, book 174 #4, Jan. 1854, Ala. Supreme Court, ADAH; *Farmer* v. *Fiske, supra* note 8; *Morton* v. *Bradley, supra* note 37; *Mangham* v. *Cox & Waring*, docket #2952, book 1856, 1st div., no. 32, Ala. Supreme Court Records, *ADAH*; see also *Sessions* v. *Cartwright*, drawer 342 #142, Nov. 1851, Adams Cty. Cir. Ct., Miss., *HNF*; *Cotton* v. *Rogolio, supra* note 37.

56. *Martin* v. *Bosley*, drawer 49, folder 3E, 1805, Adams Cty. Cir. Ct., Miss., HNF.

57. This seems to be an unusual twist on the perennial "rules vs. standards" debate, an instance where a rule gives more leeway than a standard. See Duncan Kennedy, "Form and Substance in Private Law Adjudication," 89 *Harvard Law Revue* 1685 (1976).

58. *Fortier* v. *LaBranche*, docket #3289, New Orleans, June 1839, SCA-UNO, appeal reported in 13 La. 355 (1839). Similarly, a slave buyer was denied rescision of the sale in *Smith* v. *McDowell* when the court found that the slave had only been returning (twice) to his former owner's plantation to see his wife. Docket #4431, New Orleans, Jan. 1843 SCA-UNO, appeal reported in 3 Rob. 430 (La. 1843).

59. *Bocod* v. *Jacobs*, 2 La. 408, 410 (1831). Trial transcript is docket #2101, New Orleans, June 1831, SCA-UNO. *Nott* v. *Botts*, docket #3123, New Orleans, Mar. 1839, SCA-UNO, appeal reported in 13 La. 202 (1839).

60. *Kirk* v. *James*, docket #7049, Apr. 1855, Adams Cty. Cir. Ct., Miss., HNF, appeal reported in 29 Miss. 206 (1855). James's trading business had him in the courts often; he defended three suits for breach of warranty in the Adams County Circuit Court in 1849–50 alone.

Four juries heard Kirk's suit against James. The first jury found for James, and Kirk was granted a new trial; two successive trials ended in mistrial. In 1853 the fourth jury found for Kirk, and Judge Stanhope Posey overruled James's motion for a new trial. James then lost his appeal to the Mississippi High Court of Errors and Appeals.

61. *James* v. *Kirk,* 29 Miss. at 208. In fact, habitual drinking was often considered as a "relative vice" in Louisiana cases. Justice Handy was unmoved by James's argument, affirming the lower-court judgment for Kirk. In this case, he ruled, the Louisiana rules were not mere evidentiary regulations unenforceable in Mississippi; they were express stipulations of the contract itself. Ibid. at 211.

62. *Trapier* v. *Avant,* box 21, 1827, S.C. Supreme Court Records, *SCDAH.* Trapier's slaves drowned crossing in Avant's ferry; disputed facts included whether crossing in a paddleboat rather than a "flat" was contrary to custom and whether Avant's ferryman had been negligent, or even present, at the time of the drowning.

63. Ibid.

64. For a useful discussion of the application of another tort liability rule, the fellow-servant rule, to slaves, see Paul Finkelman, "Northern Labor Law and Southern Slave Law: The Application of the Fellow Servant Rule to Slaves," 11 *National Black Law Journal* 212 (1989). Finkelman argues that it was precisely because of the limits on slaves' agency—in this case, their ability to avoid dangerous work conditions—that Southern courts refused to apply this rule to slaves.

65. In the trial records, the slave's name appears as both "Sam" and "Landon"; in the supreme court report it is reprinted as "London."

66. *Gorman* v. *Campbell,* docket #1175, June 1853, Ga. Supreme Court Records, GDAH, appeal reported in 14 Ga. 137 (1853).

67. Judge Lumpkin of the Georgia Supreme Court overturned the lower court verdict, finding for the slave owner. 14 Ga. 137 (1853); see Finkelman, "Northern Labor Law and Southern Slave Law," 230; see also *Wilder* v. *Richardson,* 23 S.C.L. (Dud.) 323, 324 (1838) ("To run away is an act arising from the volition of the slave"); *Horlbeck* v. *Erickson, supra* note 8 ("The slave being a moral agent, and having volition, adventured from the impulses of his nature") (both hire cases).

68. I found no instances of parties in the courtroom explicitly comparing slaves to animals, although very occasionally a party cited cases involving unsound pigs or horses to bolster his legal argument. *Scarborough* v. *Reynolds,* 46 S.C.L. (13 Rich.) 98 (1860) (plaintiff argued that a slave with a crooked arm was unsound, citing cases in which lame horses were ruled unsound); *Barnes* v. *Blair,* 16 Ala. 71, 72 (1849) (citing horse cases).

69. *Outlaw & McClellan* v. *Cook,* Minor 257, 257–58 (Ala. 1824); *Hogan* v. *Carr & Anderson,* 6 Ala. 471, 472 (1844). See also *Mayor & Council of Columbus* v. *Howard,* 6 Ga. 213, 219 (1849) ("If a man hires a horse, he is bound to ride it moderately"); John E. Stealey, "The Responsibilities and Liabilities of the Bailee of Slave Labor in Virginia," 12 *American Journal of Legal History* 336 (1968).

70. *Cozzins* v. *Whitacker, supra* note 10; *Walton* v. *Jordan,* docket #2099, Mar. 1857, Ga. Supreme Court, GDAH, appeal reported in 23 Ga. 420 (1857). *Stevenson* v. *Reaves,* docket #4043, book 171, Barbour Cty. Cir. Ct., Jan. 1854, Ala. Supreme Court Records, ADAH, appeal reported in 24 Ala. 425 (1854).

71. *Hopkins* v. *Tilman,* docket #2268, Sept. 1857, Ga. Supreme Court Records, GDAH, appeal reported in 25 Ga. 212, 213 (1858); *Laurence* v. *McFarlane, supra* note 9.

72. *Buhler* v. *McHatton, supra* note 14.

73. Cross-examination of Hugh M. Coffee, plaintiff's witness, *Perkins* v. *Hundley, supra* note 9.

74. *Wallace & Wallace* v. *Spullock*, docket #3608, Dec. 1860, Ga. Supreme Court Records, GDAH, appeal reported in 32 Ga. 488 (1861).

75. Cobb, *Law of Negro Slavery*, 231.

76. *George* v. *Bean*, docket #7418, Dec. 1855, Chickasaw Cty. Cir. Ct., MDAH record group 32, drawer 105, appeal reported in 30 Miss. 147 (1855).

77. *Brocklebank* v. *Johnson, supra* note 13; *Dinkins* ads. *Parkerson*, Box 34, 1839, S.C. Sup. Ct. Records, SCDAH.

78. *Cotton* v. *Rogollio, supra*; *Barnaby* v. *Tomlinson*, drawer 31, 1805, Adams Cty. Cir. Ct., Miss., HNF.

79. *Bush* v. *Jackson*, docket #4012, book 174 no. 14, Jan. 1854, Ala. Supreme Court Records, ADAH. See also *Tilman* v. *Stringer*, docket #2486, 1858, Ga. Supreme Court Records, GDAH ("counsel for defendant objected to the witness' stating any thing as to what the negro said in regard to her situation and that she complained—in the ground that it was hearsay—the Court overruled the objection and allowed the testimony. . . . stated that the negro complained of head ache and said she had pains in her back and side and shoulders.").

80. *Hill* v. *Winston*, drawer 336 #25, May 1849, Adams Cty. Cir. Ct., Miss., HNF.

81. See Thomas D. Morris, "Slaves and the Rules of Evidence in Criminal Trials," in this volume.

82. *Fondren* v. *Durfee*, 39 Miss. 324 (1860).

83. *Bates* v. *Eckles & Brown*, Jan. 1855, Ala. Supreme Court Record Book 153, ADAH, appeal reported in 26 Ala. 655 (1855).

84. 26 Ala. at 659-60; *Blackman* v. *Johnson*, 35 Ala. 252 (1859); see also *Stringfellow & Hobson* v. *Mariott*, 11 Ala. 573 (1836) (admitting slave's declarations to prove *scienter* on the part of the vendor); *Barker* v. *Coleman*, 35 Ala. 221 (1859).

85. Fede, "Legal Protection for Slave Buyers," 323.

86. See, e.g., *Ferguson* v. *Nelson*, drawer 356 #25, May 1859, Adams Cty. Cir. Ct., Miss., HNF (white horse warranted as "sound and gentle" turned out to be "unsound and scary"); *Brown* v. *Jones*, Misc. Ct. Cases, Briefs, Etc., 1820-1873, SG 2803, Ala. Supreme Court Records, ADAH (horse warranted sound).

87. Oakes, *Slavery and Freedom*, 139.

88. Ibid., 160.

89. Patricia Williams, *The Alchemy of Race and Rights: Diary of a Law Professor* (Cambridge: Harvard University Press, 1991), 219.

90. Clifford Geertz, *Local Knowledge* (New York: Basic Books, 1983), 219. I accept Geertz's "two propositions, that law is local knowledge not placeless principle and that it is constructive of social life not reflective, or anyway not just reflective, of it." Ibid., 218.

10

Slave Auctions on the Courthouse Steps: Court Sales of Slaves in Antebellum South Carolina

Thomas D. Russell

IN JUST OVER ONE hundred auction sales at the beginning of twenty-two different months in 1845 and 1846, Jeremiah Cockrell, sheriff of Fairfield District, South Carolina, sold 311 slaves, 15,450.5 acres (24.1 square miles) of land, 99 cows, 102 pigs, 36 horses, 28 mules, 44 sheep, 3 yokes of oxen, 3 pianos, and a variety of other personal property of between eighty and ninety debtors and then distributed the total proceeds of $127,589.50 to more than 225 creditors. Cockrell was an agent of the courts, and the courts acted as the state's greatest auctioneering firm. Fifty percent of South Carolina's antebellum sales of slaves took place at court sales, which included sheriffs' sales like Cockrell's and also probate and equity court sales. These sales by operation of law were all auction sales. Because not all noncourt sales were by auction, the courts' slave auctions comprised the majority of South Carolina's slave auctions. Cockrell and the courts were thus at the center of the domestic slave trade.[1]

By no sensible standard can court sales be regarded as marginal or unimportant to antebellum social, economic, or legal life. For example, the 311 slaves that Sheriff Cockrell sold during the two-year period comprised 2.3 percent of the district's total slave population in 1845. On average, Fairfield District's sheriff sold 1.2 percent of the district's slaves during each of the two years. Excluding the sales of houses and lots, he sold forty-two different parcels of land, an average of 7,720 acres per year. Using the 1850 federal census figures as a rough approximation of the 1845–46 figures, Cockrell thus sold an average of 2.2 percent of the district's farmland each year.[2]

Through law the sales channeled power into the lives of those whose property was sold and, further, into the lives of those sold as property.

The large amount of cash that Sheriff Cockrell handled as a result of these auctions reflects the magnitude of his sales and, therefore, the power of the courts. For purposes of comparison, the total tax revenue and total expenditures of South Carolina's state government are useful figures. The total state tax revenue during 1845 and 1846 was $607,321. The state's expenditures amounted to slightly more, a total of $611,102; one-third of this amount paid salaries in the judicial, legislative, and executive branches; another tenth maintained the state's militia and arsenals. Cockrell's receipts—that is, the money that passed through his hands—equalled just over 20 percent of the state's entire tax receipts. The Fairfield sheriff handled and disbursed one-fifth of the amount of money that the state's treasurer managed.[3]

Another indicator of the great volume of Sheriff Cockrell's sales comes from his livestock sales. During the two years, Cockrell sold about the same number of animals as human beings. Again using the 1850 census figures as an approximation of the 1845–46 figures, the sheriff sold 0.8 percent of the horses, 0.4 percent of the cows, 4.5 percent of the oxen, 0.6 percent of the mules, and 0.3 percent of the sheep each year. His livestock sales were substantial, although the percentage of the district's livestock that he sold, with the exception of the three yokes of oxen, did not reach the yearly averages for slave (1.2 percent) and land (2.2 percent) sales. One possible explanation for the smaller fraction of livestock sold is that debtor-farmers might have had proportionally less livestock than solvent farmers. Another explanation is that slaves—the farmer's most liquid and valuable capital assets—were usually among the first property the sheriff offered for sale. Although statute allowed a debtor-slaveholder to reserve slaves from sale until other property was sold, sale books indicate that typically the sheriff would not sell the farmer's livestock, farm implements, and household goods until the end of the sale and would not sell them at all if receipts from the other property sold met the debt.[4]

This basic finding must force historians to discard certain presumptions regarding the relationship of slavery, economy, and law. For example, analysts of the economics of slavery, now alert to the central role of the courts in the conduct of slave sales, can no longer regard the economic transactions of slavery as taking place within a realm of purely private ordering. Courts were neither marginal nor unimportant with regard to slave sales, and so economic historians must grapple with the role of legal institutions. Similarly, other historians of slavery can no longer justify treating the relationship of master and slave as largely hermetic. Masters were powerful, but through the operation of law, many additional actors, institutions, and norms joined the relationship of slaveholder and slave.

The basic quantitative finding of this essay is important for scholars interested in legal aspects of slavery's history. Obviously, the finding of the courts' central role in the domestic slave trade supports the efforts of those who argue that one must comprehend the operation of law in order to understand slavery more fully. More interestingly, the finding supports the idea that in the United States the history of law and issues of race are necessarily and intimately linked. For example, this finding supports Sanford Levinson's effort to center slavery in the constitutional law canon.[5] Levinson's project is a good one, but this essay's finding can serve as a vaccine against the next possible step, which would be to presume that the constitutional aspects of slavery were the most important legal aspects of the peculiar institution's history. Some germ—perhaps the supremacy clause?—causes constitutional scholars to take their subject somewhat too seriously; this article's quantitative finding is a reminder that to the extent that law was important in the everyday lives of slaves, it was not the law offered by the United States Supreme Court but rather the law as administered by local trial court judges, masters in chancery, sheriffs, ordinaries, magistrates, justices of the peace, and other miscellaneous and now-forgotten low-level legal officials.

*   *   *

For most people today, auctions of any sort are unusual events. But in antebellum South Carolina, especially in the cities of Charleston and Columbia, auctions were common. Any newspaper—the *Charleston Courier*, for example—was likely to carry at least a column, often more, of daily advertisements for auction sales. These were predominantly commercial sales conducted by merchants. The merchants sold their wares at auction not just in unusual situations of damaged, used, or one-of-a-kind goods, but in the ordinary course of business. These sales included every type of merchandise. Of course, not all the property was goods: there were slave auctions as well.[6]

Included with and often mingled among the auction advertisements were notices of auction sales that courts had ordered or would supervise. Auctions were the typical and traditional manner for sales of property that agents of courts or other state legal institutions supervised. For example, after the War of Independence, the new state's Commissioners of Confiscated Estates sold the seized property of Tories at public outcry. From time to time legislation authorized auction sale of state-owned land. Officials of the court of the ordinary, now the probate court, supervised and sometimes conducted sales of decedents' estates. Masters or commissioners in equity frequently conducted public sales as part of the resolution of suits—technically called "bills" or "petitions"—in the equity court. Like the sales of ordinaries, these were most often sales of the estates of dead persons that were necessary either to pay debts or to partition the estate among heirs. Litigants turned to the equity court when the estates were large or when the matter involved issues more complicated than the court of the ordinary could manage. Even coroners conducted sales under some circumstances, such as when the sheriff was a party to the case or, in some instances, when sheriffs simply refused to conduct the sale.[7]

When slave sales by operation of law have attracted scholarly concern, probate sales have received the most attention. Among scholars interested in legal, social, or economic history, the few who have commented upon courts' slave sales have usually noticed only sales occasioned by the death of the slave owner and the subsequent division of the decedent's estate. Historians, often uninterested in or uncomfortable with the mundane details of nineteenth-century law, have largely ignored sheriffs' and other court-ordered sales. When they have noticed such sales, they have generally minimized these sales as unimportant.[8]

Probate sales—the sales most often noticed by historians—were not the most important type of sales by operation of law. Sheriffs sold more property than other agents of the state. Antebellum sheriffs, it is important to understand, had roles different from the gunslinging crimefighter of cinematic or operatic fame. The great bulk of sheriffs' work concerned civil litigation, not peacekeeping functions such as catching stagecoach robbers and horse thieves. To be sure, sheriffs had a role in the history of antebellum criminal justice, but the duties that consumed most of their efforts were civil rather than criminal in character.[9]

The conduct of sales was among a sheriff's important duties. Most of these sales were execution sales: sales connected with execution of a court's judgment. Execution sales nearly always involved debt. Indeed, the sheriff's office was crucial to antebellum economic transactions. The sheriff and the common-law courts played a key role in the conduct and security of credit transactions, a role that did not begin only after the debtor failed to pay a preexisting loan but, rather, that began with the initiation of the loan. In addition to selling the property of debtors, the sheriff also auctioned property for other reasons. He conducted tax sales when property owners did not pay taxes, usually selling only the use of the property for a term of years, not the absolute ownership of the property.[10]

In specific circumstances the sheriffs could also auction free blacks and convert them into property. In 1820 the South Carolina legislature prohibited free blacks from entering the state and authorized the sheriff to sell, for a term of up to five years, any free black who entered the state, stayed more than fifteen days after being ordered to leave, and failed to pay the twenty dollar fine for overstaying her or his welcome. In December 1822, as part of the stiffening of laws that followed the thwarting of Denmark Vesey's Charleston rebellion, the legislature authorized the auction sale of "every free male negro or person of color, between the ages of fifteen and fifty years" who was either not a South Carolina native or had not lived in the state for more than five years and who did not pay a fifty dollar tax—a huge sum at the time. Other free blacks—females and those males who met the nativity or residency tests—were subject to a móre modest two dollar annual tax. The statute directed the sheriff to sell "[s]uch free negroes, mulattoes and mustizoes, as shall neglect or refuse to pay the tax imposed by law," for a term long enough to pay the tax.[11]

In 1831, for example, Fairfield District tax collector James Beaty directed Sheriff Yongue to arrest Legs and Christina Bird, two free blacks who had failed to pay $9.60 in taxes. The sheriff's fees for making the arrest and other costs were added to the delinquent tax bill, nearly doubling the sum for which the Birds were liable. Fortunately for the Birds, before they were sold, someone helped them by paying the tax bill and associated costs. Thus the powers and responsibilities of sheriffs included the auction conversion of free blacks into property. Generally speaking, however, sales of free blacks who were illegally present in the state or who failed to pay the annual tax on their freedom were extremely rare events.[12]

The more ordinary sales that sheriffs conducted every month involved the property of debtors. South Carolina sheriffs' sales took place on the first Monday of each month, a day known as Sale Day. Sometimes sales would continue on Tuesday as well. This article documents the human and wealth consequences by aggregating data drawn from records of these sales. In addition to exploring sheriffs' sales, this article charts the empirical contours of sales that other legal officials either ordered or supervised, specifically probate and equity court sales. Like sheriffs' sales, these took place on Sale Day.

This article also presents a large body of quantified data for the sales of about twenty-one hundred slaves between 1823 and 1865. These data come from the sale books of sheriffs, masters in chancery, and probate courts in five different South Carolina districts: Edgefield, Fairfield, Marlboro, Newberry, and Union. The different sale books include similar details regarding the sale of slaves and other property. The sheriff's sale book was one of three record books "of good material and strongly bound" that the state legislature directed the sheriff to keep. The sheriff was to record all relevant details of executions, levies, advertisements, and sales, including the names of the parties, descriptions of property sold, dates of sales, purchasers' names, sale prices, and statements about the distribution of proceeds. Sheriffs usually identified the slaves they sold by name and only rarely indicated a slave's age. The records of masters in chancery—the equity court officials who ordered sales—and probate courts contained the same or analogous information. Probate records also generally contained inventories and appraisals of decedents' estates.[13]

The data that form the basis of the quantitative conclusions of this article are not from a statistically random sample. Not all the original sources of the sales data still exist, and the five districts that supplied the

TABLE 1

DATA SAMPLE: DISTRICTS, SLAVES SOLD, AND MONTHS

	Sheriffs'		Probate		Equity Court	
	SLAVES SOLD	MONTHS OF DATA	SLAVES SOLD	MONTHS OF DATA	SLAVES SOLD	MONTHS OF DATA
Edgefield	—	—	420	184	—	—
Fairfield	504	142	—	—	63	49
Marlboro	445	377	384	180	65	100
Newberry	93	15	—	—	—	—
Union	88	40	—	—	45	81
Total	1,130	574	804	364	173	230

data are but a sample of the districts with extant data. Execution of a true, statistically random sample of the extant records would have had three principal effects. First, a research design that included a random sample would have greatly magnified the cost and time necessary for this study. Second, a random sample would not have produced longitudinal data for individual districts; without such contiguous data, it would be impossible to describe trends over time within individual districts.[14] Third, a statistically random sample would draw a bevy of complicated statistics into an otherwise relatively simple, quantitative study.

The five districts that supplied the data comprised one-sixth, or 16.6 percent, of the total number of South Carolina districts in 1860. In 1820 twenty-eight South Carolina districts existed; by 1860 division of two existing districts had raised the number of districts to thirty. In the five decennial censuses between 1820 and 1860, these five districts accounted for just under one-sixth of the state's total population, an average of 16.4 percent. Overall, the five districts averaged a somewhat smaller proportion of the state's slaves, comprising altogether 15.7 percent of the state's slaves.[15]

Edgefield District was representative of not only South Carolina but the South as a whole, according to historian Orville Vernon Burton. Burton is the author of, in his own true words, "a total, almost encyclopedic, history of nineteenth-century Edgefield families and their communities." After careful, serious accumulation and comparison of statistical evidence, Burton has concluded that Edgefield District "was representative of rural South Carolina in the mid-nineteenth century"; that the "demographic patterns (age and gender structure, death and birth rates) were also remarkably like those of rural South Carolina as a whole"; and that the district's "black population as a proportion of the total paralleled that of South Carolina for most of the nineteenth century." Furthermore, Edgefield "was representative of the large Piedmont section of the up-country," which stretched from Georgia through South and North Carolina and into Virginia, and the district's violence was also typical of the South. Burton also found that a number of other historians, including Richard Hofstadter and Clement Eaton, had described events in Edgefield as typical of the South as whole. However, unlike Burton's history, my conclusions are not founded upon the analysis of one district.[16]

Four of the five districts—Edgefield, Fairfield, Union, and Newberry —were in the South Carolina up-country. The up-country is a section of the Piedmont that forms a rough triangle in the northwestern part of the state. Edgefield, which had at all times the greatest population of the five districts, supplied data for fifteen consecutive years of probate sales. As table 1 indicates, during these years of probate sales, 420 slaves were sold at Edgefield's courthouse. Fairfield District lies above the fall line and sand hills that divide the low country from the lower Piedmont and is just north of Richland District, which contains Columbia. Columbia, at almost the geographic center of the state, is the city where the state's

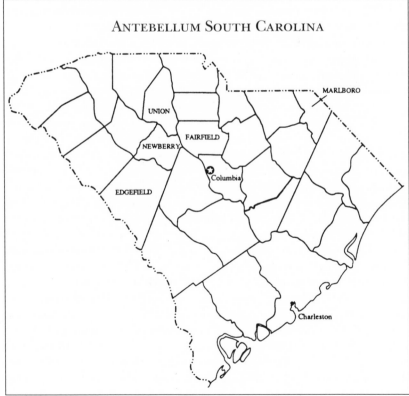

Ellen Lougee

legislature has met since 1790. Newberry, third in terms of population, lies between Fairfield and Edgefield, with Union District lying above Newberry, to the northwest of Fairfield.[17]

Fairfield, which provided data for sheriffs' and equity court sales accounting for more than one-quarter of the 2,107 slave sales this article considers, differed most importantly from Edgefield by its greater proportion of slaves. Fairfield was the second largest of the five districts. In 1850 Edgefield, the largest district, had a total population of 39,262, while Fairfield had 21,404. Edgefield's population in 1820 was 48.6 percent slave, with this proportion growing to 60.3 percent by 1860; Fairfield in 1820 had proportionally fewer slaves—45.1 percent—but over the next four decades, that proportion grew steadily and reached 70.3 percent in 1860.[18] Fairfield was thus somewhat wealthier and even more deeply committed to slavery than Edgefield and the other districts. In this way Fairfield matched some of the common stereotypical views of the Old South, notions that have grown since the Civil War.

The other two up-country districts that supplied data for this study, Newberry and Union, were both smaller than Fairfield, with proportions of slaves that were generally intermediate between the very high concentration of Fairfield and the high concentration of Edgefield. As table 1 indicates, only a small portion of the data comes from Newberry District: just fifteen months during 1832 and 1833. Union District supplied just over 120 months of data, with a total of 133 slave sales.[19]

The institution of slavery prospered in each of the five districts during the antebellum years. The trends in slave population growth indicate well how slavery fared in the various districts. From 1820 to 1860 a majority of South Carolina's residents were slaves. During these years the slave populations of each of the five districts grew steadily in size, with the increase in the slave populations of the districts outpacing the statewide growth in slave population. In 1820 12.8 percent of South Carolina's slaves lived in these five districts; by 1860, that fraction had grown to 17.6 percent. By the 1850 and 1860 censuses, a majority of the residents in each of the five districts were slaves, with proportions ranging from 52 percent slave in Marlboro and Union Districts in 1850 to just over 70 percent in Fairfield in 1860. In 1820 the ratio of slave to total population in the five districts averaged 80 percent of the state proportion; by 1860 the ratio of slaves to total population in the districts was greater than the overall state figure by about 7 percent.[20]

Marlboro District, the only one of the five districts not in the up-country, was a small district with a richness of extant records. This low-country but not tidewater district is tucked between the Great Pee Dee River and the westward bend that the South Carolina/North Carolina border makes about 120 miles from the Atlantic Ocean. Marlboro's population nearly doubled from 6,425 in 1820 to 12,434 in 1860. During this time, the proportion of slaves increased from 47.2 percent to 55.4

percent. As table 1 indicates, the district supplied data for all three types of sales. The records yielded complete sheriffs' sales book data for each month during the years from 1826 to 1856, with the exception of 1851 and a few other scattered months. In addition, Marlboro supplied 180 months of probate data and 65 months of equity-court sales data. In total, Marlboro District supplied data for the sales of 894 slaves.[21]

The five districts are a sample of the state's total number of districts, and the sales data are a sample of all the sales that took place within the districts. The three types of sales took place on a monthly schedule; often each of the three types was held on the same Sale Day. If each of the three types of sales occurred every month between 1823 and 1865 in each of the five districts, there would have been a total of 7,740 sales: 2,580 of each type. There was not, however, a sale of each type each month in each district. The sampled data include 1,168 of the possible universe of 7,740 sales, or 15.1 percent. Sales data from every South Carolina district would total 45,144 sales statewide. The sample comprises 2.6 percent of this largest imaginable collection of sales data.

No statistical test can offer the assurance that these sales data were representative of the state as whole. Any direct comparison is impossible because, with the partial exception of Charleston district—which will be discussed below—there are no collected data for sales by operation of law in other districts. The sample is sufficiently large to warrant the frank guess that the data represent well the rest of the state. Furthermore, if the sampled districts were relatively more prosperous than the rest of the state, then they would have probably had a lower rate of sales by operation of law. This is because in more prosperous districts there would have been fewer sales due to financial distress. Thus, if the sample is unrepresentative, the bias likely diminishes the count and importance of sales by operation of law. It is quite possible that the sale of slaves by law was even more important than I have argued here.

The next issue is whether the South Carolina courts' slave sales were representative of the rest of the South. No one can say yet. Often, or perhaps typically, historians regard South Carolina as exceptional. What marks the Palmetto State's peculiarity in the historiography is its *ultra*-ness: ultra-Southern, ultra-slave, ultra-aristocratic, ultra-anti-Yankee. For historians who seek to document differences between the antebellum North and South, South Carolina is certain to provide a striking contrast.[22] This may mean that South Carolina cannot represent the rest of the South; but if unrepresentative, then the *ultra*ness of South Carolina in its aristocratic and paternalistic tendencies would tend to suggest that there would be fewer rather than greater numbers of slave sales by operation of law when compared with other states that guarded less jealously the prerogatives of the slave master. But this can only be a guess. At the very least, no differences in other states' laws or legal institutions suggest that South Carolina's high volume of court sales of slaves was exceptional within the South. So the pattern of slave sales by operation of law in South Carolina was probably much like that in other slave states.

* * *

For debts sufficiently great that even the sale of slaves would not generate receipts sufficient to satisfy the creditor, Sheriff Cockrell sold everything except certain property that the statute made exempt from sale. For each family, goods exempt from sale included two beds and bedding, two bedsteads, a spinning wheel with two pairs of cards, a loom, one cow and calf, cooking utensils, and ten dollars worth of provisions, as well as the tools of a farmer or mechanic. This statutory exemption did not include land and was not, therefore, a homestead exemption like that enacted by the Republic of Texas during the 1830s. Not until 1851, ten years after Mississippi became the first state to adopt a homestead exemption, did the South Carolina legislature pass its own exemption law. South Carolina's act exempted fifty acres of real estate and up to five hundred dollars in personal property from levy and sale. But in response to the credit constriction that followed the Panic of 1857, the legislature repealed the homestead exemption; legislators yielded to the pressure of merchants and small farmers, all of whom sought to loosen the flow of credit by renewing creditors' entitlement to take debtors' homesteads.[23]

Sheriff Cockrell's Fairfield District sales included every sort of property, as did similar sales that masters in equity and probate officials ordered. In cases of full sale, the sale books provide fascinating inventories of antebellum households. The diversity of the property sold at these sales makes containment of the analysis difficult. What did it mean to property owners to be divested fully of their households, left only with the nucleus of property that the statute allowed? Consider the buyers. How did they feel as they carted off their new, but previously owned, possessions or moved into property formerly occupied by the debtor? Did the ghosts of previous title walk the rooms? What did J. D. Starke and his wife see when they peered into the looking glass that he brought home on March 2, 1846 after the sale that broke up N. S. Perry's household?[24] Did Perry's image linger on the silvered glass? Fleeting as Perry's image, the answers to these questions are probably beyond the reach of historians.

The sales confronted debtors with the opportunity to reflect, perhaps despairingly, on the meaning of property. Like the property owners, slaves were also in a desperate situation. The sale books record nothing of slaves' reactions to their sale. Henceforth, this section will narrow in focus to consider slaves, while expanding temporally and geographically to include sales in five districts during the period from 1823 to 1865.

Slaves were the central assets of the Southern economy. At sales they

were the most important assets sold: more important than the accumu-
lated personal property of households; more important than the crops,
farm implements, and livestock; and more important than the land itself. Roger Ransom and Richard Sutch have estimated that in 1859, in
the South's major cotton-growing states, capital investment in slaves represented 44 percent of the total wealth, with real estate, including both
land and buildings, representing around 25 percent of all wealth. By
1860, on the eve of the Civil War, Ransom and Sutch estimate the value
of slave capital to have been more than three billion dollars.[25]

Among assets, the centrality of slaves, even, or especially, over the
land, cannot be stated too strongly. As Gavin Wright, the leading economic historian of the antebellum South, puts it, "even a few slaves would
dominate the portfolio of all but the wealthiest capitalist or landlord."
Slavery was profitable, and, Wright explains, "the essence of the
profitability of slavery was the financial value of slave property." He com-
pares the outlook of slaveholders to that of "homeownership today—
most families," he notes, "buy one house to live in and do not frequently
buy and sell in response to fluctuations in price; yet these households
maintain an active and sometimes intense interest in the value of their
homes." Although recent research suggests that slave owners sold their
slaves more frequently than Wright implies, his analogy between slave
and home ownership is useful and accurate. The wealth of slave owners
increased as the value of their slave assets climbed. Much like California's
housing price curve during the 1970s and most of the 1980s, the slave
price curve in the 1850s was especially steep. Indeed, Wright argues for
protection of these upward gains as the cause of the Civil War.[26]

Most important among assets, slaves also lay at the foundation of
Southern social order. In *Slavery and Freedom*, James Oakes describes the
antebellum South as one of the few slave societies in history. There have
been many societies with slaves, but the mere presence of slaves did not
constitute a slave society. "A slave society," Oakes explains, "was one in
which a relatively high proportion of slaves signaled the central place of
slavery in the social hierarchy, the economic structure, and the political
system." He nicely illustrates the point hypothetically. Imagine the pre-
revolutionary North without slaves and imagine the antebellum South
without slaves. The society fundamentally altered in this hypothetical is
a slave society, the other a society with slaves. In a slave society, "[s]ocial
standing was determined by whether one was slave or free, and, if free,
whether one owned or did not own slaves," Oakes explains. "The most
important economic activities, the basis of a society's wealth, derived
from slavery."[27] The centrality of slaves in the Southern economic and
social order supports this study's predominant concern with their sale.
The number of slaves sold by operation of law is the best measure of the
social consequences of sales by operation of law.

* * *

After Sheriff Cockrell's election in 1844, he initially sold few slaves. During the first two months of his term, Sheriff Cockrell sold only one slave; at that rate, he would have sold six slaves over the course of a year. But during the next calendar year, 1845, he sold 183 slaves, or 1.4 percent of the district's enslaved population. In 1846 he sold about one-third fewer slaves—128—and in 1847 and 1848, the percentage of the slave population that he sold declined further still. It is not difficult to account for the large number of Sheriff Cockrell's sales during 1845 and 1846, as these were years of great agricultural distress in South Carolina.[28]

Figure 1 illustrates the annual sales of three different Fairfield District sheriffs. Sheriff Yongue began his term in 1831 and served until 1835. In the forty-five months of Yongue's term for which sale records are extant, he sold forty-two slaves, with an average annual rate of sale of around 0.1 percent, never selling more than 0.2 percent of Fairfield's slave population. The sharply peaked curve to the right of Sheriff Yongue's sales are those of Cockrell, with a maximum rate of sale of 1.4 percent of the population in 1845, and thereafter a sales rate that declined to about 0.3 percent in 1846. Finally, to the right of Cockrell's

FIGURE 1

FAIRFIELD SHERIFFS' SALES ANNUAL SALES OF SLAVE POPULATION

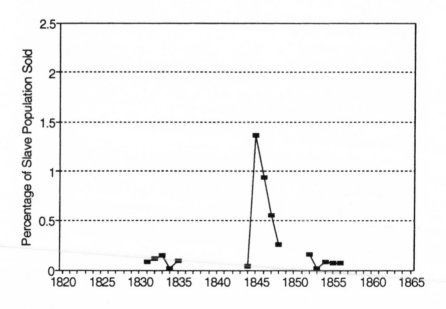

curve is the term of Sheriff Ellison (1852–1856), during which time he, like Yongue, never sold more than 0.2 percent of the district's slaves.

The records of Marlboro District present a slightly different picture, as figure 2 illustrates. With the exception of 1851, sale records exist for each month between 1823 and 1856. Additional records exist for some months between 1857 and 1861. As with Sheriff Cockrell's sales, there is a relative maximum during the harsh, drought years of 1845 and 1846. With a district slave population of approximately five thousand, the Marlboro District sheriff sold thirty-four slaves in 1845 and forty-nine in 1846. In the latter year, like Sheriff Cockrell, Marlboro's sheriff sold just under 1 percent of the district's slaves. The absolute maximum for the Marlboro sheriffs' sales of slaves came earlier, in 1830. That year the sheriff sold 97 of the district's 4,333 slaves, a total of 2.2 percent. Overall, sheriffs sold an average of 0.3 percent of the slave population each year in both Marlboro and Fairfield Districts.

Sheriffs' sales were not, of course, the only type of sale by operation of law, and sheriffs were not the only agents of law who auctioned slaves at the direction of court officials. In terms of volume, the next most important type of sale after sheriffs' sales were those supervised by the court of the ordinary, that is, probate sales.

FIGURE 2

MARLBORO SHERIFFS' SALES
ANNUAL SALES OF SLAVE POPULATION

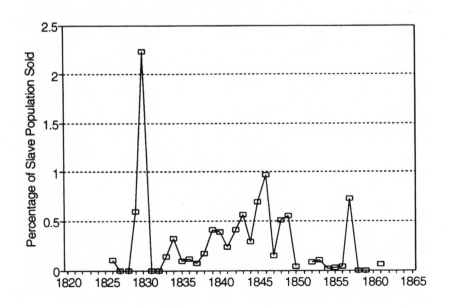

FIGURE 3

MARLBORO PROBATE SALES
ANNUAL SALES OF SLAVE POPULATION

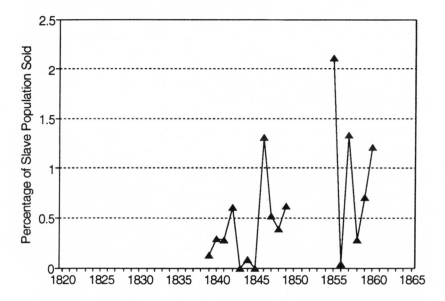

Figure 3 illustrates slave sales the probate court ordered in Marlboro District. Maximum sales came in 1855, with just over 2 percent of the slave population sold. However, this high figure may not be entirely trustworthy, as incomplete sales data for that year made extrapolation of annual sales volume necessary. As with the sheriffs' sales data for both Fairfield and Marlboro, there was a peak in sales volume in 1846, with 1.3 percent of the district's slaves sold at probate sales. This relationship is unsurprising, as more probate sales would likely occur during times of economic distress. As the estates of decedents proved insufficient to meet the demands of creditors, creditors would force a sale of the property. A similarly high sales figure occurred with the Panic of 1857, when the contraction of credit in New York and London caught South Carolina banks in an overextended position that forced them to suspend payments in specie.[29] That year probate sales again accounted for the sale of 1.3 percent of the slave population.

Figure 4 combines sales curves from figure 2 and figure 3 and illustrates the percentage of the slave population sold at both Marlboro sheriffs' and probate sales between 1839 and 1860. Both curves depict variability in sales volume from year to year. Considered together, the curves suggest some relationship between the sales volume at different types of sales, especially with the relative peaks that come around 1846 and 1857;

FIGURE 4

MARLBORO SALES
PROBATE AND SHERIFFS' SALES

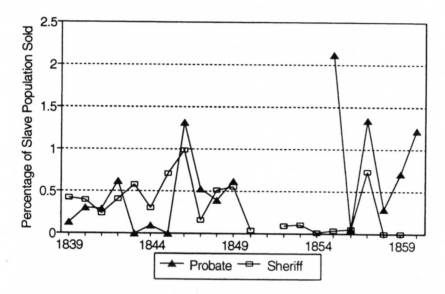

perhaps the same factors that brought about sheriffs' sales also led to probate sales. This combined depiction of these curves, which would not have been possible with a random sample, also begins to illustrate the great cumulative volume of slave sales by operation of law.

Table 2 is a more complete representation of the cumulative volume of sales by operation of law. The table presents Marlboro District data from each of the three types of sales this article considers for the seven-year period between 1855 and 1861. Listed beneath the year is a figure for the district's slave population. These population figures are simple linear interpolations based on the decennial census figures.[30] Next, opposite sheriff, equity court, and probate, are the number of slaves sold at each type of sale during the specified year. Beneath this figure is the number of months for which data were available. The last row for each sale type indicates the annual percentage of the slave population sold at the particular type of sale.

For years in which not all the monthly sales were available, the annual sales figure is an extrapolation based on those months with extant data. For example, if four months of sales data were available and these data recorded the sale of ten slaves, the annual percentage would derive from an estimated annual sale of thirty slaves. Extrapolated figures are underlined in table 2.

Table 2 adds data from the third type of sales, those made on order

TABLE 2

MARLBORO DISTRICT SLAVE SALES BY OPERATION OF LAW

Year	1856	1857	1858	1859	1860
Slave Population	6,376	6,505	6,634	6,764	6,893
SHERIFF					
slaves sold	3	8	0	0	N/A
months of data	12	2	2	2	
% of population	0.05	0.74	0.00	0.00	
EQUITY COURT					
slaves sold	0	16	8	29	0
months of data	12	12	12	12	12
% of population	0.00	0.24	0.12	0.42	0.00
PROBATE					
slaves sold	3	87	19	48	14
months of data	12	12	12	12	2
% of population	0.05	1.34	0.29	0.71	1.22

of the equity court. South Carolina maintained two parallel sets of courts, equity and common law. Equity court sales originated with the filing of bills or petitions in equity. Sheriffs' sales originated in the common law courts. Even for lawyers, the differences between the courts are often quite mystical. The simplest distinguishing characteristic between the two courts was the remedies available in each. Most simply, at common law plaintiffs could seek and, if successful with the suit, win damages in the form of money from the defendant. When cash would not suffice or when, for some other reason, the remedy available to the plaintiff at law was inadequate, the plaintiff might turn to the equity courts in search of an alternative remedy. Foreclosure is an equitable remedy, something that the equity court may order in response to the claim of the petitioner (the plaintiff's name in equity court) that someone has failed to pay a debt secured by a mortgage. Put briefly, foreclosure enabled the creditor to preclude forever the debtor's equitable right to regain legal title to the property by repaying the debt at some point after it was due. South Carolina mortgages were of real estate and sometimes of slaves as well. Sheriffs did not foreclose on property or hold foreclosure sales because sheriffs took their orders from the common law courts, not the equity courts. Sheriffs held sales when the plaintiffs had liens: claims on property that arose after the plaintiff received a judgment in a civil suit. Thus, foreclosure was associated with equity courts and execution of liens with sheriffs and the common law courts. Despite the technical differences the three types of sales by operation of law arose from essentially the same circumstances: death or nonpayment of debts or both together.[31]

TABLE 3

SLAVE SALES BY OPERATION OF LAW: TOTALS AND AVERAGES

	Slaves Sold	Months of Sale	Percentage of Slave Population Sold (Avg.)
EDGEFIELD			
Probate	420	184	0.12
FAIRFIELD			
Sheriff	504	142	0.32
Equity	63	49	0.11
MARLBORO			
Sheriff	445	377	0.30
Equity	65	100	0.11
Probate	384	180	0.46
NEWBERRY			
Sheriff	93	15	0.86
UNION			
Sheriff	88	40	0.45
Equity	45	81	0.12
TOTAL	2,107	1,168	0.73

Table 2 cumulates data from sales occasioned most often by debt or death. For example, looking down the column for 1857 in table 2, one can see that the Marlboro sheriff sold eight slaves during the two months for which data are available. Similar sales over the course of the year would have resulted in the sheriff selling 0.7 percent of the district's 6,505 slaves; however this extrapolation is merely a guess. At equity court sales, for which twelve full months of data for 1857 are extant, the commissioner in equity sold sixteen slaves, or 0.2 percent of the slave population. During the same time the probate court ordered sales of 1.3 percent of the slave population, a total of eighty-seven slaves. In total, at least 111 slaves were sold at Marlboro District sales by operation of law—likely more if complete sheriffs' sale data were available. These 111 slaves comprised 1.7 percent of the total slave population of the district.

Table 3 further aggregates and averages the five-district data for probate, equity, and sheriffs' sales. These data represent the sale of 2,107 slaves between 1823 and 1865. Of this total 1,130 were sold by sheriffs, 804 by probate, and 173 by equity courts.[32] In the three different types of sales the percentage of each district's slaves sold yearly varied considerably, from none sold during certain years in some districts to a high of 2.2 percent of the total slave population of Marlboro District sold by the sheriff during 1830.

Most importantly, table 3 includes average figures for the annual percentage of the slave population sold at each type of sale in the different districts. As stressed above, some of the annual-sale percentage figures in table 2 include adjustments for those years for which the sale data were incomplete. But table 3 does not simply average those annual figures; rather, it derives averages from only those months for which actual sale data were available. The convenient extrapolations of table 2 are not included in the calculation.

Table 3 indicates that the Marlboro District sheriffs' sales averaged 0.30 percent of the slave population each year. The Marlboro probate court sold more slaves than the sheriff, averaging about 0.46 percent of the slaves, while the equity court sold proportionally fewer, just 0.11 percent. The highest figure is for the Newberry District sheriff, who averaged an annual sales rate of 0.86 percent, but this figure is based on sales during only fifteen months, when the sheriff sold ninety-three slaves. The lowest figures in the group are the sales rates for equity courts, with Fairfield and Marlboro District equity courts having identical average annual rates of 0.11 percent.

Figure 5 further averages the annual-sale percentage figures from table 3. This pie-shaped figure represents the relative proportions of the three types of sales. Although there were occasionally other sales by operation of law besides probate, sheriffs', and equity-court sales, this figure presumes that these sales were not significant. If there were significant

FIGURE 5

SLAVE SALES BY OPERATION OF LAW
RELATIVE PROPORTION OF SALE TYPES

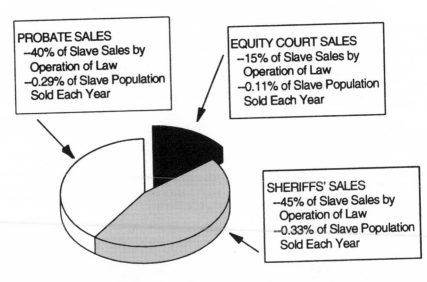

PROBATE SALES
--40% of Slave Sales by Operation of Law
--0.29% of Slave Population Sold Each Year

EQUITY COURT SALES
--15% of Slave Sales by Operation of Law
--0.11% of Slave Population Sold Each Year

SHERIFFS' SALES
--45% of Slave Sales by Operation of Law
--0.33% of Slave Population Sold Each Year

numbers of other types of sales by operation of law—tax-execution sales like the one that threatened the Bird family, for example—this would only support my general argument regarding the importance of the human and wealth consequences of sales by operation of law. The largest of the three pie wedges represents sheriffs' sales, which comprised 45 percent of all slave sales by operation of law. The average, adjusted for the number of months of collected data, of the four different sheriffs' sale averages in table 3 is 0.33 percent of the slave population sold each year. In other words, between 1823 and 1865 sheriffs sold one-third of one percent of the slave population each year; that is, from a population of one thousand slaves, the sheriff would sell three.

The second greatest volume of slaves sold occurred at probate sales. Probate accounted for 40 percent of the slave sales by operation of law: 0.29 percent of the slave population each year. Again, with one thousand slaves, three would be sold each year at probate sales. Finally, the exploded pie section in figure 5 represents equity-court sales, which accounted for 15 percent of slave sales by operation of law, or 0.11 percent of the slave population annually—approximately one of every one thousand slaves.

Aggregated, averaged, and added, sales of slaves at the three types of sales by operation of law—sheriffs', equity court, and probate—in the districts of Edgefield, Fairfield, Marlboro, Newberry, and Union amounted to a total of 0.73 percent of the slave population sold each year. From situations that typically began with either debt or death—sometimes both—the agents and instruments of law brought the power of law to bear, each year, on about seven out of every thousand slaves (and their owners) by selling them.

Seven out of a thousand may seem a small figure; can less than one percent of anything amount to much? Some present-day comparison may help put this figure in context. In the United States during 1990, an estimated 2,162,000 people died: a crude death rate of 8.6 deaths per thousand. This death rate, which is about 18 percent greater than the annual rate of slave sales by operation of law, answers the question of whether an event that affects less than 1 percent can amount to much.[33]

But death rates may not be the best figure with which to compare average slave rates of sale, because sale was something that could and would happen more than once in a slave's lifetime. A crime that can happen more than once to present-day residents of the United States is motor-vehicle theft. The 1990 rate of such offenses known to the police—6.6 per thousand, or 0.66 percent— was lower than the death rate. These figures equal about 90 percent of the rate of slave sales by operation of law.[34]

Reported rates of rape were much lower than motor-vehicle theft rates, with 0.41 reported rapes per thousand inhabitants—both men and women—or 0.041 percent. Surveys in which the census bureau asks people directly whether they have been victimized yield much higher rape rates than police reports. The 1990 victimization-survey rate indicates that 0.1 percent of females twelve years or older reported that they were victims of attempted or completed rape. So the rate at which agents of law sold slaves was about 85 percent of the 1990 death rates, 10 percent above car-theft rates, and seven times the victimization-survey rape rate for women. In order for the rate of slave sale by operation of law to be so small as to be unimportant, car theft, rape, and death have to be too small to be worthy of notice as well.[35]

* * *

A different way to comprehend the volume of slave sales by operation of law is to consider them as a proportion of all slave sales. The number of slave sales that courts of law and equity ordered or supervised was far from insignificant or unimportant in relation to all slave sales. Indeed, an average annual sales percentage rate of 0.73 percent of the slave population is quite high in proportion to the best existing estimates of the annual sales percentage from all sources, not just sales by operation of law.

Herbert Gutman's 1976 observation that there are few good estimates of the volume or frequency of slave sales—especially local sales—remains true today. Until recently the only systematic efforts to derive a comprehensive estimate of all types of slave sales came from data from one Maryland district, Anne Arundel, during the 1830s. A variety of historians have manipulated this district's data and have calculated annual slave-sales figures ranging from 1 percent to 3.46 percent.[36]

Recently another historian has essayed some figures for total slave sales, this time for the 1850s. These data, as chance—or the plethora of extant records—would have it, come mostly from South Carolina, in particular the low-country districts of Charleston and Sumter. The new figures appear in Michael Tadman's *Speculators and Slaves*, a fine book that has replaced Frederick Bancroft's *Slave Trading in the Old South* as the best book on the domestic slave trade. Tadman does not offer a figure for total annual sales, but buried in his footnotes are data that make possible the calculation of this figure. Tadman's total estimate for South Carolina slave sales in the 1850s is 14,600. Among total sales in the 1850s, Tadman's estimate of 67,500 court sales makes sales by operation of law a majority of all slave sales: 59.2 percent. Although Tadman's data indicate that sales by operation of law comprised a majority of slave sales, Tadman never calculates this figure, and he never mentions or seems to notice the preponderance of sales by operation of law. In all, Tadman's figures yield an annual sales rate of 2.9 percent of the South Carolina slave population per year.[37]

Sales by operation of law are troubling to parts of Tadman's argument. When he looked at the manuscript records of slave traders and counted the sources of their slave purchases, he found that slave traders made only between 4 and 5 percent of their slave purchases at judicial sales. Tadman describes this large discrepancy between the supply of slaves at judicial sales and the purchases of traders as "not particularly surprising." However, he accounts for this difference rather poorly. Tadman argues that traders found unsuitable the long credit available to purchasers at judicial sales. But it is hard to imagine why traders who dedicated their business lives to speculative profit in slave selling would recoil from credit terms that often allowed repayment over three years at 7 percent simple interest rates fixed by statute and held at 7 percent by the very courts that made the sales. Those were good terms then, just as they are now. It is true that debt posed great problems for many in the nineteenth century, but typical complaints were not that purchases were available on terms that were too easy. And men of business would not be the group most likely to reject credit for ideological reasons.[38]

The reasons for the discrepancy between Tadman's figures for sales by operation of law and those of this article are unclear. Tadman appears to have handled his data well. In the absence of a sound reason for disregarding Tadman's figures for sales by operation of law, the best approach is to incorporate them into the calculation of total sales volume. This article's calculation of the final figure for sales volume thus incorporates Tadman's figure of 1.47 percent of the Charleston District's slave population sold each year at sales by operation of law. This figure is combined with this article's lower figure of 0.73 percent, but combined in a conservative, weighted fashion that uses Tadman's figure only for the low-country Charleston District and this article's lower figure for the rest of the state. The result is a composite average of 0.85 percent of the state's slave population sold each year by operation of law.[39]

Over the four decades before the Civil War, the annual average of 0.85 percent of South Carolina's slaves sold at court-ordered or court-supervised sales roughly equalled the number of slaves sold locally and interregionally at nonjudicial sales. Returning to the calculation of the total slave-sales volume from all sources, as depicted in table 4, we find that over time the total average sales rate was 1.70 percent, with sales by operation of law accounting for half of all sales. As table 4 indicates, during the antebellum decades in South Carolina there were about 232,000 slave sales, with court sales of slaves numbering 115,000.

At first blush these sales figures may not seem particularly substantial.[40] Annual rates for sales are figures of convenience. The real effects of sales on slave lives and slave families must take into account the additive risk of sales that slaves experienced over time. Figure 6 charts the cumulative risk of sale that South Carolina slaves faced over time. The figure has two curves. The upper curve is the cumulative risk to an individual slave of sale from all sources, using an annual average sales rate of 1.70 percent. The lower curve cumulates the risk of sale from sales by operation of law, with an average annual rate of 0.85 percent.

A number of things are important about figure 6. First, although

TABLE 4

TOTAL SLAVE SALES IN SOUTH CAROLINA

	1820s	1830s	1840s	1850s	
COURT SALES					
Interregional	4,890	5,474	6,067	6,709	
Local	19560	21,897	24,268	26,837	
SUBTOTAL	24,450	27,371	30,335	33,546	115,702
NON-COURT SALES					
Interregional	7,420	28,536	11,301	32,323	
Local	7,824	8,759	9,707	10,735	
SUBTOTAL	15,244	37,295	21,008	43,058	116,605
Total Decennial Sales	39,694	64,665	51,343	76,604	
Population Mean	286,938	321,220	356,011	393,695	
Annual Rate (%)	1.38%	2.01%	1.44%	1.95%	
Average Annual Rate (%)					1.70%

the rates of sale used to compute the cumulative risk of sale are constant, risk of sale actually varied through the course of a slave's lifetime. For example, younger slaves faced greater risk of commercial sale. Second, despite the constant rates, the curves are not flat. Thus, although the annual risk of sale is 1.70 percent, after twenty years an individual slave's chance of having been sold during those twenty years would not be twenty times the annual rate, or 34 percent. The actual figure would be less, about 29 percent. This is not an unfathomable mystery of probability. The 29-percent figure represents the chance that an individual would be sold at least once during a twenty-year period. The difference of 5 percent represents multiple sales of slaves; during the twenty-year period, some slaves were sold more than once, others more than twice.[41]

* * *

The courts of South Carolina operated much like commission-merchant firms. Profit motivated the individuals who comprised the institutions. In firms, vendue masters—as commercial auctioneers were called in South Carolina—took a percentage of the sale amount as a commission. Fees also drove the work of sheriffs and other officials who conducted sales. Like auctioneers they all worked on commission. As table 5 indicates, sheriffs earned a variety of fees from litigants as they served writs, executed judgments, housed slaves and prisoners, and conducted sales. For sales, sheriffs received a commission of 2 percent of the sale amount

FIGURE 6

CUMULATIVE LIKELIHOOD OF A SLAVE'S BEING SOLD AT
LEAST ONCE
(SALES BY OPERATION OF LAW AND ALL SALES)

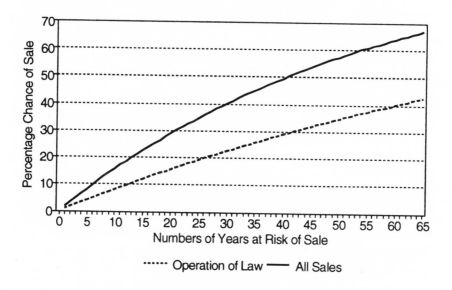

Numbers of Years at Risk of Sale

⋯⋯ Operation of Law —— All Sales

up to three hundred dollars and 1 percent on sale proceeds above three
hundred dollars. They also collected an additional 0.25 percent on the
amount of money that they paid out—for example, on the disbursement
of the proceeds to creditors. On the sales receipts alone, sheriffs received
commissions from 1.25 to 2.25 percent.

Just as commissions motivated auctioneers, commissions and fees
inspired the work of the sheriff. The state's legislators recognized the
fee-driven character of the sheriff's office when they changed the sheriff's
oath of office in 1839. An act of 1785 required the sheriff to swear to
serve the state faithfully, to the best of his ability, and also added the
republican pledge to "do equal right to all persons, high and low, rich
and poor, without malice, favour or affection." In addition the sheriff
promised "to truly execute all process" and not take "any other or greater
fees than allowed by law." This oath changed in 1839. The new oath,
which Sheriff Cockrell took in 1844 when he began his first term, dropped
the republican language regarding equality and focused instead on the
fees. The law required Cockrell to say, "I, Jeremiah Cockrell, swear, (or
affirm, as the case may be,) that I am under no promise, in honor or law,
to share the profits of the office, to which I have been elected, and I will
not, directly or indirectly, sell or dispose of said office, or the profits . . .

TABLE 5
SELECT FEES OF SHERIFFS, ACT OF 1840

SHERIFF'S ACTION	SHERIFF'S FEE
Receiving writ	$ .25
Serving writ	$1.00 plus mileage
Mileage (going not returning)	$ .05/mile
Commitment & Release of Prisoner	$ .50
Search for persons/goods not found	$ .50
Dieting white persons in gaol	$ .30/day
Dieting slaves/free blacks in gaol	$ .18/day
Levying execution	$1.00 plus mileage
Commissions—sums received	
Under $300	2.0 %
Over $300	$6.00 plus 1%
Commissions—money paid out	0.25 %
Execution lodged/no levy	$ .50
Serving *capias ad satisfaciendum*	$1.50
Advertising	$1.00 plus printer's bill
Executing deed	$3.00
Executing bill of sale	$2.00

thereof during the period fixed by law, if I so long live—so help me God!" This new oath recognized that, as with commission merchants, profits motivated the sheriff in the performance of his duty.[42]

Profit motive alone did not make the South Carolina courts commission-merchant firms. The courts begin to resemble a statewide auctioneering firm when considered as an institution that coordinated a large assembly of sheriffs, masters in chancery, ordinaries, and other state officials in each of the state's districts, an assembly which, on the first Monday of every month, conducted and drew profit from sales by operation of law. Using coordinated procedures and operating according to centralized rules, sheriffs and the agents and officials of probate and equity courts conducted one-half of all the South Carolina slave sales.

The agents, coordinated in statewide action, profited from the sales; but the state's legal system, as an institution, benefited as well. Just as commercial firms benefited from the important, albeit intangible, goodwill of the firm, so agents of law benefited from the maintenance and growth of goodwill toward the institutions and personnel of the legal system. Legitimacy—the confidence that people had in the court system—was the measure of the legal system's success in the distribution of its product. Just as the managers of commercial firms sought to expand their goodwill and profit, actors within the legal system worked to establish and sustain its legitimacy and power, even as they profited personally from the fees and commissions received in the course of their official duties.

The goodwill that measured the legitimacy of the legal system could not be taken for granted. On more than one occasion during the eighteenth century, lack of confidence in the courts, in particular dissatisfaction with the treatment of debtors, inspired groups of South Carolinians to shut down the courts. Such revolts would have seemed out of place in the relatively stable and harmonious post-Revolution domestic political environment of South Carolina. Nonetheless, lack of confidence could lead to less demonstrative rejections of the court system. From the standpoint of creditors, lack of confidence in the courts might induce them to restrict the supply of credit. For example, if creditors felt uncertain about the ability of the courts to liquidate property of debtors who failed to repay debts, they might choose to lend less money and instead to divert it to different investments.[43]

Like the managers of commercial firms and stock exchanges, the managers of the legal system aggregated individuals working in a variety of contexts into an institution that offered what can be called a *product*. Liquidation of the assets of defendants, debtors, and decedents was the clearest goal of court sales. Liquidity, the capacity to turn assets into cash, was the most important characteristic of the product that the courts offered. The courts' sales offered ready mechanisms for the conversion of assets into cash that could be distributed to interested parties, particularly creditors.[44]

In addition to liquidity, sales by operation of law offered other important benefits. Antebellum court sales standardized the time, place, and manner of sales. This standardization reduced the costs that the recipients of sales proceeds would have faced had they conducted the sales themselves. The standardization of advertising practices and the routinization of Sale Day also attracted buyers for the property the courts sold. The legislature and the courts provided the rules by which the sales would be conducted, and agents of the courts monitored the conduct of the sales. Courts were also able to provide some assurance to buyers by means of title-security functions as well as preservation of transaction records in sturdy volumes that the public could consult.[45]

With regard to the selling of slaves, courts were what would today be called a very powerful *market actor*. Once again, Gavin Wright's useful analogy between the value of slave property and the present-day regard for home sales is an instructive comparison. If, for example, one-half of present-day real-estate sales were sales that courts ordered or conducted, this stunningly large proportion of sales would not escape the notice of those with houses to buy or sell.

One indication of the court's success in conducting the slave auction business is the extent to which the involvement of the courts has remained largely unnoticed. For example, to remain unnoticed and un-seen is a goal of stock exchanges like those in New York or Tokyo. The New York Stock Exchange (NYSE) is a firm with rules that define and limit trading of securities; but many would think of the NYSE as merely a place where trades take place. The rules and institutional structure of the NYSE are successful insofar as they remain transparent. Whether the slave-selling courts are seen as being more like commission-merchant firms or more like commodities or stock exchanges, their goals were, from the organizational point of view, the same ones that motivated com-mission merchants and exchange managers. As with commercial firms and stock exchanges, the courts' sales generated both individual and institutional profit.

* * *

The large share of court-supervised slave sales makes clear that scholars interested in any aspect of slave selling can no longer allow slave sales by operation of law to remain unseen. Scholars cannot look to and analyze commercial sales only. They cannot exclude court sales as if they were unimportant or of only marginal importance. This is particularly a prob-lem for cliometric analyses of the economics of slavery. For historians interested in looking at "the market" for slaves, the reflexive tendency to exclude sales by operation of law as unimportant and marginal is insup-portable. With regard to volume, prices, and importance, sales by opera-tion of law must occupy a central place in the history of slave selling. Economic historians must think seriously about the role of legal institu-tions and about the motives of those who managed the courts and other agencies of law. Law and economy were closely linked in transactional life; slave sales did not take place in a free realm where only the prefer-ences of buyers and sellers were important. The volume of slave sales by operation of law was too large not to have affected all aspects of slave selling.

Slave sales by operation of law not only generate the question of where one should look if interested in finding and collecting data on the conduct of slave sales; they also suggest the importance of courts and their sales in creating and sustaining the norms of transactional life. This issue is beyond the scope of this article, but if, for example, one seeks to study the historical transformation in the very meaning of the market, court sales must figure prominently. The agents of courts as well as the judges, chancellors, and justices not only supervised the conduct of sales, but they also influenced the interpretive context within which South Carolinians viewed transactions of economy. For example, if credi-tors or sellers colluded and thereby affected the outcome of a sale, this might produce litigation.[46] The litigation would give judges and chan-cellors the opportunity to offer their own notions of what was proper and then back their interpretations with the imperative force of a judicial decree and sheriffs' writs. The volume of the courts' slave sales could establish these sales as benchmarks for valid procedures of exchange. Slave sales were central forges for the conceptual outlook of South Carolinians with regard to economy.

Slave sales by operation of law expressed social disregard for black families and slave humanity. Slaves thus sold experienced contradictions of American liberalism: racism and economics at odds with both their individuality and their place in families and communities. This is not news. However, no scholar has identified or considered the central role of law's institutions in these powered clashes of slavery, economy, humanity, and family. Indeed, the role of law and sales by operation of law in the destruction of slave families has remained largely invisible. This is unfortunate, for the examination of how people have used law to wield power, whether against one another or in defense or promotion of themselves, and how others have experienced law against themselves is among the most interesting tasks of legal history. Legal history recalls and considers law's imperative power.

Finally, the slave auction is perhaps the most powerful and disturbing image from the history of the United States. But the usual image conjured by the phrase *slave auction*—that of a commercial sale taking place in a large city such as Charleston, South Carolina, or Richmond, Virginia—is misleading. The auction image from the commercial slave marts neglects and omits the most important actors and institutions in the slave auctioneering business. A more accurate vision of the slave auction would make clearer the full involvement of law and legal officials. The site of these sales was not an auction block beside an urban wharf, but rather the steps of any district's courthouse. The stirring metaphor of the slave auction ought, then, to bring to mind an image of courts and law and a vision of these courthouse steps, on which each month one-half of all slave sales took place.

Notes

1. Fairfield County, Sheriff, Sale Book, 1844–48, South Carolina Department of Archives and History (hereinafter cited as SCDAH).

2. The 1845 figures for slaves are the average of the 1840 and 1850 census figures. *Sixth Census or Enumeration of the Inhabitants of the United States . . . in 1840* (Washington, DC: 1841), 229; J[ames] D[unwoody] B[rownson] De Bow, *Statistical View of the United States. . . Being a Compendium of the Seventh Census* (Washington, DC: Nicholson, 1854), 302, 304. The Sixth Census of 1840 did not enumerate acres of improved and unimproved farmland.

3. Lacy K. Ford Jr., *Origins of Southern Radicalism: The South Carolina Upcountry, 1800–1860* (New York: Oxford University Press, 1988), 302, 308–11.

4. "An Act for Establishing County Courts, and for Regulating the Proceedings Therein," no. 1281, § 37, *Statutes at Large of South Carolina*, 12 vols. (Tho-

mas Cooper et al eds., Columbia, S.C., A. S. Johnson, 1836–) 211, 229 (1785), (hereinafter cited as S.C. Stat.) ("no lands or tenements, or slaves, shall be taken in execution . . . where other goods and chattels are shewn by the defendant or debtor to the sheriff or other officer, sufficient to satisfy the demands of such sheriff or other officer.")

5. Sanford Levinson, "Slavery in the Canon of Constitutional Law," in this volume; Paul Brest and Sanford Levinson, *Processes of Constitutional Decisionmaking: Cases and Materials*, 3d ed. (Boston: Little, Brown, 1992), 129–33, 177–227.

6. See, for example, *Charleston Courier*, June 23, 1818, p. 3; June 17, 1845, p. 3; March 2, 1846, p. 3; May 1, 1834, p. 3.

7. "An Act for Disposing of Certain Estates, and Banishing Certain Persons, Therein Mentioned," no. 1153, S.C. Stat. 4, 516 (1782); *Haig v. Commissioners of Confiscated Estates*, 1 S.C. Eq. (1 Des.) 144 (1787); *Wainwright v. Read*, 1 S.C. Eq. (1 Des.) 573 (1787); "An Ordinance for the Sale of Sundry Lands Belonging to the Public," no. 1469, S.C. Stat. 5, 132 (1789); "An Act to Provide for the Sale of Certain Lands Belonging to the State," no. 4361, S.C. Stat. 12, 544 (1857); "An Act Concerning the Office and Duties of Ordinary," no. 2781, § 18, S.C. Stat. 11, 62 (1839); § 26, ibid. See also *M'Guire v. M'Gowan*, 4 S.C. Eq. (4 Des.) 486 (1814); *Young v. Teague*, 8 S.C. Eq. (Bail. Eq.) 13 (1830); "An Act Concerning the Office, Duties, and Liabilities of Coroner," no. 2782, § 41, S.C. Stat. 11, 78 (1839) (coroner to perform duties of sheriff where sheriff is a party to the action).

8. See, for example, William J. Cooper Jr. and Thomas E. Terrill, *The American South: A History* (New York: McGraw-Hill, 1991), 215–21; Robert W. Fogel and Stanley L. Engerman, *Time on the Cross: The Economics of American Negro Slavery* (Boston: Little, Brown, 1974), 55; Herbert G. Gutman, *Slavery and the Numbers Game: A Critique of Time on the Cross* (Urbana: University of Illinois Press, 1975), 132–37; Edward W. Phifer, "Slavery in Microcosm: Burke County, North Carolina," *Journal of Southern History* 28 (1962): 153–56; William Calderhead, "How Extensive Was the Border State Slave Trade: A New Look," *Civil War History* 18 (1972): 42, 47–48. A very important early exception is Kenneth M. Stampp, *The Peculiar Institution: Slavery in the Ante-Bellum South* (New York: Vintage Books, 1956), 237–44. Another historian who has noticed the importance of slave sales by operation of law is Bobby Frank Jones, "A Cultural Middle Passage: Slave Marriage and Family in the Ante-Bellum South," (Ph.D. diss., University of North Carolina, 1965), 189–94.

9. Edward L. Cahn, dir., *Law and Order*, screenplay by John Huston and Tom Reed, (Los Angeles: Universal Studios, 1932); John Ford, dir., *My Darling Clementine*, screenplay by Samual G. Engel and Winston Miller (Los Angeles: Twentieth-Century Fox, 1946); Giacomo Puccini, *La Fanciulla del West*, libretto by Carlo Zangarini and Guelfo Guinini (Milan: G. Ricordi, 1910). For a comparison of the office of sheriff in England and colonial Virginia, see Cyrus Harreld Karraker, *The Seventeenth-Century Sheriff: A Comparative Study of the Sheriff in England and the Chesapeake Colonies, 1607–1689* (Durham: University of North Carolina Press, 1930): 93–156, which notes that the colonial sheriff had greater political and economic functions and a lesser judicial role than his English counterpart.

10. Creditors secured themselves by filing lawsuits against their debtors at the time of the loan. If the debtors failed to repay the debt, then the creditor

was already in the position of an execution creditor, which meant that the next step was simply to have the sheriff execute the judgment and sell the debtor's property. On the preponderance of debt actions in civil-trial courts, see Thomas D. Russell, "Historical Study of Personal Injury Litigation: A Comment on Method," 1 *Georgia Journal of Southern Legal History* 109, 118 (1991); see also idem, "The Antebellum Courthouse as Creditors' Domain: Trial-Court Activity in South Carolina and the Concomitance of Lending and Litigation," 40 *American Journal of Legal History* (forthcoming); "An Act to Raise Supplies for the Year One Thousand Eight Hundred and Thirty-Nine," no. 2772, § 11, S.C. Stat. 11, 1 (1839).

11. "An Act to Restrain the Emancipation of Slaves, and to Prevent Free Persons of Color from Entering into this State," no. 2236, § 2, S.C. Stat. 7, 459 (1820); "An Act for the Better Regulation and Government of Free Negroes and Persons of Color," no. 2277, § 2, S.C. Stat. 7, 461 (1822); see, for example, "An Act Prescribing the Duties of Certain Officers in the Collection of Supplies, the Payment of Salaries," no. 2884, § 2, S.C. Stat. 11, 246 (1843); "An Act to Raise Supplies for the Year," no. 2922, § 2, S.C. Stat. 11, 285 (1844).

12. Tax Collector's Execution, May 29, 1831, Fairfield County, Sheriff's Executions, Tax Collections, SCDAH.

13. Edgefield County, Judge of Probate, Sale Book, WPA typescript, South Caroliniana Library, University of South Carolina [hereinafter cited as SCL]. Fairfield County, Sheriff, Sale Books, 1831–35, 1844–48, 1852–56; idem, Master in Equity, Sale Book, 1841–63, SCDAH. Marlboro County, Sheriff, Sale Book, 1823–63; idem, Master in Equity, Sale Book, 1856–69; idem, Ordinary/Probate Judge, Inventories, Appraisements, and Sales, 1840–60, SCDAH. Newberry County, Sheriff, Sale Book, 1832–33, SCDAH. Union County, Sheriff, Sale Book, 1823–26; idem, Master in Equity, Sale Book, 1823–34, SCDAH. "An Act Concerning the Office, Duties, and Liabilities of Sheriff," no. 2780, § 6, S.C. Stat. 11, 39–40 (1839).

14. For a general introduction to longitudinal historical studies of courts, see Lawrence M. Friedman, "Opening the Time Capsule: A Progress Report on Studies of Courts Over Time," 24 *Law and Society Review* 229 (1990).

15. "South Carolina County Records," W.P.A. typescript, SCL, 2; Francis Walker, ed., *The Statistics of the Population of the United States, . . . Ninth Census* (Washington, D.C.: U.S. Government Printing Office, 1872), 60–61. (hereinafter cited as *Ninth Census*). Beginning with the Reconstruction Constitution of 1868, South Carolina's districts were called counties. 1868 S.C. Const., art. II, § 3, in Francis Newton Thorpe, *The Federal and State Constitutions* (Washington, D.C.: U.S. Government Printing Office, 1909), 3285.

16. Orville Vernon Burton, *In My Father's House Are Many Mansions: Family and Community in Edgefield, South Carolina* (Chapel Hill: University of North Carolina Press, 1985), xvii, 4–6.

17. This description from Ford, *Origins of Southern Radicalism*, viii–ix.

18. *Ninth Census*, 60–61.

19. For a local history of Newberry, see Thomas H. Pope, *The History of Newberry County, South Carolina: Volume One: 1749–1860* (Columbia: University of South Carolina Press, 1973).

20. *Ninth Census*, 60–61.

21. Ibid.

22. See, for example, William H. Pease and Jane H. Pease, *The Web of Progress: Private Values and Public Styles in Boston and Charleston, 1828–1843* (New York: Oxford University Press, 1985); Michael Hindus, *Prison and Plantation: Crime, Justice, and Authority in Massachusetts and South Carolina, 1767–1878* (Chapel Hill: University of North Carolina Press, 1980); on the issue of Southern distinctiveness, see Carl N. Degler, *Place over Time: The Continuity of Southern Distinctiveness* (Baton Rouge: Louisiana State University Press, 1977).

23. "An Act to Prohibit Sheriffs and Their Deputies, under Certain Penalties, from Purchasing Executions Lodged in their Offices; and for Other Purchases Therein Mentioned," no. 2315, § 4, S.C. Stat. 6, 214 (1823); Henry W. Farnam, *Chapters in the History of Social Legislation in the United States to 1860* (Washington, D.C.: Carnegie Institution, 1938), 150–51; Lawrence M. Friedman, *History of American Law*, 2d ed. (New York: Simon and Schuster, 1985), 244; "An Act to Increase the Amount of Property Exempt from Levy and Sale," no. 4041, § 1, S.C. Stat. 12, 77 (1851); Ford, *Origins of Southern Radicalism*, 322–23.

24. Fairfield County, Sheriff, Sale Book, March 2, 1846, p. 44, SCDAH.

25. Roger Ransom and Richard Sutch, "Capitalists without Capital: The Burden of Slavery and the Impact of Emancipation," *Agricultural History* 62 (1988): 133, 138–39, 151.

26. Gavin Wright, *The Political Economy of the Cotton South: Households, Markets, and Wealth in the Nineteenth Century* (New York: W. W. Norton, 1978), 41–42, 141–44. See also James Oakes, *The Ruling Race: A History of American Slaveholders* (New York: Vintage Books, 1982), 171–79. On the myth of the reluctance of slaveholders to sell their slaves, see Michael Tadman, *Speculators and Slaves: Masters, Traders, and Slaves in the Old South* (Madison: University of Wisconsin Press, 1989), 111–32.

27. James Oakes, *Slavery and Freedom: An Interpretation of the Old South* (New York: Alfred A. Knopf, 1990), 38.

28. In 1844 Fairfield's white men—who since 1810 had enjoyed universal suffrage—elected Cockrell to a four-year term. In a state in which the legislature tightly controlled the appointment of state officials, sheriffs were among the relatively small number of local officials of state government directly elected by each district's voters. Ford, *Origins of Southern Radicalism*, 102, 215, 304–5; "An Act Prescribing the Mode of Electing Clerks, Sherifs, [sic] and Ordinaries," no. 2779, § 7, S.C. Stat. 11, 35 (1839); Alfred Glaze Smith, *Economic Readjustment of an Old Cotton State: South Carolina, 1820–1860* (Columbia: University of South Carolina Press, 1958), 2–8, 50–54, 110.

29. J. Mauldin Lesesne, *The Bank of the State of South Carolina: A General and Political History* (Columbia: University of South Carolina Press, 1970), 109–113; Ford, *Origins of Southern Radicalism*, 330–31.

30. *Ninth Census*, 61. This volume has a very helpful summary of each county's population figures for each of the first nine censuses.

31. The most common equitable remedies are injunctions, where the equity court tells someone to do or not to do something, and specific performance, where the court tells someone to perform a particular contract. On the differences between remedies in equity and at law, see Robert Wyness Millar, *Civil Procedure of the Trial Court in Historical Perspective* (New York: The Law Center of New York University, 1952), 419–21, 474–80, and Steven Wechsler, "Through the Looking Glass: Foreclosure by Sale as *De Facto* Strict Foreclosure—An Em-

pirical Study of Mortgage Foreclosure and Subsequent Resale," 70 *Cornell Law Review* 850, 855–62 (1985).

32. Note that these numbers do not represent the relative frequency of these types of sales.

33. The age-adjusted death rate from all causes was 515.1 per 100,000. According to the National Center for Health Statistics, "Age-adjusted death rates control for changes and variations in the age composition of the population; therefore, they are better indicators than crude death rates for showing changes in mortality risk over time and for showing differences between race-sex groups within the population." U.S. Department of Health and Human Services, National Center for Health Statistics, *Monthly Vital Statistics Report*, 39:13 (August 28, 1991), 3-4.

34. Table 3.128 in Timothy J. Flanagan and Kathleen Maguire, eds., *Sourcebook of Criminal Justice Statistics—1992*, U.S. Department of Justice, Bureau of Justice Statistics, (Washington, D.C.: U.S. Government Printing Office, 1992), 373.

35. Ibid. Table 3.19, ibid., 275. These figures rely on a definition of rape that underreports the incidence of nonconsensual sex. See Susan Estrich, *Real Rape* (Cambridge: Harvard University Press, 1987), 10–15.

36. Herbert G. Gutman, *The Black Family in Slavery and Freedom, 1750–1925* (New York: Vintage Books, 1976), 145, 569 n.25. The paucity of empirical estimates of slave sales is especially surprising in light of the well-understood threat that sale posed to slave lives and families, see ibid., 35–36, 128–29, 145–49, 285–90; John W. Blassingame, *The Slave Community: Plantation Life in the Antebellum South*, rev. ed. (New York: Oxford University Press, 1979), 173–77; William Calderhead, "How Extensive Was the Border State Slave Trade? A New Look," *Civil War History* 18 (1972): 42; Fogel and Engerman, *Time on the Cross*, 1:53; Gutman, *Slavery and the Numbers Game*, 126; Herbert G. Gutman and Richard Sutch, "The Slave Family," and letter from Engerman, 4 November 1974, in Paul A. David et al., *Reckoning with Slavery: A Critical Study in the Quantitative History of American Negro Slavery* (New York: Oxford University Press, 1976), 106. The Anne Arundel data are revisited in Herman Freudenberger and Jonathon B. Pritchett, "The Domestic United States Slave Trade: New Evidence," *Journal of Interdisciplinary History* 21:3 (Winter 1991): 447–77, 467 n. 28.

37. Tadman, *Speculators and Slaves*; Frederic Bancroft, *Slave Trading in the Old South* (Baltimore: J. H. Furst Company, 1931). Most importantly, Tadman has disposed of the myth that slaveholders only reluctantly sold their slaves. Tadman, *Speculators and Slaves*, 111–32. He also presents convincing estimates of the total interregional movement of slaves. "Calculating the Structure of the Interregional Movement," app. 3 of ibid., 237–47. And Tadman displays considerable knowledge of domestic slave selling. Especially impressive is his identification of about 150 slave-trading firms that operated in South Carolina in the 1850s. "South Carolina Slave Traders of the 1850s: A Digest of Evidence," app. 4 of ibid., 248–76.

For the 1850s Tadman estimates total statewide judicial sales of 67,500 slaves, with 54,000 sold locally, and 20 percent of the total sold at court sales—13,500—sold out-of-state. In addition, he estimates that non-court local sales, sales that took place not by operation of law and resulted in the slaves remaining within the state, were 40 percent of local sales. His figure for these local sales is thus 21,600. The final sales component are noncourt, interregional sales. The total interregional movement of South Carolina slaves he estimates at 65,053 for the 1850s. Sixty percent of this, or 39,000, he attributes to sales, the remainder to planter migration. Because 13,500 of these sales were court sales, 25,500 were noncourt, interregional sales. See ibid., 120 n. 16.

The 2.9 percent total sales figure divides Tadman's figure for sales evenly over the decade and then further divides these figures by the average population between the censuses of 1840 and 1850. Tadman's estimates for statewide total judicial sales appear very large, particularly his probate totals. Using Charleston District records, Tadman derives sales figures that he extends to the whole state. But where the present article has found that sales by operation of law accounted each year for sales of 0.73 percent of South Carolina's antebellum slave population, Tadman's figures yield a figure between 1.23 and 1.47 percent of the 1850s slave population. Table 5.2, ibid., 119. The figure 1.47 is based on the population mean of the decennial censuses of 1850 and 1860. The slave population of Charleston District declined very sharply between these censuses, from 54,775 to 37,290. Because much of this decline took place close to 1860, the lower figure of 1.23 percent uses the 1850 census figure. Tadman's rates of sale are 70 to more than 100 percent higher than those derived from Edgefield, Fairfield, Marlboro, Newberry, and Union District records.

38. Tadman, 113–14; "An Act for the Reduction of Interest from Eight to Seven Pounds for Each Hundred Pounds," no. 1031, S.C. Stat. 4, 363 (1777); Joseph Brevard, 1 *An Alphabetical Digest of the Public Statute Law of South Carolina* xiv (Charleston, John Hoff, 1814); David McDowell to Elizabeth Calmese Kincaid, January 1, 1840, Kincaid-Anderson Papers, SCL.

Although Tadman is correct in identifying long, inexpensive credit as the usual possibility at equity court and probate sales (Tadman, *Speculators and Slaves*, 137 n. 5), the medium of exchange at sheriffs' sales was cash. Even if Tadman were right that traders preferred to pay cash, they could have exercised that preference at sheriffs' sales. Tadman also suggests that traders avoided court sales because of the mixed lots sold at these sales. He says that court officials often sold lots of slaves that included groups, such as family fragments composed of mothers with small children, rather than selling slaves individually, as the traders would have preferred. Ibid., 136. My work in progress suggests that a greater fraction of slaves were sold individually at court sales than at other sales. Furthermore, prices were relatively lower than at non-judicial sales. Thus, Tadman's explanation for the low rate of purchase by traders at judicial sales is unconvincing. But because judicial sales are not central to his argument, this lapse does not mar his thorough and thoughtful treatment of other aspects of slave selling.

39. Michael Tadman, letter to author, May 22, 1991. I rechecked and confirmed his data for probate sales. Charleston County, Inventories, Appraisements, and Sales, vol. C (1850–53); vol. D (1854–57); and vol. E (1856–60), SCDAH. I also checked and confirmed his data for equity court sales. Charleston County, Master-in-Equity, Sales Book, 1851–59, SCDAH. I am grateful to Ms. Carolyn Hamby (1960–1996) for her assistance in confirming Tadman's data.

On average the Charleston District slave population comprised 16.6 percent of South Carolina's total slave population between 1820 and 1860. The recalculation of the total sales percentage by operation of law uses this percentage to weight Tadman's higher figure:

(0.166 x 1.47 percent) + [(1 - 0.166) x 0.73 percent] = 0.85 percent.

40. An annual sales rate of 1.70 percent is lower, after all, than the estimate of 1.92 percent in *Time on the Cross*, a book that came to be regarded as minimizing the degradation of slavery. Fogel and Engerman, *Time on the Cross*, 1:53.

41. On the age-specific risks of commercial sale, see Tadman, *Speculators and Slaves*, 25–31, 43–44, 233–35; see also Gutman and Sutch, "The Slave Family," 111 n. 26. Gutman and Sutch employ the correct formula for computing the risk of sale. Where 0.0170 is the annual risk of sale, 0.9830 is the probability of *not* being sold. Where n = the number of years at risk,

$1 - (0.9830)^n$ = the cumulative risk of sale.

In this way the risk of sale was more like the earlier quoted rates of rape than death. After death a victim does not rejoin the potential pool of victims. But those who survive rape, like those who experienced sale as slaves, face continuing risk with each successive moment of their lives.

42. "An Act for Establishing County Courts, and for Regulating the Proceedings Therein," no. 1281, § 28, S.C. Stat. 7, 224 (1785); "An Act Concerning the Office, Duties, and Liabilities of Sheriff," no. 2780, § 2, S.C. Stat. 11, 38 (1839).

43. Robert M. Weir, *Colonial South Carolina: A History* (Millwood, NY: TKO Press, 1983), 108–9; Michael Hindus, *Prison and Plantation: Crime, Justice, and Authority in Massachusetts and South Carolina, 1767–1878* (Chapel Hill: University of North Carolina Press, 1980), 3–15; Ford, *Origins of Southern Radicalism*, 145–214. See Pauline Maier, "Popular Uprisings and Civil Authority in Eighteenth-Century America," in Lawrence M. Friedman and Harry N. Scheiber, eds., *American Law and the Constitutional Order: Historical Perspectives*, enl. ed. (Cambridge: Harvard University Press, 1988), 69–84.

44. Jonathan Macey and Hideki Kanda, law professors at the Cornell University and the University of Tokyo respectively, have presented a framework useful for the evaluation of the product courts offered. Macey and Kanda examine the product that present-day, organized security exchanges—specifically the New York Stock Exchange and the Tokyo Stock Exchange—offer to firms with publicly traded stock. The product is the listing of the stock on the exchange. Macey and Kanda "unbundle" this product into four components. Exchanges, they say, offer "(1) liquidity, (2) monitoring of exchange trading, (3) standard form, off-the-rack rules to reduce transactions costs and (4) a signalling function that serves to inform investors that the issuing companies' stock is of high quality." Liquidity, they note, is "the most widely understood function of an organized exchange." Jonathon Macey and Hideki Kanda, "The Stock Exchange as a Firm: The Emergence of Close Substitutes for the New York and Tokyo Stock Exchanges," 75 *Cornell Law Review* 1007, 1010–11 (1990). Robert W. Hamilton, *Fundamentals of Modern Business: A Lawyer's Guide* (Boston: Little, Brown, 1989), 516–17.

45. These functions "all reduce the agency costs that are endemic to the modern publicly held corporation." Macey and Kanda, "The Stock Exchange as a Firm," 1012.

46. See, for example, *Carson v. Law*, 19 S.C. Eq. (2 Rich. Eq.) 296 (1846).

APPENDIX: SLAVE SALES BY OPERATION OF LAW, 1823–1865

Number of Slaves Sold and Percentage of Slave Population Sold, by District, Year, and Type of Sale

(Italic figures are extrapolations from incomplete yearly data.)

	1820	1823	1824	1825	1826	1827	1828	1829	1830	1831	1832	1833	1834	1835	1836
EDGEFIELD	12,198	13,143	13,458	13,774	14,089	1,4404	14,719	15,034	15,349	15,568	15,787	16,006	16,225	16,444	16,662
Probate															
months															
FAIRFIELD	7,748	8,947	9,347	9,747	10,147	10,547	10,946	11,346	11,746	11,822	11,898	11,974	12,050	12,125	12,201
Sheriff										7		18	2	1	
months										8	12	12	12	1	
percent										*0.09*	0.12	0.15	0.02	*0.10*	
Equity															
months															
MARLBORO	3,033	3,423	3,553	3,683	3,813	3,943	4,073	4,203	4,333	4,312	4,290	4,269	4,247	4,226	4,204
Sheriff					4	0	0	25	97	0	0	6	14	4	5
months					12	12	12	12	12	12	12	12	12	12	12
percent					0.10	0.00	0.00	0.59	2.24	0.00	0.00	0.14	0.33	0.09	0.1
Equity															
months															
Probate															
months															
NEWBERRY	5,749	6,519	6,776	7,032	7,289	7,546	7,803	8,059	8,316	8,475	8,634	8,792	8,951	9,110	9,269
Sheriff											83	10			
months											12	3			
percent											0.96	*0.45*			
UNION	4,278	5,144	5,433	5,721	6,010	6,299	6,588	6,876	7,165	7,284	7,403	7,522	7,641	7,759	7,878
Sheriff		7	14	6	61	11									
months		4	12	12	12	12									
percent		*0.41*	0.26	0.10	1.01	0.17									
Equity		31	0	3	0		0	0							
months		11	12	12	12		12	10							
percent		*0.66*	0.00	0.05	0.00		0.00	*0.00*							

	1837	1838	1839	1840	1841	1842	1843	1844	1845	1846	1847	1848	1849	1850	1851
EDGEFIELD	16,881	17,100	17,319	17,538	18,057	18,575	19,094	19,613	20,132	20,650	21,169	21,688	22,206	22,725	22,859
Probate							0	4	10	6	24	0	37	6	15
months							*3*	12	12	12	12	12	12	12	12
percent							*0.00*	*0.02*	0.05	0.03	0.11	0.00	0.17	0.03	0.07
FAIRFIELD	12,277	12,353	12,429	12,505	12,679	12,853	13,027	13,201	13,376	13,550	13,724	13,898	14,072	14,246	14,375
Sheriff								1	183	128	77	33			
months								*2*	12	12	12	11			
percent								*0.05*	1.37	0.94	0.56	*0.26*			
Equity															
months															
MARLBORO	4,183	4,161	4,140	4,118	4,266	4,414	4,563	4,711	4,859	5,007	5,155	5,304	5,452	5,600	5,729
Sheriff	3	7	17	16	10	18	26	14	34	49	8	27	30	2	
months	12	12	12	12	12	12	12	12	12	12	12	12	12	12	
percent	0.07	0.17	0.41	0.39	0.23	0.41	0.57	0.30	0.70	0.98	0.16	0.51	0.55	0.04	
Equity															
months															
Probate			5	12	12	27	0	4	0	66	27	21	28		
months			11	12	12	12	12	12	12	12	12	12	10		
percent			*0.13*	0.29	0.28	0.61	0.00	0.08	0.00	1.32	0.52	0.40	*0.62*		
NEWBERRY	9,428	9,586	9,745	9,904	10,182	10,461	10,739	11,018	11,296	11,574	11,853	12,131	12,410	12,688	12,789
Sheriff															
months															
UNION	7,997	8,116	8,235	8,354	8,558	8,762	8,965	9,169	9,373	9,577	9,781	9,984	10,188	10,392	10,433
Sheriff															
Equity															
months															

	1852	1853	1854	1855	1856	1857	1858	1859	1860	1861	1862	1863	1864	1865	Tot. & Ave.
EDGEFIELD	22,992	23,126	23,259	25,319	23,526	23,660	23,793	23,927	24,060	24,194	24,327	24,461	24,594	24728	
Probate	42	119	0	91	58	4	4	0							420
months	12	12	12	12	12	12	12	1							184
percent	0.18	0.52	0.00	0.39	0.25	0.02	0.02	0.00							0.12
FAIRFIELD	14,504	14,632	14,701	14,890	15,019	15,148	15,276	15,405	15,534	15,663	15,792	15,920	16,049	16,178	
Sheriff	2	3	13	10	12										504
months	1	12	12	11	12										142
percent	0.17	0.02	0.09	0.07	0.08										0.32
Equity	22	11	18	12	0										63
months	12	12	12	12	1										49
percent	0.15	0.08	0.12	0.08	0.00										0.11
MARLBORO	5,859	5,988	6,117	6,247	6,376	6,505	6,634	6,764	6,893	7,022	7,152	7,281	7,410	7,540	
Sheriff	5	6	1	2	3	8	0	0		4					445
months	12	12	12	12	12	2	2	2		11					377
percent	0.09	0.10	0.02	0.03	0.05	0.74	0.00	0.00		0.06					0.30
Equity					0	0	16	8	29	0	0	0	0	12	65
months					2	12	12	12	12	12	12	12	12	2	100
percent					0.00	0.00	0.24	0.12	0.42	0.00	0.00	0.00	0.00	0.96	0.11
Probate				11	3	87	19	48	14						384
months				1	12	12	12	12	2						180
percent				2.11	0.05	1.34	0.29	0.71	1.22						0.46
NEWBERRY	12,889	12,990	13,901	13,192	13,292	13,393	13,494	13,594	13,695	13,796	13,896	13,997	14,098	14,199	
Sheriff															93
months															15
percent															0.86
UNION	10,475	10,515	10,556	10,596	10,637	10,678	10,719	10,760	10,801	10,842	10,883	10,924	10,965	11,005	
Sheriff															88
months															40
percent															0.45
Equity															45
months															81
percent															0.12

Part IV

Comparative
Law of Slavery

11

Seventeenth-Century Jurists, Roman Law, and the Law of Slavery

Alan Watson

ISSUES OF SLAVERY and slave law were of considerable theoretical interest to continental European jurists in the seventeenth century. They lived in a different world from American colonists of European descent because they had no direct experience of slaveholding and no immediate financial involvement. This interest of theirs stemmed from the fact that their education was in Roman law; and not only was Roman law the most revered system but slaves were prominent in it. For the jurists' attitudes we must remember that (at least in theory) there were no slaves in territories such as the Dutch Republic, Germany, or France. (And what slaves there, were were the innocuous domestic servants of colonists back for a visit.) The writings of the jurists had implications for slavery in the Americas partly because their views might be translated into actual law, and mainly because respect for them could influence contemporary and later opinion on theoretical issues of the morality or otherwise of slaveholding. And this theoretical opinion could then have practical implications. We must not forget that since these jurists wrote mainly in Latin, a language understood by a large proportion of the educated, their ideas could have an impact across local, national, and continental boundaries.

In this paper I will not expressly consider the impact of juristic writing on slavery in the Americas. Rather I shall consider aspects of the intellectual "baggage" that some jurists of the seventeenth century themselves brought to the task of framing their opinions.[1] Scholars do not develop their theories just as they like: they are also bound by what they do and do not know, by what they have and have not read, by the intellectual cultural tradition in which they work, and by the outside world.[2] I will not stress the idiosyncracies of individuals, but what the jurists of the time had in common, as part of their heritage. A prime purpose of this paper is, in fact, to alert scholars of American slavery to this common, European, legal heritage.

Romanist Ideology

Scholars who rise to the top of their profession usually have a fondness for their discipline, and are even tempted to exaggerate its virtues and downplay its weaknesses. Thus, at the outset (1.1.15) of his *Institutions of the Law of Scotland* (first edition, 1681), Lord Stair writes: "The Law of *Scotland*, in its Nearness to Equity, plainness and facility in its Customes, Tenors and Forms, and in its celerity and dispatch in the Administration and Execution of it, may be well paralleled with the best Law in Christendom." And William Blackstone's complacency in his admiration for the law of England, as set out in his *Commentaries on the Law of England* (first edition, 1765–69) is notorious.[3]

But the primary training of the continental jurists with whom we are concerned was in Roman law, as already mentioned, and their high esteem of it is a commonplace. Thus, Hugo Grotius of Holland has:

> When no general written laws, privileges, by-laws or customs were found touching the matter in hand, the judges were from times of old admonished by oath to follow the path of reason according to their knowledge and discretion. But since the Roman laws, particularly as codified under Justinian, were considered by men of understanding to be full of wisdom and equity, these were first received as patterns of wisdom and equity and in course of time by custom as law.[4]

And the Frisian, Ulrich Huber:

> But because the laws of the State of Rome spread with her ancient empire through the whole of Europe, and because they surpass all other known systems of law in sagacity and justice, Roman law kept its force among almost all Christian peoples, so much so that it has been adopted by many of them; not, however, without every free nation taking away or adding what seemed to it good. Among some nations also it has no binding power, but rather serves as a pattern of wisdom and legality, without the judges being actually bound by it.[5]

This praise for Roman law is especially significant because these quotations from both jurists are taken from treatises on their own local law.

This admiration of theirs was for Roman private law in general, not just for one branch of it. The Romans were among the world's greatest slave users and had a highly developed law of slavery. Admiration for Roman law in general induced later jurists to be less critical of Roman slave law.

I deliberately say "to be less critical," not "to praise." A good example of what I mean is provided by another scholar from Holland, Johannes Voet, *Commentarius ad Pandectas* ("Commentary on Justinian's *Digest*") (first edition, 1698, 1704). Because he was producing a commentary that in fact was geared towards the law of his own time, slave law is naturally deemphasized, since it did not exist in Holland. Still, in the main passage in 1.5.3, "On the Status of Humans," which occupies less than one page in a standard edition, he manages to emphasize that the rights of owners came to be restricted to moderate punishment and that, though slavery between Christians has been ended, yet where barbarians enslave Christians, so Christians by the *ius talionis* (law of retaliation) enslave barbarians, and sometimes in such circumstances Roman law applies, as by Ordonnances of the Belgian Federation. Almost half of Voet's text is devoted to persons in Gelderland, Zutphen, and elsewhere where slavery did not exist, but who were attached to the soil, and who, he said, in fact were free from none of the stains of slavery. In none of this is there a condemnation of slavery or criticism of Roman slave law. Rather, there is almost pride—not in the institution but in the quality of the rules. Masters' rights to punish, Voet says, were restricted to moderate punishment; when by *ius talionis* Christians took barbarians as slaves, it was the Roman rules that applied at times; and in any event, though slavery did not then exist, contemporary and neighboring states had a status that was not much different.

Even more instructive is Voet's treatment of the *Senatus consultum Silanianum* of A.D. 10 in *Commentarius*, 29.5. This decree of the Roman senate is, in my opinion, the most horrifying manifestation of law as applying to slaves at Rome, to the extent even that (so far as I am aware) it was not accepted in any American colony of a European power. The main provision was that when an owner was murdered in his home, all the slaves normally resident there were to be tortured and then executed. The full horror is that the jurists interpreted this as they did any other piece of law.[6] It was quite irrelevant that a slave could have shown that he had had no part in the crime and could not have prevented the murder. Moreover, by typical legal logic the jurists could reach conclusions quite hostile to the spirit of the decree: thus, for example, if someone was killed at home, those slaves whom he possessed in good faith—thinking he was owner—or in whom he had a life-rent were spared because the victim was not in fact the owner. By similar reasoning, a son who had been given in adoption was not treated as owner even though he was murdered in his real father's house. The common people at Rome were appalled by the savagery of the law.[7] But of this nothing appears in Voet. His emphasis is all on the justification of the *Senatus consultum*: that otherwise no home would be safe and that slaves ought to guard their master's life with their own.

Thus, because of their love for Roman law, leading jurists of the seventeenth century presented Roman slave law—the slave law that was known to them—more kindly than it appears in the Roman legal sources. This should not surprise us or be taken as an indication that they had a personal, if indirect, interest in the maintenance of slavery in the American colonies. Exactly the same overgenerous estimate of slave law in the Roman legal sources appears in the writings of twentieth-century Roman law scholars.[8]

Juristic Bias

But if subsequent jurists tend to represent Roman slave law as less harsh than it appears in the sources, then it must also be said that the Roman sources themselves give a distorted, gentler, picture of the institution.

To the outsider looking in, every legal system, especially a past system, presents only a partial profile. Our information is incomplete and shows us only the concern of certain groups. This is very true for Roman law. We have almost no information on Roman private law except what is contained in the legal sources, especially Justinian's *Code* (which contains the legal rulings of the emperors) and *Digest* (which contains excerpts from the writings of the classical jurists). The *Digest* is twice as large as the *Code* and more important. The jurists in the earlier days were gentlemen who treated legal interpretation as a hobby that brought them social prestige and political prominence, and from the second century they were imperial bureaucrats. They were in general not interested in law in the round, nor in law reform, nor what went on in court, nor in the structure of the system. In their interpretation of the law they discussed the problems that interested them, not necessarily those that actually often arose. For example, in the whole of the *Digest* there are only two texts that expressly mention the market.[9] The jurists were just not concerned about policing arrangements or in administrative matters.

This tunnel vision has three consequences for our knowledge of Roman slave law. First, the sources say almost nothing about policing issues that relate to slavery and thus are in marked contrast to those, say, for English or Dutch America. Only one *Digest* text, reporting a letter of the Emperors Severus and Antoninus to the prefect of the city guard, reveals that the prefect had the duty to hunt down runaway slaves and return them to their owners.[10] But often it is policing regulations that are most informative about unpleasant and nasty restrictions in the society.

Second, just as the jurists were uninterested in what went on in court and in issues of proof, so likewise were they uninterested in the difficulties of showing that an owner had punished a slave beyond reason. That the difficulties were well-nigh insuperable is revealed only incidentally by a few imperial rulings in the *Code*.[11] The absence of such discussion tends not to bring the issue before the mind of a later reader. Not one legal text even mentions sexual abuse of slave children by their owner.

Third, the juristic emphasis on complex situations and the absence of focus on matters just because they were important in the society means that relatively very little is said about the condition of the poorer sort of slave. Roman slaves were of many types. At the high end of the scale, slaves might be set up by their owners as doctors, ship masters, bankers, or business entrepreneurs with even hundreds of other slaves in their *peculium*. The peculium was a fund in the ownership of the master but under the control of the slave, who might even be allowed to use it to buy his freedom. At the low end of the scale were the slaves who toiled in the poisonous air of the silver mines or who labored in chains in the fields. But all the interesting legal questions concern the slaves at the upper end of the scale: the measurement of the peculium, the effect of a contract made by a slave, a ship captain operating beyond his instructions, a surgeon cutting carelessly, the complexities of manumission, the division of a slave's acquisitions when he or she was owned by one person but another had a life-rent. Slave miners and agricultural workers scarcely have the opportunity to appear as heroes or villains of legally interesting situations, so are seldom the subject of discussion by the jurists. Consequently, the slaves that appear in the *Digest* are those (and usually only those) who are relatively affluent. In addition, they are those who had been well treated in the past (or they would not have figured in such situations) and who were likely to continue to be favorably treated by their owners.

Natural Law and the Ius Gentium

For most of our history the most powerful legal theories in the Western world have been theories of natural law. Such theories almost always insist that, independently of any acceptance by a state, there exists a higher law binding as law whether because of its innate and obvious morality, its being in accordance with reason or nature, or its deriving from God's will. The moral goodness of natural law is its primary characteristic. This description, however, does not fit the definition of natural law given in Justinian's *Institutes* and *Digest*, which derives from the classical jurist Ulpian. This must be emphasized at the beginning of this section because, however the Justinianian definition is approached and modified by later jurists, the notion of inherent moral rightness will tend to be attached to it because of the impact of theories of natural law.

For Justinian, law is divided into three kinds: natural law, the law of all peoples (*ius gentium*), and civil law. He defines natural law as the law that nature teaches all animals. It is not restricted to humans but is common to all animals. This definition, which has no philosophical interest, was, I believe, used to deny significance to natural law, because for the jurists law was always purely positivist. Nor has the definition practical value. As Grotius puts it:

> The distinction, which appears in the books of Roman law, between an unchangeable law common to animals and man, which the Roman legal writers call the law of nature in a more restricted sense, and a law peculiar to man, which they frequently call the law of nations, is of hardly any value. For, strictly speaking, only a being that applies general principles is capable of law, as Hesiod rightly observed.[12]

His heading introducing the passage reads: "That the instinct common to other animals, or that peculiar to man, does not constitute another kind of law." That the natural law as defined by Justinian was not law but instinct was a commonplace for seventeenth-century jurists.[13]

Justinian proceeded to define *ius gentium* as the law established by reason and common to all people. Civil law was the law peculiar to a particular state.

The uselessness of the Justinianian definition of natural law, coupled with the strength of natural-law theories, caused later jurists to reassess the situation. A standard position in the seventeenth century would be as follows.[14] The term *natural law* is used, it is claimed, properly and improperly. The improper sense is that found in Justinian's *Institutes* 1.2pr,[15] which defines not law but instinct. The proper sense is the natural law of men, dictated by right reason, hence discovered easily, thus found in all (civilized) nations, and it is always fair and good. *Ius gentium* has a primary and a secondary meaning. The primary meaning is that just designated as natural law, properly so called. The secondary meaning is what we nowadays call international law.

But Justinian had described slavery as part of *ius gentium*, found everywhere, though contrary to nature.[16] In the Roman texts this "contrary to nature" had no moral significance. Under the reinterpretation common in the seventeenth century, the *ius gentium* found in this passage was natural law in its proper sense. Hence, slavery could be described, as indeed on this basis it was, as part of natural law. Both because of the jurists' reinterpretation of the Justinianian definition and because of the moral force of theories of natural law, slavery could be regarded as consistent with reason, consented in by nations, and fair and good.

Servare, to save

But there is yet another Roman strand to the intellectual baggage of these seventeenth-century jurists, and this emerges from the very next text in Justinian's *Institutes* and *Digest*, following on his remark that slavery is an institution of the law of nations that is found everywhere and is contrary to nature: "Slaves (*servi*) are so called because commanders order their captives to be sold, and thereby they are accustomed to save (*servare*) rather than kill them."

The tone of this text is not entirely clear. When the Roman jurists said that slavery was contrary to nature, they were in no way suggesting it was immoral or blameworthy.[17] But this succeeding text may be self-justification or self-praise. Whichever it is, it pointed out a problem to the seventeenth-century jurists. In their day, as before, wars, whether local or extensive, of short or long duration, were frequent, and many prisoners, military and civilian, were taken.

But what was to be done with the prisoners? The problem was precisely that they could not be enslaved. The nobility could be ransomed.[18] But that left the great majority. Simply to keep them as prisoners was wasteful both of supplies and of soldiers to guard them. Yet to return the soldiers even at the end of the war was dangerous because there was no telling when the war might restart, even if with some rather different contenders. Moreover, some prisoners were, or could become, mercenaries and if freed might later fight for a different army against their captors. One rather obvious way out of the dilemma was simply to kill those prisoners who could not be ransomed or exchanged.

Grotius' main treatment of the right over prisoners of war is instructive.[19] He opens by claiming that slavery is contrary to nature, but "it is not in conflict with natural justice that slavery should have its origin in a human act, that is, should arise on an agreement or a crime." He continues that "without exception all who have been captured in a formal public war become slaves from the time they are brought within the lines." Not only prisoners of war but also, he says, their descendants born of a slave woman are slaves. Even the incorporeal property of captives belongs to the master. He continues:

> All these rights have been introduced by the law of nations, with which we are dealing, for no other reason than this: that the captors, mollified by so many advantages, might willingly refrain from recourse to the utmost degree of severity, in accordance with which they could have slain the captives, either immediately or after a delay, as we have said before. "The name of slaves [*servi*]," says Pomponius, "comes from the fact that commanders are accustomed to sell prisoners and thereby to save them [*servare*] and not to kill them." I have said "that they might willingly refrain"; for there is no suggestion of an agreement whereby they may be compelled to refrain, if you are considering this law of nations, but a method of persuading them by indicating the more advantageous course.
>
> For the same reason this right is transferred to others, just as the ownership of things. Further, it has been agreed that ownership should be extended to children; the reason is that otherwise if the captors had

used their full right, the children would not have been born. Whence
it follows that children who were born before the catastrophe do not
become slaves, unless they are themselves captured.

And he explains: "The rights under consideration, moreover, have not
been introduced by the nations in vain. This we may perceive from what
happens in civil wars, in which we find that on many occasions captives
have been killed because they could not be reduced to slavery. The fact
is noted by Plutarch in his *Otho* and by Tacitus in the second book of his
Histories." Grotius goes on to consider whether such captives have the
right to flee and to resist their master.

So far we have been dealing with the main and major portion of
Grotius's treatment. He accepts that the law of nations is that prisoners
of war and their descendants do become slaves. He accepts this with
approval because otherwise the prisoners would simply be killed. He
strengthens this position by arguing, on the basis of classical authors,
that when enslavement is not permitted, as in civil wars, the prisoners
are, in fact, simply killed. For Grotius, it seems, enslavement by capture
in a formal, public war is ethically correct.

But there remain two short sections in his chapter. In section 8 he
points out that not all nations have observed this rule. And section 9
begins:

> Christians furthermore have as a whole agreed that those who are cap-
> tured in a war which has arisen among themselves do not become slaves
> so as to be liable to be sold, constrained to labor, and suffer the fate of
> slaves in other respects. In this they are surely right, because they have
> been, or should have been, better instructed in the teachings of Him
> who has sanctioned all charity, than to be unable to be restrained from
> the slaughter of unfortunate men in any other way than by the conces-
> sion of a lesser cruelty.

The chapter goes on to end very weakly. In the passage just quoted, the
words "because they have been, or should have been, better instructed"
are noteworthy. Grotius knew from personal experience that Christianity had not always taught generosity towards Christian prisoners, and he
was too much of a historian to be unaware of numerous instances where
Christian victors massacred Christian prisoners of war who could not be
ransomed. In 1625, when *De Jure Belli ac Pacis* was first published, the
Thirty Years' War was in progress, and the atrocities of the St.
Bartholomew Day massacre of the Huguenots (1572) and those committed during the Dutch Revolt from 1565 onward were fresh in memory.

"Or should have been" gives the game away. It appears a cruel joke
to claim slavery of Christians was abolished because of Christ's teaching
of all charity, so that men ought not to be persuaded away from slaughter by permitting them a lesser cruelty. In fact, Christians had not always

been so persuaded. Grotius is aware that enslavement could be a benefit. Cornelis van Bynkershoek claimed that the practice of massacring prisoners of war had grown almost obsolete; but, he goes on, "this fact is to be attributed solely to the voluntary clemency of the victor, and we cannot deny that the right might still be exercised if anyone wished to avail himself of it." He also says, "Since the conqueror may do what he likes with the conquered, no one doubts that he also has the power of life and death over him."[20]

The structure and emphasis in Grotius's chapter is as important for reconstructing his thought as is the substance itself. His opening is that slavery is contrary to nature but not to natural justice. Enslavement of prisoners of war is part of the law of nations. And he himself has previously reinterpreted his sources so that natural law is this very same law of nations. He proceeds to detail the conditions of this slavery, and he maintains that it was introduced for humanitarian reasons. He sticks closely to the short treatment in the Justinianian texts, and he uses Roman legal authority. He writes always in the present tense, as if this law still exists. Indeed, it should do or it would not be *ius gentium*. Close to the end of the chapter, however, he explains that not all nations have had this law, and that it is now obsolete for Christians to take Christian slaves. His rationale for this is weak in itself and seems to have been unconvincing even to him.

Ulrich Huber puts the matter even more clearly in his *Praelectiones Juris Civilis* ("Lectures on the Civil Law") on the *Institutes* 1.3 (first published in 1678):

> As we just said, slavery is not necessarily at odds with reason. For the Christians themselves only late disapproved of slavery, nor is it disapproved of in the Old or New Testament. Likewise laws of Charlemagne, Louis the Pious, and Lothar on slaves survive in the *Laws of Charlemagne and the Lombards*. Indeed, there exist rulings of King William of Sicily and of the Emperor Frederick on runaway slaves in *Neapolitan Decisions*. But from that time, that is A.D. 1212 or not much later, Christians stopped enslaving one another, which is also the case among the Muslims and Turks according to Busbequius, *Letter 3*, where he also argues that slavery was not rightly removed from among us. The specious pretext of charitableness was adduced, but in vain. The result was a flood of free persons whom wantonness and need drove to wickedness or beggary. The ministrations of the enlarged family were reduced. Add that slaughter in war became more frequent when slavery was removed, which the Romans put to the test in civil wars in which the captives were not made slaves. Tacitus, *Histories* 2, cap. 44, Plutarch, *Otho*, and *Dig.* 49.15.21.1. This reasoning is not without weight. See Berneggerus on Tacitus, *Germania*, question 134.

For Huber it was a "specious pretext" to claim that the abolition of enslavement of coreligionists was on account of benevolence. Moreover, for Huber the result was bad, leading "a flood" of free persons to crime or beggary.[21] The passage suggests that Huber would have found the enslavement of Christian prisoners preferable to their becoming criminals or beggars.

Conclusions

The European jurists of the seventeenth century wrote about slave law either when discussing Roman law or their own system. For them slavery was an abstract issue but one to which they brought considerable intellectual baggage. They approached the subject through Roman law, and because they admired Roman law in general, they were less critical of slave law than they might have been. Moreover, for historical reasons the Roman legal texts put the stress on the more benign aspects of slavery and downplayed the horrors. For reasons unconnected with slave law, the jurists of the seventeenth century reinterpreted the Justinianian definitions of natural law and *ius gentium* in such a way that natural law properly so called was the law based on reason, found among (civilized) nations. Since slavery was assuredly part of the *ius gentium* it was also part of natural law. And it was impossible to exclude the notion of fairness and justice from natural law. Indeed, they claimed, slavery was a benefit in so far as it was an alternative to killing prisoners of war.[22]

Notes

1. The same baggage is found in eighteenth-century writers: see, e.g., J. G. Heineccius, *Elementa Juris Naturae et Gentium* ("Elements of the Law of Nature and of Nations").

2. See, e.g., D. Daube, "Fashions and Idiosyncracies in the Exposition of the Roman Law of Property," now in D. Daube, *Collected Studies in Roman Law*, vol. 2 (Frankfurt am Main: Klostermann, 1991), 1325–39.

3. See, above all, Jeremy Bentham, *A Fragment on Government* (1776).

4. Hugo Grotius, *Inleiding tot de Hollandsche Rechtsgeleertheyd* ("Introduction to the Jurisprudence of Holland"), 1.2.22. This was written between 1619 and 1621 but published in 1631.

5. Ulrich Huber, *Heedensdaegse Rechtsgeleertheyt* ("Contemporary Jurisprudence"), 1.2.24 (first published in 1686).

6. See, e.g., Alan Watson, *Roman Slave Law* (Baltimore: The Johns Hopkins University Press, 1987), 134–38; *Slave Law in the Americas* (Athens, Ga.: University of Georgia Press, 1989), 7–10.

7. Tacitus, *Annales*, 14.42–45.

8. See Alan Watson, "Roman Slave Law and Romanist Ideology," now in Alan Watson, *Legal Origins and Legal Change* (London: Hambledon Press, 1991), 279–91.

9. One, *Digest of Justinian* [hereinafter cited as *Dig.*] 1.12.1.11, says that the supervision of the pig market is within the charge of the urban prefect. The other, *Dig.* 42.4.7.13, mentions the market only incidentally. I am here ignoring the famous aedilician edicts concerning warranties in sale of beasts and slaves.

10. *Dig.* 1.15.4.

11. See Watson, *Legal Origins*, 287–91.

12. Hugo Grotius, *De Jure Belli ac Pacis* ("On the Law of War and Peace"), 1.2.11.1 (first published 1625).

13. See the discussion in Alan Watson, "Some Notes on Mackenzie's *Institutions* and the European Legal Tradition," 16 *Ius Commune* 303–7 (1989).

14. See again, Watson, "Some Notes on Mackenzie's *Institutions.*"

15. Justinian's *Institutes* (an elementary textbook, issued with the force of statute in 533) is hereinafter cited as *J. Inst.*

16. *J. Inst.* 1.3.2; *Dig.* 1.5.4.1.

17. For the argument see Watson, *Slave Law in the Americas*, 115–19.

18. For ransoming as standard practice see, e.g., Robert Ward, *An Enquiry into the Foundation and History of the Law of Nations in Europe*, vol. 1 (1795), 178–80.

19. Grotius, *De Jure Belli ac Pacis*, 3.7.

20. Cornelius van Bynkershoek, *Quaestiones Juris Publici* ("Public Law Questions"), 1.3 (published 1737).

21. For the Dutch horror of beggars and vagabonds, see Simon Schama, *The Embarrassment of Riches* (Berkeley: University of California Press, 1988), 15–24.

22. I do not intend to relate here how these ideas were taken over by other scholars and theologians, who then influenced thinking in America, but for one detail see Watson, *Slave Law in the Americas*, 158 n. 19.

12

The British Constitution and the Creation of American Slavery

Jonathan A. Bush

THE ADOPTION OF SLAVERY by early American colonists cannot be called a surprise. Surely it is no surprise that planters in the English Caribbean colonies were attracted to the huge profits of sugar monoculture and to a flexible labor institution long entrenched in the nearby Spanish and Portuguese colonies. And it is no surprise that planters in the mainland southern colonies similarly turned to slavery when, toward the end of the seventeenth century, the supply of "free" (that is, indentured) laborers fell and their price rose, and when the supply of slaves increased and their price, at least temporarily, fell. Indeed, there are few settings in which notions of race, commodity production, market, labor coercion, and empire are more germane. As a result the switch to slave labor has been richly if variously explained by social and economic historians.

It is, however, a different and more difficult matter that English and colonial law came to accept slavery, given the strong rhetoric in English legal culture rejecting slave status and celebrating freedom. No less remarkable is that the law adopted slavery in the way that it did: quietly, without ever formally introducing the new institution—an "unthinking decision," in Winthrop D. Jordan's apt phrase.[1] Instead, a startlingly new labor regime, repudiated at home for centuries, was introduced by rapacious planters and merchants; as local practice it was enshrined in provincial statute and allowed indirectly under common law—from start to finish, a passive, almost stealthy process of legal accommodation.[2] This essay explores the route by which slavery came to be legal in a system that had long rejected unfree labor and that outwardly seemed to retain that view.

The Problem of Slave Law In British America

For a number of decades now, scholars have examined nineteenth-century slave law, Northern as well as Southern, for the legal reasoning and intellectual underpinnings of slavery. The diverse work these scholars produced shares the assumption that the law was an important social institution buttressing slavery and that the precise configurations of slave jurisprudence therefore matter.

This article approaches slave law from a different perspective, arguing that in the critical first century of English colonial slavery, the common law had very little of importance to say about slaves. Unlike many other slave societies, colonial America never developed a systematic law of slavery. Early American slave law, which was largely piecemeal and reactive, played an insignificant role as seventeenth-century colonial planters turned to slavery. Rather than focus on what little substantive law of slavery existed, this paper instead explores how emigrants from the densely legalistic culture of England dared erect and maintain *de jure* slavery without direct legal authority, and in spite of English common law's apparent repudiation of slavery.

The claim that existing common law was not an impediment to slavery—indeed, on the surface it was barely relevant to slavery—seems paradoxical. "English society was intensely 'law-minded,' obsessed with legal considerations, legal rights, and legal remedies."[3] Early seventeenth-century Englishmen regarded law and litigation as a principal means of dispute resolution, and the volume of litigation in royal courts continued to grow. Litigants sought more than speedy resolution; they seem to have viewed the law as an important means of social interaction. In the words of one leading historian, litigation "had everything that war can offer save the delights of shedding blood. It gave shape and purpose to many otherwise empty lives . . . [and] remained the most popular of indoor sports."[4] The swaggering, quarrelsome frontier entrepreneurs who clawed their way to the top of colonial Southern and Caribbean society shared these values, and they too were "law-minded," using local courts and law to consolidate property and position.[5] And without question, slaves and indentured servants were valuable investments for planters, capable of yielding enormous profits even as they raised unusual legal issues. For these practical reasons we might expect planters to have invested in slaves only with the guarantee that the law would permit and enforce slavery, and a slave law to have developed not long after the inception of slavery as an institution.

In approaching the issues in this way, I argue that colonists lacked sufficient legal authority to erect and maintain slavery and that the resulting slave law in both England and the colonies was incomplete. Historians correctly tend to shy away from such arguments about omissions. After all, most negative claims can be answered by showing that the allegedly missing phenomenon either did occur to some degree, perhaps by some other name, or else did not occur, and then arguing that it is anachronistic to expect that it should have. Because of these difficulties, the claim that slave law was deficient requires that we survey in some detail the major areas of colonial and English law relevant to slavery.

Part 2 sets out the paradox of colonial slavery without initial authority or systematic legal rules. Of course, colonial courts and legislatures addressed slavery, frequently, in thousands of colonial statutes and cases relating to slaves, but the results were haphazard. Colonial slave law was incomplete because the concern of local courts and legislatures was primarily with public law, the policing of slavery. The formal legal institutions generally ignored the applicability of private law to slaves. Meanwhile, Parliament and the common law courts in Westminster did little to remedy the inadequacies of local slave law, offering a few rules about the slave trade and almost nothing about slaves and slavery. Neither colonial nor metropolitan lawmakers addressed slavery in the thorough way that the common law had long addressed other relationships and forms of property, or that the other European powers had addressed their New World slave systems.

The core issue, however, is not why there was a paucity of systematic law on slavery but rather how the colonists erected and sustained slavery using what they asserted were familiar legal doctrines and rationales. Part 3 explains the substantive deficiencies of English and colonial slave law by turning to the unexpected but familiar ground of constitutional law. Ultimately, the basis for colonial slavery, and the explanation for the seeming absence of common law directly on the matter, lies in the constitutional relationship between the English Crown and its colonies.

The colonies began as lands in the king's possession but not under Parliament or common law. Instead, they were dominions, governed by the royal prerogative and either annexed to the Crown or granted to lords proprietary. This prerogative framework permitted divergent local practices. Thus, despite the common law's traditions of antislavery rhetoric, doctrinal conservatism, and centralization, there were few obstacles to prevent the colonists from making their own local slave law, fashioned from bits and pieces of common law doctrine. Predictably, the legal results were incomplete and intellectually underdeveloped. The quantity and quality of slave law, however, were less significant than the fact that the colonists would presume to fashion such radically new doctrine and that, despite the traditions and precedents of English common law, there were few obstacles restricting the colonists from doing so.

In this light, colonial constitutional law represents more than the familiar political backdrop to the American Revolution. It also provided the basis on which plantation slavery could develop with full legal protection, but only minimal legal obstruction. Thus through constitutional doctrines slavery indirectly became an area in which it is possible to speak of the early "Americanization" of the common law. Under the evolving colonial constitution, slaveholders got to keep both their common law birthright and their slaves. The reliance on constitutional law, rather than on the concept of unfree status as such, reflects notions of the colonists' right to adapt the precepts of the common law, which in turn had obvious and enormous importance for the development in the eighteenth century of a distinct American political identity. In the end, colonists awkwardly and often implicitly fitted the issues raised by their slaveholding into the traditional categories of the common law. Debt, contract, and tort actions, gifts, and bequests became possible for property in slaves. But that result was only possible because the colonial constitution of the old British Empire provided a rationale for legal divergence and thus a lawyerly way to reconcile American slavery with American freedom.

The Lack of Systematic Slave Law and Its Significance

THE INADEQUACIES OF COLONIAL SLAVE LAW

Both nineteenth-century Southern judges and Northern abolitionists agreed that slavery had never been legally created or initially authorized. Historians agree. Slavery simply evolved in practice, as a custom, and then received statutory recognition.[6] Actually, the process of "recognition" was implicit, involving no articulation of first principles. For the first few decades of English colonization, there was likely no slavery in practice and certainly no mention of slavery in law. Suddenly, legal documents began to refer to slaves. In 1636 the governor and council of Barbados decreed that "Negroes and Indians, that came here to be sold, should serve for Life, unless a Contract was before made to the contrary." A Maryland act of 1638, for example, noted matter-of-factly that "all Christians—except slaves" shall have the full rights of Englishmen at home. A Rhode Island statute of 1652 cited "the common course practised among English men to buy negars, to that end that they may have them for service or slaves forever." The famous Fundamental Constitutions, drawn up by John Locke and the Earl of Shaftesbury in 1669 for the nascent South Carolina colony, guaranteed that "Every Freeman of Carolina, shall have absolute power and authority over Negro Slaves."[7] Almost from the outset, slavery was assumed in this way, *ex nihilo*, but it was nowhere authorized, justified, explained, or systematically described.

It is commonly thought that, however illegitimate its origins, colonial slavery soon acquired a legal framework sufficient for its purposes. But the reality is that even in the eighteenth century, slavery was principally acknowledged in law by an extensive set of police measures. There were few legal provisions for commercial and other private law aspects of slavery. Nor could the existing categories of property, tort, and contract suffice. Colonial lawmakers learned, as jurists had recognized in slaveowning Rome and as American lawyers continued to realize in the nineteenth century, that the legal issues posed by chattelized humans and thinking property often could not be accommodated within ordinary legal categories. But the response was slow, and slave law failed to develop a significant analytic apparatus until the last few years of the colonial period. There are no thoughtful opinions of appellate judges on slave law until the last third of the eighteenth century. Daniel Boorstin has noted "how few books on the laws of slavery came out of the South."[8] In fact, there were few treatises, Northern or Southern, on American slave law, and they all date from slavery's last decades. There were also no systematic slave codes in the English colonies, in contrast to such other New World texts as the French *Code noir* or the *Codigo negro caroleno* of Santo Domingo.[9] In short, whatever the timing and extent of slavery in each English colony, at every step English colonial law seemed to take slavery more or less for granted.

The literary evidence adds almost nothing to this picture of colonial jurisprudential indifference. In all of the rich English polemical literature of the seventeenth century discussing oppression or slavery in domestic political contexts, there is no serious discussion of slave law and little defense of New World slavery. Similarly, seventeenth-century mercantilists rarely defended the slave trade or examined Africa, even though they clearly assumed that the African slave trade was important. Travelers to the colonies and the colonists themselves wrote about crops, taxes, political disputes and claims, slave purchases, and occasionally slave life, but did not defend or attack black slavery on political or legal grounds or describe its rules. The contrast is illustrated by the startling omission of blacks from the writings of Robert Beverley and Hugh Jones, two leading contemporary observers of colonial Virginia. Both devoted major passages to land, crops, governance, peoples, and especially to the customs of the defeated American Indians, emphasizing the exotic bravery of the "noble savage." But both said almost nothing about blacks (free or slave), other than to insist with evident irritation that slaves were treated better than reports in England alleged, better in fact than free English woodsmen at home.[10] That seventeenth-century planters and traders were increasingly racist needs little proof here, but they rarely wrote about Africans or slaves or used race as an important rationale for slavery, unlike their nineteenth-century successors. In fact, there seems to have been a distinct lack of curiosity about plantation slavery and African slaves among all but a few European travelers, merchants, and other observers, including lawyers. This is especially remarkable in light of the consistent literary fascination of Europeans with the customs of the Far East and of Native Americans.[11]

Yet, from the very inception of slavery, practical questions requiring legal answers arose every day: which heir should take how many slaves;

what were the limits to a master's punishment of his slave; did a lessee have to pay when the slave died within the term of the lease. Whatever the substance of the answers, it was clear that colonial slave law had to be home-grown. Although English law had never abolished the category of "villeinage"—common law serfdom—it was in complete desuetude,[12] and common law had no other category for slaves. Later, Southern judges occasionally invoked medieval villeinage to support the general proposition that bondage and the common law were compatible, and abolitionists cited villeinage to argue that it was the only form of unfreedom permitted by the common law, but both sides saw that slavery was not in any historical sense a direct continuation of villeinage.[13] Nor could the substantive rules of villeinage support plantation slavery by way of metaphor or analogy. Medieval common law almost from the outset had distinguished between villeinage land tenure and a villein's personal status, even though the tenants of villeinage land typically were unfree villagers. Local custom protected the tenant in villeinage, and in time the common law did as well. As for unfree personal status, common law had always limited the lord's right to kill or maim his serf, and it assumed that the villein would have rights to religion as well as family integrity and formation (subject to certain payments). It permitted the villein to act in such legal capacities as executor to a will. In short, under all formulations of villeinage—even Sir Edward Coke's ahistorical and slavish "villein in gross"[14]—the villein was protected in ways that went far beyond the essentially unlimited nature of colonial slavery.

In theory, proslavery forces could have invoked other bodies of common law to account for slavery. The common law of personal property, for instance, contained doctrines applicable to ownership and transfer of things as well as damage to and by those objects. Certain of these doctrines were transferable to property in slaves. Similarly, the body of harsh Tudor law on vagrants, apprentices, and servants contained doctrines applicable to the governance of slaves. But neither English personal property law nor labor law contained the *a priori* first step that would permit humans to be deemed property or slaves. On the contrary, at the heart of early modern labor law was the paradox that, despite its severity and assumption that (free) labor ought to be compelled to work, the law also regarded all non-villein labor as meaningfully free, and it celebrated that freedom. The practical unfreedom implied by Tudor-Stuart labor law may have resembled slavery, but by its own terms that law addressed laborers of "free" status and was part of a legal system that knew neither slavery nor slaves.[15] The result was that neither villeinage nor other substantive bodies of common law could have been transferred whole to the New World to justify and then sustain slavery.

The only other ready-made slave law in the seventeenth century would have been Roman law, upon which the various colonies belonging to Portugal, Spain, France, and the Netherlands had relied in order to support and implement their slave systems. But such wholesale reception of

Roman slave law was impossible in an English colony. Whatever the influence of Roman law on particular English doctrines or on common law generally, a full reception by a colonial legislature would have faced fatal constitutional, political, and ideological difficulties. A handful of Roman slave doctrines were used and retained into the nineteenth century, particularly *partus sequitur ventrem*, the rule by which the child of a mixed-status union follows the mother.[16] But even then it was clear that American slave law had very little in common with Roman law,[17] and aside from the rule of maternal descent, there is little evidence of Roman borrowings. In short, the colonists neither brought with them nor borrowed a systematic law of slavery. A new law had to be constructed.

Of course, the colonists did produce a legal response to the practical questions associated with a slave regime. It came not in the form of systematic codes or treatises, but in a large quantity of local case law and statutes. Beginning in the mid seventeenth century, legislators in Barbados and the Chesapeake colonies responded to the public "problem" of black labor by defining slave status with increasingly harsh clarity. Rarely did this emerging public slave law address questions of private law. Typically, colonial slave statutes responded to some perceived threat to the stability of the slave regime, and were limited, reactive, and negative. As for local private law, the reported cases are short and conclusory, almost entirely devoid of analysis or reasoning. They usually record transactions of value such as the sale or manumission of a slave, debts secured on slaves and other assets, and the probate of estates including slaves.[18] But nowhere in the statutes or caselaw is there anything remotely like a jurisprudence of slavery.

Contemporaries would not have seen this lack of systematic thinking about slavery in formal sources as a failure of the legal imagination. On the contrary, it reflected the colonists' view that the aim of applied law was dispute resolution and local order rather than the articulation of grand principles.[19] Similarly, we can read little significance into the failure to write on slave law. In many colonies, it was only late in the eighteenth century that the trappings of modern legal practice appeared, with regular appeals, a professional bar and published judicial opinions. Until the same period, common law treatises written in the colonies or England rarely discussed anything but the ancient forms of action and the duties of various officeholders and courts; even after that, there were few Southern academic jurists, law schools, or texts.[20] Neither the conventional silence of treatises nor the brevity, limited distribution, and practical orientation of colonial decisions necessarily meant that discourse concerning slavery was not transpiring, only that there was no incentive to transcribe or publish more thorough case reports. But, whatever the reason, a consequence of the lack of reported discussions was that any courtroom discourse that did occur about slavery was unlikely to have been transmitted to a wider audience.

Moreover, there were reasons outside of the law for the apparent lack of colonial slave law. Most important was that normative thinking about slavery occurred outside of legal forms. In addition to law, colonial Southerners found social legitimation in other systems such as honor and religion, which supported slavery. The master-slave relationship, which implied the complete removal of the slave from the public sphere, was particularly open to elaboration outside of law. And the developing political culture of plantation slavery, emphasizing values of personal autonomy and paternalism, made it likely that slaveowners would use law as but one means of implementing their mastery. Within the private world of the master, the formal underdevelopment of slave law was off-set by private "rulemaking," described in plantation manuals and rule books and enforced with whipping and other punishments, including death.[21] For all these reasons the failure of colonial law to generate a formal slave jurisprudence cannot by itself be taken as proof of a desire to avoid confronting slavery.

But if these considerations suggest there was no lack of rules for the governance of slaves, the lack of a systematized and specifically legal response to slavery often left masters without answers to practical questions. The familiar example is the uncertainty as to what kind of property a slave was. The common law provided essentially two choices—real property or personal (chattel) property. Once an item of property was classified as either real or personal, lawyers and owners everywhere would have known how to treat the item in any contingency. Categorization helped implement the routine transactions planters entered: purchasing slaves on credit from the Caribbean, pledging them to London creditors, transferring them to kin. Many colonies and states flip-flopped, but eventually almost all described slaves as chattels. The important point, however, is that neither category worked very well. Jurisdictions that classified slaves as real property typically came to add that, unlike other forms of real property, a slave was a chattel for certain purposes.[22] But where slaves were termed personal property, it was often said that they were still realty for purposes of inheritance or transfer by an underage heir.[23] Notwithstanding these analytic difficulties, the English colonies were slow to turn to new hybrid categories and more systematic jurisprudence, preferring to reason by analogy and with ad hoc exceptions.[24] And so, of the colonial statutes concerning private slave law, many were private acts confirming or breaking entails of real property to which slaves were annexed.[25] Only by fiat could the law accommodate the gordian knot of family, creditors, and doctrinal consistency.

Colonial slave law was characterized not only by inadequate categorization, but also by a complete failure to address topics relevant to everyday life. With its focus on responding to threats of slave disorder and recording valuable transactions, colonial slave law never provided for most areas of private law. Such matters as work, family, religion, wages and slave property (the Roman *peculium*), bequests to slaves, most torts against and by slaves, adoption (of a master's illegitimate child), and so on were essentially absent from local jurisprudence, and left to private ordering.

English Law as a Source of Substantive Slave Law

In theory there was always the possibility that Westminster would come to the rescue. Common law courts, Parliament, or some thoughtful legal author could have offered answers for the new legal questions. The lessons of the French, Spanish, and Portuguese empires are suggestive, not because they each used different civil law doctrines to maintain slavery, but rather because each imperial power authorized or imposed by legislative decree a body of slave law.[26] In the case of the English settlements, the colonists were, after all, governed by English common law and statutes, despite bitter disputes over precisely what that governance meant. Had Westminster lawmakers wished to fashion a law of slavery, their common law contained the raw materials: an extraordinarily refined law of property and a modest but serviceable law of persons, which provided for various kinds of dependent exploited labor. Lawmakers also knew of the long legal tradition of regulating laborers, foreign trade, and new territorial acquisitions. Neither jurisdictional limitations nor deference to local practice would have prevented English lawmakers from addressing colonial slavery, just as their late nineteenth-century descendants ultimately did not shrink from prohibiting slavery in their African empire. More important, throughout the eighteenth century, English lawmakers repeatedly used statutes to create new or redefine existing property interests in other settings, ranging from the right to trade opium to ownership of hunting dogs.[27]

But Westminster did not affirmatively address slavery in any substantive way in the seventeenth or early eighteenth centuries. In fact, the resulting legal problem can be seen in stronger terms than simply legal neglect or oversight. Not only *could* English lawyers and legislators have intervened to clarify the law; under one view, they were *bound* to recognize slavery affirmatively, or else the institution would likely fail. To a seventeenth-century lawyer, the supremacy of the common law meant that any institution grounded on custom and local legislation alone, like slavery, was very vulnerable. Neither the authority of colonial statutes, nor a tradition of coercive labor practices at home would have been sufficient to permit slavery to interpose itself into common law. Without actual or implied adoption by the common law, the claim of local planters to "legislate" about slavery was a mere problem of *ultra vires*, unless the practice was "reasonable" within the stringent test of the common law, and no common law authority ever said that slavery met the formal test of a reasonable custom. Chief Justice Holt acknowledged in a famous slave case that slavery was in fact the custom of the colonies, but, as he said elsewhere, it is not open to private parties to dictate legal change to the courts in this backdoor way.[28] In light of this, the inaction of English courts and Parliament concerning slavery is a matter of considerable importance.

Yet the extraordinary fact is that there are only one dozen published decisions in which common law courts addressed colonial slavery before *Somerset* v. *Stewart* (1772), even though at least one and probably closer to two million Africans had already been brought as slaves to the English colonies in the Caribbean and America.[29] None of these few cases are very significant, though they have been studied with microscopic care from the time of *Somerset* to the present. Most are actions in trover or trespass, one is in assumpsit.[30] The traditional view of these cases is that they represented the beginnings of the final, glorious ascent of the common law toward *Somerset*, abolition, and equal justice under law. Special praise is given to the celebrated trover cases in which Chief Justice Holt reasoned that "as soon as a negro comes into England, he becomes free; one may be a villein in England, but not a slave." He later asserted, "[F]or the common law takes no notice of negroes being different from other men. By the common law no man can have a property interest in another." These cases, historian David Ogg once said, are "an extraordinary change of judicial opinion . . . [and] one of the most revolutionary of all the judicial pronouncements of the century."[31]

Scholars today are more skeptical of this whiggish interpretation and less likely to ascribe much importance to this trickle of slave cases. The reported cases contain dubious rhetoric, contradict each other, and in a few instances—including the cases in which Chief Justice Holt reasoned for freedom—were neither published nor widely known in their own day. The famous rhetoric of Holt was dicta, and the cases rejecting trover for slaves were decided on narrow pleading grounds and irregularly "reversed" soon after. In an earlier ruling Holt had concluded to the contrary that Africans were indeed commodities. And in no case—including *Somerset*—did the common law ever meddle with, ratify, reject, or otherwise directly address slavery in the colonies, as opposed to England, other than to accept it as the apparent custom of the colonies.[32]

In fact, there are many reported cases concerning the English slave-trading monopoly, indebted tobacco or sugar planters, the duties charged on various plantation commodities, and trade to Africa and America, all matters whose circumstances frequently involved black slaves. Yet few of these cases even mention the institution, much less elaborate on the law applicable to slavery or articulate special rules. The same pattern characterizes cases arising in specialized jurisdictions, such as the Admiralty Court. Here again the facts often concerned contested ownership of slave cargo, but many decisions did not itemize slaves or any other part of the cargo, the convention being to refer to "cargo" without differentiation, and few described special legal rules applicable to slaves. Of course, legal discussion often develops outside of reported cases, and there is some evidence that such exchanges on slave law occurred in the late seventeenth century. But even assuming such a debate did occur, the paucity of cases, recorded discussions, and formal rules for slavery is revealing.[33]

Ironically, abolitionists later praised English law for this consistent silence. Nowhere, they said with Holt's rhetoric in mind, did English law recognize slavery or race. Therefore, the common law must be a system of neutral rules and equality under the law. That may be so, but the silence of the seventeenth- and early eighteenth-century common law coexisted not only with licit slavery throughout the British Empire, but also with the retention of black slaves in England. The paucity of cases reaching final disposition in the central courts, as well as the noncommittal stance of the common law until *Somerset*, did not imply that the air of England was too free for a slave to breathe, as the celebrated rhetoric put it. Rather, it meant that the status of colonial slaves brought to England, and free blacks as well, was inconclusive, depending in any single case upon private, negotiable considerations. Most blacks in England—and there may have been fifteen thousand by 1772—were neither clearly slave nor clearly free but up for grabs, in law and often in fact as well.[34] In favor of freedom in a given case was a slave's ability to find refuge if he fled; in favor of slavery was a master's ability to bind or induce his slave to stay, or to recover him if he fled. In short, the abolitionists misstated the history. Legal silence did not mean that the law did not know slavery or that the question of status never arose, but it did create uncertainty.

Nor do other official sources of English law supplement the slender body of case law. To be sure, a number of statutes regulated such mercantile and revenue matters as plantation commodities and rights to trade with Africa, but neither statutes nor parliamentary debate addressed, in serious or sustained fashion, the new forms of labor in the New World.[35] More significantly the Privy Council, with its advisory boards and committees, knew of the new labor practices in the colonies: "Blacks [are] the most useful appurtenances of a Plantation and perpetual servants," the Council for Foreign Plantations observed in 1664.[36] But the Privy Council and its entities were concerned with defense and trade, and only secondarily with internal colonial economic and social institutions. Neither council nor boards issued substantive slave law, and the reactive authority to evaluate colonial legislation on any topic was routinely exercised only toward the late seventeenth century. By then slavery was firmly in place and far too valuable a form of property for the council to disallow.

Inevitably, the council had to address slavery as part of its authority to oversee the affairs of the empire. Among the most significant conciliar rulings was the decision, first reached in 1677, that slaves were goods or commodities within the Navigation Acts, and thus that the slave trade had to be carried by English ships and crews.[37] But despite their status as property under both colonial law and the Navigation Acts, blacks coming into England were not enumerated or dutiable like other commodities.[38] In other words, the council's decision was less a general claim about the legal status of blacks than a revenue ruling with almost no social implications. In fact, the council and boards sent proprietors and colonial officials thousands of orders, opinions, and instructions, aimed at taxing, registering, slightly easing the plight of, and ensuring the proper flow of and title to blacks.[39] Like the 1677 ruling, these texts also are problematic sources of legal reasoning and slave law. Even those texts that relayed decisions reached after judicial-type consideration usually did not include legal reasoning, and none of the texts substantively addressed slavery. Rather, they were confined to protecting the slave trade or weighing whether some colonial regulation was acceptable to London. Nowhere did the Crown or council explain the premise that the law, having seen classic villeinage fade away, could create or permit a new class of unfreedom. For that we will have to look outside of slavery, to constitutional law.

Other, unofficial legal genres present a picture consistent with this, offering almost nothing about colonial slavery or about blacks, in the New World or in England. Nothing, for instance, is to be found in even the most imaginative of English legal genres, the "readings," or lectures, at the Inns of Court. Among the regular topics were such standard texts of freedom as Magna Carta, chapter 29; other subjects seemingly relevant to the slave trade included the medieval Statute of Merchants and Statute of Westminster I, ch. 4 (on shipwrecks). Significantly, the readings often dealt with complex, even impossible, hypotheticals, including the figure of the (extinct) villein. The tradition of readings continued until approximately 1670, by which time Barbados had completely adopted slave labor and Virginia, Maryland, the Leeward Islands, and Jamaica were importing growing numbers of slaves. Yet no known readings alluded to contemporaneous African slaves.[40]

The same silence largely characterizes the treatises. Thomas Wood's *New Institute of Imperial or Civil Law*, for instance, does contain a rare reference to slaves by tracking Holt on the unavailability of trover, but Wood offers no opinion either way in his more important work, the *Institute of the Laws of England*, even in its later, posthumous editions, published after *Somerset*.[41] Most other English "institutional" writers, writing within a stylized textual tradition that aimed at legal breadth and virtuosity, said little about modern slavery: where convention called on them to address the so-called law of persons and its distinctions, beginning with free/unfree, they addressed the outdated villeinage, servants, apprenticeship, even freedom in the sense of "free from arrest," but not black slavery.[42]

Once again, Wood approached colonial issues by mentioning certain legal innovations associated with indentured apprenticeship, but not until the 1760s was plantation slavery addressed, and then by Blackstone, the last great systematizer, in language that nurtured the abolitionists and prefigured Mansfield's *Somerset* decision.[43]

A few legal sources did mention slavery, some even discussing it in considerable detail. But the slavery they described was ancient Greek and Roman, occasionally updated to describe medieval enslavement of infidels captured in war, and their discussions were stylized and irrelevant, aside from whatever prestige they conferred on the new slavery by their acceptance of a homologous but clearly different institution. This is true of English authors like Swinburne and Zouche and of prestigious and widely read works of the great international lawyers like Grotius and Pufendorf.[44]

The apparent silence of English law toward slavery was not based on social or cultural blindness. Far from being hidden from English eyes, slavery, both as an idea and practice, was familiar and widely discussed by the laity. Englishmen spoke, almost obsessively, about slavery in the sense of political subjugation. They fought wars and emigrated to ensure their freedom, argued endlessly about liberty and rights, and denounced the Spanish for having enslaved Indians in the New World; in fact, polemicists described almost every perceived political, economic, or religious threat as seeking specifically to enslave the righteous English.[45] Nor was hostility to slavery confined to articulate disputants and political metaphor. Public opinion was familiar with both the possibility of legal slavery at home, as the notorious and quickly repealed 1547 Vagrancy Act underscores,[46] and with the broad range of licit but possibly contested coercive labor institutions, such as houses of correction and bridewells, mandatory apprenticeships, galley slavery, transportation to Ireland and the colonies, and impressment.[47]

Public opinion also was well acquainted with blacks and the growth of black slavery. Blacks had been in London since at least the late sixteenth century, and by the mid seventeenth century their presence came to be well known.[48] Even more widely known was the systematic use of slaves in the colonies. Indeed, it is a measure of how broadly diffused information was about slavery and conditions in the plantation colonies that many of the poorest English and Irish men and women—prospective emigrants—resisted private blandishments and public campaigns to remove them to the colonies because they expressly did not want to be worked like slaves.[49] But despite this very broad social awareness, English law, in both official and private sources, said almost nothing about the seventeenth century's enormously valuable "new property," the African slave.

COLONIAL SLAVERY STATUTES

With English law thus largely indifferent to slavery, only one body of significant slave law existed in the English colonies: the incomplete and analytically inadequate colonial statutes. Consider the Virginia Slave Code of 1705, which formed the basis of all subsequent Virginia slave law and is widely considered the legislative consolidation of slavery in Virginia.[50] Substantively the act is not a "code"; it is neither comprehensive nor systematic. The act lists, under four dozen more or less random titles, the activities that slaves and indentured servants cannot do, must do, or cannot do with whites, the things that whites cannot do for slaves, and that blacks cannot do even if free.[51] Among the topics are the correction of slaves, slave flight, weaponry in the possession of slaves, illegitimacy and intermarriage, and the baptism of slaves. Other leading common law slave "codes" are similar in the public law topics they address as well as in their lack of structure. The influential Barbados Act of 1661, which formed the basis of later slave statutes in Jamaica (1664), South Carolina (1696), and Antigua (1702), covered such matters as slave crime, noncriminal policing of slaves, flight, and rebellion. Supplemental Barbadian statutes later addressed black-white commercial dealings and the enforcement of black deference. But even these elaborate statutes from other jurisdictions are not truly codes. Like the ancient Anglo-Saxon dooms, they are more akin to lengthy police measures, listing crimes, consequences, and trial procedures but little more. Furthermore, the various Caribbean "slave codes" left practical legal problems unanswered and unclear.[52]

Essentially reactive and penal, colonial slave law was similar to other contemporary bodies of new or reformed law. Like English military law, domestic criminal law, and the law governing Irish plantations, colonial slave law relied upon brutality and death as "the defining characteristics of this era of substantive British law."[53] But the police problem common to each of these areas was surely most acute in the context of slavery, as the fearful legal responses of masters imply. Hence the predictable types of provisions contained in the statutes. These provisions have been classified and tracked from one code to the next, ameliorative trends—on paper—have been identified, and many monographs have explained the real or perceived pressures which impelled legislators to respond how and when they did.[54] Taken together, these codes appear to recognize, organize, and legitimize the practice of slavery. But the general tenor of the codes is more important than any particular provision or penalty. At their core, the statutes respond in similar ways to a similar problem—determining who was a slave and how slaves could be kept unfree and unthreatening. Whether we consider such statutes individually or as additions to a notional slave "code," they were largely police measures. Granted, they went well beyond criminal policing to address public law, broadly defined. That is, the codes were concerned with such seemingly private matters as a master's right to punish, educate, or manumit his slave, or a slave's right to sell produce, precisely because the codes assumed these behaviors affected the safety of whites and the political etiquette between whites and others (Indian, black, and mulatto).[55] The codes assumed rather than addressed slave status, and sought to patrol the public boundaries between free and slave, and between white and nonwhite.

FREEDOM'S BOUNDARIES: THE MEDIEVAL COMPARISON

Where colonial slave law merely defined a racial and status boundary, Roman slave law, long before, had aimed to be comprehensive, particularly on private law issues of manumission and succession. As a result, the English colonial codes are comparable in structure not to Roman law, but rather to the early common law texts whose teachings on villeinage the colonists knew to be inapt. Most important of these medieval English treatises was the great systematic text attributed to Bracton, dating from the thirteenth century. Antebellum judges and counsel occasionally cited Bracton—Southerners typically to adduce his discussions of villeinage, Northerners to note Bracton's passages (themselves taken from Roman law) on the natural liberty of all men and the law's "preference" for freedom.[56] But the similarity between Bracton and colonial slave law is one of structure, not simply of familiarity or quotation.

Like colonial law, medieval common law texts such as Bracton's did not contain the efficient, concise statements of legal disabilities that the Roman model offered. On the contrary, medieval legal authors seemed to avoid discussing certain legally marginalized groups, including women, foreign merchants, Jews, the Irish, lepers, various kinds of serfs, and children born out of wedlock. There are a number of reasons for these omissions, though medieval moral discomfort is not among them. For present purposes, it suffices that Bracton had almost nothing to say about most of these groups, despite their importance to the Crown on fiscal or ideological grounds. In short, the text illustrates legal omission regarding outsiders.

Bracton was *not* silent about one legally unfree group. He had a great deal to say about villeins. Almost all of it, however, concerned the boundary between serf and free: can a serf bring various actions, can a free litigant sue his serf vendor, and so on. Bracton had little to say about labor, the lord-villein relationship, or the economic, religious, and family rights of serfs. Most of what he writes is not a substantive law of unfreedom, but what might be termed "boundary law." As for other outsiders such as Jews and Irishmen, whom medieval common law ousted from its protection and sometimes also called "unfree," Bracton said almost nothing at all.[57]

One reason that the common law texts treated medieval villeins so differently from Jews and Irishmen was the respective numbers of each group. Yet another consideration was the problem of demarcation. Unfree manorial peasants were in most respects very similar to free peasants. In village society free and unfree mixed: they intermarried, leased land to each other, and stood surety for each other.[58] A legal system that wished to retain a status barrier between the free and unfree had to deploy elaborate legal tests to differentiate them. Precisely because unfree peasants were so much like free peasants, the legal topic of rightless villeins became an elaborate set of doctrines.

Meanwhile, such rightless persons as the Jews and the Irish required no legal elaboration to be defined and isolated. They were demonstrably different. In the case of Jews, most wished to stay that way. Some purchased exemptions from the legal disabilities of Jewishness, but only a small handful sought the exemption that was almost always open—voluntary conversion. As for the Irish, a few of them, too, purchased or otherwise obtained the privilege of English liberties, but most could no more change their legal identity than they could their background. And so the jurists had very little work to do to define membership in these communities. English law simply took a seemingly commonsense test of Irishness and appropriated the self-definition of the Jewish community; little legal elaboration was necessary to distinguish either community from the English.[59]

The silence of the medieval texts as to some unfree persons but not others brings us back to colonial slavery. The relative indifference of American law to slave questions is in part explained by the English majority's perception of groupness and difference. Winthrop D. Jordan has shown that English antiblack racism was very much in evidence by the late sixteenth century.[60] Thus, a social and intellectual category, the marginalized black, was in place perhaps a century before the encounter between English whites and African or Mediterranean blacks began on any meaningful scale. By the late seventeenth century, what had been chiefly a psychological category had become a major legal and economic category in the colonies, black slavery. And for most of the time from the seventeenth century through the American Civil War, the notion that African Americans were different and inferior served as the cornerstone of American slavery and seemed to need no elaboration. Just as they once had seen the Irish and Jews, the English and their colonial kin now saw Africans as self-evidently different. The law thus could assume rather than assert or explain the premise of slavery.

But in the course of developing this simple legal definition of slavery the English needed rules, especially in the form of "boundary" statutes to address miscegenation, manumission, runaways, and black-white behavior. Often these lists were sealed with some form of harsh polemi-cal claim, such as the 1696 South Carolina legislature's declaration that slaves are "of barbarous, wild, savage natures, and such as renders them wholly unqualified to be governed by the laws, customs, and practices of this province." In part, rules were necessary to police slaves and slavery. But the additional implication of Bracton's extensive treatment of villeinage may be that status markers and boundaries are hard to impose on complex social practice. The colonial boundaries of skin color and white racism did not always succeed in separating the races, particularly before the eighteenth century. There were instances of black slaves and white servants seeing their plights as common and running away together, or fighting together for the rebel Nathaniel Bacon, or drinking, trading, working together, or consensually making love. For masters the general answer to these boundary challenges was the same: keep slaves as slaves and not free by keeping blacks separate. This explains the prominence of colonial penal statutes, miscegenation laws, restrictions on manumis-sion, and similar acts.[61]

On one level, the significance of these boundary or policing rules is how little else there was to colonial American slave law. As one leading scholar has observed, "[T]he striking thing about southern legal culture in the nineteenth century is how little of it there was,"[62] and this legal underdevelopment of rules, analysis, and institutions was even more char-acteristic of slave rules in the colonial period. In response to this, most scholarly effort has been spent attempting to identify where the law found its understanding of slavery. Various substantive bodies of doctrine, such as villeinage, Roman slave law, the newer bodies of law on apprentice-ship and indentured servants, and the law of chattel property have all been proposed.[63] In one sense these explanations are all true. Many fea-tures of colonial slave law were taken intact from old law: the mother rule, the policing system with its use of hue-and-cry, branding, and sum-mary criminal procedure for slave trials. Colonial lawyers were analyti-cally opportunistic, borrowing doctrines from all these bodies of law. But at the same time none of the doctrinal candidates really explains the foundations of slave law.

In fact, what is significant is not the sources of colonial slave law, but that it existed at all, in its rude and incomplete form. First, by what au-thority had local lawmakers dared to create slavery and a body of slave law? Second, why was it that lawyers and lawmakers back in England failed to supplement the flawed colonial legal effort, as they had in other con-texts? The two questions are related, and for their explanation we must focus on the royal servants and common lawyers in Westminster.

The Constitution of the Old British Empire

There is another legal explanation for both slave law—essentially, the policing measures applied in the colonies—and the paucity of explicit authorization and sophisticated legal discussion. It derives not from any branch of substantive law, but rather from what later imperial lawyers knew as the constitutional law of the British Empire. Recall Chief Justice Holt's decision in *Smith* v. *Brown and Cooper* that trover was unavailable to recover a black slave. We have seen that the case was in fact decided on narrow pleading grounds, and contemporaries may not have even learned of it for a number of years. But the chief significance of the case lies elsewhere, in the advice that Chief Justice Holt gave the unsuccessful plaintiff: "[y]ou should have averred in the declaration, that the sale of the negro was in Virginia, and, by the laws of that country, negroes are saleable; *for the laws of England do not extend to Virginia, being a conquered country their law is what the King pleases . . .*"[64] In other words, the critical doctrine was not slave law as such, but the common law's more general response to legal issues arising in conquered lands, a response that pre-dated the meager caselaw about slavery.

Among the clearest cases in the development of this doctrine of colonial conquest was *Blankard* v. *Galdy*, a debt action that arose in Jamaica and was decided in King's Bench, also before Chief Justice Holt, in 1694.[65] The defendant's plea was that the debt stemmed from the purchase of the office of provost-marshal in Jamaica, and that purchase of such an office violated English statutory law. The court rejected the plea, holding that the statute did not apply to the colony. In the case of conquered territory, such as Jamaica, English law could be imposed, but it did not apply until the conqueror had specifically imposed it. Until then, local laws—perhaps the former law of the subjugated population, more often the laws of the conqueror's troops and settlers—continued in effect. The implication was that divergent local institutions like colonial slavery were valid, under this theory of tacit delegation.

Behind this legal framework for the Caribbean conquest were centuries of related doctrines. Medieval "just war" theory had distinguished between Christians and infidels, for purposes both of making war and of judging behavior in war, and that legal tradition had been revitalized in the sixteenth century. Coke, in *Calvin's Case*, had distinguished between aliens in general and the "perpetual enemies" of a Christian kingdom.[66] Most important, there were the renewed Tudor attempts to conquer Ireland. These efforts in Ireland were important precursors to subsequent New World colonization.[67] Thus, when Englishmen conquered new lands, the Crown could impose the common law on the new territories. But it need not do so, and the Crown at its discretion could impose common law doctrines selectively. It could annex the territories to the Crown and govern them as a feudal sovereign, directly or through a grantee, or permit even the old, preconquest rulers to remain in place.

The hard, practical result of conquest doctrine was that by imposing common law land tenure on portions of Ireland, the lawyers rationalized the seizure of huge tracts from indigenous Irish owners.[68] Of equal importance, however, was the constitutional question of who had the power to make the substantive decisions. Who decided when common, martial, or local law applied, and on what basis? The answers to these questions were also clarified by the conquest of Ireland. Conquered land, the theory went, was under the king alone, and not under the realm headed by that Tudor fiction, the king-in-Parliament. By the early seventeenth century, there was reluctance to entrusting Ireland or the new American colonies solely to the Crown.[69] But opposition soon turned to other royal extravagances, and the Crown's claims to prerogative colonial rule gained acceptance, with only occasional flickers of resistance. Dominion status meant that new lands were not under Parliament or the common law until such time as the king extended those boons to a territory. Arguments drawn from feudalism and the law of war supported this constitutional conclusion.

Of course, the matter was more complex than this. Each of the Old World "dominions" had acceded to or been seized by the Crown under different legal circumstances. Lawyers distinguished between dominions of the king and of the Crown, between lands in the royal demesne and Crown lands held on other terms, between conquered and inherited lands, and among Ireland, the Channel Islands, Scotland, and so forth. Older medieval instances like Gascony, Calais, and the palatinates had themselves differed, and seventeenth-century lawyers examined the cases anew. In fact, each case was *sui generis*. Scotland was variously called a subordinate or independent kingdom, and it retained its own law. Ireland was termed a "kingdom and colony," but in law it had been neither. Ireland was conquered, incompletely and repeatedly, and was incorporated into the common law to the extent that writs of error lay from Dublin to the king's bench in England. In most of the other Old World dependencies, the general rule was that appeals and other petitions lay to the Council.[70]

The critical point for the development of colonial slavery is that, however the medieval precedents were glossed, the seventeenth-century versions of conquest doctrine allowed *all the colonies* a private space in which planters and merchants could deploy slave labor with little oversight from England. The leash was never so long that the colonists could take major or costly policy initiatives against the wishes of the Crown. Quite the contrary, Westminster demanded the right to review local legislation and to reject unsuitable legislation. Often Westminster was able to make its claims and policies stick. But the momentum was with the colonists.[71] By using the decentralized private space allowed them by prerogative constitutionalism, the colonists were able to erect a regime of slave law.

Once this constitutional scheme was set in motion, little attention was required to sustain or clarify prerogative rule in the colonies, notwithstanding the ongoing political battles between Westminster, governors, and local councils and elites. The parliamentarians of the Civil War, for instance, absorbed but did not curtail the prerogative power in colonial affairs, even though they abolished most prerogative justice at home.[72] Similarly, seventeenth- and eighteenth-century English jurists rarely discussed the rights of the Crown to govern foreign territories. Even royal supporters, such as William Noy and John Brydall, and the systematizers, like Matthew Hale and Thomas Wood, made little mention of the Crown's foreign claims and were content to enumerate other royal rights such as war and peace, customs, fountain of justice and honors.[73] Of course, after the Glorious Revolution, it could hardly be maintained that the royal prerogative was independent of Parliament, but even the post-1689 prerogative, reduced to "only such part of the ancient discretionary right of the Crown as Parliament saw fit to leave untouched," permitted, in practice, colonial autonomy outside those areas of trade regulation habitually addressed by Parliament.[74] The prerogative thus permitted English planters to adopt the radically new institution of slavery and later to legitimize that slavery through law, without articulating a category of unfreedom that would clash with the strong rhetoric of the rights of Englishmen.

The prerogative also allowed a second form of privatization, private ordering in the colony, in addition to the more obvious sense of privatization on each master's plantation. Legal autonomy of this sort was not new to the common law: medieval villeinage, like the colonial case, also used privatization to permit unfreedom. Serfdom was a matter of manorial custom. It was a private matter, between the lord and serf. Thus, most common law texts did not describe serfdom at all. Serfdom was what the local lord had always been able to get away with, softened in practice by whatever limits the peasants could get away with; in short, it was custom, permitted at the boundary of the law. If a person could not establish his freedom according to the common law tests, he was unfree. He was under his lord and not common law. To use an anachronism, what the common law did was develop a public-private distinction. Whoever could not prove his freedom was vulnerable because he was subject to private ordering only. The serf was "privatized" and excluded from common law.

Thus, the privatization of the medieval manorial serf is a model for colonial autonomy under the prerogative. Prerogative theory held that the early colonies were military or commercial enterprises, under the quasi-feudal lordship of their promoters and indirectly under the king, and that the royal as well as proprietary colonies were not necessarily under common law. As Charles Andrews put it, "[I]n reality these settlements were not colonies; they were private estates." Hence, early governors adopted laws at variance with the common law, like Dale's *Lawes Divine, Morall and Martiall* in Virginia.[75] The irony of all this was that, long before the seventeenth century, private ordering had come to apply only to certain frontier zones; generally, it had fallen into sharp disfavor, and the centripetal rules of the common law had made that body of law essentially the only one that mattered. Everywhere in sixteenth- and seventeenth-century Europe, the trend was toward the breaking of old private and feudal social relations.[76] Thus, when seventeenth-century lawyers applied conquest law to the new colonies, they were taking a highly unusual step. Legal decentralization, where it was permitted, was a privilege aimed at creating and sustaining private preferences, typically in the hope of huge colonial profits. Viewed from "above," from Westminster, common law judges saw private ordering, with which they would be reluctant to meddle.

But from "below," from the perspective of Jamaica, for example, private space under the prerogative permitted not only local customs but the legitimation of those customs. The planters not only made local arrangements to regulate their affairs, including their slaves; they did so, significantly, in forms and with a vocabulary that echoed the common law. In other words, autonomy meant not only privatization but self-governance. These local slave *laws* represent private ordering that came to acquire in its own right the legitimating force of a legal order. From "below," a description of colonial slave law was not simply that "we employ the following practice" or "we govern our practice with local law" but "our law permits it, and their law permits us to permit it." Elsewhere, the civil law slave colonies deployed differing rationales for their slave laws, chiefly involving reception or legislative grant of a substantive body of slave law. In the common law colonies the basis was conquest and royal prerogative and the legal autonomy that they permitted.

Inevitably, the legal basis for common law colonial slavery was more complicated than this. Neither the conquest doctrine nor Coke's dicta in *Calvin's Case* about infidels can fully explain the legal steps taken to support slavery, despite the great weight often assigned by historians to his language.[77] In the first place, the rhetoric about infidels tended to disappear by 1685.[78] More important, jurists like Coke and Davies had all along feared that the conquest doctrine, even when applied overseas, held potentially dangerous consequences for a range of domestic constitutional issues. Refinements to the conquest doctrine were needed, and the tools lay readily at hand in the international *jus gentium* tradition, which recognized a variety of theories for territorial claims and whose distinctions seemed both eminently usable as a classification tool and an accurate description of how the colonies had come into British hands.[79] One result was that, along with conquest, other rationales such as discovery, descent, and cession, were deployed. Barbados, for instance, was deemed to have been not conquered but rather found and settled, and so a legal theory different from conquest was used to explain its precise legal relationship to the Crown.[80]

Courts also refined and embellished conquest doctrine itself. They asked, first, whether the Crown had authorized or subsequently ratified the seizure of a given territory or if the participants had ventured completely on their own. Second, recalling the Crown's right to extend common law to conquered land, courts asked whether common law had in fact been extended to or applied in a given colony. Often, it was no easy matter to disentangle colonial prescriptive claims and idiosyncratic charter language to determine whether common law had been offered to or imposed on a given colony and, if so, which legal doctrines the grant included. Where colonists were guaranteed common law, it might mean substantive common law adjudicated locally, but it might include access to the courts at Westminster. Indeed, in the fluid political and legal world of the colonies, where charters were withdrawn, treaties not followed up with promised instructions, and case reports almost nonexistent, who would properly date the local reception of the common law or delineate its extent? Using conquest theory's notion of "reception," for instance, which law ought to apply to a legal question arising in St. Kitts, which changed hands seven times around 1700 in the Anglo-French wars?

Moreover, even where colonists had brought or been granted their common law, the claim met with skepticism in England. As Blackstone later put it:

> [B]ut this [a colonial right to common law] must be understood with very many and very great restrictions. Such colonists carry with them only so much of the English law as is applicable in their own situation and the condition of an infant colony.

Inevitably, formulas like this invited litigation over how much common law was appropriate and which colonies were still not of age. Finally, conquest doctrine was oddly ambiguous in settings where common law had *not* been imposed by the Crown, by extending hope to both the conquered people and the English conquerors that their respective rules would be applied. Given the piecemeal reception of common law, for instance, were Dutch inheritance customs to apply in newly won New York, to the possible disinheritance of His Grace's English subjects? Whatever the answers to any of these scenarios, by using a nuanced legal approach to foreign acquisitions, jurists neutered conquest doctrine, removing its explosive domestic political associations and leaving a malleable analytic tool.[81]

In short, starting from *Calvin's Case, The Case of Tanistry,* and *Blankard* v. *Galdy,* and behind them the *jus gentium,* a constitutional framework of considerable complexity was crafted. The framework shared the characteristics of much of the best law: it addressed issues where the practical stakes were enormous, and it offered rules that were endlessly complex, intellectually fascinating, and completely inconclusive, further encouraging litigation and judicial elaboration. So it proved to be. Whenever new territory was added to the expanding empire, its particular constitutional status had to be determined—or relitigated—decades later. Newfoundland was not deemed a legal settlement but a mere fishing outpost under a commodore-governor; Tangier and Bombay were in the private hand of the Crown, having been a marriage gift to Charles II, but Bombay was soon granted, with full rights of governance and defense, to the East India Company. South Carolina, Pennsylvania, and Maryland were granted to private proprietors under charters that, like their medieval models, gave the lords proprietary a wide ambit in organizing and governing the new colonies. Over time additional classifications were developed: protectorates, ceded territories, dependencies, appendages, imperial possessions, and so forth.[82] The full consequences of the various statuses took decades or longer to work out. Thus, cases addressing the legal status of long-subdued Ireland and Wales appeared as late as the end of the seventeenth century, and Lord Mansfield reexamined the status of Jamaica over a century after it was seized by Britain.[83]

Additionally, regardless of the constitutional status of a colony, the applicability of statutory law was different than that of common law. After all, many statutes predated the colonies, and these acts could be understood either as clearly not intending application outside of England or as clearly incorporated into common law and applicable wherever common law was carried or given. Of those statutes post-dating colonial foundation, some expressly cited a colony or clearly implied colonial application while others might but need not be applied to the colonies. In time a typical response to the problem of whether English statutes applied was the formula that, in addition to all common law, a colony received all statutes made prior to the founding of the colony; statutes enacted subsequent to foundation did not apply unless they expressly named that colony. However clear this formula was, its flaws were obvious: it meant that ancient, wholly irrelevant statutes were applicable, but that desirable new acts like the Habeas Corpus Bill did not apply. Another response was to distinguish among types of legislation. Some acts, precolonial or recent, were said to be declarative of common law; others made new law; and still others fell in a third category, defined by Lord Mansfield as statutes that were in affirmance of common law but were mere police measures and so not applicable to the colonies. Overall, the result was that the empire was a complex constitutional and administrative patchwork, under which the applicability of common law or British statutes and the prospect of conciliar review were highly irregular and often unclear—as contemporaries saw.[84]

But for purposes of slave law, the differences between the various colonial legal regimes were insignificant. The same constitutional result, allowing slavery, can be reached in conquered land that had not yet been given parliamentary status or common law but that was permitted some common law remedies; in settled land where postsettlement parliamentary statutes did not specifically include the colony; and in any colony that was able to resist the practical consequences of strong prerogative rule. The critical point thus is not that conquest or discovery or infidel status was used to authorize slavery, but that under *all* of the variants of prerogative governance, almost any local practice could be adopted by or made acceptable to English law. There was no difference in the essential status of slavery between settled Barbados, conquered and ceded Grenada, discovered and proprietary Maryland, and conquered Jamaica and Virginia. Everywhere planters fashioned legal support for slavery, while the common law did not have to talk about it.

In "blaming" the prerogative rather than common law in this way for colonial slavery, there is a risk of our yielding to the powerful rhetoric of the common law, as colonists themselves did. It was an article of political faith to the colonists that common law was their birthright, the mark and guarantee of their freedom, and the best possible form of private governance. Early colonial charters and letters of instruction often contained clauses asserting that settlers should be subject to rules "as neere to the Common Lawe [of] England, and the equity thereof as may be"—though how close the results were to English common law has been debated.[85] Consistently, however, from the early seventeenth century to the eve of the Revolution, the colonists sought more than an approximation of common law rights. Through their local legislatures and in petitions to Whitehall for amendments to their charters, the colonists asserted the full common law rights of Englishmen.

Of course, there was irony in the colonists' invoking common law while relying on the prerogative for their ownership of slaves. Claiming to possess the rights of Englishmen, the colonists consistently and firmly insisted they were not at the mercy of the prerogative. They opposed conquest theory, either by denying that their respective colonies had in fact been conquered or by asserting that the territory was conquered but by them and their ancestors, English settlers who brought their rights with them.[86] In this view, conquering or settling prerogative lands in no way diminished the colonists' common law rights because, as Coke had written in another context,

> the common law hath so admeasured the prerogatives of the king, that they should not take away, nor prejudice the inheritance of any: and the best inheritance that the subject hath, is the law of the realme.[87]

Prerogative law was for conquered, discovered, or annexed peoples, the argument ran; Englishmen abroad and their descendants brought and retained common law. Notwithstanding this rhetoric and the attraction of the common law for English colonists, prerogative status allowed for slavery, while the status of slavery under the common law was unclear.

And so colonists benefited by being under the royal prerogative, which allowed them to erect a system of slavery while also asserting common law status. But in the last decades prior to the Revolution, this attempt to have it both ways proved untenable. In the 1760s London reversed its long-standing policy of decentralization and neglect and tried to impose taxes and tighter control. To the colonists the older policy had represented not benign neglect but recognition of their right to local self-government. And between these two understandings there was no legitimate decision rule, for, notwithstanding the various judicial and bureaucratic formulas we have examined, "[t]here never had been any constitutional theory to explain and shape Britain's relations with its dependencies in the West"—no authoritative theory, in any event.[88]

Suddenly the traditional arguments were felt to be an inadequate defense to perceived English abuses. Claims about the common law rights of Englishmen could not be decisive given the difficulties in determining which rights applied in which colonies. The familiar alternative argument that Parliament would check an overbearing executive was also useless because the American colonies sent no representatives to Westminster and felt they were not represented there. More important, it was Parliament that had passed the hated new Stamp Act, Declaratory Act, and so on. One response was to reject the relatively new theory of parliamentary sovereignty, either because the colonies were not represented directly or because some steps were beyond the competence of any legislature, and with it to reject in part the common law that appeared to sanction parliamentary sovereignty. A variant of this was to accept parliamentary rule, conditional upon the grant of a colonial bill of rights guaranteed by Parliament. Another variant, employed during the crises over the Stamp Act and the Townshend duties, was to accept sovereignty in principle but to reject Parliament's authority to impose the particular tax in question, by distinguishing between legislation in general and tax measures, between internal and external taxation, or between measures intended to raise revenues and those raising revenues only incidentally.[89] A very different response to the crisis of authority was to replace common law rights with the new natural rights, the rights of man, as the Declaration of Independence and *Common Sense* were to do. Those who followed this course ran the risk that the natural right to be free (from Britain) might be invoked by American slaves too, and James Otis is only the best known of many abolitionists on the eve of the Revolutionary War who reminded opponents of imperial "enslavement" of the hard reality of plantation slavery.[90]

Yet a third, unexpected alternative to the inadequacies of the colonists' old common law rhetoric was to rely on the royal prerogative. Thus the Continental Congress in October 1774 "solemnly assured George

III that they wished 'not a diminution of the prerogative,'" and thus such leading authors as James Wilson, James Iredell, John Dickinson, and John Adams advanced various formulations by which the colonies *were* conquered or settled lands and *were* under the king but not Parliament. Behind this radical appropriation of royalist rhetoric was the knowledge that prerogative status in practice meant distance and constitutionalization of the colonies' practical autonomy. Some proponents suggested an explicit linkage between acknowledging the prerogative and a right to be represented in and ruled by (at least in domestic matters) their colonial legislatures; in so arguing they prefigured later theories of the empire and Commonwealth as a partnership of essentially independent states under queen and Privy Council. But it was impossible to make local legislatures a necessary, as opposed to beneficial, part of prerogative theory. As a result, colonists using any formulation of the prerogative were resting their claims to autonomy on a theory that held they had no rights at all, as subjects in territories conquered or otherwise annexed to the unchecked power of the Crown. To borrow Carl Becker's characterization of the shifts in revolutionary rhetoric, "[T]his was precisely what could not be avoided."[91]

Of course, the attempt of both colonial and metropolitan dissidents to blame Parliament and turn instead to the Crown proved short-lived, as did any claim for American rights within the British system. By the time of the Declaration of Independence, the strategy was completely reversed: blame the king rather than Parliament for all abuses.[92] But that is to focus only on the end of the story, the surprising but least significant part. The more revealing point of the revolutionaries' use of prerogative rhetoric is that it illustrates what the colonists had in fact been doing all along with respect to their law and their slaves. Long before the 1770s, the colonists espoused the rights of Englishmen. That much is familiar, and it is traditionally read as a part of the political and ideological matrix from which the Revolution developed. Slavery, however, presented the exceptional setting in which the colonists could not afford the full common law. Even as the colonists pressed toward Attorney-General Richard West's conclusion in 1720 that "[t]he Common Law of England, is the Common Law of the Plantations," what they wanted was not the common law as understood in England, with Holt's possibility that slavery would be unrecognized and unprotected.[93] What the colonists needed was the right to pick and choose common law doctrines to secure their non-common law asset, the slave.

Given the widespread confusion among lawyers and political leaders over how the prerogative applied to particular colonies, and the realization that much common law was unnecessary to the needs of colonial society, the colonists sought selective reception of the common law. Such selectivity was not improper, for prepositivist lawyers of the eighteenth century understood the common law to include not only syllogistic rules but also a storehouse of principles, historical parallels, a vocabulary, and a methodology. Necessarily, the rules that colonists sought included security of property and the right not to be taxed arbitrarily as well as other "rights of Englishmen." But the remaining details could be worked out later by courts and legislatures.[94] In the end, the common law as received, to the extent that it addressed slavery, varied among the colonies as to whether a master might entail his slave, or convey the slave by bargain-and-sale, or sue by trover or detinue. The important point is that, as received and then extended, nowhere did the colonial common law *systematically* address slavery. It was the doctrine of prerogative governance that allowed the retention of local customs like slavery and the selective "reception" of various usable common law doctrines that facilitated the retention and management of slavery.

Conclusion

Slave law in the English colonies was not found in a systematic text like the *Code noir* or *Las siete partidas*. Accordingly, it lacked the breadth and analytic richness that characterize such texts. But slave law in the English colonies also consisted of more than an assemblage of local ordinances and truncated case decisions. In fact, the most significant step in colonial slave law had, on its face, nothing to do with slavery. It was, instead, a new version of the already old notion that substantive common law need not be the law of English foreign settlements. This step was largely unstated—indeed, it was often denied by the colonists, who claimed that they had brought the common law with them from England, *jus sanguinis*. But common law, when it crossed the Atlantic, was received selectively, which prerogative theory allowed. In this sense the colonists were, like some of their descendants, "federalists." In the case of the colonists, their prerogative framework permitted them to create a property interest in persons as well as a private realm for slave governance. Centrifugal constitutionalism was consonant with the rough ethos of a far-flung mercantile empire, and in the plantation colonies it permitted enslavement to be legitimated into law.

This evolving constitutional relationship explains the formal underdevelopment of English slave law, in contrast to the systematic slave laws of the other colonial powers and the self-evident "success" of English slavery on the ground. Colonial constitutional law explains why the English courts faced only a handful of slave cases over a century. Like their medieval predecessors in the matter of villeinage, English jurists saw slavery as a private matter, under local men and local custom and under the oversight of a lord—here, the king. And unlike medieval judges and legal authors, colonial judges faced relatively few thorny questions of demarcation. Increasingly, white racism, black skin color, and local policing statutes did that for them.

Notes

Portions of this paper were delivered to the Critical Legal Studies Conference, Cambridge, Mass., April 12, 1992, and published in 5 *Yale Journal of Law and the Humanities* 417 (1993), whose permission to publish I gratefully acknowledge. I also thank J. H. Baker and Paul Finkelman for their gracious assistance.

1. Winthrop D. Jordan, *White over Black: American Attitudes toward the Negro, 1550–1812* (Baltimore: Penguin Books, 1968), 44.

2. For some historians the initial legal acceptance of slavery is less problematic, given the practical exploitation of colonial labor in the early and mid seventeenth century and the multiplicity of legal doctrines available to masters. See, e.g., David Eltis, *Economic Growth and the Ending of the Transatlantic Slave Trade* (New York: Oxford University Press, 1987), 31; Edmund S. Morgan, *American Slavery, American Freedom: The Ordeal of Colonial Virginia* (New York: W. W. Norton, 1975), 296–305; Stanley Elkins and Eric McKitrick, "Institutions and the Law of Slavery: The Dynamics of Unopposed Capitalism," *American Quarterly* 9 (1957): 3, 14, reprinted in *Comparative Issues in Slavery*, ed. Paul Finkelman (New York: Garland Press, 1989), 141, 152; Paul Finkelman, "Exploring Southern Legal History," 64 *North Carolina Law Review* 77, 91 (1985). This understates, in my view, the enormous importance of traditional common law reasoning about freedom and the frequent resistance of legal thinking to change.

3. E. W. Ives, *The Common Lawyers of Pre-Reformation England. Thomas Kebell: A Case Study* (Cambridge: Cambridge University Press, 1983), 7.

4. Lawrence Stone, *The Crisis of the Aristocracy, 1558–1641* (Oxford: Clarendon Press, 1965), 242. Recent figures on the levels of litigation are contained in J. H. Baker, *The Reports of Sir John Spelman*, 2 vols., Selden Society, 94 (London, 1978), 2:51–62; Marjorie Blatcher, *The Court of King's Bench, 1450–1550: A Study in Self-Help* (London: Athlone Press, 1978), 17–20, 138–39, 170–71; C. W. Brooks, *Pettyfoggers and Vipers of the Commonwealth: The "Lower Branch" of the Legal Profession in Early Modern England* (Cambridge: Cambridge University Press, 1986), 48–57, 75–79.

5. Morgan, *American Slavery, American Freedom*, 124–27, 148; Bernard Bailyn, "Politics and Social Structure in Virginia," in *Seventeenth-Century America*, ed. Joseph H. Smith (Chapel Hill: University of North Carolina Press, 1959), 90, 96. The habit of litigiousness persisted into the eighteenth century. Rhys Isaac, *The Transformation of Virginia, 1740–1790* (Chapel Hill: University of North Carolina Press, 1982), 90, 93–94.

6. For nineteenth-century opinion, see Thomas R. R. Cobb, *An Inquiry into the Law of Negro Slavery in the United States of America* (1858; reprint, New York: Negro Universities Press, 1968), sec. 83, p. 82; William Goodell, *The American Slave Code in Theory and Practice* (1853; reprint, New York: Negro Universities Press, 1968), 258–65; *Miller v. McQuerry*, 17 F. Cas. 335, 336 (C.C.D. Ohio 1853). For historians, see Wesley Craven, *White, Red, and Black: The Seventeenth-Century Virginian* (New York: W. W. Norton, 1971), 75; David Brion Davis, *The Problem of Slavery in the Age of Revolution, 1770–1823* (Ithaca: Cornell University Press, 1975), 473-74; David Brion Davis, *The Problem of Slavery in Western Culture* (Ithaca: Cornell University Press, 1966), 247; Paul Finkelman, *The Law of Freedom and Bondage: A Casebook* (New York: Oceana Press, 1986), 1, 10; Jordan, *White over Black*, 72, 81;

Morgan, *American Slavery, American Freedom*, 330; Kenneth M. Stampp, *The Peculiar Institution* (New York: Vintage Books, 1956), 21–22; Alan Watson, *Slave Law in the Americas* (Athens, Ga.: University of Georgia Press, 1989), 11–12, 64, 85, 103; Whittington B. Johnson, "The Origin and Nature of African Slavery in Seventeenth Century Maryland," *Maryland Historical Magazine* 73 (1978): 236, 236-38, reprinted in *Colonial Slave Society*, ed. Paul Finkelman (New York: Garland Publishing, 1989), 82–84; William M. Wiecek, "Somerset: Lord Mansfield and the Legitimacy of Slavery in the Anglo-American World," 42 *University of Chicago Law Review* 86, 127 (1974).

7. The Barbados decree is reprinted in Richard S. Dunn, *Sugar and Slaves: The Rise of the Planter Class in the English West Indies, 1624–1714* (New York: W. W. Norton, 1972), 228; the Maryland act is cited in James Oakes, *Slavery and Freedom* (New York: Vintage Books, 1990), 68; Rhode Island's act is cited in Jordan, *White over Black*, 70; Section 110 of the South Carolina Fundamental Constitutions is reprinted in Finkelman, *Law of Freedom and Bondage*, 20 n. 6.

8. Finkelman, "Exploring Southern Legal History," 97 (citing Boorstin).

9. Cobb, *Inquiry into the Law of Negro Slavery* (1858); Goodell, *American Slave Code* (1853); John C. Hurd, *The Law of Freedom and Bondage in the United States*, 2 vols. (1858–62; reprint, New York: Negro Universities Press, 1968); George M. Stroud, *A Sketch of the Laws Relating to Slavery in the Several States of the United States of America* (1827; 2d ed., 1856, reprint, New York: Negro Universities Press, 1968). The French and Spanish codes are cited in Watson, *Slave Law in the Americas*, 52, 59, 85. The *Code noir* dates from 1685 and 1742, and the *Code negro caroleno* from 1785.

10. Davis, *Problem of Slavery in Western Culture*, 151; Peter Fryar, *Staying Power: Black People in Britain since 1504* (Atlantic Highlands, N.J.: Humanities Press, 1984), 16–17; Duncan J. MacLeod, *Slavery, Race and the American Revolution* (Cambridge: Cambridge University Press, 1974), 65. See Robert Beverley, *The History and Present State of Virginia* (1705; reprint, ed. Louis B. Wright, Charlottesville, Va.: University Press of Virginia, 1947), 272; Hugh Jones, *The Present State of Virginia* (1724; reprint, ed. Richard L. Morton, Chapel Hill: University of North Carolina Press, 1956), 75–76, 130. See also Philip D. Morgan, "British Encounters with Africans and African-Americans, circa 1600–1780," in *Strangers within the Realm: Cultural Margins of the First British Empire*, ed. Bernard Bailyn and Philip D. Morgan (Chapel Hill: University of North Carolina Press, 1991), 157, 214–15.

11. Davis, *Problem of Slavery in Western Culture*, 10, 13, 110, 201, 204–19, 452–57; Jordan, *White over Black*, 3–43, 90–91; Seymour Drescher, *Capitalism and Antislavery: British Mobilization in Comparative Perspective* (New York: Oxford University Press, 1987), 20; Dunn, *Sugar and Slaves*, 13; Stephen Greenblatt, *Marvelous Possessions: The Wonder of the New World* (Chicago: University of Chicago Press, 1991), 22, 54–55; Anthony Pagden, *European Encounters with the New World: From Renaissance to Romanticism* (New Haven: Yale University Press, 1993), 11; Thomas Hahn, "Indians East and West: Primitivism and Savagery in English Discovery Narratives of the Sixteenth Century," *Journal of Medieval and Renaissance Studies* 8 (1978): 77–114. David Brion Davis and Winthrop Jordan have described the important European discovery and scientific literatures about Africans and blackness prior to 1700. But even those early discussions were not as sustained, or as interesting to a wide readership, as comparable writings about

the native peoples of the Americas. Davis has demonstrated that there was some interest in discussing slavery as public policy in the seventeenth century, but the evidence in his own magisterial work is largely drawn from the eighteenth century.

12. See R. H. Hilton, *The Decline of Serfdom in Medieval England*, 2d ed. (London: Macmillan, 1983), 55–58; Margaret Post, ed., *Calendar of Patent Rolls. Elizabeth I*, vol. 8, *(1578–1580)* (London: Her Majesty's Stationery Office, 1986), 16–18.

13. See, e.g., *Opinion of Dulany* (1767), reprinted in 1 H. & McH. 559, 560–61 (1809); *Somerset* v. *Stewart*, Lofft, 1, 3, 20 How. St. T. 1, 35–49 (K.B. 1772) (argument of counsel Hargrave); *Chamberline* v. *Harvey*, 5 Mod. 186, 189 (K.B. 1697) (argument of counsel); *R.* v. *Allan* [The Slave, Grace], 2 Hagg. Adm. 94, 107–8, 115 (Adm. 1827); Cobb, *Law of Negro Slavery*, sec. 90, p. 87; Davis, *Problem of Slavery in the Age of Revolution*, 482-83, 487-88; Thomas D. Morris, "'Villeinage . . . as It Existed in England, Reflects But Little Light on Our Subject:' The Problem of the 'Sources' of Southern Slave Law," 32 *American Journal of Legal History* 95, 125–27 (1988); A. E. Keir Nash, "Fairness and Formalism in the Trials of Blacks in the State Supreme Courts of the Old South," 56 *Virginia Law Review* 64, 69 (1970) (proslavery judges reject continuity of villeinage and slavery, thus placing slaves outside of basic legal protections accorded villeins).

14. Edward Coke, *The First Part of the Institutes of the Laws of England*, 2 vols., (1628; reprint, New York: Garland Publishing, 1979), vol. 1, sec. 181, pp. *120a–b. Earlier discussions of the notion, by Littleton and Smith, are cited in Jonathan A. Bush, "Free to Enslave: The Foundations of Colonial American Slave Law," 5 *Yale Journal of Law and the Humanities*, 417, 424 n. 18 (1993).

15. See Robert J. Steinfeld, *The Invention of Free Labor: The Employment Relation in English and American Law and Culture, 1350–1870* (Chapel Hill: University of North Carolina Press, 1991); Jonathan A. Bush, "'Take This Job and Shove It': The Rise of Free Labor," 91 *Michigan Law Review* 1382, 1388–98 (1993).

16. This rule was the opposite of the long-established common law father rule, which applied both to personal freedom; see, e.g., Coke, *First Part of the Institutes*, vol. 1, sec. 187, p. *123; *Bacon* v. *Bacon*, Cro. Car. 601, 602 (K.B. 1641). See Paul R. Hyams, *Kings, Lords, and Peasants in Medieval England: The Common Law of Villeinage in the Twelfth and Thirteenth Centuries* (Oxford: Clarendon Press, 1980), 176–81. The rule of maternal descent for slavery was first enacted in Virginia in 1662; see 2 *The Statutes at Large; Being a Collection of All the Laws of Virginia* 170, William W. Hening, comp. (Richmond, 1819–23) (hereinafter cited as Va. Stat. (1619–1820)). See Davis, *Problem of Slavery in Western Culture*, 277-78 (surveying adoption of mother rule); Susan M. Stuard, "Ancillary Evidence for the Decline of Medieval Slavery," *Past and Present* 149 (1995): 3, 10–13.

17. For the lack of reliance on Roman law in slave matters, see R. H. Helmholz, "Use of the Civil Law in Post-Revolutionary American Jurisprudence," 66 *Tulane Law Review* 1649, 1660-61 (1992); Morris, "'Sources' of Southern Slave Law," 114-24. But see Watson, *Slave Law in the Americas*, 64–65, *supra note* 13, 348, at 351–53. See, e.g., *Somerville* v. *Johnson* (Md. Chanc. 1770), reprinted in 1 H. & McH., 348, 351–53 (reference to Roman law in context of life tenant's claim to issue of slave).

18. Some of the connections between race, slavery, and legislation are explored in Alden T. Vaughan, "The Origins Debate: Slavery and Racism in Seventeenth-Century Virginia," *Virginia Magazine of History and Biography* 97 (1989): 311–54, reprinted in *Roots of American Racism* (New York: Oxford Uni-

versity Press, 1995), 136–74. T. H. Breen and Stephen Innes, *"Myne Owne Ground": Race and Freedom on Virginia's Eastern Shore, 1640–1676* (New York: Oxford University Press, 1980); Craven, *White, Red, and Black*, 73–109; Morgan, *American Slavery, American Freedom*, 154–57, 295–337; Warren M. Billings, "The Cases of Fernando and Elizabeth Key: A Note on the Status of Blacks in Seventeenth-Century Virginia," *William and Mary Quarterly*, 3d ser., 30 (1973): 467–74; T. H. Breen, *Tobacco Culture: The Mentality of the Great Tidewater Planters on the Eve of the Revolution* (Princeton: Princeton University Press, 1985), 96–97. For the reactive quality of slave law, see Dunn, *Sugar and Slaves*, 228. For the use of private law to record property interests in slaves, see Morgan, *American Slavery, American Freedom*, 178.

19. William H. Bryson, "Law Reporting and Legal Records in Virginia, 1607–1800," in *Judicial Records, Law Reports, and the Growth of Case Law*, ed. J. H. Baker (Berlin: Duncker und Humblot, 1989), 319, 328–29.

20. See A. W. B. Simpson, "The Rise and Fall of the Legal Treatise: Legal Principles and the Forms of Legal Literature," 48 *University of Chicago Law Review* 632 (1981); reprinted in *Legal Theory and Legal History* (London: Hambledon Press, 1987), 273; Finkelman, "Exploring Southern Legal History," 112–13; Erwin C. Surrency, "The Beginnings of American Legal Literature," 31 *American Journal of Legal History* 207 (1987).

21. Breen, *Tobacco Culture*, 85–86; Morgan, *American Slavery, American Freedom*, 312; James Oakes, *The Ruling Race* (New York: Alfred A. Knopf, 1982), 24–25, 155–67; Gary A. Puckrein, *Little England: Plantation Society and Anglo-Barbadian Politics, 1627–1700* (New York: New York University Press, 1984), 86–87; Stanley Elkins and Eric McKitrick, "Slavery in Capitalist and Non-capitalist Culture," *American Quarterly* 9 (1957): 159, 167, 175; reprinted in *Comparative Issues in Slavery*, 161, 169, 177. See also Peter C. Hoffer, *Law and People in Colonial America* (Baltimore: Johns Hopkins University Press, 1992), 91.

22. These included bargain-and-sale, attachment for debt, recording transfer, disbursal by an executor, enfranchising the owner, transfer by gift, and suit in detainer, trover, and conversion. See Davis, *Problem of Slavery in Western Culture*, 248–51; Warren M. Billings, "The Law of Servants and Slaves in Seventeenth-Century Virginia," *Virginia Magazine of History and Biography* 99 (1991): 45, 61 n. 50; M. Eugene Sirmans, "The Legal Status of the Slave in South Carolina, 1670–1740," *Journal of Southern History* 28 (1962): 462, 464–65, reprinted in *Colonial Slave Society*, 388, 390–91; William M. Wiecek, "The Statutory Law of Slavery and Race in the Thirteen Mainland Colonies of British America," *William and Mary Quarterly*, 3d ser., 34 (1977): 258, 264, reprinted in *Colonial Slave Society*, 452, 458; see also Act of 1727 in 4 Va. Stat. (1619–1820) 222, repealed by Act of 1748 in 5 Va. Stat. (1619–1820) 432. See also A. Leon Higginbotham Jr., *In the Matter of Color: Race and the American Legal Process. The Colonial Period* (New York: Oxford University Press, 1978), 170.

23. See Davis, *Problem of Slavery in Western Culture*, 248–51; Stampp, *Peculiar Institution*, 197; Wiecek, "Statutory Law of Slavery," 258, 264; see also Elmer B. Russell, *The Review of American Colonial Legislation by the King in Council* (1915; reprint, New York: Octagon Books, 1976), 106–7, 135, 160.

24. A similar claim is made for the nineteenth century in Mark Tushnet, *The American Law of Slavery, 1810–1860* (Princeton: Princeton University Press, 1981), 40, 92–93, 157–58.

25 See *The Laws of Virginia, Being a Supplement to Hening's The Statutes at Large: 1700–1750*, at 57, 60, 265, 341, 344, 352, 362, 376, Waverly K. Winfree comp., (Richmond, Virginia State Library, 1971); Bailyn, "Politics in Virginia," 110–11.

26. See Watson, *Slave Law in the Americas*, 46-47, 83, 85, 91, 93, 103-4; Elsa V. Goveia, "The West Indian Slave Laws of the Eighteenth Century," in *Caribbean Slave Society and Economy*, ed. Hilary Beckles and Verene Shepherd (New York: New Press, 1991), 346, 349, 354–56, 358–59.

27. Susan Staves, "Chattel Property Rules and the Construction of Englishness," 12 *Law and History Review* 123 (1994).

28. *Smith* v. *Brown and Cooper*, Holt 495, 2 Salk. 666 (Q.B. 1702?). The general problem is stated in J. H. Baker, *An Introduction to English Legal History*, 3d ed. (London: Butterworths, 1990) 540, and in condensed form in Bush, "Free to Enslave," 441–44. See the cases discussed in J. H. Baker, "The Law Merchant and the Common Law before 1700," 38 *Cambridge Law Journal* 295, 299 (1979) reprinted in *The Legal Profession and the Common Law* (London: Hambledon Press, 1986) 341, 345; see Daniel R. Coquillette, "Legal Ideology and Incorporation IV: The Nature of Civilian Influence on Modern Anglo-American Commercial Law," 67 *Boston University Law Review* 877, 937–38, 943 (1987). Concerning colonial customs, see especially the *Case of Tanistry*, Davies 28, 31–33 (Irish K.B. 1606); James Q. Whitman, "Why Did the Revolutionary Lawyers Confuse Custom and Reason?" 58 *University of Chicago Law Review* 1321, 1355 n.136 (1991).

29. The rough estimates are based on Philip D. Curtin, *The Atlantic Slave Trade: A Census* (Madison: University of Wisconsin Press, 1969), 9, 52–72, 118–53.

30. Most are abstracted in Helen T. Catterall, ed., *Judicial Cases Concerning American Slavery and the Negro*, 5 vols. (Washington, D.C.: Carnegie Institution, 1926–37), 1:2–14; others are cited in *Somerset* v. *Stewart, supra* note 13, Lofft 3–4, 8, 17, 19, 20 How. St. T. at 51–55 (especially in Hargrave's argument); Davis, *Problem of Slavery in Western Culture*, 205–06; James Oldham, *The Mansfield Manuscripts and the Growth of English Law in the Eighteenth Century* (Chapel Hill: University of North Carolina Press, 1992), 2:1225, 1236–37; see also *Noel* v. *Robinson*, 1 Vern. 453 (Ch. 1687) (citing Sgt. Maynard's case). There were also a few Scottish cases, cited in *Somerset* v. *Stewart, supra* note 13, 20 How. St. T. at 1–12 n., and a larger but undetermined number of slave-related cases in local courts. See, e.g., Fryar, *Staying Power*, 23–24, 74–75; M. Dorothy George, *London Life in the Eighteenth Century* (1925; reprint, Harmondsworth, Middlesex: Penguin Books, 1966), 141.

31. *Smith* v. *Brown and Cooper, supra* note 28, at Holt 495 (first Holt quotation); *Smith* v. *Gould*, 2 Ld. Raym. 1274, 1274–75 (Q.B. 1706) (second Holt quotation); David Ogg, *England in the Reigns of James II and William III* (Oxford: Clarendon Press, 1955), 73–74.

32. Baker, *Introduction to English Legal History*, 541. For departure from Holt's language, see *Somerset* v. *Stewart, supra* note 13, Lofft 8 (counsel for slave owner calls Holt's language mere dicta and seeks narrow, procedural ruling); *Pearne* v. *Lisle*, Ambl. 75 (Ch. 1749) (Lord Hardwicke disregards Holt on trover, on basis of informal advisory opinion by himself and Lord Talbot in 1729). For difficulties with the cases, see Davis, *Problem of Slavery in the Age of Revolution*, 480 n.19; Drescher, *Capitalism and Antislavery*, 32; Oldham, *Mansfield Manuscripts*, 2:1225, 1236–37; William M. Wiecek, *The Sources of Antislavery Constitutionalism in America*,

1760–1848 (Ithaca: Cornell University Press, 1977), 23–25; Edward Fiddes, "Lord Mansfield and the Somersett Case," 50 *Law Quarterly Review* 499, 501–2 (1934); James Oldham, "New Light on Mansfield and Slavery," *Journal of British Studies* 27 (1988): 45, 49, 54, 62–65; Wiecek, "Somerset," 90, 93–95. For seeming judicial acceptance of slavery in the colonies, see *Smith* v. *Brown and Cooper*, *supra* note 28 (Holt, C. J., acknowledges Virginia custom).

33. See, e.g., *De Jonge v. Isaac* (Adm. 1763), reprinted in 23 British Maritime Cases 1648–1871, at 216 (1978); *The Africa* (Adm. 1762), 23 British Maritime Cases 228; see also R. G. Marsden, ed., *Law and Custom of the Sea, vol. 2, A.D. 1649–1767*, Naval Record Society, 50 (London, 1916), 95–101; *Select Pleas in the Court of Admiralty: Vol. II, The High Court of Admiralty (A.D. 1547–1602)*, ed. Reginald Marsden, Selden Society, 11 (London, 1897), xvi; *Robertson* v. *Ewer*, 1 T.R. 127 (K.B. 1786); *Hale and Fleetwood on Admiralty Jurisdiction*, ed. M. J. Prichard and D. E. C. Yale, Selden Society, 108 (London, 1993), ccxxiv–xxv. For early discussions of slave cargo, see Bush, "Free to Enslave," 453 n. 131. For the possibility of unreported discussions, see ibid., 454.

34. On legal uncertainty, see Davis, *Problem of Slavery in Western Culture*, 211; Drescher, *Capitalism and Antislavery*, 27–29, 32–35, 185–91; Fryar, *Staying Power*, 23–24, 62–64, 68, 72, 78, 115–17; Oldham, *Mansfield Manuscripts*, 2:1238; James Walvin, *The Black Presence* (New York: Schocken Books, 1971), 14–16, 23–25; Seymour Drescher, "Manumission in a Society without Slave Law: Eighteenth-Century England," *Slavery and Abolition* 10 (1989): 85, 87–97; Fiddes, "Lord Mansfield," 509–10; Morgan, "British Encounters with Africans," 164–65. For estimates of the black population, see *Somerset* v. *Stewart*, *supra* note 13, Lofft at 10, 15, 17, 20 How. St. T. at 79; Baker, *Introduction to English Legal History*, 541 n. 48; George, *London Life*, 140. But see Drescher, *Capitalism and Antislavery* 27–29, 185–86 n. 10; Folarin Shyllon, *Black People in Britain, 1555–1833* (London: Oxford University Press, 1977), 102 for considerably lower estimates.

35. See, e.g., 5 Geo. II, c. 7; 9 Will. III, c. 26; Wesley F. Craven, *The Colonies in Transition, 1660–1713* (New York: Harper and Row, 1968), 295; Leo F. Stock, ed., *Proceedings and Debates of the British Parliaments Respecting North America*, 5 vols. (Washington, D.C.: Carnegie Institution, 1924–41), *1, 1542–1688*.

36. Cited in Jordan, *White over Black*, 85.

37. Public Record Office, "Journal of the Lords of Trade and Plantations," "Letter from Philip Lloyd to Attorney-General or Solicitor-General," both 17 July 1677, and "Opinion of Solicitor-General," 24 July 1677, in W. Noel Sainsbury and J. W. Fortescue, eds., *Calendar of State Papers, Colonial, America and West Indies, 1677–1680* (London, 1896; Vaduz: Kraus Reprint, 1964), nos. 337, 339, pp. 118, 120 (1677 decision).

38. Drescher, *Capitalism and Antislavery*, 27; Peter Mathias, *The First Industrial Nation: An Economic History of Britain, 1700–1914* (New York: Charles Scribner's Sons, 1969), 97, 100.

39. See, e.g., the published calendars of the Privy Council; George Chalmers, ed., *Opinions of Eminent Lawyers on Various Points of English Jurisprudence, Chiefly Concerning the Colonies, Fisheries, and Commerce*, 2 vols., (London, 1814; reprint, in 1 vol., Burlington, Vt.: C. Goodrich, 1858), 144–45; Leonard W. Labaree, ed., *Royal Instructions to British Colonial Governors, 1670–1776*, 2 vols. (1935; reprint, New York: Octagon Books, 1967), 2:505–8, 665–79; Russell, *Review of Colonial Legislation*.

40. Personal communication with Professor J. H. Baker, September 1992 and March 1993; *Chamberline* v. *Harvey, supra* note 13, at 189; but see *Smith* v. *Gould, supra* note 31, at 1274–75. For the stock examples discussed in the inns, see Samuel E. Thorne and J. H. Baker, eds., *Readings and Moots at the Inns of Court in the Fifteenth Century: Vol. II, Moots and Readers' Cases*, Selden Society, 105 (London, 1990), lxxii.

41. See Thomas Wood, *An Institute of the Laws of England*, 3d ed. (1724; reprint, New York: Garland Publishing, 1979), 539–40; idem, *Institute*, 4th ed. (London, 1728), 539–40; and idem, *Institute*, 5th ed. (London, 1734), 539–40; Drescher, *Capitalism and Antislavery*, 187 n. 19 (citing 10th ed. of Wood's *Institute*). On Wood, see Daniel R. Coquillette, "Ideology and Incorporation III: Reason Regulated—The Post-Restoration English Civilians, 1653–1735," 67 *Boston University Law Review* 289, 344–45 (1987).

42. See Bush, "Free to Enslave," 446–49.

43. Wood, *Institute*, 3d ed., 51; Blackstone, *Commentaries on the Laws of England*, 1:*127, *416-17, *423-25, 2:*402. For the evolution of Blackstone's views on slavery, see Davis, *Problem of Slavery in the Age of Revolution*, 485-86; Wiecek, *Antislavery Constitutionalism*, 27.

44. Bush, "Free to Enslave," 448–52.

45. See Robin Blackburn, *The Overthrow of Colonial Slavery, 1776–1848* (London: Verso, 1988), 42; Drescher, *Capitalism and Antislavery*, 17; John Locke, *Two Treatises of Government*, 3d ed. (1698; reprint, ed. Peter Laslett, New York: New American Library, 1960); Morgan, *American Slavery, American Freedom*, 6–8; Steinfeld, *Invention of Free Labor*, 95–97. Ironically, many eighteenth-century American colonists later thought in the same terms, seeing the home government as seeking to enslave them. Bernard Bailyn, ed., *Pamphlets of the American Revolution 1750–1776: vol. I 1750–1765* (Cambridge: Harvard University Press, 1965), 140–41.

46. 1 Edw. VI, c. 3, repealed by 3 & 4 Edw. VI, c. 16. As Blackstone puts it, "the spirit of the nation could not brook his [a slave's] condition, even in the most abandoned rogues." Blackstone, *Commentaries on the Laws of England* I:*424. See, generally, C. S. L. Davies, "Slavery and Protector Somerset: The Vagrancy Act of 1547," *Economic History Review*, 2d ser., 19 (1966): 533–49.

47. See Blackburn, *Overthrow of Colonial Slavery*, 36–37; Abbot E. Smith, *Colonists in Bondage: White Servitude and Convict Labor in America, 1607–1776* (Chapel Hill: University of North Carolina Press, 1947), 176–77; Steinfeld, *Invention of Free Labor*, 97–98. The best evidence for this popular antislavery tradition may be the behavior of juries in sixteenth-century villeinage cases, which consistently found for freedom on even implausible facts or fictitious suits. See J. H. Baker, "The Roots of Modern Freedom: Personal Liberty under the Common Law, 1200–1600" (unpub. ms. 1992), 19–20.

48. See, e.g., Michael Craton, *Sinews of Empire: A Short History of British Slavery* (Garden City, N.Y.: Anchor Books, 1974), 32, 35; Finkelman, *Law of Freedom and Bondage*, 10 (citing 1624 testimony of "John Phillips A negro Christened in England 12 yeers since"); Fryar, *Staying Power*, 5, 8–13, 19, 21, 24; Walvin, *Black Presence*, 12–13, 63–65; Davies, "Protector Somerset," 548 n. 3; Fiddes, "Lord Mansfield," 500 n. 4; David B. Quinn, "Turks, Moors, Blacks, and Others in Drake's West Indian Voyage," *Terra Incognitae* 14 (1982): 97, 100, 104, reprinted in *Explorers and Colonies: America, 1500–1625* (London: Hambledon Press, 1990), 197, 200, 204.

49. See, e.g., Hilary D. Beckles, *White Servitude and Black Slavery in Barbados, 1627–1715* (Knoxville: University of Tennessee Press, 1989), 71, 189–90 n. 74; Jordan, *White over Black*, 80–81; Morgan, *American Slavery, American Freedom*, 128; Steinfeld, *Invention of Free Labor*, 101–2; Breen, "Changing Labor Force," 3, 5; David T. Konig, "'Dale's Laws' and the Non-Common Law Origins of Criminal Justice in Virginia," 26 *American Journal of Legal History* 354, 367 (1982).

50. See, e.g., Breen and Innes, *"Myne Owne Ground,"* 5; Billings, "Law of Servants and Slaves," 61–62.

51. 3 Va. Stat. (1619–1820) 259, 269, 447; 4 Va. Stat. (1619–1820) 126, 168; see Craven, *Colonies in Transition*, 297 (reactive quality of Virginia slave law generally); Smith, *Colonists in Bondage*, 227, 264, 275–76.

52. My discussion relies on statutes cited in Dunn, *Sugar and Slaves*, 238–44; Goveia, "West Indian Slave Laws," 346–62; Wiecek, "Statutory Law of Slavery," 258, and Philip J. Schwarz, *Twice Condemned: Slaves and the Criminal Laws of Virginia, 1705–1865* (Baton Rouge: Louisiana State University Press, 1988), 19.

53. Peter Linebaugh, *The London Hanged* (Cambridge: Cambridge University Press, 1992), 53.

54. See Dunn, *Sugar and Slaves*, 238–45; Watson, *Slave Law in the Americas*, 82; Goveia, "West Indian Slave Laws," 350–54; Bradley J. Nicholson, "Legal Borrowing and the Origins of Slave Law in the British Colonies," 38 *American Journal of Legal History* 38–54 (1994); Wiecek, "Statutory Law of Slavery," 258.

55. See Davis, *Problem of Slavery in Western Culture*, 239–41, 248; Dunn, *Sugar and Slaves*, 253; Jordan, *White over Black*, 108; Stampp, *Peculiar Institution*, 207, 212; Watson, *Slave Law in the Americas*, 66, 69–72.

56. Henry Bracton, *De Legibus et Consuetudinibus Anglie*, ed. George E. Woodbine, trans. & intro. Samuel E. Thorne, 4 vols. (Cambridge: Harvard University Press, 1968-77). For the "preference for freedom," see Coke, *First Part of the Institutes*, vol. 1, sec. 193, p. *124b; John Fortescue, *De Laudibus Legum Anglie* [c. 1468–71], ed. and trans. by S. B. Chrimes (1942; reprint, New York: Garland Publishing, 1979), ch. 42, pp. 103–04. The doctrine's relationship to New World slavery is discussed in Bush, "Free to Enslave," 438–39 n. 75. For antebellum uses of Bracton, see *Fisher's Negroes* v. *Dabbs*, 14 Tenn. (6 Yer.) 119, 124 (1834); Cobb, *Inquiry into Law of Negro Slavery*, sec. 71, p. 70. For familiarity with Bracton in the colonial period, see William Hamilton Bryson, *Census of Law Books in Colonial Virginia* (Charlottesville: University of Virginia Press, 1978), xvi, 36; Bailyn, ed., *Pamphlets*, 26; Gordon S. Wood, *The Creation of the American Republic, 1776–1787* (New York: W. W. Norton, 1969), 299 n. 66.

57. For Bracton and villeinage, see Hyams, *King, Lords, and Peasants*. On medieval Jewish status, see Bush, "'Take This Job and Shove It,'" 1407–09. On the Irish as legally unfree, see G. J. Hand, "Aspects of Alien Status in Medieval English Law, with Special Reference to Ireland," in *Legal History Studies 1972*, ed. Dafydd Jenkins (Cardiff: University of Wales Press, 1975), 129, 132–34; G. J. Hand, "The Status of the Native Irish in the Lordship of Ireland, 1272-1331," 1 *Irish Jurist*, n.s. (1966): 93.

58. See, e.g., Edward Miller and John Hatcher, *Medieval England: Rural Society and Economic Change, 1086–1348* (London: Longman, 1978), 132–33; Helen M. Cam, "Pedigrees of Villeins and Freemen," in *Liberties and Communities in Medieval England* (London: Merlin Press, 1963), 124, 131–35.

59. For Jewish disabilities, see in Robert Chazan, ed., *Church, State, and Jew in the Middle Ages* (New York: Behrman House, 1980), 188–89. H. G. Richardson,

The English Jewry under Angevin Kings (London: Methuen, 1960), 28–32; Paul Hyams, "The Jewish Minority in Mediaeval England, 1066–1290," *Journal of Jewish Studies* 25 (1974): 270, 276–77; Robert C. Stacey, "The Conversion of Jews to Christianity in Thirteenth-Century England," *Speculum* 67 (1992): 263, 269–71. For medieval regulation of Ireland, see Steven G. Ellis, *Tudor Ireland: Crown, Community, and the Conflict of Cultures, 1470–1603* (London: Longman, 1985), 24; G. J. Hand, *English Law in Ireland, 1290–1324* (Cambridge: Cambridge University Press, 1967), 205–10.

60. Jordan, *White over Black*, ch. 1.

61. See Wiecek, "Statutory Law of Slavery," 270 (citing 1696 South Carolina act). For black-white activities, see Beckles, *White Servitude*, 100–02, 111–12; Breen and Innes, *"Myne Owne Ground,"* 27–30, 95–96, 98–100, 104–07; Morgan, *American Slavery, American Freedom*, 311, 327, 336; Peter Wood, *Black Majority: Negroes in Colonial South Carolina from 1670 through the Stono Rebellion* (New York: W. W. Norton, 1974), 54, 96, 218, 243–44; Paul Finkelman, "The Crime of Color," 67 *Tulane Law Review* 2063–112 (1993); T. H. Breen, "A Changing Labor Force and Race Relations in Virginia, 1660–1710," *Journal of Social History* 7 (1973): 3, 7–8, 11–12; Douglas Deal, "A Constricted World: Free Blacks on Virginia's Eastern Shore, 1680–1750," in *Colonial Chesapeake Society*, ed. Lois G. Carr, Philip D. Morgan, and Jean Russo (Chapel Hill: University of North Carolina Press, 1988), 275, 277.

62. Finkelman, "Exploring Southern Legal History," 113.

63. Billings, "Law of Servants and Slaves," 48–57 (citing Sir Thomas Smith); Davies, "Protector Somerset," 542–43, 547; Richard Huloet, *Abecedarium Anglico-Latinum* (1552; reprint, ed. R. C. Alston, Menston, England: Scolar Press Ltd., 1970), s.v. "apprentice"; Morris, "'Sources' of Southern Slave Law," 106, 112; Huloet, *Abecedarium*, s.v. "slave"; Jonathan L. Alpert, "Origin of Slavery in the United States—The Maryland Precedent," 14 *American Journal of Legal History* 198-209 (1970); Craven, *Colonies in Transition*, 295–96; Frank W. Craven, *The Southern Colonies in the Seventeenth Century, 1607–1689* (Baton Rouge: Louisiana State University Press, 1949), 217; Billings, "Law of Servants and Slaves," 45; Nicholson, "Legal Borrowing and the Origins of Slave Law," 42–48; Beckles, *White Servitude*, 71, 74; Jordan, *White over Black*, 50–51.

64. *Smith* v. *Brown and Cooper, supra* note 28, 2 Salk. at 666 (emphasis supplied). Holt's own published report of the case uses substantially similar language.

65. *Blankard* v. *Galdy*, 2 Salk. 411, Holt 341, 4 Mod. 215 & 221, Comber. 228 (K.B. 1694). See Joseph H. Smith, *Appeals to the Privy Council from the American Plantations* (New York: Columbia University Press, 1950), 470–71.

66. *Calvin's Case*, 7 Co. Rep. 1a, 17a–b (K.B. 1608). See Barbara A. Black, "The Constitution of Empire: The Case for the Colonists," 124 *University of Pennsylvania Law Review* 1157, 1177–81, 1186 (1976) (revisionist view of Coke's entire position); Bush, "'You're Gonna Miss Me When I'm Gone,' Early Modern Common law Discourse and the case of the Jews," [1993] *Wisconsin Law Review* 1225, 1257–58 (examining Coke's dicta on infidels and perpetual enemies).

67. Nicholas P. Canny, *Kingdom and Colony* (Baltimore: Johns Hopkins University Press, 1988); Nicholas P. Canny, "The Permissive Frontier: Social Control in English Settlements in Ireland and Virginia, 1550–1650," in *The Westward Enterprise: English Activities in Ireland, the Atlantic, and America, 1480–1650*,

eds. K. R. Andrews, N. P. Canny, and P. E. H. Hair (Detroit: Wayne State University Press, 1979), 17–44.

68. *The Case of Tanistry, supra* note 28; Nicholas P. Canny, *From Reformation to Restoration: Ireland, 1534 to 1660* (Dublin: Helicon, 1987), 160–62, 175–77; Hans S. Pawlisch, *Sir John Davies and the Conquest of Ireland* (Cambridge: Cambridge University Press, 1985), 9–13, 55–83; David T. Konig, "Colonization and the Common Law in Ireland and Virginia, 1569–1634," in *The Transformation of Early American History,* eds. James A. Henretta, Michael Kammen, and Stanley N. Katz (New York: Alfred A. Knopf, 1991), 70, 74–75, 77–78.

69. See for example, *Commons Debates 1621,* ed. Wallace Notestein, Frances Helen Relf, and Hartley Simpson, 7 vols. (New Haven: Yale University Press, 1935), 4:256. Robert Zaller, *The Parliament of 1621* (Berkeley: University of California Press, 1971), 209 n. 91; Black, "Constitution of Empire," 1188–91. See also A. Berriedale Keith, *Constitutional History of the First British Empire* (Oxford: Clarendon Press, 1930), 11–13.

70. See Ellis, *Tudor Ireland,* 139–41; Kent McNeil, *Common Law Aboriginal Title* (Oxford: Clarendon Press, 1989), 113 n. 20; Ralph A. Griffiths, "The English Realm and Dominions and the King's Subjects in the Later Middle Ages," in *Aspects of Late Medieval Government and Society,* ed. J. G. Rowe (Toronto: University of Toronto Press, 1986), 83–105; Jenny Wormauld, "The Creation of Britain: Multiple Kingdoms or Core and Colonies?" *Transactions of the Royal Historical Society,* 6th ser., vol. 2 (London: 1992), 175, 185. See also Black, "Constitution of Empire" (surveying the MacIlwain-Schuyler debate and the reliance of American revolutionists on medieval English legal models).

71. Some of the instruments of oversight are printed in *Royal Instructions to British Colonial Governors,* 1:133–40. See also Dunn, *Sugar and Slaves,* 158.

72. Indeed, they had no choice: with the execution of Charles I, the prerogative necessarily had to lapse into desuetude or revert to Parliament. See Keith, *Constitutional History,* 10, 48–58; Charles H. McIlwain, *The American Revolution: A Constitutional Interpretation* (1923; reprint, Ithaca: Cornell University Press, 1958), 9, 21–31.

73. See John Brydall, *Jura Coronae* (1680; reprint, New York: Garland Publishing, 1979), 7–10; William Noy, *A Treatise of the Rights of the Crown* (1634; 1715 ed. reprint, New York: Garland Publishing, 1979); Wood, *Institute,* 3d ed. (1724), 21. Hale surveyed only the medieval models, and not contemporary colonies. Matthew Hale, *The Prerogatives of the King,* ed. D. E. C. Yale, Selden Society, 92 (London, 1976), 43. Blackstone, *Commentaries on the Laws of England,* 1:*98–105, attempted to survey all prerogative claims, but by his day they were increasingly irrelevant in the politicized mainland colonies.

74. McIlwain, *American Revolution,* 3.

75. See William Strachey, *For the Colony in Virginea Britannia: Lawes Divine, Morall and Martiall* (1612; reprint, ed. David H. Flaherty, Charlottesville: University of Virginia Press, 1969) (reprint contains Dale's 1611 Laws); Francis Jennings, *The Invasion of America: Indians, Colonialism, and the Cant of Conquest* (New York: W.W. Norton, 1975) 109 (Andrews quotation).

76. Blackburn, *Overthrow of Colonial Slavery,* 40. See, e.g., Stone, *Crisis of the Aristocracy,* 199–270; Frederick Pollock and Frederic W. Maitland, *The History of English Law before the Time of Edward I,* 2d ed., 2 vols. (Cambridge: Cambridge University Press, 1968), 1:512.

77. See, e.g., Morton J. Horwitz, *The Transformation of American Law, 1780–1860* (Cambridge: Harvard University Press, 1977), 5–6; James H. Kettner, *The Development of American Citizenship, 1608–1870* (Chapel Hill: University of North Carolina Press, 1978), 28, 45.

78. *East India Co.* v. *Sandys* (Case of Monopolies), 10 How. St. T. 371–505 (1683–85). Whatever was left of the doctrine was sharply criticized in *Fabrigas* v. *Mostyn,* 2 Black., W. 929, 20 How. St. T. 81, 162, (C.P. 1773), *aff'd in* 1 Cowp. 161, 20 How. St. T. 183, 214 (K.B. 1775) (argument of counsel); *Campbell* v. *Hall,* Lofft 655, 716, 741, 744, 1 Cowp. 204, 209, 20 How. St. T. 239, 323, 325 (K.B. 1774). See Bush, "'You're Gonna Miss Me When I'm Gone,'" 1250, 1259–64.

79. Black, "Constitution of Empire," 1177–81, 1186, 1198; Konig, "Colonization and the Common Law," 77–78. For *jus gentium* doctrines on the rights of conquerors and settlers, see, e.g., Hugo Grotius, *The Rights of War and Peace* [1625] trans. A. C. Campbell (1901; reprint, Westport, Conn.: Hyperion Press, 1979), II.2–4, pp. 85–116.

80. *Anon.,* 2 P. Wms. 75 (Ch. 1722); *Wytham* v. *Dutton,* 3 Mod. 159 (K.B. 1687); *Dawes* v. *Pindar,* 2 Mod. 45 (K.B. 1675).

81. *Blankard* v. *Galdy, supra* note 65; *Campbell* v. *Hall, supra* note 78, Lofft at 658, 1 Cowp. at 205, 20 How. St. T. at 321, 323 (citing 1762 articles of surrender by which French islanders became British subjects but retained right to their former government, laws, and customs "until His Majesty's pleasure be known"); *Fabrigas* v. *Mostyn, supra* note 78, 1 Cowp. at 177–81, 20 How. St. T. at 211, 233–38 (distinguishing between "transitory" and "local" writs in determining whether a native-born Minorcan should have access to common law remedy against the governor); Blackstone, *Commentaries on the Laws of England,* I:*107; Dunn, *Sugar and Slaves,* 22–23, 117–18 (St. Kitts); McNeil, *Common Law Aboriginal Title,* 117, 138–39, 147–57 (Barbados and Pitcairn Island); David E. Narrett, *Inheritance and Family Life in Colonial New York City* (Ithaca: Cornell University Press, 1992), 54, 69, 83–84, 98, 198 (Dutch testation practices in English New York).

82. See for example, *Campbell* v. *Hall, supra* note 78 (status of Grenada after 1762 conquest); *Collett* v. *Keith,* 2 East 260 (K.B. 1802) (Cape of Good Hope); David Ogg, *England in the Reign of Charles II,* 2d ed. (Oxford: Clarendon Press, 1956), 2:659–62, 668–69; *Appeals to the Privy Council,* 268. For the American proprietary grants, see Craven, *Southern Colonies,* 190, 338–41; Keith, *Constitutional History,* 39–43; Russell, *Review of American Colonial Legislation,* 36.

83. T. C. Barnard, "Planters and Policies in Cromwellian Ireland," *Past and Present* 61 (1973): 31–69. See also Nicholas P. Canny, "The Marginal Kingdom: Ireland as a Problem in the First British Empire," in *Strangers within the Realm,* 35, 60. For belated discussions of constitutional status, see, e.g., *Craw* v. *Ramsey,* Carter 185, Vaug. 274, 2 Ventr. 1 (C.P. 1670), rev. sub nom. *Collingwood* v. *Pace,* 1 Ventr. 413, 1 Lev. 59 (Ex. Ch.); Wormauld, "Creation of Britain," 175–94. See also *R.* v. *Vaughan,* 4 Burr. 2494, 2500 (K.B. 1769) (Lord Mansfield reexamining Jamaica); *Atty Gen.* v. *Stewart,* 2 Meriv. 143 (Ch. 1816-17) (Grenada); Bush, "Free to Enslave," 462 nn. 165, 169. The complex *Ramsey* cases are discussed in Kettner, *Development of American Citizenship,* 36–42.

84. Well before New World colonization, the lawyers, with a view to Ireland, had recognized the different status of statute law. Samuel E. Thorne, Introduction to *A Discourse upon the Exposicion and Understandinge of Statutes, with Sir Thomas Egerton's Additions* (San Marino, Cal.: Huntington Library, 1942), 34–35.

The classic formulation was set out in Blackstone, *Commentaries on the Laws of England*, I:*107; see Konig, "Colonization and the Common Law," 70–71. See Jack P. Greene, *Peripheries and Center: Constitutional Development and the Extended Polities of the British Empire and the United States, 1607–1788* (Athens, Ga.: University of Georgia Press, 1986), 43–44; Smith, *Appeals to the Privy Council*, 473–75. For the resulting constitutional uncertainty, see J. C. D. Clark, *The Language of Liberty, 1660–1832* (Cambridge: Cambridge University Press, 1994), 2; John P. Reid, *In a Defiant Stance* (University Park: Penn State University Press, 1977), 101.

85. Warren M. Billings, "The Transfer of English Law to Virginia, 1606–50," in *The Westward Enterprise*, 215, 216 (quoting supplemental instructions from Virginia Co. in London to provincial council in 1606).

86. See, e.g., Richard Bland, *The Colonel Dismounted* (1764), 20–21 and James Otis, *The Rights of the British Colonies Asserted and Proved* (1764), 34–35, both reprinted in Bailyn, ed., *Pamphlets*, 292, 319 and 408, 444; Keith, *Constitutional History*, 185. That the colonists should be deemed settlers with English rights rather than occupants of conquered land had ample precedent. Chalmers, ed., *Opinions of Eminent Lawyers*, 206–07 (citing 1720 opinion).

87. Edward Coke, *Second Institutes* (1642; reprint, New York: Garland Publishing, 1979), Magna Carta, ch. 30, p. *63, discussed in Kettner, *Development of American Citizenship*, 27 n. 44. But see *Campbell v. Hall*, supra note 78, Lofft at 741, 744, 1 Cowp. at 209, 20 How. St. T. at 289, 323 (Mansfield rejects Coke's view).

88. Bernard Bailyn, "1776 in Britain and America: A Year of Challenge—A World Transformed," 19 *Journal of Law & Economics* 437, 464 (1976).

89. McIlwain, *American Revolution*, 19–20; see Clark, *Language of Liberty*, 103–05; Greene, *Peripheries and Center*, 133; Kettner, *Development of American Citizenship*, 134; Pauline Maier, *From Resistance to Revolution: Colonial Radicals and the Development of American Opposition to Britain, 1765–1776* (New York: W. W. Norton, 1991), 245; Edmund S. Morgan, *The Birth of the Republic, 1763–89*, rev. ed. (Chicago: University of Chicago Press, 1977), 18, 25–26, 33, 35, 42, 62–64; Edmund S. and Helen M. Morgan, *The Stamp Act Crisis* rev. ed. (New York: Collier Books, 1962), 112–16; Clinton Rossiter, *The Political Thought of the American Revolution*, pt. 3 of *Seedtime of the Republic* (New York: Harcourt, Brace & World, 1963), 19–32; Wood, *Creation of the American Republic*, 177, 350–52; Thomas C. Grey, "The Origins of the Unwritten Constitution: Fundamental Law in American Revolutionary Thought," 30 *Stanford Law Review* 843, 867 (1978); Martin S. Flaherty, "Note: The Empire Strikes Back: *Annesley v. Sherlock* and the Triumph of Imperial Parliamentary Supremacy," 87 *Columbia Law Review* 593 (1987). See also J. R. Pole, *The Gift of Government: Political Responsibility from the English Restoration to American Independence* (Athens, Ga.: University of Georgia Press, 1983), 44–45; Wormauld, "Creation of Britain," 185.

90. See Carl L. Becker, *The Declaration of Independence* (1922; reprint, New York: Vintage Books, 1942), x, 20–22; McIlwain, *American Constitution*, 192; MacLeod, *Slavery, Race, and the American Revolution*, 13–14, 17–18, 21; Wiecek, "Somerset," 114.

91. Becker, *Declaration of Independence*, 133. For use of the prerogative on the eve of the Revolution, see, e.g., *Opinion of Dulany*, supra note 13, at 564–65; John Phillip Reid, ed., *The Briefs of the American Revolution* (New York: New York

University Press, 1981), 8–9, 76, 78–79; Greene, *Peripheries and Center*, 134–35; McIlwain, *American Revolution*, 2 (quoting Continental Congress); Bailyn, ed., *Pamphlets*, 134–35; Pole, *Gift of Government*, 36; Rossiter, *Political Thought of the American Revolution*, 17–18; Robert L. Schuyler, *Parliament and the British Empire* (New York: Columbia University Press, 1929), 136; Black, "Constitution of Empire," 1193; Grey, "Origins of the Unwritten Constitution," 887–88.

92. Becker, *Declaration of Independence*, 18–20; Maier, *From Resistance to Revolution*, 200–10.

93. Chalmers, ed., *Opinions of Eminent Lawyers*, 206 (quotation). West concluded with a lawyerly qualification "Let an Englishman go where he will, he carries as much of law and liberty with him, *as the nature of things will bear.*" Ibid. (emphasis added).

94. For selective reception, see Edward S. Corwin, *The "Higher Law" Background of American Constitutional Law* (Ithaca: Cornell University Press, 1955), 47–48; Keith, *Constitutional History*, 184–85; Smith, *Appeals to the Privy Council*, 473–75; Wood, *Creation of the American Republic*, 296–98; J. R. Pole, "Reflections on American Law and the American Revolution," *William and Mary Quarterly*, 3d ser., 50 (1993): 123, 124, 138. See also *Fabrigas* v. *Mostyn*, supra note 78, 1 Cowp. at 162, 20 How. St. T. at 137–38, 167, 172, 225, 227 (testimony that subjects in conquered Minorca freely selected from English and Spanish legal doctrines, as befitting the case).

13

Thinking Property at Rome

Alan Watson

IT IS A COMMONPLACE among writers on slavery that there is an inherent contradiction or a necessary confusion in regarding slaves as both human beings and things. In law there is no such contradiction or confusion. Slaves are both property and human beings. Their humanity is not denied but (in general) they are refused legal personality, a very different matter.

Things as property may be classed in various ways, and the classification may then have an impact on owners' rights and duties. A thing may be corporeal or incorporeal, immovable or movable. Some movables may be classed as *res se moventes*, things that move of their own accord, animate beings, such as horses and cattle; others, again, as inanimate property. A subdivision of *res se moventes* might be of—in Aristotle's term—"thinking property,"[1] that is, human beings. And the ownership of thinking property may in the eyes of the law create rights and duties that are somewhat different from those arising from the ownership of other *res se moventes*.

This paper is devoted to an examination of some problems that occur when slaves are considered as "thinking property." I will not deal with the rather different issues that arise when slaves are to some extent accorded legal personality, such as when they may appear as witnesses, create a legally valid marriage, or be prosecuted for crime. The subject, therefore, concerns issues such as whether a person is liable for injuries caused to a slave whom he had hired, by the negligence of a fellow worker;[2] and whether a hirer of a slave is liable if he permitted the slave to do work forbidden by the contract, and the slave was injured.[3]

This paper is restricted to Rome because it was there that the law of thinking property was most developed. I will deal with only five examples, chosen because I have not examined them before and because I think I have something new to say.[4]

A Slave Gives a Mandate to Buy Himself

A first issue will be selected from mandate which was the contract that came into being when one person asked another to do something for him gratuitously, and the latter agreed.[5] When a slave made a contract, all the rights under it accrued to his owner, but in early law no liability attached to the owner; and the slave, not having legal personality, could not be sued. By the last century of the republic a slave's contract could make his owner liable in some cases to some extent. Most commonly, the owner's liability was restricted to the amount of the slave's *peculium*—a fund that belonged to the owner but which he allowed the slave to use as if it were his own—and the extent to which the owner had benefitted.

> *Digest of Justinian*, 17.1.19 (Ulpian, *On Sabinus, book 43*).[6] If my slave gave a mandate for the purchase of himself so that he might be redeemed, Pomponius elegantly discusses whether he who redeemed the slave can sue the seller to take the slave back, since the action on mandate is reciprocal. But Pomponius says it would be most unfair that I should be forced, through his own act, to take back my slave whom I wanted to alienate in perpetuity; nor should I in this case be more liable on mandate than that I sell him to you.

Ulpian was a jurist and imperial bureaucrat who was murdered in A.D. 224, Pomponius was a jurist active in the mid second century. The text is not quite in proper form. "He who redeemed the slave" (*is, qui servum redemerit*) must mean "he who bought the slave to redeem him" because the slave has obviously not been redeemed. Otherwise, since he would now be free, he could not be returned as a slave to his former owner. If Aulus is the first owner of the slave and Balbus is the purchaser, then there are two contracts between Aulus and Balbus. First, there is a mandate from Aulus to Balbus to buy the slave—let us call him Pamphilus—with subsequent redemption. In mandate the "principal" has to indemnify the "agent" for any loss he suffers, and the "agent" is liable for fraud but usually not for negligence. Second, there is a contract of sale of the slave, Aulus being the seller, Balbus the purchaser.

The slave has been delivered to Balbus, but Balbus has repented of his agreement. He no longer wants to free the slave but to return him to Aulus. Balbus seems not to have an action on the contract of sale that is perfectly valid and seems irreproachable; but what about mandate, since the action is reciprocal? Balbus should not suffer loss from executing Aulus' mandate; so can he recoup by returning the slave and getting back the purchase price?[7]

If Aulus personally, not the slave, had given Balbus a mandate to buy Pamphilus and then free him,[8] and if Balbus had bought but not freed Pamphilus, Aulus would have an action on mandate against Balbus to the extent of his interest. Balbus should go through with the mandate but be entitled to reimbursement from Aulus. But in actuality the initiative is the slave's, and the mandate is by the slave. We are not even told whether Aulus knows of the mandate. To what extent, then, has the slave, Pamphilus, made his owner, Aulus, liable?

There is no reasonable, principled, answer in the absence of fraud and the issue of fraud is not raised. Balbus should, perhaps, go through with freeing the slave and then sue Aulus on the mandate up to the level of the slave's peculium.[9] But Balbus is unwilling to do so, possibly because there are insufficient funds in the peculium. And Aulus obviously has no burning desire to free the slave and is not pressing Balbus to fulfill the mandate. The desire that the mandate be carried out is that of the slave. Balbus is in a difficult legal position: a mandatary may withdraw from the contract so long as nothing has been done on it, but thereafter he is liable to the mandator if he does not go through with it. Balbus has willfully left the mandate incomplete, so he has no real title to sue Aulus.

Pomponius' solution is simply to hold that, in the circumstances, Aulus' liability to Balbus on mandate is restricted to selling the slave Pamphilus to Balbus. That is to say, the mandate is valid, but Balbus, the mandatary, has no action against Aulus. Ulpian describes Pomponius' discussion as elegant. So in the event is his solution.[10] It would, indeed, have been unjust that a mandate between the slave and Balbus, primarily and obviously in the interest of the slave, would have put the burden on Aulus when Balbus was unwilling to complete the mandate. Pomponius, it should be stressed, claims that "it would be most unfair": a policy argument. Policy arguments are very uncommon in Roman law; but here no solution could otherwise be found.[11]

A different approach to the problem, or a related one, was taken by the most famous of the Roman jurists, Papinian, who was executed in A.D. 212:

> *Dig.* 17.1.54pr (Papinian, *Questions, book 27*). When a slave gives a mandate to a third party to buy him, the mandate is void. But if the mandate was to this end that the slave be manumitted, and the purchaser did not manumit him, the owner will both recover the price as seller, and also there will be an action on mandate on account of affection: suppose the slave was his natural son or brother (for the jurists have agreed that in actions on good faith account is to be taken of affection). But if the buyer gave the price from his own money (nor can he otherwise be released by the action on sale) the question is frequently asked whether he can validly bring an action on account of the *peculium*. And it seems more correct and expedient to hold that the pra-

etor had not contemplated contracts of this kind by which slaves might take themselves away from their owners by bad cause.

Again, Papinian is considering the situation where the slave has taken the initiative in giving a mandate to Balbus. A simple mandate by Pamphilus to Balbus to buy him is, Papinian says, void. This would not of itself affect the validity of the subsequent purchase. If the slave's mandate to Balbus is both that Balbus buy him and manumit him, and if Balbus buys but does not free the slave, then Papinian holds both that the contract of sale is valid and Aulus has an action for the price and also that the mandate is valid and Aulus will have an action on it. The mandator's action lies for his interest in having the mandate carried out.[12] Hence, since he has recovered the money due to him by the *actio venditi*, the action on sale, we are expressly told that the *actio mandati* will lie on account of affection. (Incidentally, the text shows that in an action of good faith, the award which will always be in money, may be for more than the plaintiff's financial loss.)

Papinian next turns his attention to the issue of a remedy to Balbus to the extent of the slave's peculium. This action cannot relate to the contract of sale since that was properly carried out. Thus, the mandate must be performed by Balbus. Hence, the slave is presumably manumitted by Balbus, and the question is whether Balbus can bring the action on mandate against Aulus for his expenditure in fulfilling the mandate (the purchase price), restricted to the amount of the peculium. So this is not now the situation discussed by Pomponius. Papinian's solution is crude but effective. Balbus has no *actio mandati* because the praetorian remedies designed to give some protection to third parties contracting with slaves were not envisaged for cases where a slave was wrongfully removing himself from his owner.[13] There is no principle here: in other situations where a slave acted wrongfully in making a contract, the owner could be liable up to the amount of the peculium.

If we consider together the opinions of Pomponius and Papinian, whether or not we think their views are consistent with one another, the following picture emerges.

For Papinian, a slave's mandate to a third party simply to buy him is null. This is reasonable as a result because either party can freely withdraw from the mandate until there is some performance or reliance on it.[14] Performance is, in fact, the making of the contract of sale, and thereafter all issues between the parties can be resolved by rights under that contract. There is no need to discuss particular issues, such as whether a slave can legally bind his owner by such a mandate. But the slave's mandate might be more extensive: that Balbus buy him and then free him. For Pomponius, if Balbus buys and does not free, there is a valid mandate. Aulus is liable to Balbus on mandate, but in the absence of complete performance by Balbus, Aulus' liability is restricted to the sale. The

result seems equitable, but no legal principle is discoverable for the precise extent of liability on mandate. On similar facts Papinian discusses
only Balbus' liability to Aulus. Aulus has both the action on the sale for
payment of the price and the action on mandate for any further interest
in performance of the mandate, based on a personal affection for the
slave. This would seem to be in accord with standard legal principles.
Where Balbus both buys and frees the slave, Papinian holds that the
mandate is valid but would refuse Balbus an action on that contract against
Aulus because that is not the kind of slave's contract that praetors had
envisaged would make an owner liable to third parties. This is again a
policy argument, such as, I have said, is found very rarely in Roman law;
but no principle seems to exist that could determine the issue. I tend to
believe, though cannot prove, that the policy argument appears simply
because there was no principle.

A Slave's Contract for His Prisoner-of-War Owner

A second issue concerns a contract of stipulation taken by a slave from a
third party. The *stipulatio* was a formal, unilateral, verbal contract of strict
law where one party asked the other if he promised to give or do something, and the other immediately responded, necessarily using the same
verb. The promisor was very much bound by the wording of the stipulation; and it was a basic rule that one could not make a stipulation on
behalf of another, except on behalf of the person in whose power one
was.[15] Since neither a person in power nor a slave could acquire anything, a stipulatio taken by a son or daughter in power or a slave immediately accrued in normal circumstances to the *paterfamilias* or the owner.
But there could be problems: for example, if a slave had two owners, or
if he were the object of a usufruct.[16] Thus:

> *Dig.* 45.3.18.2 (Papinian, *Questions, book* 27) A slave whose owner had
> been captured by the enemy stipulated for something to be given to
> the owner. Although whatever he had simply stipulated for or received
> from another would belong to the heir of the prisoner and the law is
> otherwise in the case of a son [of a prisoner-of-war] since he was nei-
> ther in power at the time he took the stipulation nor would he later
> (like the slave) be included in the inheritance,[17] yet in the present case
> the question may be raised whether the heir acquired nothing from
> this stipulation, just as where a slave forming part of the inheritance
> stipulated on behalf of the deceased or of the future heir. But in this
> case the slave will be equated with the son. For even if a son of a captive
> took a stipulation for his father, the matter will be in suspense, and if
> the father died among the enemy, the stipulation will be seen to be
> without effect, because he stipulated for another, not for himself.

A Roman who was captured by the enemy immediately lost his citizenship and, indeed, was regarded as a slave of the enemy. If he died in captivity, then for succession purposes—only for succession purposes—he was regarded as having died at the moment of captivity so that (never having lost his citizenship) his succession would open up in the usual way. If he returned from the enemy in an honorable way, then he returned with *postliminium*. Postliminium is perhaps the subtlest part of Roman legal science. The former prisoner's rights were treated in different ways: thus, marriage (with two exceptions) was dissolved by capture and did not revive by postliminium;[18] guardianship (*tutela*) that he exercised was ended by captivity, revived by postliminium, but not retroactively; *patria potestas*, obligations and property rights, were suspended by captivity, but if the captive returned with postliminium they were revived as if he had never been a prisoner.[19]

The main issues in our text concern a stipulatio taken by a slave whose owner (Aulus, again) has been captured by the enemy. If the wording was "Do you promise to give to me?" "I promise," then there is no real problem: the slave acquires the rights for his owner even if the owner's identity cannot be determined at the moment. Thus, if Aulus returns with postliminium, his property rights revive retroactively, and Aulus is entitled under his slave's stipulatio. If Aulus dies in captivity, he is regarded for succession purposes as dead from the moment of capture; hence, at the time of the stipulatio the slave belongs to the inheritance, and the rights under the stipulatio go to the heir, should one be recognized.[20]

The problem arises when the wording was "Do you promise to give to Aulus?" "I promise." If Aulus returns with postliminium, then his property and contractual rights revive retroactively and the stipulatio is validly in his favor. But what if he has died in captivity? Then in at least one sense, the slave has made the stipulation for an outsider—indeed, a nonperson—in whose power he is not. But ought the heir be allowed to have right under the contract?

To help with the problem, Papinian has recourse to the effect of a stipulation made by a *filius familias*, a son-in-power. Where the stipulatio is framed in the simple form (*simpliciter*) by the son, the result is not the same because, we are told, "he was neither in power at the time he took the stipulation nor would he later [like the slave] be included in the inheritance." This does not give a direct answer to the fate of the stipulation, and there is something not quite right with the first alternative.[21] As the text makes plain further down, and as is confirmed by other texts, the effect of the stipulation is in suspense: if the father returns with postliminium, the stipulation is valid in his favor.[22] Hence, *patria potestas* must, for Papinian, have been restored retroactively. Where the father does not return, then since the son cannot be regarded as part of the inheritance, the stipulation will be valid for the benefit of the son.

But the real issue arises when the stipulation was taken "for Aulus." Until the mortal fate of Aulus is sealed, the matter is in suspense. When the promisee is the son and the father returns with postliminium, then the stipulation is valid and accrues to Aulus; if the father has died in captivity, the stipulation is for a third party and is void. Papinian adds—actually very lamely—that here a slave can be equiparated to the son. Accordingly, if Aulus does not return, his inheritance does not acquire right to the stipulation because when the stipulation was made it was made for the benefit of a third person and so is void. Papinian does not further disclose his reasoning to that decision.

The text seems rather confused, but the author's thought process can be recovered. The question at issue is the status of a stipulation by a slave made expressly in the name of his owner when the owner has become a prisoner of war. The difficult case is where the owner dies in captivity. Papinian has no answer that can be reached by straightforward legal principle. So he takes two standard approaches together. By one he proceeds from the simpler case—the stipulation *simpliciter*—to the case that concerns him. By another he tries the approach by analogy: in many—though not all—ways, a master's rights from a slave's transaction are the same as a father-of-a-family's rights from a son's transaction.

But in this instance neither of these two approaches turns out to be fruitful. The simpler case provides no guidance for the difficult alternative in the more complex case. The analogy with the son also breaks down in the simpler case: this time the result of the *stipulatio* would differ according to whether it was made by a slave or son. So now Papinian has a real dilemma: no help from the simpler case or by analogy. So he cuts the Gordian knot by an assertion: that the analogy does work for the complex case even when the owner died a prisoner! But he can produce no convincing argument for the approach.

The text is thus very revealing. Papinian was faced with a tricky issue that he had real difficulty in resolving. He should indeed then have cut out his discussion of the simpler case and the analogy with the son, but they had been part of his mental workings, and they were retained. He might have used a more direct approach for the difficult alternative, which would have been at least as persuasive and which would have given the same result. When Aulus has died in captivity, his inheritance is treated as passing at the moment of capture. Hence, when the stipulation was made "for Aulus" at the time when he was a captive, it was, Papinian might have argued, made after his death and was not part of the inheritance.

A Slave's Compromise with a Villain

My third example of bargains made by "thinking property" relates to *transactio*, compromise. Transactio was a compromise (that involved no formalities) of a legal dispute, whether the action was pending, running its course, or even—if an appeal was possible—already decided. It was the abandoning of a claim in return for something given or promised, or the abandoning of a particular defense in return for some other concession.[23]

> *Dig.* 47.2.52.26 (Ulpian, *On the Edict, book* 37). If my slave who had free administration of his *peculium* made an agreement not on account of a gift with a person who stole a thing from the *peculium*, this seems a valid compromise. For although the action on theft is procured [*quaeratur*] for the owner, nonetheless still the matter concerns the slave's *peculium*. But even if the whole double penalty of theft was paid to the slave there is no doubt the thief would be released. It is in harmony [*consequens est*] with this that if it happened that the slave received from the thief what appears satisfactory on that account, there seems to be a real compromise.

The limits of a slave's administration of his *peculium* were precisely those set by his owner, except that even if he were granted full powers of administration (*libera administratio*) he could not make a valid gift.[24]

The text concerns a very particular type of issue, and this accounts for the emphasis in the text. *Sed et si,* "but even if," introduces a more extreme case. *Cui consequens est,* "it is in harmony with this," then proffers a decision that is now easy, given the previous case. But why is payment to the slave of the full double damages for a theft a more difficult case for the release of the thief's liability than a compromise made to the slave?

The situation is this: Someone has stolen a thing from the peculium of a slave (Pamphilus), whose owner (Aulus) has granted him free administration of it. The private-law action on theft (*actio furti*) for double the value of what was stolen is in the air, is pending; otherwise a *transactio* could not be involved. This action can be brought only by the owner. Ulpian emphasizes that the action was procured, "was created for," the owner. At this stage Pamphilus makes a deal with the thief, Gnaeus, a deal in which the slave does not intend to make a gift. The issue is whether this is a valid *transactio*, because if it is, the result is that Aulus' action is barred. Ulpian holds the *transactio* valid.

"But even if"—introducing the more extreme case—the slave has received the full amount that the owner would have been awarded in the *actio furti*, the arrangement will have been valid. The point is that if the *actio furti* has gone to fruition, the award will have gone directly to Aulus and will only fall into the peculium if Aulus so wishes. Indeed, the money will not form part of the peculium until it is actually delivered to the slave by the owner.[25] In contrast, where on account of the theft the thief pays the double value—the amount that would have been awarded had there been an *actio furti*—to the slave, the money will automatically be in the peculium. Since the full amount of the claim is paid, a technical transactio is not involved. The arrangement simply wipes out the owner's action automatically.

The slave's peculium is in the ownership of his owner. But it may make a huge difference to the slave's owner, both in terms of law and of practical life, whether a sum of money is in the peculium of the slave or not. In terms of law, between master and slave the owner can arbitrarily strip the slave of all or part of the peculium. But the owner's position with regard to outsiders is very different. He cannot arbitrarily withdraw anything from the peculium in a way that would deprive a creditor of any recovery on the slave's contract or delict.[26] Hence, if some other party has an action against the owner because of a contract with the slave, he may well receive much more if the money from the thief has gone into the peculium than if it has not. In terms of practical life, the master would be affected if, for example, he has agreed with the slave to free him on payment of a fixed sum from the peculium. Such an agreement would seem to be common—it would be good for the slave's morale and would encourage him to work harder, and the owner could use the money to buy a replacement.[27] The agreement, of course, would have no legal effect, but most owners would not depart from it lightly or arbitrarily. Such behavior would make not only that slave less tractable but the others also. So in practical terms here, it is much better for the owner that this money, not earned by the slave, not go into the peculium, but that the slave earn more and so build up the peculium.

It is in this sense that an arrangement is more extreme where Pamphilus receives all that might have been won in an *actio furti* than where he made a compromise. It is also more extreme in the sense that even where there is no technical compromise, transactio, but only a single payment of what might have been recoverable in Aulus' action, Pamphilus' behavior excludes the possibility of Aulus bringing a law suit.

For modern scholars, with their interest in recovering the classical law of Ulpian from any subsequent manipulation up to and including its inclusion in the Byzantine *Digest* of Justinian, there is more to the text. The substance of the text is thought by some scholars to have been altered. Above all, *non donationis causa*, "not on account of a gift" is said to be suspect.[28] H. F. Jolowicz claims: "Only Byzantine subjectivism could make the validity of a compromise depend on the slave's intention; a classical lawyer would compare the amount received under the compromise with the value of the claim and decide accordingly whether there was a gift or not.[29]

The argument seems quite misguided. First, there is no independent evidence that Byzantine jurists were more interested in the subjective state of a party's mind than were the Roman classical jurists. Second, there are just too many situations—all of which could fruitfully have been studied for this paper—where a slave's state of mind is considered relevant for one to think they are all the result of interpolation.[30] Third, Ulpian is not stressing Pamphilus' state of mind. He is simply stating only that a gift was not intended: if a gift were involved, the problem would have been other. Fourth, the issue that interested Ulpian was something quite different: could an act by a slave bar his owner's action when the result was that anything obtained went into the *peculium* and not, as would otherwise have been the case, directly to the owner? Fifth, for a classical lawyer, as for most other lawyers, the validity of the compromise would not depend on the amount received compared with the value of the claim but on the reasonableness of the compromise. That reasonableness could depend on the financial state of the thief and the *chances* of recovery. That in the circumstances the compromise is to be regarded as reasonable is indicated by *non donationis causa*.

A Mandate to a Slave to Pay a Debt to His Owner

A fourth example may again be chosen from the contract of mandate:

> *Dig.* 17.1.22.8 (Paul, On *the Edict,* book 32). If I gave a mandate to your slave that he should pay on my behalf what I owe you, Neratius writes that although the slave, having obtained a loan entered it into your account books as received from me, nonetheless if he did not take the money from the creditor expressly to give it on my behalf, neither am I released nor can you bring the action on mandate against me. But if he had borrowed expressly that he would give on my behalf, in both cases the answer is the opposite. Nor does it matter whether someone else or the same slave received in your name what was paid on my behalf. And this is the more correct view because as often as the creditor receives his own money the debtor is not released.

Paul was a junior colleague of Papinian in the imperial service, and Neratius was consul in A.D. 97. There are several situations discussed in the text, though I will deal only with the first two. The unifying factor is the reason given in the last sentence: a debtor is not released when the money received by the creditor for the debt is already the creditor's own.

It is important to note that although the mandatary, the agent, must act for free, there is no legal difficulty in accepting that a slave may bind himself to act gratuitously under a mandate for another. He may thus make his owner liable to an *actio mandati* (up to the limit of the peculium).

The simplest situation is the second one: Marcus owes Aulus money, and he gives Aulus' slave a mandate to pay his debt to Aulus. The slave, Pamphilus, to fulfill the mandate, borrows the money from Cornelius expressly in the name of Marcus. Since Cornelius delivers the money to Pamphilus expressly on behalf of Marcus, Cornelius does not, as otherwise would be the case, make Aulus the owner on delivery. It is not Cornelius' intention to make Aulus owner of the money. The slave delivers the money to Aulus and marks off in Aulus' account books the payment of Marcus' debt. Paul holds that Marcus' debt is extinguished and that Aulus has an action on mandate against Marcus. The *actio mandati* lies for any loss falling to Aulus on account of the mandate—that is to say, because of any liability to Cornelius on the loan. The legal status of the loan is not simple. There is no legal relationship between Marcus and Cornelius! When X gives a mandate to Y to buy from Z, and Y acts, there is a contract of mandate between X and Y and a contract of sale between Y and Z but no contract between X and Z since, in general, Roman law did not recognize direct agency.[31] Nor in this case can there be an action *in rem* of any kind to Cornelius against Marcus. A third person generally cannot acquire ownership through delivery to himself for another person unless he is the general agent, *procurator*, or in the power of that other.[32] But as I said, the slave has not acquired ownership of the money for his owner, Aulus, since Cornelius had no intention of giving to Aulus. Hence, there is no contract of loan for consumption, *mutuum*, between Aulus and Cornelius since that contract required transfer of ownership to the borrower.[33] Rather, so long as the actual coins received by the slave can be identified, Cornelius will have the action claiming ownership, the *vindicatio*; thereafter Cornelius will have the general remedy of the *condictio* against Aulus, claiming that Aulus acquired something of which restitution ought to be made. Aulus' *actio mandati* against Marcus is in respect to Aulus' liability to Cornelius under a *vindicatio* or *condictio* as a result of Marcus' mandate to Aulus' slave.

The first situation in the text now becomes simpler. When Pamphilus receives the money from Cornelius, without specifying that he is receiving it on behalf of Marcus, he receives ownership automatically for his owner, Aulus. There is thus a *mutuum* between Cornelius and Aulus, and Aulus will be liable up to the limit of the slave's peculium. Even though Pamphilus marks off in Aulus' account books that Marcus' debt is paid, Marcus is not released because in fact the debt has not been paid. Since Pamphilus did not expressly receive the loan on behalf of Marcus, he is not regarded as having acted on the mandate, hence his owner Aulus, cannot bring the *actio mandati* against Marcus.

A Runaway Slave's Purchase of Slaves

Mandate also provides us with a final example. The text in question, which is the first one printed below, presents some very odd features.

> *Dig.* 17.1.22.9 (Paul, *On the Edict*, book 32). My runaway slave, when he was in the hands of a thief, acquired money, and procured slaves with it, and Titius received them by delivery[34] from the seller. Mela says that by the action on mandate I would obtain that Titius restore them to me because my slave seemed to have given Titius a mandate to take by delivery, provided he had done this at the request of the slave. But if the seller had delivered to Titius without his request then I would bring the action on sale that the seller deliver them to me, and the seller would recover from Titius by a *condictio*, if he had delivered slaves to Titius which he did not owe, when he thought he owed them.[35]

Mela was a jurist of the very early empire. The first oddity is that on the text as it stands the legal decision is quite straightforward and the facts seem unworthy of the seriousness of the treatment. A second oddity is that we are given facts that are irrelevant to the decision, and Roman juristic texts normally only give details that are in point for the case.[36] Thus, on the facts stated it is quite irrelevant for the decision that the slave acquires the money after he runs away and not before. Third, if the slave has bought the others and not given the seller a mandate to deliver them to Titius, it is strange that the seller does so deliver them *under the impression that he is bound to deliver them to Titius*. So many oddities cry out for an explanation.

But first we should consider the text at its face value. We are not told whether the money involved is part of the peculium, nor does it matter. A slave who runs away forfeits any right to administer the peculium.[37] Strangely, a runaway slave was regarded as still in the possession of his owner,[38] but even if that were not so, the important point is that the acquisitions of a runaway slave (like those of other slaves in most circumstances) become the property of his owner. Certainly, while the slave is in the hands of a thief—even someone who subsequently takes the slave— this is the case. The money used to buy the slaves is the money of the runaway slave's owner. If Titius receives the slaves from the seller at the request of the runaway, Pamphilus, he will be acting on Pamphilus' mandate. A contract of mandate will thus exist between Titius and the slave's owner, Aulus. If delivery has been made in proper form, with the required ceremony of *mancipatio*, Titius will have become owner. The reference in the second alternative to a *condictio* shows that, in the situation envisaged, Titius has become owner of the slaves because the seller has clearly ceased to be such. Where the slaves are delivered to Titius without Pamphilus' approval, no contract of mandate exists between Titius and the runaway's owner, Aulus; but the latter could have recourse to the contract of sale made by Pamphilus and the seller on account of the failure to deliver the slaves. That seller, in his turn, could bring a *condictio* against Titius for *indebiti solutio*, the payment of a debt that was not owed.

There is nothing difficult or surprising or particularly subtle in all this, as a glance at two other texts will show:

> *Dig.* 12.1.11.2 (Ulpian, *On the Edict,* book 26). If a runaway slave lent you money, the question is raised whether the owner has a *condictio* against you. And, indeed, if my slave who had been granted administration of his peculium lent to you, there will be a *mutuum.* But a runaway or another slave, lending against the wishes of his owner, by lending does not make the recipient owner. What therefore is the position? A vindicatio can be brought for the coins if they still exist; or if they have ceased to be possessed because of fraud an *actio ad exhibendum* [action for production] is available. But if you have used them up without fraud I will be able to sue you by *condictio.*
>
> *Dig.* 12.1.31.1 (Paul, *On Plautius,* book 17). In ignorance and good faith I bought your slave from a thief. He, with his peculium which belonged to you, acquired a man who was delivered[39] to me. Sabinus and Cassius think you can bring a condictio against me for the man, but if I were out of pocket for the transaction your slave has made, I have in turn an action against you. This is correct . . .

Sabinus and Cassius were jurists of the early empire.

Thus, to return to *Dig.* 7.1.22.9. The rulings and discussion are banal if we take the text as it stands. After examination the unnecessary details and oddities appear still odder. But an explanation is perhaps at hand: in the transmission of the text a detail has possibly been lost. I should like to suggest that Titius is the person with whom the runaway slave has been living.

Such a suggestion would explain why the seller, without a mandate from the runaway, delivered the slaves to Titius, thinking he was bound to do so: he thought, mistakenly, that Titius was the runaway's owner. This would also explain why we are told that the runaway was in the hands of a thief: that is the relationship between the runaway and Titius.[40] It then also becomes interesting, if eventually not legally relevant, that the runaway acquired the money in question when he was in Titius' hands.

So the legal issues become what are Aulus' legal rights when his runaway slave, Pamphilus, in the hands of Titius buys slaves with money that he acquired when he was with Titius, and the seller delivered the slaves to Titius?

The short answer is that Aulus' rights under any contracts made by his slave, even with Titius, are unaffected by the fact that Titius is regarded as the thief of Pamphilus. Thus, if the bought slaves were delivered to Titius at the request of Pamphilus, a contract of mandate exists between Aulus and Titius, and he can bring the *actio mandati* against Titius on account of the delivered slaves. It is perhaps because in the end Aulus' contractual rights are unaffected by the situation in theft between Titius and Aulus that Titius' position as thief has fallen from the text.

That the issue of rights between the thief of a slave and his owner was of interest to the jurists is well illustrated by *Dig.* 47.2.68.4 (Celsus, *Digest*, book 12):

> It is settled that, when a stolen slave steals from the thief, the thief will have on that account an action against the owner so that wrongful deeds of such slaves not only do not go unpunished but also are not a source of profits to the owners.

Celsus was active at the beginning of the second century A.D. Buckland's observation on this text is well-known and acceptable.[41] His claim was that this is "a grotesque case, but correct in principle."[42] Likewise, it is grotesque but correct in principle that a runaway slave in the hands of a thief can put the thief under an obligation to his owner on mandate, the contract founded on "duty and friendship."[43]

In conclusion, it should be noted that there was very little Roman law that was specific to slavery. In some areas a slave was treated as a human being; in these his legal position was very much akin to that of a son in paternal power. In others he was treated as property; in these his legal position was not much different from that of cattle.[44] Yet still, as "thinking property" slaves in some areas caused the law to be very complex. This complexity was avoided in English-speaking America.

Notes

I am grateful to John L. Barton for his helpful criticisms. Many of the issues in this paper concern the contract of mandate which was the subject of my D.Phil. thesis. While writing that, I also received much aid and advice from John. For that and for many years of friendship, I wish to dedicate this paper to him. I also must thank Paul Finkelman for much advice.

1. *Politics*, 1.4–6.

2. For the U.S. see, e.g., *Farwell v. Boston & Worcester Railroad Corp.*, 45 Mass. (4 Met.) 49 (1842); *Ponton v. Wilmington & Weldon Railroad Co.*, 51 N.C. (6 Jones) 245 (1898). Cf. Mark Tushnet, *The American Law of Slavery* (Princeton, N.J.: Princeton: University Press, 1981), 45ff; A. Watson, review of Tushnet, 91 *Yale Law Journal*, 1037 (1982).

3. For the U.S. see, e.g., *Gorman v. Campbell*, 14 Ga. 137 (1853). Cf. Tushnet, *American Law of Slavery*, 50ff; Watson, review, 1040ff; Paul Finkelman, "Slaves as Fellow-Servants: Ideology, Law and Industrialization," 31 *American Journal of Legal History* 269 (1987).

4. Thus, of necessity, I will not deal with any text from the republic or any of the standard cases, since these are covered by my five volumes on *The Law in the*

Later Roman Republic (Oxford: Clarendon Press, 1965–74); *The Contract of Mandate in Roman Law* (Oxford: Clarendon Press, 1961); *Roman Slave Law* (Baltimore: The Johns Hopkins University Press, 1987).

5. See, e.g., in general, V. Arangio-Ruiz, *Il mandato in diritto romano* (Naples: Jovene, 1949); Watson, *The Contract of Mandate.*

6 The *Digest* (hereinafter cited as *Dig.*) was part of the codification of Roman law issued by the Byzantine emperor Justinian I with the force of statute which much later came to be called the *Corpus Juris Civilis.* The *Digest,* published in A.D. 533, is a huge collection of excerpts from writings of jurists who lived between the first and mid third centuries A.D. Modern edition, ed. The Digest of Justinian, 4 vols., Latin text edit by Theodor Mommsen and Paul Krueger, English translation by Alan Watson (Philadelphia: University of Pennsylvania Press, 1985).

7. Any action on mandate to Balbus would in fact be for recompense in money, not to compel Aulus to take back the slave.

8 Perhaps, for some reason, it would have been more appropriate for Balbus to be the exslave's patron.

9. On the sale of a slave the peculium remained with the seller, unless otherwise agreed.

10. It is noticeable that he does not say that the mandate to Balbus was only to buy the slave, but that Aulus' liability on mandate was only to sell the slave.

11. See Alan Watson, *The State, Law and Religion: Pagan Rome* (Athens, Georgia: Georgia University Press, 1992), 64ff.

12. See, e.g., Watson, *The Contract of Mandate,* 111ff.

13. The *praetors* were among the highest of the elected Roman officers of state, and among their duties was control of the main courts. At the beginning of his year of office, a praetor issued an edict setting out the types of actions he would allow. Technically, this was not legislation, but in practice the edict was a most powerful source of law. The praetor (as here) could grant new actions, or change the scope of existing remedies. Praetors took over most of the Edict of their predecessors.

14. A more complex and principled explanation is provided by a rescript, *Code of Justinian* 4.36.1pr, of the emperors Diocletian and Maximinian, dated A.D. 293:

> If a slave gave an outsider a mandate to buy himself, an action is thought to exist although neither from the person of the slave [because a free person could not give this mandate] nor from the person of the owner [since whoever gives a mandate that something be bought from him gives a mandate in vain], and this for the very best reason because the point is not that the action arises from the mandate itself, but that on account of the mandate the action arises on a different contract. It is settled that an action is acquired for the owner.

The remainder of the rescript seems rather confused but the action in question seems to arise from the subsequent sale.

The *Code* (hereinafter cited as *Code J.*) is that part of Justinian's codification that contained the rulings of the emperors.

15. See, e.g., W. W. Buckland, *Textbook of Roman Law,* 3d ed, ed. by P. Stein (Cambridge: Cambridge University Press, 1963), 439.

At Rome a person was in paternal power so long as his or her father—or remoter paternal ancestor—was alive, unless he or she had been formally released from power. Only persons, male or female, free from paternal power could own property. Hence, when a person in paternal power made a contract, all the rights and benefits under it went to the father.

16. See, e.g., *Dig.* 41.1.37.4, 5, 6; 41.1.43pr., 2; 41.1.45. For issues that could arise from ownership of a common slave, see, e.g., M. Bretone, *Servus communis* (Naples: Jovene, 1958). Perhaps my favorite example is in *Dig.* 45.3.9.1: a slave owned in common by Titius and Maevius took a stipulation "for Titius or Maevius." Cassius, who is followed by Julian and approved by Ulpian, held that the stipulation was ineffective. The slave cannot be creditor; and since it does not appear whether Titius or Maevius is the creditor, neither can sue.

17. A slave, being property, would on his owner's death be part of the inheritance. In contrast, a son would on the death of his father become free from paternal power (unless there was a more remote male ancestor) and, indeed, would usually be one of the heirs.

18. See Alan Watson, *Studies in Roman Private Law* (London: Hambledon Press, 1991), 37ff.

19. See, in general, L. Amirante, *Captivitas e postliminium* (Naples: Jovene, 1950).

20. We need not go into details, but it should be noted that, except for slaves of the deceased or persons who became free of paternal power on that death, Romans did not become heirs either on intestacy or under a will until they accepted the inheritance.

21. Indeed, interpolations are suspected in the text: cf. Amirante, *Captivitas*, 93. As the remainder of this section of this paper will show, I treat the text as genuine. But the suggested interpolations do not affect the basic argument.

22. See, e.g., *Dig.* 45.1.11; 46.4.11.3; *Institutes of Gaius*, 1.129. The *Institutes of Gaius* are an elementary students' textbook written around A.D. 161.

23. *Dig.* 2.15; *Code J.* 2.4. See also Buckland, *Textbook*, 525; M. Kaser, *Das römische Privatrecht* 1, 2d ed. (Munich: Beck 1971), p. 642.

24. *Dig.* 2.14.28.2.

25. For the nature of the peculium and acquisitions to it, see, above all, W. W. Buckland, *The Roman Law of Slavery* (Cambridge: Cambridge University Press, 1908), 187ff.

26. We need not go into details, but for such remedies, the *actio de peculio*, *actio tributoria*, and the *vocatio in tributum*, see Buckland, *Textbook*, 533f.

27. See Alan Watson, *Slave Law in the Americas* (Athens, Ga.: University of Georgia Press, 1989), 53ff; Alan Watson, *International Law in Archaic Rome: War and Religion* (Baltimore: The Johns Hopkins University Press, 1993), 67f.

28. I agree that one would expect it to have appeared before, not after, *cum eo*. But apart from doubts I might have about consistent elegance in Ulpian's style, a scribal slip cannot be excluded. It is not easy, in my view, to explain why an interpolationist would misplace the phrase.

29. *Dig.* 47.2: *de furtis* (*Digest*, ed. Jolowicz, 79 n. 26). See that note also for other suggestions of interpolation.

30. See, e.g., *Dig.* 18.1.12; 41.1.37.4, 5, 6; 41.2.1.10, 19.

31. See, e.g., Buckland, *Textbook*, 533ff; A. Kirschenbaum, *Sons, Slaves and Freedman in Roman Commerce* (Jerusalem: Magnes Press, 1987).

32. See, e.g., Watson, *Studies*, 109ff.

33. See, e.g., Buckland, *Textbook*, 468f.

34. All the references in the text to acquisition of ownership by delivery, *traditio*, would in Paul's original have referred to *mancipatio*, a formal ceremony that then was needed for the transfer of slaves.

35. Roman actions always lay for money. It is shorthand to write that the action was for the slaves.

36. See the discussion in my book *The Spirit of Roman Law* (Athens, Ga.: University of Georgia Press, 1994).

37. See, e.g., *Dig.* 12.1.11.2;

38. See, e.g., Buckland, *Roman Law of Slavery*, 269f.

39. Again, references in the text to *traditio* would originally have concerned *mancipatio*.

40. The position of Titius is not that of an American abolitionist. Rogues would help slaves to run away, taking with them valuables of the owner. The bargain was that the rogues, in return for payment to them by the slaves of their owners' valuables, would secure freedom for the slaves. The machinations and the law were complicated, with law usually trying to catch up with the villain's latest ingenuity. The classic discussion is David Daube, "Slave Catching," now in his 1 *Collected Studies in Roman Law*, 501 (1991). A slave who ran away committed theft of himself (though he could not be sued by his owner), and anyone who helped him became an accomplice, liable in full to the standard action on theft, *actio furti*.

41. See, e.g., *Dig.* 47.2 (*Digest*, ed. Jolowicz, 106 n. 4); Watson, *Roman Slave Law*, 59.

42. Buckland, *Textbook*, 581.

43. *Dig.* 17.1.1.4.

44. See Alan Watson, *Roman Law and Comparative Law* (Athens, Ga.: University of Georgia Press, 1991), 39ff.

14

Thinking Property at Memphis: An Application of Watson

Jacob I. Corré

ANYONE FAMILIAR WITH Alan Watson's scholarship will take for granted the wide range of learning, the elegant expression, and the analytic rightness exhibited in his contributions to this volume. His new analysis of some difficult problems in Roman slave law has inherent value, as does his sketch of the European intellectual history of slavery as a theoretical institution around the time that it was being entrenched as a real system in the Americas. Yet it must be said that at first blush something is disturbing about the presence of Watson's work in this collection. Watson emphasizes the absolute evil of slavery but nevertheless implicitly invites us to think about the foundations and implications of its practice in highly conceptual terms—as a lawyer's puzzle, if you will. Given the moral horror of slavery, it would be easy to decline the invitation politely and move on. Besides, what can a collection of Roman jurists and seventeenth-century natural lawyers teach us about the confrontation between law and slavery in the United States—particularly when Watson suggests that the legal systems of the American South generally avoided the complexities that "thinking property" generated in Roman law?[1]

It would be a mistake to ignore the questions raised by Watson's work as they apply to the law of slavery in the United States. In particular I want to suggest that the conceptual problems that necessarily arise in relegating a thinking agent, a human being, to the status of property also haunted the jurists charged with regulating and protecting slavery in the American South. Discovering how they handled these problems can deepen our understanding of the legal aspects of a culture that sustained and was sustained by an atrocity. The cases treated in "Thinking Property at Rome" support a thesis, which Watson has suggested elsewhere, that any slaveholding society will manifest "a continuous tension in law between the treatment of the slave as property and the recognition that he is human or at least has volition."[2] That thesis by itself, Watson notes, may not tell us much, but testing it in particular legal contexts can be revealing. I will focus on the implications of the problem examined in *"Thinking Property at Rome"* for our understanding of United States slave law by examining certain aspects of the slave law of Tennessee.[3] The cases below show Watson's "continuous tension" in action at a time and place far removed from those studied in his paper.

Tennessee 1835–1871: Some Problems in the Dualistic Conception of a Southern Slave

In the thirty years before legalized slavery ended, and for a number of years thereafter, the supreme court of Tennessee decided several cases that raised questions that could not be treated satisfactorily without revealing the juristic limitations of treating a slave as ordinary chattel. More than once the judges of that court spoke explicitly on the inadequacy of such treatment and the problems in finding an alternative conception. A vision of the owner-slave relationship grounded on principles of agency had the virtue of implying a realistic account of the slave's mental capacities, but it could not accommodate the slave's lack of legal rights. A model of the relationship based on notions of property had the converse problem. It made sense of the slave's personal status in legal terms, but it could not be coherently adopted in cases where the slave had exercised his rational capacities in a manner that seemed significant from a moral or juristic point of view.

The cases that raised this tension most clearly dealt with the vicarious liability of a slave owner for his slave's wrongful acts and with a free man's converting the labor of another's slave. I will discuss both cases involving negligence and cases involving intentional wrongdoing by the slave. The problems raised in the negligence cases relate both conceptually and functionally to the problem of applying the common law fellow-servant rule in the context of injured slaves: conceptually, because both depended in part on the legal character of the relationship between owner and slave; functionally, because the slave of one owner might negligently injure the slave of another owner in a work-related incident, thus raising both questions at the same time. Throughout the latter half of the nineteenth century, employers were normally not liable to servants for injuries caused by fellow servants. Chief Justice Shaw of the Massachusetts Supreme Judicial Court wrote the leading opinion on this point in *Farwell* v. *Boston & Worcester R.R.* Paul Finkelman has shown that Southern courts consistently rejected this rule in the context of injured slaves; the owners of the slaves were allowed to sue the employer of the coworker who injured the slave on a theory of *respondeat superior* liability.[4]

The decisions of the Tennessee Supreme Court in these areas did not reveal an overt proslaveholder bias. In fact, in most of these cases it could not have been clear that a particular outcome would benefit the class of slave owners as a whole or that the case was actually decided in the best interests of slave owners generally. Perhaps we should not be surprised that the conceptual problems were clearest when the economic and social interests were murky. But it simply cannot be said that the economic interests of the slave-owning class invariably overwhelmed the analytic difficulties generated in attempting to describe a slave in legal terms. Decisions were made that can best be understood on conceptual grounds.

Vicarious Liability of Slaveholders for Wrongs Committed by Slaves

The opinion of Justice Nathan Green in *Wright* v. *Weatherly* (1835) expressly acknowledges the inadequacy of any legal characterization of the slave that focuses solely on either the slave's legal status as property or his human capacity for agency. The facts as they are given to us were extremely simple. Wright's slave, Andrew, got into a fight with Weatherly's slave, Jerry. Andrew stabbed Jerry, and Jerry died. Weatherly brought an action on the case against Wright to recover Jerry's value. At trial in the circuit court for Rutherford County, the court instructed the jury that a master was liable for a slave's trespass "whether the act be done when in the master's service or not, and whether with or without the master's knowledge." The jury found for Weatherly and awarded him $550, its assessment of Jerry's value.[5]

Wright sought error in the supreme court of Tennessee, and that court reversed the judgment. Justice Green's opinion is worth quoting at length:

> This court is of opinion that this action cannot be sustained. There are but two classes of cases known to the common law which have any analogy to this case. Either we must look upon the slave as occupying the same relation to the master as the servant does in England or we must regard him in the light of property only, and hold the master liable as he would be for mischief which might be committed by a vicious domestic animal. These are the analogies the common law furnishes us, and by the application of neither of these can this action be supported. To consider the slave as property only, the owner would only be liable in case he were acquainted with the vicious propensities and habits of his slave, and, with such knowledge, should permit him to run at large.

That is not the case here. But it is manifest that this case has very little analogy to the case of mischief done by a slave. Although he is, by our law, property, yet he is an intelligent moral agent, capable of being a subject of government, and, like all other men, liable to answer for his own wrongs to the injured party, but for the fact that all his personal rights as a citizen, and his liabilities as such, are destroyed and merged in the ownership of the master, who controls his person, owns his property, and is entitled to the fruits of his labor.

If we consider him in the light of a servant only, the master would not be liable for the injury charged in this declaration; for, in England, although a master is liable to answer for any damages arising to another from the negligence or unskilfulnes of his servant acting in his employ, yet he is not liable in trespass for the wilful act of his servant, done without the direction or assent of the master. But here, too, it is manifest, there is scarcely an analogy in the two cases. In England the servant is a free man; he is a subject of the government; he has legal rights and liabilities, and the master is only liable, in any case, because the servant in his employ, and injuries resulting from his unskilfulness or negligence while thus employed, are, in some degree, the consequence of the master's act in employing one so unskilful or negligent. But a wilful trespass committed by the servant, without the direction or assent of the master, does not fall within the above reason, and, therefore, the servant is made to answer himself for the wrong.[6]

Under either analogy the trial court's instructions had been wrong, and the declaration failed to allege proper grounds for vicarious liability. Therefore, Green saw no reason to decide which rule to apply and which of two equally unsatisfactory characterizations of the slave to adopt. Instead, he concluded that the case was "entirely new, and one to which no principle of common law is applicable." Green argued that some remedy in these cases was "loudly called for," that such a remedy would be "fair and equal among the slaveholders themselves," and that it was "imperiously required" in relation to injuries suffered by the majority of citizens, who did not hold slaves. He even suggested that Tennessee at least adopt the civil-law rule, which he said, somewhat misleadingly, was that the master is liable for the slave's wrongdoing to the extent of the slave's value. But a court could achieve none of this. The relief had to come from the legislature.[7]

Although one Texas judge claimed that Green's opinion was "presented with the perspicuity, accuracy, and conciseness which characterizes the legal opinions of that learned judge,"[8] the ultimate rationale of the decision in *Wright* v. *Weatherly* is unclear. Two interpretations are possible. On the one hand, Green's analysis at the beginning of the opinion indicates his belief that Wright should be absolved from liability on either a proprietary or an agency theory of the relationship between owner and slave: The lack of evidence that Wright knew of his slave's violent tendencies would preclude liability under the property-based analogy to liability for harm done by dangerous domestic animals; the indisputable evidence that the slave had committed an intentional wrong immunized the master from liability under the agency-based analogy to the common law of masters and servants. Therefore, there was no need to rule as to the proper analogy and characterization of the relationship. On the other hand, Green's statements toward the end of the opinion evidence a judgment that neither the agency nor the property characterization of the owner-slave relationship could be properly applied. Since those were the only common law grounds for imposing vicarious liability, Weatherly's claim had to fail because it simply did not state a common law cause of action, even if "the injured party ought, in justice, be entitled to damages."[9] Green may have been relying on both theories or neither.

Under either interpretation the problem of describing the owner-slave relationship in a conceptually coherent manner looms large in Green's decision. However that relationship be described, it is not the kind that could result in vicarious liability for an unauthorized, intentional wrong by the slave. It is significant that in this case a slaveholder was bound to lose whatever the outcome. It is therefore hard to view Green's analytic hand-wringing as a mere ruse to justify a decision that the economic interests of the slave-owning class required. On a global level it might be said that the decision did benefit slaveholders. Under the rule no slaveholder would be liable for an unauthorized, intentional wrong that his slave committed against a free person, and when slaves injured slaves there would simply be a transfer of wealth between members of the slave-owner class. But ultimately such an explanation cannot satisfactorily explain the motives behind the decision in *Wright v. Weatherly*. Paul Finkelman has demonstrated, in his important study of the fellow-servant rule as applied in the context of injured slaves, that Southern courts were perfectly capable of applying different rules, depending on whether the injury was suffered by a slave or a free person.[10] Had the Supreme Court of Tennessee wanted only to protect slave owners, it could have given judgment for Weatherly while reserving the question of the liability standards when slaves injured free persons. Moreover, the court would not have announced its belief that the decision was contrary to justice and ought to be reversed by the legislature. The decision in *Wright v. Weatherly* is best understood as a product of the difficulties entailed in thinking about "thinking property."

The Tennessee legislature never answered Green's call for legislation in this area. The supreme court of Tennessee did ultimately define a liability standard by which to judge the vicarious liability of owners for the wrongs of their slaves: The slave owner was liable for the slave's wrongs whenever he commanded that the slave commit the wrongful act, or at least had sufficient knowledge of the specific wrong. This was a hybrid rule that contained elements of both an agency-based law of master and servant and of a property-based law of domestic animals. But agency law exerted the stronger influence. In one case the master was held liable even though there was no clear evidence of intentional wrongdoing by the slave, only negligence, and even though it was not clear that the master actually knew about the relevant acts.[11] The formulation of the rule in this case bore a close resemblance to the common law master-servant rule.

In *Wilkins* v. *Gilmore* (1840) the court considered a trespass action between a slave-owning landlord and his tenant. The landlord, Wilkins, had become unsatisfied with the tenant, Gilmore. In March 1839 someone entered Gilmore's leasehold and tore the roof off the house that his family was occupying. There was sufficient evidence to show that the vandal was Wilkins's slave and that he had acted on his master's command. The supreme court of Tennessee affirmed an award of actual and exemplary damages against Wilkins. The court ruled that masters were liable for the torts of their servants or slaves whenever the servant or slave acted "by the command or encouragement of the master." Blackstone was the principal authority for the rule, and the court did not note any distinction in its very brief opinion between the law as it would apply to servants and to slaves.[12]

By 1859 the Tennessee court was willing to impose vicarious liability on the slaveholder even without sufficient proof that the slave had acted on the instructions of the owner, although it stopped just short of adopting wholesale the master-servant rule, which would have imposed liability on the master in all cases of negligent acts committed in the scope of "employment." In *Byram* v. *McGuire*, McGuire's mule escaped from its enclosure and was found dead the next day on Byram's property. McGuire sued Byram in trover and in case for negligence. The evidence showed that after the mule had wandered onto Byram's land, Byram's slaves tied it to a tree "to keep him from doing mischief." That evening Byram returned to his land and, upon seeing McGuire's mule and learning how it had gotten there, ordered his slaves to return the mule to McGuire. Byram's slaves "in [Byram's] presence and hearing, and apparently with his sanction, declined [the order], assigning as a reason that [McGuire] would soon be after [the mule]." That evening the mule was chained to the tree and it suffocated during the night. It was unclear whether Byram or his slaves had chained the mule, as well as whether the mule's death had been the product of willful or merely negligent conduct.[13]

The Tennessee court affirmed a judgment (apparently on both counts) of actual and exemplary damages in McGuire's favor. The court held that a slave owner was liable for the wrongful acts of his slaves if those acts were committed in his presence. "Presence" would be imputed whenever the slave owner must have known about the acts. The court in fact suggested that liability could be imposed on the owner whenever the slave was acting for the owner's benefit, regardless of the owner's knowledge.[14] Nevertheless, the court heavily emphasized the degree of Byram's complicity in, or at least knowledge of, the events at issue. Given the ambiguity of the opinion, it is not possible to conclude that the Tennessee Supreme Court would necessarily have held the owner liable if a slave acted negligently but without the owner's specific instructions or knowledge.

Wilkins and *Byram* both show the Tennessee Supreme Court inclining toward an agency-based conception of the relationship between slaveholder and slave. Still, the court was never able to overcome Green's doubts about the agency analogy completely.

The pure-property analogy, on the other hand, had no future in the vicarious-liability cases. *Sweat* v. *Rogers* (1871) demonstrates the court's rejection of the property-based theory of vicarious liability grounded on analogy to the law of domestic animals. Rogers sued Sweat in an action on the case, alleging that in 1861 two of Sweat's slaves had burned down his storehouse and robbed him of the goods that had not been destroyed in the fire. The first two counts in the declaration alleged that the slaves "were of bad character for stealing and pilfering, and that Sweat, being their owner, was cognizant of their vicious character and habits, and allowed them to go abroad, and did not prevent them from practicing their stealing propensities." The third count alleged that the slaves had acted "with the knowledge, indulgence, permission, allowance and instigation of [Sweat]." Citing *Wright* v. *Weatherly,* the court ruled that the allegations in the first two counts were insufficient to support the action because they did not contain "the necessary allegations to make the defendant liable for the trespasses and felonies of his slaves." The third count, however, stated a good claim.[15] The court must have interpreted *Wright* as having rejected a theory of vicarious liability founded on the law of domestic animals. The first two counts had alleged that Sweat had let his slaves go free with actual knowledge of their dangerous tendencies. These allegations would have sufficed in a domestic-animal case, but they were insufficient in the case of slaves. But *Sweat* v. *Rogers* is important as much for its evidence about pleading practice as it is for the evidence gained from its actual holding. To the very end it was not clear in Tennessee whether a litigant should, for vicarious-liability purposes, conceptualize the slave as the property of the owner, as the owner's agent, or as some never clearly articulated hybrid of the two. A zealous lawyer had to plead on all theories, but in the end we can say that the pure-property theory lost: The law of Tennessee, like the law of Rome, was sensitive to the slave's cognitive powers.

This does not mean that a pure-agency theory won. The broadest implications of such a theory—that the owner would be liable for the negligent acts of a slave whenever the slave was laboring for the owner, regardless of the owner's knowledge—never won the clear approval of a Tennessee court.[16] In these cases vicarious-liability law as applied to slaveholders approached asymptotically the common law of master and free servant but did not converge with that law. Nor did these rulings explicitly contemplate the contradiction that the legal nature of the owner-slave relationship engendered, as Green had in *Wright* v. *Weatherly*.

Liability for Conversion of a Slave's Services and Death of a Slave: Jones V. Allen

In *Jones* v. *Allen* (1858) the Tennessee Supreme Court once again spoke to, but could not resolve, the broad questions implicit in the hybrid legal status necessitated by the volitional capacities of a slave.[17] *Jones* involved a potential conflict between two distinct interests of slave owners. Admittedly, this created an economic levelling in which the theoretical problems could most easily come to the fore. But *Jones* simply cannot be explained in terms of the bare economic interests of slaveholders.

Jones held a cornhusking in the fall of 1857. He solicited the help of his neighbors and, in particular, sent a message to Allen requesting aid. Allen's slave, Isaac, came to the cornhusking. Jones gave whiskey to Isaac and the other hands (some of whom were free, others slaves) while they worked. Between ten and eleven P.M., Jones gave the slaves supper. After supper he ordered them to go home, and then he retired for the night. A few slaves, Isaac among them, lingered for about thirty minutes. During this time an uninvited white man named Hager, the only man on the scene who was drunk, stabbed Isaac to death without provocation.[18]

Later on it came to light that Allen had never received Jones's message. Isaac had been at the cornhusking without his owner's permission. Allen sued Jones on two counts, trover (the declaration alleging conversion) and a special action on the case. The gravamen of the action on the case was (1) that Jones had allowed Isaac to come onto his land without Allen's written consent; (2) that he had employed Isaac in cornhusking, which usurped Isaac's labor; and (3) that Isaac had died while so employed. At that time a statute in Tennessee forbade any person to

> knowingly permit any slave or slaves to come, collect, or assemble at his or their dwelling-house, negro-house or houses, without a written pass from the owner, overseer, or person in whose employ such slave or slaves may be, setting forth his or their business, and time of absence . . . under penalty of ten dollars.

Other statutes prohibited all assemblages of slaves without their owners' permission and constituted all owners and overseers as patrols to control the forbidden movement of slaves.[19]

At trial Jones offered to prove a local custom that those who held cornhuskings permitted the slaves of others onto the premises without inquiring whether the slave had permission, written or otherwise, to be there. The trial court rejected this evidence and instructed the jury that Jones was charged in law with knowledge as to whether Isaac was at the cornhusking with Allen's consent. The jury returned a verdict for Allen on the trover count and awarded damages of $1,050.[20]

In the error proceedings before the Tennessee Supreme Court, Jones's counsel argued that the evidence regarding the customs of the cornhuskings should have been admitted. According to the reporter the argument presented an agency theory of the owner-slave relationship in the starkest possible terms:

> The court erred in excluding this testimony, because if such were the well established usage or custom of the country and of the neighborhood of these parties, Allen's consent to the presence and services of his boy Isaac at Jones', would have been the legal presumption protecting Jones in accepting from him reasonable labor of that character, and in order to take himself out of such legal presumption, or its operation, Allen must have done so by announcement, or some other manner of dissent, made known to the neighborhood or to Jones. In this country, the legitimate presumption, in the absence of proof to the contrary, is, that the master permits those accommodations by his servants for his neighbors, which are usual and customary, and which are esteemed necessary to a good neighborhood. The rejected testimony shows corn shuckings to be prominent among that class of customs.
>
> This position is distinctly within the analogies of the law of agency. Indeed, a slave performing services for another under such circumstances, may very well be regarded as the servant or agent of the master, acting in pursuance of his implied consent and authority.[21]

Jones was thus to be shielded from liability because Isaac, by his presence, was capable of projecting that he had Allen's permission to be at the cornhusking. Such an argument would have been impossible without an implicit emphasis on the volitional capacities of a slave. That emphasis transformed itself into an explicit appeal to the law of agency.

Against this theory Allen's counsel argued that Jones was liable on the conversion count because he had "permitted and encouraged" Isaac to work without Allen's actual license. On the case count, Allen's counsel argued that Jones was breaking the law by allowing Isaac to be on his land without Allen's permission. Jones's liability for Isaac's death followed from the statutory violation because the death was a consequence of the violation, regardless of whether it had been caused by a third party.[22]

The supreme court reversed the judgment in Allen's favor. The opinion is not entirely clear on the matter, but it appears that the court did not go so far as to adopt explicitly the pure-agency theory offered by Jones's counsel, at least not for the purpose counsel had proposed. The court did, however, rely on a view of slaves as moral and legal agents in addressing the question of whether Jones had violated Tennessee statutes by permitting Isaac to participate in the cornhusking without Allen's written consent:

> [T]hese statutory provisions must be understood and expounded, according to the manifest intention of the Legislature. We are not to forget, nor are we to suppose that it was lost sight of by the Legislature, that, under our modified system of slavery, slaves are not mere chattels, but are regarded in the two-fold character of persons and property. That as persons, they are considered by our law, as accountable moral agents, possessed of the power of volition and locomotion. That certain rights have been conferred on them by positive law and judicial determination, and other privileges and indulgences have been conceded to them by the universal consent of their owners. By uniform and universal usage they are constituted the agents of their owners, and are sent on their business without written authority. . . . The simple truth is, such indulgences have been so long, and so uniformly tolerated, the public sentiment upon the subject has acquired almost the force of positive law. Would it not be absurd to suppose that the police regulations above noticed, had reference to such usage?

The court therefore concluded that the statute had not been violated and that Jones would be immune from liability if Allen had assented verbally to Isaac's presence at the cornhusking.[23] This holding implies that a slave could be the agent of his owner for the purpose of communicating the owner's permission to a third party to use the slave's labor.

The court did not decide whether Jones could presume such verbal consent from the customs of the community in the absence of an express refusal by Allen to be bound by the custom (or an express refusal to allow his slaves to work for others in particular instances). It ultimately ruled that the conversion judgment was erroneous, even on the joint assumptions that Allen had not assented to Isaac's presence, that Jones had actually known that Isaac had come without permission, and that the assembly statutes had been violated. The court held that Jones was not liable for conversion merely because he "passively acquiesced in [Isaac's] remaining, and in his continuing to husk corn." The only affirmative acts alleged against Jones involved "furnishing the slave with supper and a dram." These acts were insufficient to establish a conversion, so the action in trover had to fail. The only remedy, if there was a remedy at all, was an action on the case; and since the jury had not found for Allen on that count, the supreme court of Tennessee reversed the judgment outright.[24] Thus, by reading the law of constructive conversion extremely narrowly, the court avoided passing on the broadest implications of the pure agency theory put forth by Jones' counsel.

Still, it seems hard to deny that the court took seriously the conceptual implications of the slave's volitional capacity. The judgment turned at least in part on the slave's status as "thinking property." That the judgment went against the slave owner is also evidence against a decisional motive centered exclusively on the protection of the slave-owning class. We are not even told whether the defendant Jones owned slaves, because that fact was entirely irrelevant under the court's analysis. It is true that a decision which had the effect, if not the express purpose, of protecting a local custom that allowed slave owners to consent tacitly to the use of their slaves by others might have benefited the class of slave owners as a whole. To the extent that agricultural producers who owned slaves also relied on "donated" labor at husking time, they would be relieved of the burdens of checking for permission slips; the owner who assented to the use of his slave would be relieved of the burden of writing one. But as in the case of the vicarious liability of slave owners, nothing would have stopped a court from developing different rules for cases where the seeker of assistance was a slaveholder and cases where he was not. At some level, the opinion must evidence at least a residual concern for the analytic integrity of the legal system.

Summary

It is important to emphasize the modesty of the claims being made here. I claim only that the conceptual tensions which Watson sees as part of the picture in the development of Roman slave law (and as a general feature of legal systems that regulate slavery) also played a part in the development of United States slave law. In some instances United States slave law moved in directions charted by judges who were consciously, and conscientiously, trying to deal with a unique form of property—property that could think and act on those thoughts. There was nothing admirable about this, and I do not mean to suggest that the judges in Tennessee or anywhere else ought to be applauded for struggling to recognize the humanity of the slave. The slaves never won in any of these cases. And any man who could recite the story of the slaying of Isaac in *Jones* v. *Allen* and launch without recoiling into a detailed discussion of the different measure of damages available in trover and case deserves no praise.[25] The limited point is that sometimes someone besides the slaveholders, individually or as a class, did win. They won because the jurists of the South, no matter how committed they were to slavery, were also committed, or at least reflexively inclined, to some minimal standard of legal intelligibility.

It is surely correct, as Watson argues, that the problem of "thinking property" is quite distinct from the problems that arise when a slave is granted legal personality, although the line between the two will be hard to draw in some cases. Many of Watson's examples are best seen as belonging to what we would call the law of agency, as are the cases I have discussed.[26] Some might claim that treating a slave as his owner's agent amounts to granting the slave a limited form of legal personality. But a decision to recognize the legal significance of a slave's purposeful activity is not the same as a decision to allow a slave to participate in the formal institutions of a legal system. The examples I have discussed are, like Watson's, better viewed as problems of thinking property, not as problems of legal personality.

Watson concludes that "thinking property" caused Roman law to become very complex in some areas, while English-speaking America avoided this complexity. This claim, I think, says less about differences between the two legal cultures than it does about the different roles that slaves played in ancient Rome and the antebellum South. The key here is that Roman slaves were routinely assigned more complicated tasks than slaves in the United States. Roman slaves were doctors, bankers, or even scholars. The most difficult cases in Roman law emerged when slaves performed functions that slaves in the United States were likely never to have performed.[27] The relative crudity of the legal analyses discussed above was the product of the relatively unsophisticated economic role that the Southern slave was forced to play. The intellectual problems faced in Rome and Memphis were similar in many ways. We are very fortunate to have Alan Watson remind us to seek out these large connections.

Notes

I thank Julie Bentz, Paul Finkelman, James Lindgren and Richard McAdams for their helpful comments.

1. Alan Watson, "Thinking Property at Rome" and "Seventeenth-Century Jurists, Roman Law, and the Law of Slavery," both in this volume.

2. Alan Watson, "Slave Law: History and Ideology," 91 *Yale Law Journal* 1034, 1047 (1982), reviewing Mark V. Tushnet, *The American Law of Slavery, 1810–1860: Considerations of Humanity and Interest* (Princeton: Princeton University Press, 1981). Much the same point is made in Watson's most recent extended study of Roman slave law. Alan Watson, *Roman Slave Law* (Baltimore: Johns Hopkins University Press, 1987), 46 (even when the slave is treated as a thing "the human qualities of the slave will continually emerge.").

3. The slave law of Tennessee is the subject of a very fine study by Arthur Howington. Arthur F. Howington, *What Sayeth the Law: The Treatment of Slaves and Free Blacks in the State and Local Courts of Tennessee* (New York: Garland Press, 1986). Howington's book deals with manumission, slaves and free blacks as criminal defendants, and white violence against slaves and free blacks; it concentrates on the procedural due process that the Tennessee courts afforded to blacks. Howington does not discuss the problems and cases analyzed below. His work does show that the Tennessee courts recognized the significance of the slave's

humanity in other areas of law. Howington, however, is not specifically concerned with the conceptual complexities to which this recognition gave rise. See, generally, pp. iv–v, 1–3, and 247–48.

4. *Farwell* v. *Boston & Worcester R.R.*, 45 Mass. (4 Met.) 49 (1842). Paul Finkelman, "Slaves as Fellow Servants: Ideology, Law, and Industrialization," 31 *American Journal of Legal History* 269 (1987). At least some of these cases emphasized that the slave's status as chattel precluded application of the fellow-servant rule because a slave, as chattel, could not be anyone's fellow servant. Finkelman, "Slaves as Fellow Servants," 298–304. In contrast, I argue below that Tennessee developed a law of vicarious liability for slaveholders, significant elements of which conceived the owner-slave relationship in agency terms. The apparent tension between these two conclusions merits more attention than I can give it in this comment. For reasons discussed below, I do not believe that the material interests of slave owners can explain why different characterizations of the owner-slave relationship prevailed in different kinds of cases. It bears mentioning that no Tennessee court had occasion to decide a fellow-servant case in the slave context, although Tennessee cases between owner and hirer usually (but not always) came out in favor of the owner. See Finkelman, "Slaves as Fellow Servants," 284 n. 60. The same was not true in the cases of vicarious liability and conversion that I discuss below. For another interesting discussion of the application of fellow-servant rule to slaves (a discussion that Finkelman supersedes on critical points), see Tushnet, *The American Law of Slavery*, 45–49, 183–88.

5. *Wright* v. *Weatherly*, 15 Tenn. (7 Yer.) 367, 378, 367–68. (1835).

6. Ibid. at 378–80. Justice Green also authored an important testamentary manumission case, *Ford* v. *Ford*, 26 Tenn. (7 Hum.) 75 (1846), noted for its apparent recognition of the slave's humanity. Arthur Howington has studied this case at length. Arthur F. Howington, "Not in the Condition of a Horse or an Ox: *Ford* v. *Ford*, the Law of Testamentary Manumission, and the Tennessee courts' Recognition of the Slave's Humanity," *Tennessee Historical Quarterly* 34 (1975): 249. See also Howington, *What Sayeth the Law*, iv, 2–3, 12.

7. *Wright* v. *Weatherly*, *supra* note 5, at 380. Green was evidently referring to the so-called noxal liability of slave owners under civil law. His citation to "Cooper's Justinian 362" refers to the first edition (1812) of Thomas Cooper's translation of the *Institutes of Justinian*. (The second edition was not published until 1841.) I have not seen the first two editions of Cooper, but in the third edition (1852) the title "On Noxal Actions" (book 4, title 8) appears at pages 354 through 357. The principal texts in the *Institutes* on noxal liability are *J. Inst.* 4.8.1–3. See also *Dig.* 9.4.2 (Ulpian, Ad Edictum 18).

Green's description of noxal liability is misleading. In cases of noxal liability the owner had the option of paying the damages specified by the applicable law or *surrendering the wrongdoing slave*. The slave's monetary value did not act as a cap on the owner's liability if the owner chose to pay damages. If the slave had committed a wrong with the owner's knowledge, the owner was fully liable for all damages, although what would count as knowledge in this regard was a matter of some doubt. See *Dig* 9.4.2–4.

Noxal liability for the torts of a slave should not be confused with the owner's general liability for a slave's contractual undertakings. As Watson notes, in Roman law the master's contractual liability was limited to the slave's peculium.

Watson, "Thinking Property at Rome." For more detailed discussions of noxal liability, see Watson, *Roman Slave Law,* 68–75, and William W. Buckland, *The Roman Law of Slavery* (Cambridge: Cambridge University Press, 1908), 98–130.

8. *Ingraham and Wife v. Linn, Administrator,* 4 Tex. 266, 267 (1849) (Wheeler, J.). In *Ingraham,* the supreme court of Texas adopted the rule that the owner was not liable for intentional harms committed by his slave. The Texas court explicitly found that the common law master-servant analogy was appropriate, although it mentioned that Green had doubted the analogy in *Wright.* Ibid. at 269.

9. *Wright* v. *Weatherly, supra* note 5, at 380.

10. Finkelman, "Slaves as Fellow Servants," 274–304.

11. *Byram* v. *McGuire,* 40 Tenn. (3 Head) 529 (1859), discussed below. It is worth noting that under civil law the owner's knowledge was also critical in determining whether he could escape full liability for his slave's wrongs by making a noxal surrender. See the discussion in note 7.

12. *Wilkins* v. *Gilmore,* 21 Tenn. (2 Hum.) 139, 140–41 (1840). According to the court, the trespasser was either a slave or a white man wearing blackface. It is interesting that the court did not apparently consider the possibility that the trespasser was a free black. Citing William Blackstone, *Commentaries on the Laws of England,* (4 vols. (Oxford: Clarendon Press, 1765) 1: 431–32.

13. *Byram* v. *McGuire, supra* note 11, at 531.

14. Ibid. at 532–34.

15. *Sweat* v. *Rogers,* 53 Tenn. (6 Heisk.) 117, 118–19 (1871). *Wilkins* v. *Gilmore* required an allegation in intentional wrong cases that the slave had acted according to the "command or encouragement" of the owner. In *Sweat* the plaintiff had prevailed at trial, but the supreme court ordered a new trial based on the erroneous admission of statements by the slaves against the owner. The court claimed that the statements admitted had been made after any conspiracy had terminated, not that the statements of slaves were inadmissible *per se* against their owners. Ibid. at 121–23.

16. By way of contrast, the common law master-servant rule clearly governed vicarious liability for the acts of an overseer. That standard blended with the quotidian wickedness of slave law to produce very strange distinctions. When a slave was beaten to death by the overseer of a person who had hired the slave, the liability of the overseer's master (i.e. the lessee of the slave) depended on the overseer's state of mind. If the purpose of the beating was to discipline the slave and the overseer had accidentally killed the slave, the hirer could be held vicariously liable. This rule followed logically from the rule that permitted the corporal punishment of slaves. The improvident administration of legal violence was only negligence, so the overseer's master was liable. If the overseer was acting with a nondisciplinary motive, the master was absolved so long as he had not authorized the act. *Puryear* v. *Thompson,* 24 Tenn. (5 Hum.) 396 (1841). The lawyers thought the slave cases appropriate analogies in *Puryear.* The hirer's counsel cited *Wright* v. *Weatherly,* and the owner's counsel relied on *Wilkins* v. *Gilmore.* Ibid. at 397. The court cited neither case in its opinion.

17. *Jones* v. *Allen,* 38 Tenn. (1 Head) 626 (1858).

18. Ibid. at 632–33.

19. Ibid. at 632–36 Laws of Tennessee, 1803, 13, § 3.

20. Ibid. at 632–34.

21. Ibid. at 627–29, quoted at 628–29.

22. Ibid. at 630–32.

23. Ibid. at 636–37. The precise role that the allegation of the statutory violation played in reviewing the judgment on the trover count is unclear. It was probably related to the question raised by the possibility that the slave could be his owner's agent for the purpose of communicating the owner's consent to the use of the slave. The argument would be that if the slave's presence could not be lawful without written consent, *a fortiori* the use of his labor could not be lawful without written consent. The problem with this argument is that the violation of the statute did not depend on the absence of the owner's actual consent but instead on the failure of that consent to take a particular form. On the other hand, the question in conversion was the existence of the consent, not its form. Ibid. at 638.

There was a separate question about whether the defendant could escape liability only when the owner had given his actual consent (in any form), or whether consent could be implied from the slave's representations or even from the fact of his presence alone. The court ducked this question by holding that Jones would not be liable in trover even if he knew that Isaac was at the corn-husking against his owner's wishes. Ibid.

24. Ibid. at 638, 639.

25. Ibid. at 635.

26. Watson, "Thinking Property at Rome," at p. 420–423 (mandate for purchase and redemption of slave) and at p. 428–429 (mandate to slave to pay debt of owner).

27. Watson, "Thinking Property at Rome." See Thomas Wiedemann, *Greek and Roman Slavery* (Baltimore: Johns Hopkins University Press, 1981), 73 (Pliny the Elder's attack on physician slaves); ibid., 131–32 (case of fraud by slave banker related by the early Christian theologian Hippolytus); ibid., 127–28 (Suetonius' identification of significant slave grammarians).

Notes on Contributors

PAUL FINKELMAN is the Joseph C. Hostetler-Baker & Hostetler Visiting Professor at Cleveland Marshall College of Law, at Cleveland State University. He is the author of *Dred Scott v. Sandford: A Brief History With Documents* (1997), *Slavery and the Founders: Race and Liberty in the Age of Jefferson* (1996), *An Imperfect Union: Slavery, Federalism and Comity* (1981) and, with Spencer Waller and Neil Cohen, *Baseball and the American Legal Mind* (1994).

DERRICK BELL is Visiting Professor at New York University Law School. He is the author of numerous books on race and rights including *Faces at the Bottom of the Well: The Permanence of Racism* (1992), *And We Are Not Saved: The Elusive Quest for Racial Justice* (1977), *Race, Racism, and American Law* (1973, 1980, 1992), and *Gospel Choirs: Psalms of Survival in an Alien Land Called Home* (1996).

WILLIAM W. FISHER, III is Professor Law at Harvard Law School and the author of *American Legal Realism* (1993).

SANFORD LEVINSON holds the W. St. John Garwood & W. St. Garwood, Jr. Centennial Chair at the University of Texas School of Law. He is the author of *Constitutional Faith* (1988), *Responding to Imperfection* (1994) and with Paul Brest, *Processes of Constitutional Decisionmaking* (1992).

JAMES OLIVER HORTON is Professor of American Studies and History at George Washington University and Director of the Afro-American Communities Project at the Smithsonian Institution, and author of *Free People of Color* (1993). He is co-author (along with Lois E. Horton) of *In Hope of*

Liberty (1996), *A History of the African American People* (1995), and *Black Bostonians* (1979).

Lois E. Horton is Professor of Sociology and American Studies at George Mason University. She is co-author (along with James O. Horton) of *In Hope of Liberty* (1996), *A History of the African American People* (1995), and *Black Bostonians* (1979).

Michael Kent Curtis is Professor of Law at Wake Forest University School of Law. He is the author of *The Constitution and the Flag* (1994) and *No State Shall Abridge: The 14th Amendment and the Bill of Rights* (1985).

Thomas D. Morris is Professor of History at Portland State University. He is the author of *Free Men All: The Personal Liberty Laws of the North* (1974) and *Southern Slavery and the Law, 1619-1860* (1996).

Judith Kelleher Schafer is Associate Director of the Murphy Institute of Political Economy at Tulane University and Visiting Professor of Law at Tulane Law School. She is the author of *Slavery, the Civil Law, and the Supreme Court of Louisiana* (1994).

Ariela Gross is Assistant Professor of Law at the University of Southern California Law Center. She received her Ph.D. in history and her J.D. from Stanford University.

Thomas D. Russell is Assistant Professor of Law at the University of Texas School of Law. He received his Ph.D. in history and his J.D. from Stanford University.

Jonathan A. Bush is Associate Professor of Law at Santa Clara University School of Law and the Ruth Meltzer Senior Research Fellow at the United States Holocaust Museum.

Alan Watson is the Ernest P. Rogers Professor at the University of Georgia. He is the author of *The Trial of Jesus* (1995), *The Spirit of Roman Law* (1995); *The State Law and Religion: Pagan Rome* (1992); *Slave Law in the Americas* (1989), *Roman Slave Law* (1987); and *Roman Law: Law Making in the Later Roman Republic* (1974).

Jacob I. Corré is Visiting Professor at Chicago-Kent College of Law.

Index

Slavery and the Law
was typeset in New Baskerville,
a faithful rendering of John Baskerville's
classic transitional face of mid-eighteenth-century
Britain. New Baskerville combines the graceful openness
of early penmanship with the vertical emphasis of the then
emerging Modern types. The titling face is Americana.

TYPOGRAPHY BY GREGORY M. BRITTON